FUTURE SEEKERS II

FUTURE SEEKERS II

Refugees and Irregular Migration in Australia

Mary Crock, Ben Saul and Azadeh Dastyari

THE FEDERATION PRESS
2006

Published in Sydney by:
The Federation Press
PO Box 45, Annandale, NSW, 2038
71 John St, Leichhardt, NSW, 2040
Ph (02) 9552 2200 Fax (02) 9552 1681
E-mail: info@federationpress.com.au
Website: http://www.federationpress.com.au

National Library of Australia
Cataloguing-in-Publication entry

Crock, Mary E.
Future seekers II: Refugees and Irregular Migration in Australia.

Includes index.
ISBN 1 86287 602 9 (*after January 2007*: 978 1 86287 602 6)

1. Refugees – Government policy – Australia. 2. Refugees – Legal status, laws, etc – Australia. 3. Emigration and immigration law – Australia. 4. Detention of persons – Australia. 5. Australia – Emigration and immigration. I. Saul, Ben. II. Dastyari, Azadeh. III. Title.

325.210994

Typeset by The Federation Press, Leichhardt, NSW.
Printed by Southwood Press, Marrickville, NSW.

Future Seekers II is the ideal book for the concerned citizen wanting to know if Australia now strikes the right balance between compassion and national interest in our treatment of asylum seekers arriving without visas. Like its predecessor *Future Seekers*, this book is user friendly with chapter summaries of key points and statistics which put Australia's concerns and responsibilities in a global context. Written by legal academics able to communicate with a broad public, this book provides a comprehensive, reliable overview of Australian law and policy.

Fr Frank Brennan SJ AO

What the critics said of *Future Seekers* (2002):

[The] book is a valuable overview of the policy and the law affecting asylum seekers in Australia. ... It is refreshing to hear views that challenge the populism coming from governments ... The authors manage to reinforce the importance and centrality of human rights in the debate.

Adelaide Law Review

This book will help bring some of the truth into the public domain. It should be compulsory reading.

UNSW Law Journal

Future Seekers is well timed, and a must read for those who wish to have a concise overview of issues surrounding Australia's asylum seekers.

Law Society of ACT

Foreword

Future Seekers II provides a valuable analysis of how Australian law and practice continue to evolve with regard to asylum-seekers, refugees and migrants.

The issues it raises are not just for experts and lawyers, but ones that should concern each and every one of us.

As long as conflict, persecution and the abuse of basic human rights exist in this world, there will be those who need international protection. Helping such persons – who are both victims and survivors of persecution – demands understanding and an active engagement not only by States, but by all sectors, including the general public.

The fundamental challenge is how to provide security in a world in which global terrorism and transnational crime are real concerns, while maintaining the essential openings for those in need of protection to have access to it.

Gaps in the international protection regime are not new – leaving as they do many who need and deserve our help without it. Stateless persons in Asia, persons internally displaced by natural disasters like the Pakistan earthquake, women and girls trafficked for prostitution in Europe – the litany of those who "fall between the cracks" is long and tragic.

At the United Nations Summit which took place in September 2005 there was wide-reaching agreement on the need to prevent recurrence of failures to provide protection, such as those which occurred in Rwanda in 1994 and Srebrenica in 1995. This renewed commitment to the "Responsibility to Protect" must become more than rhetoric. Practical ways of closing the gaps must be found and acted upon.

Refugees and migrants have long enriched Australian society. When someone genuinely in need of international protection reaches out, we must all decide whether we will turn a blind eye or hold out a helping hand.

This book will help its readers to understand whether the world we live in is evolving into one that we would want our children to grow up in.

Neill Wright
UNHCR Regional Representative
Canberra, Australia
December 2005

Contents

PART 3: IMMIGRATION DETENTION

PART 4: CONCLUSION

About the Authors

Mary Crock, BA (Hons) LLB (Hons) PhD (Melbourne University), has worked in the area of immigration and refugee law since 1985. She is an Associate Professor and Associate Dean (Post Graduate Research) in the Faculty of Law, University of Sydney. She is chief examiner in the various Specialist Accreditation programs in immigration law across Australia; and editor of the *Immigration Review* (Butterworths). She has served in executive positions for the Law Council of Australia (International Law Section) and the Refugee Council of Australia; worked as adviser to the Australian Senate (Inquiry into Australia's Refugee and Humanitarian Program, 2000) and as consultant to HREOC (on immigration detention). She helped to establish and run the Victorian Immigration Advice and Rights Centre Inc in Melbourne (1989-92). Her books include: *Protection or Punishment: The Detention of Asylum Seekers in Australia* (1993); *Immigration and Refugee Law in Australia* (1998); *Future Seekers: Refugees and the Law in Australia* (2002) (with Ben Saul); and *Nation Skilling: Immigration, Labour and the Law* (2003). She has written many articles on immigration and refugee issues, including works on judicial review and "court stripping" (various); immigration detention (2003); interdiction and the *Tampa* Affair (various); and children and refugee status (2004). She teaches administrative law, migration law, refugee law and related subjects for both undergraduate and postgraduate law students at the University of Sydney. In 2006 she will also publish two reports on a three-year project involving the study of unaccompanied and separated children and refugee protection.

Dr Ben Saul, BA (Hons) LLB (Hons) DPhil (Oxon), is a Lecturer in the Faculty of Law at the University of NSW, Director of the Charter of Rights Project at the Gilbert+Tobin Centre for Public Law, and an Associate of the Australian Human Rights Centre. Previously, at Oxford he taught international law, lectured at the Refugee Studies Centre, trained diplomats, and coordinated the Oxford Public Interest Lawyers and the Public International Law Discussion Group. His books include *Defining Terrorism in International Law* (Oxford University Press, 2006) and (with Mary Crock) *Future Seekers: Refugees and the Law in Australia* (Federation Press, 2002). He has published widely in law journals, presented numerous lectures and seminars, and been involved in parliamentary inquiries and public debates on human rights issues. Ben is a member of the NSW Legal Aid Commission's Human Rights Committee, the Steering Group of the Law Council of Australia's International Legal Issues Focus Group, and the Management Committees of the International Law Association (Australian Branch) and the Refugee Advice and Casework Service. He was a legal expert for the UN Committee on the Inalienable Rights of the Palestinian People, monitored election violence in Sri Lanka for the International Commission of Jurists, and serves on the International Law Association's International Committee for the Compensation of Victims of Armed Conflict. Ben is admitted as a lawyer in Australia and was previously a Legal Officer at the Australian Law Reform Commission and Chair of the NSW Attorney-General's Juvenile Justice Advisory Committee. He received the 2003 Human Rights Award from Washington College of Law.

Azadeh Dastyari, BA, LLB (Hons) (Syd), is an Assistant Lecturer at Monash University and a member of the Castan Centre for Human Rights Law. She has taught International Refugee Law at Monash University and Immigration and Refugee Law at the University of Adelaide. She is a co-founder of RAVN, the Refugee Advocacy Volunteer Network at the University of Sydney, and a member of the founding collective for North West Friends of Refugees. Azadeh has translated for people in immigration detention and has worked closely with various NGOs since 1999, including in voluntary capacities with Amnesty International, the Public Interest Advocacy Centre and the Refugee Advocacy and Casework Service

Acknowledgements

Many people have assisted us in writing this book by providing information, advice and comment. For statistical information and assistance with UNHCR photographs, we are particularly grateful to Ariane Rummery and Sylvana Whyte from UNHCR in Australia. We acknowledge also the assistance (for statistical data) of Robyn Bickett and Judyth O'Neill from DIMA and Keiko Forster, Swaysee Lee and Souvira Kheuaphim from IOM. Kaye Barnard, Gordon Thomson and Charlene Thompson provided information about Christmas Island and Andrew Bartlett and Karen Lee assisted us with data on both Christmas Island and Nauru – not the least by allowing author Mary Crock to accompany them on a visit to Christmas Island in November 2004.

The following people provided much needed advice, research assistance and/or general support for the project: Jane McAdam, Ron McCallum, Lorien Vecellio, Sam Dastyari, Danielle Gavshon, Jessie Hohmann, Alison Davidian, Leah Friedman, Catherine Chang, David Marr, Stephen Watkins, Glen Jeffreys, Libby Hogarth, Pamela Curr, Zachary Steel, Frank Brennan, Parastou Hatami, Christian Carney (Refugee Advice and Casework Service), Gerard and Jacqueline Crock, Ella and Naser Dastyari, Peter Bladin, Eva Sallis (Australians Against Racism), Howard Glenn and Kate Gautier (A Just Australia), and Jack Smit (Project Safecom).

Special thanks are due to Phil Oakley (formerly of Christmas Island), Andrew Bartlett and Thomas Mann for the generous donation of some wonderful photographs.

Finally, we are grateful for the patience and expertise of our publisher, Chris Holt, and for Clare Moss, Trish Valliappan and Kathy Fitzhenry of Federation Press who produced the book. Any opinions expressed belong to the authors alone. Sadly, we also accept sole responsibility for any errors that remain!

Abbreviations

ACM	Australian Correctional Management Pty Ltd
CEDAW	Convention on the Elimination of All Forms of Discrimination Against Women 1981
CROC	Convention on the Rights of the Child 1989
DIMA	Department of Immigration and Multicultural Affairs (1996-2001, 2006-)
DIMIA	Department of Immigration, Multicultural and Indigenous Affairs (2001-2006)
HREOC	Human Rights and Equal Opportunity Commission
IAAAS	Immigration Advice and Application Assistance Scheme
ICCPR	International Covenant on Civil and Political Rights 1966
IDC	Immigration Detention Centre
INS	Immigration and Nationality Service
IRPC	Immigration Reception and Processing Centre
MIMA	Minister for Immigration & Multicultural Affairs
NATO	North Atlantic Treaty Organisation
Refugee Convention	Convention Relating to the Status of Refugees 1951 and Protocol 1967
RRT	Refugee Review Tribunal
Torture Convention	Convention against Torture and Other Cruel, Inhuman or Degrading Treatment or Punishment 1984
UDHR	Universal Declaration of Human Rights 1948
UNCAT	United Nations Committee Against Torture
UNHCR	United Nations High Commissioner for Refugees

List of illustrations

Part 1
An Overview of Asylum Seekers, Refugees and Irregular Migration in Australia

1

Immigration, Refugees and Australian Nationhood

Australia is often described as a country of immigrants. Ignoring the prior ownership of the indigenous peoples, it was "created" by colonialists who were consciously aware of the potential in the late 19th century for building a new nation in a certain image. More than 100 years after Federation, Australia's population growth continues to rely heavily on importing human capital. In 2003, 23% of Australia's population of 20 million was born overseas and almost the same proportion again had a parent born abroad - similar to the proportion of foreign born at Federation in 1901. More than 620,000 of the post-Second World War migrants came as "refugees". Australia continues to offer the third largest offshore refugee resettlement program in the world. Generally, its programs for accepting, integrating and rehabilitating people injured by war, persecution and trauma are considered as good as any in the world. Why, then, does the very word "refugee" evoke such varied and emotional responses in Australia?

The turn of the millennium was a particularly ambivalent time. In the first half of 1999, Australians generously gave temporary refuge to 4,000 men, women and children displaced by the Balkan conflict in Kosovo. Turmoil in East Timor later saw Australia open its doors to refugees from that country. At the end of 2004, the catastrophic loss of life across the Indian ocean region caused by a tsunami saw Australians open their hearts and their wallets in extraordinary gestures of generosity and compassion.

The contrast in the reception afforded to asylum seekers - people entering Australia in search of protection as refugees - could not be more pronounced. Can this be the same country where refugee claimants who arrive without visas are regularly detained in remote and forbidding detention centres? Where a failed refugee claimant who cannot be returned to his claimed country of origin could be incarcerated for seven years before winning (qualified) freedom? Where a stateless child born in immigration detention could be locked up for three years before the public outcry grew loud enough to secure her release? How to explain the panic engendered by the arrival of refugee boats? Worse still is the indifference shown to the loss of hundreds of lives at sea following the sinking of boats carrying asylum seekers from Indonesia.

It is not difficult to explain hostile responses to asylum seekers. Non-citizens who enter Australia without permission and seek protection as refugees are an obvious challenge to a government's immigration laws and border controls. Numbers cannot be planned in advance and there is none of the pre-screening for good health and character of "regular" migrants. At the same time, many Australians' concerns about such loss of control have deep historical roots that reflect the country's geography and its political and cultural orientation towards Britain and Europe.

On a practical level, Australia is one of very few countries in the world that has achieved almost perfect control of people moving into and out of its territories. It is the only island continent in the world that shares no borders with any other country. Broad expanses of inhospitable land and highly concentrated urban developments make it relatively easy to monitor arrivals and departures. When a boat load of Chinese arrived in northern New South Wales in 1999, a local official wryly observed that they were easily spotted: "They don't fit into Kempsey, I can tell you".

As many have noted, Australia's white (European) colonisers found themselves small in number in an alien land. The local inhabitants, the vegetation and the animals were strange and difficult to understand. This cultural isolation encouraged reflection and introspection about how the "new" Australian society was to look. The ability to control immigration has been matched with a long historical preoccupation with the selection of "appropriate" migrants: laws to restrict "coloured" migration were among the first to be made by the new Commonwealth Parliament after Federation in 1901.

Having said this, conflicting views were expressed during the drafting of the Australian Constitution in the 1890s about how membership of the country was to be defined. Attempts to protect human rights were defeated, not least because some colonies wanted to preserve racially discriminatory labour laws. The Constitution ultimately made no mention of Australian citizenship, an omission of continuing significance because of the powers given to the Parliament to make laws to confer (and revoke) membership of the Australian community.

The fact that the "White Australia Policy" survived until well after the Second World War demonstrates that fears of invasion from the populous (Asian) north are deep seated and of long standing. Just as importantly, there has always been a general expectation that governments can and should control immigration. High Court Justice Sir Isaac Isaacs expressed it this way in 1923:

> The history of this country and its development has been, and must inevitably be, largely the story of its policy with respect to population from abroad. That naturally involves the perfect control of the subject of immigration, both as to its encouragement and restriction with all their incidents. (*R v Macfarlane* (1923) 32 CLR 518 at 557)

As explored in chapter 3, Australia's experience of irregular migration has been modest and spasmodic compared to the rest of the world. However, a number of events converged at the start of the present millennium to make the issue of asylum seekers more pressing than might otherwise have been the case. The first issue was the scale of "unauthorised" boat arrivals. Whereas Australia had experienced years of boats arriving with small numbers of asylum seekers, people smugglers operating out of Indonesia in the late 1990s became bolder and more ambitious, particularly as their trade became more lucrative and the risk of detection increased.

The Australian Parliament responded in October 1999 by downgrading the protection offered to unauthorised arrivals recognised as refugees, and limiting the range of people eligible to seek asylum. Refugees who entered Australia without a visa became eligible for three-year temporary visas where they had formerly been granted permanent residence. They lost the right to sponsor their families to join them and were no longer eligible for the full range of social security and resettlement benefits. Temporary protection prolonged the uncertainty felt by refugees about their future, causing considerable fear. These changes did nothing to reduce the numbers arriving, however. (The restrictions on family reunion may in fact explain the escalation in boat arrivals after 1999.)

If it became clear by 2001 that "something had to be done", the imminence of a federal election in that year created political conditions in which public anxieties could be manipulated for electoral advantage. The world-changing events of the terrorist attacks in America of 11 September 2001 provided the final impetus for dramatic change.

When a cluster of boats arrived in August 2001 carrying 1,212 people, the government declared that it would end incursions by people smugglers from Indonesia. Matters came to a head when 433 people (mainly Afghans) were rescued from a sinking boat by a Norwegian container ship, the *Tampa*, on 26 August 2001. The government provoked a major international incident by refusing to allow the *Tampa* to dock and land the boat people on the Australian territory of Christmas Island. The rescuees wished to claim protection as refugees in Australia. The affair escalated when the government ordered Australian commandos to take control of the *Tampa* to prevent it from unloading its human cargo.

The *Tampa* incident, discussed in chapter 7, has been described as a crisis manufactured by the government to increase its support in the impending 2001 election. The government's hard line certainly increased its popularity in opinion polls. The Labor Opposition was caught off-guard. Slow to respond to the unfolding drama, it agreed that the unauthorised boat arrivals were alarming and awkwardly declared that it supported the government in all of its actions. Labor first opposed but later agreed to pass legislation retrospectively to validate the boarding and take-over of the *Tampa* by Australian soldiers.

With the terrorist attacks in the United States on 11 September 2001, public opinion hardened even further. Australian politicians were quick to draw links between the incursions of boat people and the prospect of terrorist attack. As explored in chapters 7 and 8, the Opposition ultimately agreed to pass no less than seven immigration statutes in one day, supporting a guillotine motion by the government that pushed the measures through Parliament with little discussion.

The *Tampa* affair was resolved at an international level after the intervention of senior United Nations officials, who brokered an agreement between Australia and its Pacific neighbours. The asylum seekers were detained and shipped to the tiny Pacific Island nation of Nauru and to New Zealand. These countries agreed to house the asylum seekers while their refugee status was assessed. As explored in chapter 8, these arrangements were later extended to become what was dubbed "the Pacific Solution" (later renamed "the Pacific Strategy"). Asylum seekers were intercepted at sea and relocated for refugee processing in Nauru, Papua New Guinea and New Zealand. The arrangements cost many times the amount expended on processing refugee claims in Australia, even if the costs of detaining asylum seekers in Australia are included.

The human costs of this interdiction and deflection program were enormous. On 19 October 2001, in the middle of the federal election campaign, a boat carrying hundreds of asylum seekers sank on its way to Australia with the loss of 353 lives. This shocking catastrophe – the largest single loss of life at sea in the region since the Second World War – was initially virtually unnoticed and un-mourned in much of Australia, such was the animosity felt for would-be asylum seekers. Many of the dead had relatives in Australia and would not have been on the doomed boat but for Australia's temporary protection regime, which precludes family reunification through regular sponsorship and thus encourages further irregular migration (see chapter 4).

Australia received 8,316 boat people between June 1999 and July 2001 – a little over 11 per day. The vast majority sought asylum and were found to be refugees – the victims, not perpetrators, of terrorism and persecution. Indeed between 1 November 1999 and 31 May 2001, around 85% of the 5,936 asylum seekers in detention were recognised as refugees and granted temporary protection visas.

Since 2001, much has happened, yet at the same time little enough seems to have changed. Allegations have continued of abuses within the asylum process; of the enforced separation of families; of death and serious harms suffered by failed asylum seekers returned to their countries of origin; and of lack of support for refugees who are released from detention suffering from mental illness as a result of their long-term incarceration. The detention centres continue to be plagued with repeated hunger strikes, suicide attempts, mass disturbances and even deaths.

In 2004-05, major scandals erupted following the discovery of two cases involving Australians detained (and in one case deported) on the basis that both were unlawful non-citizens. The first was that of an Australian resident woman suffering from schizophrenia, Cornelia Rau, who was detained for over nine months in a Queensland prison and in Baxter detention centre in South Australia. The case highlighted the poor diagnosis and treatment of mental illness in Australia's detention centres (see chapters 11 and 12). Even greater alarm was caused by the revelation that an Australian citizen of Philippine descent – Ms Vivienne Solon-Alvarez – had been detained and removed from the country: see chapters 3, 9 and 12. As inquiries were instituted into these cases, it was revealed that no less than 201 Australian citizens and permanent residents had been mistakenly arrested and detained as unlawful non-citizens between 1993 and 2005 – one of whom may have been detained for seven years according to the federal Ombudsman (see chapter 9).

These cases also suggest how desensitised the public had become to detention, since Australians only took notice of these cases because they involved citizens or permanent residents. Detention of non-residents had seemingly become routine, unremarkable and unexceptional. The case of Peter Qasim, a young man detained without charge or trial for seven years, attracted little concern until his cause was championed by Australian entrepreneur Dick Smith and others.

These cases, together with disturbing accounts of the damage inflicted on children kept for long periods in detention, eventually led to a revolt in the government's own ranks. Liberal backbenchers led by Petro Georgiou MP threatened to introduce a Private Members' Bill (inviting the Parliament to amend the *Migration Act 1958* (Cth), instead of waiting for the government to do it). This initiative and the barrage of bad press finally moved the government to make some concessions in late June 2005. The federal Ombudsman was given the power to review the case of anyone detained for more than two years. The more than 200 cases of wrongful arrest and detention were also referred to this office for investigation. At the same time, the migration laws were changed to enable the release of children and women into the community, declaring that children are only to be detained as a last resort. Other changes allow many refugees holding temporary protection visas to change their status to permanent residence. In the immigration bureaucracy, changes were made in the leadership team, with the Secretary and other members of the management team being replaced.

Nonetheless, Prime Minister Howard was at pains to stress that the government's commitment to immigration control has not wavered. Mandatory detention of most adults without valid documentation continues in Australia, as does the incarceration of asylum seekers in detention centres hosted by Australia's Pacific neighbours under the "Pacific Strategy". More resources are being spent on building a much larger detention centre on Christmas Island. In August 2005, the government used its Senate majority to remove most offshore islands from the "migration zone", ensuring that potential asylum seekers reaching Australia's offshore territories are not afforded the same rights as those who arrive on Australia's mainland (see map in chapter 7). In April 2006, embarrassment caused by the arrival of asylum seekers from West Papua led to proposals to institute further restrictive measures across the north of Australia. In May of that year a Bill was introduced to entrench the

"Pacific Strategy" for all unauthorised arrivals - even those who are able to reach the Australian mainland.

Unfortunately, attempts to highlight the harms caused by Australia's refugee and detention policies have left the country deeply divided. Support for the government's hard line suggests that some Australians accept border control as necessary for the security of the nation. While many Australians are very upset about the human impact of their government's detention laws and policies, many others deeply resent suggestions that they are callous and uncaring about refugees.

Modern Australia has never experienced the full horrors of prolonged war and oppression on its own territory. The good fortune of most Australians makes it harder to comprehend the "push" factors influencing a refugee's decision to flee, and to empathise with their situation. When asylum seekers are segregated from the community - locked away in remote detention centres - their humanity is hidden along with their plight. It is not difficult to promote the idea that these invisible people are a threat, or are less deserving than the "real" refugees who wait patiently in refugee camps in Kenya, Pakistan or Jordan.

In many respects it is easier to make out the case for excluding these people than to argue for compassion and leniency. In an age where fear of terrorism is rampant, compassion is easily derided as weakness and naiveté. At the same time, the number of people in need around the world is numbingly large: according to UNHCR, there were 9.2 million refugees in the world at the end of 2004, included among 19.2 million people whose human rights and ability to survive were "of concern".

Australia argues that its controlled refugee intake shows that it is "doing its bit" to help, and that it cannot possibly accept everyone in need. It also argues that encouraging asylum seekers by offering them protection undermines "orderly" international resettlement programs. The argument is that refugees should have a right to seek protection from persecution, but should not be allowed to select their country of refuge. Because most asylum seekers who reach Australia have transited through other countries, the argument is that these people are at best "secondary movement" refugees seeking a "preferred immigration outcome".

The problem for Australia's refugees is that the dominant rhetoric of blame and exclusion does not match the reality with which they live. Some refugees travel directly to Australia without permission because they *must* do so to escape persecution. Their choices can be very stark: leave by whatever means or possibly face serious harm, torture or death. Others may have tried to gain assistance through UNHCR or at foreign embassies in countries of so-called "first asylum". The hard reality is that these avenues often fail to deliver the protection a person needs. There is no "immigration queue" for these people, no "proper channels" available which will provide them with safety.

For the most part, international law does not regard some refugees as being more "deserving" than others (exceptions are made for certain criminals, including terrorists). Most importantly, refugees are not considered "illegal" because they enter a country without authorisation. On the contrary, under international law it is wrong to impose penalties on refugees because they have entered a country of refuge without permission. As a former judge of the Federal Court, Marcus Einfeld, said on the ABC's *7.30 Report* (12 April 2001):

> People do not arrive illegally. That is a mistake. A person is entitled under Australian and international law to make an application for refugee asylum in a country when they allege that they are escaping from persecution ... That is simply the law.

The refugee problem is not an easy one to solve. As explored in chapter 4, people smuggling and the trafficking in human beings are often highly exploitative criminal enterprises. In this uncertain age, there is also an obvious need for countries to ensure that irregular migration does not allow the admission of terrorists. However, Australia's "solutions" are doing more harm than they are preventing.

The imbalance of the laws and policies is particularly acute in the area of immigration detention. Detention is defended as necessary to deter unlawful immigration. Whether or not immigration detention does deter (it probably does not), questions arise about the sense, humanity and legitimacy of causing pain to one individual to deter others. This is particularly so where detainees are children or other vulnerable persons.

If one aim of this book is to unravel the complexities of the refugee phenomenon and Australia's responses to it, it is also concerned to explore the wider implications of measures controlling immigration and membership of the Australian community. At this point the shortcomings of Australia's Constitution become an issue. When the drafters of the Constitution left the matter of conferring or denying citizenship with the Parliament, they also omitted any Charter of Rights from the Constitution. In 2004, the High Court confirmed that these omissions can have a devastating impact on those "outside" the Constitution.

In 2004-05 the High Court heard a series of cases involving children born in immigration detention and individuals born as Australian citizens who lost that status when Australia relinquished the colonial territory on which they were born. The Court rejected arguments that citizenship in Australia could ever be a birthright (or *jus soli*) and confirmed that the Parliament has almost untrammelled power to determine who is or is not a citizen. For those who are not citizens (or whose citizenship is revoked) - constitutional "aliens" - the Court confirmed that the Constitution does not prevent laws requiring detention regardless of age or justification. The Court also upheld the constitutionality of detaining non-citizens without any time limits (potentially allowing indefinite detention) and without any guarantees about the conditions of detention: see chapters 9 and 10. Public discussion of these cases and their implications for all Australians has not been extensive, but these cases underscore the importance of taking an holistic approach to issues first raised by refugees.

The development of a dissident refugee support movement in and after 2001 signalled a new direction in the refugee debate - towards subversion and civil disobedience of laws regarded by some as unbearably harsh. Bipartisan support for the key planks of Australia's border protection and detention laws has radicalised resistance to those laws, as the Labor Opposition has done little to distinguish its asylum policies from those of the government, or to provide a humane alternative. Refugee support groups have proliferated as concerned citizens of all political persuasions have joined organisations such as A Just Australia, Chilout and Rural Australians for Refugees. As more Australians become disturbed by the human impact of the government's policies, the movement for genuine reform can only continue to gather pace.

Australia has yet to find the right balance between compassion and national interest in its treatment of refugees and irregular migrants; indeed, a humane response to refugees is arguably in the national interest. The issues continue to define Australia's national character. If being "un-Australian" means anything, then surely the policies of mandatory, indefinite detention are deeply un-Australian, as are the temporary protection laws which keep members of refugee families separated. This book recognises that a full and informed public debate cannot proceed without a basic understanding of the facts and the law about refugees.

***

In 2002, two of the authors published *Future Seekers: Refugees and the Law in Australia* to help Australians understand Australia's response to refugees and asylum seekers. This book builds on that work. Recognising that public understanding of refugee issues has become more sophisticated, this work includes both a deeper analysis of refugee law and a consideration of broader issues relating to irregular migration and the status of non-citizens. While Australia's experience of forced migration is modest in world terms, its response has wider significance. This is so, both because Australian citizens and residents have been mistreated by the immigration bureaucracy and because Australia's laws and policies are influencing the practice of other countries.

Like *Future Seekers*, this book provides basic information about the scope and challenges of global and regional movements of refugees, asylum seekers, and irregular and forced migrants. It gives an overview of Australian and international laws governing the reception, detention, processing, admission and expulsion of asylum seekers and refugees. It also explores the relationship between refugees, human rights and immigration control, within the social, political and cultural contexts in which the law operates.

Part 1 of this book looks at who comes to Australia irregularly and how they arrive (chapters 2 and 3), including through people smuggling and trafficking (chapter 4). Part 2 examines how the law identifies and treats "refugees" who arrive directly in Australia, with or without permission. The procedures for determining refugee status are described in chapter 5 while who is recognised as a refugee (Australia's "jurisprudence" on the refugee definition) is discussed in chapter 6. Australia's border control strategies, including the deflection of asylum seekers from Australian territory, are explained in chapter 7. The outcomes for refugee claimants, including temporary protection and the removal of failed asylum seekers, are considered in chapter 8.

Part 3 is devoted to the subject of controlling irregular migration. Chapter 9 outlines the basic mechanisms of enforcement, including how the system has failed in recent years. Chapters 10 and 11 focus on immigration detention, examining who is detained, the legality of detention and the conditions of detention. Chapter 12 explores how Australia's laws and practices compare with those of other Western democracies. The book concludes by reflecting on the broader implications of Australia's laws and policies on refugees and irregular migration.

2

Compassion and Common Sense: Refugees and Immigration Control

Key Points in this Chapter

- Australia has settled more than 620,000 refugees and displaced persons since the 1940s.
- Australia's quota of humanitarian entrants has been set at between 12,000 and 13,000 in recent years. This program includes refugees and others with humanitarian needs.
- In 2005, Australia contributed almost US$13 million to the global refugee agency, the United Nations High Commissioner for Refugees (UNHCR) – making it the 15th largest donor country in the world.
- A refugee is defined in the UN Refugee Convention of 1951 as someone outside their country of origin who is unable or unwilling to return there because of a "well-founded fear of persecution" in their home country for reasons of race, religion, nationality, membership of a particular social group, or political opinion.
- An asylum seeker is a person seeking recognition and protection as a refugee.
- The international legal definition of a refugee is narrow and excludes many who need protection (such as victims of environmental disasters).
- Australia has a legal duty not to return refugees to persecution in their countries of origin and must guarantee their basic human rights.
- Australia has a legal duty to protect victims of torture and other human rights abuses who do not qualify as refugees.
- The obligation to protect refugees does not extend to refugees who are threats to national security or public order.
- Refugees come to Australia through government programs, or may arrive without visas and seek protection from within the country.

Regulating immigration to Australia

Long before Prime Minister John Howard's famous election statements around the time of the *Tampa* affair ("We will decide who comes into this country and the circumstances in which they come"), the right to control immigration was an established principle of international law. The very definition of state sovereignty implies that nations have the right to decide whom they allow on to their territory, and whom they exclude from it. In legal terms, sovereignty is the authority of a group of people, organised through a government, to control exclusively a particular territory.

As noted earlier, Australia has relied on the controlled admission of foreigners to build up its population. In more recent years, immigration has been used to promote economic growth, create new jobs and opportunities, increase knowledge and understanding of different cultures, and make society more youthful, sophisticated and vibrant. As in most countries, it is difficult to imagine Australia as a modern democracy without immigration of some kind. The global movement of people - as tourists, students, temporary workers or permanent migrants - has become an accepted and ubiquitous fact of life. Even so, debates still rage about how many migrants Australia should accept. Policy makers have to take into account the country's capacity to settle new migrants, the availability of employment and other opportunities, overall population size, environmental factors and potential social security costs.

Within the scheme of planned immigration, refugees and asylum seekers are in an awkward position. Displaced from their homes and homelands, refugees can find themselves without the protection of their country of origin or nationality and with no "right" (in the form of a visa) to travel to another country. On one hand, it is not difficult to see why refugees can be deeply unpopular - the subject of fear and suspicion. On the other, the impossibility of their position explains why many countries have been prepared to endow refugees with limited rights, even where they enter a country without authorisation.

In Australia, the cross-border movement of people (both citizens and non-citizens) is controlled by detailed laws and regulations. The federal government has powers under the Australian Constitution (1901) to make laws with respect to "immigration and emigration" (the "immigration power"); naturalisation and aliens (the "aliens power"); and external affairs. These powers to legislate have been interpreted broadly by Australia's High Court to permit Parliament to make far-reaching laws controlling refugees, and to allow non-citizens to be treated with fewer rights and protections than citizens (see chapter 1).

The federal *Migration Act 1958* (Cth) and the related *Migration Regulations 1994* (Cth) establish a detailed system requiring every non-citizen who enters or remains in Australia to possess a visa. The legislation sets out the criteria that have to be met before a visa can be issued. While non-citizens in many instances are expected to apply for their visas *before* entering Australia, the regulations also allow people to apply for visas after arrival. In essence, it is a matter of government policy as to who is allowed to apply for what type of visa at what point in time or place. One of the most important concessions made with respect to refugees is that "protection" visas can be granted after entry into Australia, even where a non-citizen has entered or is in the country illegally. It is important to note in this context that, while some aspects of refugee protection may be unplanned (see below), it is not true to say that Australia's refugee system is un-*regulated*.

In theory, all non-citizens without a visa must be detained and removed from Australia as soon as possible. In practice, complex rules determine who is actually detained and removed: see chapter 9. Much depends on how non-citizens enter Australia; what visa (if any) they have held; and what other circumstances affect their application. The federal Department of Immigration and Multicultural Affairs (DIMA) administers the migration laws and determines whether to admit foreigners to Australia. (Until January 2006 the Immigration Minister also had responsibility for Indigenous Affairs.) DIMA is responsible for assessing whether or not a person is a refugee, and its officials wield considerable discretionary power to make decisions that deeply affect people's lives.

Australia's migration laws attempt to ensure that non-citizens applying to enter the country are treated equally and fairly – regardless of where they come from. As in many countries, this was not always the case. Until the early 1970s, the White Australia Policy discriminated against non-Europeans of "colour" who wanted to settle in Australia. Australia now takes pride in its non-discriminatory immigration policy. Current laws aim to give an equal opportunity to all non-citizens who apply to enter and non-discrimination is the foundation of Australia's modern, culturally diverse community. It also reflects the value Australians place on treating other human beings equally and fairly – particularly the less fortunate. These principles are reflected in the special concessions made for non-citizens determined to be refugees.

Refugees have been an integral part of Australia's immigration intake since the end of the Second World War. Nowadays, approximately 13,000 places are set aside each year for the "humanitarian" component of Australia's permanent immigration program. The Humanitarian program is used to resettle refugees and other groups of humanitarian concern, such as people subject to serious discrimination or human rights violations in their home country. (While Australia's resettlement program for refugees is the third largest *formal* resettlement program in the world, it is very small compared to the millions of refugees who have entered host countries such as Pakistan, Iran and Kenya in recent years.) It is in this context that residence status is granted both to refugees who apply for admission from overseas and to refugees who seek protection after they arrive in Australia.

Australia's Migration Program

Each year Australia accepts a pre-determined quota of migrants from overseas, either for temporary or permanent residence. The intake aims to maximise the social, cultural and economic benefits of migration to Australia, and varies from year to year. Migrants must satisfy a variety of criteria, including English language competency, health and public interest requirements, and minimum financial means.

Australia admitted 120,000 migrants in 2004-05, including:

- 42,000 people in the "Family Stream" (relatives of Australian citizens and permanent residents);
- 72,100 in the "Skill Stream" (work-related or business migrants);
- 900 "Special Eligibility" category (migrants with special sporting, professional or artistic skills); and
- 5,000 places for skilled migrants for people who commit to living and working in regional areas.

In addition, the government allocated 13,000 places for humanitarian cases:

- 6,000 are for *offshore* applicants recognised as refugees under international law; and
- 7,000 for *offshore* applicants under the Special Humanitarian Program and for applicants with *onshore* protection needs.

Offshore refugees

Australia's offshore humanitarian program involves the grant of visas to two broad groups of people in need of protection: refugees and those who enter under the Special Humanitarian Program (SHP). Refugees are identified predominantly by UNHCR (or other designated relief agency) and then referred to Australia. The Refugee visa category includes the sub-categories of Refugee, In-country Special Humanitarian, Emergency Rescue and Woman at Risk. SHP entrants are people outside their home country who suffer discrimination amounting to a gross human rights violations in their home countries. They must be sponsored by an Australian citizen, permanent resident or by an organisation that is based in Australia. They may or may not be "refugees" in the strict legal sense explained below. The table on the following page shows the origin of refugees and humanitarian entrants brought to Australia under the *offshore* humanitarian program in recent years.

These statistics show that there have been substantial changes in the source countries of humanitarian entrants in recent years. At the height of the influx of boat people at the end of the 1990s, complaints were made repeatedly that the unauthorised arrivals were taking the place of "genuine refugees" who were languishing in UNHCR refugee camps. The rhetoric heightened awareness of the neglect of long-term refugees in African and Middle Eastern camps. In response, the intervening years have seen a dramatic rise in the intake of UNHCR recognised refugees from Africa. In 2003-04, 71% of all offshore refugees came from Africa

Offshore Resettlement Program: 1998-99 to 2003-04

Region	1997-98	1998-99	1999-00	2000-01	2001-02	2002-03	2003-04	2004-5
Europe	5,307	4,736	3,424	3,462	2,709	1,158	354	20
Middle East & SW Asia	2,952	2,919	2,208	2,155	2,743	4,656*	2,867**	3174
Africa	1,473	1,552	1,736	2,032	2,801	5,628	8,353	8486
Asia	685	295	113	316	189	201	221	415
Americas	50	24	21	27	16		7	1
OPCs*						311	90	
Other						15		
Total	10,467	9,526	7,502	7,992	8,458	11,656	11,802	12,096

* Includes 311 Afghans and Iraqis processed in PNG and Nauru - see OPCs.
** Includes 90 Afghans and Iraqis processed in PNG and Nauru.

Source: DIMA Fact Sheets 60 (2005) and 40 (2002)

compared with 47% in 2002-03 and 23% in 1999-2000. By 2004-05, the nationalities receiving the highest number of offshore visas were Sudanese (5,220 visas), Iraqi (1,589), Afghan (1,291), Liberian (868), Sierra Leonean (751), Burundian (660), Burmese (313), Congolese (300), Iranian (278) and Somalian (201), with 625 visas going to other nationalities.

Onshore refugees

The second aspect of Australia's humanitarian program involves the grant of protection visas to non-citizens who claim refugee status after their arrival *from within* Australia. Most of these applicants arrive on valid visas as tourists or students, or on other short-term visas, and then seek to *change their status* to that of permanent resident on the basis that they are refugees. A smaller number enter Australia without valid visas and then seek protection as refugees.

People who lodge a claim for recognition as a refugee are referred to as "asylum seekers". They are, in fact and law, seeking asylum, refuge or protection in Australia. Their fate depends on whether or not they can prove that they meet the international legal definition of a refugee. These are the people who are charged with "jumping" the immigration "queue". Whatever their mode of entry into Australia, they make their application for protection and await a decision inside Australia rather than overseas. As a strict matter of law, these are also the *only* refugees that Australia is *obliged* to protect under international law. An *onshore* asylum seeker has many obstacles to overcome before gaining the entitlement to protection as a refugee.

The notion of obligation towards people who come uninvited and without authorisation is challenging and confronting for many people, especially in Australia where strict immigration control has been the norm for many years. Some people also resent the fact that refugee protection is established by international law, which constrains the operation of Australia's domestic laws.

Australia's historical experience of both asylum seekers and irregular migration is discussed in chapter 3. In spite of the rhetoric about being "swamped" by asylum seekers and refugees, the humanitarian intake quota of approximately 12,000 places (increased to 13,000 in 2004-05) has not always been filled in recent years. In 1998-99, 640 places were unallocated while in 1999-2000 there were 2,040 places left unfilled. Although the quota was exceeded by 1,733 places in the following year (2000-01), there is no evidence of a major overrun of the program caused by the surge in onshore applications. The available statistics are not easy to interpret because of the tendency to include temporary visa grants - including 5,900 non-renewable "temporary safe haven" visas - as part of the permanent migration program.

In September 2001 the law was changed to block the grant of offshore visas to anyone who had spent seven days or more in a country where the applicant could have accessed UNHCR processes or sought "effective protection". These changes underscore the importance to the government that refugee and humanitarian applicants "go through the proper channels" - even though these channels often fail to deliver real solutions for refugees, such as where protection is not "effective" in practice. These changes narrowed the range of asylum seekers eligible for permanent refugee resettlement in Australia. It was not until 2004-05 that concessions enabled temporary protection visa holders to access permanent status (see chapter 7).

Humanitarian Program, Grants by Category, 1998-2005

Category	1998-99	1999-00	2000-01	2001-02	2002-03	2003-04	2004-5
Refugee	3,988	3,802	3,987	4,160	4,376	4,134	5,511
Special Humanitarian	4,348	3,051	3,116	4,258	7,280	8,297**	6,755***
Special Assistance	1,190	649	879	40			
Onshore Protection	1,830	2,458	5,577	3,885	866	788	895
Safe Haven		5,900					
Temporary Humanitarian			164	6	3	2	17
Total	11,356	15,860*	13,733	12,349	12,525	13 851	13,178

* Includes 5,900 Safe Haven visas 4,000 offshore Kosovars

** Includes 1,900 onshore East Timorese and 31 others onshore.

*** Includes 148 grants to East Timorese and 22 others onshore

Source: DIMA Fact Sheet 60

Playing off the "onshore" and "offshore" refugee programs

Australia linked the onshore and offshore refugee and humanitarian programs in July 1996, reducing the number of offshore humanitarian visas issued for every protection visa issued to an asylum seeker within Australia. The change encouraged unhelpful rhetoric about "good" (offshore) and "bad" (onshore) refugees, playing off the protection needs of one group against the other.

In response, UNHCR criticised Australia for creating different classes of refugees, with different rights and entitlements. The Refugee Council of Australia argues that linking the two programs resulted in "confusion and manipulation". If asylum seekers are jumping a queue, it is arguably a problem of Australia's own making. Ironically, by reducing the number of places for offshore asylum seekers, the linkage could *encourage* people to come directly (without permission) to Australia to seek asylum, rather than waiting in countries of first asylum to be selected for resettlement.

There is some evidence that the linkage has also created tension between different refugee communities within Australia. Communities which have sponsored relatives as refugees from abroad find themselves in conflict with others who relied on people smugglers to bring their relatives into the country. The government's policy has the effect of placing unnecessary emotional pressure on refugees in Australia.

The debate about the respective merits of "offshore" and "onshore" refugees raises many issues about the nature of international protection and the interface between refugee law and immigration control. A central problem is that asylum seekers in Western countries like Australia are many times more likely to gain recognition as refugees than are those who apply for this status from within UNHCR controlled refugee camps. Government officials in refugee-receiving countries argue that this is because Western countries are too generous in their administrative processes. Hence, it is argued that mobile asylum seekers gain an unfair advantage over their counterparts in UNHCR camps. Others point out that UNHCR is grossly underresourced in its status determination work in the large camps established to deal with mass refugee flows. The integrity of decision-making in those situations can be compromised by factors ranging from physical and temporal constraints to corruption.

Indeed, the very purpose of the offshore and onshore processes can be completely different. In a camp situation, refusal of status may mean exclusion from a resettlement program but little else in the short term. In countries of asylum like Australia, denial of status carries with it the risk of return to the country from which the claimant has fled.

At the very least, the characterisation of (onshore) asylum seekers as less deserving of protection as refugees than their overseas counterparts is confusing and misleading. It does not convey the very important differences between the offshore programs – which are founded on (Australia's) free choice to bring in migrants – and the onshore program, which is reactive and based on international protection *obligations*. This essential difference lies in the way international law constructs the status of "refugee" and then attaches protection obligations to that status. As explained below, the most important obligation under the 1951 Refugee Convention is that countries refrain in all but exceptional circumstances from returning a "refugee" to a country where he or she faces persecution for a Convention reason.

The changing meanings of "refugee"

The term "refugee" has an ordinary, everyday meaning that is quite different from its technical, legal definition. Its popular meaning connotes a person fleeing from danger, intolerable circumstances or conditions, however caused. There are many reasons why people need to flee to safety, such as to escape oppression, threats to life or liberty, deprivation, poverty, war or civil strife, or natural or human-made disasters.

International law first sought to define the term "refugee" in the 1920s, when the League of Nations negotiated legal instruments to assist persons fleeing from oppressive regimes, such as Bolshevik Russia and later Nazi Germany. In those early instruments, "refugees" were defined by their nationality or ethnicity, rather than by more abstract ideas about the underlying causes of flight. Even when international instruments in the 1930s began to recognise social and political upheavals as causes of flight, these remained tied to particular refugee crises and nationalities.

The modern international law definition of "refugee" in the 1951 Refugee Convention was drafted under the auspices of the United Nations after the Second World War. Instead of tying the meaning of a "refugee" to specific refugee flows based on nationality or ethnicity, the 1951 Convention establishes a more universal definition based on the concept of "persecution".

The 1951 Refugee Convention

The legal meaning of "refugee" applies to a much narrower range of people than its everyday meaning. It excludes all but victims of quite politicised forms of persecution. The Refugee Convention was a response to the persecution of Jews and others during the Second World War, and reflects an attempt to ensure that no person would ever again be left without the protection of a country when faced with persecution. At the same time, however, it is full of political compromises.

Even so, since being temporally and geographically extended by a 1967 Protocol, it provides the most widely accepted international legal definition of a refugee, forming the basis of many countries' domestic refugee definitions. A "refugee" is any person who:

> owing to well-founded fear of being persecuted for reasons of race, religion, nationality, membership of a particular social group or political opinion, is outside the country of his nationality and is unable or, owing to such fear, is unwilling to avail himself of the protection of that country; or who, not having a nationality and being outside the country of his former habitual residence as a result of such events, is unable, or, owing to such fear, is unwilling to return to it.

This definition limits protection to people who can show that they fear *persecution* on one of the five "grounds" – race, religion, nationality, membership of a particular social group and political opinion. It is not enough that a person is afraid to return for fear of persecution. There must be evidence that the person's fear is "well founded" from an objective standpoint. As a matter of domestic and international law, this definition offers a very narrow gateway to protection for people who may have fled a country in fear for their lives. Its narrow focus on persecution may exclude from protection people who are fleeing generalised violence, war or serious human rights abuses, although some regional organisations offer extended protection and "complementary" forms of human rights-based protection have emerged in some countries (see chapter 6). By requiring that a refugee be outside their country of origin, the Convention definition also excludes people displaced *within* their home country (known as "internally displaced persons") (see chapter 6). As explained in chapters 6 to 8, the *Migration Act* was amended in September 2001 to further refine and limit the way this definition is interpreted in Australia.

Assistance in interpreting the definition in the Refugee Convention comes from policy guidelines (such as the *Handbook on Procedures and Criteria for Determining Refugee Status*) issued by the UNHCR Executive Committee, currently made up of representatives from 66 countries, including Australia. The procedures for individually determining whether a person in Australia is a refugee are described in chapter 5. In general, a *refugee* is a person who has already been officially assessed as satisfying the international definition of a refugee, either by UNHCR or a national government. In contrast, an *asylum seeker* is a person who has not yet been officially recognised as a refugee, but who is applying to have his or her status as a refugee recognised under the international definition.

Ordinarily, asylum seekers must establish an individual basis for their fear of persecution. However, in situations where there are sudden, mass exoduses of tens or hundreds of thousands of people, it is often not practical to assess each case individually. In these circumstances, it will usually be obvious that members of large groups are fleeing for the same reasons, and so it will be possible to declare a "group determination" of refugee status. Each member of the group will automatically be regarded as a refugee, unless there is evidence to disprove the need for protection. Australia has never been faced with a situation of mass influx, although temporary protection has been granted to whole groups of people fleeing violence in Sri Lanka, Kosovo and East Timor.

Overseas, a major problem with group determination of refugee status has been preventing the militarisation of refugee camps. Refugees must (normally) be civilians to receive protection and soldiers serving in conflicts are not considered refugees (although deserters or conscientious objectors may still be eligible). In some Rwandan refugee camps in the mid-1990s, and in East Timorese refugee camps in West Timor in the late 1990s, militants hid among the refugee population, or controlled refugee camps through intimidation.

Australia's obligations under the Refugee Convention

By signing and ratifying the Refugee Convention, Australia agreed that:

- it will not return refugees to a country where they could face persecution (or the threat of persecution) on one of the five refugee grounds (race; religion; nationality; membership of a particular social group; or political opinion). This is known as the principle of *non-refoulement*, or non-return to persecution. Exceptions are made for refugees who represent a threat to national security or who have protection somewhere else;
- protection must be given to all refugees without discrimination;
- it will not penalise refugees for entering the country "illegally", because people fleeing from persecution cannot be expected to leave their country and enter another in the "regular" manner;
- it will only expel refugees in exceptional circumstances to protect national security or public order, because expulsion may have very serious consequences for the individual;
- refugees should be treated as a social and humanitarian problem and should not be a cause of political tension between states;
- it will cooperate with other nations to find satisfactory solutions to refugee problems, because the grant of asylum can place unduly heavy burdens on some countries;
- it will cooperate with UNHCR to manage refugees globally;
- it will give the same human rights to refugees that it affords to its citizens and non-residents, including rights to work, education, housing, welfare, freedom of movement and freedom of opinion.

Of these obligations, the promise not to send back refugees is the most confronting, as well as the most important. This obligation explains why boat people who reach Australia cannot be simply turned around or towed back out to sea. If the boat people are refugees, such action would breach Australia's obligations under the Refugee Convention – a treaty ultimately built on common decency and humanitarianism.

Even at the height of the *Tampa* affair, there was never any question that the asylum seekers rescued at sea should have their claims for refugee status determined. The real issues were where and by whom the claims should be processed. Unfortunately, Australia's anxiety about the electoral impact of complying with its international legal obligations towards refugees led it to adopt more and more laws restricting asylum in Australia. In April 2006 there were even suggestions of interdiction programs to stop West Papuans from seeking asylum in Australia – in direct contradiction of Australia's non-refoulement obligation under the Refugee Convention. These laws are explained in chapters 5 to 8.

Criticisms of the Refugee Convention

Since the 1990s, many criticisms have been levelled at the Refugee Convention. Governments complain about the cost of determining individual refugee claims and about the social and financial impact of granting asylum to large numbers of refugees. In 1990, Western countries were spending 10 times as much on national refugee determination procedures as they were allocating to UNHCR to protect the entire global refugee population. The situation has improved little in the intervening years. Valid arguments are also made about the role that organised crime plays in conveying asylum seekers to countries of refuge and about the inequity of a system that privileges mobile, wealthier refugees over those who wait for years in the often harsh conditions of UN refugee camps.

Internationally, Australia has been vocal in calling for reform of the Refugee Convention, to prevent its "manipulation" by economic migrants or those fleeing civil violence rather than persecution. Yet, as UNHCR observes, few countries have supported Australia's position, and Amnesty International fears that "any renegotiation would see a diminution of international standards". At a formal legal level, most countries have adopted the opposite approach to Australia, by supporting the strengthening of the Refugee Convention through UNHCR's "Agenda for Protection" process and "Convention Plus" initiative.

From the perspective of asylum seekers, concerns about the Convention focus on the narrowness of the refugee definition, and the tendency of countries to restrictively interpret their *non-refoulement* obligations. Again, concerns have been raised about the fairness of a system that favours individuals who fear harm because of their politics or ethnicity, over persons who may face death for reasons that do not fall within one of the five narrow Convention grounds. As chapter 3 shows, Australia recognises a smaller proportion of asylum seekers as refugees than many other democratic countries, suggesting that it interprets the refugee definition more narrowly than other countries.

The failure to set minimum criteria for processing refugee claims is also a major problem, with procedures left largely to the discretion of governments (Australia's procedures are discussed in chapter 5, and those of other democracies in chapter 12). The indeterminacy of the refugee definition raises further difficulties. Because there is no central authority that can decisively rule on its interpretation, real inconsistencies can develop between the way different countries interpret the definition and views differ on even the most basic precepts underlying the Convention. At a practical level, the Convention has no mechanism for holding countries responsible for breaches of the Convention.

Balancing sovereignty and rights

The essential difference between the perspectives of governments and refugees is that governments invariably want to take responsibility for fewer refugees, while asylum seekers complain that the doors to freedom are too few and too narrow. Without denying the strength of some of the criticisms of the Convention from both sides, some of the complaints underscore elements that are timeless and universal in the refugee experience. People who leave home to seek refuge in a foreign country have always presented a challenge, a source of annoyance and discomfort. The Refugee Convention is often described as a product of the "Cold War", designed to allow Western countries to use international law to trumpet their freedoms to the Eastern bloc. But the Convention also has a more principled foundation, as a collective expression of horror at the human rights abuses perpetrated during the Second World War.

Central to protecting human rights is the idea that no person should be returned to a situation where his or her fundamental rights are threatened. The principle of *non-refoulement* in refugee law was created with the recent memory in mind of refugees being denied protection by countries of first asylum, with catastrophic consequences. Without international obligations, the pressure of domestic politics is likely to weigh even more heavily than it does now against protecting refugees. The crisis that developed in April 2006 surrounding the grant of refugee protection to 42 West Papuans is testament to this (see further chapters 3 and 7).

The simple truth is that the Jewish and other asylum seekers turned away before and during the Second World War were not wanted any more than today's asylum seekers are wanted when they arrive without permission. It was to deal with just such a situation that the Refugee Convention was created: to require countries to provide protection to refugees physically on their territory. This is reflected in Prime Minister John Howard's insistence that the *Tampa* refugee claimants not be permitted to land on Australian soil, which would have activated Australia's asylum process. Some argue that the concept of protected exile is outdated in this age of international diplomacy. Even so, it is still the case that flight remains the only option for many who are faced with extremist regimes or the uncontrolled violence of civil war.

The basic *non-refoulement* obligation in the Refugee Convention provides the strongest argument for maintaining the treaty. Without it, the ambiguity of state practice would provide a shakier foundation for the assertion that *non-refoulement* is part of customary international law. Even the most strident critics of the Convention acknowledge that reopening the instrument for debate would almost certainly result in a lessening of the legal protections available to refugees.

Of course, the immediate protection of refugees from *refoulement* is not the sole function of the Refugee Convention and the mandate of UNHCR is much wider. It is unsurprising that countries like Australia are most comfortable with refugee protection in the context of accommodating and resettling refugees located in other countries. In theory, the establishment of an effective regime for the protection of refugees would remove the need for individuals to seek asylum in other countries. Until a perfect system can be devised, however, a mechanism for protecting asylum seekers remains necessary. The Refugee Convention provides such a basis, and should be used as such in building mechanisms for more equitable burden-sharing. Human rights instruments, such as the Convention against Torture and the ICCPR, provide important complements to the Convention regime.

The problem of "secondary movement refugees"

A common criticism of the Refugee Convention is that it was designed for a much simpler time when refugee problems were localised and refugee movements were limited to direct border crossings. Today, advances in transport and technology and the ready market in people smuggling mean that refugees may seek asylum after travelling through many countries. If refugee law was designed to allow people who have lost the protection of their countries to obtain "substitute protection" from an asylum state, it was never meant to allow refugees to secure a preferred immigration outcome. The challenges posed by mobile refugees are many: understandably, richer countries deeply resent the use of asylum law to by-pass stringent immigration controls. Just how to deal with the problem, however, is another question.

Australia has adopted a variety of mechanisms to prevent refugees from "forum shopping". It has entered into bi-lateral agreements with Indonesia and, as noted earlier, restricted the availability of protection where an asylum seeker has spent seven or more days in a country in which they could have either sought asylum or sought UN assistance (see above and chapter 8).

Although statistics on the impact of these measures are not available, it is unlikely that they have had any more success in Australia than similar initiatives in other countries. Once an asylum seeker applies for protection in one country, countries through which the person may have transited (or even resided) become very reluctant to take them back. If the only country with a legal duty to admit the asylum seeker is the country of alleged persecution, the asylum state can be left with no option other than to process the claim. For asylum seekers denied entry at the border, the various agreements between countries can result in these people being treated like human pinballs. In Australia, the reality of being refused readmission to another country can be indefinite detention: see chapters 8 and 10. Some of the difficulties in using devices to deflect refugees and asylum seekers are discussed in chapters 6, 7 and 9.

Conclusion

Historically, Australia has acted as a model global citizen in its assistance to refugees. Relative to population size, Australia and Canada have been two of the largest recipients of refugees since 1945. Australia is still one of only 10 countries among the 191 member states of the United Nations that persistently provides an annual offshore refugee resettlement quota in addition to accepting onshore arrivals. In recent years, Australia has offered protection to people from 55 different countries.

Unfortunately, over this same period, in the case of *onshore* refugees, Australia has significantly undermined its tradition of compassion and humanitarian assistance. The new reality of Australian refugee law owes much to changes in the movement of people around the world that are sharply at odds with traditional expectations of immigration control. Refugees are increasingly aware of the protections offered by international law. Ease of international travel – by regular or irregular means – has made refugees more mobile than ever before. It is to these matters that this book now turns.

References and further reading

Patrick Barkham, "The other Howard's way won't work here", *Guardian* (UK), 25 January 2005

Mary Crock, "The Refugee Convention at 50: Mid-life Crisis or Terminal Inadequacy? An Australian Perspective" in Susan Kneebone (ed), *The Refugees Convention 50 Years On: Globalisation and International Law* (Ashgate, Hampshire, 2003)

DIMA, "Fact Sheet 60: Australia's Refugee and Humanitarian Program": <www.-immi.gov.au/facts/60refugee.htm>

DIMA, "Overview: Migration to Australia": <www.immi.gov.au/migration/index.htm#migration>

Guy Goodwin Gill, "Definitions and Descriptions" in *The Refugee in International Law* (2nd ed, Clarendon Press, Oxford, 1996)

Refugee Council of Australia, "Submission to the 2000-2001 Refugee and Humanitarian Program Size And Composition Review: Views from the Community Sector": <www.refugeecouncil.org.au/html/resources/subhumpro.html>

Dennis Shanahan, "Border protection has led to a bigger (legal) migrant intake", *The Australian,* 15 July 2005

Senator Amanda Vanstone, "Media Release: Migration Program", 9 February 2005: <www.minister.immi.gov.au/migration>

3

The Essence of Control: Australia's Experience of Irregular Migration and Asylum Seekers

Key Points in this Chapter

- Australia's history and geography have given the country an enviable ability to control immigration. Most non-citizens in Australia without permission are people who "overstay" the time limit on their visa.
- People who arrive in Australia by boat without authorisation make up only a small fraction of those present in Australia without permission.
- The highest numbers of "unlawful non-citizens" come (in order) from Britain, the United States and China.
- Over the past 10 years, almost equal numbers of unauthorised arrivals have travelled by boat as by aeroplane.
- Most refugee claimants who travel by plane enter lawfully with a visa. However, Australian law permits some unlawful non-citizens to apply to DIMA for refugee status if they fear persecution at home.
- A higher proportion of people who have come to Australia by boat, as opposed to by plane, have been recognised as refugees.
- Australia's experience of asylum seekers coming by boat has been recent and episodic, reflecting disturbances in the region and the opening of people-smuggling routes. Groups of boat people first came to Australia from Vietnam in the late 1970s, then from Cambodia in 1989. Boat people came from China after the Tiananmen Square massacre and the crackdown on the pro-democracy movement. The late 1990s saw people smuggled through Indonesia from Iran, Iraq, Afghanistan, Sri Lanka and other troubled countries. In 2006, a small number arrived from West Papua.
- Australia takes in few undocumented arrivals and asylum seekers, both in absolute terms and per head of population.
- Since 2001, there has been a significant drop in the number of refugees globally, which was also reflected in Australia's experience.

Irregular migrants in Australia

Australia is an island continent that shares no land borders with any other country. It is geographically remote and remains difficult to access. It is also a large country with a small population of 20 million, concentrated in coastal urban centres, entry into which (by air or by sea) is highly regulated. As noted in chapter 1, these factors have meant that Australia has always enjoyed remarkable control of its borders and immigration processes. This continues to be the case, even though pressures of globalisation and ease of travel mean that Australia has not completely escaped the growth of undocumented immigration and the increase in mobile asylum seekers.

The population of non-citizens in Australia without permission has remained fairly stable over recent years at around 50–60,000 people. This number is made up of two broad groups, which are each divided in turn into two sub-groups. The first category covers non-citizens in Australia without a valid visa and includes persons who arrive without a visa and individuals who stay longer than the time allowed on their temporary visas. The second group covers non-citizens whose visas are cancelled, either because of something they did or said *before* coming to Australia, or because of their behaviour *after* coming to the country.

The largest group is the "visa overstayers". These are non-citizens who come as tourists, students or visitors and remain after their visas expire. Of the estimated 47,800 non-citizens in Australia without permission in mid-2005, 40,600 (or 85%) arrived on visitor visas. In mid-2005, 600,000 non-citizens were in Australia on temporary visas. Many overstayers only extend their stay in Australia by a few days or weeks before leaving voluntarily. However, 32% of the overstayers in mid-2005 had been in Australia for more than 10 years, 44% between three and 10 years, 10% between one and two years, and 14% for less than one year.

In 2004-05, DIMA located only 18,341 unlawful non-citizens, or about one-third of all visa overstayers estimated to be living in Australia. The nationals most frequently located in that year were Chinese (2,735) followed by Indonesians (1,233), Koreans (1,164), Malaysians (1,068) and Indians (1,022). Nationals of the United Kingdom, who comprise the highest number of overstayers, ranked sixth in the number of overstayers located, with only 919 people detected. The next largest groups of nationalities located were Fijians (751), Filipinos (715), people from Hong Kong (580) and Thais (567). Nationals of the United States, who are the second largest group of overstayers, did not rank in the top 10 nationalities of overstayers detected in 2004-05. These statistics suggest that persons with Anglo-Saxon features continue to be less "visible" to immigration control officials. Conversely, if the experience of Vivian Solon-Alvarez is any indication, Australians of colour and of non-Anglo-Saxon background are more likely to have their immigration status questioned (see further chapter 9).

Top 10 Countries of Origin of Overstayers at 30 June 2003*

Country	Male	Female	Total
UK	3,700	2,500	6,200
USA	3,400	2,300	5,700
China, PRC	2,700	1,200	3,900
Philippines	2,100	1,100	3,200
Indonesia	2,000	1,100	3,100
Japan	1,500	1,400	2,900
Rep Korea	1,600	1,200	2,800
Malaysia	1,400	700	2,100
Germany	1000	700	1,700
Thailand	800	900	1,700

Source: DIMA Fact Sheet 86 (statistics removed in 2004-05)

A government review in 2000 found that most visa overstayers probably work illegally to support their stay in Australia, mostly in the hospitality, agricultural, manufacturing, retail and construction industries. In February 2004, a free telephone "dob in" hotline was launched to encourage people to contact DIMA should they become aware of illegal workers or visa overstayers. Despite this, only 3,870 illegal workers were located by DIMA in 2004-05, although employers have been increasingly issued with warning notices by DIMA. Paradoxically, labour shortages in some Australian industries have led employers to lobby the government to regularise the employment status of unlawful non-citizens. Acknowledging their economic contribution, in late 2005 the US President proposed to offer three-year guest worker visas to the 13 million unlawful immigrants in the United States. Workers are also less likely to be exploited if they have the protections of legal status.

Australia's experience of *unauthorised* arrivals (those who arrive without a valid visa) is much more limited, although it is this second subgroup that attracts most attention and resources. While roughly equal numbers of unauthorised arrivals have come to Australia by plane as by boat, "boat people" have generated most concern. Australia's response is not unique: boat people always seem to cause inordinate concern for countries, whether because of the potential for larger scale incursions by un-checked invaders, or because of some deeper cultural fear.

The statistics on "boat" arrivals in Australia are given most often from 1989. Australia has always received very small numbers of stowaways (14 in 2004-05) and seafarer deserters (36 in that year) from the many passenger and cargo ships arriving by sea in Australia each year (340,000 passengers and crew arrived by sea in 2004-05). The first boat carrying predominantly asylum seekers arrived on 30 November 1989, after a pause of some 10 years. In fact, Australia's first real experience of "boat people" and direct asylum seekers occurred after the Vietnam War.

Between April 1976 and April 1981, 2,087 Vietnamese arrived in boats on the north coast of Australia. These people were treated very differently from the asylum seekers who have arrived in more recent years. All were granted permanent residency, either immediately upon arrival or in the course of amnesties that were offered in 1976 and 1981. None was placed in immigration detention.

Between 1989 and July 2004, 13,593 non-citizens arrived in Australia without permission on 159 boats. On board the first boat (code named the "Pender Bay" - see below) were 26 Cambodians (one child was later born in detention). In the years immediately following the numbers of people transported on individual boats ranged from 10 to 110. Between 1989 and 1992, the number of boat people totalled 654, with a further 30 children born in detention. This block of post-Vietnam boat people are of particular significance because, although small in number, they represent the genesis of Australia's policy of mandatory immigration detention. By the time the "issue" of the Cambodian boat people was resolved (through a deal involving their repatriation and sponsored return), the first arrivals had spent more than four years in detention. The whole affair cost Australian taxpayers millions of dollars and saw the development of major conflict between the (Labor) government and the federal courts, which led in turn to restrictions on judicial oversight of immigration matters that have continued ever since.

At the height of the influx of asylum seekers in 1999-2000, a total of 1,695 people were refused entry at Australian airports and 4,175 people arrived without visas on 74 boats. In 2000-01, 1,508 people were refused entry at airports and 4,141 people arrived without authority on 54 boats. The number of unauthorised arrivals dropped sharply in 2001-02, following the *Tampa* affair and the institution of a blockade against asylum seekers known as "Operation Relex". Over that financial year 1,277 people arrived on seven boats (most before December-January), with 1,193 coming by plane. The number of unlawful air arrivals dropped further in 2002-03 when 937 people were refused entry at Australia's airports, rising to 1,241 in 2003-04 and 1,632 in 2004-05 (amounting to about 0.01% of the 10.4 million air arrivals that year).

While some people are refused immigration clearance at airports because they had no passport or visa or carried "improper" documents (8% of those refused in 2004-05), most are refused entry because they were judged not to be "bona fide" travellers (75%). That is, they were found to be at risk of overstaying their visa or otherwise likely to breach the conditions imposed on their visit (such as by illegally working or studying). A small number of people is refused entry for other reasons such as failing health or character checks (17%). Almost all unlawful air arrivals are removed within 72 hours (98% in 2004-05), usually on the next available flight. The airlines which bring these people to Australia are usually fined, with 993 infringement notices imposed on airlines in 2004-05, down from a high of 5,048 in 1999-2000.

The Australian government also has "Airline Liaison Officers" at 18 key airports overseas, who work with local authorities and airlines to identify people who do not have permission to enter Australia. This pre-emptive screening process resulted in airlines refusing to board 179 people in 2004-05. The problem with this procedure is that it could prevent asylum seekers from reaching Australia to make a refugee claim, even though proper documentation is not legally necessary to claim asylum in Australia. It places Australia at risk of breaching its international obligations not to return a person to a place of persecution, by rejecting them at a "virtual" frontier. In the *Prague Airport* case (2004), the UK House of Lords found that the UK practice of installing its immigration officers at Prague airport in the Czech Republic was racially discriminatory towards Roma ("gypsy") people who sought to leave that country to seek asylum in the UK.

Although no unauthorised boats successfully landed on Australian soil in 2002-03, there has been a modest number of boat people since that time who have made it through Australia's defences. In 2003-04 the *Hao Kiet* made landfall in Darwin with 53 Vietnamese on board. All sought asylum and were transferred to Christmas Island for the processing of their claims (even though they had a legal right to be processed on mainland Australia). All were eventually found to be refugees. Another boat, the *Minasa Bone*, also arrived at Melville Island north of Australia carrying 14 Turkish men. All were returned home without being allowed to enter Australia. In March 2004 a group of 15 people landed on the Ashmore Islands in the Indian Ocean. These people were all returned to Indonesia without being allowed to lodge asylum claims. The number of people either apprehended en route to Australia or arriving by boat has remained low. A handful of asylum seekers from West Timor were taken to Christmas Island for processing in 2005 and 43 people arrived from the Indonesian province of West Papua in January 2006. The decision to grant refugee status to 42 members of this group caused a major international incident, with Indonesia objecting vehemently. When Indonesia withdrew its ambassador from Australia, there were fears that it would also renege on arrangements associated with the border control measure of 2001. (Indonesia has been accommodating hundreds of refugees and asylum seekers who would otherwise have ended up in Australia.) As explored in chapter 7, Australia responded swiftly (if controversially) to the concerns expressed.

Although the total figures in the 1999-2002 period were higher than in most of the previous 10 years (as the table opposite shows), they were not alarmingly high by world standards. What concerned authorities were the numbers arriving in each boat and the (uncontrolled) mode of their arrival. A further 1,547 would-be unauthorised arrivals were deflected from Australia under the so-called "Pacific Strategy" after August 2001. In mid 2006, initiatives were taken to extend this program to cover all unauthorised boat arrivals, including those reaching mainland Australia (see further chapter 7).

Non-citizens in Australia without Permission 1989-2005

Year	Plane Arrivals	Boat Arrivals	Overstayers
2004-05	1,632	0	47,800
2003-04	1,241	82	51,000
2002-03	937	(14 excluded)	59,800
2001-02	1,277	1,193	60,000
2000-01	1,508	4,141	60,102
1999-2000	1,695	4,175	58,745
1998-99	2,106	920	53,143
1997-98	1,550	157	51,000
1996-97	1,350	365	45,100
1995-96	663	589	—
1994-95	485	1,071	—
1993-94	2,448 arrivals by air from 1989 to 1993	194	—
1992-93		194	—
1991-92		78	81,164
1990-91		158	—
1989-90		224	—
Total	12,437	13,503	N/A

Source: DIMA

Costs associated with immigration compliance

The greatest expense generated by Australia's immigration enforcement and compliance operations relates to the detention of unlawful non-citizens in Australia and the operation of the Pacific Strategy (see chapter 7). According to DIMA, $218 million was spent on the latter operations between August 2001 and July 2004: see Fact Sheet 76. However, the Minister for Immigration has also stated that more than $230 million was spent on building detention centres in 2000-02: see MPS 33/2002. Further, statistics supplied to a Parliamentary Estimates Committee in February 2004 suggest that the total costs of running mainland detention centres in 2003 amounted to $87 million: see further chapter 10.

From the data that is made public, it is difficult to work out how much the government is spending on immigration compliance and border control. Considering the number of irregular migrants intercepted, it is fair to say that the program is financially very expensive. In the budget papers for 2006-07, Immigration was allocated a total of $1.149 billion, of which $992,488,000 was set aside for "contributing to Australia's society and its economic advancement through the lawful and orderly entry and stay of people". As the table on the following page shows, large amounts are expended on compliance and border security measures, although substantial savings appear to be claimed in the moves to process people in Nauru (see amounts in parentheses). Unfortunately, the human cost of the program is also considerable - and not only because a substantial proportion of the irregular migrants intercepted are found ultimately to be refugees or in need of humanitarian assistance. This was acknowledged in 2006 with the allocation of $2.6 million for "long term detention health services delivery strategy".

Extracts from DIMA Summary of Expense Measures in the 2006-07 Budget (with Projections to 2009-10)

Measure	2006-07 $'000	2007-08 $'000	2008-09 $'000	2009-10 $'000
Detention services – implementation of review	5,803	5,126	–	–
Identity security – establishing new strike teams	344	353	357	364
Immigration compliance activities – enhancement	9,565	10,880	10,983	11,115
Long-term detention health services delivery strategy – implementation	2,652	2,049	1,567	1,586
Migration legislation – amendments	6,453	4,532	4,584	4,637
National security – enhancing the Regional Movement Alert List	2,582 add 787 (Capital injection)	2,539 add 154 (Capital injection)	2,198 add 156 (Capital injection)	2,289 add 158 (Capital injection)
Offshore processing strategy – Nauru	(4,336) (4,895) Admin; 559 DIMA expense	(9,577) (10,143) Admin; 566 DIMA expense	(9,821) (10, 396) Admin; 575 DIMA expense	10,072 (10,657) Admin; 559 DIMA expense
Prospective illegal immigrants – arrangements in transit countries	3,286	3,334	3,381	3,428
Securing border against Illegal Foreign Fishing – detention services	13,443	13,519	11,272	11,407
Detention facilities – new long term onshore detention strategy	11,997 (Capital expenditure)	(1,707) (Capital expenditure)	(36,637) (Capital expenditure)	(85,278) (Capital expenditure)
Systems for people-ensuring well trained and supported staff (IT improvements)	70,036	23,583	23,067	19,636

Available through <www.budget.gov.au/>

Comparative experiences of irregular migration

By world standards, Australia has never had a serious undocumented immigration problem. It was estimated that there were 3 million irregular migrants in the European Union in 2004-05, with up to 500,000 new undocumented arrivals each year. In 2005, the Pew Hispanic Centre estimated that the United States hosted up to 11 million unauthorised migrants, with 750,000 illegal migrants entering each year. Britain detected around 38,000 irregular migrants trying to enter it in 2003.

Although these countries have larger populations than Australia, as a proportion of population most still receive many more undocumented migrants than Australia, partly because of the porous land and sea borders which the US and the EU share with neighbouring countries such as Mexico, Turkey and the North African region (including Morocco and Tunisia). While Australia's good fortune is no reason for it to lessen its vigilance, the relatively small size of the problem in Australia raises questions about the proportionality of its restrictive responses.

The available evidence is that irregular migration is prompted more by "push" factors (such as war, disaster or lack of opportunity) and by opportunity (the ability to move) than by anything a receiving state does or does not do. Australia's geographical isolation, lack of land borders and the limited means of gaining access to the country have been the principal reasons for its success in controlling immigration. In recent times, it is also clear that the interdiction program to stop boats coming from Indonesia was instrumental in stopping the flow of asylum seekers through that country. On the other hand, the evidence is more mixed about the deterrent effect of Australia's mandatory detention regime.

Refugees and irregular immigration

A fair proportion of the world's undocumented migrants leave their country of origin to escape persecution or because life in their home country has become intolerable. Australia is one of a number of developed countries sought out by such people because of its reputation as a place of peace and prosperity, where the human rights of individuals are respected and refugees are recognised and protected.

Yet, it is also true that more and more people are using onshore refugee protection regimes as an alternative migration route, as the options for legal migration become increasingly narrow and unattainable. Unscrupulous agents sometimes lure potential migrants with promises of riches and high lifestyles. For victims of such scams the reality of the refugee determination processes in many countries is a rude shock. The system in Australia is no exception.

After arriving in Australia, many non-citizens who enter without a visa or on false documents lodge applications for asylum. Most air arrivals claim asylum after entering the country rather than immediately upon arrival: only 40 applications for protection visas were made at Australian airports in 2004-05. Asylum claims are processed by DIMA as part of the onshore refugee program. The determination process attempts to work out which applicants meet the international definition of a refugee, and which do not: see chapters 5 and 6. Some applicants who fail to meet the refugee definition are nevertheless identified as people facing particular risks and may be accepted on humanitarian grounds: see chapter 6.

As noted earlier, Australia has the third largest formal resettlement program of refugees per capita in the world. Refugees under this program are processed offshore in refugee camps overseas. In terms of the total number of "refugees" cared for by Australia each year, however, Australia's record does not look so generous for the simple reason that few people seek asylum from within the country. According to UNHCR, 3,100 people applied for asylum in Australia in 2004, compared with 40,200 in Britain, 61,600 in France, 35,610 in Germany, 25,500 in Canada and 52,360 in the US. The table below shows the number of asylum claims submitted in some of the main industrialised countries between 2000 and 2004:

Asylum Applications Lodged 2000-04

Country	Asylum Claims	Per 1000 residents
Australia	38,700	2
Austria	144,810	17.9
Belgium	118,350	11.5
Canada	175,230	5.6
Czech Republic	52,550	5.1
Denmark	38,590	7.2
France	279,190	4.7
Germany	324,150	3.9
Ireland	45,730	11.7
Italy	64,660	1.1
Netherlands	118,330	7.4
Norway	67,010	14.8
Slovak Republic	41,120	7.6
Spain	35,020	0.9
Sweden	127,350	14.4
Switzerland	99,430	13.9
United Kingdom	393,830	6.7
United States	411,660	1.4
All EU 25 countries	1,923,640	4.2
All 5 Nordic countries	248,430	10.3
Total (50 countries)	2,793,660	2.1

Source: UNHCR

The number of asylum claims in *industrialised* countries only reflects a small proportion of the total number of refugees needing protection world wide. In many *developing* countries, there are enormous refugee camps "ware-housing" hundreds of thousands of refugees. Most camps are run by UNHCR and other relief agencies. The people in these camps do not usually apply for asylum in the countries where the camps are located. Normally they wait for a chance to safely return to their home countries. However, they are still a large financial burden on the limited resources of the temporary host countries. The top two asylum countries at the end of 2004 were Iran, which was home to approximately 1,046,000 asylum seekers, and Pakistan, which supported 960,600 people. As the following table shows, Australia does not rate amongst the leading countries for accommodating refugees. The countries with the greatest arrivals of asylum seekers in 2004 were Chad (131,000) (due to attacks on civilians by Arab militias and government soldiers in the Darfur region of Sudan), Burundi (20,700), Yemen (16,600), Uganda (15,500), Rwanda (14,100), the Syrian Arab Republic (12,000) and Liberia (5,500).

Main Countries of Asylum, 2004

Iran	1,046,000
Pakistan	960,600
Germany	876,622
Tanzania	602,100
United States	420,900
China	299,400
United Kingdom	289,100
Serbia and Montenegro	276,700
Chad	259,900
Uganda	250,500

Source: UNHCR

The number of people recognised as refugees varies greatly according to the nationality and circumstances of those seeking asylum. Over the years, many more people have failed in their refugee claims than have succeeded. Asylum seekers from Iraq and Afghanistan in the late 1990s – before foreign intervention in those countries – represented exceptions, with success rates close to 100%.

This does not mean that all those who fail are abusing the system. Many fear persecution if they are forced to return home. However, for various reasons they do not meet the strict terms of the Refugee Convention. Unlike other countries of asylum, Australia does not have an onshore visa program for these near-miss cases (although it did have until 1989). The only option now is to seek the personal intervention of the Minister for Immigration: see chapters 5 and 6.

Changing attitudes to boat people

Australia has experienced the arrival of boat people in fairly well-defined phases. The first group arrived in northern Australia in the late 1970s and early 1980s, fleeing after the end of the Vietnam War in 1975. Around 2,000 Vietnamese arrived in Australia by boat in 1981. These unauthorised arrivals were in addition to the 43,000 refugees Australia agreed to resettle as part of a regional crisis management plan known as the Comprehensive Plan of Action (CPA).

The Vietnamese refugees included people who had worked with the defeated South Vietnamese government, who were allies of American or other Western forces, or had fled Vietnam after being suspected of collaboration. All considered themselves at risk of persecution by the new communist government of Vietnam (formerly North Vietnam). These boat people were accepted automatically as refugees by Australia and made new lives in the community. As a combatant in the Vietnam War, Australia felt obliged to help protect Vietnamese at risk of persecution as a result of their assistance to Western armed forces. Public sympathy for the refugees was high. Politicians were careful not to sensationalise the refugees' irregular mode of entry into the country.

In 1979, a new conflict erupted in the region when the Vietnamese army invaded Cambodia, deposing the genocidal government of Pol Pot. People fleeing this conflict – and persecution by the Khmer Rouge – also came to Australia as boat people. Most fled when the Vietnamese army withdrew from Cambodia and the United Nations organised elections under the Paris Peace Plan, with which Australia was closely involved. Although this UN operation was a significant foreign affairs achievement, it seems to have coloured Australia's approach to the Cambodian refugees who arrived in Australia from 1989. From this time, Australia became increasingly hostile to, and obsessed with, boat people.

The Cambodian boat people were not immediately accepted as refugees. Senator Evans and Prime Minister Bob Hawke labelled them "economic migrants" on the basis that conflict in Cambodia was under control. The Cambodians were placed in detention centres. When refugee advocates challenged their removal in the courts and later sought their release from detention, the Parliament passed laws making the detention of unauthorised arrivals mandatory, and limiting the role of the courts in reviewing detention decisions: see chapter 10.

A further complicating factor in the late 1980s was the unrest in the People's Republic of China. Following the violent repression of the pro-democracy movement in 1989, Australia gave shelter to many refugees from that country. Sympathetic measures were taken by the Hawke government to grant protection to almost 30,000 Chinese nationals, who were either in Australia as students at the time or who arrived shortly after the repression began, although not all of these were strictly refugees.

Boat people, however, continued to be treated with suspicion. The events in China were compounded by the decision in the early 1990s to close the refugee camps in South East Asia which were housing the remaining Vietnamese refugees and others displaced economically by the war. As a refugee resettlement country, Australia was part of this regional CPA process. Slum clearing measures against Sino-Vietnamese people in southern China brought the next boat people to Australia. Australia's response was to pass laws preventing these people from seeking refuge in Australia, on the basis that individuals covered by the CPA were either not refugees or had other countries where they could receive protection.

Ethnicity of Boat People from 1989 to January 2001

Iraqi	2,773		Indian	28
Afghani	2,478		Kurdish	20
Chinese	1,855		East Timorese	18
Sino-Vietnamese	1,112		Kuwaiti	17
Iranian	572		Macau	13
Cambodian	318		Romanian	12
Turkish	195		Indonesian	11
Palestinian	138		Polish	11
Bangladeshi	95		Moroccan	9
Vietnamese	82		Lebanese	9
Sri Lankan	81		Jordanian	6
West Papuan	51		Other	113
Syrian	40		Stateless	3
Pakistani	36		Unknown	3,120
Algerian	28		Australian births	109
			Total Arrivals	**10,225**

Recent boat people: Central Asia and the Middle East

The boat people who arrived in Australia towards the end of the 1990s represented a new phase, since they came from countries more remote from Australia. These asylum seekers fled from the oppressive regimes of Saddam Hussein in Iraq and the Taliban in Afghanistan. In 2000-01, 2,271 Afghans and 992 Iraqis arrived without permission by boat, while a further 213 Afghans and 869 Iraqis arrived in the second half of 2001. The treatment of people in both of those countries was considered so serious by Australia that it became one of the justifications for invading Afghanistan in 2001 and Iraq in 2003, as part of the US-led coalition.

Unlike the earlier boat people from Cambodia and China, the overwhelming majority of arrivals since 1998 have been recognised as refugees. Ninety-five per cent of Afghans and 90% of Iraqis were approved as refugees in 1999-2000. Almost half of all asylum seekers from Iran and Palestine were also granted refugee status in 1999-2001. Overall,

87% of people who arrived unauthorised by boat between 1999 and 2003 were granted refugee status.

The higher acceptance rate of the more recent arrivals does not mean that Australia has been more generous. On the contrary, Australia has downgraded the protection offered to refugees who arrive without permission. Boat people continue to be detained until their claims for refugee status are assessed. Those accepted as refugees now only receive temporary protection and enjoy fewer rights: see chapter 7. Compared with other countries, Australia's rate of recognising asylum seekers as refugees remains low.

The serious human rights violations, war crimes and crimes against humanity committed by the Taliban regime in Afghanistan and by Saddam Hussein's Baathist party in Iraq are well known. Since the fall of those regimes, persecution of particular religious and ethnic groups, and of some women, continues in various forms in both countries, whether at the hands of the authorities or by private armed groups. In Afghanistan, the Hazara people (predominantly Shia Muslims) have long been marginalised by Afghan governments and discriminated against by other Afghans. They suffered particularly from violence, persecution and displacement at the hands of the Taliban regime (Sunni Muslims). The new Afghan government has little power outside the capital cities and the country continues to be ruled by warlords and plagued by ongoing military and tribal violence.

Many refugees returned to Afghanistan after the fall of the Taliban in 2001. However, this does not necessarily signal that the country is safe. As Amnesty International reports, most refugees are returning from Iran and Pakistan because they have no viable alternative protection in those countries. In December 2003, new information about the instability led UNHCR to reprocess the claims of Afghans who had been found not to be refugees but who had remained on Nauru. In 2004, UNHCR and Australia recognised that there are still strong grounds for believing that Hazaras could be subject to persecution if returned to Afghanistan. DIMA began reassessing the refugee claims of Afghan nationals in mainland detention centres in July 2004.

East Timorese asylum seekers in Australia

Before the escalation of conflict in East Timor in late 1999, around 1,600 East Timorese had applied for asylum in Australia. Many of these had been waiting for up to 10 years without success. Australia argued for many years that, because Portugal was the former colonial power controlling East Timor, the East Timorese held Portuguese nationality and should apply for protection in Portugal.

The Federal Court rejected this argument in 1998, noting that East Timorese are not automatically regarded as Portuguese citizens; that there was no clearly recognised right to citizenship; and that the fact of nationality itself may not guarantee protection from persecution.

Although the government appealed the decision, the eruption of conflict in East Timor in late 1999 put international pressure on Australia to accept the East Timorese as refugees, which it did – but only on a temporary safe haven basis: see chapter 8. The conflict in East Timor led the government to create a broader visa class for non-citizens needing temporary safe haven in Australia.

In the post-election violence in September–October 1999, an estimated 250,000 people were displaced within East Timor, while a further 290,000 people fled into West Timor. Very small numbers of refugees were brought to Darwin during this time, until the Australian-led INTERFET force made East Timor secure.

In the meantime, Australia passed a law ensuring that people could not apply for refugee status in Australia where they have the capacity to seek or hold citizenship in another country: see chapter 7. This law may prevent the courts from further considering the effectiveness of Portuguese nationality for East Timorese asylum seekers. As East Timor struggles to re-establish itself as a liberal democracy, with outbreaks of violence in mid-2006, asylum claims may continue to be made by East Timorese.

Boat people from West Papua

By far the most controversial asylum seekers to have arrived in Australia by boat in recent times are the handful of people who have made it to mainland Australia from West Timor (in 2005) and West Papua (in February 2006). Of the 43 West Papuans, 42 were granted refugee status almost immediately, causing something of a diplomatic rift in relations with Indonesia (the remaining person was also recognised as a refugee but told that he should seek protection in Japan). Indonesia had been very upset by what it saw as Australia's change of heart over the issue of Indonesian sovereignty in East Timor. It asserted that the grant of refugee status to West Papuans signalled Australia's renewed intervention in internal Indonesian affairs. It feared that Australia was throwing its support behind the separatist movement in the province of West Papua.

As explored in chapter 7, the affair highlights the challenges posed by the international protection regime for refugees. The grant of asylum is rarely free of politics. According to John Wing and Peter King (see CPAC Report 2005), military operations in the Papuan Highlands caused the displacement of more than 11,000 Papuans between 2003-05, with much destruction of personal and community property. They allege that activists have been killed, tortured and gaoled for up to 15 years for dissent – even in the form of raising the Papuan flag.

Australia has been sensitive to the situation in West Papua for many years. When Indonesia gained its independence from the Netherlands in 1949, Papua was not part of the post-colonial settlement. It was not until 1962 that Australia began to support Indonesian claims to this region. Under the government of Robert Menzies in the 1950s, emphasis was placed on the fact that the predominantly Christian Papuans had little in common with Muslim Indonesia. A UN-organised plebiscite to decide the province's political future was plagued by irregularities. Since 1962, the view has been that it is preferable strategically to support Indonesian sovereignty over the province. As in East Timor (where there are rich oil and gas reserves offshore), the issue in Papua is partly economic. The province is rich in mineral deposits and has become a very significant source of revenue for the government in Indonesia. Australia is well aware of these matters and has no desire to support the independence movement in West Papua, even if it is concerned about the human rights abuses occurring in the province.

Illegal fishers from Indonesia

A recent group of "boat people" causing concern are Indonesians fishing without permission inside Australia's Exclusive Economic Zone (EEZ), which extends 200 nautical miles into the ocean from Australia's coastline. While limited forms of traditional fishing are allowed in parts of Australian waters under agreements with Indonesia and Papua New Guinea, organised commercial foreign fishing presents quarantine, conservation, environmental and security risks, with fishers particularly targeting shark fin and reef fish for Asian markets.

Illegal foreign fishers are detained under the *Fisheries Management Act 1991* on enforcement visas for up to seven days while the authorities investigate any fisheries offences and decide whether to prosecute. On release from fisheries detention, their enforcement visas expire and they become unlawful non-citizens liable to detention and removal under the *Migration Act 1958.* Most illegal foreign fishers are detained in Darwin or on Horn Island in the Torres Strait, and in 2005 the government announced that a temporary facility on a former military base would be developed into a permanent detention centre.

In 2004-05, 1,485 illegal foreign fishers were apprehended for suspected fisheries offences, of which 1,417 were removed and the few remaining were subject to prosecution or were convicted. There are around 70 prosecutions each year, with sentences ranging from 30 days to two years in prison. Usually only the master (not the crew) is charged. The boats, catch and gear are forfeited, although the owners may pay a bond to retrieve a vessel before it is destroyed. Those not charged are removed from Australia as soon as practicable, with an average detention period of 7-10 days since 2004 (down from 4-6 weeks previously). Few of these people apply for asylum in Australia. For a discussion of the detention arrangements for these people, see chapter 9.

Decline in the number of refugees

Fewer asylum seekers sought protection in Australia between 2002 and 2005. The Australian government has attributed this drop to its restrictive policies such as immigration detention and temporary protection visas.

Whilst these restrictive policies may have had an obvious impact on boat arrivals, the decline in the number of asylum seekers in Australia is consistent with a reduction in the number of refugees globally. Similar trends can be seen in countries that have not adopted the Australian model of detention and temporary protection.

The total population of concern to UNHCR fell from 20.8 million people at the end of 2002 to 19.2 million at the end of 2004. UNHCR also recorded a drop in the global number of refugees from 10.6 million to 9.2 million persons. This was the fourth consecutive year in which the global refugee population had dropped sharply. Over the two years between 2002 and 2004, the global refugee population fell by 24%.

In 2004, the largest decreases in the refugee population were in Southern Africa, followed by West Africa, Europe, the Americas, Africa as a whole, South-West Asia, North Africa and the Middle East. In contrast, Central Africa and the Great Lakes region, East Africa and Horn of Africa, Asia, and the Pacific all recorded increases refugees.

UNHCR reports that the number of asylum seekers arriving in industrialised countries (368,000) fell sharply for the third consecutive year in 2004. Germany (35,610) recorded its lowest number of asylum seekers for a decade; the United States (52,360) and Switzerland (14,250) both experienced the lowest number of asylum seekers since 1987; and The Netherlands (9,780) recorded its lowest arrival of asylum seekers since 1988. UNHCR attributed these reductions to changes in the source countries of Iraq, Serbia and Montenegro, and Afghanistan, while emphasising that improvements in refugee source countries were fragile and that those countries required continuing aid and resources.

Between the hype and the reality

The media hype often surrounding the arrival of boat people exaggerates the significance of people entering Australia by sea without permission. The vast majority of unauthorised non-citizens in Australia are visa overstayers who entered the country lawfully - mainly by air. Most people who apply onshore for refugee status arrive on a valid visa and then apply to change their status. Of those who arrive without a visa, most have traditionally come by air rather than by boat. It was only in 1999-2001 that unauthorised boat arrivals outnumbered unauthorised air arrivals. The number of boat arrivals decreased again significantly in 2002-04, in line with a global drop in refugee numbers.

Why then is there so much concern about boat people? There is no evidence that they present a greater threat to Australia than other unauthorised non-citizens. On the contrary, statistics suggest that boat people are much more likely to be recognised as refugees than people who enter Australia lawfully. For example, only 21 out of 937 people who arrived in Australia by plane without permission in 2002-03 applied for asylum. In comparison, the overwhelming majority of people who arrive by boat and seek protection and are recognised as refugees. This has been the case throughout the history of boat people in Australia.

References and further reading

Australia's Fisheries Management Authority, "Illegal foreign fishing - Illegal, unreported and unregulated foreign fishing (IUU)": <www.afma.gov.au/management/compliance/illegal/default.htm>

Australian Senate Legal and Constitutional Legislation Committee, Questions Taken on Notice Additional Estimates Hearing: 17 February 2004

Background Briefing: "Politically Pesky Papuans" ABC Radio National, 9 April 2006, <www.abc.net.au/rn/talks/bbing/stories/s1608850.htm>

DIMA publications available at: <www.immi.gov.au>

DIMA, *Managing the Border: Immigration Compliance* 2004-05 Edition

DIMA, "Fact Sheet 86. Overstayers and People in Breach of Visa Conditions"

DIMA, "Immigration Dob-In Line"

DIMA, "Fact Sheet 75. Processing Unlawful Boat Arrivals"

MIMIA, "MPS 33/2002 Offshore Processing Developments and Related Savings"

UNHCR, "2004 Global Refugee Trends Overview of Refugee Populations, New Arrivals, Durable Solutions, Asylum-Seekers, Stateless and Other Persons of Concern to UNHCR", 17 June 2005: <www.unhcr.org/Statistics>

UNHCR, "Asylum Levels and Trends in Industrialized Countries: 2004 Overview of Asylum Applications Lodged in Europe and Non-European Industrialized Countries in 2004"

John Wing and Peter King, *Genocide in West Papua: The role of the Indonesian State apparatus and a current needs assessment of the Papuan people.* Report published by the Centre for Peace and Conflict Studies, the University of Sydney, 2005, <http://www.arts.usyd.edu.au/centres/cpacs/WestPapuaGenocideRpt.05.pdf> (CPAC Report 2005)

Cases

Prague Airport Case [2004] UKHL 55

4

People Smuggling and People Trafficking

Key Points in this Chapter

- People smuggling and people trafficking both involve the unauthorised movement of people across national borders. "Trafficking" involves the enslavement or exploitation of those people after their arrival.
- People smuggling and people trafficking are lucrative criminal enterprises, worth an estimated US$10 billion per year internationally. People smugglers allegedly charge between $3,800 and $40,000 per person for organising travel to Australia.
- The travel provided by people smugglers can be unsafe. The most tragic recent example in Australia's region is the sinking of the "SIEV-X" on 19 October 2001 with the loss of 353 lives.
- Australia's efforts to combat people smuggling include border control measures; criminal offences with harsh penalties; overseas advertising and "disruption" campaigns; and improved boat and document identification mechanisms.
- Periodic incidents of people smuggling into Australia are partly due to a breakdown in the international system of protection for refugees. Although people smuggling is exploitative and criminal, it exists because there is a strong demand for it among people fleeing from persecution who do not have ready access to "regular" migration.
- No reliable statistics on people trafficking in Australia are available. This may be because those trafficked usually enter by plane, on a visa. They do not immediately identify themselves by claiming asylum.
- In October 2003 Australia introduced an anti-trafficking package, which created two new visa sub-classes to protect victims who assist in the investigation and prosecution of people traffickers.

Defining "smuggling" and "trafficking"

The Department of Immigration defines "people smuggling" as the organised illegal movement of people to another country, for profit, "when there is a lack of economic opportunity, a reduced availability for legitimate migration and the lure of better lifestyle": see Fact Sheet 83.

This definition fails to mention that many people who are smuggled are refugees in need of protection. In some cases, paying people smugglers is necessary to escape from persecution to a safe country. Australia's stance on asylum seekers who arrive without visas highlights the problem of a growing criminal industry that exploits the misery and desperation of people at risk in their home countries. Most of the recent boat people paid people smugglers to bring them to Australia. These people were often told by people smugglers that they would be allowed to stay in Australia when they arrived, even if they were not refugees.

People smuggling is different from "people trafficking", although the two can be related. Trafficked persons are often smuggled into countries. The main difference is that trafficked people are brought into a country by people intending to exploit or somehow benefit from them, such as by forcing them into prostitution or forced labour. In contrast, smuggled migrants usually have no continuing relationship with the persons responsible for their transport to the country. There is, however, considerable confusion and inter-changing of these terms. One reason for this is because in many cases trafficked and smuggled people are fleeing for the same reasons. Trafficked people are also distinguishable in many cases because they have no control over their travel (including choice of destination). In practice, trafficked and smuggled people can both be legitimate refugees. In international law, the UN Protocol on Trafficking in Persons (2000) defines people trafficking as:

> the recruitment, transportation, transfer, harbouring, or receipt of persons, by means of threat or use of force or other forms of coercion, of abduction of fraud, of deception, of the abuse of power of a position of vulnerability or of the giving or receiving of payment or benefits to achieve the consent of a person for the purpose of exploitation. Exploitations shall include, at a minimum, the exploitation of the prostitution of others or other forms of sexual exploitation, forced labor or services, slavery or practices similar to slavery, servitude or the removal of organs.

Australia has had, and continues to have, experience of both smuggled and trafficked people. In general, less attention has been paid to trafficking victims than to people smuggling. This may be because smuggling events are more visible, particularly in recent years when smugglers have conveyed increasingly large numbers of people to the country on leaky boats. Most trafficked people enter the country by plane with apparently valid (temporary) visas.

There is no doubt that people smuggling and people trafficking are significant problems. In the past 10 years the industries are believed to have become the third highest global income source for organised criminal groups, worth up to US$10 billion annually according to the International Organisation for Migration (IOM). The problem is growing because the criminals involved perceive smuggling to be low risk relative to potentially high profits. Up to 4 million people seek to migrate illegally around the world each year (according to the IOM in 1996), providing a large potential market for smugglers. It is alleged that people smugglers have charged between $3,800 and $40,000 per person for arranging illicit travel to Australia. The Australian Federal Police estimates that most people pay smugglers between US$1,500 and US$2,500 for a passage from Indonesia to Australia, with much more charged from the Middle East. Organised criminal groups in southern China, Singapore, Malaysia, Philippines, Lebanon, Jordan, Thailand and Indonesia have brought people from Afghanistan, the Middle East and North Africa to Australia.

Smugglers (and traffickers) are usually involved in other forms of crime, including document fraud, illegal prostitution and migration agent malpractice. Both forced and voluntary migrants make use of smugglers, whether to flee persecution, war, famine or environmental disaster, or to seek employment or a better life: see Andreas Schloenhardt, "The Business of Migration". Smuggling and trafficking have grown and been arranged by organised crime because of factors such as the restriction of legal migration in developed countries, the growing demand for migration and the relatively low risks of detection: see Schloenhardt.

The international community has recently taken steps to combat people smuggling and trafficking. In 2000, the UN adopted a Convention Against Transnational Organized Crime, with two protocols attached: the Protocol against the Smuggling of Migrants, and the Protocol against Trafficking in Persons. Both Protocols require countries to criminalise people smuggling and people trafficking and to combat document fraud. Transnational organised crime was identified by the UN Secretary-General in 2005 as a key threat to human security, which all countries should take active steps to combat. As explained below, recent changes to Australian law reflect and implement these international obligations.

The human cost of smuggling

Smuggling operations can result in dreadful loss of human life, as when 58 people perished in a sealed cargo container on a truck entering the UK in 2000. In Australia's region, illegal travel has proved just as dangerous. The first Vietnamese boat people had to endure dreadful hardships and dangers in crossing the South China Sea in the 1970s. The more recent voyages from Indonesia to Australia's Ashmore Reef and Christmas Island and other Indian Ocean territories have also been hazardous. While the waters in these areas are not patrolled by the same number of vicious pirates who preyed on the Vietnamese refugees, pirates do operate in the Indian Ocean and near Indonesia. Other hazards of the journey have been the poor condition of the boats, overcrowding and treacherous seas and weather.

With the peak in the number of boat arrivals in the late 1990s, would-be asylum seekers faced heightened dangers induced by policy changes and intelligence initiatives in Australia. As explored in chapter 7, during this period the Australian government began to explore avenues to "disrupt" the flow of refugees by making it more difficult for smugglers to operate out of Indonesia. Former diplomat Tony Kevin argues that the incidence of larger smuggling operations after 1999, with more and more people being crammed onto un-seaworthy craft, reflected the elimination of smaller smuggling operations. The concentration of the "enterprise" into fewer hands would eventually make it easier for the Australian and Indonesian governments to engage in "sting" operations so as to drive the smugglers out of business.

In December 2000, Minister Ruddock announced that two boats, carrying 163 people, sank near Ashmore Reef. Although the passengers survived that incident, two women lost their lives when a boat caught fire off the same reef in the following year. According to one young survivor, the boat was being skippered by asylum seekers who were little more than boys, after the original captain and crew abandoned the vessel to avoid apprehension by Australian authorities. Initial reports suggested that the boat people set fire to the ship deliberately. Later indications were that the engine probably caught fire due to overheating when an attempt was made to out-run the Australian coast guard: see chapter 7.

The "SIEV-X" sinking

The most tragic maritime disaster in Australia's recent history involved a boat commanded by people smugglers that sank in international waters on 19 October 2001 with the loss of 353 lives. This incident occurred in the immediate aftermath of the *Tampa* affair that marked the beginning of an overt campaign by Australia to prevent asylum seekers from reaching its shores. Some people in Australia believe that the "SIEV X" disaster, as it became known, was a direct by-product of the harsh change in policy. As explored further in chapter 7, the precedent was set when a cargo vessel named *MV Tampa* was refused access to Australia when attempting to off-load 433 asylum seekers rescued from a sinking Indonesian boat. The company with whom the *Tampa* was registered lost precious time and money when the boat was caught up in a spectacular display of military and political strength by the Australian government. When the SIEV X foundered at sea, many believe that the *Tampa* affair had discouraged vessels in the area from rescuing the shipwreck victims.

By the middle of 2001, the practice of the Australian government was to track the progress of boats leaving Indonesia that were thought to be carrying asylum seekers. Such boats are referred to as "Suspected Illegal Entry Vessels" (or "SIEVs") and are given an identifying number. Although originally designated SIEV 4, the official version is that Australia's search and rescue authorities were not aware of the position of the ill-fated vessel when it sank. Accordingly, it became known as "SIEV X" (the unknown boat).

Inquiries into the disaster reveal that SIEV-X left Bandar Lampung in Indonesia on 18 October 2001 bound for Christmas Island. The boat was severely overloaded, leaving port with around 430 passengers and crew – more than four times the number of passengers it could safely carry into the heavy seas of the Sunda Strait. In spite of concerns about the boat's condition, only 10 passengers refused to board. There are claims that Indonesian police were protecting the people smugglers, forcing some passengers onto the boat at gunpoint. To add to the mystery, a small group of asylum seekers – Mandeans from Iraq – were permitted to disembark on an island in the Sunda Straight.

Fears about the boat's seaworthiness proved well founded. Almost from the start of the voyage passengers were required to bail out water flowing in through a long crack in the hull. On 19 October 2001, the engines on the boat stalled and the boat began to take in large amounts of water. The boat capsized and sank, leading to the deaths of 146 children, 142 women and 65 men.

Clinging to wreckage for more than 19 hours, survivors later claimed that during their overnight ordeal, various ships passed within sight and earshot of the wreckage. Some asylum seekers claimed that two vessels stopped and shone their lights on the survivors in the water before turning away without offering assistance. Although the evidence now points to SIEV X going down in an area covered by Australian search and rescue operations, a Senate inquiry into the disaster found no evidence of Australian knowledge of, or complicity in, the disaster.

The asylum seekers on the boat were Iraqi, Palestinian, Afghan and Algerian. UNHCR claims that at least 26 of those who drowned had been recognised as refugees before their voyage and had waited for years for another country to resettle them. Many of the women and children who drowned had family in Australia, commonly a father or husband who had been granted temporary protection (which does not allow family reunion). One Iraqi man in Australia on a TPV lost 14 members of his immediate and extended family.

One survivor of the disaster was Sondos Ismael, who received media attention after she lost three daughters in the tragedy. Mrs Ismael's husband, Ahmed Al Zalimi, had temporary protection as a refugee in Australia. After the accident, Mrs Ismael was taken to Indonesia where she sought in vain to be reunited with her husband so that the couple could mourn the loss of their children together. Mr Al Zalimi was informed that, because he only had temporary protection, he had no travel rights and would not be permitted to return to Australia if he left for Indonesia. Mrs Ismael was finally reunited with her husband in Australia in March 2002, five months after the death of their children.

All of the survivors from the SIEV-X were found to be refugees. Seven were accepted by Australia and admitted on temporary protection visas. The others were granted protection in Finland, Sweden, Norway and Canada. Australia was the only country to grant temporary protection to refugees from SIEV-X, thereby prolonging their uncertainty about the future.

The 19 October voyage of the SIEV X was organised by Egyptian-born Abu Quassey. Following the sinking of the vessel, this man served an eight-month prison sentence in Indonesia for visa offences. Egypt and Australia then both attempted to extradite Quassey but, according to the Indonesian Justice Minister, Egypt was more serious in its attempt. As a result, Abu Quassey was extradited to Egypt where he was sentenced in December 2003 to five years in jail for homicide for negligently causing death and another two years for aiding illegal migration. He was also ordered to pay a fine of 500 Egyptian pounds. On appeal, Quassey's sentence was reduced to five years and three months in prison.

The failure of the Australian government to extradite Quassey led to allegations that it did not wish an Australian court to examine Australia's alleged links to people-smuggling disruption programs. Australia responded that it could not seek to extradite Abu Quassey because its extradition agreement with Indonesia covers only crimes common to both countries, and Indonesia has no offences for people smuggling.

Abu Quassey's assistant, Khaleed Shanayf Daoed, was arrested and extradited from Sweden in May 2003. He was sentenced to nine years in jail by the Queensland Supreme Court in July 2005. The trial shed little further light on the events behind the tragedy of four years passed.

SIEV X: A Survivor's Account

Since the incident, we have been living the tragedy daily. I saw a couple crying, asking each other for forgiveness. The wife was saying "This cannot be true, it must be a nightmare". There were people crying out for water, others asking for forgiveness before they died. Even now, we cannot sleep because of the tragedy, it is more than we can bear.

The waves were three or four metres high, a mixture of fuel and saltwater. Anyone who swallowed it and was able to vomit was okay, but those who could not vomit died immediately by suffocation. It was a battle against the sea and the rain. By morning, most people had stopped talking, but many did not lose hope in God and continued to pray to God for salvation.

We saw many different tragedies, the floating dead bodies, those crying for their brothers, fathers, wives, children, etc. It was unimaginable ...

True, I lost three children and my wife, but the other 150 children [sic] are like my own too. Those who perished with their families have found reprieve; but as for us, we are mere empty shells, our souls went with them ...

I saw my entire family crying. To this day, I remember the scene ... my wife holding the 20 day old child and crying, not knowing what to do, and the children crying ...

When the boat capsized, I lost my sanity. I was weeping over my misfortune, that I did not die with them. I began searching for them. Every time I saw a child, I thought it was one of my children. My wife and children stayed under the boat, they never came out. I was not wearing a lifejacket. I was hitting at my head and lamenting my loss and praying for my own death. I was dragged under water three times, I do not know what kept pushing me up to stay alive.

Anywhere I placed my arm, a drowned child or woman would emerge and lift my arm and the surviving women would cry more.

I boarded the boat with 15 other family members, 9 drowned and 6 remained. We clung on to a plank of timber for 20 hours drifting in the water. Something I witnessed left a very strange impression, a baby with umbilical cord still attached to the mother was amongst those who drowned. There was 150 children on board, only 4 survived.

[The man broke down and could not continue his account.]

Source: Transcript of video interview with SIEV-X survivors at Bogor one week after the shipwreck. Translated by Keysar Trad. Submitted by Tony Kevin to the Senate Select Committee into a Certain Maritime Incident.

Australia's response to people smuggling

Legislative measures

The Australian government has taken a variety of steps to prevent people smuggling. In June 1999, it introduced 20-year jail terms and fines of up to $220,000 for people convicted of organising the illegal entry of five or more non-citizens in a group. Individual instances of smuggling became punishable by a maximum 10-year jail term and fines of up to $110,000. Other legislative changes increased government powers to seize, sell and destroy smuggling boats, while increased funding and powers were given to Coastwatch, Customs and the Navy to detect, pursue, intercept and search boats carrying suspected unauthorised entrants.

Two years later, these powers were increased further by the *Border Protection (Validation and Enforcement) Powers Act 2001*. This Act introduced a mandatory minimum sentence of five years for adults found guilty of people smuggling offences (eight years for repeat offenders). These powers were the legislative framework within which Australia conducted its interdiction and disruption operations from August 2001: see chapter 7.

The government also increased the number of immigration staff at key overseas posts and airports, and improved liaison with international intelligence agencies and foreign governments in the Asia-Pacific and the Middle East. New systems were trialled to identify false documents, and airline and customs staff were specially trained. In 2004-05, the government committed $9.7 million towards developing biometric technology to combat identity fraud at Australia's borders. The penalties imposed on airlines bringing people to Australia without proper travel documents were also increased from $2,000 to $3,000 per entrant. As discussed below, another key event occurred in May 2004 when Australia ratified the UN Convention Against Transnational Organised Crime.

Despite the strong legal framework against smuggling, there have been very few criminal convictions for smuggling offences. In 2004-05, there were 94 allegations of people smuggling but only one new prosecution, along with three convictions and five cases pending. In the previous year (2003-04), there were 128 allegations of smuggling but only eight new prosecutions and three convictions. The small number of prosecutions partly reflects the difficulties involved in obtaining evidence of transnational criminal activities spread across multiple jurisdictions.

Dissuasion through advertising

In October 1999 the Minister for Immigration launched an Overseas Information Campaign to discourage people from coming to Australia without permission. Videos featured pictures of crocodiles, sharks and snakes infesting Australia; a smuggling boat being burnt; an individual drowning in the ocean; and people being detained behind prison fences in the hot desert sun. The message of the advertisements stamped over the screen at the end of each segment was "It's Not Worth the Risk".

This advertising campaign could be seen as misleading because it stated baldly that boat people detected in Australia are simply detained and then removed. The campaign did not acknowledge that asylum seekers have the right to seek protection in Australia - even if they break domestic immigration laws. (In contrast, posters at Heathrow airport in the United Kingdom advise new arrivals of how to claim asylum.) The campaign also failed to note that many boat people are eventually recognised as refugees and accepted into the community. In fact, the vast majority of boat people who have made it to Australia over the years have succeeded in their attempts to stay in the country.

Another anti-smuggling campaign the following year tried to deter asylum seekers by stating that Australians are racist towards people who arrive without permission. Both campaigns were withdrawn following complaints that the messages conflicted with the tolerant, multicultural image Australia fosters for tourists, business and other lawful migrants.

Boat people and "queue jumping"

One of the most powerful criticisms levelled at boat people and onshore asylum seekers is that they are "queue jumpers" who take the place of "genuine" refugees waiting patiently for resettlement in camps overseas. In reality, *there are no queues* for many asylum seekers overseas. In many countries of persecution, Australia has no embassy or diplomatic representation, so it is not possible for people to apply for resettlement in Australia through official overseas channels. Although there are more than 200 countries in the world, Australia has only 80 overseas missions. Of these, only 30 contain immigration officers - that is, staff authorised to issue visas. Most are concentrated in Western countries from which Australia traditionally draws most of its migrants. The scarcity and placement of Australia's embassies means that very few of the world's refugees are able to seek asylum in Australia through Australia's "official channels". Although UNHCR and relief agencies also provide channels for protection, the system as a whole cannot efficiently guarantee protection to everyone who needs it.

Time is also a crucial factor: people living in fear are often unable to wait for long periods for an official response. At many Australian embassies, the wait for the outcome of applications can stretch back for months or even years. For example, in 1999 the Australian High Commission in Kenya had only two-and-a-half full-time immigration staff to deal with asylum applications from 34 African countries, and that office alone had 9,000 outstanding applications waiting to be determined.

Most refugees eventually granted protection under Australia's offshore program have waited overseas for an average of 15 months for their asylum applications to be processed. Until recent changes in those countries, people fleeing persecution in Iraq or Afghanistan who applied for protection at the Australian High Commission in Pakistan waited more than one year and four months for a refugee visa, one year and 11 months for a humanitarian visa, and one year and eight months for a women-at-risk visa.

The system run by UNHCR is also beset with problems that compromise the effectiveness of international protection. Serious allegations of bribery, corruption and sexual harassment have arisen in some UNHCR offices. Access to UNHCR offices can also be impossible where any travel in a troubled country is unsafe. Finally, persecutory governments are unlikely to provide people with the travel documents, such as passports, necessary to apply for a visa at an Australian embassy. As a result, people fleeing persecution may try to reach safety in any way possible, including travelling directly to safe countries.

The most significant break-down of protection for refugees has occurred in "countries of first asylum" - meaning the first country to which a refugee flees and usually adjacent to the refugee's home country. For example, refugees who fled to Iran from Afghanistan or Iraq have periodically been given ultimatums by Iran to voluntarily leave the country or be deported. According to UNHCR, 82,000 Afghans were forcibly deported from Iran in the first six months of 2001. At that time, it was patently unsafe for many of these refugees to return to Afghanistan.

Countries of first asylum can also be dangerous places for refugees in their own right. The difficulties experienced by some Afghan refugees living in Pakistan in recent years are examples in point. In mid-2000, prominent Afghan writers, academics and former politicians living in Pakistan were attacked by Islamic extremists. The Pakistani government was unable to offer them the security they needed.

One of Pakistan's worst sectarian killings in recent times took place in Quetta, a city with a large Afghan refugee population. In July 2003, three gunmen attacked a crowd of 2,000 worshippers at Friday prayers in Asna-Ul-Asharia mosque, killing 53 people and wounding many more. The mosque is one of the city's main centres of worship for Afghan Shiites. The killing followed a similar incident in Quetta in June 2003 where 12 Hazara police cadets were killed and nine critically injured in a racially motivated attack. Quetta is not the only city that has witnessed violence against Hazaras in Pakistan. Thousands of Shi'a Muslims have been killed in Pakistan over the past two decades in sectarian violence fuelled by extremist sects of Sunni Muslims.

One reason for the breakdown of protection in countries of first asylum is the failure of the international community - including Australia - to equitably share the burden of assisting refugees. As the Refugee Council of Australia points out, in 2001 Iran hosted over 1.4 million Afghan refugees - many of whom had been there for 20 years - as well as a further 500,000 Iraqi refugees from the early 1990s. At the end of 2003, Pakistan hosted more than 1.1 million refugees.

As noted in chapter 3, these countries provide protection to huge numbers of refugees. The international community has failed to adequately assist them - even though refugees are a global legal responsibility. Iran received only about US$12 per refugee from the global community in 1999, while Pakistan received US$17 per head. This situation changed after the fall of the Taliban regime and the toppling of Saddam Hussein, which allowed many refugees to return to Afghanistan and Iraq. Even so, these countries continue to suffer from the economic and social costs of hosting so many refugees and displaced persons. In contrast, Australia spent an estimated $100 million on 4,000 Kosovar refugees in 1999, or about $25,000 per person. Its interdiction and deflection operations since August 2001 have cost over $2 billion, taking into account infrastructure costs in building and maintaining offshore detention and processing centres. These operations have involved less than 2,000 asylum seekers.

With serious inequalities in the distribution of international assistance to refugees, it is little wonder that countries of first asylum like Iran and Pakistan - themselves poor countries - find it difficult to continue helping refugees. The decision by wealthy countries to close their doors to refugees exacerbates the problem. A British Home Office report found in 2004 that tough asylum policies had led to more people trafficking and people smuggling because they force refugees to utilise all available avenues to escape from persecution.

In countries of asylum like Australia, it is sometimes argued that refugee determination processes, together with the visas given to successful claimants, act as a lure for refugees. The complaint is that asylum seekers should not be allowed to "forum shop" so as to find the country most likely to offer the best rewards. Refugees should only be entitled to immediate protection from persecution: they should not be allowed to use asylum processes to achieve an "immigration outcome".

It is true that the Refugee Convention does not confer any express right on asylum seekers to "choose" their preferred country of asylum. Nonetheless, these arguments ignore the tremendous risks involved in entering developed countries like Australia by irregular means. Entrusting one's life to people smugglers is never a soft option. It is also misleading to suggest that Australia's refugee status determination system allows for "immigration" outcomes. Protection is rarely granted unless a claimant is either recognised as a refugee or able to demonstrate compelling humanitarian reasons for permission to stay. Australia's attempts to "level the playing field" for asylum seekers are discussed further in chapter 7.

If some refugees do seek out Australia, it is difficult to blame them. As immigration laws around the world have been tightened, it has become increasingly difficult for asylum seekers to gain protection. For this reason, it is understandable that asylum seekers seek refuge in countries that are prepared to honour their international commitments.

The solution is not for Australia to impose further restrictions, but to work cooperatively with other countries to find global solutions. This means actively encouraging other countries to offer full protection to asylum seekers in accordance with their international obligations, so that an unfair burden is not placed on those countries that do fulfil their commitments to refugees. The greatest demands are placed on poor countries that are less capable than Australia of meeting the challenges posed by forced migration. In accordance with the UN Millennium Development Goals, Australia could also increase its foreign aid and development budget to assist poorer countries to cope with refugee flows.

People trafficking

People who are *trafficked* can be (doubly victimised) Convention refugees. They may be individuals facing persecution or gross abuse of human rights who are taken from one bad situation into another. Trafficked people face exploitation and/or may not even consent to being brought into a destination country. They may be unaware that they are being smuggled into a country using illegal means. It is not unusual for people who are desperate for a better life for themselves or their children to believe the false promises of traffickers. When large populations are displaced or de-stabilised by natural disasters, civil unrest, internal armed conflict or poverty, people's vulnerability to exploitation or abuse increases. In many cases, shattered families are desperate to get the most vulnerable family members (often their children) to safety and will employ any means to achieve this end. In other cases, disasters displace or separate children from their families, making them susceptible to organised crime rings.

In the aftermath of the 2004 Indian Ocean tsunami disaster, many organisations, including the UN, were concerned about the presence in the disaster areas of criminal elements. It was feared that crime rings might take advantage of the disaster by stealing and selling orphaned children for adoption or into slavery. The disaster wrought by Hurricane Katrina in the United States in August 2005 gave rise to similar concerns.

Trafficking in Australia

Globally, it is very difficult to obtain clear data on the number of people involved in trafficking, and estimates are both rough and variable. The US State Department's Trafficking in Persons (TIP) Report (2002), for example, stated that the global number of "people bought, sold and held against their will in slave-like conditions" ranged from 700,000 to as many as 4 million in 2002. The UN estimates that 200,000 women and children are trafficked annually in Asia, mainly for sexual exploitation. Globally, sex trafficking is worth from US$5-7 billion per year (UN).

The Australian government and non-government organisations have also found it difficult to estimate the scale of the trafficking problem. In 2004, Australia was labelled a "Tier 1" country by the US State Department TIP Report. This means that Australia has a "significant" trafficking problem with more than 100 victims, although it complies with the minimum standards required to tackle the problem. Australia expressed its disappointment with this assessment, stating that the problem was much smaller. In contrast, one international network, ECPAT ("End Child Prostitution, Child Pornography and Trafficking of Children for Sexual Purposes"), estimates that crime syndicates have been trafficking up to 300 Thai women into Australia each year. ECPAT assesses the overall number of trafficking victims to be considerably higher if women of other nationalities are included. Some reports refer to as many as 1,000 sex slaves being brought into the country annually, worth over $50 million per year in profits to sex traffickers.

While it is impossible to get a clear fix on the size of the problem in Australia, a sizeable number of young non-citizen women are apprehended in brothels each year and found to be working illegally. In 2002-03, immigration officials located more than 134 people working illegally in the sex industry, four of whom complained they were trafficked. This increased to 353 people located in 2003-04, before decreasing to 290 located in 2004-05, almost all of whom were removed from Australia except the small number issued bridging visas. Most of the illegal sex workers located in 2004-05 were female (94%) and came from Asian countries: 25% from Thailand, 22% from China, 19% from the Republic of Korea, 18% from Hong Kong and 9% from Malaysia. Most had held visitor visas (54%) or bridging visas (31%).

Both the number of illegal migrant sex workers located and the proportion of them who were identified as being trafficked are likely to be much lower than their real levels. As noted in chapter 3, DIMA detects only a small percentage of the unlawful migrants in the community as a whole, and there is little reason to think that the rate of detection in the sex industry (particularly in illegal brothels) is any higher than in the general community. As for the number of sex workers trafficked, cultural factors (such as a sense of shame) and fear of reprisals by criminal groups result in considerable underreporting of trafficking.

Although many young women are trafficked to work in brothels and in forced prostitution, people are also trafficked to work as domestic servants, in sweatshops, on building sites, or to perform other jobs. The difficulties in identifying such people as victims of trafficking are obvious. As exploited workers, victims of trafficking may also be protected by the International Convention on the Protection of the Rights of All Migrant Workers of 1990, which applies even to irregular migrants.

Linking trafficking to unlawful status

Trafficking is often associated with illegal migration and organised crime. This colours government approaches to the issue since trafficking victims are often considered first as illegal migrants or even as criminals themselves. Trafficked persons are often charged with immigration violations, frequently detained in prisons or detention centres, and/or deported. The circumstances in which people leave their home countries often make it impossible for them to obtain authentic papers. Organised criminal groups supply false travel documents. In some instances, these documents are either destroyed or re-circulated in the trafficking organisation soon after the person reaches a destination country. This simultaneously makes the victim both vulnerable to traffickers and "unlawful" under the local law. In Australia, unlawful status brings with it mandatory detention and liability to be removed from the country "as soon as is practicable": see chapter 9.

The treatment of Vivian Alvarez-Solon (see chapter 9) illustrates the vulnerability of such people. Her story is punctuated with incidents suggesting that she was identified as a sex slave from the Philippines. If this encouraged the authorities to remove her from Australia, it also fostered the view that no one would care about her removal.

Australia's response to traffickers and trafficked people

Recently, there has been a shift in attitude so that trafficked persons have become recognised as victims rather than simply as unlawful non-citizens. However, both the law and government funding still focus on apprehending trafficked persons mainly because of their unlawful status. In 1999, amendments to Chapter 8 of the Commonwealth *Criminal Code* created offences relating to slavery, sexual servitude and misleading recruitment practices for sexual services. In 2002, the government created an aggravated offence of people smuggling, which covers cases involving deceptive recruiting, slavery and sexual servitude. This offence is punishable by up to 20 years' imprisonment.

In enforcing these laws, in 2004-05 DIMA referred 36 matters (involving 41 victims) to the Australian Federal Police for investigation, while 67 matters (involving 75 victims) were referred in 2003-04. These were significant increases over the 17 referrals (involving 29 victims) in 2002-03, the two referrals in 2001-02 (involving five victims) and three referrals in 2000-01 (involving eight victims), and four cases in 1999-2000. None of these referrals involved a child or young person. In the Senate Estimates Committee in February 2001, DIMA was aware of only one trafficking incident involving a child, dating back to 1995.

In October 2003, the Australian government announced a four-year, $20 million package to further combat people trafficking. It includes activities in the region by AusAID (which administers Australia's overseas aid programs) and the establishment of a 23-member Australian Federal Police strike team to investigate trafficking and sexual slavery. A senior immigration official has been stationed at the Australian Embassy in Bangkok to investigate people trafficking. Attempts are being made to improve cooperation with regional governments to combat the problem through education and capacity building in local policing. The package also establishes a comprehensive victim support scheme run by the Australian Federal Police. The scheme is targeted at trafficked persons who are returned from Australia and is designed to break the cycle of poverty and exploitation that feeds trafficking as an industry.

One of the most important elements of the support scheme was the creation of special visa sub-classes for trafficked persons - Class UM and Class DH visas. These visas provide for temporary stays of two years which can be converted to permanent residence where the need for protection is ongoing. Although a welcome initiative, there is still an unfortunate linkage between protecting trafficked persons and prosecuting their traffickers. Trafficking victims only gain protection if they cooperate in the prosecution of their traffickers. To obtain temporary protection, a person must hold a criminal justice stay visa (available for witnesses in a criminal trial). The Minister must be "satisfied" that the trafficking victim contributes significantly to, and cooperates closely with, the prosecution case. Permanent protection is only available if the person would also be in danger if returned home.

These new visas focus primarily on the prosecution of traffickers as criminals, rather than on the needs of victims. There is no permanent or temporary visa available for trafficking victims who decline to assist in a prosecution. Victims sometimes do not help in criminal investigations because they are too afraid to cooperate, fearing reprisals against themselves or their families at home. The knowledge of how criminal networks operate frequently outweighs the assurances given by law enforcement or immigration officials. In other cases cooperation may not be possible because traffickers cannot be found. Trafficking victims comprise some of the most vulnerable in society, coming frequently from countries where governments cannot be trusted. Assisting a foreign government official can therefore be daunting and create great anxiety.

Australia currently offers a victim support scheme coordinated by the Office of the Status of Women. Of the $20 million government initiative, $5.6 million over four years has been allocated for these purposes. The scheme aims to rehabilitate a highly vulnerable group of people, and to apprehend and convict those responsible. Victims are assisted with living and other expenses, including income support, accommodation, basic legal advice, medical treatment, counselling, training and social support. Again, the support services are only available for victims who agree to assist with investigations or prosecutions. In mid-2005 it was difficult to assess the effectiveness of these initiatives, although they certainly improve previous arrangements.

Australia adopts the UN Protocol on Trafficking

The UN Protocol to Prevent, Suppress, and Punish Trafficking in Persons, Especially Women and Children, supplementing the UN Convention Against Transnational Organized Crime, was signed by 120 countries in 2000. The Protocol aims to prevent and combat trafficking, protect and assist its victims, and promote cooperation against trafficking.

Australia signed the Protocol and enacted it into domestic law in the *Criminal Code Amendment (Trafficking in Persons Offences) Act 2005* (Cth). The Act creates new trafficking offences, including for trafficking children into and from Australia and for the domestic trafficking of people wholly within Australia. It also extends the existing offence of deceptive recruiting for sexual services and creates a new offence of debt bondage. Telephone intercept warrants are now available for investigating these offences, while special provisions protect child witnesses in proceedings involving sexual crimes.

In addition to this Protocol, there are other international instruments relevant to people trafficking which Australia has ratified, including the International Labor Organization (ILO) Convention (105) on the Abolition of Forced Labor, the UN Supplementary Convention on the Abolition of Slavery, the Slave Trade, and Institutions and Practices Similar to Slavery, the 1948 Universal Declaration of Human Rights and the 1986 Convention on the Elimination of All Forms of Discrimination Against Women. However, Australia has yet to ratify some significant conventions and to make them part of domestic law, including the ILO Convention (182) to Eliminate the Worst Forms of Child Labor and the UN Convention on the Protection of the Rights of All Migrant Workers and Members of Their Families. Further, Australia has signed but not ratified the UN Convention on the Rights of the Child on the Sale of Children, Child Prostitution, and Child Pornography.

References and further reading

Attorney General's Department, "Trafficking in Persons": <www.ag.gov.au/agd/WWW/ncphome.nsf/Page/Trafficking_in_Persons>

Claire Brolan, "An Analysis of the Human Smuggling Trade and the Protocol Against the Smuggling of Migrants by Land, Air And Sea from a Refugee Protection Perspective" (2000) 14 *International Journal of Refugee Law* 561

DIMA, "Fact Sheet 73: People Smuggling" <www.immi.gov.au/facts/73smuggling.htm>

DIMA Fact Sheet 74a, <http://sievx.com/articles/psdp/DIMIA74a_boatarrivals.pdf>

Tony Kevin, *A Certain Maritime Incident: the sinking of SIEV X* (Scribe Publications, Melbourne, 2004)

Janet Phillips, "People Trafficking: Australia's Response", Australian Parliamentary Library, Research Note No 20, 16 November 2004

Andreas Schloenhardt, *Migrant Smuggling: Illegal Migration and Organised Crime in Australia and the Asia Pacific Region* (Martinus Nijhoff, The Hague, 2003)

Andreas Schloenhardt, "The Business of Migration: Organised Crime and Illegal Migration in Australia and the Asia Pacific Region" (1999) 21 *Adelaide Law Review* 81

Senate Select Committee on A Certain Maritime Incident, <http://www.aph.gov.au/Senate/committee/maritime_incident_ctte/report/index.htm>

"Siev X" website: <http://sievx.com>

Rebecca Tailby, "Organised Crime and People Smuggling/Trafficking to Australia", *Trends and Issues in Crime and Criminology*, No 208, Australian Institute of Criminology, May 2001

UNHCR refugee camp at Farchana, Sudan (8 January 2004)
© UNHCR/ H Caux

A Sudanese refugee seeks shelter from a sandstorm near the Chadian border town of Tine (7 February 2004) © UNHCR/ H Caux

Officials bring asylum seekers ashore, Christmas Island © Phil Oakley

Asylum Seekers boarding Australian Hercules aircraft,
Christmas Island © Phil Oakley

Part 2
Asylum and Refugee Status

5

Seeking Asylum: Refugee Status Determination Procedures

Key Points in this chapter

- Australian immigration officials are under no statutory duty to tell people arriving without permission that they have a legal right to apply for asylum. However, they must ask questions to see if a person may be a refugee.
- Asylum seekers must apply for a "protection visa". Applications are assessed by DIMA officers to determine a person's refugee "status" in a two phase process that involves a "screening-in" interview followed by a fuller determination process.
- A special scheme has been created to provide "application assistance" to asylum seekers, with most attention given to helping persons in detention.
- Applicants have a right to know about and respond to any adverse material affecting their case. However, there are aspects of the initial determination process that can make it difficult for asylum seekers to make out their claims – particularly where claimants are young and vulnerable.
- Applicants denied a protection visa have a right to appeal to the Refugee Review Tribunal (RRT). This Tribunal is described as "inquisitorial" because proceedings are controlled by the member asking questions of the applicant and of any witnesses the Tribunal considers relevant. Claimants have no right to be represented at hearings and have no right to chose or to examine or cross-examine witnesses. Not all members have legal training and there are questions about the independence of the Tribunal from DIMA.
- Australia has passed laws which restrict the ability of Australian courts to judicially review refugee and migration decisions, in particular by introducing "privative clauses", time limits on applications for review, and costs orders.

AUSTRALIA'S REFUGEE DETERMINATION PROCESS FOR UNAUTHORISED ARRIVALS

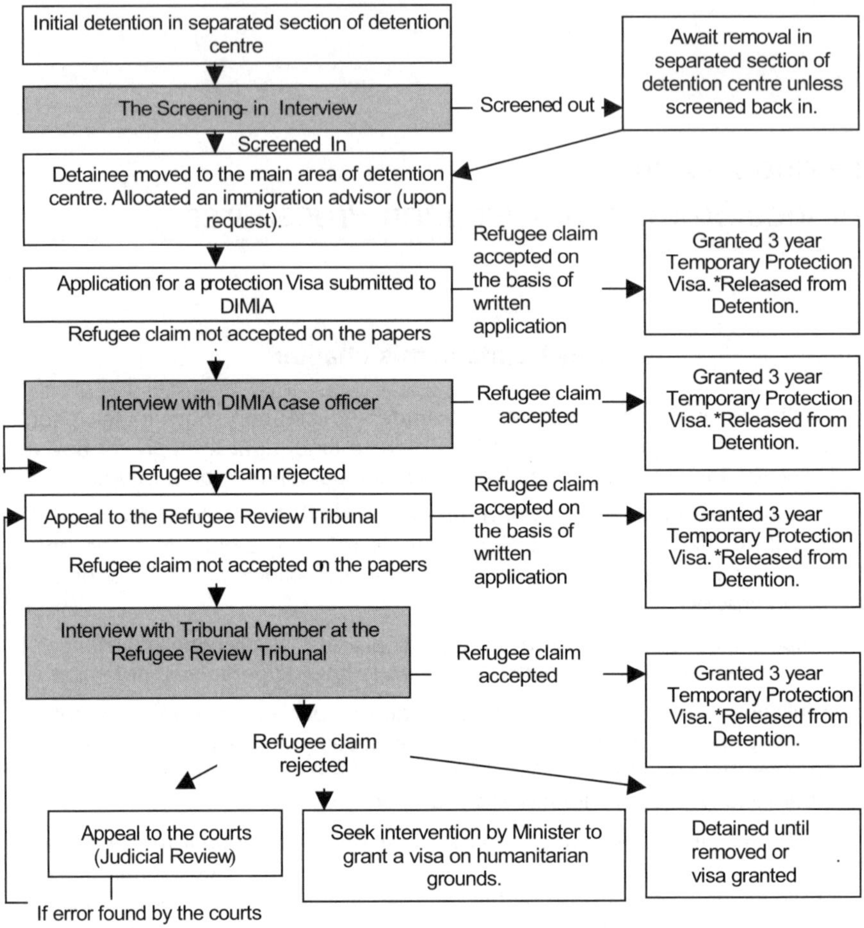

* The Minister has discretion to grant a permanent as opposed to a temporary protection visa. However this discretion is rarely exercised.

Source: Senate Legal and Constitutional References Committee (2000)

Who gains protection: an overview

Between 1999 and 2004, a total of 13,588 protection visas were granted by DIMA either at the primary application stage; on appeal to the Refugee Review Tribunal (RRT); or following review by one of Australia's federal courts. The majority of the visas granted (8,912) were three-year temporary protection ("subclass 785") visas (TPVs): see Senate Estimates, February 2004. The statistics given do not reveal how many of those granted TPVs were subsequently granted permanent protection (a small number of TPV holders have also applied for non-humanitarian visas).

Applicants in detention are often more successful in their claims for refugee status than those in the community. In 1999-2000, for example, 84% of primary applications for protection by those in detention were successful. In contrast, only 5% of people who sought refugee status from within the community – these are people who arrived in Australia on a valid visa – succeeded in their primary claims. Of those who appealed to the RRT, 64% of detainees succeeded on appeal, while 13% of applicants in the community had adverse decisions overturned. These statistics reflect the obvious point that individuals who can travel freely are less likely to meet the persecution requirements of the Refugee Convention.

The application process

People in Australia who wish to seek asylum must apply for protection visas using standard application forms obtained from DIMA. An application must be written, in English, and must demonstrate that the claimant meets the international legal definition of a refugee. In practice, refugee status is determined on a case-by-case basis, although families can be included as the dependants of a principal applicant. The relevant form is divided into four parts, with Part C dealing with Convention claims and Part D setting out the details of dependants. Each family member may claim protection in separate Part C forms, with the stories of each being relevant to the assessment of the family as a whole.

The legal requirements that have to be met for a person to be designated a "refugee" are explained in chapter 6. It is sufficient to note here that the complexity of the process explains why status determination is so costly and time consuming, and also why most people need professional help in making a claim.

Screening in

One complaint made by refugee advocates – and acknowledged as a serious shortcoming by the Australian Senate in 2000 – is that the law places no duty on immigration officials to tell people that they have a right to claim refugee status. As explained in chapter 9, non-citizens who enter Australia without a visa or permission are immediately detained. This is how many asylum seekers end up applying for asylum from within detention centres. When unauthorised arrivals are first taken into custody, they are isolated from other detainees as part of a pre-screening process. They are interviewed by DIMA officers without being given access to independent advice. They are told nothing about the determination process and will sometimes have no idea of the significance of what they are saying. The same procedures are followed in all cases: no exception is made for separated or unaccompanied children seeking refugee protection. "Separated children" is the phrase used by UNHCR to describe children (aged 17 years or less) who are not travelling with a family member or responsible guardian. Unaccompanied children are those who are travelling completely alone – without any responsible adult.

Only people who tell a story that fits within the Refugee Convention definition are allowed to apply for refugee status. For example, people who speak of fear, torture or of being hurt will be screened in, while those who say simply that they want a future for their children could be screened out. The screening process has caused concerns that immigration officials are failing to recognise refugees who have not spoken up about their claims, or articulated them in legal language. Many asylum seekers are suspicious of authority figures because they have been ill-treated by the authorities in their own countries.

The screening process is particularly concerning in the case of separated or unaccompanied children. In most cases, children who arrive within family groups are not subjected to an individual screening in process. Their claims are inferred from the interview with their parents. However, separated or unaccompanied children are interviewed and assessed in their own right. There are many reasons why children may not articulate reasons for their flight, including a relatively poor understanding of the refugee determination system and a lack of awareness of the dangers that faced them in their home country.

The Human Rights and Equal Opportunity Commission (HREOC)'s 2004 report on children in immigration detention and an international study concluding in 2006 document the screening out of two orphaned siblings aged 14 and 10. The older sister was unable to articulate much at all during her initial interview. Her understanding of what was happening was so poor that she did not even know that she had been excluded from the asylum process. According to observers at the detention centre, the 14-year-old girl would dress carefully each morning, take her chair outside and wait with her younger brother to be called for another interview like all the other people. However, as the children had not been screened in, she and her brother were never called. The two children were only admitted to the full status determination process upon the intervention of advocates – six months after the children's arrival in the country.

Legal assistance

While the initial screening process for detainees is done without the claimant having access to legal advice, once admitted into the process most asylum seekers in detention (as well as some applying from within the community) are given access to government-funded assistance if they sign a form requesting such help. Migration agents (some of whom are lawyers) are allocated to detainees without charge under a special legal aid scheme known as the Immigration Advice and Application Assistance Scheme (IAAAS). Asylum seekers in detention cannot choose their agent, but are assigned advisers who win the right to act after a competitive tendering process where the service providers quote a fixed amount for each case.

Asylum seekers who apply from within the community - that is, most claimants - are free to choose and retain their own advisers. However, funds are available to some people in the community under the IAAAS, including people from different cultural backgrounds; who are illiterate; in remote locations; and/or affected by physical or psychological disabilities due to the harms they have experienced. At later stages in the determination process, the IAAAS also provides assistance to prepare applications for merits review to a tribunal if the initial application is refused. In 2002-03, the IAAAS provided $1.3 million in assistance, two thirds of which went to applicants in the community, and one third to 256 applicants in detention.

Government-funded legal assistance is not available where an applicant appeals to the Federal Court, the Federal Magistrates' Court or to the Minister's personal discretion under s 417 of the *Migration Act 1958*. In practice, legal assistance is still provided for court actions, either directly from Legal Aid offices or from lawyers funded by Legal Aid. Nevertheless, after changes to federal legal aid guidelines in 1998, legal aid has become much more difficult to obtain. Legal Aid Commissions cannot provide assistance to asylum seekers for initial applications, merits review applications, or judicial review applications except where the law is unsettled or the proceedings challenge the lawfulness of detention.

Unfortunately, as noted by the UK Law Society, of all fields of legal practice, refugee advice "is probably the one most dogged by incompetence and malpractice", to the detriment of asylum seekers. The introduction of the IAAAS raised the standard in Australia to some extent, although this came at the cost of greatly reduced legal aid assistance. Bad advice remains a besetting problem for asylum seekers, since not all contract winners send refugee experts to the detention centres. Contractors are not required to have legal training, although all must be registered as "migration agents".

The Refugee Council of Australia observes that the number of people needing assistance far exceeds the capacity of service providers; service providers are not paid for some essential services; and there is a lack of transparency about the tendering process. As the Law Council of Australia notes, legal assistance for asylum seekers remains underfunded. While many law societies and courts have set up pro bono legal schemes for asylum seekers wishing to challenge visa refusals in the courts, access to good advice remains a major problem. The high number of litigants appearing without legal counsel is one of the most troubling consequences of this problem. This situation is likely to get worse after laws were passed in 2005 to penalise those involved in bringing an "unmeritorious" immigration application in a federal court: see further below.

Full status determination proceedings

In essence, the refugee application form lodged after a person has been screened in to the status determination process requires an asylum seeker to tell her or his story. The claimant is encouraged to frame his or her case within the terms of the Refugee Convention, with specific questions asked about what the claimant fears and why. Although claimants have an advantage if they can produce documentary evidence to back up their story, the reality is that many refugees arrive with little more than the clothes on their backs. Many come on false passports or with no identity documents. Where people have fled a country in fear of immediate harm, it is quite normal that they have little to offer other than their story and the physical or psychological scars of their ordeal.

A case officer from DIMA, acting with the delegated authority of the Minister, assesses the individual's written application and decides whether the applicant meets the definition of a refugee. If further clarification is needed, the case officer may interview the applicant, although applicants have no right to be given reasons for being refused an interview. The case officer may also seek information about the situation in the applicant's home country from other sources, including the Department of Foreign Affairs and Trade, other governments and human rights groups.

Applicants are given the chance to respond to any adverse information that affects their case. Migration agents - some of whom are lawyers with specialised knowledge of immigration and refugee law - can also make written submissions on behalf of an applicant. Departmental officers are obliged to treat applications confidentially and normally no contact is made with governments in the countries from which asylum seekers have fled. However, in the case of a defecting Chinese diplomat in 2005, Mr Chen, the Chinese consulate was inappropriately contacted by Australian authorities before any decision to grant asylum. Further, in the same year Vietnamese asylum seekers alleged that Australia provided information about their cases to the Vietnamese government, resulting in the persecution of family members in Vietnam. If an applicant meets the international refugee definition, satisfies "good character" requirements, and demonstrates that he or she could not have sought protection in another safe country, the case officer will grant the applicant a protection visa. Otherwise, the applicant will be refused protection.

Evaluating credibility

The process of determining individual refugee claims is notoriously difficult. Asylum seekers will often try to improve their chances by embellishing their stories or even telling outright lies. Officers can have a difficult time trying to work out what really happened to a person and whether a lack of truthfulness indicates the deep fear of a refugee or just opportunism and lack of credibility.

Unfortunately, little sympathy is shown for the procedural and psychological difficulties facing asylum seekers when they first arrive in Australia. Among the seven Acts passed by federal Parliament on 26 September 2001 (following the *Tampa* affair) was legislation that weakens the position of asylum seekers who lie, or who appear tentative, confused or obfuscatory when interviewed by Australian officials on arrival. The law allows officers to require asylum seekers to swear or affirm that what they assert is true in fact. Failure to comply with a request can be used in making an adverse finding about the credibility of the claimant at any stage in the determination process. The law also allows an officer to draw adverse inferences if the officer "has reason to believe" that the claimant is "not sincere" in making a statement (s 91V of the *Migration Act*). Adverse inferences may also be drawn from the claimant's demeanour, or where claimants refuse or are unable to produce documentary evidence of their identity, nationality or citizenship.

The stress under which asylum seekers are operating at the point of first contact with the authorities in any country of asylum makes it inevitable that claimants will present as nervous and unsure of themselves. In addition, there are obvious difficulties in "reading" the intentions and understandings of persons coming from radically different cultural and linguistic backgrounds. Even if an asylum seeker does lie or dissimilate, it does not follow that the person is not a refugee. The more desperate a person's situation, the more likely it is often that the person will lie – particularly when they have not been given adequate legal advice and/or are relying on misconceived advice given by smugglers or other asylum seekers. It is almost standard practice for asylum seekers to arrive without valid travel or identity documents, because escape from their country of origin is often impossible without false papers.

The legislation of September 2001 aimed to protect the refugee decision-making process from judicial supervision. It was rushed through Parliament without the benefit of scrutiny by specialist parliamentary committees and in the face of concerns expressed by UNHCR and community groups. The new provisions carry a real danger of placing Australia in breach of its international legal obligations not to return Convention refugees to persecution. The legislation may protect bad decisions, made on the basis of cultural or psycho-social misunderstandings. More problematically, it can also encourage officers to make bad decisions by fostering the idea that people who lie should have their refugee claims rejected automatically.

Fair process

Government cost-cutting measures have led to economies being made in the determination process which place further pressures on some refugee claimants. Of the asylum seekers who are not detained (those who arrived on temporary visas and who remain in the community), only about 10% are interviewed in the initial determination phase. This means that claims can be rejected solely on the basis of a written application, even where an application is filled in by someone who has little idea about what they are doing.

Other complaints about the initial determination process relate to the quality of the information used by the immigration authorities about what is happening in the claimant's country of origin, and the weight that is given to this material compared to the first hand account of the applicant. Some refugee advocates assert that immigration authorities tend to understate the seriousness of persecution in source countries, to suggest that claimants' fears are unfounded. Often a claimant will find it impossible to contradict the official version, even though they know it is wrong.

The problem is that official acceptance of the stories of asylum seekers often turns on the view that the Australian government takes of the country of origin. This was illustrated in the dramatic change in the acceptance rate of asylum seekers from Afghanistan that occurred between late 2001 and early 2002. As soon as the US bombing campaign started and the US declared that the Taliban had been ousted, Afghan asylum seekers suddenly found their claims being rejected on the basis that it was safe for them to return. Australia was one of the first countries of asylum to adopt this position. Of course it was not safe for many of the asylum seekers to return, particularly those from vulnerable minority groups, and the policy change meant that many asylum seekers ended up spending months and even years in detention fighting these prematurely optimistic rulings. Again, an about-face in decision-making coincided with Australia's public acceptance that Afghanistan was still an unstable and unsafe country for many people.

Institutionally, some have questioned whether it is appropriate for the Department of Immigration to process refugee claims. Core objectives of that Department include border control and preventing the unauthorised entry of people into Australia. These objectives can conflict with the international obligation to protect refugees from persecution and thus to allow them entry into Australia, even when they come without permission. As many people have suggested, it would be preferable to transfer primary decision-making about refugee claims from the Department of Immigration to the Attorney-General's Department, which is responsible for ensuring implementation of Australia's international obligations. That Department would not suffer from the same conflict of interest as DIMA, and such a move might help to alleviate the culture of rejection and suspicion of asylum seekers which seems to permeate DIMA decision-making.

Administrative Appeals Tribunal and the Refugee Review Tribunal

Applicants refused protection may challenge the factual basis of the decision in an independent tribunal, usually in the RRT but also in the

Administrative Appeals Tribunal (AAT) in circumstances involving security issues or important questions of law. A single member of the RRT reviews the merits of the refugee status decision in a setting less formal and adversarial than that of a court. It examines all over again ("de novo") whether the applicant meets the refugee definition and is not required to assess the reasons given for the primary decision. The RRT must make its decision based on the facts and law at the time of its decision, so it is able to take into account changes in an applicant's situation or in their country of origin.

Where the RRT is unable to make a decision favourable to the applicant on the written evidence available, it must give the applicant an opportunity to be heard in person. The RRT can overturn the decision of the immigration officer and grant a protection visa to the applicant if it believes that the initial decision was wrong based on the facts of the case. The RRT can also uphold the immigration officer's decision to reject an asylum claim, in which case the applicant must pay a A$1,400 fee and leave Australia within 28 days. If an applicant does not leave within time, DIMA will remove the person by force (unless the applicant appeals to the courts). In 2004-05, one in three DIMA decisions appealed to the RRT were set aside, indicating a high rate of error in departmental decision-making at first instance (see further the first table on p 80 below).

Asylum seekers have no right to be represented (by a lawyer or anyone else) when they appear before the RRT, although legal and other advisers can be present as observers and can contribute to the hearing at the discretion of the Tribunal member. Asylum seekers must appear in person and answer questions put to them by the presiding member. Interpreters are provided for those who do not speak English. RRT hearings are closed to the public and the RRT is bound not to release any details that might identify an asylum seeker.

Where applicants are living in the community, this system works well enough. Advisers can listen to an asylum seeker's answers and request breaks if they think that an asylum seeker is stressed or needs time to collect his or her thoughts. Before a hearing ends, Tribunal members leave the room to allow the adviser to speak in private to the asylum seeker to make sure that the person has said everything that he or she wants or needs to say in support of their claim. This adjournment is referred to by the Tribunal as the "natural justice" break. Members will also ask advisers at the end whether they have anything they want to add. It is at this point that discussions often occur between the Tribunal and the adviser about the finer points of refugee law, what court cases the member should be considering, and other matters. The member will then advise the claimant and her or his adviser that they have seven days in which to lodge any further submissions.

Problems with RRT hearings appear to arise frequently in cases where hearings are conducted using conferencing technology. The RRT "sits" in two centres: Melbourne and Sydney. This means that claimants elsewhere often have their hearings via video link-up or telephone conferencing. For asylum seekers in remote detention centres, these arrangements can be impossibly alienating, given that many claimants come from countries with little experience of such technology. To begin with, the RRT member and the interpreter can be situated in one city and the legal adviser in another. Once the hearing begins, there is often no communication at all between the adviser and the claimant. The confusion and anxiety of the asylum seeker can be palpable (although RRT members try to handle the situation as well as can be expected). How a Tribunal member can properly extract information and assess credibility in such circumstances is difficult to comprehend. Hearings conducted on Christmas Island are of particular concern because of the uncertainty of the telecommunications facilities on this remote territory. It has been proposed that that island is to be developed as a remote processing centre to replace the facility on Nauru.

In principle, the RRT was established as an appeal system that could operate without the need for lawyers. Members are supposed to be neutral arbiters of a claimant's legal status. The theory is that all the asylum seeker has to do is to answer the questions put by the Tribunal honestly and fully. The problem is that asylum seekers often need assistance to articulate matters that, as a matter of fact and law, are critical to recognition of their status as refugees. Claimants will often say things that are important to them, but that do little to support their claims. Conversely, they can fail to mention experiences of critical importance, because they are unaware of their legal significance. Claimants may also be reluctant to criticise the countries from which they have fled because of either fear of reprisals back home or general uncertainties about the trust they should place in authority figures in a strange country. Comments that claimants want to make a new life in Australia because of its beauty and freedoms are classic examples. Such statements can reveal a "courtesy bias", where the claimant is trying to say things that please Australians. In practice such statements can work against the claimant because they will be assessed as opportunists rather than as individuals who have fled in fear.

In other cases, claimants have answered questions put by the RRT without understanding either the point of the question or the significance of their answer. One example is where a claim alleging political and religious persecution was denied on the grounds of unsatisfactory answers to questions about elements of what the claimant stated to be his religion. The claimant may have been unaware during the hearing that his answers were being used as proof that he did not practise that religion. This situation could have been avoided if the RRT hearing was conducted with the more active involvement of an adviser. Mandating the physical presence of all the relevant parties in the hearing room would also provide obvious improvements on the system.

In 2000, and again in 2006, a Senate Committee recommended a range of measures to improve RRT decision-making, including that:

- DIMA officers should not serve as RRT members, due to the risk of bias;
- information should be provided to applicants about the workings of the RRT;
- further training be given to RRT members;
- the changing workload of the RRT be identified;
- Tribunal members should be drawn from a wider cross-section of society;
- the Principal Member of the RRT have judicial experience;
- the RRT be able to sit with single members or as a panel of 2-3 members.

None of these recommendations has been implemented. Instead, in June 2005 the government announced that it would amend the *Migration Act* to include processing time limits for asylum seekers. The RRT is now required to achieve a result within three months from the date of application for review. The Minister for Immigration is now required to table in Parliament any failure to meet the time limit.

Review of decisions in the courts

Asylum seekers whose refugee claims are rejected can seek judicial review of RRT decisions in the federal courts, but they will only succeed in very limited circumstances. Judicial review does not represent another opportunity to present all the facts and evidence relevant to a refugee claim. Rather, it is about checking whether an error of law has occurred during the process - either in the way a case was heard or in the way the law was interpreted. A serious error of law is required to be shown before the courts will intervene. The role of the courts is thus different from the role of the RRT, which *can* review the facts and all the circumstances of a case and grant a protection visa. Judges can only review points of law and the Court cannot itself grant a protection visa. It can only uphold an earlier refusal to grant a protection visa, or direct that an application be reassessed by the RRT.

For some time, the Federal Court (and the subordinate Federal Magistrates Court which also reviews refugee cases) has been limited in its ability to review the legality of immigration or refugee decisions. In 1994 Parliament changed the law to narrow the grounds on which the Federal Court could provide a remedy for "unlawful" migration decisions. It removed the ability of the Federal Court to intervene even if a decision: breached the common law rules of natural justice; was so unreasonable that it could have been made by no reasonable person; was made in bad faith; appeared to be biased; took irrelevant considerations into account or did not take relevant considerations into account; or constituted an abuse of power.

The 1994 legislation did not stop people from going to the Federal Court, although it became increasingly difficult for applicants to win in that jurisdiction. More problematically, an increasing number of failed refugee claimants chose to seek judicial review in the High Court because that was the only court that was not limited in its ability to review the lawfulness of refugee decisions. As explained below, this is because the High Court has constitutional powers to review administrative decisions that cannot be taken away by Parliament.

In 1995-96, 18% of cases filed in the original jurisdiction of the High Court were migration matters. By 1999-2000, this had increased to 47% of filings – an increase of 161% in five years. In 2002-03, migration cases comprised 82% of the High Court's matters, although that figure is exaggerated because the government prohibited "representative" migration actions in that year and thus forced one action to be split up and filed as 1350 separate matters. By 2003-04, the High Court reported that migration matters accounted for 50% of all special leave applications (up from 39% in 2002-03) and 93% of all applications for constitutional writs (which are special remedies arising directly under the Australian Constitution).

The large increase was disastrous for the Australian justice system. The High Court has only seven judges. It is responsible for deciding all the most important legal matters in the country, from the interpretation of the Australian Constitution through to hearing the most important criminal appeals. The High Court issues barely 100 written judgments each year. Yet since 1994 it has been increasingly asked to determine what are really first level (trial) appeals in refugee cases. This has happened because of the limitations placed on the Federal Court, arguably to punish its judges for using the law to assist refugee claimants.

"Privative clause"

On 26 September 2001, Parliament passed legislation that repealed the 1994 provisions in the *Migration Act* and inserted what is known as a "privative clause" that applies both to the federal courts and the High Court. The new provisions state baldly that a "privative clause decision":

(a) is final and conclusive; and
(b) shall not be challenged, appealed against, reviewed, quashed or called in question in any court; and
(c) is not subject to prohibition, mandamus, injunction, declaration or certiorari in any court on any account (that is, the regular administrative law remedies of the Common Law).

A "privative clause decision" is defined as an administrative decision made under the *Migration Act* or *Migration Regulations* (s 474(2)). Most refugee protection visa decisions are now classified under the Act as "privative clause decisions".

This new legislation is very restrictive, but it has not had the effect that a simple reading would suggest. In spite of the words used, privative clauses do *not* generally prevent all judicial review. The High Court always has the power to check the legality of actions taken by "officers of the Commonwealth" because s 75(v) of the Constitution entrenches this role for the Court. The phrase "officer of the Commonwealth" includes tribunals like the RRT and even the Minister for Immigration. The High Court also has original jurisdiction where any issue is raised that involves an international treaty to which Australia is a party (s 75(i) of the Constitution). As s 75(i) and (v) are constitutional grants of jurisdiction, Parliament cannot restrict this jurisdiction without putting the change to the Australian people through a referendum (which requires a double majority of both voters and States in order to succeed). Unless otherwise legislated, the Federal Court has similar (not identical) powers to those of the High Court.

In 2003, the High Court significantly reduced the scope of the privative clause in the case of *Plaintiff S157/2002* (2003). The Court confirmed that, in spite of the "privative clause", it could check the legality of any Tribunal decision and that the High Court could overrule decisions affected by "jurisdictional error".

The privative clause used in the *Migration Act* reflects a device used as long ago as 1945. In *R v Hickman* (1945), the High Court ruled that privative clauses can validly restrict the scope for judicial intervention provided that three criteria are met. The protected decision must involve "a bona fide attempt" to exercise the power conferred on the decision-maker; it must relate to the subject matter of the legislation; and it must be "reasonably capable of reference to the power" given to the decision-maker. This is known as the *Hickman* principle.

The *Hickman* principle really comes down to a matter of how the legislation is interpreted. The courts have reconciled such clauses with the Constitution by holding that provisions do not actually "oust" review by the courts – they simply reinforce the notion that courts only review matters of basic legality rather than matters that might reveal judicial preferences on matters of fact or opinion. The High Court confirmed in *Plaintiff S157* (2003) that privative clauses do *not* expand the jurisdiction of the decision-makers so as to *deem legal* any action taken by them (as argued by the government). Instead, the High Court stressed that determining the limits (or interpretation) of any law made by Parliament will always be for *judges* to determine (and no one else). The Court regarded the *Hickman* principle as merely a principle relevant to the statutory interpretation of privative clauses, rather than as a decisive test to be followed to the exclusion of all other factors.

The new provisions in the *Migration Act* do not just limit judicial review: they also specify that primary decisions cannot be reviewed by the Federal Court in any circumstances. This means that asylum seekers whose claims are rejected by DIMA must appeal to the RRT within 28 days if they want to maintain their right to judicial review by the Federal Court. In theory, if they do not appeal to the RRT, the only Court empowered to consider an application for review is the High Court. In

Plaintiff S157, however, the High Court found that, as jurisdictional error fell outside of the privative clause scheme, it was open to the Federal Court and the Federal Magistrates Court to review decisions for jurisdictional error.

Privative clauses are not peculiar to the migration area. They are used in many jurisdictions to limit access to the courts. They are inserted most often to restrict judicial review of rulings made by inferior courts of law established with a specialised jurisdiction; or to protect bodies that are charged with making specialised findings of fact (such as medical tribunals). In this way standard privative clauses do not offend against the notion that the bodies making final determinations on points of law should be courts. This is fundamental to the so-called separation of executive, legislative and judicial powers in the Constitution.

The new migration legislation is unusual because the bodies whose decisions the legislation attempted to protect from judicial review are neither inferior courts nor fact-finding tribunals. The RRT and the other migration tribunals make findings that typically involve issues of both fact and law in the interpretation and application of domestic legislation and principles of international law. Importantly, they are not courts.

This explains why the Law Council of Australia objected vigorously to the introduction of the privative clause. The desirability of judicial oversight of administrative tribunals such as the RRT also explains why the Labor Opposition resisted passing privative clause legislation for over two years: the government's first legislative attempt was defeated in Parliament in 1998. Yet, after the *Tampa* affair and the terrorist attacks of 11 September 2001, the Opposition changed its position and supported the legislation.

Apart from the privative clause provisions, further legislation was passed in 2001 to reduce the role played by the courts in the refugee determination process. As noted earlier, the right to bring class actions or representative proceedings in the Federal Court or the High Court was removed. Class actions are legal proceedings brought by groups of people who have the same or a similar complaint about the lawfulness of decisions made or of legislation relied upon. A 35-day time limit was also imposed on applications for constitutional review in the High Court and to limit the range of people eligible to challenge an adverse decision. This raises constitutional questions about whether the High Court's jurisdiction can be made subject to statutory time limitations by the Parliament.

In 1994, some commentators predicted accurately that the old "court stripping" provisions in the *Migration Act* would not reduce applications for judicial review, but rather result in the High Court being flooded with applications. The new privative clause has not stopped people from challenging adverse refugee decisions in the courts either. Nor has it stopped all judges from finding ways to overturn refugee decisions that they believe offend basic principles of natural justice and fairness. Indeed, the many legislative changes made in and after September 2001 are so complex and convoluted that they invite litigation.

In 2005 further measures were introduced in an attempt to discourage applications for the judicial review of adverse migration decisions. To remove pressure from the Federal and High Courts, the Federal Magistrates Court was given expanded powers to review the basic legality of migration decisions other than "primary" (DIMA) decisions. Another attempt was made to introduce time limits for the judicial review of migration decisions in all of the Courts (including the High Court) and to extend unsuccessfully the privative clause to include "purported" decisions in a narrow range of cases. ("Purported" decisions are defined as decisions affected by jurisdictional error - making any such amendments of dubious constitutionality.)

Unmeritorious litigation

More problematic are initiatives to discourage unmeritorious migration litigation. The *Migration Litigation Reform Act 2005* (Cth) lowers the bar at which the federal courts can summarily dismiss an application for judicial review for being vexatious or time wasting. The Act enables a judge to dismiss, without hearing, any application that he or she considers to have "no reasonable prospect of success". This departs from the carefully constructed common law test, which requires that a case be "manifestly groundless", "hopeless" or "bound to fail" before it can be summarily dismissed. This higher threshold ensures that cases are not disposed of prematurely, before all the evidence has become available during the proceedings on the merits. As then Chief Justice Barwick of the High Court stated in the *General Steel Industries* case (1964), "great care must be exercised to ensure that under the guise of achieving expeditious finality a plaintiff is not improperly deprived of his opportunity for the trial of his case".

In contrast, requiring a reasonable prospect of success risks depriving applicants of a fair opportunity to mount a case. Particularly where public interest test cases are run to challenge accepted interpretations of the law, there may be "no reasonable prospect of success" in the immediate case, but the litigation may contribute importantly to the future evolution of the common law. Discouraging litigation where there is no reasonable prospect of success risks chilling the progressive development of the law, and stymieing the correction of bad precedents.

The Act also introduces personal cost orders into the *Migration Act*. A person must not encourage another to commence or continue migration litigation if it has no reasonable prospect of success and either: (i) the person does not properly consider its prospects of success; or (ii) the purpose of the litigation is unrelated to the objectives of the court process. A person who encourages such litigation can be made personally liable for the court costs. The word "encouraged" is not defined. The threat of cost orders seems designed to discourage lawyers from becoming involved in legally uncertain migration matters. However, the law may apply more broadly to impose cost orders on anyone "encouraging" litigation - including friends, interpreters, community sector volunteers, journalists, local members of Parliament and others who play a part in instituting litigation or helping in the process of litigation. Cost orders may prove particularly burdensome for pro bono and non-profit community organisations which assist asylum applicants.

The importance of judicial review

Internationally, UNHCR recommends that asylum seekers should be entitled to at least one level of review - administrative *or* judicial - of refugee decisions. In Australia, review by the RRT alone would satisfy that standard, yet Australia also extends a further right of *judicial* review to asylum seekers. While international human rights law establishes a right to due process or procedural fairness in *civil* and *criminal* proceedings in court (ICCPR, Art 14), there is no express right to procedural fairness in *administrative* proceedings, such as decisions by DIMA or the RRT about refugee status. For its part, the Refugee Convention only requires that refugees enjoy the same access to the courts as nationals of the asylum country *once* the person has been recognised as a refugee.

Nevertheless, as one of the world's oldest liberal democracies, which inherited the British common law tradition, Australia has always offered a higher standard of justice than most countries, including the right to full judicial review. UNHCR's recommendation about review is only a *minimum* international standard, intended to apply equally to authoritarian countries and democracies. Similarly, international human rights law establishes *minimum* standards of due process, and it has long been expected by Australians that procedural fairness also applies to administrative action by government officials.

In this context, applying privative clauses to migration decisions involving non-citizens undermines the principle of equal treatment that is fundamental to the rule of law and the common law, and may infringe the human right to freedom from non-discrimination. The idea of equality before the law demands that Australia's justice system, including the basic right of judicial review of administrative action, must extend to all persons within Australia's jurisdiction, regardless of their migration status. Procedural fairness and natural justice are elementary protections designed to prevent the arbitrary exercise of political power, whether against citizens or non-citizens.

As a practical matter, judicial review also plays an important part in improving Australia's own refugee determination system. As the Law Council of Australia argues, judicial review of refugee decisions is essential because it encourages consistent decisions, correct interpretation of the law, and helps the law to keep pace with changing international circumstances. Further, applicants' rights in tribunals are severely restricted, since there is no right to legal representation or to call witnesses or cross-examine witnesses. Review encourages the independence of tribunals and helps prevent a negative culture of rejection of asylum seekers.

Limits of judicial review

Admittedly, over-reliance on judicial review can be damaging at many levels of a refugee determination system. At best, all a court can do when reviewing a decision is to "vacate" or quash a ruling and send a matter back to the earlier decision-maker to be redetermined in accordance with the law. In practice, cases are returned to the RRT and the whole hearing process has to be repeated. An asylum seeker who holds no visa will remain in detention in spite of an apparent "win". Moreover, a rehearing does not guarantee a different outcome, particularly where the court remits a matter because the RRT has committed a procedural error. Tribunal members learn quickly how to conduct hearings in ways that will keep the courts quiet. If a member does not believe a claimant, or is convinced that conditions in a country of origin are safe, the rehearing will not assist the asylum seeker.

The other problem with judicial review is that claimants may languish for many years in detention waiting for their cases to be heard or reheard. As explained in chapter 11, delays can have a devastating impact on the mental health of the detainees. In recent years there have been cases where asylum seekers have gone back and forth between the RRT and the courts for years. In these cases a break in the procedural deadlock only occurs with the intervention on compassionate grounds by the Minister. The high profile case of the Bakhtiyari family led to no less than 20 legal challenges in an effort to find safe haven in Australia. They were deported to Pakistan (from whence they returned to Afghanistan) in early 2005.

Misuse of judicial review

As applications for judicial review by asylum seekers rapidly increased in recent years, the government often asserted that many asylum applicants are abusing the judicial review process to unjustifiably prolong their stay in Australia. In particular, the government claims that the vast majority of review applications do not succeed. As discussed above, the government responded by attempting to limit access to the courts and to reduce the remedies available once cases reach court.

Undoubtedly, a proportion of judicial review applications lack merit, and some are encouraged by unscrupulous migration agents or lawyers. On the other hand, the problem with the government's approach is that it continues to simplistically restrict access to judicial review, rather than to address the underlying reasons why so many asylum applicants seek judicial remedies.

First, Australia has a comparatively low rate for accepting asylum seekers as refugees relative to other developed countries. This is caused by a number of factors: restrictive interpretations of the "refugee" definition; poor quality decision-making by DIMA and the RRT; and lack of appropriate legal advice. Some asylum seekers go to court in the hope of securing a more favourable interpretation of the "refugee" definition that accords with more generous international practices.

Second, applicants in need of protection may not strictly satisfy the refugee definition, yet there is no regular procedure available to them for claiming complementary protection (for example, based on a fear of torture, or serious human rights abuses). There is therefore an incentive for such applicants to pursue judicial review as a means of avoiding return to serious harm.

Finally, the fact that a judicial review application fails does not mean that the application for protection itself lacks merit. Courts can only review applications for errors of law, not fact, so that cases wrongly decided on the merits may still be unsuccessful in judicial review proceedings.

Minister's discretion to overrule a negative decision

Under s 417 of the *Migration Act*, the Minister has power to make a decision in favour of an applicant where the RRT or a court has rejected an application for review. The Minister can exercise this power when he or she believes that it is in the public interest to do so, but the Minister cannot be compelled to reconsider a rejected application. Nor can reconsiderations be reviewed by the courts: hence the description of the ministerial discretion as "non-compellable and non-reviewable".

The former Minister for Immigration, the Hon Phillip Ruddock MP, used this power much more frequently than Ministers either before or after him. From taking office in 1996 to the end of 2002, Minister Ruddock used his discretionary powers 1,916 times. His predecessor, Senator Nick Bolkus used his power only 311 times between 1993 and 1996. Under Minister Vanstone, the discretion to intervene was devolved to different members of the government. Minister Vanstone retained control of the detention cases, while the Minister for Multicultural Affairs was charged with the review of cases involving persons who were not detained.

One explanation for the higher use of discretion is that the system as a whole became much tougher under the Coalition government, so that more people needed to seek the Minister's merciful intervention. Not all of Minister Ruddock's acts of mercy involved refugees (the discretion extends across all visa classes). However, by far the greatest majority (1,046 cases) were interventions to substitute a decision more favourable than that given by the RRT. There were allegations that Mr Ruddock favoured particular ethnic communities. Such claims are probably inevitable given the way the power is focused so completely in one person and the significance of the decisions made.

In 2003, allegations were made about the Minister's discretionary powers being used to approve visas in return for political donations. The so-called "cash for visas" scandal led to a Senate Select Committee inquiry in late 2003. Four cases of alleged impropriety were investigated but none was substantiated. Despite the inconclusiveness of the inquiry, the Committee's Report made an important contribution to Australia's migration debate. It found that there are serious problems of accountability and transparency in the exercise of the ministerial discretion; that the system is susceptible to bias or a perception of bias; and that it may cause hardship to the vulnerable applicants it is designed to aid. Finally, the Committee questioned whether the regular use of a personal discretion to deal with compassionate and humanitarian issues is appropriate and adequate. It also questioned whether the problems with alleged abuse (and heavy reliance on) discretion illustrated deep, systemic problems in Australia's migration laws, particularly in respect of refugee claimants.

In 2005, the Minister for Immigration was granted additional non-compellable, non-reviewable discretions. The first is to specify alternative arrangements for a person in detention and has been used to release children and families from immigration detention centres. Another is to grant bridging visas to people in long-term immigration detention - a measure designed to address the plight of detainees who cannot be returned to their home countries. The Labor Party, Greens and Democrats called immediately for a reexamination of these extra powers. While everyone welcomed the release of children from detention, questions were raised about conferring further non-reviewable powers on the Minister in light of the earlier controversies.

Statistics on appeals and judicial review

The number of appeals lodged in respect of refugee decisions has varied over time in response to a variety of factors. In periods where decision-makers are presented with asylum seekers from well-publicised and shocking conflicts, one might expect fewer appeals because most claimants are recognised at first instance. More appeals will be lodged as more people are rejected. This appears to be the pattern of appeals for the "wave" of asylum seekers who arrived in Australia in the late 1990s. What is interesting is the increase in the rate of refusals in the politically charged period leading up to the *Tampa* affair in 2001. Given that there was no change in the character of the applications being made throughout this period, the statistics raise questions about the true independence of the refugee status determination system in Australia - both at the primary level and on appeal to the RRT. The decline in the following years probably reflects the drop off in the number of asylum claims after the successful blockade against boat people travelling through Indonesia.

In 1998-99, 5,427 cases were appealed from DIMA to the RRT. The number of appeals rose to 6,131 in 1999-2000 and 6,670 in 2000-01. The following year saw these figures drop to 4,929 appeals, with 4,877 cases recorded in 2002-03. The RRT heard 3,344 appeals from DIMA in 2003-04. Again, this significant reduction in the number of cases heard reflects the drop in the number of asylum seekers lodging refugee claims with DIMA. The first table on the following page shows the success rate of appeals to the RRT:

Outcome of reviews	2001-02	2002-03	2003-04	2004-05
Primary decision affirmed	4,647 (79%)	5,388 (86%)	4,685 (81%)	1,899 (63%)
Primary decision set aside	710 (12%)	359 (6%)	739 (13%)	1,009 (33%)
Withdrawal by review applicant	299 (5%)	426 (7%)	377 (7%)	72 (2%)
Otherwise resolved	131 (2%)	78 (1%)	87 (1%)	53 (2%)
Total finalised	5,865	6,251	5,810	3,033

Source: RRT Annual Reports

Primary decisions "set aside" indicate a successful appeal for the applicant, resulting in the grant of a protection visa. Where the primary decision is "affirmed" or the applicant withdrew his or her review application, the refugee claimant has failed. The RRT Annual Report states that cases described as "otherwise resolved" include applications lodged outside the applicable time limit.

The following table summarises the numbers of migration *and* refugee cases resolved by the Federal Court between 1993 and 2005. Again, when a claimant "withdraws", the implication is that he or she concedes defeat (although this is not always the case where agreements are negotiated between the parties). Withdrawal by the government generally means that the case goes back to the RRT for rehearing. This is also the result where a claimant "wins" in court.

Federal Court Resolution of Migration and Refugee Cases

Year	Claimant withdrew	Govt withdrew	Claimant won	Govt won	Total
1993-94	66	92	20	84	262
1994-95	126	108	18	67	319
1995-96	173	133	15	81	402
1996-97	336	116	17	202	671
1997-98	278	128	49	283	738
1998-99	255	199	74	387	915
1999-00	262	111	77	473	923
2000-01	396	205	71	611	1,283
2001-02	410	131	75	811	1,427
2002-03	526	53	48	879	1,506
2003-04	890	136	102	2,451	3,579
2004-05	896	264	112	2,099	3,371

Source: DIMA Fact Sheets 9 and (former) 86

On average, an application for review in the Federal Court or the Federal Magistrates Court took 5.3 months in 2002-03, an improvement on the 10-month average recorded in 1995-96.

Applications to the High Court increased from 65 applications in 1998-99 to 128 applications in 1999-2000. In early 2002 there were more than 4,000 applicants involved in class actions before the High Court. In 2003-04 more than 2,000 applications for constitutional writs were lodged at the High Court. Many of the applications filed in 2002-03 followed the decision of the Court in *Plaintiff S157* that limited the effect of the privative clause and allowed the review of all decisions marred by jurisdictional error. Most of the applications were subsequently remitted to either the Federal Court or the Federal Magistrates Court. During 2003-04, the number of migration applications dropped to 513.

International appeal mechanisms

Australia has signed and ratified a number of international treaties that allow individuals to make complaints to United Nations committees. Two such committees are the UN Human Rights Committee and the UN Committee Against Torture - both of which have made rulings criticising Australia's treatment of asylum seekers. In particular, as discussed in chapter 10, a number of decisions have criticised Australia's mandatory detention of asylum seekers, including the cases of *A v Australia* (1997), *C v Australia* (2002), and *Baban v Australia* (2003).

In another case, in May 1999, the UN Committee Against Torture decided that Australia's decision to refuse refugee status to a Somali asylum seeker, "SE" (a code name given to protect his identity), exposed him to the risk of return to torture - contrary to Australia's obligations under the Torture Convention. The UN Committee based its conclusions on the advice of international experts on refugees and torture. *SE v Australia* was important because it showed that international supervision of Australia's asylum procedures helps to identify and improve problems with those procedures. In July 1999, the Minister for Immigration used his discretionary power to intervene in the Somali man's case, permitting him to lodge a repeat application for refugee status. However, the man remained in detention. After suffering further rejections and questions being raised about his credibility, SE left Australia of his own accord.

In the case of *Winata v Australia* (2002), the UN Human Rights Committee considered the situation of two non-citizen parents who overstayed their visa in Australia, unsuccessfully applied for asylum, and who were subject to deportation. The couple had a 13-year-old Australian citizen son, who had lived his entire life in Australia, spoke only English and would have had difficulty moving to Indonesia. The Committee found that deporting the parents would arbitrarily interfere in their family life and the rights of the child, violating Australia's international obligations.

The difficulty with using international mechanisms to advance a domestic application for asylum is that they are usually only available in extreme cases - when all other domestic avenues of appeal and review have been exhausted. Complaints to international bodies typically take a very long time to resolve and, even when a decision is made, it is not binding on the domestic government in a strict legal sense. International mechanisms rely on political pressure and public embarrassment to encourage governments to change their practices. If a government chooses to ignore the rulings made, however, the complainant's victory can be hollow and illusory.

Australia has been sensitive to international criticism as interfering in its sovereignty and democratic processes. As a result, Australia has often criticised UN human rights bodies, despite voluntarily signing up to the treaties which create them. While democratic government often protects individual liberties, sometimes the freedoms of non-citizens are not of paramount concern in a majoritarian democracy. This is particularly so in Australia, which, unlike most other common law countries, lacks a constitutional Bill of Rights or a statutory Human Rights Act (as in the UK), which could protect the rights of foreigners and minorities. For this reason, international scrutiny of Australia's treatment of irregular migrants assumes particular importance, especially since international bodies have expertise in human rights law that is absent in Australia's legal system.

References and further reading

Administrative Review Tribunal: <www.aat.gov.au>

Jacqueline Bhabha and Mary Crock, *Seeking Asylum Alone: Unaccompanied and Separated children and Refugee Protection: A Comparative Study of Laws, Policy and Practice in Australian, The United Kingdom and the United States of America* (Themis Press, Sydney, 2006)

Guy Coffey, "The Credibility of Credibility Evidence at the Refugee Review Tribunal" (2003) 15(3) *International Journal of Refugee Law* 377

DIMA "Fact sheet 61. Seeking Asylum within Australia": <www.immi.gov.au/facts/61asylum.htm>

DIMA "Fact Sheets 9. Litigation Involving Migration Decisions": <www.immi.gov.au/facts/09litigation.htm>

Federal Court of Australia, Annual Reports: <www.fedcourt.gov.au/aboutct/ar.html>

Federal Magistrates Court of Australia, Annual Reports: <www.fmc.gov.au/pubs/html/annual.html>

High Court of Australia, Annual Reports: <www.hcourt.gov.au/publications_01.html>

Law Council of Australia, Submission to the Inquiry into the Migration Litigation Reform Bill 2005 (April 2005): <www.lawcouncil.asn.au/get/submissions/2412116656.pdf>

Refugee Review Tribunal: <www.rrt.gov.au>

Senate Legal and Constitutional References Committee Report, *Administration and Operation of the Migration Act 1958*, 2 March 2006, <http://www.aph.gov.au/senate/committee/legcon_ctte/ migration/report/index.htm>

Senate Legal and Constitutional Reference Committee, *A Sanctuary Under review: An Examination of Australia's Refugee and Humanitarian Determination Processes,* June 2000

Senate Select Committee on Ministerial Discretion in Migration Matters (31 March 2004)

Cases

A v Australia, Communication No 560/ 1993, UN Doc CCPR /C/59/D/560/1993 (30 April 1997) (UN Human Rights Committee)

Baban v Australia, Communication No 1014/2001, UN Doc CCPR/C/78/ D/1014/2001 (12 August 2003) (UN Human Rights Committee)

C v Australia, Communication No 900/1999, UN Doc CCPR/C/76/D/900/1999 (28 October 2002) (UN Human Rights Committee)

General Steel Industries Inc v Commissioner for Railways (NSW) (1964) 112 CLR 125

Plaintiff S157/2002 v Commonwealth (2003) 195 ALR 24

SE v Australia, Communication No 120/1998, CAT/C/22/D/120/1998) (20 May 1999) (UN Committee Against Torture)

Winata v Australia (2002) Communication No 30/2000, UN Doc CCPR/C/72/ D/930/2000 (16 August 2001) (UN Human Rights Committee)

6

Who is a Refugee? The Refugee Definition and "Protection"

Key Points in this Chapter

- There is a difference between the ordinary meaning of the term "refugee" and its narrower legal meaning. Under the 1951 Refugee Convention, a refugee is someone who is outside their country of origin and has a well founded fear of persecution, because of their race, religion, nationality, political opinion or membership of a particular social group.
- In September 2001 changes to Australian law narrowed the way the Refugee Convention definition of "refugee" is interpreted in Australia by inserting definitions of the terms "persecution", "particular social group" and "non-political crime". The law also makes it easier to reject the refugee claims of asylum seekers whom officials "have reason to believe" are not telling the truth.
- The Australian courts have generally taken a conservative approach to refugee cases, with some exceptions. The High Court has found that some women fleeing domestic violence can be refugees and that homosexuals can be refugees even if they could avoid persecution by hiding their sexuality.
- Australia has a right to refuse refugee protection to serious criminals, including terrorists and people who have committed war crimes. Refugees can be deported if they commit serious crimes, threaten national security or if they gain residence or citizenship by lying about crimes they have committed.
- The refugee definition does not protect many people who fear serious harm or human rights abuses in their home country, since persecution is only one kind of harm against which people may require protection.
- Australia does not recognise the concept of "complementary protection" for people who fall outside the refugee definition, but who still need protection from serious harm. In contrast, the 25 countries of the European Union offer such protection. As discussed in chapter 5, the only mechanism for "near miss" cases in Australia is the Immigration Minister's non-compellable, non-reviewable discretion to intervene in hard cases.

The legal definition of "refugee"

As explained in chapter 2, the term "refugee" has a technical, legal definition that is quite different from its ordinary, everyday meaning. The legal definition of refugee can be found in the 1951 Convention relating to the Status of Refugees. According to Art 1A(2) of the Convention, a "refugee" is any person who:

> owing to well-founded fear of being persecuted for reasons of race, religion, nationality, membership of a particular social group or political opinion, is outside the country of his nationality and is unable or, owing to such fear, is unwilling to avail himself of the protection of that country; or who, not having a nationality and being outside the country of his former habitual residence as a result of such events, is unable, or, owing to such fear, is unwilling to return to it.

This definition limits protection to persons who can show that they fear persecution on one of the five "grounds" - race, religion, nationality, membership of a particular social group and political opinion. It is not enough that a person is afraid to return for fear of persecution. The use of the qualifier "well-founded" before the word "fear" means that there must be evidence that the person's fear is "well founded" from an objective standpoint. This is why status determination processes around the world rely on reports by governments and NGOs, media articles and other information about what is happening on the ground in the countries from which refugees have fled.

Australia has incorporated some aspects of the Refugee Convention into its domestic law through the *Migration Act 1958*. To qualify for a protection visa in Australia, the Minister for Immigration must be satisfied that an asylum seeker is a person to whom Australia has "protection obligations" under the Refugee Convention: see *Migration Act*, s 36(2)(a). Thus, the Australian courts must interpret the Refugee Convention definition of "refugee" to determine who is owed a protection under domestic law. As explained below, the *Migration Act* was amended in September 2001 to refine the way in which the international definition is read in Australia.

Interpreting the Convention definition of "refugee"

The task of interpreting the definition of "refugee" has grown in complexity as governments, UNHCR, courts, tribunals and academics around the world have provided views about the Refugee Convention. No specialised international court has jurisdiction specifically to interpret the refugee definition, and UNHCR can only issue non-binding guidelines about its preferred approach to definition (see the UNHCR *Handbook on Procedures and Criteria for Determining Refugee Status* (1992)). As a result, interpretation of the definition varies between countries and even between different decision-makers, tribunals and courts in the same country.

In Australia, the most important starting point was in 1989, when the High Court determined the case of *Chan Yee Kin* (1989). That case involved a failed asylum seeker from China whose application for judicial review came before the High Court just as the Chinese government brutally repressed pro-democracy demonstrators in Beijing's Tiananmen Square. These events help to explain why the case became famous, even though the refugee involved was not a demonstrator but had been in Australia for nearly 10 years.

Well-founded fear and the "real chance" test

Chan Yee Kin's case set the boundaries for refugee determinations in Australia by establishing the "real chance" test. The High Court ruled that a "well-founded fear of persecution" has two aspects. First, it means that a person has fled their country with a (subjective) fear in their mind. Second, it means that (viewed objectively) the fear has a reasonable basis in that there is a *real chance* that the person could be persecuted if sent back. Although issues have arisen in later cases about how to determine whether there is a *real chance* that a person will be persecuted, the High Court has resisted attempts to either revise or refine its 1989 test.

"Persecution"

The High Court also said in *Chan Yee Kin* that "persecution" should be interpreted as an ordinary Australian would view the word - as harassment, threatened harm or other offensive behaviour. This finding has been the subject of considerable debate since 1989. For example, when Chinese came to Australia claiming refugee status for opposing China's "One Child" policy, it was questioned whether laws of general application can ever be considered as "persecution". Although the Full Federal Court ruled that persecution required someone to be singled out, the High Court found that this was the wrong approach. The High Court said in *Applicant A* that persecution is about the harms people suffer rather than about the legal means by which the harms are perpetrated. It ruled that forced and coerced abortion and forced sterilisation will always amount to persecution if carried out by, or with the implicit consent of, a government. It is the actions that constitute persecution, not the general policy that couples should only have one child.

In *Ibrahim* (2000), Justice McHugh stated (at [65]) that persecution will ordinarily be constituted by:

- unjustifiable and discriminatory conduct directed at an individual or group for a Convention reason;
- which interferes with the basic human rights or the dignity of that person or the people in the group;

- which the country of nationality authorises or does not stop; and
- which is so oppressive or likely to continue that the person threatened cannot be expected to tolerate it, so that flight from, or refusal to return to, that country is the understandable choice of the individual.

At the same time, the High Court has avoided an exhaustive or precise definition of the term, noting that such an approach would be inappropriate (if not impossible). Whether a particular act or threat will constitute persecution will depend on the circumstances of each case: see also *Gersten* (2000) at [45]; and *Kord* (2002) at [35]. This is the approach taken in the UNHCR *Handbook on Procedures and Criteria for Determining Refugee Status* (1992).

Interestingly, when the Australian Parliament sought to define "persecution" in the *Migration Act*, Justice McHugh's formulation was adopted. Section 91R of that Act stipulates that Art 1A(2) of the Refugee Convention will only apply where a refugee claimant can show that the "essential and significant" reason (or reasons) for the persecution feared is (or are) one or more of the five Convention reasons (race, religion, nationality, membership of a particular social group or political opinion: see below). Persecution is then defined as involving "systematic and discriminatory conduct" and "serious harm", which is defined in turn as including:

- a threat to the person's life or liberty;
- significant physical harassment or ill-treatment of the person; and
- significant economic hardship, denial of access to basic services, or denial of capacity to earn a livelihood of any kind where any of the foregoing threatens the person's capacity to subsist.

The provisions also exhort decision-makers to disregard any conduct engaged in by an asylum seeker in Australia unless the person can satisfy the Minister that the behaviour was not designed to enhance her or his refugee claim. This aspect of the definition effectively places the onus of proof on the refugee claimant, and contradicts UNHCR's recommendation that refugee claimants be given the "benefit of the doubt" in determining a request for asylum.

HREOC has argued that s 91R(3) of the Act potentially excludes claims involving mental torture and serious non-physical harms. HREOC argues that "persecution" should be interpreted in conformity with Australia's obligations under international human rights treaties. HREOC also believes that conduct engaged in by an asylum seeker in Australia should not be disregarded as envisaged by s 91R(3) of the Act. HREOC argues that the post-arrival behaviour of asylum seekers *should* be considered unless the Minister is satisfied that they were acting for the sole purpose of fraudulently claiming protection.

State involvement in persecutory behaviour

Another issue that has arisen in interpreting the UN definition of a refugee is the extent to which persecution must involve the state or government of the country from which an asylum seeker has fled. Court decisions around the world have split into two groups on this point. One view is that the Refugee Convention should be read foremost as an instrument designed to protect people against gross human rights abuses, regardless of the public or private status of the perpetrator. The second view is that the Convention was never designed to deal with all kinds of harm to people. Rather, its function is to protect individuals from a limited range of harms, allowing countries of refuge to provide substitute protection where a state is unable or unwilling to protect its nationals. In Australia, a majority of the High Court has favoured this "accountability" approach (although some judges prefer the "human rights" approach). In practice, this means that the existence of a government or a state is necessary before someone can be a refugee within the meaning of the Refugee Convention. Hence, the High Court has confirmed that people fleeing general violence, such as civil war, will not be recognised as refugees unless they can demonstrate some personal fear of a governmental authority: see *Ibrahim*'s case.

"For reasons of"

Since 1989, many other important rulings on the definition of a refugee have been made by the High Court and by Australia's federal courts. It is not possible to detail all the cases here (some are discussed below), but there are some important basic issues to be aware of. One is the requirement that refugees fear of persecution *by reason of* one of the five Convention grounds: race, religion, nationality, membership of a particular social group, or political opinion. It is not enough to fear persecution or even certain death if an individual is not targeted for one (or more) of these five reasons. In *Kuldip Ram* (1995) the Federal Court found that decision-makers should try to look *through the eyes* of the imagined persecutor so as to determine whether the refugee claimant (a) is being targeted; and (b) why she or he is being targeted for persecution. Justice Burchett said (at 317):

> Persecution involves the infliction of harm, but it implies something more: an element of an attitude on the part of those who persecute which leads to the infliction of harm, or an element of motivation (however twisted) for the infliction of harm. People are persecuted for something perceived about them or attributed to them by their persecutors …

The five Convention grounds

Each of the five Convention grounds has raised different legal issues over the years. Common arguments about the definition include the extent to which claimants must demonstrate that they are being targeted for persecution because they possess some physical or other "immutable" (or unchangeable) attribute. Certainly, in the early cases on the definition, preference was shown for people who were obvious targets - either because of their skin colour, religion or publicly manifested political opinion. This tendency to recognise people who are "obvious" targets eventually led people to question whether the Convention was favouring men - or more importantly failing to see that women acting in less "public" ways could also be refugees: see below.

In cases involving race or nationality, the central question is often not whether a person is being singled out because of their race or nationality, but whether the experiences of the person can be described as "persecution". For example, in *Uma Chand* (1997), the Federal Court ruled that "democratic deficiencies" in a country, such as where one racial group is preferred over another for education and employment opportunities, will not necessarily amount to persecution.

Cases involving claims of religious persecution and political opinion are also marked by differences of interpretation. Again, it seems that much turns on the treatment of claimants in their state of origin and the extent to which their religious beliefs or political opinions are publicly displayed. The greater the harm suffered and the more public the religious or political activities of the person, the easier it has been to gain refugee protection.

Opinion has differed about claimants who have asserted a right to proclaim their religion or to proselytise. In *NABD* (2005), the High Court ruled that decision-makers may draw a distinction between regimes that persecute all members of a religion and those that only persecute individuals who attempt to convert others. Thus, a person who chooses to evangelise will not necessarily be a refugee if the person could survive and practise his or her religion in private. Of course, these cases all turn on their facts: decision-makers typically look at a diverse range of matters including the situation in the claimant's country and the personal attributes and situation of the claimant.

These cases raise the complicated issue of the divide between "public" and "private" behaviour. The decision in *NABD* (2005) suggests that religious cases are treated differently from cases involving sexual orientation: see below. This may be because sexual preference is often difficult to disguise and is so fundamental to a person's identity as to be "immutable".

The final and most controversial of the refugee "grounds" is persecution for "membership of a particular social group". This was inserted into the definition at the suggestion of Sweden to broaden the categories of people eligible for protection. Opinion has differed over the extent to which this "safety net" category broadens the definition beyond that envisaged by the other four categories. The Australian courts have been comparatively generous in interpreting this category. At the same time, the dominant view in the High Court is that the definition should not be interpreted to save all persons at risk of serious human rights abuses. The Court has been careful not to allow this safety net to open the floodgates to refugees.

In practice, this means that the High Court favours an interpretation of the phrase "particular social group" that requires people to belong to a defined group in a given society. In *Applicant A* (1997), the Court confirmed that social groups can be made up of people who identify themselves as a group through voluntary association or through some unchangeable characteristic. It further found that such groups can also exist where they are *perceived* to exist. However, it also stated that a group cannot be defined solely by shared experiences of persecution, because this would result in a circular argument whereby anyone suffering similar persecution could claim that they were members of a social group (that is, comprising other persecuted people). Over the years, debate occurred over whether a group has to be recognised *within* a given society. In *Applicant S* (2004), the High Court confirmed that the test is an objective one. In other words, it is not necessary that a society perceives individuals as belonging to a social group: it is enough that an outside observer can recognise the social pattern.

In 2001, the Australian Parliament refined the definition of "particular social group" to exclude people who fear persecution based on the past persecution of a family member for reasons other than one of the five Convention grounds. These changes are aimed at family members targeted by governments for breaches of civil or criminal law committed by another family member. In practice, this can force asylum seekers to meet the refugee definition in their own right, without considering that a family member not included on the application has already been recognised as a refugee. This impact of the provision is particularly harsh on families separated en route to Australia because women and children typically base their protection claims on the persecution experienced by their husbands and fathers. Family members who arrive as a unit will be assessed on the claims of the primary applicant.

Women and refugee status

Globally, many women are victims of political, economic and social repression. In spite of the overrepresentation of women as refugees, the refugees chosen for resettlement in host countries are predominantly male. Unfortunately, international law does not distinguish between male and female asylum seekers. The Refugee Convention does not include gender as a separate ground of persecution and pays no special attention to the ways in which women might fear different harms. There has, however, been progress in international policy and domestic law, with "gender specific" guidelines for decision-makers created by UNHCR (*Guidelines on the Protection of Refugee Women*) and DIMA (1996, being revised in 2006).

UNHCR notes that, in addition to "standard" forms of persecution, women may experience gender-based discrimination or inhumane treatment amounting to persecution. Examples are women who are punished for refusing to conform to strict codes of social behaviour (such as wearing restrictive clothing or being forced into arranged marriages, or participating in activities reserved only for men) and women subjected to sexual violence, domestic violence or coercive birth control. Such women may be considered to be refugees where a government cannot - or will not - provide adequate protection against the persecution.

Two elements of the refugee definition had to be "reconsidered" for this recognition to take place. First, the harms experienced by women had to be accepted as being persecution. Second, women had to be accepted as a "particular social group" susceptible to the harms described. In 1984, the European Parliament accepted that women facing cruel or inhuman treatment because of their objection to social codes should be considered as a "particular social group" within the refugee definition. Many countries now have special guidelines dealing with gender-based persecution, including Australia, the United States, Canada, Germany, the Netherlands and Switzerland. Female genital mutilation has also been recognised as persecution in France, Canada and the United States.

In Australia, the courts' response to the issue of gender in refugee claims has been mixed. In the main, courts have confirmed that the refugee definition works best for people who flee their countries in fear of public and visible types of persecution. As noted earlier, in many overseas cultures, the people who are most frequently targeted for their politics and even their nationality or religion are men.

Refugees and China's One Child Policy

An example in point is the High Court's ruling on cases involving those fleeing from China's One Child Policy. What really happens to people in China who refuse to comply with the One Child Policy is not always clear. However, in some instances, persuasive evidence has emerged of highly coercive birth control practices in the implementation of the policy. These include husbands and wives being subjected to forced sterilisation, forced abortion and, in extreme cases, of babies being killed at birth.

The current Australian position is that women seeking protection from the One Child Policy are not refugees: see *Applicants A and B* (1997). In the Australian courts the harm Chinese women suffer falls outside the refugee definition because most women who fall pregnant in contravention of the policy are not acting collectively and politically as agitators in an identifiable group. If anything, they are perceived to be acting as domestic subversives - people to whom the refugee definition does not extend. The High Court ruled that a "particular social group" cannot be defined solely by the shared experiences of persecution suffered by members of the group: there must be some other catalyst to bind the group together.

The decision in *Applicant A* (1997) was softened in 2000 by the decision in *Chen Shi Hai* (2000). There, the High Court held that a child born in contravention of the One Child Policy *was* eligible for asylum in Australia. This is because "black children" (as these children are called) are readily identifiable in Chinese society, being singled out from birth because of the illegal behaviour of their parents. Having no control over how they are characterised, black children have an "immutable" status that makes them a recognisable social group. Technically, this decision provides little relief for the mothers who bear such children, because the mothers themselves are not considered refugees. In practice, however, Chinese families in Australia who seek refugee status on the basis of their "black child" should now gain protection. Very few such claims have been made.

The quality of Australia's response to Chinese refugee claimants (and of Australia's status determination system generally) was called into question in the late 1990s following the terrible experience of one Chinese woman, Zhu Qing Ping. Zhu Qing Ping was deported from Australia in 1997 after her refugee claim failed. She was eight and a half months pregnant and protested that her child would be forcibly terminated if she was returned to China and pleaded to be allowed to stay in Australia until after the birth of her second child. Upon her arrival, the woman's child was forcibly aborted just 10 days before it was due. The then Minister for Immigration, Phillip Ruddock, remarked that it had not been established whether her abortion on return to China was forcible or not. A Senate Committee found that the abortion was carried out without the woman's consent: see Senate Legal and Constitutional References Committee (2000); and Crock (2000). The woman returned to China accompanied by her first child, a daughter born in detention in Australia. Today both of the women's children would be recognised as refugees pursuant to the decision in *Chen Shi Hai*.

One Child Policy cases stir concerns in Australia about floods of applications from China. At the same time, few Australians feel comfortable about the fate of the Chinese woman and her aborted child. The problem could be ameliorated if Australia adopted a policy similar to that of the United States. American law allows up to 1,000 people each year to be admitted to America if they fear the One Child Policy. A similar approach in Australia could easily accommodate the tiny number of One Child Policy claims that have been made in Australia to date.

Another way of assisting women affected by the One Child Policy would be to extend Australia's protection obligations to include the requirements of the UN Torture Convention. Women fleeing the One Child Policy may experience torture as it is defined in this Convention. There is little evidence, however, that Australia is willing to extend its protection obligations in either of these ways.

Domestic violence, rape and refugee status

Domestic violence is one of the most serious violations of women's and children's human rights. Violence against women is endemic in many countries. Nevertheless, the ability of women to find refuge from violence in the home varies enormously between countries according to whether governments are prepared to recognise the needs of the victims and to act against the perpetrators of violence. Australian law has slowly begun to recognise that victims of domestic violence can be refugees. The courts in rare cases are prepared to make allowances where the persecution faced by a woman has an official aspect. This can happen where the woman faces harm from a state authority - for example, a woman accused of adultery who would be stoned under Islamic law if returned to her country.

In *Khawar's* case (2002) the High Court recognised a woman victim of domestic violence as a refugee because of the refusal or inability of state authorities to protect her. Here the High Court appears to be following the lead of the English courts. The cases of *Islam* (1999) and *Shah* (1999) involved women victims of domestic violence in Pakistan. The House of Lords held that a "particular social group" could include those who feared persecution because of their gender. While not laying down a general rule, the majority of judges found "evidence of institutionalised discrimination against women by the police, the courts, and the legal system, the central organs of the State". In *Khawar* (2002), the High Court focused less on the cause of the woman's fear (the threat of violence from her husband) and more on the failure of the state to protect her from the harm feared and whether this inaction implied state complicity in the violence.

Claims by women asylum seekers should also be dealt with sensitively in other ways. In many cultures, very personal harms such as rape or sexual assault are the cause of great shame and embarrassment. Such women need a caring environment and sensitive support in order to talk about persecution of such a distressing nature. Immigration staff may not appreciate how the trauma of rape can lead victims to describe their experiences in an inconsistent and contradictory manner. Where this occurs, an applicant's credibility is adversely affected, even though there are good reasons why their stories appear to lack credibility. DIMA's gender guidelines of 1996 recognise this and exhort officers to conduct interviews in a culturally sensitive manner. Whether practice reflects these guidelines, however, is open to question in some cases.

Immigration authorities in Australia and overseas have begun to acknowledge the particular difficulties facing victims of rape. In America there have been a number of cases where the US Court of Appeal has been sensitive to issues of credibility and granted asylum to women who have been victims of rape or sexual violence (see *Angoucheva v INS* (1997)).

Another example is the Canadian case of *G v Minister for Citizenship and Immigration* (1999). The case involved domestic violence and acknowledges how credibility should not be confused with the conflicting evidence often presented by trauma victims. Ms G was a married woman from the Caribbean who had suffered brutal and constant domestic violence for her entire married life. At the original hearing, the decision-maker informed her lawyer that they would not question her credibility. However, in rejecting her application for asylum, they strongly attacked her credibility and claimed her testimony was "not clear and consistent". On appeal, Judge Campbell heavily criticised this approach and ruled there had been a denial of procedural fairness.

Homosexuality and refugee status

Homosexuality has been recognised in many countries as a ground for refugee status in cases where people have been persecuted because of their sexual orientation. UNHCR argues that people facing serious discrimination or inhumane treatment because of their homosexuality, in countries where governments do not offer adequate protection, should be recognised as refugees because such people are often clearly both "persecuted" and members of a "particular social group".

In Australia, people who fear persecution because of their sexual orientation may also be recognised as refugees. However, they face difficulties unless they can demonstrate that their government actively persecutes gay and lesbian people. In the past, many homosexual asylum seekers were rejected in Australia if it was found that they could act discreetly and thus avoid persecution. In the case of *S395/2002* (2003), the High Court overturned lower court rulings that homosexuals could not claim refugee status if they could hide their sexual preference. The case was a world leading judgment by a final appellate court on issues of discretion and homosexuality.

Children and refugee status

There remains one group of people whose protection claims have yet to gain the recognition they deserve: children. In many respects, young people stand today in a similar situation to women refugee claimants some years ago. Although children represent more than half of the world's refugees, the jurisprudence on applying the refugee definition to children is largely underdeveloped. There are a number of reasons for this. While women and children dominate the world's refugee camps, they tend to be less mobile than men and so are not as prevalent among refugee populations moving between countries. Just as importantly, there is a tendency to subsume the status of women and children within family groups. While there has been a recent move to recognise the special needs of women, the same changes in thinking have yet to occur in relation to children: see Bhabha and Crock (2006).

In Australia, jurisprudence on children and refugee status is recent and poorly developed. While there are a few instances where children have been the focus of refugee claims (*Chen Shi Hai* (2000) is a good example), in most cases the claims of child asylum seekers are not spelled out separately, and children thus win or lose under the claims of the accompanying adults.

However, children can be refugees in their own right. For the Convention to be recognised as relevant to a child's claim, the specific nature of the harms that can and do befall children must be carefully considered. Just as the Convention definition has been "read down" to accommodate the particular experiences of women, it is necessary to make similar concessions for children.

The RRT has recognised the inherent difficulties associated with children's evidence (in its *Guidelines on Children Giving Evidence*). DIMA has also issued guidelines based on the 1989 Convention on the Rights of the Child and relevant UNHCR guidelines as a framework. These guidelines address both the processing of refugee claims and the refugee definition in cases involving child claimants.

One obvious problem with literally interpreting the refugee definition is that young children may be vulnerable, yet incapable of expressing any fear. As is often the case with child soldiers, it is an attribute of childhood that children do not experience fear in the same way as adults because of their underdeveloped cognitive state. The inability of a child to express subjective fear should not be a barrier to recognition of refugee status. In assessing the child's refugee claims, UNHCR guidelines recommend that "particular regard should be given to circumstances such as the child's stage of development, his/her possibly limited knowledge of conditions in the country of origin, and their significance to the legal concept of refugee status, as well as his/her vulnerability".

Similarly, the RRT *Guidelines on Children Giving Evidence* acknowledge that a "child applicant in a refugee matter may not be able to express a subjective fear of persecution in the same manner as an adult applicant". They also recognise that children may be unable to present evidence in support of their claims because of their age, gender, cultural background or other circumstances. The guidelines state that greater allowances should be made for inconsistencies in children's evidence.

DIMA guidelines also state that if there is reason to believe that the parents of a minor have a well-founded fear of persecution, then the child may also have such a fear. This raises a different problem concerning the kind of harms that children face. In many refugee claims, the focus is placed on what would happen to the adults in a family group, whereas in fact the children may be just as at risk of harm. Too often, questions are not asked about what would happen to the children.

Even where such questions are asked, legal issues can be raised about whether the harms can be related to the refugee definition. An example is where a child is returned to a country where trafficking in children, the recruitment of children as soldiers or the general exploitation of children are known problems. Does the vulnerability of a child to these forms of harm make the child a refugee? The answer probably should be "yes" if the child can be identified as belonging to a "particular social group" at risk of such harms. Such groups may comprise "unaccompanied children" or "children of dissidents".

There have been recent cases where the Australian courts have considered whether children travelling alone (unaccompanied minors) can constitute a "particular social group". The High Court's decision in *Applicant S* (2004) is helpful, clarifying that the existence of a social group should be determined using the test of an objective observer of a particular society. It is not necessary that a group be overtly acknowledged as such within a society. Even so, there are many cases where the claims of children have not been spelt out, even though there is evidence that they would face greater dangers than their parents.

Importantly, Art 22 of the Convention on the Rights of the Child requires states to ensure that child asylum seekers and child refugees "receive appropriate protection and humanitarian assistance" in enjoying their rights under the Convention and other human rights treaties. States must also assist the UN, international agencies and NGOs to help reunify such children with their families: see further Crock (2005); Bhabha and Crock (2006) and Crock (2006).

Exclusion from refugee status

A very small number of asylum seekers who arrive in Australia are alleged to have committed war crimes, human rights violations or other serious crimes in their home countries. Any influx of people fleeing war, civil unrest or persecution may contain some people who are seeking to escape responsibility for their crimes. Under international law, people who have committed serious crimes are expressly excluded from protection as refugees. Article 1F of the Refugee Convention excludes a person from refugee status where there are "serious reasons for considering" that the person has:

(a) committed a crime against peace, a war crime, or a crime against humanity, as defined in international treaties;

(b) committed a serious non-political crime outside the country of refuge before his admission to that country as a refugee;

(c) been guilty of acts contrary to the purposes and principles of the United Nations.

Australia is allowed to remove these people once they have been properly identified and evidence of their crimes has been established. The person need not be convicted of a criminal offence, as long as there are "serious reasons for considering" that the person has committed such conduct. The usual practice in many countries is to first consider the "inclusion" clauses (that is, whether a person has a well-founded fear of persecution for a Convention reason) before then applying the exclusion clauses. This is necessary because all the elements of a person's experience of persecution may not emerge if the exclusion clauses are applied first. Some countries, however, examine exclusion before inclusion in exceptional cases.

Exclusion under Art 1F(a) is based on the international crimes clearly identified in international treaties. In contrast, there is no internationally agreed list of crimes for exclusion under Art 1F(b), allowing national governments a discretion in deciding when a crime is both "serious" and "non-political". Since the 19th century, persons who commit "political" crimes have been excluded from extradition to another country to face prosecution for crimes committed there. The "political offence exception" aimed to prevent political rebels from being unfairly or oppressively treated by their home governments. Many courts have thus interpreted the meaning of "non-political" crimes in *refugee exclusion* cases by referring to the meaning of "political" crimes in *extradition law* cases.

While national courts have adopted different approaches, many liberal democracies consider crimes to be "non-political" where the targets of violence include innocent civilians, or where the means used are atrocious, indiscriminate or disproportionate to the end sought. People who commit such acts may, therefore, be excluded from refugee status. However, people accused of "political" crimes by authoritarian governments may be entitled to refugee status if they have been unjustly accused. Sometimes, "political crimes" are simply expressions of basic rights like freedom of thought or opinion.

The most ambiguous ground for excluding a person from refugee protection is that involving "acts contrary to the purposes and principles of the United Nations": see Art 1F(c). The principles and purposes of the UN are listed in Arts 1 and 2 of the UN Charter (1945), and include many of the aspirations of a peaceful and just international community. Because many of these aspirations are vague hopes rather than precise legal concepts, it is accepted that this ground of exclusion should be narrowly interpreted and cautiously applied, to prevent the unfair or oppressive exclusion of refugees. The small number of cases under Art 1F(c) has excluded serious drug traffickers, serious human rights violators and suspected terrorists.

Australian decision-makers take into account the exclusion grounds in Art 1F of the Refugee Convention in determining whether an applicant meets the refugee definition. DIMA has an alert list containing 7,000 names of suspected war criminals and a War Crimes Screening Unit was established in 2002-03. Decision-makers may also take into account allegations made by international criminal tribunals, INTERPOL, ASIO or other intelligence agencies, foreign governments or groups in the community about a person, although information from the latter two sources is not always reliable. In 2004-05, DIMA imposed additional screening on 881 visa applicants (of all visa types) suspected of war crimes, although 738 cases were cleared and it was only recommended that seven cases be refused.

Allegations were raised in the media in late 2005 that Australia had allowed some suspected foreign war criminals to enter and remain in

Australia. It can be difficult to track suspects who may conceal their identities and falsify documents, while evidence against them may also be hard to locate and test. Indeed, there is a danger that refugees may be excluded on the basis of unproven allegations, given the sensitivities surrounding crimes of this nature. In addition, people who associated with suspected criminals should not necessarily be excluded themselves.

In 2001, definitions were inserted into the *Migration Act* of "non-political" and "particularly serious" crimes in relation exclusion under Art 1F(b) of the Refugee Convention: see *Migration Act*, ss 91T and 91U. The amendments expand the circumstances in which refugees convicted of criminal offences (abroad or in Australia) can be excluded from protection and returned to their country of origin. The clause defining "serious Australian offences" is of particular concern given the clamp down on asylum seekers convicted of offences in immigration detention. The changes facilitate the removal of refugees involved in riots and other disturbances in custody. The problem here is that under the Refugee Convention, exclusion is only permitted for "serious non-political crimes" *outside the country of refuge* – and not for offences committed *after* entering the country (withdrawal of protection after entry is discussed below). In any case, offences such as escaping from detention are arguably *political* acts (not non-political as required by the Convention) and may not be *serious* enough to trigger exclusion under the Convention (which refers more to violent acts endangering life). By adding a ground for exclusion not found in the Convention, the law places Australia at risk of breaching its protection obligations.

In addition to considering the exclusion clauses during the asylum process, under Australian law the Minister for Immigration may refuse to grant a visa or cancel a visa (including a protection visa) if a person does not pass a "character test": see s 501 of the *Migration Act*. There are four grounds for failing the character test, including where: (a) a person has a substantial criminal record (meaning a sentence of imprisonment for 12 months or more); (b) a person is suspected of associating with a criminal or criminal group (including in the past); (c) a person's past and present criminal or general conduct makes them not of good character; or (d) there is a significant risk that in Australia the person would (i) engage in crime, (ii) harass, molest, intimidate or stalk another person, (iii) vilify a segment of the community, (iv) incite discord in the community or in a segment of it, or (v) endanger the community or a segment of it (through disruption or violence).

If the Minister for Immigration intends to refuse to grant or to cancel a protection visa under Arts 1F, 32 or 33(2) of the Refugee Convention, the Minister may issue a certificate in the national interest declaring that the person is an excluded person: see s 502 of the *Migration Act*. Security or intelligence information can be protected from disclosure even to the person affected by a decision under s 501: see s 503A of the *Migration Act*. A controversial example of this occurred in 2005, when an American peace activist, Scott Parkin, was detained and removed from Australia without being told why he was considered to be a security risk to Australia, and even though he had recently been cleared for a visa before coming to Australia. For those already on a visa, only 1% of the 23,365 visas cancelled in 2004-05 were cancelled on character grounds, with 47 people removed in that year.

Since the character test also applies to decisions to *grant* visas (including protection visas), it effectively establishes very wide, additional exclusion grounds which are not found in the Refugee Convention. It is not known how many protection visas were refused under the broader character grounds in s 501. Most refugee applicants who are excluded are excluded by the application of Art 1F in the asylum determination process. Even if s 501 supplies an additional basis for refusing a protection visa, the Minister has a discretion not to exercise the power. Even so, it is of significant concern that Australian law allows refugees to be refused protection in wider circumstances not permitted under international law.

Exclusion of terrorists from asylum

Since the late 1990s, there has been growing international pressure automatically to exclude terrorists and suspected terrorists from asylum. The UN General Assembly and the UN Security Council have urged states not to grant asylum to those who plan, facilitate or participate in terrorism and to prevent refugee status being abused by terrorists: see Security Council Resolution 1373 (2001). They have also urged that terrorism should not be regarded as a political offence exempt from extradition.

The difficulty with automatically excluding terrorists or suspected terrorists from refugee status is that terrorism is not listed as a separate ground of exclusion under Art 1F of the 1951 Refugee Convention. Nor is terrorism a separate international crime under Art 1F(a). Accordingly, exclusion must be based on an individual assessment of whether a person falls within Art 1F of the Convention - not by automatic exclusion of all suspected terrorists, which risks denying procedural fairness. As a UK tribunal stated in the case of *Thayabaran*: "The question is not whether the appellant can be characterized as a terrorist, but rather whether the words of the exemption clause apply to him". Those who commit terrorist acts may be excluded where those acts amount to a war crime, crime against humanity or a serious non-political crime; or where the acts are contrary to UN purposes and principles.

Further, there is no internationally accepted *definition* of terrorist offences that could serve as a principled basis of exclusion, despite the best efforts of the international community since the 1930s. National definitions of terrorism are widely divergent, potentially leading to incongruous exclusion results. Article 1F is an *international* standard which cannot be determined by reference to unilateral national definitions of terrorism, some of which criminalise a very wide range of activities, including legitimate political resistance. Since some national definitions criminalise relatively minor conduct, reliance on such definitions in exclusion decisions endangers refugees in need of protection. While there may indeed be cogent policy reasons for defining terrorism, until the international community agrees on a definition, reference to the term is of little legal or practical use in excluding undeserving persons from international protection.

At the end of the Second World War, the drafters of the Refugee Convention were well aware of the security concerns of states. The Convention has always ensured that those who carry out serious terrorist-type acts are excluded. The 1946 Constitution of the International Refugee Organization (IRO) had excluded from the IRO's mandate persons who "participated in any terrorist organization" after the war. Yet, the drafters of the Refugee Convention decided *not* to exclude terrorists explicitly, indicating that the exclusion provisions of the Convention were considered sufficient.

There is little evidence that international refugee law has been misused by suspected terrorists to gain admission to other states or as a means of safe haven. In America, none of the 11 September 2001 hijackers was a refugee or asylum seeker. Terrorists are far more likely to pursue legal migration channels to infiltrate a state than to use asylum procedures, since asylum seekers are subject to rigorous identity and security checks, document verification, administrative scrutiny and suspicion of credibility, and, in some states, mandatory detention.

It is important to reject unjustified linkages between terrorists and asylum. Refugee law does not provide safe haven for terrorists and does not prevent the prosecution of suspects. As UNHCR notes, "any discussion on security safeguards should start from the assumption that refugees are themselves escaping persecution and violence - including terrorist acts". Attention should focus on *the security of refugees themselves,* not just the security threats posed by refugees.

Withdrawal of protection

Once asylum seekers are recognised as refugees and accepted into the community, they can only be removed in exceptional circumstances. These include instances where the refugee represents a threat to national security. Under Art 33(2) of the Refugee Convention:

> [*Non-refoulement*] may not ... be claimed by a refugee whom there are reasonable grounds for regarding him as a danger to the security of the country in which he is, or who, having been convicted by a final judgement of a particularly serious crime, constitutes a danger to the community of that country.

This provision, which allows the withdrawal of protection, is distinct from the Art 1F exclusion clauses, though governments (including Australia as discussed above) sometimes confuse them. Indeed, Art 14(5) of the EU Qualification Directive (see chapter 12) provides that the grounds for withdrawal of protection in Art 33(2) of the Refugee Convention may be used to exclude persons *before* they are granted refugee status. This effectively establishes a fourth exclusion clause.

Article 33(2) means that, like other foreign nationals living permanently in Australia, refugees can have their permission to remain in Australia revoked and may be removed if they commit serious crimes, threaten national security, or commit rare offences such as treason, treachery, sabotage, sedition, incitement to mutiny or assisting prisoners of war to escape. Many of these offences are archaic, little used and ill-suited to a modern democracy like Australia. Indeed, a review of the federal criminal law in 1991 recommended that most of these offences be reformed and narrowed, and that some of them be abolished altogether.

As a result of recent changes to citizenship laws, even refugees who become Australian citizens may have their citizenship revoked if they obtained their citizenship fraudulently, or if their original entry to Australia was fraudulent. A failure to reveal crimes committed in the past can count as fraud in these cases. In 2005, it was even proposed by some backbenchers that people who are naturalised as citizens should have their citizenship stripped from them if they are involved in terrorist activities. Not only would this create a category of second-class citizens, whose ongoing citizenship depends on good behaviour (unlike citizens by birth in Australia), it also risks making some people stateless, contrary to international law.

People subject to expulsion under Art 33(2) are still entitled to complementary forms of human right protection, such as the absolute prohibition on Australia returning a person to torture (see below). In some cases, it is not possible to remove criminal non-citizens if other countries refuse to accept them. In other cases, Australia will refuse to send people back if they are likely to be executed or receive an unfair trial, because Australia considers the death penalty and arbitrary justice to be unacceptable violations of human rights.

Where it is not possible to deport alleged criminals, Australia may decide to prosecute or detain them in accordance with Australian law. As discussed in chapter 9, in the *Al-Kateb* case (2004), the High Court found that where a person is not entitled to remain in Australia, but cannot be removed, Australian law could permit them to be detained indefinitely.

Gaps in protection: internally displaced persons

By requiring that a refugee be outside their country of origin, the Convention definition excludes people displaced *within* their home country (also known as "internally displaced persons" or IDPs). IDPs leave their homes for similar reasons as refugees, but because they do not cross international borders, they are not recognised as refugees and do not receive the same rights and protections under international law. IDPs include people forced to flee their homes to escape armed conflict, general violence, human rights abuses or natural or human-made disasters.

It is estimated that there are around 25 million IDPs around the world, following the escalation of internal conflicts after the end of the Cold War and/or natural disasters. Recent sources of displacement include the Indian Ocean tsunami in 2004; Hurricane Katrina in the southern United States in 2005; the clearing of slums in Robert Mugabe's Zimbabwe; ethnic cleansing in the Dafur region of Sudan; and Israel's military demolition of Palestinian houses in the Occupied Territories.

Traditionally, it was assumed that national governments would look after the welfare of people displaced within their own borders. However, this assumption, which was based on the historical deference of international law to national sovereignty, may be flawed where a government itself is the source of displacement. A government may be unable to protect displaced persons (since it lacks resources, or effective control over territory in a conflict), or it may be unwilling to protect (because it deliberately targets or discriminates against certain groups). In these circumstances, international protection may become necessary as a substitute (or complement) to national protection. Displacement by natural disasters may be aggravated by underlying separatist conflicts, such as when government relief efforts became politicised after the tsunami in Aceh (Indonesia) and in Tamil Tiger controlled areas of Sri Lanka.

While the UN adopted *Guiding Principles* on internal displacement in 1998, these are *non-binding* standards to guide governments and international organisations, and there is little international political interest in adopting binding legal rules to protect IDPs. In practice, the UN General Assembly sometimes tasks UNHCR with responsibility for the welfare of IDPs, particularly where related to refugee protection. In addition, at the World Summit in 2005, the international community agreed on the principle that there is a national and international "responsibility to protect" people at risk of grave human rights abuses, although it remains to be seen whether (and how) this translates into concrete international interventions to protect vulnerable populations of internally displaced persons.

Gaps in protection: human rights abuses

Since the drafting of the Refugee Convention over 50 years ago, the causes of refugee movements have become more numerous and more varied. In recent years refugee outflows have resulted primarily from civil wars and ethnic, tribal or religious violence. This change prompted the UN General Assembly to extend UNHCR's mandate to protect people fleeing war whose states are unable or unwilling to protect them – even though such persons do not fear persecution under the Convention definition.

Regional arrangements in some parts of the world have formally *expanded the definition of a refugee* to include a broader range of people. The 1969 Organisation of African Unity Convention in Africa and the 1984 Cartagena Declaration in Latin America define a refugee to include many war victims. However, this broader concept of a refugee has not been accepted in the same way in Western Europe, North America or Australia, which remain less willing to protect victims of war and civil conflict. Even in the European Union, where human rights concerns provide a basis for legal protection (including temporary protection), persons fleeing war or violence may not be entitled to formal refugee status and its accompanying rights.

It should be remembered that the right of every person *to seek asylum* from persecution was central to the major human rights treaties adopted after the Second World War. The Universal Declaration of Human Rights (UDHR 1948) (Art 14) and the International Covenant on Civil and Political Rights (ICCPR 1966) (Arts 6, 7, 9 and 12) recognise the fundamental importance of the right to seek asylum. However, political difficulties in securing international agreement on protecting refugees meant that *the right to enter another country* in order to seek asylum was not enshrined in the Refugee Convention.

Many people who do not qualify as refugees but who are nevertheless unable or unwilling to return to their country of origin may still require urgent humanitarian assistance from other countries. Countries offer such protection because they recognise that otherwise people may lose their lives or freedom, even though they do not technically fall within the refugee definition.

In addition, states may have other obligations under international or regional human rights treaties that prevent them from deporting persons who, while not Convention refugees, nevertheless need international protection. For example, the 1984 Convention against Torture prohibits the removal of a person to a place where he or she faces a substantial risk of being tortured, while the ICCPR and the 1950 European Convention on Human Rights extend this prohibition to persons who face *cruel, inhuman or degrading treatment or punishment*. Other relevant treaties include the 1989 Convention on the Rights of the Child and, more generally, the protections of international human rights law.

These international human rights treaties were signed voluntarily by Australian governments and subsequently approved by Australian Parliaments. The obligations on Australia to protect human rights have not been forced on the Australian people against their will by some outside body and therefore they do not infringe Australia's sovereignty. There are good reasons why Australia agreed to these treaties, because they protect the same fundamental human rights and values that the Australian community upholds.

Nonetheless, these treaties have not been made fully part of Australian domestic law by the Parliament and Australia lacks any Bill of Rights like those found in other Western democracies. Accordingly, those treaties cannot be relied upon directly in Australia as a basis for protection. This is in spite of the fact that the obligation to refrain from sending a person back to torture has been recognised under international law as a fundamental duty that cannot be suspended (or "derogated" from) under any circumstances - even in the "war on terror".

As the European Court of Human Rights found in the case of *Chahal v UK* (1996), the prohibition against returning a person to torture cannot be suspended even in a time of public emergency threatening the life of the nation. By way of contrast, in the case of *Suresh v Canada* (2002), the Canadian Supreme Court placed Canada in breach of international law by allowing the deportation of a suspected terrorist to a country where he was at risk of torture. The case involved the exceptional situation where Canada believed its national security was at risk.

If Australia breaches its obligations, affected persons can only seek remedies at the international level, such as by making an individual complaint to the UN Committee against Torture or the UN Human Rights Committee in Geneva (Australia currently has a representative serving his second term on this Committee, Professor Ivan Shearer, who followed another distinguished Australian lawyer, Justice Elizabeth Evatt). Even then, the findings of UN committees are not enforceable; the process requires domestic avenues of redress to be first exhausted; and such claims can be expensive and take a long time.

Protection against torture

The Torture Convention defines torture as any act by a public official which causes severe pain or suffering (either physical or mental) to another person, for any of the following purposes:

- to obtain information or a confession from the person;
- to punish an act the person has committed or is suspected of committing;
- to intimidate or coerce the person or a third person;
- to discriminate against the person.

Common forms of torture include sensory and sleep deprivation, use of psychotropic drugs, electric shocks, burning, mutilation, psychological abuse, isolation and solitary detention, beatings, sexual violence and rape, starvation, exposure to heat and cold, sham execution, near fatal immersion in water and suffocation, being forced into crippling positions, and being forced to watch the brutalisation of family or friends.

The Convention against Torture has a number of limitations. First, only acts committed by public officials are regarded as torture, even though private military or criminal groups may commit similar violence. Second, acts committed for purposes other than those listed are not covered, such as violence to humiliate or degrade a person. Third, the treaty does not list specific acts of torture, leaving room for governments to argue that certain uses of force or interrogation do not constitute "severe" pain or suffering.

Finally, many of the provisions in the Convention only apply to *torture* and not to *cruel, inhuman or degrading treatment*. Thus, there is no duty on governments to criminalise cruel, inhuman or degrading treatment or to compensate persons who suffer it; information obtained from a person by such methods may be used against a person to incriminate them in criminal proceedings; and persons at risk of such treatment may be returned to a place where it may occur (unlike for torture).

Even before 2001, Amnesty International estimated that torture was used by 120 governments. After 11 September 2001, the use of torture appears to have accelerated around the world. A number of trends have emerged. First, some governments have argued that aggressive interrogation techniques, used against suspected terrorists, do not amount to torture and are therefore permissible. Second, some governments have "contracted out" the torture and interrogation of terrorist suspects to less scrupulous countries, or irregular armed forces not bound by international law, particularly through "irregular rendition" to avoid procedural protections. Third, some lawyers have attempted to justify the torture of suspected terrorists in some situations (such as the "ticking bomb" scenario), including US government lawyers, some Australian academics and even a Harvard law professor.

Complementary protection

Some countries have a tradition of extending protection to persons who need it, even though they do not meet the formal refugee definition. This practice is known as "complementary protection" or "subsidiary protection", but historically has been described also as humanitarian protection, "Refugee B status", or protection of *de facto* refugees. There is, however, no universal system of complementary protection. The most comprehensive transnational scheme is found in the European Union, which in 2004 adopted a Directive on "subsidiary protection". This Directive provides a legal status that is similar, but not identical to, Convention refugee status to persons who fear return to:

- the death penalty or execution;
- torture or inhuman or degrading treatment or punishment; or
- a serious and individual threat to a civilian's life or person by reason of indiscriminate violence in international or internal armed conflict.

Australian law used to allow the grant of visas on humanitarian grounds. However, from the early 1990s, the idea of complementary protection became dependent on the Immigration Minister exercising a special discretionary power, which the Minister cannot be forced to exercise and which cannot be reviewed by the courts. This *ad hoc* system does not provide sufficient guarantees against return to torture or other serious harm, and may place Australia in breach of international law.

It would be preferable for Australia to establish a new visa category for complementary human rights protection - as in the EU - while retaining the Minister's humanitarian discretion for exceptional, last resort cases. While there is no internationally agreed definition of "complementary" or subsidiary protection, it generally refers to the grant of protection status based on international human rights treaties, such as the Convention against Torture, the Convention on the Rights of the Child or the ICCPR. As chapter 12 shows, in recent years the European Union has introduced a formal legal protection status for those who need complementary protection on human rights grounds, and this is a model Australia could adopt.

In spite of various cases that have caused controversy and/or led to the lodging of complaints with the UN Torture Committee, the political will to introduce a comprehensive visa scheme for near-miss refugee cases still appears to be missing. (Although in 2006, the Labor Opposition called for Pacific islanders at risk of displacement from rising sea levels (due to climate change) to be offered humanitarian resettlement in Australia.) In 1951, the drafters of the Refugee Convention regarded refugee protection as part of international human rights law, and not as a disconnected area of law. Just as human rights law has evolved and become more sophisticated since 1951, so too could countries develop refugee law by recognising and incorporating these developments in the human rights field.

References and further reading

Jacqueline Bhabha and Mary Crock, *Seeking Asylum Alone: Unaccompanied and Separated children and Refugee Protection: A Comparative Study of Laws, Policy and Practice in Australian, The United Kingdom and the United States of America* (Themis Press, Sydney, 2006)

Mary Crock, *Seeking Asylum Alone: Unaccompanied and Separated Children and Refugee Protection in Australia* (Themis Press, Sydney, 2006)

Mary Crock, "Lonely Refuge: Judicial Responses to Separated Children Seeking Refugee Protection in Australia" (2005) 22(2) *Law in Context* 120

Mary Crock, "A Sanctuary Under Review: Where to From Here for Australia's Refugee and Humanitarian Processes" (2000) 23 *UNSWLJ* 246

DIMA, *Policy and Advice Manual 3*

DIMA, *Refugee and Humanitarian Visa Applicants: Guidelines on Gender Issues for Decision-Makers* (1996)

Gender guidelines for a number of jurisdictions can be found at the Centre for Gender and Refugee Studies at the University of California Hastings: <http://cgrs.uchastings.edu/law/gender_guidelines.php>

HREOC, "Submissions to the Refugee Review Tribunal Regarding s.91R(3) Migration ACT 1958": <www.hreoc.gov.au/legal/guidelines/refugee_review.html#1>

Jane McAdam, "Complementary Protection and Beyond: How states deal with human rights protection" (2005) *UNHCR New Issues in Refugee Research*, Working Paper 118

RRT, *Guidelines on Children Giving Evidence* <www.rrt.gov.au/newsarchive.htm>

Ben Saul, "Exclusion of Suspected Terrorists from Asylum", Institute for International Integration Studies (Trinity College, Dublin), Discussion Paper No 26, July 2004

Senate Legal and Constitutional Reference Committee, *A Sanctuary Under review: An Examination of Australia's Refugee and Humanitarian Determination Processes,* June 2000

UN *Guiding Principles on Internal Displacement,* UN Doc E/CN.4/1998/53/Add.2 (1998), noted in UN Commission on Human Rights resolution 1998/50, <www.umn.edu/humanrts/instree/GuidingPrinciplesonInternal Displacement.htm>

UNHCR, *Guidelines on the Protection of Refugee Women,* EC/SCP/67, July 1991, <www.unhcr.org/women>

UNHCR, *Handbook on Procedures and Criteria for Determining Refugee Status,* January 1992, <www1.umn.edu/humanrts/instree/refugeehandbook.pdf>

Cases

Al-Kateb v Godwin (2004) 219 CLR 562

Angoucheva v INS, 106 F 3d 781 (7th Cir 1997)

Applicant A v Minister for Immigration and Ethnic Affairs (1997) 142 ALR 331

Applicant NABD of 2002 v Minister for Immigration and Multicultural and Indigenous Affairs (2005) 216 ALR 1

Applicant S v Minister for Immigration and Multicultural Affairs (2004) 206 ALR 242

Chan Yee Kin v Minister for Immigration and Ethnic Affairs (1989) 87 ALR 412

Chen Shi Hai v Minister for Immigration and Multicultural Affairs (2000) 170 ALR 553

Gersten v Minister for Immigration and Multicultural Affairs [2000] FCA 1917

Islam v Secretary of State for Home Department [1999] 2 AC 629

Minister for Immigration and Multicultural and Indigenous Affairs v Kord (2002) 125 FCR 68

Suresh v Canada (Minister of Citizenship and Immigration) [2002] 1 SCR 3

Kuldip Ram v Minister for Immigration and Ethnic Affairs and the RRT (1995) 130 ALR 314

Minister for Immigration and Multicultural Affairs v Ibrahim (2000) 204 CLR 1

Minister for Immigration and Multicultural Affairs v Khawar (2000) 178 ALR 120

S395/2002 v Minister for Immigration and Multicultural Affairs (2003) 203 ALR 112

Thayabaran (UK Immigration Tribunal, No 12250)

Uma Chand (unreported, Federal Court, Branson J, 17 March 1997)

7

Protecting Australia: Border Control and the Deflection of Asylum seekers

Key Points in this Chapter

- Australia passed laws in 1999 and 2001 to improve "search and seizure" powers.
- The government has taken steps to divert asylum seekers from Australia, including by funding UNHCR to assess the refugee claims of asylum seekers in Indonesia who would otherwise come to Australia.
- In August 2001 the government took a stand against people smuggling by refusing permission for asylum seekers rescued by the *MV Tampa* to land in Australia. The *Tampa* affair became the basis for "the Pacific Solution", later renamed the "Pacific Strategy". Asylum seekers intercepted en route to Australia or at an "excised offshore place" are processed offshore (at Australia's expense). Countries participating in the scheme are (or were) Nauru, Papua New Guinea (PNG) and New Zealand. The scheme is prohibitively expensive and has drawn considerable criticism.
- Retrospective legislation was enacted to validate (or legalise) the action taken by the Australian authorities in the *Tampa* case.
- Parliament empowered the Minister for Immigration to declare parts of Australian territory ("excised offshore places") to be outside the "migration zone". Asylum seekers who land on "excised" territory no longer have a right to make a valid visa application in Australia unless the Minister for Immigration exercises his or her power to allow an application to be made. In July 2005, islands off the coast of Queensland, Western Australia and Northern Territory were also excised from Australia's migration zone. Australia's excision provisions now affect approximately 4,891 islands.
- The interdiction program, code-named "Operation Relex", resulted in the apprehension and deflection of 1,830 people on 12 boats between August 2001 and May 2002. This program remains in operation.
- Special visa classes have been created for asylum seekers recognised as refugees under the determination processes devised for the Pacific Strategy.
- In May 2006 Indonesia's reaction to the grant of asylum to fugitives from West Papua led to initiatives to extend the "Pacific Strategy" to cover all unauthorised boat arrivals. The proposal is to deflect all asylum seekers arriving in Australia by boat (without visas) to Nauru or some other destination for the processing of refugee claims. The measures would catch both those interdicted en route to Australia and those who make landfall on the mainland. The proposals are very controversial because they have no precedent anywhere in the world and because many assert that they place Australia in breach of basic aspects of the UN Refugee Convention.

Deterring and deflecting refugees and irregular migrants

There can be no doubt that years of media hype and government rhetoric (from both sides of the political divide) about invasions and loss of border control have engendered deep fears in the Australian public. This is despite the relatively low number of people who have entered Australia without authority. Conscious of how much of the public feels, the federal government has gone to extraordinary lengths to stop asylum seekers from coming to Australia – at great cost to the country.

This chapter explores the mechanisms that have been put in place to restrict, discourage and to prevent people from seeking asylum in Australia. It tracks the legislative changes made in and after 1999 in response to a surge in the number of unauthorised arrivals seeking access to Australia. These began with the *Border Protection Legislation Act 1999* (Cth) which made a raft of significant amendments to the *Migration Act 1958*. For example, it reintroduced temporary protection for certain persons recognised as refugees in Australia: see chapter 8.

This chapter focuses on the measures taken to improve "border control" and to limit access to refugee procedures in Australia. These include so-called "safe third country" provisions, based on the idea that refugees should not be eligible for asylum in Australia if they could seek protection elsewhere. Such measures later became the basis for more extensive initiatives to force refugees to exhaust all options before seeking protection in Australia.

Deflection measures also included agreements made with countries of transit to stop the flow of asylum seekers to Australia. It was not until 2001 and the drama of the *Tampa* affair, however, that Australia instituted a full "interdiction" program, effectively setting up a blockade to prevent asylum seekers on boats from making landfall. However, even before that time efforts were made to reach agreements with countries in the region to stop asylum seekers from reaching Australia.

This chapter turns finally to the events surrounding the interception of the *MV Tampa* (including the associated court cases) and associated measures to stop the boats and to establish offshore refugee processing centres in Nauru and Papua New Guinea. It concludes with a critique of these laws and policies, otherwise known as the "Pacific Strategy". Particular attention is paid to the proposals introduced in May 2006 to extend the operation of the Pacific Strategy to cover *all* unauthorised boat arrivals – both those intercepted en route to the country and those who make landfall in mainland Australia.

Border protection

In late 1999, growth in the number of unauthorised boat arrivals led the Australian Parliament to enact broad legislation aimed at reducing people smuggling. The *Border Protection Legislation Act 1999* permits Australian authorities to board and search ships and aircraft in Australia's territorial sea, the "contiguous" and "exclusive economic" zones and even on the high seas. It enables "hot pursuit" of ships whose captains have not complied with a request to board and authorises pursuit of "motherships" which are "reasonably suspected" of being used for illegal activities. The zones referred to here are terms of international law of the sea and refer to areas measured outwards from Australia's coastline over which the law permits different levels of sovereign control.

The law also allows ships to be moved or destroyed if they are unseaworthy or pose a serious risk to navigation, quarantine, safety, public health, property or the environment. Customs officers are now permitted to carry and use firearms and other defence equipment. Other changes enable the forfeiture, seizure and disposal of ships and aircraft used in contravention of immigration laws. The amendments also enabled asylum seekers apprehended en route to Australia (who would arrive without permission) to be brought to the mainland and detained as unlawful non-citizens, pending consideration of any refugee claims.

The 1999 laws also facilitated the carriage to Australia of asylum seekers rescued at sea. In this respect they were largely consistent with Australia's obligations under the international law of the sea. However, as the government discovered in August 2001, the laws did not allow Australia to *prevent* people rescued at sea from being landed in the country: see further below.

The concept of protection elsewhere

The most potentially restrictive aspects of the 1999 amendments were those designed to force potential asylum seekers to seek protection in countries other than Australia if at all possible. The concepts were not new. In the early 1990s a Labor government had passed laws preventing certain groups of people from claiming asylum in Australia if they had access to protection in a nominated country. These laws stopped the admission of Sino-Vietnamese boat people resettled in China after the Vietnam War under what was known as the Comprehensive Plan of Action. In 1999, however, the provisions were broadened to introduce a general rule barring asylum claims from people who could have access to protection in any country other than their country of origin. These were referred to as "safe third countries".

Such "third countries" may be countries where an asylum seeker enjoys the right of citizenship or the right of residence. The proviso is that such countries must be considered to offer either outright protection or procedures to determine a refugee claim. The 1999 law deems Australia "not to have protection obligations" to anyone who has failed to take "all possible steps" to find safe haven in any country in which the asylum seeker has spent seven or more days en route to Australia. This means that if a person has resided in another country for a continuous period of seven days before coming to Australia, the law potentially excludes that person from refugee protection here. It also excludes anyone who has nationality in two or more countries or who has a right to enter and reside in any safe country (however temporary the right of stay). The laws allow the Minister for Immigration to draw up a list of safe countries deemed incapable of producing refugees.

In 2001, the idea that Australia should not protect anyone who could have sought protection elsewhere was extended to cover all the visa subclasses in Australia's offshore refugee and humanitarian program. Although subject to the Minister's discretion, the offshore visas now privilege applicants processed by UNHCR or who apply from countries where there is no possibility of gaining effective protection. A stay of seven days in a country where UNHCR has a presence can now be enough to disqualify asylum seekers from receiving a protection visa.

The UNHCR Executive Committee (ExCom) recognises "safe third countries" or "protection elsewhere" as bases for allowing countries to share the burden of refugee protection. However, ExCom has spelt out basic standards that should be met before an asylum seeker is turned away. A decision to return a person to a safe third country must carry assurances that the person will:

- be readmitted to that country;
- enjoy effective protection there against return to persecution;
- be able to seek and receive asylum; and
- be treated according to international standards.

Australia's safe third country provisions do not appear to meet these basic standards for the simple reason that there are no guarantees that a so-called "safe" third country is in fact safe. The law does not require agreements between Australia and the "safe" countries in question, so that countries could decide to reject refugees referred back, sending these people to persecution or even death.

Having said this, the practical impact of these provisions seems to have been limited since many countries of transit refuse to readmit asylum seekers who have passed through on their way to Australia. Indeed, in Europe, similar safe third country laws have created a phenomenon of "refugees in orbit", with refugees being refused protection on the basis that they could find safe haven elsewhere. In the worst case scenario, the result can be that refugees are deported through a chain of countries back to their country of origin, where they face persecution.

Under the Australian law, the Minister for Immigration may declare that certain countries have effective asylum procedures. A potential problem is that declarations about the safety of particular countries may be affected by political favouritism based on diplomatic, trade or security interests, rather than on humanitarian factors. When immigration officers deport asylum seekers in the belief that they have protection in a third country, there is no opportunity for refugee lawyers and the courts to intervene if it is suspected that the country is not safe.

In some cases, countries considered safe may not be safe for members of particular minority groups, a fact that may not be recognised in the assessment of the overall safety of a country. In other instances, Australia's decision to refuse to consider a refugee claim where a safe third country is available may be misunderstood as a ruling that the asylum claim lacks merit. This can lead to a refusal of protection in the third country. Another difficulty is that it is often hard to prove through which countries an asylum seeker has travelled and how long the person spent there, so that it may not be possible accurately to identify the safe third country. In practice, asylum seekers often choose not to seek protection in a "safe third country" because of difficulties with asylum procedures in that country. The only way to find effective protection may be to travel to places like Australia.

The practicality of Australia's safe third country laws is questionable, for the simple reason that other countries in the region do not have comparable refugee protection systems. As noted earlier, where asylum seekers reach the mainland, Australia often does not even try to return the human cargo delivered by the people smugglers. It knows that the transit countries will refuse admission to non-citizens who had no authorisation to pass through their territory in the first place. This was demonstrated during the *Tampa* incident in August–September 2001 when Indonesia refused to take back asylum seekers who had transited unlawfully through that country: see further below.

Stemming the flow: regional agreements to stop refugees

In the late 1980s and early 1990s, the arrival of boat people from Cambodia, China and from other countries in the region prompted the then Labor government to conclude inter-country agreements (most notably with China) that ultimately stopped the flow of would-be asylum seekers at the source. More recent governments were slower to explore these options, although they did eventually adopt similar tactics.

Australia's experience of boat people peaked in the late 1990s as people-smuggling channels were opened up through Indonesia for asylum seekers from Iraq, Afghanistan and the Middle East. These developments led the Australian government to seek the cooperation of Indonesia to curtail the number of asylum seekers passing through Indonesia from reaching Australia. Indonesia was and is of particular significance for asylum seekers wishing to access Australia because of its geographic proximity to the Australian territories of Christmas Island (approximately 340 kms from the Indonesian island of Java) and Ashmore Reef (around 150 kms from the Indonesian island of Roti).

Indonesia is not a party to the Refugee Convention and has not established institutions and procedures for granting refugee status. Even so, as the largest Muslim country in the region it has been a country of choice for many asylum seekers with Islamic backgrounds - both as a destination and as a transit point.

There can be little doubt that Indonesia has faced difficulties in regulating unauthorised immigration. To begin with, it has many internal problems that have prevented it from tackling asylum seekers en route to Australia as a priority. With 1.3 million internally displaced people, Indonesia faces the challenge of two major separatist movements (in Aceh and West Papua). It has been plagued at times by ethnic violence and the failure of centralised control over its police and military. In more recent times it has had the added burden of rebuilding many areas devastated by the Indian Ocean tsunami of December 2004.

In 2000 Australia developed a regional cooperation arrangement with Indonesia, under which Indonesia is paid to intercept asylum seekers before they can travel to Australia. Australia pays the International Organisation for Migration (IOM) to interview the people taken into custody and inform them of their options. The regional cooperation arrangement with Indonesia also allows Australia to intercept boats and force them to return to Indonesia.

Should asylum seekers in Indonesia wish to return voluntarily to their home countries, Australia pays the IOM for the cost of voluntary removal. Those who wish to make a refugee claim are referred to UNHCR for assessment and resettlement. Australia bears the cost of detaining asylum seekers in Indonesia. Asylum seekers who are recognised as refugees by UNHCR must wait in Indonesia until a signatory country to the Refugee Convention accepts them for resettlement. There has been argument about whether UNHCR should allow itself to be used as a contractor by Australia for the offshore processing of asylum claims which would otherwise be Australia's responsibility.

As discussed below, Australia's decision to grant asylum to 42 people from West Papua in March 2006 caused serious tensions with Indonesia. The regional co-operation agreement was thought by some to be at risk.

The *Tampa* affair

The agreement with Indonesia in 2000 did not immediately curb the number of boats carrying asylum seekers to Australian shores, although it did raise the stakes as smaller operators appear to have been forced out of the smuggling "game". After 2000, the boats became increasingly unseaworthy, carrying more and more people crammed on board. The Australian government's concerns peaked in August 2001, with Prime Minister Howard intervening personally to halt the developing trend.

The immediate impetus for the government's action was the discovery on 26 August of a boat carrying 433 asylum seekers. The ship was in distress and apparently on the verge of sinking in the ocean 75 nautical miles north of Australia's Christmas Island. Because of the emotional nature of the dispute that these events were to generate, the

Australian courts decided ultimately that these asylum seekers should be referred to by the value neutral term of "rescuees".

At the request of the Australian search and rescue authorities, the asylum seekers were taken aboard by a 49,000 ton Norwegian container ship named the *MV Tampa*. The captain, Arne Rinnan, moved initially to return the rescuees to the Indonesian port of Merak (about 246 nautical miles north), but then changed course for Christmas Island when the rescuees objected. The Australian government then formally requested Captain Rinnan to head for Indonesia and ordered the ship to remain outside of Australian territorial waters. The captain refused - citing the medical condition of some of the rescuees and his inability to feed and care for 433 people on a vessel equipped to house 30 people and licensed to carry no more than 50 people. (The rescuees included three pregnant women and one person with a broken leg. Early reports suggested that many of the rescuees were dehydrated and that some were unconscious.) Australia even threatened to charge Captain Rinnan with people-smuggling offences if he brought the rescuees to Australia.

When the ship came within four nautical miles of Christmas Island, the Australian government sent 45 Special Air Service (SAS) troops to board and take control of the *Tampa*, preventing any of the occupants from disembarking. The Island's port was closed, with barriers erected to prevent the ship from docking. This hostile action was seen by many as being at odds with Australia's obligations under the international law of the sea. Coastal states are supposed to allow safe passage to friendly ships in distress who have acted so as to prevent loss of life at sea - a primary obligation of all seafaring vessels.

Amid the blaze of publicity that surrounded these dramatic events, legal actions were instituted in the Federal Court of Australia by the Victorian Council for Civil Liberties and a private solicitor, Eric Vadarlis. The applicants asked the court to order that the rescuees be brought into Australia's migration zone; that they be told of their rights under the *Migration Act*; and that they be permitted to make refugee claims. The applicants also sought the release of the rescuees on the ground that they were being detained unlawfully, since there was no legislative basis for the actions taken against the *Tampa*. The court allowed Amnesty International and the Human Rights and Equal Opportunity Commission (HREOC) to intervene as friends of the court or "amicus curiae".

In his decision in *Vadarlis v Minister for Immigration* (2001), Justice North of the Federal Court found that the applicants did not have the right to ask the court for orders about the rights of the rescuees under the *Migration Act*. He ruled that the applicants' inability to get direct instructions from the rescuees was fatal to this part of the action. (With the SAS in control of the *Tampa* and the owners of the vessel unable or unwilling to act as intermediaries, none of the litigants was allowed to communicate with the rescuees. It later transpired that the government was secretly monitoring all communications with the ship.) However, he held that the rescuees *were* being detained by the SAS, and that the detention and proposed expulsion from Australian territory were illegal. The judge ordered that the *Tampa* rescuees be returned to Australia and that they be permitted to lodge refugee claims.

When the case was appealed to the Full Federal Court (*Ruddock v Vadarlis* (2001)), Justice North's ruling was overturned by two of the three appeal judges, giving victory to the government. Justice French decided that the government had the legal authority to board the *Tampa* because of the nature of the executive power vested in it by s 61 of the Australian Constitution. He ruled that the power to expel non-citizens was part of the *unwritten* executive power of government that is an implied part of national sovereignty. He held that such powers are only displaced if there is clear legislation that covers the field. He ruled further that the actions taken by the SAS did not constitute immigration detention. He stated that their actions were "incidental to the objective of preventing a landing and maintaining as well the security of the ship". Justice Beaumont agreed with Justice French, but went further, ruling that the court could not release the rescuees from unlawful detention because the rescuees had no legal entitlement to enter Australia.

In dissent, Chief Justice Black agreed with the original judgment of Justice North that the asylum seekers must be released from unlawful detention. He doubted whether an independent executive or prerogative power to exclude aliens still existed, since the area of immigration control had been so well legislated over the years. Even if such a power did exist, he found that it was overridden by legislation enacted by Parliament to comprehensively regulate the entry and expulsion of non-citizens (the *Migration Act 1958*). Since that statute did not provide for the detention of non-citizens outside of Australian territory, he reasoned that the detention of the rescuees must be unlawful.

Underlying the reasoning of the minority opinion was the view that in a modern democracy based on the rule of law, invasive powers of detention must be conferred by Parliament, rather than exercised at the whim of the executive. It is noteworthy that the four Federal Court judges in total who considered the case were split two against two on the issue of unlawful detention. An appeal to the High Court, however, failed.

The aftermath of the *Tampa*: The "Pacific Strategy"

The first decision (by Justice North) in the *Tampa* case was made on 11 September 2001, a few hours before terrorists hijacked four planes in North America, crashing into the Pentagon in Washington DC and obliterating the twin towers of the World Trade Center in New York. The disaster could not have come at a worse time for Australia's boat people, many of whom were Afghani nationals. Within hours, commentators began to implicate Afghanistan's brutal Taliban government and the elusive terrorist Osama bin Laden in the attacks on America. If the *Tampa* rescuees incited any public sympathy before 11 September, there was a hardening in attitude as pictures of the devastation in New York were played and replayed on Australian television. The rescuees were transformed overnight from victims into potential terrorists. Not surprisingly, when Australians were asked "Do boat people increase the risk of terrorism?", a resounding majority of those polled answered "yes". Few seemed to heed Opposition leader Kim Beazley's remarks that most well-organised terrorists would clearly prefer plane travel to the hazards of leaky boats piloted by unscrupulous people smugglers.

In Parliament, the *Tampa* affair spawned a raft of legislative measures. Acts passed on 26 September 2001 included provisions to validate the actions taken by the Australian authorities in the *Tampa* affair and to radically strengthen the powers of the Australian authorities to intercept and deflect potential asylum seekers. The *Border Protection (Validation and Enforcement Powers) Act 2001* was unprecedented, yet the popular pressure generated by the terrorist attacks meant that it was opposed only by the Democrats, the Greens and independent Senator Brian Harradine. The Act retrospectively validates any action taken by the government in relation to the *Tampa* and other ships stopped between 27 August and the date of Royal Assent to the Act. It also prevents the commencement *or continuance* of any civil or criminal proceedings challenging actions covered by the legislation. In this way, the Act made any further appeal of the *Tampa* decision futile.

This Act extended the search powers granted to federal officers in 1999. It conferred extraordinary powers on officers to search, detain and move persons aboard ships that have been pursued, boarded and detained by Australian authorities. There is no requirement that officers boarding a ship act in "good faith". The law is not limited to actions taken within Australia's territorial sea, despite extraterritorial enforcement jurisdiction being limited under the 1982 UN Convention on the Law of the Sea.

What is clear is that the law goes beyond UN initiatives. The Protocol against the Smuggling of Migrants by Land, Air and Sea (supplementing the Convention against Transnational Organised Crime) encourages states to fully exercise their jurisdiction to combat people smuggling – but not to exceed their jurisdiction. Nor are there any moves to expand the maritime jurisdiction under international law, despite Australia's proposal in late 2004 to establish a 1,000 nautical mile Maritime Identification Zone beyond the 200 nautical mile limit of Australia's Exclusive Economic Zone (see further below).

Other measures in the 2001 *Border Protection Act* are more extreme. In response to the *Tampa* litigation, s 7A of the *Migration Act* confirms the power of the executive (that is, the government and its administration) to act outside of any legislative (or parliamentary) authority. This power allows the authorities to eject any persons who have crossed Australia's borders, regardless of whether they are foreigners or citizens. To reinforce the toughness of the government's stance and to ensure judicial compliance, the amendment also imposes mandatory minimum prison terms for (adult) persons convicted of people-smuggling offences. First time offenders attract a mandatory sentence of five years, and repeat offenders eight years.

Mandatory sentences are without precedent in the federal courts and could attract constitutional challenge.

On the other side of the ledger, the border protection legislation allows for judicial review by the High Court and for the payment of compensation to persons who suffer economic loss as a result of the boarding and interdiction of a vessel. The law could, therefore, allow the owners of the *Tampa* and of other innocent vessels stopped by the authorities to recover damages suffered due to the interdiction.

The 2001 laws form the legislative basis for what became known as the "Pacific Solution" and later as the "Pacific Strategy". The renaming of the policy seems to have been a response to critics who asserted that the Pacific Solution was not, in fact, a "solution" to anything and that the phrase had disturbing resonances with Hitler's "Final Solution".

The "excision" of territory for immigration purposes

Australia's Pacific Strategy is based on three major initiatives (to which the proposals of May 2006 may well be added in due course). The first is the declaration that certain offshore territories are deemed "not" Australia for immigration purposes. The second and third relate to the interception of asylum seekers and their deflection to other countries for the purpose of having their refugee status determined.

The removal of certain territory from Australia's "migration zone" was a novel move by any standards. The Minister may make regulations declaring *any* islands off the mainland of Australia to be "excised offshore places". People on these islands are thereby excluded from Australia's "migration zone" for the purposes of applying for an Australian visa. The *Migration Amendment (Excision from Migration Zone) Act 2001* excised Christmas Island, Ashmore Island and Cartier Islands on 8 September 2001. Cocos (Keeling) Islands were excised on 17 September 2001.

People entering Australia at excised offshore places are deemed *not* to have entered Australia's migration zone for the purpose of applying for a visa. The law blocks asylum claims from anyone who is labelled an "offshore entry person". The practical effect is that these people now fall outside Australia's refugee protection system and have no right to access Australian tribunals. Instead, they are shipped to Pacific islands to have their refugee claims assessed by UNHCR or by Australian officials.

The government made many attempts between 2001 and 2005 to excise further areas from Australia's migration zone but was frustrated by the Opposition and minor parties in the Senate, which has a power to disallow regulations. The ad hoc methods adopted in the excision of territory was revealed in December 2001, when the government temporarily excised four islands off Western Australia after a boat was sighted sailing towards them. The excision was lifted when it became apparent that the vessel was a fishing boat carrying eight crew members.

On 4 November 2002, a boat carrying 14 Kurdish asylum seekers from Turkey reached Melville Island. A few hours after their arrival, the government retrospectively excised Melville and many other islands off the northern coastline from the migration zone, to prevent people arriving on them from applying for protection. The boat was towed by the Australian Navy back to Indonesia, where the men were taken into immigration detention. The Senate disallowed the regulations less than two weeks after they were introduced, but the government argued that the Kurdish asylum seekers had not validly applied for protection because the excision order was valid at the time of their arrival. In Indonesia, the IOM assisted eight of the Kurdish asylum seekers to apply to UNHCR for protection; the other six asked to return home.

In July 2005, the government used its new Senate majority to excise Coral Sea Islands Territory, Queensland islands north of latitude 21 degrees south, Western Australian islands north of latitude 23 degrees south and Northern Territory islands north of latitude 16 degrees south. According to the Senate Legal and Constitutional References Committee (2002), which had earlier considered similar excision proposals, this means that more than 4,891 islands are now excised. The map opposite shows the territory excised from Australia's migration zone.

The excision of territory is controversial because it goes much further than the policy of interdiction of asylum seekers on the high seas, which the United States Supreme Court upheld as lawful (in a much criticised decision) in relation to Haitian asylum seekers in that country. *Interdiction* prevents boats of asylum seekers from reaching the territorial waters of a state. In contrast, Australia's policy of *excision* allows it to expel boat-loads of asylum seekers even when they have reached Australian territory and would ordinarily be subject to the general law.

Both interdiction and excision potentially conflict with Australia's obligations under international law, which require countries to fulfil their legal obligations both within their territory and in relation to any action taken outside their territory, including on the high seas. Under international law, the construction of a "migration zone" in domestic law cannot exclude the application of *non-refoulement* obligations under the Refugee Convention. For example, in *Amuur v France* (1996), the European Court of Human Rights found that an "international zone" created (by French law) at Paris airport to detain unlawful immigrants did not exclude France's international human rights obligations. It should be noted that Australia has not attempted to argue that the excision of its island territories relieves Australia of its international obligations under refugee law. The purpose of the law is to limit the operation of the *Migration Act* to reduce the procedural entitlements of asylum seekers.

As explained below, in May 2006 legislation was proposed that would render these excision provisions irrelevant. This is because the plan is to deny all persons arriving in Australia by boat without a visa the right to seek asylum here. The laws would apply equally to persons apprehended en route to Australia and those who make landfall on mainland Australia.

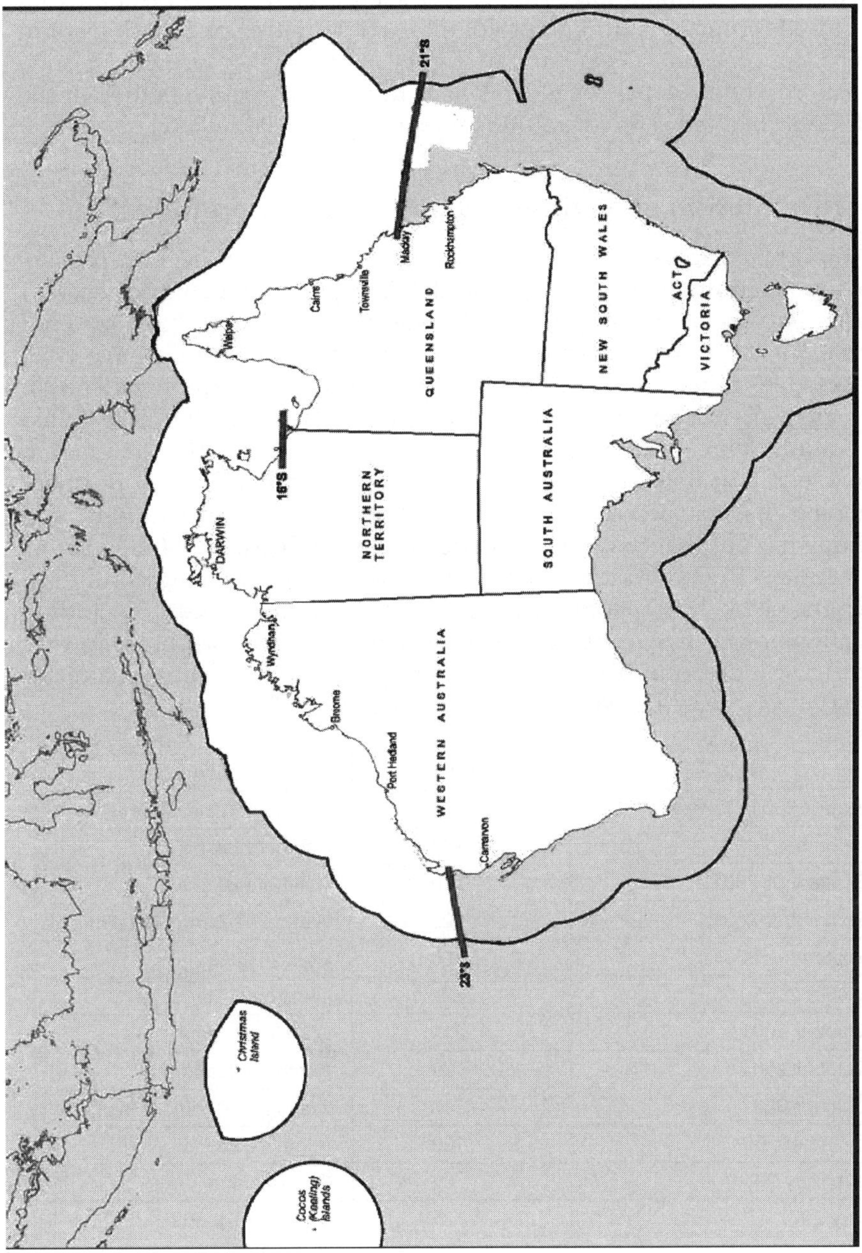

Note: The black line around Australia denotes the 200 nautical mile Exclusive Economic Zone (EEZ). The areas shaded white between the EEZ and the Australian coastline have been excised from the migration zone.

The 2001 laws also limit the range of refugees eligible for protection by introducing a variety of "deflection" mechanisms. For example, the Minister may declare that a country provides access to effective procedures for assessing a person's protection needs; provides protection pending the determination of a refugee claim; provides protection to a recognised refugee pending their voluntary repatriation or resettlement in a third country; or meets human rights standards in providing such protection. The laws bar legal challenges to the new regime (although the High Court maintains its constitutional power of judicial review).

The interdiction of asylum seekers: "Operation Relex"

An important aspect of the Pacific Strategy is to deny asylum seekers access to Australia by processing and detaining them in countries such as Nauru, Papua New Guinea and Indonesia. Boats that have entered Australian waters or landed on excised Australian territories have been redirected to other countries, even when boats were barely seaworthy. The naval interdiction program begun on 3 September 2001 was called "Operation Relex" and, as of mid-2006, "Operation Relex II" remained in force. Operation Relex placed the Australian Navy in a difficult position: stretching its resources, interfering politically in its operations and straining its compliance with international law on the safety of life at sea.

Human Rights Watch has also criticised the poor living conditions experienced by boat people during the interdiction process, including allegations of excessive use of force by naval personnel. The following table shows the number of people stopped from reaching mainland Australia between August 2001 and May 2002:

Date	People	Arrived
26 August 2001 (*Tampa*)	433	Waters off Christmas Island
8 September 2001	231	Ashmore Island
10 September 2001	130	Ashmore Island
12 September 2001	129	Waters off Ashmore Island
15 September 2001	65	Cocos Island
6 October 2001	222	Christmas Island
20 October 2001	219	Christmas Island
28 October 2001	29	Ashmore Island
31 October 2001	149	Waters off Ashmore Island
8 November 2001	160	Ashmore Island
9 December 2001	62	Cocos Island
27 May 2002	1	Ashmore Islands

Source: DIMA Fact Sheet 76 (2004) (removed from its website in 2005)

In addition, four boats were intercepted at sea and returned to Indonesia after arriving in Australian waters in 2001. Two of the boats arrived in October 2001, the first carrying an estimated 238 passengers and the second approximately 215 people. The further two boats arrived in December 2001 and were believed to be carrying 147 people. Although the flow of boats carrying asylum seekers has slowed to a trickle, it has not stopped altogether. In July 2003 a boat carrying 53 Vietnamese arrived in the Northern Territory. All were sent to Christmas Island for the processing of their refugee claims under the *Migration Act*. After appeals to the RRT and applications to the Federal Court, all were found ultimately to be refugees. In January 2006, 43 West Papuans reached the mainland and were transferred similarly to Christmas Island. As explored further below, the swift recognition of the refugee claims of 42 members of this group became a matter of controversy because of Indonesia's reaction to the ruling. What the Indonesians failed to appreciate is that refugee law serves neutral, apolitical, humanitarian purposes. It is not intended to prejudice relations between governments.

Although an effective deterrent for asylum seekers who might be contemplating risking illegal entry into Australia, the Pacific Strategy is not sustainable in the long term unless places are found for the resettlement of those recognised as refugees by UNHCR and Australian authorities. Accordingly, changes to the law in Australia included the creation of two protection visa classes for "offshore entry persons" recognised as refugees.

The first (subclass 447) is designed for asylum seekers apprehended on board boats bound for Australia. In many instances those who are returned to Indonesia have been taken in for refugee processing by IOM and UNHCR. The subclass 447 visas allow temporary stay in Australia of three years. The second subclass of visas (451) is designed for asylum seekers apprehended *before* they board boats for Australia, such as those planning to depart from Indonesia, Sri Lanka, Pakistan or other transit countries. As explained earlier, in addition to the arrangements on Nauru and Manus Island, Australia is paying UNHCR to process asylum seekers intercepted in Indonesia under an agreement with Indonesia. The subclass 451 visas allow temporary stay in Australia of five years.

At one level, these new visas are broader than the Refugee Convention because they do not rely solely on the Convention definition of refugee. They provide temporary protection for refugees; persons fearing gross abuse of their human rights; and women at risk of "victimisation, harassment or serious abuse because of [their] sex". Because the applicants are not in the "Australian migration zone" when they apply, however, there are extra obstacles to the grant of these visas. In both instances, the visas are granted at the Minister's discretion and only in compelling circumstances, having regard to a range of criteria. This means that the Minister does not have to grant the visa even if an applicant meets all the criteria. The factors that must be taken into account by the Minister (or the Department as delegate) are:

- the extent of the applicant's connections with Australia;
- the degree of persecution feared;
- whether a female applicant has the protection of a male relative;
- whether another country can provide protection;
- the community's capacity to support a person's stay; and
- whether granting a visa is contrary to Australia's interests.

Applicants must also pass character, security and health tests and show that they do not owe a debt to the government. The latter requirement can rule out asylum seekers who have previously sought refugee status in Australia. Such people often owe a debt to the government since they are liable for the cost of their detention and/or their $1,400 "post application fee" (levied against failed refugee claimants). Health tests can be waived by the Minister, but this is also discretionary. The regime is stricter than that applying to other overseas refugee and humanitarian visas.

Subclass 447 visas allow a stay of three years, with no automatic right to apply for permanent residence. Visa holders can only apply for a subclass 866 permanent protection visa if the Minister is satisfied that it is in the public interest to allow the application. This means that a 447 visa holder applying for further protection must go through the entire onshore refugee determination process every three years unless ministerial discretion is exercised to grant permanent residence. If they cannot meet the definition of refugee, only the Minister's discretion can protect them from return to persecution. The 451 visa holders are in a similar position, but they can apply for an 866 protection visa without the leave of the Minister. The difficulty is that they cannot apply until four and a half years after the grant of the 451 visa (although the Minister may waive this requirement).

Asylum seekers in Indonesia

Many of the asylum seekers who were turned away from Australia in October and December of 2001 remained in Indonesia in June 2006. They are held by IOM at the expense of the Australian government and are processed by UNHCR. Asylum seekers in Indonesia are held in various locations. In June 2006 this included Jakarta, Bogor, Situbondo and Mataram. The head of the IOM in Indonesia in 2003, Richard Danziger, admitted to the ABC program *Four Corners* that conditions are probably better in the IOM centres of Nauru and Manus Island than in Indonesia. One reason given for the poor conditions was an attempt to avoid causing too much envy towards the refugees amongst the Indonesian population.

The poor living conditions and the frustration of being stranded in Indonesia for many years have led to a number of disturbances. In 2003, Afghan asylum seekers in West Nusa Tenggara province began a hunger strike which ended after the protesters were hospitalised. In January 2004, asylum seekers in Mataram Lombok also held a hunger strike with some asylum seekers sewing their lips together. The strike ended when UNHCR agreed to review their cases based on up-to-date information about the situation in Afghanistan and finalise their cases by March 2004. A further hunger strike was held in August 2004 by a dozen Afghan asylum seekers living for more than two years in a hostel in southern Jakarta. The protesters stitched their lips together and refused food in response to UNHCR's ruling that Afghanistan was safe for return.

The Nauru experiment

A central element of Australia's Pacific Strategy was the agreement it reached with countries in the Pacific region to accept asylum seekers interdicted en route to Australia who could not be returned to Indonesia. The first of these countries was the tiny island republic of Nauru and the second was Papua New Guinea, where Manus Island was designated as the site for a detention and processing centre.

Nauru was a protectorate of Australia until 1968 and retains close connections with Australia, including sharing the same currency. Whilst originally rich in phosphate, Nauru has been devastated by mining and subsequently by political corruption. Nauru has little drinkable water, few remaining natural resources and is effectively bankrupt.

Nauru allowed Australia to establish a processing centre in September 2001 to host the *Tampa* asylum seekers while their refugee claims were assessed. In exchange, Australia pledged $30 million in aid and development programs. Nauru has since been granted aid of $41.5m for 2001-03 and $22.5m for 2003-05. According to Oxfam (2002), Nauru had been scheduled to receive a mere $3.4 million in aid from Australia in 2001-02. The pledge of $30 million was greater than all of the AusAID funds provided to Nauru between 1993 and 2001 and represented 18% of the total AusAID budget to all Pacific Islands in 2001-02 ($164.6 million). Nauru has a population of only 12,000 people.

For practical purposes, the processing centre in Nauru is a detention centre. Detainees are not permitted to leave the compound without permission. In an attempt to respect the Bill of Rights in Nauru's Constitution, which prohibits arbitrary detention, the Australian and Nauruan governments have argued that the camps are not detention centres, but "visa precincts". They claim that the asylum seekers are not detained but only subject to visa conditions that limit their right of movement in Nauru to the confines of the camps.

The centre on Nauru is managed by IOM. UNHCR has assessed the claims of some of the asylum seekers – in essence, half of those taken from the *Tampa* and from a boat named the *Aceng*, absent the 130 women and children from the *Tampa* sent directly to New Zealand in 2001. The Australian government has processed all the others.

Although the asylum seekers on Nauru have been assessed, many who were refused refugee status have refused to return to their countries for fear they would still be in danger at home. Others who felt it was safe to return have done so. In September 2004, there were 65 adults and 17 minors detained on Nauru, with more than half being Iraqis and around one third Afghans. One year later, 27 people remained in Nauru, including eight Afghans and 13 Iraqis. By the end of 2005, all but two Iraqis had been resettled in Australia.

Prolonged detention left many asylum seekers on Nauru in despair. In December 2003, detainees began a hunger strike, with some sewing their lips together, to protest their detention and to mark their refusal to return home after their asylum claims were rejected. The hunger strikers complained of the use of inappropriate translators by DIMA in their assessments and disputed the safety of returning to Afghanistan.

The hunger strikes ended after the Australian government and UNHCR began reviewing the applications of Afghani nationals on Nauru in January 2004. The government denied that it was influenced by the protests and asserted that the reexamination of the Afghani cases was influenced by updated country information on Afghanistan that reported the instability and danger of returning certain groups to the country. The cases of 197 Afghans were reexamined with 168 being recognised as refugees and only 29 being denied refugee status.

Iraqi detainees on Nauru also began a hunger strike in June 2004, protesting that Iraq was not safe for return. The Minister again declared that the hunger strikes would not make a difference to their asylum applications yet, in August 2004, she asked DIMA to reassess these cases as well. In December 2004 it was announced that 27 of the 41 Iraqis reassessed were refugees. These included 11 people assessed by UNHCR. For the first time in 2004, a migration agent, Marion Lè, was allowed access to the camps on Nauru and assisted some asylum seekers in their claims. The brevity of her visit and the number of cases reopened meant that she could not help everyone. A great many of those given this modest assistance were recognised as refugees and resettled in Australia.

In September 2005, the Australian government sent experts to Nauru to assess the mental health of the 27 remaining asylum seekers. Many of them were believed to be depressed and reliant on sedatives for sleep. In an interview with the *Age* in April 2005, many of them reported giving up all hope of securing freedom or seeing loved ones again. By December 2005 all but two had gained their freedom – 13 of them as refugees – with the last detainees being resettled in Australia on humanitarian visas after three and a half years in offshore detention.

According to the IOM, the vast majority of the 1,232 people detained on Nauru were Afghans (785) and Iraqis (387), with small numbers of Iranians (18), Sri Lankans (6), Bangladeshis (6), Pakistanis (8) and Palestinians (19). Of these, 756 people were *resettled* (513 men and 243 women, of whom 268 were children) and 473 *voluntarily returned* to their country of origin (458 men and 15 women, of whom 20 were children). Of those resettled, Australia took 483 people, New Zealand 229, Sweden 18, Canada 16, Denmark six and Norway four. Of those who voluntarily returned, 420 people went to Afghanistan, 17 to Iran, 23 to Iraq and six to Pakistan. (One Afghan also died in Nauru.)

Papua New Guinea

An agreement was signed with Papua New Guinea (PNG) on 11 October 2001 to build a detention facility on Manus Island in exchange for A$1 million. The PNG facility has a potential capacity of 1,000 places. UNHCR refused Australia's request for assistance in the processing of asylum seekers in PNG, leaving DIMA solely responsible.

Several hundred asylum seekers were taken from Australia to PNG to be processed. There were grave concerns about the conditions in the detention facility on Manus Island. The Royal Australasian College of Physicians called for the removal of asylum seekers (in particular pregnant women and young children) because malaria is endemic. Although 12 detainees and five staff contracted malaria, the facility remained in place until all of the detainees had been processed.

In July 2005 there were no asylum seekers on Manus Island as the detainees had all been repatriated, resettled in third countries or accepted by Australia. The last remaining asylum seeker on Manus Island, Aladdin Maysara Salem Sisalem, was granted a temporary protection visa to enter Australia in May 2003. Mr Sisalem spent more than 18 months in detention in PNG and was the sole detainee on the island for 10 months. Australian officials took Mr Sisalem to Manus Island after he reached the Torres Strait Islands by boat and requested asylum.

In the first six months of Mr Sisalem's solitary detention, the Australian government spent more than $216,666 a month for his detention. An estimated total of $1.3 million was spent accommodating, feeding and caring for Mr Sisalem. Overall costs, including power, water and maintenance projects which benefited the local community, along with some back pay, came to more than $4 million.

The "new" Pacific Strategy: The response to Indonesian concerns about West Papuan refugees

The government's response to the furore that erupted in May 2006 over the grant of refugee status to 42 refugees from the Indonesian province of West Papua was the Migration Amendment (Designated Unauthorised Arrivals) Bill 2006. This is one of the most significant pieces of legislation affecting refugees and asylum seekers to be introduced into the Australian Parliament since September 2001 at the height of the *Tampa* affair. Put simply, the processing of *all* asylum seekers who arrive without authorisation by boat is to be done "offshore" in places like Nauru. The result is that these asylum seekers will undergo an inferior assessment process and those found to be refugees will have no automatic right to refugee protection in Australia.

The legislation is without precedent in Australia or internationally. It places Australia at grave danger of breaching fundamental obligations it has assumed under international law. The changes will impact directly on the ability of people in need who are legally entitled to protection (and deserving of compassion) to gain immediate and long-term protection.

The thrust of the Bill is that future boat people will not be eligible to apply for any visa within Australia. This is so, whether they are intercepted before reaching the Australian mainland or whether they reach Australia. The Minister will have a non-compellable, non-reviewable power to admit boat people to the refugee determination system on mainland Australia. The underlying policy is to transship all unauthorised boat arrivals to offshore centres to have their claims for refugee status assessed. Statements by Minister Vanstone suggest that her first preference is for Nauru. The immediate effect of the change is that refugee status decisions will be made offshore by Australian government officials, presumably officers of DIMA. Those assessed as having protection needs will be eligible for "resettlement" in third countries, although in theory these people could also be considered for a range of "offshore" humanitarian visas, some of which are broader in their decisional criteria than onshore protection visas.

If the processes used on Nauru between 2002-05 are a guide, there will be no access to independent merits review by the RRT. Claimants will have no right to government-funded legal advice although they will have access to interpreters employed by the Australian government.

The consequences are serious. Between 1993 and early 2006, the Refugee Review Tribunal overturned 7,885 departmental decisions refusing refugee status. That represents more than 7,885 individuals (some cases involved families) who could have been removed to situations of serious harm and even death but for the appeal process.

Prior experience of the offshore assessment regime established on Nauru is that the system produced fewer successful refugee claims. For example, the percentage of unaccompanied children whose claims were rejected on Nauru was dramatically higher than in Australia. International Organisation for Migration statistics suggest that 32 of 55 unaccompanied children were returned to Afghanistan in 2002-03. Of 290 such children who made it to Australia, none was returned over this period.

The legislation is of concern both at the level of principle and in its likely practical impact. It places Australia at risk of returning people to persecution, in violation of the *non-refoulement* principle which is the cornerstone of the international refugee protection regime. It also undermines the principle that parties to the Refugee Convention should assume full responsibility for refugees on their own territory, unless there are serious reasons (such as mass influx or humanitarian emergency) for alternative arrangements.

Any action by Australia that could expose asylum seekers to persecution, torture, or inhuman or degrading treatment or punishment is in breach of its obligations under the 1951 Refugee Convention, the International Covenant on Civil and Political Rights (ICCPR) and the UN Convention against Torture.

Australia's proposed new laws offend these basic principles because they pose serious threats to the ability to ensure that refugees are not returned to countries where they face persecution. While Australia may not be relinquishing total responsibility for the asylum seekers affected, the asylum seekers are to be consigned to a degraded processing system. This in turn is likely to lead to a failure to recognise genuine refugees.

The only exceptions to the principle of *non-refoulement* of genuine refugees is where there are reasonable grounds for regarding the refugee as a danger to the country or where the refugee has been convicted in Australia of a particularly serious crime and so constitutes a danger to the Australian community. This recognises the pre-eminence of states' rights to protect their territorial and societal integrity. Again, these exceptions are designed to operate on a case-by-case basis. The Convention does not permit states to make blanket assertions about state security that have no basis in fact.

Non-discrimination and the prohibition on penalising asylum seekers

Another fundamental premise enshrined in the Refugee Convention is that states must not discriminate between refugees on the basis of race, religion or country of origin (Article 3 of the Refugee Convention). The fact that the refugees affected by these changes are coming from particular countries in Australia's immediate vicinity may place Australia in violation of this principle. This principle is also enshrined in the ICCPR and other human rights instruments. Parenthetically, non-discrimination on the basis of race is a principle that is central to Australia's domestic immigration laws.

Article 31 of the Refugee Convention states plainly that states should not penalise refugees for entering their territory illegally where they have come directly from a country in which they face persecution. The proviso is added that the refugees must present themselves to authorities without delay and show good cause for their illegal entry or presence. Again, this is a fundamental aspect of the Convention as it underscores the right of people in distress to seek protection, even if their actions constitute a breach of the domestic laws of a country of asylum. Article 31 recognises that the circumstances compelling flight commonly force refugees to travel without proper documentation. Irregular movement and lack of documentation do not say anything about the credibility of a protection claim.

The proposed laws would apply to asylum seekers coming directly from the country of claimed persecution. Because they establish a second determination regime that is markedly inferior to that operating on mainland Australia, the laws could be regarded as punitive in breach of Article 31.

Durable solutions and state responsibility

The new policies are designed to group refugees recognised through processes conducted offshore together with those recognised by UNHCR in the course of its fieldwork operations. Attempts will be made accordingly to have the Australian refugees "resettled" through the auspices of UNHCR.

In this respect the laws are fundamentally at odds with the principle that states signatory to the Refugee Convention should assume full responsibility for refugees on their own territory unless there are serious reasons for alternative arrangements to be made. In most instances, UNHCR processing is conducted in countries that have either not become parties to the Refugee Convention (Indonesia is a regional example in point) or which are unable to cope with the sheer scale of human movement on their territory (Kenya is an example in point). In either case, UNHCR comes in at the invitation of the government in question as a gesture of humanitarian aid and in response to perceived need.

There are currently approximately 9 million Convention refugees "on the books" of UNHCR. Less than 1% can expect to achieve resettlement in third countries. For Australia to purport to add its tiny number of refugees (tiny in absolute as well as relative terms) to UNHCR's burden is unconscionable.

The Tampa is no precedent

As a postscript to this discussion of the role played by UNHCR, it is false to see the involvement of UNHCR and IOM in the resolution of the standoff generated by the *Tampa* affair as a precedent for these laws. On that occasion, UNHCR intervened in a situation of humanitarian crisis, operating as a broker to negotiate a solution for the asylum seekers rescued at sea from a vessel in distress. It agreed to assist in the processing of asylum seekers taken from the *Acheng*, because these people were collected and delivered to Nauru at the same time as the *Tampa* rescuees. UNHCR declined involvement in the processing of asylum seekers intercepted and deflected to Nauru after this time.

There are other factors that make this period very different from the scenario now envisioned by the Australian government. As well as being a situation of crisis, the individuals were intercepted before reaching Australian soil. Moreover, according to rhetoric of the time, many were characterised as "secondary movement" refugees or, in crude terms, refugees who had passed through safe countries and who were looking for "immigration outcomes" rather than simple protection. Deflecting responsibility for asylum seekers fleeing directly to Australia and who land on Australian territory is a dramatically different proposition. This has particular relevance for asylum seekers from West Papua who come directly to Australia without passing through any other states. Australia is one of the nearest countries and an obvious country of refuge.

International relations issues

Indonesia's vocal concerns about Australia's refugee protection regime have a very practical (financial) base. In February 2006, Indonesia became a party to the ICCPR and is now required to report within one year on its human rights record. An adverse report can have ramifications for the grant of foreign aid under regional ASEAN arrangements. Australia's actions therefore have potential financial ramifications for Indonesia. Professor Shearer (Australia's representative on the UN Human Rights Committee) has suggested that this is a reason for the furore caused by the West Papuan defectors.

The proposed laws will do little to address these concerns. Indeed, the involvement of other countries in the region in the messy business of refugee processing may only make matters worse. Asylum (again) is a non-political act.

Reasons for processing boat people in Australia

It is difficult to understand fully why Australia turned so resolutely against the boat people arriving in 2001. In the aftermath of the *Tampa* affair, concerns about security were certainly acute. The prevailing rhetoric about boat people as a menace seems to have gained traction in the public's mind. Many Australians also seemed to believe that the government's actions were lawful and that any "real" refugees caught up in the affair would be properly looked after. The involvement of UNHCR and the IOM in the Pacific arrangements bolstered this perception. For its part, the government was careful to craft statements about boat people so as to avoid the language of refugee protection. Even in 2005, two elections after the *Tampa* Affair, boat people are almost always referred to as illegal immigrants rather than as asylum seekers.

There are sound reasons why Australia should reverse its policy and allow boat people in its waters to land and have their refugee claims processed. Refugee determination procedures in Nauru and Indonesia are qualitatively inferior to those in Australia, increasing the risk that genuine refugees will fail to be recognised. These shortcomings are well demonstrated by the outcomes of reprocessing the claims of failed asylum seekers on Nauru. The arrangements can also be criticised because of the inferior ability of offshore assessing bodies to run health and character checks on the refugee claimants.

From the perspective of the refugee, failure to gain Convention status clearly places them at greater risk of being returned to face death or serious abuse of their human rights. Importantly, the arrangements also pose problems for asylum seekers who *are* recognised as refugees. This is because the scheme does not guarantee that such refugees will be accorded the protections to which they are entitled under international law. As the Oxfam report *Adrift in the Pacific* noted in 2002, Nauru is not a party to the Refugee Convention. While PNG is a party, it has made reservations which mean that it does not accept the following Convention obligations: paid employment (Art 17); housing (Art 21); public education (Art 22); freedom of movement (Art 26); non-discrimination against refugees who enter illegally (Art 31); expulsion (Art 32); and naturalisation (Art 34).

An obvious problem with the Pacific Strategy is that it offers no long-term solution for refugees. Under the original Memoranda of Understanding with Nauru and PNG, all refugees were supposed to be resettled in other countries within six months. These agreements have been extended year after year. Moreover, there can be little doubt that Australia is better equipped to offer protection than Indonesia, the transit country of most of the recent asylum seekers. The same is true of transit countries such as Pakistan.

A further compelling argument in favour of repatriating the processing of boat people to the Australian mainland is economic. Put simply, Australia will not be able to support the extravagant financial costs of these extraterritorial initiatives for very long. As noted in chapter 1, the estimated cost of the *Tampa* affair in September 2001 was $120 million. In 2002-03 alone, $90 million was spent on offshore asylum seeker management. In comparison, only $5 million was spent on administering the entry of 4,000 refugees under the offshore humanitarian program (assisted passage and medical clearance costs) in that year.

Legal and financial questions aside, Australia's stance has little to commend it in ethical terms. The vast majority of the Afghan and Iraqi asylum seekers were genuine refugees in dire need of protection. Of the 131 asylum seekers from the *Tampa* taken in by New Zealand, all were accepted as refugees and granted permanent residence and the right to sponsor family members. New Zealand resettled a further 77 people from the *Tampa* after they were processed on Nauru. Of this total of 208 *Tampa* rescuees accepted by New Zealand, 76 were granted citizenship by 2005.

Finally, if one objective of the Pacific Strategy is to deter further people smuggling and undocumented arrivals, this is likely to fail in the long term. Asylum seekers can still gain access to some form of refugee processing system, paid for by Australia, with the ultimate prospect of refugee resettlement in a third country. Short of terminating refugee processing altogether, even the slimmest hope of protection – including that offered by the restrictive Pacific Strategy – is enough to motivate asylum seekers to risk their lives to reach safety.

References and further reading

Australian Government, Department of Defence "Australian Defence Force Operations": <www.defence.gov.au/globalops.cfm>

Moira Coombs, "Excising Australia: Are we really shrinking?" Australian Parliamentary Library Research Note No *5 2005–06* (31 August 2005): <www.aph.gov.au/library/pubs/RN/2005-06/06rn05.htm>

Mary Crock, "In the wake of the Tampa: conflicting visions of international refugee law in the management of refugee flows" (2003) 12 *Pacific Rim Law and Policy Journal* 49

DIMA, "Fact Sheet 76. Offshore Processing Arrangements", <www.immi.gov.au/facts/76offshore.htm>

DIMA, "Fact Sheet 81. Australia's Excised Offshore Places", <www.immi.gov.au/facts/81excised.htm>

Michael Gordon, *Freeing Ali: The Human Face of the Pacific Solution* (UNSW Press, Sydney, 2005)

John Howard, Transcript of Doorstop Interview: *Boat people; APEC; deployment terms and conditions*, Sheraton Hotel, Brisbane, 19 October 2001 <www.pm.gov.au/news/interviews/2001/interview1399.htm>

Minister for Defence, "ADF Operations - More Money to get the Job Done": <www.minister.defence.gov.au/HillTpl.cfm?CurrentId=3805>

Parliamentary Library Department of Parliamentary Services, "Excisions from the Migration Zone—Policy and Practice": <www.aph.gov.au/library/pubs/rn/2003-04/04rn42.pdf>

Senate Legal and Constitutional References and Legislation Committees Question Taken On Notice Additional Estimates Hearing: 11 February 2003 Immigration And Multicultural And Indigenous Affairs Portfolio (86) Output 1.5: Offshore Asylum Seeker Management

UNHCR Executive Committee Conclusion 58 (XL) 1989: *Problem of refugees and asylum seekers who move in an irregular manner from a country in which they had already found protection*

UNHCR, Position on Readmission Agreements, "Protection Elsewhere" and Asylum Policy, August 1994, published in (1997) 3(2) European Series 465

Various (2002) 13 *Public Law Review* 85 (The "Tampa" Issue)

Debbie Whitmont, "To Deter and Deny: The inside story of Operation Relex - the defence forces' mission to stop asylum-seekers reaching Australian shores" ABC TV (*Four Corners*), Broadcast: 15 April 2002, Transcript at <www.abc.net.au/4corners/stories/s531993.htm>

Cases

Ruddock v Vadarlis (No 2) (2001) 115 FCR 229

Vadarlis v Minister for Immigration and Multicultural Affairs (2001) 22(20) Leg Rep SL1

8

Refugee Outcomes: Temporary Protection, Permanent Settlement and Removal or Return

Key Points in this Chapter

- Under international law refugees should be afforded the same rights and assistance as any other foreigners legally resident in a country.
- While Australia recognises the need to assist refugees in establishing themselves in the community, the level of support for resettlement varies according to their mode of entry. Those who arrive without visas or who are intercepted and processed offshore receive fewer benefits than refugees brought in under the offshore humanitarian program.
- In October 1999, Australia introduced temporary protection visas (TPVs) for all asylum seekers who arrived in Australia without permission. People on TPVs are not entitled to family reunion and other benefits. In 1999 the government also experimented with special temporary entry visas known as temporary safe haven visas.
- In September 2001, further restrictions were placed on access to permanent residence for TPV holders who spent more than seven days in a country where they could have sought asylum en route to Australia. The Minister for Immigration may waive the seven-day rule.
- In late July 2004, the government began allowing TPV holders to apply for some migration visas from within Australia. In addition, the "Return Pending Visa" was created to allow for the release of some long-term detainees and to extend the options of TPV holders who failed to gain permanent protection visas.
- Birth in Australia does not guarantee Australian citizenship unless a person is born to a parent who is an Australian citizen or permanent resident, or remains in Australia for the first 10 years of their life. Citizenship also can be granted to a person who has been in Australia as a permanent resident for two years or to a person who was born in Australia and who spent the first 10 years of their life in Australia.
- Recent research has found that some asylum seekers have been removed to dangerous and even deadly situations.
- Australia has offered a reintegration package to some rejected asylum seekers and TPV holders to encourage individuals to return to their home country voluntarily.

Success and failure

Under Australian law, recognition as a refugee is an important milestone in the protection of those seeking asylum. However, it is by no means the whole story. This chapter examines the end stage of the process, beginning with a discussion of how temporary protection operates and the transition (if any) from temporary to permanent refugee protection. The chapter then reviews mechanisms introduced in 2004 to allow TPV holders and former TPV holders to access non-refugee visas in the spouse, business and general employment categories. The grant of citizenship to refugees is also discussed briefly. This chapter concludes by discussing the removal and/or voluntary return of refugees and failed asylum seekers, including recent research into the fate of failed asylum seekers who were returned to their countries of origin.

Settling refugees in the community

People who successfully apply for a visa are released from detention or are permitted to remain in the community. Apart from the right to physical safety and protection, international law guarantees refugees the same rights and assistance as any other foreigner who is legally resident in Australia. This includes freedom of thought and movement, freedom from torture and rights to work, education, adequate medical care and an adequate standard of living. The specific rights and duties of refugees under the Refugee Convention are supplemented by the full range of rights recognised in international human rights treaties, which recognise that all individuals are entitled to the same basic rights regardless of their immigration status.

Australia recognises the need to assist refugees in establishing themselves in the community. Unfortunately, negative attitudes towards onshore refugees who came as asylum seekers led to a marked reduction in the entitlements of these people. Until October 1999 all refugees (regardless of their mode of entry into Australia) were granted permanent residence, entitling them to the same benefits as ordinary migrants who settle in Australia. Onshore refugees released from detention were also entitled to some housing support, English language training and other settlement assistance to buy furniture and make a new home. After two years, they then became eligible to apply for Australian citizenship like other permanent residents.

As discussed below, this level of support is still available to refugees who are resettled in Australia from overseas. The situation for onshore refugees who arrive without a visa is, however, now quite different. Refugees who arrived in Australia without permission after October 1999 and who are granted a Temporary Protection Visa (TPV) are released from detention with two weeks' welfare payments. The burden of supporting these refugees falls largely on State governments and local religious, ethnic and community groups such as St Vincent de Paul, the Brotherhood of St Lawrence, Mercy Family Services and Anglicare.

Some refugees released from detention in capital cities with little support have been forced to stay in cheap and culturally inappropriate backpacker hostels. Some have found life without support so unbearable that they have asked to return to immigration detention. South Australian Liberal Premier John Olsen complained: "If you're taking the step to recognise them as refugees, they have also got to be funded". The Victorian government criticised the federal government in 2000 for "treating these future Australian citizens as second class citizens by dumping them in Melbourne" without support. Failing to assist these refugees may force them to resort to desperate measures to survive. Limiting the assistance available to some refugees is likely to have serious long-term consequences.

UNHCR's survey of resettlement countries in 2000 identified the main factors that are needed to help refugees resettle in another country. These include material needs such as employment, appropriate housing, access to education and language skills, and good physical health. Good settlement services are also necessary, along with support from people with similar backgrounds and from family members (including through family reunification). The major barriers to successful resettlement are the absence or inadequacy of any of these factors. Resettlement may be hindered by racism or discrimination, a lack of resources and the failure to have job qualifications and experience from other countries recognised.

It has become apparent that some sub-groups within the refugee population have special needs that must be addressed. These groups include refugee youth, older refugees and women at risk (such as single mothers and unaccompanied minors). Australia also has sophisticated medical and psychiatric services for treating refugees whose persecution involved torture or trauma, including those whose illnesses are aggravated by mandatory detention in Australia. It is conservatively estimated that about 30% of refugees have directly suffered torture, although recent research indicates that this figure may be as high as 70%.

Apart from the physical injuries resulting from torture, it has profound and ongoing psychological consequences, including depression, severe anxiety, panic, sleep interruption, guilt, loss of self-esteem, lack of trust and suspicion of authority, severe memory and concentration problems, negative thoughts and flashbacks, difficulties in social functioning and relationships, and family conflict.

The Vienna Declaration and Platform of Action (1993), adopted by countries at a major international human rights conference, establishes international guidelines for treatment and rehabilitation services for survivors of torture and trauma. In Australia, each State and Territory has support services designed specifically for the rehabilitation of survivors of torture and trauma. These services provide counselling, early health assessment and intervention, and community education. Most organisations have long waiting lists, modest budgets and have suffered from government cutbacks to health and social services. There is also a lack of interaction between specialised torture and trauma services and general health and welfare practitioners, limiting the effectiveness of treatment.

The temporary safe haven experiment

Another major change in 1999 was the introduction of visas permitting the government to evacuate refugees to Australia at short notice and strictly for temporary protection purposes. Temporary protection visas are useful and legitimate ways of dealing with refugees in cases of mass influx, where the determination of individual asylum applications is impracticable due to the large numbers of people involved. Temporary protection was given to refugees from Kosovo and East Timor for this reason and because there was a real hope that the refugees could return home safely after order was restored by the international community.

Temporary protection should, however, be a short-term measure which ultimately gives way to a durable solution. UNHCR argues that, after a reasonable period of time, temporary visa holders must have the right to claim permanent protection.

The Kosovar refugees

In early 1999, Australia agreed to take 4,000 refugees from the Kosovo conflict in the former Yugoslavia. The Kosovars were issued with temporary safe haven visas which enabled their immediate protection, easing the burden on countries closest to Kosovo.

The visas were quite different from the standard temporary protection visas given to other nationalities in the past. Previously, refugees protected for limited periods were given the right to work and to apply for other types of visas to remain in Australia after the period of temporary protection. The Kosovar temporary safe haven visas were more restrictive, depending on the discretion of the Minister for Immigration rather than on the certainty of legal rights. The visa holders were selected by the Australian authorities and were deemed to have applied for a visa upon acceptance of the offer made to them.

Unlike other refugees, while in Australia the Kosovars had no legal rights regarding their legal status or their treatment by authorities. Without the permission of the Minister (exercised personally), they were unable to apply for other types of visas to remain in Australia, even where they met regular immigration requirements for the grant of other visas. Asylum seekers against whom adverse decisions were made had no right to have the decision independently reviewed. Temporary protection was only offered for three months with one further extension of three months - even though some refugees still feared persecution after the six-month period had expired.

Although 90 per cent of the refugees had returned to Kosovo by September 1999, the remaining 10 per cent who feared for their safety were threatened with forced removal if they refused to leave Australia with a payment of $3,000. Amnesty International and other human rights groups were concerned at the lack of independent safeguards against the return of the refugees to persecution.

Of those refugees who agreed to return, Australia later allowed 82 to return to Australia as permanent residents sponsored by community groups. The absurdity was that these refugees had to come to Australia, return to Kosovo and then come back to Australia again, rather than having their applications for permanent residency dealt with while they were in Australia. This process created much anxiety and uncertainty for the refugees, and undoubtedly deterred other refugees in need of protection from applying for refugee status after they returned to Kosovo.

The temporary safe haven visas created for the Kosovars were reused later in 1999 for refugees evacuated from East Timor. The key problem with the temporary visas is that, while most of the Kosovars and East Timorese probably satisfied the international refugee definition, they were unable to apply for formal refugee status and protection in Australia. This was the case even though UNHCR recommends that temporary protection is not an alternative to permanent protection. As a result, refugees at risk can potentially be arbitrarily returned home at any time.

The safety of returning to Kosovo

Although most of the refugees went home to Kosovo as planned, a small number of them had good reasons for not wanting to return to Kosovo. Most areas of Kosovo had been made secure by the United Nations forces by the end of the temporary protection period. But some areas of Kosovo - especially Serb-dominated areas - remained unsafe. Some of the refugees in Australia had lived in these areas and felt that it was not yet safe to return. In March 2000, UNHCR stated that these areas were still unsafe and advised Australia that refugees returning to these areas would be at risk of persecution. Even in early 2001, areas of Kosovo remained unsafe, following grenade attacks and confrontations in towns like Mitrovica.

In addition, some of the Kosovars in Australia belonged to particular sub-groups of refugees which faced greater dangers than most of the refugees. UNHCR identified a number of groups who would potentially face violence, harassment and discrimination upon return to Kosovo:

- people or families of mixed ethnic or minority ethnic origin;
- people perceived to be associated with the Serbian regime after 1990;
- people who refused to join or deserted from the KLA;
- people publicly critical of the KLA or Provisional Government;
- people who refused to follow the laws of the KLA or Provisional Government.

UNHCR also noted that refugees who suffered or witnessed violence, torture or trauma may have continuing protection needs, in addition to vulnerable groups like the handicapped and ill, the unaccompanied elderly, unaccompanied minors, and female heads of households. UNHCR advised that the voluntary return of the refugees in Australia was preferable to the method of forced deportation adopted by the Australian Government.

The United Nations stated very clearly that no refugee should be forcibly returned to Kosovo against his or her will – despite NATO control of the territory. The Refugee Council of Australia pointed out that there was still no effective rule of law in Kosovo, as well as ongoing instability, at the time of their return. There was also a lack of basic infrastructure, delays and mismanagement in UN reconstruction and civil administration, and the onset of the European winter without adequate shelter.

The inefficiency of airlifting Kosovars

By evacuating 4,000 refugees directly to Australia by air, Australia helped to take some of the pressure off countries of first asylum bordering on Kosovo. As a country which supported armed humanitarian intervention in Kosovo, Australia's agreement to protect the refugees was also motivated by a recognition of its own partial responsibility for the ensuing refugee crisis.

UNHCR criticised the special treatment of asylum seekers evacuated to Western countries like Australia, although it accepted such treatment as a useful protection tool in the circumstances. UNHCR believes that all refugees should be entitled to universal standards of protection and it discourages differential treatment of refugees. Because Western countries donated funds specifically for evacuation, it is arguable that UNHCR was unable to direct the relief program according to the principles of equal treatment and protection.

The substantial amount spent evacuating a small number of refugees to Australia may have been better spent on providing for, and protecting, far larger numbers of refugees in countries closer to Kosovo. UNHCR has called the Kosovo crisis "a high visibility event" for Western countries due to the intense media coverage, and domestic political popularity was arguably a greater concern for Australia than the most efficient and effective assistance to refugees.

Temporary protection visas for onshore refugees

A defining aspect of Australia's refugee protection regime in recent years has been the granting of temporary rather than permanent protection to refugees who enter Australia without permission. The subclass 785 visa allows three years' temporary residence, while the refugee visas granted under the offshore refugee processing schemes under the Pacific Strategy (see chapter 7) provide between three and five years' temporary residence.

As the table opposite shows, the temporary protection regime has created different classes of refugees in Australia. Individuals who enter the country through the planned humanitarian entry programs have the greatest entitlements, followed closely by individuals granted the onshore subclass 866 visa. These people have immediate access rights to social security, education, settlement support, family reunion, work, language training and freedom of movement into and out of Australia. In contrast, temporary visa holders have limited or no access to most of these services and rights. The table also shows the comparative entitlements of persons released from immigration detention on bridging visas while their protection claims are being assessed.

The Refugee Council of Australia has called temporary protection for unauthorised arrivals and offshore entry persons "morally and legally questionable". Essentially, those who cannot apply under the offshore refugee program or after arrival on valid visas are penalised for seeking protection directly in Australia. This differential treatment of refugees according to their mode of entry places Australia in violation of its legal obligations under the Refugee Convention. Article 23 of the Convention provides that state parties should give refugees the same "public relief and assistance" as their own citizens. Article 31(2) also states that refugees should not be penalised for illegally entering a country. Australia argues that this provision only applies to those coming directly from a country where they face persecution. Although most refugees pass through other countries before reaching Australia, the temporary protection laws apply equally to all those entering without visas (including those who have come directly from a country of persecution). Australia's TPV holders are also denied travel documents to allow them to travel outside Australia and those who leave Australia automatically lose their right to return. This arguably violates Art 28 of the Convention, which protects the freedom of movement of refugees.

A study of the immediate and longer term consequences of temporary protection conducted by RMIT University in 2003-04 found that it can deny individuals a sense of certainty, hope and material security. It can also hamper the ability of refugees to gain employment and to access health services. Temporary protection is particularly damaging for those who are vulnerable because of harms suffered before coming to Australia. These people are not given the certainty and security they need to begin the healing process. On the contrary, future protection can depend on the perpetuation of their fears and "victim" status.

International law does not prohibit the temporary protection of refugees. However, it is UNHCR's position that it should only be used as a supplement and not an alternative to permanent protection. According to UNHCR, temporary protection is a poor alternative to permanent protection and UNHCR encourages states to consider durable solutions whenever possible. UNHCR says that temporary refuge should only be used as a practical device to meet urgent protection needs during a mass

Comparison of Visa Entitlements

<table>
<tr><th>Entitlement</th><th>Bridging Visas</th><th colspan="3">Temporary Visas</th><th colspan="2">Permanent Visas</th></tr>
<tr><td></td><td>Bridging Visa E, subclass 051 (unauthorised arrival, released from detention before process is complete)</td><td>785 (onshore unau-thorised arrivals)</td><td>451 (intercepted in inter-national waters)</td><td>447 (arrived at an excised off-shore place)</td><td>Permanent Protection Visa 866 (onshore authorised arrivals)</td><td>Permanent Humanitarian Visas 200-204 (offshore)</td></tr>
<tr><td>Settlement support</td><td>Some States offer torture and trauma counselling
No federal assistance</td><td colspan="4">Only eligible for the early health assessment and intervention</td><td>Full assistance:
information & orientation;
accommodation; household;
early health assessment & intervention;
community support</td></tr>
<tr><td>Employment</td><td>Need to show that they have a compelling need to work</td><td colspan="3">Right to work. Until 1 Jan 2003, ineligible for employment assistance programs, except for basic services (eg, touch screen job matching). From 1 Jan 2003, eligible for limited programs</td><td colspan="2">Right to work; access to all employment assistance programs</td></tr>
<tr><td>Social security</td><td>Not eligible</td><td colspan="3">Eligible for restricted entitlements: Special Benefit (Newstart rates with a more stringent income test), Rent Assistance, Family Tax Benefit, Child Care Benefit, and Maternity Allowance (Activity tested from 1 Jan 2003)</td><td colspan="2">Eligible to apply for the full range of social security benefits</td></tr>
<tr><td>Health</td><td>No Medicare unless permission to work</td><td colspan="3">Eligible for Medicare. Before 29 Aug 2000 TPV holders not automatically eligible for Medicare</td><td colspan="2">Eligible for full range of health services through Medicare</td></tr>
<tr><td>Mental health</td><td>See above
Not eligible for federal assistance</td><td colspan="5">Eligible for torture and trauma counselling</td></tr>
<tr><td>English tuition</td><td>Not eligible</td><td colspan="3">Not eligible. Only eligible for the Language, Literacy and Numeracy Program if receiving Special Benefit. Fees payable for TAFE</td><td colspan="2">510 hours of English language training (free under the Adult Migrant English Program), plus 100 hours more if necessary</td></tr>
<tr><td>Education for children</td><td>States have a discretion to waive fees; study can be precluded</td><td colspan="3">From 1 July 2002 eligible for funding through the New Arrivals Program</td><td colspan="2">Eligible for intensive English training through the Commonwealth-funded New Arrivals Program</td></tr>
<tr><td>Legal assistance for visa applications</td><td>Eligible for government-funded legal assistance</td><td colspan="3">Eligible for government-funded legal assistance in preparing fresh visa application if experiencing financial hardship and disadvantaged, eg because of non-English speaking background or disability from past torture and trauma. Unaccompanied minors (if wards of the Minister) are entitled to legal assistance under the Immigration Advice and Application Assistance Scheme</td><td colspan="2">n/a</td></tr>
</table>

Adapted from HREOC (2004)

influx of people, and until such time as applicants can have their asylum requests determined on an individual basis. Temporary protection should not be used to discriminate against people for entering a country unlawfully, including by denying them the right to family reunion.

The seven-day rule

As explained in chapter 7, measures designed to deter asylum seekers in 1999 included the introduction of a "seven-day rule" to restrict access to Australia by any asylum seeker who had spent seven days or more in a safe country before arriving in Australia. On 27 September 2001, this rule was extended to include TPV holders in Australia. Those granted a TPV after this date can only apply for another TPV when their initial protection period expires. Potentially, some asylum seekers in Australia could spend the rest of their lives on rolling temporary protection visas. Australia is the only country in the world to have adopted such a measure. Refugees affected by the seven-day rule may, however, seek a waiver from the Minister for Immigration.

Australia's geographical isolation means that many asylum seekers stop en route to Australia. The seven-day rule can apply even if the person seeking asylum stopped in a country that is not a signatory to the Refugee Convention and thus did not offer refugee protection. The many asylum seekers who stopped in Indonesia for more than seven days may be prohibited from ever applying for permanent protection if they could have sought protection but did not. Many asylum seekers may have been prevented from applying for protection en route to Australia by people smugglers who restricted their freedom of movement for fear of detection.

The denial of family reunion

The denial of family reunion to onshore refugees holding TPVs inevitably results in psychological and other forms of distress. Refugees in Australia may send money to support families offshore, but they suffer the guilt of being powerless to reduce the dangers and other privations experienced by loved ones at risk overseas. Family members may be separated for at least five years under the temporary visa system. For those processed offshore (in Nauru or PNG, for example), the separation can be even longer. As well as enduring greater processing times and delays in granting a visa, the offshore TPVs can be for five years' duration.

In signing and ratifying human rights treaties, Australia agreed that the family deserves legal protection. Article 23(1) of the ICCPR (1966) recognises that: "The family is the natural and fundamental group unit of society and is entitled to protection by society and the State". Family reunification is a crucial means of protecting the family unit when family members have been separated due to persecution. Family reunification also helps refugees settle into their new society more quickly and effectively. UNHCR principles emphasise that the family is entitled to protection by society and the state, and that family reunification should be respected by governments in any dealings with refugees.

Unfortunately, there is no international mechanism available to force Australia to adhere to its obligations under the Refugee Convention. Australia maintains that no country is obliged to do more than provide protection for individual refugees. It argues that the temporary visa scheme is not a punishment for refugees, but a permissible alternative to permanent protection. The problem is that Australia uses TPVs for refugees who have gone through a refugee determination process and differentiates between classes of refugees, based entirely on their mode of entry.

In a media statement introducing the TPV scheme, the then Minister for Immigration, Philip Ruddock, referred to the changes as tough new measures to curb the growing number of people arriving illegally. If the TPV regime aims to deter asylum seekers, it is doubtful that it will succeed. An attempt in the early 1990s to create four-year temporary protection visas for all refugees was abandoned by the Labor government. Not only did the measure *not* deter asylum seekers, it was considered to be unworkable. If the available statistics are accurate (see chapter 9), the reintroduction of temporary visas in 1999 could well have encouraged more unauthorised entrants because refugees lost the right to sponsor family members through regular migration channels.

There is circumstantial evidence that the removal of the right to sponsor families under the current laws may have encouraged asylum seekers to consign whole families to the people smugglers. This is seen in the sharp rise in the number of women and children among the boat people immediately following the (re)institution of temporary protection in 1999. According to DIMA's records (see former Fact Sheet 74a), the number of children on the boats jumped from 5% to over 30% on some boats. This represented a radical departure from the usual pattern of refugee movements in Australia (and elsewhere), whereby the father or the eldest son in the family sought refuge alone so as to become anchors for the later (legal) migration of dependants. This development can hardly be described as beneficial given the dangers inherent in boat journeys to Australia, and the problems in managing a detention population where nearly one in three detainees was a child by 2001.

The transition from TPV to permanent protection

Australia's temporary protection scheme for onshore refugees creates obvious problems when the time period of the original TPV expires. The number of asylum seekers processed and issued with TPVs between 1999 and 2002 created serious administrative stresses for DIMA. Instead of putting this caseload behind it, the Department had to start reprocessing people even before it had processed other claims for the first time. Again, the changes to the law in 2001 had the potential of leaving refugees on perpetual TPVs, requiring them to be reprocessed every three or so years. For the refugees themselves, this process can be highly demoralising and fraught with challenges – not least because of the many changes that inevitably occur over a three-year period in the refugee's original country.

Disputes have arisen as to the approach that should be taken to the question of the continuation or cessation of refugee status. The Refugee Convention states in Art 1C that a refugee will lose the protection of refugee status if a range of matters occur. These include where the refugee "voluntarily re-avails" himself or herself of the protection of a country of origin, such as where the refugee returns to a country of origin and/or applies for a passport from that country. The most controversial part of Art 1C is para (5) which allows protection to cease where there has been a *substantial change in circumstances* in the country of origin. Where refugee status ceases under Art 1C, a TPV holder will be placed in the same position as a first time asylum seeker. She or he will have to go back through the whole process of showing a well-founded fear of persecution on a Convention ground. Should Art 1C(5) not apply, however (that is, there is no substantial change in circumstances), the TPV holder will enter the process on the presumption that she or he remains a refugee. The onus is then on the government to show that the protection of refugee status should no longer be given.

Some RRT members have regarded any change in a country as triggering Art 1C(5). On this view, even if a country remains unstable, changes in the personalities responsible for persecuting a particular refugee mean that the refugee will lose that status and have to prove all over again that he or she meets the refugee definition. This approach sees refugee status tied so narrowly to the circumstances of a particular refugee that a change in the persecutor's identity will end protection.

In the Federal Court, a marked division appeared between judges. A specially convened bench of 5 Federal Court judges accepted the RRT's approach on the ground that determining whether a refugee retained that status and still deserved protection required a return to the refugee definition itself (see *NBGM* (2006)). In contrast, another Full Federal Court drew a distinction between entitlement for a visa under Australian law and the persistence of a right to protection as a refugee under Art 1C(5) of the Refugee Convention. This Full Court ruled in *QAAH* (2005) that a refugee presumptively retained refugee status unless the government could show that circumstances in the refugee's home country had altered so much as to make it safe for him or her to return. The likelihood that the two approaches will produce different outcomes for TPV holders is reinforced by the dissenting judge's finding in *QAAH* that the claimant was not a refugee, in contrast to the majority. In early 2006, the Australian government was in the process of appealing the Federal Court's decision in *QAAH* to the High Court. This appeal will be heard with the appeal in *NBGM* in mid 2006. According to the Refugee Council of Australia, of 6,000 TPV holders processed by October 2005, 50 received Return Pending Visas, meaning that their refugee claims were rejected (see below).

Light at the end of the tunnel: Change of status options

In 2004, the government acknowledged the need to provide permanent solutions for TPV holders by lifting the absolute bar on access to other visas. In August 2004, DIMA made changes that affected refugees holding subclass 785, 447 and 451 visas. The changes also benefit individuals who try without success to gain permanent refugee protection (see the discussion of the "Return Pending Visas", subclass 695, below). The changes mean that applications can be made by TPV holders for some non-refugee visas within Australia. These include spouse, student and business visas. The previous requirement that applicants leave Australia to apply for such visas was dropped. In addition, concessions were made for some visas so as to encourage TPV holders to apply for migrant visas in regional parts of Australia.

In 2004 the government also introduced the Return Pending Visa (RPV - subclass 695). This allows TPV holders who are unsuccessful in claiming permanent protection to remain in Australia for a further 18 months. Before this time, TPV holders who failed to prove that they continued to be refugees after the expiry of their protection visa had to leave immediately and were liable to be detained and deported. The RPV is not available to those whose visa was refused on character grounds or whose protection visa was cancelled or who have a substantial criminal record. The package complements incentives for TPV holders who fail to gain permanent protection to return home; see further below.

While the changes offer many refugees on temporary protection additional avenues through which to gain permanent residency, they do not signal an end to the system of temporary protection. Individuals who claim asylum in Australia will continue to be granted temporary visas. Nor do the changes resolve the uncertainties experienced by all TPV holders. Not everyone currently holding a TPV will qualify for a migration visa: refugees must be capable of either forming a relationship with an Australian or of being employed.

Refugees who are granted permanent migration visas are subject to the standard two-year waiting period for access to social security benefits. In becoming standard migrants, they also lose access to government-funded services such as torture and trauma counselling, which are available to persons holding permanent refugee visas.

The change in policy to allow refugees on temporary visas to apply for a range of migration visas is a welcome recognition of the contribution many refugees make to the Australian community and economy. However, it should be noted that refugee programs are based on humanitarian principles. There is a danger that the new scheme will discriminate against the most vulnerable refugees, such as those who are unable to find jobs in Australia or form relationships with Australians as a result of the trauma they have suffered because of their refugee experience. A more durable solution is the abolition of temporary protection in favour of permanent protection for all refugees and the establishment of a "complementary protection" regime that recognises the needs of individuals fearing grave human rights abuses: see chapter 6.

Temporary protection for some offshore refugees

The Australian government has also created temporary protection visa categories for two types of offshore refugees. A Secondary Movement Relocation visa offers temporary protection to those who moved from a safe first country of asylum to another country before applying to enter Australia. The visa lasts for five years and a person can only apply for permanent protection if there is a continuing protection need after four and a half years. The second visa category, Secondary Movement Offshore Entry, provides three-year temporary protection to those who arrived unlawfully in Australia at offshore excised places and moved from a safe first country of asylum.

The rationale for giving temporary protection to people already recognised as refugees offshore is to deter secondary movements of refugees after they have already found protection. However, in practice, a country of first asylum may not continue to provide effective protection over time, and it may be necessary for some vulnerable refugees to move again to find safety - and they should not be penalised for doing this by only receiving temporary protection. As noted earlier, these visas became more important in May 2006 when the law was changed to extend offshore refugee processing regime to all unauthorised boat arrivals.

Reasons for permanent protection

There are many obvious problems with Australia's current refugee protection regime. At a practical level, the arrangements make little sense. The Australian government needs to pay for the extraordinary cost for the reprocessing of all TPV holders. In June 2005, following sustained back-bench pressure, the government announced that it would finalise the reprocessing of all outstanding TPV holders by October of that year, imposing considerable further burdens on administrators. This goal had not been met by May 2006.

Temporary protection offers no finality for either the visa holders or refugee administration in Australia. All TPV holders must have their refugee claims reassessed if they wish to remain permanently - a process that will inevitably drag on for years, at great financial and emotional cost. Lack of finality is also a complaint made about the temporary protection visas granted to refugees who are assessed within Australia's migration zone.

Perhaps the worst aspect of the new laws, however, is their social cost to Australia. Refugees are not allowed to look forward and to get on with their lives. On the contrary, permanent safe haven depends on their maintaining their fear of persecution for at least three and up to five years.

The psychological uncertainty produced by these laws does immeasurable damage to the ability of individuals to integrate and contribute to their new country. An ongoing fear of persecution is a psychological barrier to the healing process that is crucial to resettlement.

The laws are equally damaging to the fabric of Australian society. They foster distrust of people that patently need assistance if they are to recover from past traumas. Indeed, the laws bring out the very worst in society. It is well understood that most of the recent boat people who sought refuge in Australia were Muslims from Afghanistan, Iraq and Iran. These are the people who were most likely to be given a TPV. In 2004 a Senate Committee heard that Australia granted 8,912 TPVs between 1999 and 2004. The visas were granted to 3,661 Afghans, 4,269 Iraqis and 475 Iranians, with 507 issued to other nationalities.

Race riots in Sydney in late 2005, the burning of a mosque in Brisbane in September 2001 and the sudden upsurge in violence and abuse against Muslim Australians in that year and in later years testify to the mood of xenophobia, racism and hysteria unleashed in the wake of the *Tampa* affair and the terrorist attacks in America. The new refugees require greater support rather than uncertainty if they are to settle into their new country. In the heat of the debates generated by the ongoing terrorist attacks around the world, it is easy to forget that refugees have often fled their countries of origin in fear of exactly the type of fanaticism and terrorism that has become the cause of so much fear and uncertainty in the West. It is difficult for Australia to justify invading Afghanistan and Iraq to remove brutal regimes while at the same time making it harder for the victims of those regimes to receive full and durable protection.

Permanent protection under humanitarian visas

There is a striking difference between the life of uncertainty that awaits refugees who enter Australia without authorisation and the generous support offered to refugees who enter the country under the offshore Humanitarian stream. Offshore entrants (visa subclasses 200, 201, 203 and 204) are eligible for the Integrated Humanitarian Settlement Scheme (IHSS), which provides intensive settlement support for six months. In 2005, competitive tendering was introduced for the provision of IHSS services, which include on arrival reception and assistance; accommodation on arrival and assistance in locating long-term accommodation; case coordination, information and referral; short-term torture and trauma counselling; and assisting local services to help refugees and raising community awareness. This assistance is not available to onshore refugees.

Humanitarian entrants and permanent protection visa holders are also eligible to access some mainstream settlement services designed for both humanitarian and non-humanitarian migrants, including translating and interpreting and up to 510 hours of basic English language tuition.

Refugees and humanitarian entrants under the humanitarian stream are also eligible for an additional 100 hours of language training. Most importantly, permanent protection visa holders and refugees under the humanitarian program do not have to reapply for a protection visa after three years, and have a right to travel and to sponsor family to Australia.

There are indications that the Australian government is delivering quality settlement services for refugees who arrive under the offshore program. Even so, improvements are still needed. Despite the initial support for refugees arriving within the humanitarian stream, refugees remain one of the most disadvantaged groups in the community. DIMA has identified several factors which may impair resettlement, including: low English proficiency; unemployment; accommodation and health issues; cultural adjustment; overseas skills recognition and the transition of children to Australian schools after long periods of disrupted education (DIMA, *Australia's Support for Humanitarian Entrants 2003-04*).

The competitive tendering and contracting out of the IHSS services have created problems in a system that was generally working well. In December 2005, a two-year-old child newly arrived from Burundi, Richard Niyonsave, died soon after he and his family were settled into their accommodation by the Australian Centre for Languages (ACL). While DIMA was aware that the boy had sickle-cell anaemia, the ACL case worker was apparently unaware of it. When the boy began to convulse, his father could not use the telephone to call for help, and lacked the language skills to communicate with neighbours. At around the same time, it is alleged that two refugee sisters from Africa were given no food for five days by ACL after refusing to sign a 12-month lease. Another refugee was given food vouchers without being instructed how to use them. Legally, private contractors may not be subject to the same public and administrative law remedies that are available against government agencies.

Australia is in many ways a world leader in its commitment to its offshore humanitarian program and its associated settlement support. Australia's response to offshore refugees shows that a humane alternative to TPVs is available. It is regrettable that Australia's compassionate response to offshore refugees cannot be extended to the few refugees who have had no choice but to arrive in Australia without documentation and who urgently need assistance.

Access to Australian citizenship

The final stage in the resettlement of a refugee or former refugee is the grant of Australian citizenship. In recent years, successive governments have encouraged migrants of all backgrounds to take this final step in committing themselves to Australia. Sadly, for many of the refugees who came to Australia after the Vietnam War, there were no such citizenship drives. As a result, there have been a number of recent cases of former refugees committing crimes and being deported from Australia to the country from which they had fled – as small children. Such deportations would not be possible had their families sought Australian citizenship.

In general, Australian citizenship is granted on application to refugees who have been in Australia as permanent residents for two years or more. Citizenship will be granted unless a refugee engaged in fraudulent activity in procuring a permanent visa, or is convicted of a particularly serious crime. The law also allows for the grant of citizenship to children who have spent their first 10 years in Australia. This is important because Australian law does not provide for citizenship merely by birth on Australian soil. To become a citizen, one parent must be an Australian citizen or permanent resident. In all other cases, new born children are born with the immigration status of their parents. In 2006 the government announced proposals to extend to three years the waiting period for Australian citizenship.

An attempt was made in 2004 to challenge the constitutionality of the laws that deny citizenship to children born in Australia. The High Court ruled five judges to two that the Australian Parliament is not limited in its power to regulate who is and is not a citizen of Australia. The case was brought on behalf of Tania Singh, a child born in immigration detention to asylum seeker parents. The ruling in *Singh* (2004) explains how a baby born to a Malaysian mother in Villawood IDC in Sydney could become stateless even though she was born in Australia. The child was not recognised by Malaysia as a citizen because she was born outside of Malaysia. She was not regarded as an Australian citizen because neither her mother nor her father had permanent residence in Australia.

Removal of failed asylum seekers and former TPV holders

Asylum seekers and former TPV holders whose refugee claims have been denied may be returned to their home country. As explained in chapter 9, Australia has a system of "mandatory removal". People without permission to remain in Australia are detained until they are given a visa or removed from the country. Section 198 of the *Migration Act* authorises the removal of all non-citizens who have failed in their attempt to gain a visa. Asylum seekers who come to the end of the road in Australia can elect to go "voluntarily" or can be removed by force.

Australia's removal procedures came in into question in 2005 with revelations of the wrongful removal of Australian citizen Vivian Solon-Alvarez: see chapter 9. Before that controversy, questions had been raised about the removal of asylum seekers to places where they still faced danger. For example, in 2001 Alvaro Moralez, a Colombian citizen who had escaped paramilitaries in Colombia, was refused refugee status. He subsequently chose to return to Colombia after being threatened with forced removal. Upon return, Moralez was shot within metres of his mother's apartment in Bogota, just as he claimed he would be. The government claims that Australia is not responsible for his death because he departed voluntarily. Amnesty International argues that the choices given to Moralez were not real as he was threatened with forced removal.

Australia has limited control over the fate of detainees after their removal from Australia. A 2004 study of 40 rejected asylum seekers in 11 countries by the Edmund Rice Centre, in cooperation with the Australian Catholic University, found that Australia returned at least 35 rejected asylum seekers to dangerous situations: see *Deported to Danger* (2004). The study also found cases of returnees being issued with temporary documents that expired soon after their return, leaving them without lawful status in the country to which they were returned. There were also allegations of Australia preparing false documentation for returnees. Other stories of people being returned to dangerous situations are found in Corlett (2005).

Voluntary repatriation

In recent years, Australia has offered a reintegration package to some rejected asylum seekers and TPV holders to encourage them to return home voluntarily. The first offer was made in 2002 to Afghan refugees in mainland detention centres and in Nauru, and extended in 2004 to anyone on TPVs. While the government offered similar incentives to asylum seekers and people evacuated from Kosovo as part of the Safe Haven program, the extension of the Reintegration Package to TPV holders was the first time Australia actively promoted repatriation of Convention refugees. The Reintegration Package included a cash grant of A$2,000 per person, or $10,000 per family; a one-way airfare to Kabul; the standard luggage allowance (20 kg per person); and access to limited support services on arrival. Similar assistance was offered to a small number of Iraqi detainees. By January 2003, 40 failed Afghan asylum seekers had returned under the scheme from onshore detention centres and a further 274 Afghans were returned from Nauru.

The Refugee Council of Australia criticised the lack of information provided to refugees and TPV holders about the situation in Afghanistan and their available options. The government introduced the offer while there was ongoing instability in Afghanistan and failed to provide information regarding immunisation, land mine awareness and the new currency in Afghanistan. Further, no community consultation with either refugees or advocates was organised before the offer and no funding was allocated for independent advice to refugees. The offer was announced over Christmas when most support services were closed. A second Memorandum of Understanding between Australia and Afghanistan to promote voluntary repatriation was signed in 2005.

In March 2003, the Australian government signed a Memorandum of Understanding (MOU) on consular matters with the government of Iran. The subject matter of the MOU remains confidential, but Iranian detainees were informed that agreements had been made with Iran about the fate of Iranian asylum seekers and that they may be forcibly removed from detention. Soon after, Australia announced a Reintegration Assistance Package for Iranian asylum seekers who volunteered to return to Iran. The Package included: assistance with applications for travel documents; transport to return to home communities in Iran; $2,000 per individual (adult or child) or up to $10,000 per nuclear family; and waiver of debts to the Commonwealth relating to detention and removal costs.

The Reintegration Assistance Package was open to all Iranians detained in Australia and on Nauru. Iranians who accepted the package whilst claiming asylum needed to withdraw any application to remain in Australia, in writing. The letter advising detainees of the reintegration package threatened "involuntary removal" if the option for "voluntary return" was not accepted within 28 days of the letter. Many detainees reported that the threat of forced deportation added to their already considerable emotional, financial and social insecurity. Some advocates feared that detainees may have accepted reintegration packages against their best interests. By June 2003, it was reported that six Iranians had accepted voluntary repatriation and 79 had refused. Many detainees who refused were offered one last chance to sign. When they refused again, they were told that deportation was imminent

Despite the threats of forced removal, a leaked official minute from a senior bureaucrat, John Okely, to the then Minister for Immigration, Phillip Ruddock, dated December 2002, revealed that Iran had strong reservations about accepting large numbers of forcibly removed asylum seekers and believed that Australia had not done enough to promote voluntary return. Four asylum seekers have been forcefully returned to Iran since the signing of the MOU.

By mid-2005, 437 people had accepted a reintegration allowance for voluntary return since 2002. Of these, 429 had returned voluntarily (407 Afghans, 10 Iranians, four Turks, three Pakistanis, three Sri Lankans and two Iraqis). Eight people on Nauru who accepted the package had yet to return home. In 2004-05, 14 people accepted the reintegration package (two Afghans in detention, one Afghan holding a TPV and 11 Iraqis holding TPVs), while 119 people accepted it in 2003-04 (15 Afghans in detention, 37 Afghans holding TPVs, 15 Iraqis and 22 Iranians in detention and 30 Iraqis holding TPVs).

References and further reading

Australian Citizenship website: <www.citizenship.gov.au>

Azadeh Dastyari, "Change of status options for refugees and humanitarian entrants holding temporary visas" (2004) 22 *Immigration Review* 4

David Corlett, *Following Them Home: the Fate of the Returned Asylum Seekers* (Black Inc Books, Melbourne, 2005)

"Deported to Danger: A Study of Australia's Treatment of 40 Rejected Asylum Seekers", Edmund Rice Centre for Justice & community Education and School of Education, Australian Catholic University, <www.erc.org.au/research/pdf/1096416029.pdf>

DIMA, "Fact Sheet 60 Australia's Refugee and Humanitarian Program": <www.immi.gov.au/facts/60refugee.htm>

DIMA "Fact Sheet 64 Temporary Protection Visas": <www.immi.gov.au/facts/64protection.htm>

DIMA, "Fact Sheet 66. Integrated Humanitarian Settlement Strategy": <www.immi.gov.au/facts/66ihss.htm>

DIMA, "Fact Sheet 96. Review of Settlement Services for Migrants and Humanitarian Entrants": <www.immi.gov.au/facts/96review_of_settlement_services.htm>

DIMA "Removing Unlawful Non-citizens" in Managing the Border: Immigration Compliance 2004–2005 Edition: <www.immi.gov.au/illegals/mtb/mtb-chapter11.pdf>

DIMA, "Life in Australia" : <www.immi.gov.au/settle/index.htm>

Hossein Esmaeili and Belinda Wells, "The 'Temporary' Refugees: Australia's Legal Response to the Arrival of Iraqi and Afghan Boat-People" (2000) 23 *University of NSW Law Journal: The Refugee Issue* 224

Greg Marston, "Temporary Protection Permanent Uncertainty Report" *RMIT Centre for Applied* Research: <mams.rmit.edu.au/k2vavbh0g5ik.pdf>

Janet Phillips "Temporary Protection Visas" Research Note No 51 2003-04: <www.aph.gov.au/LIBRARY/Pubs/rn/2003-04/04rn51.htm>

Refugee Advice and Casework Service, *Know Your Rights: Guide for People on Temporary Protection Visas*, April 2003

Refugee Council of Australia, "Australia's Temporary Protection Visa Regime": <www.refugeecouncil.org.au/html/current_issues/tpv.html>

Refugee Council of Australia, "Position Paper On Australia's Reintegration Package For Afghan Refugees" (April 2003): <www.refugeecouncil.org.au/html/position_papers/Repatriation_TPV.ht>ml

Cases

NBGM v MIMIA [2006] FCAFC 60

QAAH of 2004 v MIMIA (2005) 145 FCR 363

Singh v Commonwealth (2004) 209 ALR 355

The distressed KM Palapa, carrying 433 asylum seekers pulling alongside MV Tampa © News Ltd

West Papuan asylum seekers encamped at Janey Creek,
north of the Aboriginal community of Mapoon in the Northern Territory
(under guard of customs and immigration officials)
© Torres Strait Times/ Damien Barker (2006)

Protests at Woomera Detention Centre, 2002 © Tom Mann

Asylum seeker children in detention on Nauru © Andrew Bartlett

Part 3
Immigration Detention

9

Enforcing Australia's Immigration Laws: Arrest, Detention and Removal

Key Points in this Chapter

- Legally, all non-citizens without visas, including asylum seekers, must be detained and removed from Australia. The law impacts most harshly on unauthorised arrivals, as overstayers are often able to avoid detention.
- The case of Cornelia Rau raised issues about DIMA's decisions to detain (and to keep in custody for long periods) persons *"known or reasonably suspected"* of being unlawful non-citizens.
- The case of Vivian Solon-Alvarez raised questions about how the mandatory removal provisions operate in practice. Of particular concern was the failure to make adequate inquiries about her identity; and the poor oversight by senior officials of the removal process.
- "Bridging visas" (BV) are used to release people from detention pending determination of an application for a substantive visa. Those eligible are persons who once held a visa; people over 75 years of age; children (and, after June 2005, their parents in some cases); victims of torture and trauma; and unauthorised persons who remain undetected for 45 days or more after entry. Eligibility for a BV does not guarantee release and health and character checks must be passed.
- The Minister has the discretion to release from detention non-citizens who cannot be practicably removed to another country.
- Most detainees are adult males, but the introduction of TPVs saw a sharp increase in the number of women and children detained. In early 2001 almost one in every three detainees was a child.
- In June 2005, the Minister for Immigration acquired a non-compellable power to ensure that children are only detained as a matter of last resort.
- The courts cannot review the detention of asylum seekers, although they can review other forms of imprisonment. After June 2005, the federal Ombudsman was given the power to review and recommend the release of certain long-term detainees.
- DIMA has contracted private security companies to remove failed asylum seekers whose protection claims have not been accepted. Private companies are not subject to the same standards of scrutiny and accountability as government agencies.

Australia's arrest, detention and removal laws

Under Australian law, all non-citizens who enter or remain in the country without a valid visa must be detained and removed from Australia as soon as reasonably practicable. Detention ensures that people arriving without permission are available for removal if their claims are rejected. It also ensures that non-citizens are not released into the community without first undergoing character and health tests. More contentiously, mandatory detention is seen to deter people wishing to enter Australia without permission; and to encourage the departure of people who have no legitimate claims to remain in the country.

Immigration detention is an administrative measure that deprives people of their liberty even though they have not been convicted of an offence. This distinguishes it from imprisonment in the criminal justice system, which requires proof of an offence and a court-imposed sentence. Non-citizens in Australia are liable to be detained whenever an immigration official "reasonably suspects" that the person is in the country unlawfully. Detention will continue until the person is either removed from the country or granted a visa.

This chapter begins with an overview of the laws and policies governing arrest, detention and removal and the problems that have arisen in their implementation. Using the stories of Cornelia Rau and Vivienne Alvarez-Solon as case studies, it looks first at the decision to detain a suspected unlawful non-citizen; the question of longer term detention; and the operation of the "automatic" removal provisions. It argues that changes to the *Migration Act 1958* in 1994 which removed court scrutiny of immigration arrest and detention have had a devastating impact. Since 1994 there has been an epidemic of wrongful arrests, with some citizens and lawful permanent residents spending many months in detention without cause. It is argued that some mechanism for checking administrative decisions to detain people "suspected" of being unlawful non-citizens should be reintroduced, along with an independent mechanism for overseeing the removal of non-citizens from Australia.

This chapter then discusses the circumstances that govern the release of immigration detainees. The year 2005 brought extensive changes in law and policy, leading to the release on 28 July of most non-citizen families held in detention. This part examines the statistics on removals and on who is or has been detained and for how long. The last part focuses on the process of removing unlawful non-citizens.

The decision to detain a suspected unlawful non-citizen

In 2005, two scandals had a profound impact on public perceptions of Australia's mandatory detention laws as implemented by DIMA. The first concerned the German-born Cornelia Rau, a permanent resident of 18 years. The second involved Philippino-born Vivienne Solon-Alvarez, an Australian citizen for 20 years who had two Australian children. Both women suffered from mental illness and were detained on suspicion of being unlawful non-citizens. As explained below, Ms Rau spent more than 10 months in immigration detention before her plight and identity were exposed by refugee advocates and journalists. If the Cornelia Rau case embarrassed the government, things became worse when it was discovered that Ms Solon-Alvarez had been both arrested and removed from Australia.

Within a short space of time, DIMA admitted that there were no fewer than 201 other cases where citizens and lawful permanent residents had been arrested and detained between July 2000 and April 2005. Drawing a line at the Solon-Alvarez case, Mick Palmer, the former Federal Police Commissioner conducting the inquiry into the Cornelia Rau case, insisted that the 201 cases be assigned to the federal Ombudsman rather than to his modest team of investigators. In August 2005, DIMA revealed that it had paid $920,000 in compensation for the wrongful detention of 11 citizens and permanent residents since 1993, with an average (case confidential) settlement of $84,000 each. It is likely that there will be many more compensation claims when investigations into more than 200 other cases of possible unlawful detention are finalised. Of the 201 cases referred to the federal Ombudsman, 56 were kept in detention for more than three weeks, with one detainee held for up to six years, another for three to four years, and 12 for up to three years.

Although much attention has been paid to the institutional shortcomings within DIMA in the treatment of Ms Rau and Ms Alvarez-Solon (see below), questions also need to be asked about the relationship between the culture within the department and the legislative regime under which officers operate. The problem of irregular migration is not new. Powers to arrest "illegals" have always existed in Australia's immigration laws. However, two things are distinctive about the current law. One is that it now *mandates* the detention of suspected unlawful non-citizens. Section 189 of the *Migration Act* provides that where an "officer" (defined as an official of either DIMA or of a State or federal law enforcement body) *knows or reasonably suspects* that a person is an unlawful non-citizen, the officer *must detain* the person.

The second novel aspect is that s 196 of the *Migration Act* now provides that persons detained under s 189 must be kept in detention until they are either granted a visa or removed from Australia. This potentially leads to the situation where non-citizens who are not eligible for a visa but who cannot be removed from Australia could be kept in detention for the term of their natural life: see the discussion of the *Al-Kateb* case in chapter 10. The *Migration Act* also provides for the mandatory removal of unlawful non-citizens who either request to be removed or who have reached the end of the administrative process.

This dual system that ties the holding of a valid visa to both lawful status and personal freedom was not introduced into Australian law until September 1994. Before then, different provisions separated the two processes of *deciding to detain* and detention of unlawful non-citizens pending removal from the country. The removal of non-citizens was also the subject of a separate decision-making process. Non-citizens arrested on suspicion of being illegal had to be brought before a magistrate within 48 hours. If it was not possible to determine legal status in that period, suspects could be kept in detention, but they were required to be brought back before a court every seven days until their status was determined. Periodic judicial scrutiny only stopped when the order to deport was made and the detainee came to be held in custody pending removal (the second type of detention). It was a system that forced officers to move from suspicion to a firm decision if they wished to both keep someone in detention and/or have them removed from Australia. Before the courts, people could not be left in legal limbo about their immigration status.

The present regime eliminates judicial oversight of immigration detention and removal, meaning that officers no longer have to come before a court to expose the bases of their suspicions. Detainees no longer have this open process in which to put their case and to hear the evidence that DIMA has against them. Even so, the system does not change radically the personal decision-making processes that officers follow when they come across someone with an uncertain immigration status.

Cornelia Rau's story

Cornelia Rau is a German citizen who has been a permanent resident of Australia since she migrated to Australia with her family at the age of 18 months. Her misadventure with the immigration authorities in 2004-05 stemmed from her history of mental illness, which was variously assessed as "bipolar disorder", "schizoaffective bipolar" and "chronic schizophrenia", leading her to act unpredictably and erratically. The available evidence is that she vigorously resisted attempts to treat her condition through the administration of drugs and other measures.

Cornelia Rau came to the attention of DIMA in late March 2004. She discharged herself from a hospital in Sydney where she was receiving treatment and made her way to far North Queensland. On 29 March 2004 Cornelia was seen at the Han River Roadhouse at Coen where she told patrons that she was a German backpacker who had lost her passport. Concerned by her strange behaviour, the Roadhouse owner called the local police who took Ms Rau into detention on behalf of DIMA. She was then transferred to Cairns and then to the Brisbane women's correctional centre at Wacol. She was detained on suspicion of being an illegal immigrant. In the words of Minister Amanda Vanstone:

> [S]he claimed that she was German … [she] spoke German, said she was a visitor, said she had no friends and family and had with her a stolen passport. So it's a pretty fair understanding that both police and immigration would think that this person may be an unlawful [non]-citizen.

Efforts in Brisbane to identify her produced no results. Cornelia called herself variously "Anna Brotmeyer", Anna Schmidt" and other names, concealing her real identity. Although referred for mental health assessment to Brisbane's Princess Alexandra Hospital, she was ultimately returned to the prison.

In October 2004, Cornelia Rau was taken to Baxter Immigration Detention facility. She was assessed by a psychologist on 6 November but was uncooperative. No definitive findings were made about her mental health other than vague assessments that she was difficult and "attention seeking". By late November she had spent extended periods in solitary confinement in the high security management unit of Baxter. She was later moved to "Red one", a compound used for detainees who presented "management" problems. By this time her behaviour was clearly disturbed. She was screaming uncontrollably, eating dirt, failing to clean herself and otherwise acting in grossly inappropriate ways.

Reports of a strange German woman reached refugee advocacy groups in late December, with other detainees expressing concerns about her mental health. Cornelia's case was taken up by advocates who drew a journalist's attention to her plight. Cornelia's parents recognised her instantly as the "Anna" described in Andra Jackson's article in *The Age* on 31 January 2005. After the Rau family secured her release, Cornelia was admitted to the Glenside Psychiatric Hospital. Minister Vanstone then appointed retired senior police officer Mick Palmer to investigate how an Australian permanent resident who was listed as a missing person could have been detained as an unlawful non-citizen for over 10 months. The legal powers given to Palmer to conduct his inquiry were, however, very restricted, and depended on cooperation from those involved. Queensland officials, for example, refused to cooperate with the inquiry because it lacked judicial powers and could not compel evidence.

"Reasonable suspicion"

Perhaps the most biting criticism made by Mick Palmer of the officers involved in the lengthy detention of Cornelia Rau is that they became unduly fixated on the mandatory aspect of s 189, losing sight of the discretion inherent in exercising their personal judgment of a person's likely immigration status. Palmer found that the officers in the Rau case were so imbued with the notion that they *must detain* that they did not stop to reflect on the rationality of their actions in the face of the available evidence: see pp 21-22. He said (p 25):

> Comment was made to the Inquiry on a number of occasions that the operation of s 189(1) was not reviewable since it was mandatory in nature and immigration detention was administrative, not criminal. There did not appear to be - even at senior managerial level - an understanding of the distinction between the discretionary nature of the detention that must follow the forming of a "reasonable opinion".

Palmer points out that Rau was originally drawn to the attention of the immigration authorities because people were concerned about her welfare, rather than her legal status. Indeed, in her initial arrest no thought was given to the possibility that Rau might be a mentally ill woman attempting to obscure her Australian identity by disguising herself as a foreign national. Palmer itemises the names and documents (a stolen Norwegian passport) produced by Rau upon or shortly after her arrest. Palmer's timeline (pp 9-20) suggests that Rau may have tried hard at this point and later to convince the officers that she was German. She even attempted at least twice to secure a German passport. While officials made frequent contact with the German authorities in Australia and Germany in an attempt to identify Rau, attempts to identify her in

Australia as a missing person were limited to the State in which she was found, Queensland. Palmer's timeline is full of references to people expressing concerns about Rau's "irregular", "unusual" and even violent behaviour. Even so, it was not until January 2005 that a medical practitioner correctly identified her as mentally ill rather than as an "attention seeker" or simply a "difficult" detainee.

By 2005, a number of the cases involving wrongfully detained residents had come before the courts in claims for damages. Palmer noted that the courts generally supported the views he expressed about the effect of s 189 of the *Migration Act*. In *Goldie* (2002), for example, DIMA's faulty computer records suggested incorrectly that the plaintiff did not hold a valid visa. Without performing basic cross-checking that would have revealed Mr Goldie's lawful status, he was detained. The Full Federal Court found that s 189 places a strict onus on officers to make due inquiries to make sure that their suspicions of unlawful status are well founded. The Court said (at 710):

> By itself the word "suspects" would be capable of being construed to include the formation of an imagined belief, having no basis at all in fact, or even conjecture. Plainly, to empower an arrest on the basis of an irrational suspicion would offend the principle of the importance of individual liberty underlying the common law ... [T]he officer is not empowered to act on a suspicion reasonably formed that a person *may* be an unlawful non-citizen. The officer is to detain a person whom the officer reasonably suspects *is* an unlawful non-citizen.

In other words, the addition of the adjective "reasonable" before "suspicion" in the section means that there has to be an objective and rational basis for believing that a person is unlawful. It is not enough that an individual officer suspects that a person *may* be illegal. Although dealing with a different case, the ruling by the High Court in *Ruddock v Taylor* (2005) seems to confirm this interpretation: see below.

Continued detention of suspected unlawful non-citizens

Even if Rau's initial arrest and detention were justified under s 189, questions remain as to whether her detention continued to be legally justified over time. The issue here is the relationship between ss 189 and 196 of the *Migration Act*. In three cases since 2002 (two in the Federal Court and one in the High Court), the government argued that detention under s 189 continues to be lawful as long as any officer (as defined) continues to harbour suspicions about a person's immigration status. The prevailing view of these courts is that indefinite detention under s 196 cannot be justified on the basis of mere suspicion. In *VHAF* (2002), Justice Gray agreed with the approach taken in *Goldie* (2002), ruling that the government had to justify ongoing detention at every stage. He found that, where unlawful status could not be confirmed, the power to detain could not continue to be supported indefinitely. This view was endorsed unanimously by the Full Federal Court in *VFAD* (2003).

The approach of the High Court in *Ruddock v Taylor* (2005) suggests that as long as there is a reasonable basis for ongoing suspicion, detention will not be unlawful. The majority in that case (Justices Kirby and McHugh dissented) confirmed that the eventual finding that a detainee is a citizen or lawful non-citizen will not in itself render the original detention unlawful. The Court did not, however, address the question of the indefinite detention of a person whose status had not been confirmed one way or the other. Unlike either the Rau or Solon-Alvarez cases, *Ruddock v Taylor* concerned the detention of a man whose visa had been cancelled by the Minister. There was no issue that DIMA officers had acted other than with propriety in detaining the plaintiff pursuant to the Minister's direction. In other words, in the absence of bad faith on the part of the officers, there was no dispute that the officers had entertained a "reasonable suspicion" about the plaintiff's immigration status. The significance of the case lies in the High Court's ruling that a person who is lawfully detained on grounds that are found later to be baseless may not be entitled to damages for wrongful detention.

The dilemma raised by the government's interpretation of ss 189 and 196 of the *Migration Act* is that an impossible burden could be placed on detainees to prove their own legal status for immigration purposes. From an objective point of view, it is the immigration authorities (rather than the "status" holders) who ultimately have the power to determine the existence and validity of authorising documents. With no mechanism for oversight of the assessment process, a detainee could face indefinite custody on the simple assertion by an officer that they continue to have "reasonable suspicions" about the legal status of the detainee. It should be noted in this context that decisions to detain under s 189 are subject to the "privative clause" provisions in the Act. This means, on the face of it, that they cannot be challenged in a court of law other than on the basis of serious legal error.

In his report, Palmer found that DIMA officials tended to view detention under ss 189 and 196 as immutable unless nominated "events" occurred. These were the grant of a visa or removal from Australia. Although confident about their duty to detain, Palmer found that the officers considered that the process of testing their "suspicions" about a person's lawful status was administrative and without urgency. Palmer made many recommendations about the training of DIMA officers and the procedures used by DIMA and law enforcement officers. Where the Report stops is in its review of the legislative scheme under which the officials in both the Rau and Alvarez cases were working.

The primary shortcoming in the legal regime governing the arrest and detention of suspected unlawful non-citizens is that the entire process is quarantined from oversight by any body outside of the immigration administration. It would seem no mere coincidence that there has been a spate of wrongful detention cases since the changes to the Act in 1994. (Although DIMA has admitted to cases going back to 1993, the vast majority of the 201 matters referred to the Ombudsman relate to incidents that postdate 1 September 1994.) The current regime may be being misinterpreted by DIMA. However, the plain truth is that it is a system that is inherently closed and lacking in adequate accountability. There are no external mechanisms to force officers to make definitive rulings on their "suspicions". Individuals detained unlawfully are not automatically entitled to have their case reviewed. Where individuals are suffering from a mental illness so that their judgment is impaired, it is a system that has now been demonstrated to produce devastating outcomes.

The fact that the system will continue to produce such outcomes is plain from the continuing investigations of the Commonwealth Ombudsman. In March 2006, the Commonwealth Ombudsman revealed the unlawful detention of a 45-year-old Australian citizen. The man, referred to as "Mr T", was originally from Vietnam and suffered from mental illness. He was detained at Villawood detention centre three times between 1999-2003, on one occasion for more than eight months. Despite awareness of his mental state, Mr T was released by DIMA into the community without any arrangements being made for his continued support sand care. DIMA has indicated that "Mr T" will be compensated for his unlawful detention.

The removal of unlawful non-citizens

Mandatory removal is relatively new in Australian immigration law. Before its introduction in 1994, a non-citizen could only be removed from Australia if a removal order had been made. The government bore the burden of proof to show that the person did not have a right to remain in Australia and the courts had the power to review and overturn such orders. In cases like *Park Oh Ho* (1994), the High Court made it plain that damages would flow from decisions to detain or remove that did not have an appropriate legal basis.

The case of Vivian Solon-Alvarez

Ms Solon-Alvarez is a long-standing Australian citizen of Philippino descent who was removed from Australia on 20 July 2001 on the basis that she was an unlawful non-citizen. Both Palmer and the Senate Committee that examined her case in 2005 surmised that an early and radically misconceived assumption was made that the woman was a "sex slave" who had perhaps been illegally trafficked into Australia. It was assumed that she was someone that no one would miss if removed.

Ms Solon-Alvarez first came to the attention of the immigration authorities in April 2001 when she was found by a social worker in Lismore in NSW, injured and apparently destitute. She was suffering from partial quadriplegia and required walking aids. Her physical state was the result of an accident or an assault (this matter was not investigated by anyone). After a locum doctor assessed the woman as fit to travel, she was removed to Manila. In the absence of any family or other support she was admitted into a hospice for the destitute and dying run by the Mother Teresa Sisters, Missionaries of Charity, in the city of Olongapao, where she remained until her discovery in May 2005.

Palmer did not find evidence to suggest that any DIMA officer involved in the removal of Ms Alvarez "was aware that the person removed from Australia on 20 July 2001 was an Australian citizen or a reported missing person". However, the preliminary finding was that any "thorough and objective inquiry" would have established her identity. Palmer documents the convoluted steps taken to ensure Ms Alvarez's removal from Australia in the face of objective evidence that she was not physically fit to travel anywhere. He noted that on the very day that the Philippines Embassy was pressured into issuing travel documents for the woman (who, in fact was no longer a Philippino national), DIMA had received a fax from the Queensland Police Service's Missing Persons Bureau. The fax sought information about the travel from Australia of a missing person of "Philippino extraction" identified as "Vivian Solon, or Young". Several possible dates of birth were offered, including the date provided by Vivian Alvarez, 30 October 1962.

Palmer's July 2005 report contains blistering criticism of DIMA operations in the two areas of immigration detention and removal (compliance). He identifies four key failings in DIMA as being the "cause" of both the Solon-Alvarez and Rau scandals. The first are problems associated with DIMA information systems which he describes as "siloed" and "with little connectivity between systems", limiting the capacity to effectively search for information (p 189). The second major problem was in the training and selection of DIMA officers. The induction training package for compliance officers was inadequate and too much reliance was placed on on-the-job training. There was also a lack of any systematic selection process for ensuring that compliance officers possessed necessary skills and attributes (p 192).

Thirdly, Ms Rau and Ms Alvarez's problems were also attributed to "an almost complete lack of holistic case management", which was fragmented, inefficient, and lacking in accountability and oversight (p 192). Finally, Palmer was scathing about the culture within DIMA, again using the term "siloed" to described the hierarchical and segmented nature of the divisional structure. He found that the absence of communication links and information sharing lead to inefficiency and catastrophic incompetence. Support arrangements were "weak and ineffective"; staff lacked empowerment and focused excessively on process; and change was reactive and generated by crises (p 193).

In the case of Alvarez-Solon, Palmer's findings were corroborated by an inquiry into her case by Neil Comrie, a former Victorian Police Commissioner, on behalf of the federal Ombudsman. Comrie found that DIMA's handling of her case was "catastrophic" and her unlawful removal was a result of "systematic failures" in DIMA, including "inadequate training programs, database and operating system failures, poor case management and a flawed organisational culture". DIMA officers were found to have a flawed understanding of the law, and senior officers failed to act when junior officers discovered the mistake.

DIMA responded to the Rau and Alvarez-Solon inquiries by announcing a "Change Management Taskforce" to help DIMA to become more open and accountable; to deal fairly with clients; and to have well trained and supported staff. In October 2005, the government committed $230 million over five years to the reform of DIMA. The management of DIMA has been restructured, with significant staffing changes, although the former Secretary of the Department appears to have been promoted – to become Australian Ambassador to Indonesia.

Despite Palmer's criticisms, problems continued in DIMA. In September 2005, a Palestinian asylum seeker detained for five years was deported from Australia while his case was still under investigation by the UN Human Rights Committee and while the Federal Court was considering whether to issue an injunction to stay his deportation. Neither his lawyers nor the UN Committee were informed, and the Federal Court issued an injunction just as his flight departed. He was returned to Australia from Dubai after the intervention of the UN High Commissioner for Refugees.

In an earlier case, a Turkish man, Ali Tastan, was deported to Turkey after living in Australia for 30 years (including three years in immigration detention and seven years in prison for violence and drug offences). This was despite an AAT ruling that his risk of reoffending was low and that he should not be deported. Three years after his deportation, Australia sought his return to Australia after a Federal Court proceeding, based on the Court's earlier decision that a Swedish man who had lived in Australia since he was four years old could not be deported because he held an "absorbed person's visa": see *Nystrom* (2005). Since being deported, Ali Tastan appears to have been living as a homeless man on the streets of Ankara, afflicted by schizophrenia (known to the Australian authorities before his deportation) and without medical treatment. He was deported despite the AAT's finding in *Tastan and MIMA* (1999) that "[t]o deport him ... would transport him to a society where he has very few contacts and where his mental illness and associated disabilities would place him in an extremely vulnerable position" (at 327).

In 2004, Robert Jovicic, an Australian resident who was born in France to Serbian parents, was deported to Serbia on character grounds despite living all but two years of his life in Australia and having no legal status in Serbia. Jovicic was permitted to return to Australia in March 2006 only to be told that he should go back to Serbia and seek Serbian citizenship. In April 2006, it was not certain that Jovicic would be permitted to remain in Australia permanently.

Eligibility for release from detention: "Bridging visas"

Leaving aside the issue of how people come to be detained (and removed), the next question is who is entitled to be released. Detention provisions do not apply equally to all people in Australia without permission. For example, most non-citizens who enter Australia on valid visas do not end up in detention, even if they overstay their visas and lose their permission to remain. This is because of a bridging visa system that allows for the release of certain people into the community. The bridging visa is like a bail authority. It is granted to specified categories of non-citizens on the condition that they will not abscond and that they will obey the law until they leave Australia voluntarily or have their residency applications determined. The softening of the system in June-July 2005 did not change the core provisions mandating the detention of unlawful non-citizens. Rather, the range of visas available to individuals in immigration detention was increased.

People eligible for bridging visas include asylum seekers who come to Australia as tourists or students and claim refugee status. The bridging visa allows these individuals to wait out their processing times in the community. If they seek asylum within 45 days of arriving in Australia, these people are also permitted to work and are eligible for modest income support from the government.

In contrast, few non-citizens who arrive without a valid visa are eligible for a bridging visa. Detention is automatic and unavoidable unless an unauthorised arrival is an "eligible non-citizen" or meets requirements for the grant of special visas created in June 2005. "Eligible non-citizens" include people who are old (over 75 years), children, victims of torture and trauma, or non-citizens married to Australian citizens or permanent residents. However, not all "eligible non-citizens" are granted a bridging visa. The conferral of the visa is discretionary and past practice has been to detain rather than release almost all unauthorised arrivals, including the old, the young and even some victims of torture and trauma.

Bridging visas can also be granted to stateless people or others who cannot be practicably returned to their country. The Removal Pending Bridging Visa (RPBV) came into effect in May 2005 and the *Migration Regulations* were revised accordingly in June 2005. The RPBV allows the release, pending removal, of people in immigration detention who have been cooperating with efforts to remove them from Australia, but whose removal is not reasonably practicable at that time. The RPBV may therefore be used to release immigration detainees who may otherwise be detained indefinitely in Australia's detention centres: see discussion of *Al-Kateb* (2004) and *Al Khafaji* (2004) in chapter 10. The grant of an RPBV is discretionary and past practice for the release of long-term detainees has been inconsistent.

As explored in chapter 11, mandatory detention has been very damaging in practice, with many long-term detainees developing severe psychological problems. Particular concerns have been raised about the law's impact on the elderly and the young. Even where detainees are released from detention on bridging visas, the laws are not generous, with no or limited access to welfare or Medicare benefits. Some are also prevented from working and must rely on charity for basic needs such as food and shelter.

In June 2005, government backbenchers led by a Melbourne MP, Petro Georgiou, threatened to introduce two "private member's" Bills to soften the detention regime. The move was controversial because the proposed legislation was prepared without the sanction of the government and so had the potential to open destabilising divisions in the coalition parties (the Liberals and Nationals).

One of the Bills proposed that asylum seekers should only be detained where it is necessary to verify identity, assess a claim, protect public safety or ensure that a person is available for health checks or deportation (should the applicant be unsuccessful). The maximum period of detention proposed was 90 days, which could be extended indefinitely if DIMA applied to the Federal Court and was able to show that detention remained necessary. Where detention could not be justified, asylum seekers were to be released on bridging visas, in the same way as those who arrive lawfully and then seek asylum. Judicial review (in the Federal Court) of decisions to detain would also be available. The Bill also proposed that recognised refugees be granted permanent residence, rather than the temporary permits that now operate.

The limited grounds for detention proposed in this Bill largely mirrored the UNHCR Guidelines (discussed in chapter 10) and would have represented a striking improvement of Australia's detention regime. Indeed, the Bill would have gone a long way towards bringing Australia into line with every other Western democracy, none of which has a policy of mandatory detention: see chapter 12.

The second Bill dealt with those already in detention. For those detained for more than one year, a current or retired judge would determine if continuing detention was necessary on the basis of public safety or the danger of absconding. Detainees found not to present a risk were to be released into the community pending determination of their status, subject to requirements to report to the authorities if appropriate. Those released would be entitled to work and Medicare. The Bill also called for all children in detention (even those detained for less than one year) and their parents and siblings to be released pending determination of status, unless they endangered the public or would abscond.

Following heated discussions of the proposals within the government in June 2005, it ultimately reiterated its support for mandatory detention. However, the internal political pressure forced some important concessions from the Prime Minister, in the form of the *Migration Amendment (Detention Arrangements) Act 2005* (Cth). Although not all of Georgiou's proposals were accepted, the changes have been positive for some detainees.

First, and most importantly, the Prime Minister announced that by 28 June all children should be released from immigration detention centres. While a similar call in 2004 by HREOC fell on deaf ears, on this occasion there was indeed a mass release of children and families. As a result, s 4AA of the *Migration Act 1958* now affirms that as a matter of principle, children shall only be held in immigration detention as a matter of last resort: see Art 9 of the Convention on the Rights of the Child. Section 4AA(2) clarifies that the principle relates to holding children in traditional detention rather than under the community release schemes created in parallel with this policy change. The underlying idea of detention is at once affirmed and dramatically altered by amending the definition of "detain" in s 5(1) to include people directed to reside in a specified residence in the community but without direct supervision: see s 197AC. Thus as at January 2006, all children had been released from detention centres into "community detention". A community sector organisation, contracted by DIMA, provides care and residential accommodation. The Minister can stipulate different conditions for each family, such as reporting requirements. However, in general, detainees may go about their daily activities, such as shopping or attending school, without the accompaniment of a guard.

The key to the amendments are two new powers conferred on the Minister for Immigration: to grant a visa to a person in detention and to direct a detainee to be released into specified (un-supervised) accommodation: see ss 195A and 197A. The power to grant visas is particularly significant. In the exercise of the power under s 195A, the Minister is not bound by the provisions of the *Migration Act* but may grant any visa appropriate to an individual's circumstances. As is now commonplace in the immigration field, these powers must be exercised personally, cannot be compelled and are not subject to judicial review.

The current detention centres and residential housing centres will continue to be used: the first for individuals; the second for families taken into custody for breaching residential housing orders or for whom removal is imminent. Finally, the amendments require the Secretary of DIMA to report to the federal Ombudsman on those who have been detained for two years or more. The Ombudsman must review the situation of such detainees and make recommendations to the Minister as to their release or other treatment. The Ombudsman's statements must be tabled in Parliament: see *Migration Act,* Part 8C.

A system that allows immigration detainees to remain in custody for two years before the intervention of any external supervisory body still falls far short of either the Georgiou proposals or the practice of any of the Western countries that Australia uses for comparison. Liability to immigration detention now turns on the exercise by the Minister of discretionary powers. If anything, the changes in July 2005 placed even more power in the hands of the Minister and his or her delegates.

As noted earlier, the Rau and Solon-Alvarez cases saw the emergence of serial scandals surrounding Australia's immigration detention laws. By the time the Prime Minister announced the changes to the law in June 2005, no less than 201 allegations had been made of wrongful immigration detention. The cases of Solon-Alvarez and Rau suggest that immigration officials have tended to rely on racial stereotyping in their identification of suspected unlawful non-citizens. In a country as multicultural as Australia, such an approach carries inherent dangers that citizens and permanent residents will be mis-identified as unlawful non-citizens.

The detention centres

In April 2006, unlawful non-citizens on mainland Australia were detained in five Immigration Detention Centres (IDCs), Immigration Detention Facilities (IDFs) or Residential Housing Projects (RHPs) around Australia: Villawood IDC (NSW), Maribyrnong IDC (Victoria), Perth IDC (Western Australia), Baxter IDF (South Australia) and Port Augusta RHP (South Australia). The different names reflect the size and function of the detention sites. The centres tend to be based in large cities and towns, while "facilities" and "processing centres" are in more remote locations and are designed for longer stays. In April 2006, people were also detained on Christmas Island at an Immigration Reception and Processing Centre (IRPC) and at offshore processing centres on Nauru: see chapter 7. A permanent facility is under construction on Christmas Island to house unauthorised arrivals. Work on the facility began in 2004, with final construction contracts let in early 2005.

Most detainees held at the Baxter, Christmas Island and Nauru centres in recent years arrived by boat without authorisation. The facilities in Sydney, Perth and Melbourne, on the other hand, are generally used to detain visa "overstayers" or those who have breached their visa conditions. Policy changes announced in April 2006 mean that future arrivals will be detained offshore (on Christmas Island, Nauru or in PNG).

Detainees can also be held at other locations (such as hospitals, State prisons, remand centres, police stations and watch houses). Alternative forms of detention include supervision by a community organisation, foster care, and detention in a designated private apartment, motel or hotel. In March 2006, 217 non-citizens were being held in alternative places of detention, hospitals and correctional facilities. The following map shows the main detention facilities in use in 2006 (excluding Nauru and PNG):

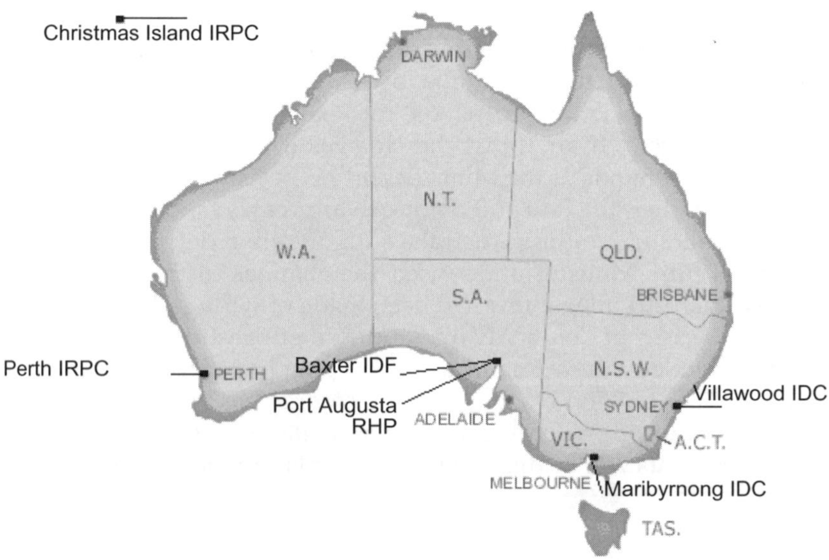

The detention of illegal fishermen

In addition to the standard immigration detention centres, facilities have been constructed to house foreign fishermen caught fishing without permission in Australian waters. One such a facility operates at Willy Creek, just north of Broome in Western Australia, on privately owned land. In 2000, this was more of a camp than a detention centre, comprising a concrete toilet block with pit toilets, some converted cargo containers (or "donghas") used for sleeping accommodation and a roughly constructed recreation centre. The detainees cooked their own food on camp fires and some were permitted to sleep on their boats which were moored in the adjoining estuary (until they were destroyed). Illegal fishermen were also detained at the gaol in Broome.

A permanent centre to house illegal fishermen has been planned for Darwin for many years. The Coonawarra Detention Centre was commissioned in 2001 and was operational by May 2003. The Senate Estimates Committee was told that the "construction and associated infrastructure" costs of the centre to that point were $7.4 million. Although the Defence Department had "used" the facility, it had not yet been used to house immigration detainees of any description. In fact, in February 2003, illegal fishermen were still being detained in unsatisfactory conditions on board their vessels in Darwin Harbour. One detained fisherman – a 21-year-old man from a village in Sulawesi, Indonesia – died on board his vessel. A coronial inquest in March 2004 found that the boat on which the man was detained held seven men; had a cabin just over 1.8 by 1.5 metres and had no on-board toilet. The man took ill in the early hours of 26 February 2003 at the height of a monsoonal storm. By the time help arrived, the man had died of "unknown causes". In 2005, a parliamentary committee was told that $9 million was needed to bring the Coonawarra centre "up to standard".

In August 2005, ABC radio reported that two new centres were planned for the detention of "suspected illegal fishermen" at Horne Island off north Queensland and at Gove in the Northern Territory. The Horne Island facility is expected to be completed in 2006 and will house up to 48 people. No location or start date had been set for the Gove centre.

Former centres

Several detention facilities have been closed in recent years (being kept as contingency facilities) in response to the decline in boat arrivals and the opening of a large facility at Baxter (near Whyalla) in South Australia. The Cocos (Keeling) Islands IRC was closed in March 2002; Curtin IRPC (north of Broome) was closed in September 2002; and both the detention centre and residential housing project in Port Hedland were mothballed in June 2004. The infamous Woomera IRPC closed in April 2003 and its Residential Housing Project was replaced with a residential detention scheme at Port Augusta. Contingency facilities continue to operate at a disused military barracks in Darwin (in the Northern Territory) and near Singleton in NSW.

The detainee population

Although people have been held by immigration authorities throughout modern Australian history, only very recently have unlawful non-citizens been detained in large numbers and for lengthy periods. In January 1985, only five people were held in detention. By January 1993, 560 non-citizens were in custody, most of them asylum seekers from Cambodia and the Peoples' Republic of China. Thereafter the numbers climbed steadily, with 1,410 detained in 1996 and 3,574 in 1999.

On 1 December 2004, 953 people were detained on the mainland; 39 on Christmas Island and 81 on Nauru. Over half of all detainees (534 of 1,031) were held at Villawood IDC and about one quarter were in Baxter IDF (252), with the remaining centres holding smaller numbers. The vast majority of detainees were men (768 of 1,031), with far fewer women (170) and children (93, or under 10%). During 2004-05, a total of 8,587 people were detained in immigration detention, with a maximum detainee population of 1,154 on any one day. Of the 7,721 people released from detention or removed in 2004-05, 199 were granted a protection visa, 1,608 were released on other grounds and 5,914 were removed from Australia.

The major policy changes in July 2005 meant that by September of that year 678 people remained in detention (excluding Nauru): 359 in Villawood, 123 in Baxter, 116 in alternative forms of detention (including prisons and other facilities) and smaller numbers in the remaining centres. No children remained in detention and the majority of detainees were men, with only 64 women. By August 2005, the detainee population on Nauru had been reduced to 32 with the grant of temporary visas to the remaining family groups and to most of the Afghan asylum seekers. By January 2006, only two people remained on Nauru. Amongst the *Hao Kiet* boat people on Christmas Island, the last 13 were recognised as refugees after the rehearing of their RRT appeals. In March 2006, 43 West Papuan asylum seekers held at Christmas Island were recognised as refugees and 42 were granted TPVs (see chapter 7).

At the end of 2004, the largest group detained in mainland Australia was Chinese, followed by the Iranians and Afghans. The largest group of detainees on Nauru were Iraqi and Afghani nationals. Those on Christmas Island were all Vietnamese (mostly from three extended families). In late 2005 asylum seekers from West Timor and (in 2006) West Papua were housed on this island. Many of the asylum seekers detained on the mainland in early 2005 reached Australia before the *Tampa* affair of 2001. They were still in detention because their asylum claims had been denied. Some were still pursuing legal challenges, while others were in custody because their countries of origin were refusing to take them back.

While asylum seekers have continued to arrive by plane, almost all recent boat arrivals have been prevented from reaching Australia. Boats carrying asylum seekers have either been returned to Indonesia or redirected to Pacific islands. As noted in chapter 8, in 2000-01, 1,834 people, arriving on 13 boats, were sent to and detained on Nauru and Manus Island.

Time spent in detention

The time people are kept in immigration detention has increased over the years, although the duration of detention has been episodic. Between 1989 and 1994 – the critical years in the emergence of mandatory immigration detention – a relatively small number of asylum seekers was held for up to four years. These were the years when the saga of the Cambodian boat people was played out: see Crock (1993). By 1998-99, 55% of all detainees had been held for less than three months, while 45% were held for more than three months. In that year, 3,574 undocumented non-citizens were detained over a total of 201,205 detainee days – an *average* stay in detention of 56 days. By early 2005, most asylum seekers who arrived in Australia by boat without valid documentation had been in detention for more than three years. Many had exhausted appeals but would or could not return home. At the end of 2005, Australia's longest serving immigration detainee was a 31-year-old Bangladeshi man detained for six-and-a-half years, whose physical and mental health has deteriorated since being in detention.

Until changes to the law in October 1999, which affected the profile of boat people coming to Australia, most detainees (around 80%) were male. Forty per cent were aged between 31 and 50 years and 35% were between 18 to 30 years old. About 5% of the detainees were children (the balance were over 50 years of age). As noted earlier, the introduction of the TPV regime in 1999 removed the ability of onshore refugees to sponsor their families to migrate to Australia. DIMA statistics suggest that this change resulted in an immediate jump in the number of children arriving by boat without permission. The following table shows the increase between 1998 and October 2004.

Table: Boat Arrivals: Adult-Child Ratios 1998-2004

Year	Adults	Children	Total	Children as % of total
1998	166	13	179	7
1 Jan 1999–31 Oct 1999	1,654	112	1,766	6
1 Nov 1999–31 Dec 1999	1,657	324	1,981	16
1 Jan 2000–31 Dec 2000	2,445	509	2,954	17
1 Jan 2001–31 Dec 2001	2,744	1,011	3,755	27
1 Jan 2002–31 Dec 2002	0	0	0	0
1 Jan 2003–1 Oct 2004	67	15	82	18

Source: DIMA

As noted earlier, these statistics demonstrate the abandonment of the traditional practice of sending one family member (usually the father or eldest son) to find a country of refuge, leaving the rest of the family to follow afterwards as legal migrants. The immediate impact was to increase the number of children taken into immigration detention. The ratio of children to adults in detention rose from 7% in 1999 to 27% in 2001, before dropping to around 10% in 2004.

Removal procedures

The term "removal" has a special meaning in the *Migration Act*, covering all expulsions of unlawful non-citizens except for those convicted of serious crimes (criminals can be "deported" from Australia). Permanent residents convicted of serious crimes are (or were) subject to special deportation proceedings: see ss 200 ff. In practice, however, most cases are processed as "removal" cases, either under the general removal powers or under s 501 of the *Migration* Act, which allows removal for "bad character". In 2003-04, two people were deported using s 200.

Removal refers to the process where DIMA locates and detains unauthorised non-citizens and arranges for their departure, or arranges the departure of people already in detention. While the majority of people who are removed from Australia are visa overstayers or those who have had their visa cancelled, some asylum seekers are also removed against their will if they are unsuccessful in their asylum claims.

Many people who have no authority to remain in Australia choose to leave the country voluntarily without any contact with Australian authorities. Those who do not leave voluntarily may be subjected to what DIMA terms "assisted departure". DIMA uses three main types of assisted departure procedures: "monitored departure", "supervised departure" and "removals".

Under *monitored departure*, a person who has breached their visa conditions or overstayed their visa is given a bridging visa to arrange their own departure and does so without any further involvement by the government. The person is responsible for paying and booking their own travel out of the country. The bridging visa ensures that those subject to monitored departure are not detained awaiting their removal and are free to remain in the community until they leave the country. Under *supervised departure*, a non-citizen must arrange their own departure including paying travel expenses. However, unlike a monitored departure, a supervised departure involves detention before the person is escorted to the airport. This is to ensure that people do in fact leave the country.

People in immigration detention are often subject to assisted departure under the "removal" category. All arrangements for their departure are made by DIMA and the removal may or may not be voluntary. Whilst DIMA pays for the cost of the removal, the non-citizen being removed is charged for their removal and must pay that debt if they hope to later re-enter Australia.

According to DIMA, between mid-1999 and mid-2004, monitored departures constituted over half of all assisted departures, while removals accounted for about one quarter and supervised departures made up almost one third. (In most of these years, fishermen comprised the vast majority of those removed who had arrived by boat.) In 2003-04, DIMA removed 12,689 non-citizens from Australia, 1,177 of whom had come to Australia by boat. This was a decline from the 1,745 people who were removed in 2002-03.

Involuntary return

Removal from Australia may be forcible if a non-citizen (including a child) does not cooperate. The threat of forced removal is highly stressful for asylum seekers, who may feel frightened of what awaits them in their home country. As discussed in chapter 8, many asylum seekers have been forcibly returned to dangerous situations. For those who decide to leave voluntarily, the decision may be made under some duress. Detainees can relent at the prospect of many years in Australia's isolated mandatory detention centres or at the threat of forced removal. One study found that many returned asylum seekers report difficulty sleeping, nightmares and persistent headaches, symptoms attributed to the ongoing implications of detention policies: see David Corlett, *Following them Home* (2005).

Recently, DIMA has engaged private security companies to remove failed asylum seekers. The Lawyers Committee for Human Rights criticised this practice for placing individuals "into the custody of the private organization which will hold him or her for an undetermined period and in conditions over which the government has no control". Once an asylum seeker has left Australia, the actions of the private company carrying out the deportation may fall outside Australian law, regulation and government supervision. Essentially this means the government is partially relinquishing its control, because the private security organisations – often foreign-owned – are not subject to the same standards of public, parliamentary and legal scrutiny and accountability as government agencies and employees. Private deportation companies used by other countries have allegedly used tranquillisers, unnecessary physical violence, and prolonged, inhumane confinement.

Many social justice advocates and Church leaders have spoken out about their grave concerns for those whose claims are rejected and are subsequently removed from Australia. A National Anti-Deportation Alliance (NADA) was established by concerned citizens to prevent the forced and wrongful removal of asylum seekers and refugees from detention centres and communities.

References and further reading

Commonwealth and Immigration Ombudsman, *Report on Referred Immigration Cases: Mr T. March 2006,* <comb.gov.au/publications_information/Special_Reports/2006/MrT_immigration_mar2006.pdf>

Commonwealth Ombudsman, "Inquiry into the circumstances of the Vivian Alvarez Matter", Report of the Commonwealth Ombudsman of an inquiry undertaken by Mr Neil Comrie, AO, APM (Report No 3 of 2005), <http://wwww.comb.gov.au/publications_information/special_Reports/2005/alvarez_report03.pdf>

David Corlett, *Following Them Home: the Fate of the Returned Asylum Seekers* (Black Inc Books, Melbourne, 2005)

Mary Crock (ed), *Protection of Punishment: The Detention of Asylum Seekers in Australia* (Federation Press, Sydney, 1993)

DIMA, "Bridging Visas": <www.immi.gov.au/allforms/pdf/1024i.pdf>

DIMA, "Detaining Unlawful Non-citizens", in Managing the Border: Immigration Compliance 2004-05 Edition: <www.immi.gov.au/illegals/mtb/mtb-chapter10.pdf>

DIMA, "Fact Sheet 82. Immigration Detention": <www.immi.gov.au/facts/82detention.htm>

DIMA, "Fact Sheet 85. Removal Pending Visas": <www.immi.gov.au/facts/85removalpending.htm>

Andrew Hamilton, "The Cambodian boat people: Are they victims of discrimination?" (1995) 6 *Law Institute Journal* 552

David Marr, "Cornelia Rau: the verdict" *Sydney Morning Herald,* 18 July 2005

David Marr, "Purgatory in Baxter" *Sydney Morning Herald,* 19 July 2005

Mick Palmer, "Inquiry into the circumstances of the Immigration Detention of Cornelia Rau Report" (July 2005): <www.minister.immi.gov.au/media_releases/media05/palmer-report.pdf>

Peter Prince, "The High Court and Deportation Under the Australian Constitution", Law and Bills Digest Group (April 2003): <www.aph.gov.au/library/pubs/CIB/2002-03/03cib26.htm>

Prime Minister John Howard, Media Release "Immigration Detention" 17 June 2005: <www.pm.gov.au/news/media_releases/media_ Release1427.html>

Cases

Al-Kateb v Godwin (2004) 219 CLR 562
Applicant VFAD of 2002 v MIMA (2002) 194 ALR 304
Goldie v MIMA (2002) 121 FCR 383
MIMIA v Al Khafaji (2004) 208 ALR 201
Nystrom v Minister for Immigration [2005] FCAFC 121
Park Oh Ho v Minister for Immigration and Ethnic Affairs (1989) 167 CLR 637
Ruddock v Taylor [2005] HCA 48
Tastan v MIMA (1999) 29 AAR 296
VHAF v MIMIA (2002) 122 FCR 270

10

Australia's Mandatory Detention Regime: The Legal Issues

Key Points in this Chapter

- Although detention is permitted by international law, arbitrary detention is prohibited. Mandatory immigration detention in Australia has been criticised internationally as arbitrary and for violating human rights.
- The High Court has found that international law does not invalidate an inconsistent Australian domestic law. However, international law may help to interpret ambiguous domestic laws.
- Mandatory detention was introduced by a federal Labor government in 1989. The High Court has upheld the constitutional validity of immigration detention since its inception but has "read down" (or limited) encroachments on the Court's review powers.
- An argument often used in Australian courts is that immigration detainees are not truly detained because they can choose to be released from detention by leaving the country. This is a legal fiction in the case of refugees and asylum seekers who cannot return to their home country.
- The High Court found in *Al-Kateb v Godwin* (2004) and *Minister for Immigration v Al Khafaji* (2004) that indefinite detention is lawful under Australian law.
- In *Behrooz v Secretary of the Department of Immigration* (2004), the High Court found that detention can be constitutionally valid even if detainees are forced to live in poor conditions. The constitutional validity of a statute is judged having regard to its purpose and not to its effect.
- There are many alternatives to detaining asylum seekers. Community release programs currently operate in virtually all refugee-receiving countries around the world.

Lawfulness of detention: international and domestic law

Immigration detention is a very modern phenomenon. With more people on the move and states in a position to monitor arrivals and departures, countries are paying much more attention to securing their borders than they have in the past. Ironically, at a time when states were less concerned with these issues, the traditional view of international law was that sovereignty permitted states to detain foreigners who entered their territories without permission. That position has been modified in the modern era by the development of international human rights law. The difficulty is that international law rarely offers enforceable remedies for individuals where a state is unwilling to acknowledge and rectify its breach of the law. Unlike in the Americas and Europe, Australia is not part of any binding regional human rights court system and, unlike all other Western democracies, Australia does not have a domestic Bill of Rights (or federal Human Rights Act) which would enable challenges to detention.

This chapter outlines aspects of international human rights laws that have been invoked either directly or indirectly by immigration detainees in Australia to challenge their detention. It then discusses relevant provisions in the Refugee Convention and analyses how the Australian courts have interpreted domestic laws in light of Australia's international law obligations. The chapter concludes by reviewing and critiquing the rationales for Australia's mandatory detention regime.

Detention and international human rights law

The right to liberty is a fundamental human right enshrined in all the major international and regional human rights instruments, from the International Covenant of Civil and Political Rights (1966) (ICCPR) and the Universal Declaration of Human Rights (1948) (UDHR) through to the European Convention on the Protection of Human Rights and Fundamental Freedoms; the African Charter on Human and Peoples' Rights; the American Convention on Human Rights; and the Cairo Declaration on Human Rights in Islam.

The UDHR (1948) prohibits arbitrary detention (Art 9) and arbitrary interference with a person's privacy (Art 12), and also guarantees the right to liberty (Art 3). While these rights are only aspirational (since the UDHR is not legally binding on States), they are made binding in the ICCPR. Article 9(1) of the ICCPR recognises that:

> Everyone has the right to liberty and security of person. No one shall be subjected to arbitrary arrest or detention. No one shall be deprived of his liberty except on such grounds and in accordance with such procedures as are established by law.

Other human rights instruments prohibit detention in even stronger terms. For example, Art 37(b) of the Convention on the Rights of the Child requires state parties to ensure that:

> no child shall be deprived of his or her liberty unlawfully or arbitrarily. The arrest, detention or imprisonment of a child shall be in conformity with the law and shall be used as a measure of last resort and for the shortest appropriate period of time.

This Convention stands out from other instruments because "refugee children" is used to cover both recognised refugees and asylum seekers.

The protection against *arbitrary* detention applies not only in criminal proceedings, but wherever a person is deprived of liberty, including for immigration purposes: UN Human Rights Committee, General Comment 8 (1982). Even *lawful* detention may be *arbitrary* if it is *unreasonable* (including where it is inappropriate, unjust or unpredictable): *Van Alphen* (1990). Detention is *unreasonable* if it is unnecessary or disproportionate to a legitimate end being sought: *Toonen* (1994).

Complaints about the extent to which Australia's immigration detention laws comply with international obligations go back many years. The first test cases were brought on behalf of Cambodian asylum seekers detained between 1989 and 1994. After the failure of a High Court challenge (see *Chu Kheng Lim* (1992), below), a complaint was made on behalf of one detainee to the UN Human Rights Committee. This is a committee in Geneva established under the ICCPR. After Australia signed the Optional Protocol to this Convention in 1992, it became possible for individuals (including those in detention) to complain to the Committee about violations of human rights in Australia.

In *A v Australia* (1997), the UN Human Rights Committee found that Australia's mandatory immigration detention policy – as it operated before 1994 – breached Art 9(1) of the ICCPR. The Committee considered the laws arbitrary because all unauthorised arrivals were detained without distinction, irrespective of the need to detain a particular person. Australia did not provide particular grounds justifying A's continued detention for four years. The Committee recommended that Australia consider alternatives to mandatory detention.

The UN Committee has not prohibited absolutely the detention of immigrants who enter without permission. The Committee accepted that detention will not be arbitrary if it is necessary in the circumstances, for example to prevent absconding, interference with evidence, or because of a lack of cooperation. However, these factors must be assessed on an individual basis, and not by detaining whole groups of people regardless of their individual risk factors. Further, both the need for detention and its duration must be a proportional response, and detention must not continue when it is no longer justified.

In *A v Australia* (1997), the UN Committee also criticised another aspect of Australia's immigration detention laws: the prohibition on courts ordering the release of detainees. Article 9(4) of the ICCPR provides that:

> Anyone deprived of liberty by arrest or detention shall be entitled to take proceedings before a court, in order that court may decide without delay on the lawfulness of his detention and order his release if the detention is not lawful.

Remedies for violations of any human right (including the right to review the lawfulness of detention) must also be effective: ICCPR, Art 2(2). If a person was unlawfully detained, he or she has an enforceable right to compensation: ICCPR, Art 9(5). These rights of review apply equally to asylum seekers as to a country's citizens, even where a person has entered a country without permission. In 1992, Australia acknowledged that some non-citizens may have been detained without authority between November 1989 and 1992. However, its legislative response was to cap compensation at $1 for every day of wrongful detention.

In *A v Australia* (1997), the UN Committee was also concerned that the law imposes no obligation on government officials to inform detainees of their right to seek legal advice, and prevented non-governmental organisations from accessing detainees to inform them of this right.

The Australian government did not modify its laws as recommended by the UN Committee. In 2003, the UN Committee again found that the detention of five children was arbitrary and in breach of international law.

In spite of these findings by the UN, and by numerous other international authorities and non-government organisations (ranging from the UN Working Group on Arbitrary Detention to HREOC, Human Rights Watch and Oxfam/Community Aid Abroad), children continued to be detained until late July 2005. Legal changes in May 2006 to deflect all unauthorised boat arrivals to be processed outside Australia again placed children at risk of serious abuse of human rights (see chapter 9 above).

Lawfulness of detention: international refugee law

International human rights law is vitally important in governing immigration detention because the 1951 Refugee Convention provides few express protections concerning the detention of asylum seekers. While Art 26 guarantees the freedom of movement of refugees, that provision only applies to refugees *lawfully* in the territory of a country – in other words, to refugees, rather than to asylum seekers who have yet to be recognised as refugees.

Article 9 allows governments to take temporary measures to protect national security in times of war or other grave or exceptional circumstances, pending determination that a person is a refugee. While this provision may permit detention, it does not currently apply to Australia, which is not affected by war or other grave emergency (notwithstanding the threat posed by terrorism in Australia). The small number of asylum seekers arriving in Australia does not amount to a mass influx which could also justify detention in closed camps.

Importantly, Art 31(1) prohibits countries from punishing people who arrive directly from a country of persecution, as long as they present themselves to the authorities without delay and provide good reasons for entering without permission. The freedom of movement of such persons can only be restricted if "necessary" and only until their status is regularised. This Article has been dismissed by Australia as inapplicable in this region for the reason that few refugees travel to Australia *directly* from a country where they face persecution. The usual experience is for asylum seekers to travel through a variety of countries before lodging a refugee claim. In the late 1990s, for example, the vast majority of the asylum seekers who arrived by boat transited through Indonesia. Again, the changes in the law in May 2006 to deflect all unauthorised boat arrivals are particularly worrying here. The main targets of the changes are people from West Papua who typically arrive in Australia from the country in which they claim to suffer persecution.

While the Refugee Convention does not impose time limits on detention, the drafters of the Convention considered that detention would only last "for a few days" to verify the identity of a person. While this may have been the intention, the subsequent practice of states party to the Convention may alter its meaning. While the practice of states party to the Convention as to the duration of detention is quite variable, there does not appear to be any clear agreement that would support lengthy periods of detention.

In the absence of clear standards in the Refugee Convention, it is helpful to turn to UNHCR's *Revised Guidelines on the Detention of Asylum Seekers* (1999), which guide states in their response to asylum seekers. Guideline 2 states that asylum seekers should not normally be detained. Guideline 3 observes that detention should only be resorted to:

- in exceptional circumstances;
- only if clearly prescribed by law;
- in conformity with international human rights law;
- after alternatives have been tried, or would be ineffective; and
- where detention is a reasonable and proportional response.

Under Guideline 5, detention is permitted only if it is necessary:

- to verify an asylum seeker's identity (when unknown or disputed);
- to determine the elements on which the asylum claim is based (to obtain essential facts, not to conduct the full merits determination);
- because asylum seekers have destroyed travel or identity documents or have used false documents *to mislead authorities* (not if a person is unable to obtain documents in their country); or

- to protect national security or public order (such as to protect the pubic from crime, but not because a person has been smuggled or trafficked).

UNHCR Guideline 5 states further that there should be automatic and independent review of a detention order, regular periodic review, and the right to challenge the necessity of detention. Detainees must also be promptly and fully notified of the decision to detain them, the reasons for detention, and their rights in detention (in a language they understand): UNHCR Guideline 5. They also have a right to be informed of their right to legal counsel, and to receive free legal assistance if possible. Detainees enjoy a right to contact and be contacted by UNHCR, national refugee bodies, other agencies and an advocate. Detention should not interfere with the making and processing of an asylum claim.

Even with the changes of July 2005, Australia's policy of mandatory detention is inconsistent with these guidelines, since there is no individual determination of whether it is necessary to detain a person on any of these grounds. Instead, Australia indiscriminately detains almost all unlawful arrivals, regardless of whether a person is a security or flight risk. Australia also resorts to detention before less invasive alternatives have been tried, such as community release subject to conditions or restrictions (see below). Mandatory detention is arguably a *disproportionate* response to the problem, since all asylum seekers arriving without authorisation are detained to contain the risk posed by just a few. The fact that children and families are no longer routinely detained is, however, a significant improvement.

Challenges to the lawfulness of mandatory detention

As refugee advocates have frequently tried to challenge mandatory detention in Australia's courts, it is inevitable that the issue has been a major source of constitutional and political dispute. Although the High Court has taken a firm stand on any attempts to exclude the courts from reviewing the basic legality of detention of any kind, it has generally tried not to become too embroiled in the politics of immigration detention. Indeed, the most recent pronouncements by the High Court (with some powerful dissents) suggest that detention should be a matter for Australia's politicians to deal with, even if this means that Australia's laws are patently inconsistent with its international obligations.

The High Court has confirmed that Australia's domestic laws cannot be altered directly by the mere invocation of international law. International law can be used to *interpret* domestic laws that are ambiguous or to develop the common law, but the general rule is that international law only enters domestic law when it is incorporated and enacted by the Australian Parliament. If the plain intention of the Australian Parliament is to create laws that infringe international human rights laws, it is constitutionally possible for this to occur.

The High Court has upheld the constitutionality of mandatory detention since its inception in the late 1980s. The key test cases have all involved asylum seekers – the earliest in 1992 concerning Cambodians. In *Chu Kheng Lim* (1992), the High Court acknowledged that no individual can normally be imprisoned without a court order. Imprisonment on its face is an act of punishment and this is a key feature of the "judicial" power that the Australian Constitution confers exclusively on the courts. However, the High Court ruled that the detention of non-citizens for immigration control purposes is not "punishment", but an administrative process designed to make people available for removal. It was in this case that Australian law first developed what some have called the "three walled prison". The Cambodians, according to the High Court, were not being detained; they were merely prevented from entering the Australian community, but were free to leave Australia for another country.

Although this characterisation of immigration detention has been soundly rejected by the UN's Human Rights Committee (see *Amuur v France* (1996) and the discussion above), the idea that immigration detainees are incarcerated by their own will persisted in Australian law. For example, Justices French and Beaumont ruled that the actions taken to stop the asylum seekers on board the *Tampa* from entering Australia did not constitute detention: see *Ruddock v Vadarlis* (2001), discussed in chapter 7. This legal fiction is particularly counter-intuitive in the context of asylum seekers and refugees who by definition cannot return safely to the country from which they fled.

In 2004, the High Court was presented with a series of cases that made the distinction between "administrative" (or protective) detention and punitive imprisonment harder to maintain. The cases involved failed asylum seekers who could not be removed to their countries of origin (*Al-Kateb* (2004) and *Al Khafaji* (2004)); asylum seekers detained in very poor conditions (*Behrooz* (2004)); and asylum seeker children arriving without visas (*Woolley* (2004)). Sadly, the High Court did not take these opportunities to limit under the Constitution the Parliament's power to legislate in these cases. As in *Chu Kheng Lim* (1992), the status of the detainees as non-citizens ("aliens" for constitutional purposes) was acknowledged as the key factor placing Parliament's enactments beyond judicial reproach.

Mr Al-Kateb is a stateless Palestinian man who, like many others around the world, has found it almost impossible to find a home. He had no entitlement to a visa allowing him to stay in Australia and the law required his removal "as soon as reasonably practicable". The problem was that, because he was stateless, he was unable to go to any other country. In upholding the law, the High Court left open the possibility that Mr Al-Kateb could be detained for the rest of his life, even though he had committed no crime. His case was heard concurrently with that of Mr Al Khafaji, who Australia had been trying unsuccessfully to return to Syria.

In all of the detention challenges, a central issue for the High Court was whether the constitutionality of a law is determined on the face of the statute or in the detail of its application. In *Behrooz*, this question arose alongside arguments that changes in the conditions of detention can transform lawful administrative detention into unlawful punishment. In the children's cases, the issue was whether the identity of the detainees as children similarly transforms administrative detention into punishment.

The government's argument in each case was that in determining the constitutionality of a statute, the Court should only consider the purpose of the law and not its effect. Thus in the *Behrooz* appeal it was argued that poor conditions do not make detention unlawful and the remedy for such treatment is to sue in tort or seek an injunction. Further, in *Woolley*, the government argued that the constitutionality of a power to detain could not depend on the identity or characteristics of the person detained (in that case, children), but solely on the existence of a legitimate purpose. The opposing view is that the constitutionality of legislation should be grounded in its substantive impact rather than in its form or a surface reading of text.

In both cases involving adult detainees (*Al-Kateb, Al Khafaji* and *Behrooz*) and detained children (*Woolley*), the question for the High Court was whether the judicial power in the Constitution qualifies the operational effect of provisions which, on their face, may have a legitimate purpose. In *Al-Kateb* and *Al Khafaji*, a slim majority of the Court (4:3) ruled that the *Migration Act* validly authorised the indefinite detention of unlawful non-citizens even where there was no real prospect of removal from Australia. The majority held that the Act was quite clear in its intention: unlawful non-citizens who have no right to enter Australia are to be detained until they are either removed from Australia or granted a visa. The clarity of the legislation, according to Justices McHugh, Hayne, Heydon and Callinan, means that the Act cannot be read "subject to a purposive limitation or an intention not to affect fundamental rights". Their Honours confirmed that, as long as a detainee can be characterised as an "alien" for the purposes of the Constitution, Parliament's power to detain is virtually unlimited.

Justice McHugh described his own ruling in *Al-Kateb* as "tragic", explaining that his ruling would not have been the same had Australia's Constitution contained a Bill of Rights enshrining a universal right not to be detained arbitrarily. He acknowledged that Australia's detention laws breached obligations assumed when Australia became party to the major international human rights treaties. However, he held that unless international law is incorporated into Australian law through an Act of Parliament, it can have little bearing on how a court interprets a statute, the terms of which are unambiguous.

Three members of the High Court in *Al-Kateb* dissented (or disagreed) with the majority. Chief Justice Gleeson and Justices Gummow and Kirby found that the *Migration Act* could be interpreted in a way that respected basic human rights. They found that where it was practically impossible to remove a non-citizen from Australia, the *purpose* of the detention provisions in the Act could no longer be fulfilled. This meant that the authority to detain a person disappeared as soon as removal became impossible. This interpretation would have allowed for mandatory detention, but in terms more consistent with international laws that prohibit "arbitrary" detention. These judges stressed that the so-called "aliens" power in the Constitution is not unlimited. They noted that detention without an administrative purpose becomes punitive, and so contravenes the rule that only courts of law can impose punishment.

The approach of the majority in *Al-Kateb* was also followed in the other refugee cases. In *Behrooz,* only Justice Kirby ruled that poor conditions in detention could transform administrative detention into punitive detention. The applicant in that case lost 6:1. In the case involving the detained children (*Woolley*), the whole court (7:0) ruled that mandatory detention meant that the personal characteristics of the non-citizen (including age, state of health and other matters) had no bearing on the operation of the law. Again, in the absence of a Bill of Rights, the Constitution offers no assistance to persons claiming that the detention of vulnerable people, including children, is wrong either as a matter of morality or under international law: see *Woolley* (2004).

The split in the High Court in *Al-Kateb* was an emotive affair. All of the judges were aware that similar issues (of failed asylum seekers who cannot be removed) had arisen in courts around the world. In other Western countries, no court of final appeal has ruled that it is constitutional to detain indefinitely a person who has committed no crime and who represents no threat to society: see chapter 12. Such courts have reached similar substantive outcomes as the minority in *Al-Kateb* (Chief Justice Gummow and Justice Kirby), though by different reasoning. Whereas the Australian decisions turned on narrow questions of statutory interpretation and limited constitutional protections, courts in other Western democracies have relied on (statutory or constitutional) Bills of Rights to preclude indefinite detention. While the ACT passed a *Human Rights Act* in 2004, and Victoria agreed to adopt one in 2006, the federal government is not interested in adopting a federal Bill of Rights.

Justice Kirby predicts that the majority ruling in *Al-Kateb* will be regarded in future like the *Dred Scott* case (1857) in the US Supreme Court (which upheld slavery) – with a mixture of curiosity and embarrassment. Arguably, even the limited choices available to the majority in *Al-Kateb* in approaching statutory interpretation could have enabled them to construct a meaning that prevented indefinite detention.

Australia's defence of mandatory detention

Mandatory immigration detention was introduced into Australian law by the Labor government in 1992. However, unauthorised arrivals, predominantly Cambodians, were detained as a matter of course from late 1989. Mandatory detention has been strengthened and maintained by the Howard Coalition government since 1996. The policy has been justified on several grounds and is designed to:

- protect the community from the dangers of unlawful arrivals;
- prevent unlawful arrivals disappearing into the community;
- facilitate the speedy processing of asylum claims;
- ensure failed asylum seekers are available for removal; and
- deter potential unlawful migrants from coming to Australia.

Each of these justifications suffers from serious flaws.

Protecting the community

First, very few unlawful arrivals present any kind of security risk or criminal threat to Australia. As ASIO reported to Parliament in 2002, not one security risk was found among almost 6,000 unlawful arrivals screened by ASIO in the preceding five years. It is difficult to see why it is necessary to detain *all* unlawful arrivals in order to contain the threat posed by very few.

Preventing absconding

Similarly, there is little evidence to suggest that many unlawful arrivals would abscond and disappear into the community. Those who enter Australia on valid visas and then apply for asylum are typically given bridging visas, yet the government has not presented evidence showing that these people regularly abscond. On the contrary, the statistics show that people who arrive without visas are more likely to be refugees. People at risk of serious danger upon return to their country of origin are more likely to comply with processing requirements than those who are free to travel the world on valid visas. Asylum seekers have everything to gain by complying with a process that will result in the regularisation of their status and the conferral of greater rights.

In other refugee-receiving countries overseas, there is evidence that the overwhelming number of asylum seekers do not abscond. This appears to be true even in relation to unsuccessful claimants subject to removal. The UK Home Office puts absconding at less than 4% of all asylum seekers who failed in their protection applications: see UK Home Office (2001) and Breugel and Natamba (2002). Further, a UK study found that the overwhelming majority of asylum seekers deemed at high risk of absconding by the authorities (including those awaiting removal) abide by the requirements that they live at a registered address, check in with local police and attend appeal hearings. Only 8-10% of the "high risk category" was likely to attempt evasion: see Breugel and Natamba (2002). Detention may increase the chances of absconding upon release because it decreases asylum seekers' level of trust in the system. Conversely, asylum seekers who are not detained may abide by immigration controls more readily because of a greater faith in the processing of their claims.

Absconding amongst asylum seekers has also been very low in the USA. A trial of supervised release in the US found that 84% of all asylum seekers appeared in court when required. The study also found that the cost of supervising asylum seekers was 55% less than the cost of detaining them: see Vera Institute of Justice (2000). The overseas statistics suggest that fear of asylum seekers absconding in Australia is exaggerated. Where absconding is a problem, it can usually be addressed by sufficiently rigorous reporting requirements or adequate supervision and monitoring in the community.

Facilitating processing

The available evidence is that detaining asylum seekers does little to speed up the processing of claims. Many claims take months or even years to be determined when a person is in detention for the obvious reason that the administrative process is more difficult to complete in remote places like Baxter, Port Hedland, Christmas Island, Woomera or Nauru. Leaving to one side the poor facilities at many of these centres, they are hard (and expensive) to reach. This means that decision-makers, lawyers and agents do not visit very often. Cases tend to be prepared and considered in batches (referred to by the authorities as "task forces").

In practice, this means that detainees experience frenetic periods of activity, first with their lawyers and then with the decision-makers in quick succession. There follows long months spent waiting for a result. In the remote centres, this task force approach is used for both primary processing and appeals. Detention frustrates the speedy processing of claims, since it makes it difficult for lawyers to visit their clients to prepare applications, and for applicants to gather information and receive the necessary support to prepare an accurate and effective application. The limited contact that detainees have with their adviser means that they often have little time to establish a relationship of trust. The agents allowed into the centres enter under contractual arrangements that demand heavy case loads, even where the detention population is not large. For example, in 2004 all asylum seekers on Christmas Island (originally 54) were being handled by one lawyer from Sydney.

Since long-term detention often triggers or aggravates mental illness among detainees, this can further obstruct the processing of claims. This became a particular problem at Baxter IDC where asylum seekers were detained for long periods in conditions that can only be described as emotionally challenging: see chapter 10. The experience of Cornelia Rau suggests how desensitised the authorities had become to mental distress in detainees by 2004. In spite of exhibiting flagrant symptoms of mental illness, her behaviour was dismissed for months as "attention seeking".

Facilitating removal of failed asylum seekers

At the end of the process, detention obviously facilitates removal of failed asylum seekers. Where processing can take many months and even years, however, it is difficult to see that this convenience justifies detention throughout the entirety of the process. There is a grave lack of proportionality between the end sought and the means used; the policy sacrifices the well being of detainees for administrative convenience, which could be attained through less harmful means.

Deterrence

Finally, detention cannot be justified as a means of deterring other unlawful arrivals. At the most basic level it is improper to use the pain and discomfort of some asylum seekers to deter others. Anyway, there is little evidence that detention has deterred genuine refugees and asylum seekers. After mandatory detention was introduced in 1992, boat arrivals actually *rose* significantly, from 78 people in 1991-92 to 1,071 by 1994-95 and 4,175 by 1999-2000. It is true that, since the *Tampa* incident in 2001, unlawful arrivals to Australia have fallen significantly. The drop in arrivals, however, is explained less by the harshness of the detention laws than by global reductions in refugee outflows and asylum claims (charted by UNHCR), as well as the interdiction of asylum seeker boats. It is worth noting that the boats from Indonesia came to an abrupt halt after the sinking of the SIEV X, with the loss of 353 lives (see chapter 4). The arrival of boats from West Timor and West Papua in 2005 and 2006 reflects local unrest and demonstrates that boat people will continue to arrive from time to time (see chapter 3 above).

People fleeing persecution (including possible death or serious injury) are unlikely to be deterred by the comparatively lesser harm of mandatory detention. In fact, some detainees report that they were unaware of where they were going, knowing only that people smugglers had been paid to take them out of danger. Moreover, to punish one group of people to deter others sends the message that Australia is not willing to protect people from serious harm.

Mandatory detention is an over-reaction to a modest challenge. Australia's experience of unauthorised arrivals has always been small both in absolute terms and compared to other countries. The sporadic spikes in arrivals (in 1978-80, 1989-93, and 1999-2001) can be explained by specific events or circumstances. For example, the surge in asylum seekers transiting through Indonesia in the late 1990s may have been due in part to retaliatory action taken by Indonesia in response to Australia's involvement in East Timor.

In contrast, Europe, the UK and the US receive hundreds of thousands of unlawful migrants per year and yet do not pursue policies of mandatory detention which do not involve assessing the risk posed by individuals: see chapter 12. The impression created by Australia's policy is that Australians are more fearful of foreigners than are Europeans or Americans – despite the lack of any objective basis for such fear.

Alternatives to detention

Changes to Australia's laws in 2005 recognise that it is unnecessary to detain *all* asylum seekers merely because they arrive without visas.

UNHCR has proposed the simple alternative of releasing asylum seekers into the community and monitoring their presence until their asylum claims have been determined. The benefit of the community release alternative is that asylum seekers are protected from the distress and trauma of unnecessary - and unlawful - imprisonment.

Community release currently operates in virtually all refugee-receiving countries around the world. As HREOC argues, Australia could release asylum seekers who arrive without permission on bridging visas, similar to those used for asylum seekers who arrive on valid visas. A bridging visa would be granted unless good reasons could be shown for detaining the person. Good reasons for detention might be:

- where the identity and intention of a person are not uncertain;
- where the person is a threat to national security or public order;
- where there is a likelihood that the person will abscond; or
- where a person breaches bridging visa conditions without excuse.

Releasing asylum seekers into the community does not threaten Australia's security or undermine its border controls. To ensure that they do not abscond and disappear into the community, asylum seekers could be rigorously monitored in the community in a variety of ways (see UNHCR Guideline 4). Mechanisms that are already in use include:

- requirements to regularly report to the authorities;
- restrictions on residency locations;
- providing a recognizance, surety or bond (like bail), which is forfeited for failure to appear at hearings or appointments; or
- asylum seekers could reside in open accommodation centres (as in the UK) with permission to leave and return during certain times.

An additional precaution suggested in 2001 is the use of electronic tags to track asylum seekers in the community. While this idea is better than detention, it carries significant civil liberties concerns and is unnecessary. The vast majority of onshore asylum seekers in Australia already await the processing of their claims within the community. Most comply with the attendance and other requirements made of them. There is no evidence that asylum seekers released into the community fail to meet their reporting obligations.

A broader community detention program could lead to significant savings for Australian taxpayers. A regime already exists which provides living allowance and application assistance to eligible asylum seekers in the community. The Asylum Seeker Assistance Scheme currently costs $44 per person per day. Forms of security such as those used for parole releasees cost approximately $8 per person per day, so the total cost would be $52 per person per day. The potential savings are obvious: see above. As explored in the following chapter, community release schemes for all asylum seekers who represent no threat to Australia would also address the problem of mental illnesses that has become so prevalent among long-term detainees since 1996.

References and further reading

Australian National Audit Office "The Management of Boat People": <www.anao.gov.au/WebSite.nsf/Publications/4A256AE90015F69B4A25690600029735>

I Breugel and E Natamba, "Maintaining contact: what happens after detained asylum seekers get bail?" South Bank University, (2002): <www.lsbu.ac.uk/php-cgiwrap/fhss/docsys/getpapers.phtml?papersid=96>

Peter Prince, "The High Court and indefinite detention: towards a national bill of rights?" *Law and Bills Digest Section* (16 November 2004): <www.aph.gov.au/library/pubs/rb/2004-05/05rb01.htm>

Refugee Council of Australia, "Alternative Detention Model": <www.refugeecouncil.org.au/html/current_issues/alternatives.html>

UK Home office Asylum Statistics 4th Quarter 2001, <www.homeoffice.gov.uk/rds/immigrationl.html>

UNHCR Revised Guidelines on Applicable Criteria and Standards Relating to the Detention of Asylum Seekers (February 1999): <www.unhcr.org.au/pdfs/detentionguidelines.pdf>

Vera Institute of Justice, "Testing community supervision for the INS: an evaluation of the Appearance Assistance Program" (2000): <www.vera.org/publications/publications_5.asp?publication_id=12>

Cases

A v Australia, Communication No 560/1993, UNHRC, 3 April 1997 [1997] IIHRL 30

Al-Kateb v Godwin (2004) 219 CLR 562

Amuur v France 19776/92 [1996] ECHR 25

Behrooz v Secretary of the Department of Immigration (2004) 208 ALR 271

Chu Kheng Lim v Minister for Immigration Local Government & Ethnic Affairs (1992) 176 CLR 1

Dred Scott v Sandford 60 US 393 (1857)

Minister for Immigration v Al Khafaji (2004) 219 CLR 664

Toonen v Australia, Communication No 488/1992, UN Doc CCPR/C/50/D/488/1992 (1994)

Vadarlis v Minister for Immigration and Multicultural Affairs (2001) 22(20) Leg Rep SL1

van Alphen v The Netherlands, Communication No 305/1988, UN Doc CCPR/C/39/D/305/1988 (1990)

Woolley, Re; Ex parte Applicants M276/2003 by their next friend GS (2004) 210 ALR 369

11

Mandatory Detention: Conditions of Detention

Key Points in this Chapter

- International law sets standards for the conditions in which people are held as well as the circumstances in which they can be detained.
- Many of Australia's detention centres are located in remote areas lacking convenient support services. They are expensive to operate and make visa processing less fair, less efficient and more costly.
- Many of the detention centres have areas where detainees who are a threat to themselves or others are held in segregated detention or solitary confinement. Solitary confinement has been used to "manage" suicidal detainees. The merits of holding vulnerable detainees under such stressful conditions are debatable.
- Until the end of 1997, immigration detention centres were run by a government agency. DIMA has now contracted out the management of its detention centres to a private prison company but DIMA remains ultimately responsible for the welfare of detainees.
- Detention can cause adverse physical and psychological damage, particularly where detainees are young and/or vulnerable. Between 2002 and 2005 DIMA recorded 506 incidents of attempted or actual self-harm involving 878 detainees. Eight people died in immigration detention centres, including one confirmed suicide, over the same period.
- Centre operations are supervised by independent bodies such as HREOC and the Ombudsman. Strong criticisms have been made of the living conditions in detention.
- The Australian government has continually rejected criticism of its mandatory detention policy.
- The policy of mandatory detention is extremely expensive and the cost of detention is increasing.

The law governing *how* people are detained

Quite apart from *whether* a country should detain non-citizens who enter or remain without authorisation, legal questions arise about *how* such people should be detained. The treatment of immigration detainees in Australia has been a subject of considerable controversy ever since mandatory detention became entrenched as policy in the late 1980s. In 2004-05 the scandal over the treatment of citizens and permanent residents wrongfully detained as illegal migrants brought the matter into such prominence that it could no longer be ignored by the government.

As a signatory to all of the major international human rights treaties, Australia has assumed a raft of obligations towards any person - whether an Australian citizen or not - held in government custody. As a result, the conditions in which people are detained must comply with minimum national and international standards of treatment. These include the full range of basic human rights (such as education and health care); special protections for families and children; a prohibition on cruel, inhuman or degrading treatment; and basic procedural rights.

In March 2000, HREOC released Immigration Detention Guidelines to serve as minimum standards for detention centres, based on international obligations regulating the treatment of anyone deprived of their liberty. They serve as a benchmark against which the treatment of detainees can be assessed. The guidelines require that detainees be accorded basic rights such as: access to legal assistance; contact with family and friends outside of detention; the provision of health care, food, shelter, education and recreation; and respect for privacy, personal security, religious freedom and human dignity. As noted in chapter 9, international human rights law is particularly explicit in the protection of children: see the Convention on the Rights of the Child. Immigration detainees who are seeking a country's protection as refugees are entitled to special treatment, starting with the right to communicate with UN-sponsored relief agencies such as UNHCR.

Responsibility for the conditions of detention

Until the end of 1997, immigration detention was regarded very much as the responsibility of Australia's executive arm of government. The Australian Protective Service, a federal government agency, managed security at the detention facilities in conjunction with the immigration bureaucracy (now DIMA). Other services at the centres, such as food, medical care, education and welfare services, were provided either directly by DIMA or through individual contractors.

At the end of 1997, the government "contracted out" the operational management of Australia's Immigration Detention Centres to a private company called Australasian Correctional Management Pty Ltd (or ACM). ACM is a subsidiary of an international security company called Wackenhut Corrections Corporation, which specialises in "human containment services" including prisons around the world. In 2001 the parent company had a turnover of more than $2.8 billion.

In 2001, the Australian government announced that the detention centre contracts with ACM would be put out to tender. Group 4 Falck Global Solutions Pty Ltd was successful in the tender process. After signing a contract with DIMA, the company was renamed Global Solutions Limited–Australia (GSL). Other GSL operations in Australia include the maximum security Port Phillip Prison for the Victorian government, and the low/medium security Mount Gambier Prison for the South Australian government.

Like ACM before it, GSL is responsible for detention centre security, accommodation, maintenance, catering, health, medical and dental care, educational and recreational activities, welfare and counselling, and transport services. DIMA staff monitor the performance of GSL at each detention centre and are supposed to take an active role in the day-to-day running of the facilities.

While the government retains ultimate responsibility for immigration detention, GSL has a duty of care towards detainees which is spelled out in contractual Immigration Detention Standards. The Standards aim to ensure detention is consistent with international obligations, including that the delivery of services is culturally appropriate. The Standards are underpinned by incentives and penalties. The government can impose fines or cancel a contract for serious breaches.

A major problem with the outsourcing of detention management to a private company is that both GSL and the government can withhold information from the public on the grounds of commercial confidentiality. Public scrutiny of detention and accountability for the treatment of detainees is limited, although media coverage of disturbances at the centres since the late 1990s has forced the government to be more open.

GSL invited the media into Baxter detention centre in July 2004. The media was given access to many areas of the centre previously not seen by the Australian public, such as the "Management Unit" where detainees with behavioural issues (including suicide attempts) are held in isolation detention. Journalists were asked not to interview detainees.

Supervising detention

The Human Rights and Equal Opportunity Commission (HREOC), the Commonwealth Ombudsman and Immigration Detention Advisory Committees established by the federal Parliament all have power to inspect detention facilities, or investigate complaints arising out of the treatment of people in detention. In practice, however, all of these bodies are hindered in their work by the immigration laws and policies and a lack of adequate resources.

The contracting out of many parts of immigration administration has increased ministerial control of detention on the one hand and made it more difficult to challenge conditions in detention on the other. For example, many of the migration agents contracted under the Immigration Advice and Application Assistance Scheme (IAAAS) are subject to strict confidentiality clauses. Speaking out about what they see in the centres places their (often lucrative) contracts at risk.

HREOC can investigate complaints made by detainees. Even before the changes of July 2005, the Ombudsman could, and did, prepare general reports on the centres. However, the *Migration Act* makes it clear that the authorities are under no duty to inform detainees that they can make a complaint to these bodies. As noted in chapter 5, this Act does not require detainees to be told anything about their entitlement to a visa either, although it does state that detainees must be given access to legal advice about detention if they ask for it.

In the past, evidence has emerged that detainees are often reluctant to complain for fear of retribution from the authorities, or of detriment to their asylum applications. HREOC has conducted regular inspections of detention facilities and its reports on inspections and complaints are available on its website: see <www.hreoc.gov.au>.

Because Australia is party to international human rights treaties, a number of UN bodies have taken an interest in the detention facilities. Over the years, complaints have been made to the UN Human Rights Committee and to the UN Torture Committee on behalf of immigration detainees. Australia has received visits from the UN Human Rights Commission and the UN Working Group on Arbitrary Detention. Non-government agencies such as Amnesty International and the US-based Human Rights Watch have also been persistent critics. Faced with adverse reports about detention from some UN bodies, Australia has often questioned the credibility of UN bodies and officials rather than engaged constructively with the UN to improve detention conditions.

The controversy surrounding immigration detention has led numerous parliamentarians and parliamentary committees to make regular tours of the facilities. Some politicians have been particularly assiduous in their oversight. Democrats Senator Andrew Bartlett stands out in this regard, being the only parliamentarian to have made multiple visits to detention centres on Nauru and Christmas Island, as well as making regular tours of the facilities on mainland Australia.

For many years, all of these reports, complaints and parliamentary visits generally inspired no great response from the Australian government. However, the controversy over Cornelia Rau and the threatened revolt by government backbenchers, led by Petro Georgiou in July 2005, finally induced a systemic change in attitude. The softening of the detention laws brought a new willingness to bring the detention centre operators to account over alleged human rights abuses.

On 29 July 2005, the Minister released a report commissioned from an investigative firm, Knowledge Consulting, on the mistreatment of five detainees in September 2004. The detainees in question were transferred from Maribyrnong detention centre in Victoria to Baxter IDC in South Australia in a bus trip of more than eight hours. In spite of GSL and

DIMA initially denying any wrong-doing, the investigators found that the detainees had been assaulted, denied food and water and even toilet breaks. GSL was fined $500,000 for breach of contract and the matter was referred to the Victorian police to consider criminal charges.

While these changes in approach are to be welcomed, the available evidence is that the change in 2005 was long overdue, and that detainees had been suffering indignities and treatment inappropriate to their status as asylum seekers. Although children are no longer routinely detained, mandatory detention is still the norm for most unlawful non-citizens. The proposal in May 2006 to expand the program for intercepting boat people and to send them to detention and processing centres is also a matter of grave concern.

Life inside the detention centres

While all of the mainland detention centres are now operated by the same company, GSL, there remain considerable differences in the way the centres are run. The most obvious difference is accessibility. The facilities in the major metropolitan centres of Sydney, Melbourne and Perth are quite open to the public. Detainees there can receive visitors and even journalists can gain admission. In contrast, the remote centres in South Australia, Christmas Island and Nauru are much more difficult to access – and not just because of their physical location. Journalists have only been admitted for formal tours on a few occasions. Visitors to these centres are rarer and are monitored more closely than in the city centres. At all centres, visitors are only admitted upon the written request of a detainee. At the remoter centres, visitors can be searched; cameras, telephones and electronic devices must be left at reception; and visitors are limited in bringing writing instruments into the centre (only transparent biros and pens were allowed at the Christmas Island facility in December 2004).

The facilities are effectively gaols, both in appearance and in the way they are run. Until August 2005, even the centre in Sydney's suburban Villawood was surrounded by double cyclone fencing, filled with four-metre high razor wire. The wire was removed in that month in a blaze of publicity that saw Minister Vanstone donning protective eyewear, heavy gloves and wielding wire cutters for the cameras. The razor wire was soon after replaced with electric fencing.

In the more remote centres at the height of the influx of asylum seekers in and after 2000, the physical appearance of the centres was forbidding, with razor wire, cyclone fencing and security cameras commonplace. The detention centres are designed so that sections can be shut down or locked up at short notice. In Villawood the different sections of the centre are referred to as "Stages" and house different categories of detainees depending on the reasons for their detention. The most restrictive part of the centre, Stage 2, holds convicted non-citizen criminals awaiting removal and others considered to be security threats.

In the newer centre at Baxter in South Australia (where the majority of long-term asylum seekers have been kept), detainees are divided into nine compounds, each of which is screened from the view of the others. Detainees must seek permission to move between the "open" compounds. The buildings are placed to create a rectangular, grassed common space. All the compounds look inwards so that the detainees are unable to see the horizon or anything outside of the centre except the sky. The compound is encircled by a 3,000-volt electric fence and has numerous security cameras. All the doors in the camp operate automatically from a central control station. The arrangements mean that detainees are supervised – and they know they are being watched – wherever they go, whatever the time of day or night.

Access to education, recreation and religious facilities

When mandatory detention became the norm for asylum seekers who arrived without authorisation in the early 1990s, little consideration was given to occupational programs for long term detainees. In fact, the deprivation of stimuli for detainees in those days was used as a form of passive deterrence, in the hope that the unrelieved boredom of life in custody would encourage detainees to give up and agree to return home. The absence of education for children in detention was a particular grievance of human rights agencies such as HREOC. By the end of the decade, all the detention centres offered tuition in English as well as classes in a variety of subjects, some of them vocational.

At the height of the influx of asylum seekers around 2000-01, many of the classes in the detention centres were taught by the detainees themselves. For example, at Curtin Detention Centre in 2000, one young Iraqi doctor who spoke perfect English was occupied almost full time in teaching English. Other detainees coordinated activities as varied as gardening, dress making, painting and computing studies.

Across Australia, most detainees are now offered tuition in English. In response to intense lobbying, most school age children had access to external schooling by 2005. The detention centres are equipped with laundry facilities for private use; class rooms; games rooms and spaces designated for religious observances. Detainees have access to communal television sets and computers. Board games and bicycles are also available in compounds where children were detained. Detainees are permitted to volunteer for various jobs around the centre and are paid in vouchers that can be redeemed at a small store in the centre. These stores trade in basic items for personal use from cigarettes to hygiene products and powdered milk for babies.

In August 2005, complaints were made that this "chores for reward" system had become so extensive that detainees were being treated as slave labour for GSL, performing work that GSL was contracted to perform. The voucher system was said to involve remuneration at a rate equivalent to one dollar for every hour worked - despite the $6 million profit GSL was expected to make in 2005.

Control measures in the centres

The measures used to control troublesome detainees have been a source of controversy for many years. At the height of the standoff over the Cambodian asylum seekers (detained between 1989 and 1994), attempts were made to make regulations allowing doctors to force feed hunger strikers. The measures were defeated largely because the doctors refused. In 2001 Minister Ruddock foreshadowed laws to permit detention centre guards to use chemical restraints - or injections of sedative drugs - without the authorisation of a doctor. On this occasion, the Labor Opposition objected and the measure was not enacted. Even so, allegations have surfaced of detainees being subjected to chemical restraints in detention.

In all of the centres, particular controversy has surrounded the use of isolation units to control difficult detainees. In Baxter Detention Centre, the compound known as "Red 1" gained notoriety after the release of the Palmer Report which detailed the abuse of mentally ill detainee Cornelia Rau.

Although considerable attention was focused on inappropriate official behaviour in the detention centres in mid-2005, many features of the legal regime governing detention suggest that endemic abuse is partly due to the system created by the Parliament. Detainees have no entrenched rights under the *Migration Act*. On the contrary, the law confers many powers on immigration officials which impact negatively on detainees. It also provides for the imposition of sanctions on detainees marked as dissenters or rebels.

For example, amendments to the Act in September 2001 allowed detainees aged 10 years and older to be strip searched. At the same time, the penalties for escaping from detention were increased from three to five years in prison. Detainees convicted of detention-related offences can be denied protection, even if they are found to be refugees. Given the role that Australia's detention system played in inciting refugees to commit such offences, real questions arise about the justice of these measures. Doubts also arise about their lawfulness in international law (see below).

Access to legal assistance

As noted in chapter 5, problems with the provision of legal assistance to asylum seekers have also affected detainees. In 1999, Australia passed a law removing the ability of HREOC to communicate with asylum seekers in detention about their legal rights. As Amnesty International noted, asylum seekers who meet the international definition of refugee "have rights but no right to know their rights". In 2001, HREOC found that the practice of "screening" asylum seekers without giving them access to any form of legal advice constituted a breach of the ICCPR: see chapter 5.

Detention in mainstream gaols

Immigration detainees have also been held in mainstream State gaols, even where they are not suspected of committing any criminal offence. As at June 2005, 14 detainees were held in State prisons, and hundreds more have spent time in State prisons, particularly in Queensland where there is no immigration detention facility. Some have been held in prisons for years, alongside serious convicted criminals, including at maximum security facilities such as Sydney's Long Bay Gaol. A 2001 report by the federal Ombudsman recommended abolishing the practice, but it was only after the Rau affair that Minister Vanstone imposed a 28-day limit on the period of detention in prisons. This period can still be overridden in "exceptional circumstances". The safety of immigration detainees may be at serious risk when held in the criminal population.

The human costs of detention

HREOC has been a constant and vocal critic of the detention policy. Its reports contain much information about life in the centres and reveal how the centres measure up to Australia's human rights obligations. Over the past few years, former inmates, guards and nurses have also spoken out about what it is like inside and some of the stories are very disturbing. In its 1998 report, *Those who've come across the seas*, HREOC found:

- unreasonable restrictions on the movement of detainees;
- limited recreational and educational opportunities;
- over-crowding and lack of privacy;
- inadequate natural lighting and ventilation;
- an absence of welfare officers and on-site interpreters;
- a lack of health care services for people with mental illnesses;
- inadequate access to legal help and advice about legal rights;
- some detention centres are very remote and difficult to access;
- conditions in detention are inadequate regarding education, trauma counselling, communications, excessive security, quality of accommodation, restrictions on movement, medical care, religious facilities, and limited recreational facilities.

While improvements have been made periodically to the conditions in detention, partly as a result of HREOC's reports, concerns remain. In 2004, HREOC reported that detention has particularly adverse effects on children (see below). Complaints have also been made by detainees of alleged assaults and unreasonable use of force by detention centre staff. In some instances, HREOC found that conditions of detention were in breach of the ICCPR and the CRC.

In addition to the episodes acknowledged by DIMA and GSL in 2005 (see above), there have been many other allegations of abuse made over the years. For example, in 1999, a nine-year-old Chinese boy detained at

Port Hedland for almost six years was forcibly fed tranquillisers to control his behaviour (caused by imprisonment for such a long period). In 2001, criminal assault charges were laid against an ACM officer from the Port Hedland centre. Detainees from the remote centres have complained not only of poor accommodation and food, but also of hostile guards. There have been persistent complaints of racism, violence, abuse and (again) the inappropriate use of solitary confinement and chemical sedation. In late 2005, 62 detainees at Villawood sent a letter to the federal Ombudsman alleging that a staff member was involved in intimidation and coercion, and illegal activities such as drug dealing and CD burning. In May 2006 the number of cases involving complaints about immigration detention (including inappropriate detention) rose to nearly 240.

On the other hand, the centres have also attracted staff who are caring in the treatment of detainees. Some nurses, psychologists and teachers have risked their careers to speak out publicly about the poor conditions and the mistreatment of detainees. Others have worked quietly inside the centres to improve the quality of life of detainees.

Many detainees have pointed out that although conditions in detention are poor, this is not their biggest concern. Rather, it is the arbitrary and indefinite deprivation of liberty that causes them the most distress. Thus, some detainees argued that, even if conditions were good, this would not compensate for their confinement in a remote gaol for months or years with limited access to the outside world. The sense of injustice is heightened because the incarceration is not linked to the commission or even the alleged commission of any crime.

Finally, detainees suffer psychological torment from the uncertainty of not knowing how long they will be held in custody, and whether they will be granted a visa or deported back into danger. In these ways the situation of detained asylum seekers differs critically from people imprisoned by the justice system, who serve time for a crime they have committed and know when their detention will end. As one long-term Iranian detainee, ultimately recognised as a refugee, said:

> Four years is a long time. It feels even longer when you have nothing to do … The stress becomes overwhelming. You can't even read anymore or hold a normal conversation. Imagine that those four years were stolen from you. Imagine that instead of doing all the things you did in those four years, you were forced to sit around waiting … Imagine that for those four years you sat around watching the people around you deteriorating. Imagine that you felt yourself going mad with the waiting … (personal communication with author)

Trauma and mental illness

The most offensive aspect of Australia's policy of detention of asylum seekers is the human cost it exacts from detainees and those responsible for their incarceration. HREOC has found that:

- many asylum seekers suffer nervousness and mental distress including depression, boredom, sleeplessness, psychosis, self-harm and suicide attempts;
- there is a high number of physical complaints, including headaches, numbness, dizziness, stomach and digestive disorders and unhealthy weight loss;
- tension within detention centres has resulted in violence between detainees and custodial officers, as well as hunger strikes, protests and break-outs;
- the overwhelming feelings among detainees are uncertainty and despair, since no one knows when - or if - they will be released;
- detention contributes to psychological distress among refugees.

Unfortunately, the period from 1998 to 2005 saw a steady deterioration in the mental health and well being of detainees. There have been numerous hunger strikes, disruptive and occasionally violent protests, attempted suicides and actual suicides. Preliminary research by the Centre for Population Mental Health Research at the University of NSW found that refugees who had spent time in detention had twice the risk of depression and three times the risk of post-traumatic stress disorder when compared to refugees who had not been in detention. Suicide Prevention Australia has argued that attempted suicide rates in detention might be at least 10 times in excess of the rate in the general Australian population.

In September 2005, academic Denise Leith received DIMA's response to a freedom of information request lodged in 2004 requesting information on the incidence of self-harm in Australia's detention centres. DIMA defines "self-harm" as "a self-inflicted injury or the act of causing harm to oneself, such as attempts and acts of cutting the body, voluntary starvation etc". Ms Leith reported that the DIMA records show 506 incident reports of attempted or actual self-harm involving 878 detainees between July 2002 and June 2005. More than half of these detainees were at Baxter (474), followed by 149 at Villawood and smaller numbers at the remaining centres. Adelaide psychiatrist Dr Jon Jureidini suggests that these figures could be understated and that he had not seen anyone over 11 years old who had not harmed themselves. He stated simply: "The primary problem is that it is an environment that drives people mad".

Government records show that eight people died in immigration detention between 1999 and 2004, including one confirmed suicide and one death due to a head injury resulting from a fall. Two of the eight individuals who died in detention were asylum seekers. One Tongan detainee, Viliami Tanginoa, had been in Australia for 17 years and died after falling from a basketball pole at Maribyrnong detention centre, which he had climbed in protest at his pending deportation to Tonga. A Melbourne coroner found that detention centre management had contributed to his death. His family is suing the government for wrongful death. Initially, they were not informed of his death or the inquest.

The psychological trauma of detention is often exacerbated by failures properly to diagnose or to treat mental illness (as in the Rau case). One Turkish detainee was returned - against medical advice - to Baxter detention centre from Glenside Psychiatric Hospital, where he was being treated after twice attempting suicide. On his return to Baxter, he attempted to overdose and had to be readmitted to hospital. DIMA policy has allowed detainees to be treated contrary to medical advice.

In *S v DIMA* (2005) the Federal Court considered the case of two detainees who suffered from severe depression and sought to be assessed under the *Mental Health Act 1993* (SA) for possible admission to a psychiatric facility. Both applicants had been detained in immigration detention facilities for approximately five years at the time of the litigation. The mental health of the applicants had deteriorated over time. DIMA admitted both applicants to Glenside Hospital before Justice Finn delivered his judgment on their case. However, his Honour ruled nevertheless that the Commonwealth owed a non-delegable duty of care to the applicants. This duty included providing a level of medical care that was reasonably designed to meet the mental health care needs of detainees, which was not met in this case.

In reaching his decision, Justice Finn questioned the Commonwealth's decision to establish the Baxter Detention Centre in a remote location. He found that the remote placement of the centre meant that the Commonwealth should bear responsibility for the resulting compromise in the medical services available to detainees. Justice Finn also criticised the standard of health care provided to immigration detainees and the means by which services were provided. His honour called for the review of the Commonwealth's arrangement for outsourcing health care. Justice Finn held the Commonwealth was responsible for "culpable neglect" in the case of the defendants.

There is also a human cost for those charged with keeping the detainees in custody. The turnover of detention centre staff in the remote centres has always been high because of the stresses inherent in managing a disturbed population of detainees. In recent years detention centre staff have taken industrial action over issues such as safety and remuneration. The system also traumatises the lawyers who are briefed by the government to assist the detainees in filing their refugee claims. The Middle Eastern detainees who have dominated the asylum seeker population in recent times have presented unsettling, tragic and violent stories. The harsh detention surroundings are inappropriate given that the focus is supposed to be on protection rather than punishment.

In mid-2005, concerns were raised about the government's fingerprinting of detainees at Maribyrnong detention centre, which were then matched with police records. While consent was required for the taking of prints, the NSW Council for Civil Liberties noted that mentally ill detainees may not be able to give informed consent, and detainees might also feel that they had no choice but to cooperate so that their asylum claims would not be prejudiced.

Solitary confinement

Many of the detention centres have a separate block where detainees who are a threat to themselves or others are segregated from the main detention population. The "Management Unit" at Baxter is an example. The Minister for Immigration conceded in June 2004 that detainees are locked in their rooms for up to 20 hours per day with a minimum of only four hours per day outside their rooms. The detainees are kept under video surveillance all day and night whilst in solitary confinement. Toilets and showers within these compounds are the only places exempt. Although detainees can receive visitors in segregated detention, this is extremely rare and only occurs where the detainees specifically request permission in advance. Detainees held in segregation are not permitted to receive phone calls after a certain time at night, while detainees in the main centre are permitted to receive phone calls all day and night.

Detaining people alone for 20 hours per day constitutes solitary confinement or isolation detention, and where it continues for prolonged periods it may amount to inhuman or degrading treatment contrary to international law. Perhaps in response to such concerns, former Minister Ruddock preferred the term "separation detention" to "solitary confinement" and this terms persists. Minister Vanstone stated in June 2004 that "separation detention" is not used for punishment but to monitor those who need greater supervision for their own safety, such as where detainees threaten violence or self-harm.

It is highly debatable that placing suicidal individuals in solitary confinement and keeping them under the constant supervision of correctional services guards (rather than doctors) does anything to relieve stress and or calm the situation. If solitary confinement is not being used as punishment, it may be more appropriate to release such individuals into the care of doctors and psychologists.

In fact, there is evidence of "separation detention" being used in circumstances and for periods of time that are grossly inappropriate. In March 2001, it was revealed that a 27-year-old Palestinian man had been detained in isolation detention for eight months (out of a total time in detention of 13 months). The man was confined after going on a hunger strike, despite allegedly suffering from depression and attempting suicide several times. In his report on Cornelia Rau, Mr Palmer reported that Ms Rau was sent into "separation detention" for five days after spitting at a guard. His report also alleges that the detention guards would watch Ms Rau as she showered in the centre, affording her no dignity or privacy.

In contrast, in NSW prisons, detainees can only be segregated for 14 days at a time – with exercise breaks – and only after violence has been committed. Further allegations were made in June 2004 that detainees at Baxter were confined in isolation cells for 23 hours a day for up to six weeks, after being involved in small altercations or suicide attempts.

Immigration Detention Standards, which are part of the Australian government's contract with GSL, forbid the use of prolonged solitary confinement and state that detainees in solitary confinement for security reasons are to be visited by a qualified medical officer daily, who should ensure that continued separation is not affecting their physical or mental health. The reality, however, is that separation detention is being used as a control mechanism to "manage" detainees, by subduing their will and/or as a means of asserting power. For individuals with a slender hold on their mental health, the effects can be devastating.

In May 2005, HREOC found that the isolation detention of 26 Iraqi and Iranian asylum seekers for eight months in Curtin detention centre in 2000-01 breached international human rights law. Such lengthy separation detention was considered unnecessary for processing new arrivals. It also meant that detainees were effectively unable to communicate with family and friends, since DIMA would only send a standard form fax stating:

> This is to let you know that [I] have arrived safely in Australia and am being detained in Immigration Detention. I am currently unable to telephone or write a letter to you but as soon as I can I will be in touch. I am in good health and being looked after. Return faxes will not be accepted.

Children in detention

As discussed in chapter 9, children were kept in immigration detention until late July 2005. The situation of children in detention became critical in early 2002 when a large number of Afghan detainees at Woomera detention centre went on a hunger strike. The protesters included children who mimicked some adults in sewing their lips together, refusing food and water to the point of hospitalisation. The protest centred on the refusal to process Afghan refugee claims pending an assessment of the situation in Afghanistan after the fall of the Taliban regime. In light of the protests, some unaccompanied children were removed from the detention centre and placed in foster care in the community.

In mid-2002, the Catholic Commission for Justice, Development and Peace released its report, *Damaging Kids*, based on documents obtained from DIMA under the *Freedom of Information Act 1982* (Cth). It revealed 264 cases of "self-harm" in detention centres over eight months, including 29 children and people younger than 20 years who had deliberately injured themselves. The report accused the government of "psychological child abuse". The Minister for Immigration responded that the numbers were inflated and that some of the incidents were minor ones.

In July 2002, attention was drawn to the plight of child asylum seekers with the (assisted) escape from Woomera detention centre of two brothers, Montazar and Alamdar Bakhtiyari. The pair was presented to the British Consulate in Melbourne and a claim was made for asylum in Britain (which was ultimately rejected). The image of the two boys being returned to Woomera made a lasting impression on many Australians.

In April 2004, HREOC released a major report into the treatment of children in detention between 1999 and 2002: *A Last Resort? National*

Inquiry into Children in Immigration Detention. HREOC identified several areas where it claims Australia contravened its international obligations. The title of the report highlights that the UN Convention on the Rights of the Child (CRC) requires states to ensure that children are only detained as a last resort and for the shortest period of time. Australia has signed and ratified the CRC and so is bound to respect this obligation.

Problematically, the *Migration Act* does not differentiate between child and adult asylum seekers. Although children are eligible for release, their parents are not. This means that, in practice, all children are detained if they arrive without permission. It was only with the changes to the law in 2005 that children came to be released as a matter of course. HREOC has found that the policy of mandatory detention puts Australia in breach of its obligations under the CRC. Detention is rarely in the best interests of a child.

The HREOC inquiry found that immigration detention is detrimental to the physical and mental health of children. It also argued that conditions in detention did not allow children to enjoy basic rights such as the right to an appropriate education, the right to be protected from all forms of physical or mental violence and the right of children who arrive without parents to be given special protection. Detention is not a climate in which children can enjoy "to the maximum extent possible" their right to development and their right to live in "an environment which fosters the health, self-respect and dignity" of children. The report was particularly scathing of the treatment of unaccompanied children in immigration detention.

HREOC recommended the release of all children in immigration detention centres and residential housing projects with their parents. Then Human Rights Commissioner, Sev Ozdowski, set a deadline of four weeks after the tabling of the report. HREOC also recommended that Australia urgently amend its immigration detention laws to comply with the CRC.

The report was dismissed by the government, although an increasing number of Australians expressed disquiet at the laws and policies governing the detention of children. The principled solution was to release both children and their parents on bridging visas, so that families can remain together and international obligations can be respected. Nevertheless, by May 2005, 59 children remained in detention and no efforts had been made to amend Australia's immigration laws to take account of the criticisms made by HREOC.

It was not until the Prime Minister intervened in late June 2005, amending the *Migration Act*, that the last children in detention finally gained their freedom. The Parliament has now affirmed the principle that a minor shall only be detained as a measure of last resort: see chapter 9.

Mass protests in detention

The introduction of mandatory detention in the early 1990s encouraged the formation of refugee activist groups around Australia. In spite of movements to lobby successive governments to take a more humanitarian approach to asylum seekers, the situation of those in detention grew steadily worse over time. Part of the problem was that governments adopted an "out of sight, out of mind" approach, resulting in the increasing isolation of both detention centres and people in detention.

The Woomera detention centre, which was mothballed in April 2003, was in the remote South Australian desert. Curtin IRPC was two hours' drive from the isolated town of Broome (WA) and Port Hedland (WA) was also remote. The newer centre at Baxter is several hours north of Adelaide. For years, detainees in these places reportedly suffered from feelings of isolation, boredom, prolonged anxiety and depression. These psychological stresses were worsened by the sometimes over-crowded and sparse conditions in the former centres of Curtin and Woomera.

Before the dramatic break-out at Woomera in June 2000, there were incidents of violence and hunger strikes amongst detainees, frustrated by the uncertain status of their asylum claims and their poor treatment. In February 2000, some asylum seekers at the Curtin centre protested by sewing their lips together. Allegations were made that, when one man attempted to hang himself, he was taken down by detention centre staff who then beat him.

The conditions at Curtin and Woomera improved after the hunger strikes and protests in 2000 and processing was also hastened. This in turn created problems as the detainees learned that protests produced results, which negotiation had failed to deliver. The politics of the situation became increasingly complex as the months drew on. With boats continuing to arrive, it was not difficult for the government to use the protests to foster community perceptions of asylum seekers as a threat. While the protests brought short term gains within the centres, they did not engender much sympathy in the Australian public.

Violent protests broke out again at Port Hedland in January 2001 and Curtin in April 2001. In March of that year, a climate of intimidation prevailed when the Australian Federal Police raided more than 50 Sydney homes in search of escapees from Villawood. Major rioting broke out again in early 2002 as a result of a decision to freeze processing of Afghan asylum claims, with hunger strikes at Woomera where detainees once more sewed their lips together. Again, these actions fostered deeply divided reactions in the public, hardening the divisions between refugee advocates and supporters of the government's hard line. Following years saw rolling protests and increasingly harsh responses from government.

In March-April 2002, approximately 50 detainees escaped from Woomera detention centre, including a mother and her three children. By October 2005, 11 Afghan and Iranian escapees had still not been located. At least one made their way to New Zealand, where they were granted refugee status and allowed to settle in the community permanently. Between 2003 and 2005, about 30 escapees were captured and charged with offences relating to their escape, with around one third being prosecuted and convicted and the remainder pleading guilty or being discharged as too mentally ill to face prosecution. In the case of one Iranian detainee, Mehran Behrooz, a South Australian judge imposed a "mercy" fine of only $100 in recognition that the medical evidence showed that his "indeterminate detention" caused a "mental condition and suicidal tendencies" which "materially diminished" his criminal culpability. The government appealed against this and other sentences.

Disturbances also broke out in Curtin and Port Hedland detention centres. Tear gas was used by guards at Curtin in a family compound. In June 2002 hunger strikes broke out again from Woomera detention centre. The hunger strikers included 13 children. In December 2004, Iranians in Baxter detention centre began a hunger strike that ended after 19 days on Christmas Eve. Many of those who participated were Christians and chose Christmas Eve to end the strike in recognition of the significance of Christmas for many Australians.

Although some of these incidents arose over the treatment of particular detainees, the major problem has been that detainees perceive the determination system to be arbitrary and unfair. Protests have persisted but occurred less frequently, perhaps as the result of the greater control and surveillance capability at the purpose-built Baxter IDC. The closure of the centres at Curtin and Woomera was also a factor.

There are many ironies in the harshness of the detention centres since 1999, when boat people transiting through Indonesia began to arrive. Not least of these is that these detainees were predominantly Convention refugees. Australia had never before detained a group of asylum seekers who succeeded in their refugee claims at the rate of the Afghan and Iraqi boat people who arrived between 1999-2001. With the overwhelming majority gaining visas, it was hard to convince those left behind that they should not also gain protection. The detainees as a whole had lived through experiences that would leave any person damaged and psychologically unstable.

For those who left families to find a safe refuge, considerable pain and frustration resulted from the discovery that, even in the very best scenario, they would not see their relatives again for four years. In the worst case, they lost not only their own chance for freedom and a new life but they also failed to find a safe harbour for their loved ones.

Government responses to complaints about conditions

Australian governments have continually rejected criticism of detention, asserting that the conditions of detention do not breach international obligations. In the absence of an Australian Bill of Rights, in 2004 the High Court found in *Behrooz* (2004) that harsh or inhumane treatment in administrative detention does not render that detention unlawful: see chapter 10. Government responses to allegations of poor conditions and treatment in detention have usually been belated and reactive, taking action only when provoked by clear and public evidence of mistreatment.

For example, in February 2001, an Australian diplomat, Philip Flood, released a report critical of detention (*Inquiry into Immigration Detention Procedures*). This was followed closely by two reports by the Commonwealth Ombudsman and a report by the Human Rights Sub-Committee of Parliament's Joint Standing Committee on Foreign Affairs, Defence and Trade (the DFAT report).

In the face of public pressure, the government immediately announced steps to improve the running of the detention centres and formed an Immigration Detention Advisory Group to improve supervision of detention. It also trialled the release of women and children asylum seekers into local communities in May 2001, which continued despite complaints by some Woomera residents. In addition, Australia agreed to implement 35 of the 94 recommendations made by HREOC's 1998 report, and partly implement a further 37 recommendations.

On the other hand, in the DFAT report on detention of June 2001, only independent Senator Brian Harradine and Australian Democrats Senator Vicki Bourne recommended the closure of remote detention centres. It was not until early 2002 that the ALP acknowledged this reality by recommending the closure of Woomera IDC.

In 2002, the UN High Commissioner for Human Rights Special Envoy to Australia and the UN Working Group on Arbitrary Detention (WGAD) investigated conditions in the detention centres. Justice Bhagwati, UNHCR's special envoy and the former Chief Justice of India, was considerably distressed by the inhuman and degrading conditions he witnessed in Woomera IRPC.

In December 2002, the WGAD report expressed similar concerns about "the psychological impact" of the detention regime, its "automatic and indiscriminate character, its potentially indefinite duration and the absence of juridical control of the legality of detention". Both reports articulated concerns about the effects of detention on children, unaccompanied minors, the elderly and the disabled. The government rejected the findings of both reports.

Response to the Cornelia Rau affair

The Rau case highlights the lack of independent assessment of both decisions to detain and decisions to keep suspected unlawful non-citizens in immigration detention. The publicity surrounding the case drew attention to the harsh realities of life in many of the detention centres, but particularly in Baxter detention centre.

In February 2005 the Minister for Immigration announced changes to the Department's procedures, including a 28-day limit on the time people can be held in State prisons; the fingerprinting of detainees (by force if necessary); more precise guidance to immigration staff on establishing a person's identity; and measures to increase access for immigration officials to State and federal law enforcement databases.

The Palmer inquiry (see chapter 9) paid particular attention to the conditions of Cornelia Rau's detention at Baxter. Palmer was highly critical of the government's handling of mandatory detention, finding (amongst other things) serious cultural problems in DIMA's immigration compliance and detention areas; inadequate mental health care facilities; and serious problems in handling difficult detainees. Palmer reported that DIMA officers were authorised to exercise extraordinary powers without adequate training or proper management and oversight, with poor information systems and no genuine quality assurance and constraints on the exercise of their powers. The report stated that any reform would need to be delivered from the top down.

The Minister for Immigration responded by acknowledging that mistakes occurred and accepting that changes need to be made within DIMA. The government also apologised to Ms Rau and promised to provide *ex gratia* assistance, including health support. As noted earlier, however, the biggest change announced by the DIMA after the Palmer inquiry is the strengthening of the role of the federal Ombudsman in immigration and detention matters. The Ombudsman is now designated the Immigration Ombudsman, in the same way that he or she performs the role of the Taxation Ombudsman. Over 200 cases of possible wrongful immigration detention which were initially referred to the Palmer inquiry were to be investigated by the Ombudsman. By May 2006 that number had increased to nearly 240. In addition, the government announced an independent review of the compliance and detention divisions in DIMA, the use of external experts to advise the Minister on the management of the detention contract, an independent assessment of IT systems, and an assessment of skills and knowledge levels amongst compliance staff.

The government's response to the report does not amount to an overhaul of the system, and the impact of the changes on the lives of individual detainees remains to be seen. However, the willingness of the government to tackle certain issues related to immigration detention and its acceptance of the findings of the Palmer report are a welcome change. Its previous responses to other critics of immigration detention, including the UNHCR and HREOC, were very different.

The financial cost of detention

In addition to the profound human costs of detention, the National Audit Office made the obvious finding that immigration detention is resource intensive in its 1998 report, *The Management of Boat People*. As at February 2004, the daily cost of detaining each detainee in immigration detention ranged from $111 at Villawood to $2,229 at Port Hedland RHP, with the remaining centres falling in between ($248 at Maribyrnong; $286 at Port Hedland IRPC; $310 at Baxter; $589 at Perth; $598 at Port Augusta; and

$725 at Christmas Island): see Senate Estimates Hearing, 17 February 2004.

Some of these figures are inflated by one-off set-up costs in 2003-04 (including at Port Augusta and Port Hedland). The figures also include transition costs associated with contractual changes from one detention service provider to another (see below) – an expense which would not be incurred if the management of the centres remained with public agencies.

Although costs can be expected to increase overall if more people are detained, the cost of detention per person has also increased significantly and beyond the level of inflation. In 1994-95, the average daily cost per detainee was $69, increasing to $105 in 1995-96. The *minimum* cost of detaining an asylum seeker in 2004 was $111. The statistics do not include the costs of border surveillance by Coastwatch, Customs or the Australian Navy, the cost of locating visa overstayers, or the costs of moving detainees between remote detention centres. For example, it reportedly cost $169,000 to relocate 46 detainees from Woomera to Port Hedland in January 2001. The Australian Democrats estimate that mandatory detention costs the Australian taxpayer $42 million per year. They also claim that a further $230 million has been spent on the building of detention centres between 2001 and 2004. At least that much again has been allocated to build a new 800-bed detention centre on Christmas Island.

Conclusion

Australia's regime of mandatory detention of asylum seekers is a grave blemish on Australia's human rights record. Despite the softening of the regime in 2005, Australia remains committed to the policy of detaining all unauthorised arrivals. Fortunately, the government now recognises that the residential housing projects near Woomera and Baxter detention centres are not the answer. Detainees in these facilities continue to lack liberty and the power to shape their own lives. Moreover, the release of women and children does little to help the men who remain behind, whose continued detention is overshadowed by the release of women and children. Whilst important steps have been made towards addressing the problems associated with detention, the government still fails to recognise the harm that detention causes to detainees and to society as a whole, which has become accustomed to their suffering.

Although the Australian government and the High Court have characterised immigration detention as "administrative" detention and not as punitive imprisonment, detainees themselves experience detention as little different from criminal punishment. Just as modern prisons originated in Bentham's ideal of complete bureaucratic control over the lives and minds of prisoners, so too are immigration centres "all seeing" (or "pan opticon") surveillance facilities. Every human movement can be observed, while troublemakers and "difficult" cases are placed in solitary confinement and denied any human contact or external communication.

In Baxter, video cameras track the movement of detainees at every hour of the day, waking or sleeping, and inappropriate behaviour is punished by sensory deprivation and close observation. It is a system of passive deterrence, designed to encourage anyone who does not have great determination to stay in Australia to return to their country of origin. The "separation detention" facilities - particularly the infamous "Red 1" centre - are striking examples of oppressive and psychologically controlling environments. Detainees know that they are being watched. They cannot see outside of the centre (the compounds face inwards), nor can they move between compounds without authorisation. For those kept in these conditions over months and even years, it is not surprising that some have developed depression and other mental illnesses. Those diagnosed with mental illnesses - and who management permit to be treated - are taken for rehabilitation to Adelaide's Glenside Psychiatric Hospital, sometimes through the intervention of their advisers or by court order (see *S v DIMA* (2005)).

Unfortunately the stories of many people in immigration detention are not heard. The revelations about the experiences of Cornelia Rau and Vivian Solon-Alvarez provide only a small glimpse into the personal tragedies that face many individuals. Their cases reflect a collective failure to see the harms that Australian laws and policies are inflicting. As explored in the next chapter, this is despite Australia's increasing isolation from countries facing much larger inflows of asylum seekers and irregular migrants. During the Palmer inquiry, it was alleged that the guards in Baxter detention centre were unmoved by Ms Rau's strange behaviour, just as the officials responsible for Ms Solon-Alvarez's removal were blind to her obvious frailty. In both instances, assumptions were made that the women were unworthy, that they were outsiders trying to subvert the fundamental and unquestionable precepts of immigration control. Ultimately, these cases - and the many others that are likely to emerge - demonstrate the necessity to change current laws and policies to restore compassion and balance in this area.

References and further reading

Commonwealth Ombudsman Reports
- see <www.comb.gov.au/publications>

Report on Referred Immigration Cases: Mr T, March 2006

Inquiry into the circumstances of the Vivian Alvarez Matter, Report of the Commonwealth Ombudsman of an inquiry undertaken by Mr Neil Comrie, AO, APM (Report No 3 of 2005)

Report of an Own Motion Investigation into the Department of Immigration and Multicultural Affairs' Immigration Detention Centres, March 2001

Own Motion Investigation into Immigration Detainees held in State Correctional Facilities, March 2001

Administrative Arrangements for Indonesian Fishermen Detained in Australian Waters, July 1998

Human Rights and Equal Opportunity Commission Reports
– see <www.hreoc.gov.au/human_rights/asylum_seekers>

Report of the National Inquiry into Children in Immigration (2004)

Report on Visits to Immigration Detention Facilities by the Human Rights Commissioner (October 2002)

Human Rights and International Law implications of Migration Bills (21 September 2001)

Human rights violations at the Port Hedland Immigration Processing Centre (28 November 2000)

Visit to Curtin IRPC (July 2000)

Human Rights violations in the Perth Immigration Detention Centre (29 June 2000)

HREOC "Immigration Detention Guidelines" (2000)

Submission on Australia's refugee and humanitarian programs (1999)

Those who've come across the seas: Detention of unauthorised arrivals (1998)

International Reports

The Report of Justice Bhagwati, Regional Advisor for Asia and the Pacific of the United Nations High Commissioner for Human Rights, *Mission to Australia*, 24 May to 2 June 2002, <www.infoxchange.net.au/ix/budi/bhagwati report.doc>

Report of the Working Group on Arbitrary Detention *Visit to Australia*, June 2002, <www.ohchr.org/english/issues/detention/visits.htm>

Parliamentary Reports on Immigration Detention
– see <www.aph.gov.au>

Senate Legal and Constitutional References Committee Report, *Administration and Operation of the Migration Act 1958*, 2 March 2006, <http://www.aph.gov.au/senate/committee/legcon_ctte/ migration/report/index.htm>

Senate Legal and Constitutional References and Legislation Committees Question Taken On Notice Additional Estimates Hearing: 17 February 2004 Immigration And Multicultural And Indigenous Affairs Portfolio (38) Output 1.3: Enforcement of Immigration Law

Senate Legal and Constitutional References Committee, "Inquiry into the operation of Australia's refugee and humanitarian program" (28 June 2000)

Joint Standing Committee on Migration "Not the Hilton: Immigration Detention Centres: Inspection Report" (September 2000)

Joint Standing Committee on Foreign Affairs, Defence and Trade "Report No 113: Statement to the Parliament on the JSCFADT Human Rights Sub-Committee's recent activities concerning conditions within immigration detention centres and the treatment of detainees" (13 October 2003)

Joint Standing Committee on Foreign Affairs, Defence and Trade "Visits to immigration detention centres" (18 June 2001)

Senate Select Committee on Ministerial Discretion in Migration Matters (31 March 2004)

Other Australian Reports

Australian National Audit Office, "The Management of Boat People" (1998), <www.anao.gov.au>

Knowledge Consulting, "Findings and Recommendations from Report of Investigation on behalf of the Department of Immigration and Multicultural and Indigenous Affairs Concerning Allegations of Inappropriate Treatment of Five Detainees during Transfer from Maribyrnong Immigration Detention

Centre to Baxter Immigration Detention Facility", <www.immi.gov.au/media_releases/media05/d05025-Report-of Investigation.pdf>

Philip Flood, AO "Report of Inquiry into Immigration Detention Procedures", February 2001

Mick Palmer, "Inquiry into the circumstances of the immigration detention of Cornelia Rau Report" (July 2005), <www.minister.immi.gov.au>

Other Further Reading

Suicide Prevention Australia, "Two Australian National Policies on Self-Injury and Suicide: A Submission to the Human Rights Commission on Children in Detention", <www.hreoc.gov.au/human_rights/children_detention/submissions/suicide_prevention.html>

Jewel Topsfield, "Hundreds in detention attempt self-harm", *The Age*, 19 September 2005

Immigration Detention Standards: <www.immi.gov.au/detention/standards_index.htm>

Cases

Behrooz v Secretary, DIMA (2004) 208 ALR 271

S v Secretary, DIMA (2005) 143 FCR 217

12

World's Best Practice: Asylum in Other Countries

Key Points in this Chapter

- Despite the greater burden of asylum seekers faced by other Western democracies, their asylum systems are often more generous than that of Australia.
- The 25 countries of the European Union have harmonised many of their asylum laws and policies concerning the refugee definition, asylum procedures, and reception and detention standards. The EU definition of a refugee is broader than that in Australian law and the EU also provides "complementary protection" status and rights to non-refugees who nonetheless fear serious human rights abuses.
- EU asylum procedures have been criticised for reducing the rights available at the border and during expedited processes. While the EU relies on the "internal flight alternative" to deny protection, the law does not provide any criteria for assessing whether internal protection is safely available in practice.
- Detention is only allowed in restricted circumstances in the EU, the US, UK, New Zealand and Canada, and is subject to much stronger judicial and procedural safeguards than in Australia.
- New Zealand receives fewer asylum claims than Australia but continues to provide permanent protection. It has good quality decision-making and provides full rights of judicial review. An increase in detention after 11 September 2001 has since declined, although there is concern about the issue of "security risk" certificates to exclude refugees.
- The United States receives much larger numbers of asylum seekers, unlawful immigrants, and refugees for resettlement than Australia. It does not routinely detain asylum seekers for long periods (although the use and manner of detention is a matter of concern). It has offered amnesties to unlawful migrants in the past. The US also has special procedures for applicants at the border. There are recent concerns about the exclusion of suspected terrorists.
- Historically, Canada has had a model asylum determination system, with full review rights as well as protection under the Canadian Charter of Rights and Freedoms. There are, however, recent concerns about Canada's return of suspected terrorists to face torture.

No country is an island

The fate of asylum seekers and refugees is an issue of global concern. In understanding how Australian refugee law works, it is helpful to compare and contrast the Australian experience with that of other asylum systems overseas. Earlier chapters outlined the much larger numbers of asylum seekers faced by other Western countries. This chapter shows that despite the greater burden shared by those countries, their asylum systems generally remain more generous and sensitive to the needs of asylum seekers than the harsher, and more punitive, Australian system. The practice of the European Union, Canada, the United States, and New Zealand is explained and evaluated here, as a way of reflecting on what the Australian system does well – and what it does badly.

Asylum in the European Union (EU)

The European Union originated in 1951 when six countries (Belgium, West Germany, France, Italy, Luxembourg and The Netherlands) established a common economic market in coal and steel. Since then, the number of EU member states has grown to 25 after enlargement in mid-2004, when 10 new member states (mainly from Eastern Europe) were admitted. Since its modest beginnings, the EU has developed into an integrated community of European democracies, founded on the rule of law and human rights standards, and governed by supranational institutions. At the same time, national parliaments retain their democratic and sovereign authority in many areas of daily life.

In the EU, refugee and immigration law was considered historically a matter of exclusive national concern, since governments were reluctant to restrict their sovereign authority to deal as they wished with migrants. As a result, national laws and policies on asylum and immigration varied widely. While nationals of EU countries gradually came to enjoy freedom of movement in other EU countries (following the 1986 Single European Act) and EU citizenship (after the 1992 Maastricht Treaty), non-EU citizens were still subject to restrictive national immigration and asylum laws. Indeed, under the 1990 Schengen Convention, the EU sought to facilitate freedom of *internal* movement in the EU by strengthening *external* border controls, through police and judicial cooperation, common visa policies and carrier sanctions.

It was only in the 1990 Dublin Convention that common EU interest turned to the issue of a common EU asylum policy. The Dublin Convention established common criteria for determining which EU country is responsible for examining an asylum request lodged in the EU. Under its rules, asylum seekers must lodge their application for asylum in the first EU country in which they arrive, and may be returned to another EU country if they either passed through its border (by air, sea or land) or made an application for asylum in it.

The Dublin Convention had the aim of preventing asylum seekers from moving, or being transferred from country to country, with their claim either being assessed several times or not at all (a person "in orbit", with no country willing to examine the claim). The second aim of this Convention was to avoid applications by asylum seekers in forums that they regard as most favourable ("asylum shopping"). EU countries retained the right to return asylum seekers to a "safe third country" outside the EU even before a determination was made. The Dublin Convention was replaced in 2003 by an EU Council regulation establishing a fingerprinting system ("Eurodac") for tracing unlawful movements of non-EU citizens.

From the early 1990s, EU countries experienced large influxes of asylum seekers and economic migrants, particularly from the Balkan wars and from Eastern Europe following the end of communism. The 1992 Maastricht Treaty flagged an asylum policy as a matter of common interest to EU countries, and in 1999 the Amsterdam Treaty required the EU Council to adopt measures to harmonise aspects of asylum by 2004.

Late in 1999, the EU Council met in Tampere, Finland, and agreed to establish a common European asylum system, leading in the longer term to common asylum procedures and uniform legal status for those granted asylum in the EU. The Tampere Council decided that "freedom" should not be reserved for EU citizens, but should be extended to those who justifiably seek to enter EU territory. The Council insisted on respect for the right to seek asylum and not to be returned to persecution, while controlling illegal migration and border protection. The most important elements of the common European asylum system initiated at Tampere included:

- the criteria and mechanisms for determining which EU country is responsible for considering an asylum claim;
- minimum standards on who qualifies as a refugee, the procedures for granting or withdrawing refugee status, and the reception of asylum seekers;
- measures on subsidiary forms of protection offering an appropriate status to persons in need of such protection.

Since Tampere, the EU Commission has drafted measures addressing each of these elements, which were duly adopted by the EU Council by mid-2004, in consultation with the European Parliament. In addition, the Council has adopted measures on temporary protection of displaced persons who cannot return to their country of origin or who otherwise need protection. The most important of these measures are considered further below. In 2000, the right to asylum became guaranteed by Art 18 of the EU Charter of Fundamental Rights, transforming the aspirational right of asylum in the 1948 Universal Declaration of Human Rights into a binding legal commitment.

The Tampere Council also urged the EU to work with countries of origin and transit to address the political, human rights and development issues (such as poverty, unemployment, poor living conditions, and conflict) which give rise to irregular movements of people. In managing migration, the Council committed the EU to combating people trafficking, economic exploitation of migrants, and document fraud, as well as to cooperating on control of EU borders. Provision was also made for provisional measures in the event of emergency situations resulting from sudden inflows of non-citizens.

EU Qualification Directive: who is a refugee in Europe?

The EU Qualification Directive lays the legal foundations for both refugee and subsidiary protection in the EU (subsidiary protection was discussed in chapter 6). It establishes minimum standards for recognising who qualifies as a refugee (and who is excluded), and provides for the minimum rights and benefits attaching to refugee status (and lesser rights for those granted subsidiary protection, particularly concerning residency, employment, documents, welfare, health, integration services, and family benefits). The Directive outlines minimum standards only and EU countries are allowed to offer more favourable conditions.

In establishing who qualifies as a refugee in the EU, the Directive closely follows the wording of the refugee definition in the 1951 Refugee Convention. It contains a number of progressive features, such as a recognition that non-state actors, and not only governments, may commit persecution. It also provides a detailed but non-exhaustive list of examples of acts constituting persecution, including mental and sexual violence, discriminatory measures, child- and gender-specific persecution, refusal to perform military service in a conflict and denial of judicial remedies. The Directive enhances the definition of a refugee by according wide meanings to most of the grounds of persecution (race, religion, nationality and political opinion) and recognising persecution based on gender or sexuality.

The Directive also recognises that asylum applications should be considered on an individual basis, rather than in groups or collectively, and urges EU countries to take into account the best interests of child asylum seekers. Persons recognised as refugees enjoy a range of basic rights, including residence permits and travel documents, freedom of movement, access to employment, education, social welfare, health care, accommodation, integration facilities and family unity.

There are, however, a number of negative features in the Directive and amendments suggested by the democratic European Parliament were not accepted. Unlike in the 1951 Refugee Convention, the Directive does not allow all persons to apply for refugee status, but is limited to non-EU nationals and stateless persons. This limitation is contrary to the non-discrimination provision in Art 3 of the 1951 Refugee Convention, and may constitute an impermissible geographical limitation on the scope of protection under the 1967 Protocol. The practical effect of the provision is that members of minority groups or other persons persecuted within, or by, EU countries cannot be recognised as refugees.

Although most EU countries are generally democratic and respect human rights, it cannot simply be ruled out that persecution may still occur. Pursuing human rights remedies in the European human rights system may take a very long time, during which time a person may continue to be persecuted at home. While the EU is premised on internal freedom of movement - allowing persons persecuted in one European country to move to another - equal rights to work and welfare are not yet enjoyed by nationals of the newly admitted EU countries of Eastern Europe. This may not make it practical to avoid persecution by moving countries within Europe, since daily survival would be so difficult.

A second problem with the Directive is that it accepts that in addition to protection by governments, refugees may also be protected by non-state parties or organisations (including international organisations) which control a country or a substantial part of its territory. This has been criticised because quasi-state authorities (including UN administrations of territory) cannot be parties to international treaties (such as the 1951 Refugee Convention or human rights treaties) and therefore are not accountable as legal actors under international law.

Another flaw in the Qualification Directive is its reliance on an arbitrary "internal flight alternative". The idea that a person fearing persecution in one part of a country should be expected to move to a safe part of that country is controversial, though accepted in international law. However, the EU does not provide any criteria for assessing whether internal protection is safely available, such as by considering whether protection is legal or merely de facto; whether vulnerable groups are properly treated; whether health care is adequate; whether protection is durable and will not result in return to persecution; and whether safety is objectively established rather than merely reasonably likely.

Importantly, internal protection should not be relied on where persecution stems from a government. The EU Directive also allows refugee status to be refused where internal protection was available, but the person cannot be returned to their country for technical reasons. This potentially leaves a person without any protection at all.

Some other problems with the Qualification Directive are that there is no tracking of failed asylum seekers to ensure that the EU made the correct decision; there is no express recognition as refugees of those who flee from generalised oppression (such as war); only "social groups" with permanent characteristics, who are *also* perceived by society as distinct groups, are recognised as within the refugee definition; and the grounds on which refugee status ceases do not provide for exceptions based on "compelling reasons" (as recognised in the 1951 Convention).

Finally, the Directive permits refugee status to be denied on national security grounds before an asylum claim has been determined. This is contrary to the 1951 Convention, which only permits exclusion on more limited grounds (see chapter 6). While a *recognised* refugee may be expelled on national security or public order grounds under Art 32(1) of the 1951 Refugee Convention, national security concerns are not a basis for excluding asylum applicants, who are not yet recognised as refugees, from the determination process.

EU minimum standards on procedures

Whereas the Qualification Directive establishes who is entitled to refugee status, the EU Minimum Procedures Directive creates basic standards governing the determination process. Again, EU countries are free to offer more generous standards in their own territory. The Directive aims to improve and harmonise procedures governing asylum claims across EU countries, and to deter irregular migration between EU countries (in part by preventing applicants from "forum shopping" between systems).

Positive features in the Directive include essential *procedural guarantees* such as the right to judicially appeal against an adverse decision, the opportunity to be heard in an interview and access to legal assistance. Asylum decisions must also be made on an individualised basis, objectively and impartially, by specially trained personnel.

Nonetheless, many of the provisions in the Procedures Directive have been criticised by UNHCR and others for reflecting a lowest common denominator approach, based on poor standards existing in some of the least generous national asylum systems in Europe. The Directive also allows EU countries to make national exceptions to some of its minimum standards, foiling the objective of common, harmonised EU standards. Particular concerns include:

- expanded use of accelerated procedures with limited safeguards;
- lack of provisions to ensure gender sensitivity of procedures;
- reduced procedural rights in subsequent and border applications;
- severe restriction of rights during preliminary examination (such as reduced time limits on submitting information, and the lack of a personal interview).

In addition, in 15 categories of cases, EU countries may derogate from the right of an applicant to remain in the country pending *review* of an initial refusal, particularly in cases considered "manifestly unfounded" or "clearly abusive". This means that while the right of appeal and review remains, it does not prevent the applicant's removal from the country.

Such a provision increases the risk of miscarriages of justice since, once they are removed, asylum seekers may not be able to conduct their appeal properly. The provision was introduced despite the fact that between 30 and 60% of refugees in the EU are only recognised on appeal, indicating the poor quality of initial decision-making in many countries. Bad decision-making is set to increase if appeals are restricted in this way. Some refugees fail the initial screening process because they are traumatised or ill-informed upon their arrival, and full review of their case may be necessary to elicit the true nature of the circumstances.

Where people apply for asylum *at the border* of a country, the Procedures Directive establishes an expedited determination process with increased use of detention and limited rights of review. Asylum seekers may be detained at the border for up to four weeks, without review of detention, or humanitarian exceptions for vulnerable groups. EU countries have a discretion whether to inform applicants about the procedure, to provide an interpreter, to allow a personal interview, or to receive free legal advice (though there is a right to consult a lawyer). Asylum seekers from "safe third countries" may be denied access altogether to the border procedure, without their claim being considered.

UNHCR notes that all asylum seekers are entitled to the same basic procedural guarantees, regardless of whether they apply at a border. Lesser protections at the border may result in rejection at the frontier without fair and effective procedures, leading to chain deportations and ultimately to return to persecution. The border procedures signal a new emphasis on immigration control over refugee protection in the EU, notwithstanding that tougher border controls inevitably encourage efforts to circumvent border controls to access asylum procedures from within.

The most controversial provisions in the Procedures Directive deal with "safe countries of origin" and "safe third countries". First, the Directive allows EU countries to expedite applications from persons who come from *safe countries of origin*, where there is deemed to be no risk of persecution or serious harm warranting protection. Safe countries of origin are identified in a common list adopted by the EU Council, or designated by EU countries themselves. The device gives rise to a presumption that a person from a safe country of origin does not need protection, although the presumption may be rebutted by evidence. It is designed to prevent the abuse of asylum by economic or social migrants. UNHCR does not oppose it, as long as there are sufficient safeguards.

In contrast, Amnesty International and the European Council on Refugees and Exiles strongly oppose this device, arguing that all asylum applications must be assessed on an individual basis, not according to general assessments about the safety of whole groups or countries. Requiring applicants to rebut the assumption of safety imposes an unfair additional burden. In practice, countries may use safe lists automatically to bar claims, without further investigation. Lists of safe countries may not take into account sudden or gradual chances of circumstances within a country. Some ostensibly "safe" countries may simply not be safe in reality. The listing of countries as safe by other governments may also be influenced by diplomatic and political factors, including economic interests, rather than human rights concerns.

The second controversial device is the use of "safe third countries", giving rise to similar concerns. EU countries may return an applicant to: (1) any country of first asylum (even if recognition as a refugee there has not ensured effective protection); (2) a specified safe third country (even if the person has only transited through that country, but otherwise has no links to it); or (3) a safe third country which agrees to admit the person (even if the person has no connection with that country).

The device is designed to reduce the onward movement of refugees, even though some have compelling reasons to move on. It limits access to the determination procedure, based on generalised lists of countries, and before an individual's personal circumstances have even been considered. The risk of creating "chain deportations", or "refugees in orbit", is very great. Nothing in the Directive guarantees that the supposedly "safe" third country will agree to admit the applicant or to accept responsibility for determining the asylum claim.

Whether some of the measures in the Procedures Directive are compatible with European human rights law remains to be seen. In the past, the European Court of Human Rights has upheld the rights of non-citizens not to be collectively expelled, without individual assessment, and to challenge the lawfulness of their detention where procedures have restricted the availability of review (see, eg, *Čonka v Belgium* (2002)). The European Court, and some national courts, have also been suspicious of attempts to limit asylum based on safe third country provisions, and have examined whether protection exists in practice rather than in a technical sense (see, eg, *Adan* (1999), *Gashi* (1999) and *TI v UK* (2000)).

Detention in Europe before 2003

Before the harmonisation of rules on the detention of asylum seekers in 2003, there were nonetheless some similarities between the detention policies of European countries. In most countries, detention was used mainly at the start of the determination procedure (to investigate travel routes and verify identity), and at the end of the process (to arrange travel documents for deportation and to prevent absconding). Unlike in Australia, EU countries did not routinely detain asylum seekers throughout the duration of the determination process.

Detention was also used where: police measures were insufficient (Sweden, Ireland, France); an asylum seeker did not cooperate to establish his or her identity and travel route (Denmark, Ireland); an asylum seeker failed to stay in a specified location (Denmark); an asylum seeker's behaviour was violent or threatening, or threatened national security (Ireland, Belgium, Spain); it was necessary to prevent crime (Sweden, Finland, Spain).

Most EU countries also had strict time limits on the duration of detention: up to four days (Spain, France, Ireland, Finland); two-three months (Finland, Austria, Germany, Luxembourg, Belgium); and between five weeks and nine months in the remaining countries. In all countries except Ireland and Luxembourg, a decision to detain could be appealed, either to a court or by administrative review.

In nine EU countries, asylum seekers had a choice of accommodation while their applications were processed. In Denmark, Finland, Luxembourg, Sweden, Portugal and France, they could choose to live outside reception or accommodation centres at their own expense (from 2% of applicants in Denmark, to 90% in France). In Belgium and The Netherlands, asylum seekers were required to stay in reception centres for the first period of the asylum process but could live outside later. In Greece, children, the elderly and the disabled could live in public establishments, while in Greece, Italy and Portugal, only a limited number of places were available in accommodation centres, forcing the remainder to find private accommodation.

Of all European countries, the UK has historically detained the greatest number of asylum seekers (around 9,000 per year), and since the late 1990s the UK has adopted an increasingly stringent approach towards asylum applicants. The UK has a tiered system of induction centres, accommodation centres and detention centres. Applicants stay in induction centres for between one and seven days, pending relocation to accommodation centres, decisions on support applications and geographic dispersal, or moving to an agreed address in the community. Information is provided about the determination process and basic health screening, and full board is provided.

Until recently, most asylum applicants in the UK lived in the community. Accommodation centres are a new concept introduced in 2002 on a trial basis, to accommodate asylum seekers throughout the entire determination process, for up to six months. The aim of accommodation centres is to reduce delays in determinations, make decision-making more efficient, reduce community tensions, reduce financial and housing fraud and illegal working, and facilitate removals.

Within accommodation centres, full board is provided, along with services, activities and support, access to legal advice and a small cash allowance. Applicants are free to come and go, although there is a residency requirement, breach of which may be regarded as damaging an applicant's credibility and prejudicing their claim. In practice, the remote location of, and lack of transport to, some proposed accommodation centres would considerably restrict the freedom of movement of applicants, and constitute a de facto form of detention.

The UK also operates detention centres for failed applicants subject to removal and, until recently, some failed applicants were even held in prisons with criminals. Between 1997 and 2002, detention places tripled from 900 to 2,800, and from 2002 the government planned to increase detention capacity by a further 40% to 4,000 places.

Part of the detention system is the Oakington Reception Centre, a fast-track appeals process for unfounded applications, which delivers decisions in seven to 10 days. Security at Oakington is nominally more relaxed than at other detention centres and free, independent legal advice is available. Up to 13,000 applicants can be processed there in a year. In the *Saadi* case (2002), the House of Lords accepted that the Oakington detention process was neither an arbitrary nor a disproportionate restriction on the human right to liberty and security, since it was reasonably necessary and justified to speedily process applications. Even so, in early 2005, video evidence emerged of racial abuse of detainees.

Detention in Europe after 2003

Detention policy in the EU was transformed in 2003 when the EU Council adopted a Directive on Minimum Standards on Procedures for Granting and Withdrawing Refugee Status. Article 17 of the Procedures Directive prohibits detention "for the sole reason" that an application needs to be examined before a determination is made. Detention pending determination is only permitted:

- following a specific decision by law that detention is objectively necessary for an efficient examination;
- where there is a strong, personal likelihood of absconding; or
- where the restriction is necessary for a quick decision to be made, in which case detention must not exceed two weeks.

Initial and subsequent judicial review must be available. It is clear from the Directive that an individualised assessment of the situation of each asylum seeker is necessary. Australia's indiscriminate policy of detaining almost all unlawful asylum seekers fails to take into account these personalised factors. Administrative convenience in decision-making is not a basis for detention in Europe (unlike in Australia), in recognition that personal liberty is essential in ensuring human dignity.

EU Conditions of Reception and Detention

In 2003, the EU Council also adopted a Directive on Minimum Standards for the Reception of Asylum Seekers, which aims to ensure a dignified standard of living for asylum seekers while they lawfully remain in the territory of an EU country. The Directive applies to all EU countries, except Denmark and Ireland, and was implemented in early 2005. It establishes *minimum* rights for asylum seekers, although EU countries may decide to provide more favourable conditions or to extend the minimum rights also to applicants for subsidiary protection.

At the start of the reception process, applicants enjoy various rights to information, including information about reception benefits and obligations (within 15 days of application), and organisations providing legal, health or reception assistance. Information must be provided in writing and in a language the applicant understands. Applicants are also entitled to documentation of their status (permission to stay while determination is pending) within three days of application.

The Directive then specifies the rights and duties of applicants concerning freedom of movement during the process. Generally, applicants enjoy freedom of movement within a country's territory, or an assigned area within the territory. Residence may be restricted for reasons of public interest, public order or for the swift processing and effective monitoring of an application, but any assigned area must not affect the right to private life or impair access to benefits. However, benefits may be conditioned upon applicant residing in a specific place. Temporary permission to leave a place of residence or assigned area must be available, and applicants must inform the authorities of their address and notify any change of address as soon as possible.

As to material conditions of reception, all forms of housing or accommodation must guarantee the basic needs of asylum seekers, the protection of family life and minors, and the possibility of communicating with relatives, legal advisers, UNHCR and NGOs. Transfers of applicants between different facilities should be kept to a minimum and applicants must have a chance to inform their legal advisers of any change. The authorities must also endeavour to prevent assaults in accommodation facilities, ensure that staff are adequately trained and involve applicants in managing the accommodation. Legal advisers, NGOs and UNHCR must be given access to the facilities.

Further, countries must provide material conditions sufficient to ensure a standard of living adequate for health and subsistence (although assistance may be means-tested and subject to repayment). The Directive allows applicants conditional access to the labour market after 12 months of waiting for a decision at first instance. Countries must also provide emergency health care and essential treatment of illness (including torture, rape or serious violence), while medical screening on health grounds may be required. Judicial review of negative decisions on the granting of benefits must be available.

There are special provisions for vulnerable persons (such as minors and unaccompanied and separated children, the disabled, elderly, pregnant, single parents with children, and persons who have been subjected to torture, rape or other serious psychological, physical or sexual violence). Minors must have access to the mainstream education system or education in accommodation centres.

The Directive generally establishes adequate standards, although it allows those countries that had higher standards before the Directive to lower their standards to the common minimum level. A number of criticisms of the Directive have been made. It does not apply to persons seeking subsidiary protection, or facing removal under the Dublin Convention. It allows too many national exceptions, undermining the harmonisation objective behind the Directive. It permits children to be educated in accommodation centres, segregated from regular schooling. Countries have a discretion to limit access to employment for certain periods and may preference their nationals in the labour market. The health provisions do not deal explicitly with issues such as HIV/AIDS, reproductive issues or cultural needs. Reception conditions are limited to first instance decisions and do not apply to the appeal process.

Most importantly, the Directive provides that reception conditions may be reduced or withdrawn in certain circumstances:

- for non-compliance in the determination process (even for trivial infractions such as a failure to report, to appear in interviews, to remain in a place of residence without informing the authorities or where an application has already been lodged);
- where an application has not been lodged as soon as reasonably practicable after arrival (even though there may be good reasons for this during the unsettling and confusing period of arrival); or
- for seriously breaching the rules of an accommodation centre or for violent behaviour (yet even criminals are entitled to the conditions necessary to ensure a basic standard of living).

Fundamental living conditions are necessary for all applicants, even those who infringe procedural or other rules, to guarantee a fair determination process and to protect and ensure human rights.

Asylum in the United States

Traditionally, the United States has maintained the largest refugee resettlement program in the world, accepting an average of 90,000 offshore refugees per year in the 1980s and 1990s. After 11 September 2001, however, the size of the program was reduced by almost two-thirds.

Non-citizens may also apply for asylum from within the US, regardless of whether they are lawfully or unlawfully present in the country. Applicants must apply for asylum within one year of arriving in the US, although exceptional circumstances may extend this period (such as changes in the country of origin or the applicant's circumstances).

US law relies predominantly on the refugee definition in the 1951 Refugee Convention but the US statutory definition of a refugee is actually broader than the Convention definition. The US definition includes past persecution, even when there is no chance of future persecution. However, the discretion to grant refugee status is less likely to be exercised favourably when there is past rather than the prospect of future persecution. Certain classes of people determined by the President may also be recognised as refugees even if they have not left their country of origin. Hence, in some circumstances, internally displaced persons may also be recognised as refugees under US law. In addition to the grounds for exclusion in the 1951 Refugee Convention, the US also excludes from refugee status persons who have been involved in, or even merely endorsed, terrorist activity – even though terrorism is not an automatic ground for exclusion under international refugee law.

There are two tracks for processing onshore asylum claims. The "affirmative" asylum process occurs where a person submits an asylum application on their own initiative, and where the person is not subject to removal proceedings. Within 45 days of application, the applicant is interviewed by an Asylum Officer of the US Citizenship and Immigration Services (USCIS), who decides if the person is entitled to refugee status. If the application is successful, the decision is usually notified within 60 days of application, a period during which applicants are not normally allowed to work (applicants may apply for work authorisation 150 days after lodging an application where the application is still pending).

If the application is unsuccessful, the applicant is referred to an Immigration Judge at the Executive Office for Immigration Review (EOIR) (within the US Department of Justice), where the claim is considered afresh, usually within six months of the initial application. At this point, the proceedings become "defensive" – the second track.

The defensive asylum process occurs where an asylum seeker (1) is referred by an Asylum Officer; (2) is placed in removal proceedings for immigration violations (such as being undocumented within the US); or (3) attempted to enter the US without proper documents but has a credible fear of persecution or torture. The defensive process may be triggered where an applicant in the affirmative asylum process fails to appear at an asylum interview without justification (failure to appear also leads to ineligibility for work authorisation). The defensive process involves an adversarial administrative hearing (referred to as an "immigration court hearing"), rather than a less formal interview.

Whether the process is affirmative or defensive, applicants have the right to representation, but the US does not fund legal aid to provide applicants with lawyers. The US does fund interpreters for the hearings which may be government employees or private contractors. Applicants are also fingerprinted and subject to security checks.

Persons recognised as refugees are granted "asylee status". This confers permission to remain indefinitely in the US, although permanent residency status can only be sought after one year. Asylee status also confers rights to work, employment assistance, social security and family reunion. Asylee status can be terminated if a person no longer fears persecution due to a fundamental change in circumstances, protection from another country or criminal activity.

Decisions of the Immigration Judge can be appealed to the Board of Immigration Appeals (BIA) by both the asylum claimant and the US government. Only asylum applicants can appeal BIA decisions to the US Court of Appeals for the circuit in which the removal hearing was held. BIA decisions can also be overruled by the Attorney General. The BIA reviews cases nationwide and the decisions of the Board are binding on all Department of Homeland Security officers and immigration judges unless modified or overruled by the Attorney General or a federal court.

Special procedures in the United States

Undocumented migrants intercepted at US ports-of-entry are usually subject to *expedited removal* procedures. Persons who fear persecution are interviewed by an Asylum Pre-Screening Officer, who determines if the person has a credible fear of persecution (under the 1951 Refugee Convention) or torture (under the 1984 Convention Against Torture). Establishing a "credible fear" of persecution is easier than establishing a "well-founded" fear, which must be shown in the next phase of the procedure. Persons with credible fears are referred to an Immigration Judge and thus placed on the defensive track.

Certain persons are also dealt with in "reasonable fear" proceedings. Where a person has (1) been convicted of serious crimes after admission to the US or (2) illegally re-entered the US after being removed or leaving while subject to exclusion, deportation or removal orders, the person may be removed without an opportunity to challenge their removal before an Immigration Judge.

However, if the person expresses a fear of return to persecution or torture, the person must be referred to an Asylum Officer, who determines if there is a reasonable fear of persecution or torture. Where there is a reasonable fear, the person is allowed to challenge the removal before an Immigration Judge. Where there is no reasonable fear, the person may appeal to an Immigration Judge.

The US also has special asylum arrangements with Canada. Under a bilateral agreement, asylum seekers must apply for asylum in the first of those two countries that they entered, even if in transit. Given the comparative generosity of the Canadian asylum system, this will increase asylum applications in the US, while reducing applications in Canada.

Asylum procedures were also affected by the response to 11 September 2001. The Immigration and Naturalization Service (INS), which fell within the Department of Justice, was replaced by a new Department of Homeland Security (DHS), dedicated to countering terrorism. While immigration judges and the BIA remained under the Department of Justice, the appeal process was reformed so that reasons no longer need be given for BIA decisions (making appeals to federal courts difficult) and questions of fact (except clear errors) may no longer be considered on appeals. In 2003 the DHS announced Operation Liberty Shield. This attempts to increase security in the US through increased screening, tighter border controls and the detention of applicants from nations where Al Qaeda or other terrorist groups are known to have operated for the duration of their processing period. Previously people were detained beyond an initial screening period on a case-by-case basis.

Detention in the United States

Historically the US did not detain most asylum seekers. Applicants in the affirmative asylum process were rarely detained, while many defensive applicants were released to relatives, community groups or on their own recognizance. From the mid-1990s, however, the US increasingly detained applicants, in response to large increases in asylum seekers and economic migrants from Latin America, Asia and Africa, and ongoing large scale migration across the Mexican border.

It was estimated in 2005 that there were up to 11 million illegal migrants in the US, with 700,000 entering each year, and illegal workers comprising almost 5% of the US workforce (Pew Hispanic Centre, 2005).

Although US politicians have taken advantage of public sentiment against illegal migrants, and adopted tough border control measures, there is little government will to remove illegal migrants once they have entered the US community. In some industries (such as agriculture and domestic services), illegal migrants supply low-wage labour, while there is little public support for mass deportations of illegal migrants. In April 2006, moves to toughen laws relating to illegal migrants led to massive popular demonstrations against the changes.

As for asylum claims, in 1995 alone, almost 149,000 claims were filed, and at the end of that year there was a backlog of almost half a million claims. From this, claims fell to 33,000 in 1999, and steadily rose to 58,000 by 2002. While the approval rate for asylum claims was 23% in 1998, the largest group of applicants, Mexicans, was the least successful (0.6%).

The number of detainees rose in the 1990s from 6,000 in 1995 to around 20,000 in 2001. After legislative changes in 1996, asylum seekers arriving at ports of entry were automatically detained pending their "credible fear" determinations. Even those found to have a credible fear remained in detention, as did persons filing defensive asylum claims. Around 40% of asylum seekers are eventually paroled (most stay with family or friends pending determination), and one quarter of these do not attend their claim hearing and disappear into the community.

Since 11 September 2001, the US has detained even more asylum seekers, ostensibly on security grounds. This includes the detention of all applicants from nations where Al Qaeda or other terrorist groups are known to have operated (see above).

In December 2001, the US began detaining all Haitians arriving by sea. To ensure that this policy was not discriminatory, it was extended in November 2002 to cover all boat arrivals (except Cubans for political reasons). However, the policy disproportionately affects Haitians. Sea arrivals are detained even where an Immigration Judge has found that the person poses no security risk or risk of absconding. These measures are applied despite the fact that most Haitians who make it to US territory are found ultimately to be refugees.

As for conditions in detention, persons may be detained in government facilities, private detention centres or in prisons. Almost half of detainees are held in private State prisons or county gaols, and there are serious concerns about the poor conditions, abuse of detainees by staff and criminal inmates, and other human rights violations.

The US government believes that releasing Haitians from detention would encourage many more Haitians to travel to the US, placing pressure on US naval resources. The policy is clearly designed to deter people from seeking refuge in the US. Detention is coupled with strict interdiction measures by the US Coast Guard, which boards and searches vessels outside US territorial waters and turns boats around. The US interdicts all people attempting to arrive by boat including Cubans and Dominicans.

Australia has modelled its interdiction and deflection programs on this aspect of US law and policy. The difference is that the US has maintained a strict "wet foot, dry foot" policy, according procedural and substantive advantages to all those who physically reach US soil. In contrast, Australia moved in June 2006 to subject all unauthorised boat arrivals to a punitive deflection regime: see chapter 7 above.

Asylum in Canada

Canada has long been recognised as one of the most generous countries for protecting refugees and asylum seekers. Canada resettles 7,000 offshore refugees annually, and reserves twice as many places for onshore asylum seekers (reversing the position in Australia). In recent years, asylum claims have ranged from a low of 22,500 in 1997 to a high of 44,000 in 2001.

Canada has not been immune from public anxiety about increases in irregular migration, particularly following increases in Chinese economic migrants in the late 1990s. Even UNHCR criticised Canada's high refugee recognition rates for discrediting the international refugee system. China argues that granting asylum to economic migrants encourages people smuggling and illegal immigration. The Canadian government has responded by toughening asylum and detention policies. This change of heart is reflected in the decreasing approval rate of asylum claims, from 70% in the mid-1990s to 56% in 1998.

Asylum applications in Canada are considered by members of the Refugee Protection Division (RPD) of the Immigration and Refugee Board (IRB). The independent members of the RPD specialise in refugee law and country of origin information. The claim is considered in a private, informal and non-adversarial oral hearing, which may be observed by UNHCR. Applicants have a right to represent themselves or be represented by a lawyer, friend, relative or other person.

If an application is accepted, the person may then apply for permanent residence status. Where a claim is rejected, the applicant is sent a written notice of reasons for the decision, as well as information about leaving Canada. The applicant has 30 days to leave Canada and 15 days to apply to a Federal Court for review. Usually, applicants can remain in Canada pending judicial review. Unsuccessful applicants may also apply to remain in Canada on *humanitarian or compassionate* grounds.

During the asylum application process, applicants are entitled to the rights enjoyed by all persons in Canada under the *Canadian Charter of Rights and Freedoms*. Applicants may be eligible for employment authorisation where they cannot subsist on their own resources. Applicants also have access to school education, and emergency and essential health services.

Pre-removal risk assessment in Canada

Where persons are subject to a removal order, they can apply for a "Pre-Removal Risk Assessment" (PRRA) to prevent their being returned to persecution, torture, risk to life, or risk of cruel and unusual treatment or punishment. PRRA is thus a form of complementary or subsidiary human rights protection, additional to the protection available under the 1951 Refugee Convention. Unsuccessful asylum applicants may only apply for a PRRA where there is new evidence. An officer from Citizenship and Immigration Canada (CIC) considers the claim and applicants may present written submissions. Certain persons are ineligible to apply for PRRA, including those subject to extradition; persons from a safe third country; repeat claimants returning to Canada within six months of departure; persons already recognised as a protected person; and persons with refugee status in another country. Persons found to be at risk have their removal stayed and may apply for permanent residence.

Detention in Canada

Under the *Immigration Act* (Canada), the authorities can detain a person who has violated the Act where it is believed the person will not appear at immigration proceedings or endangers the public. Detention is reviewed by a senior immigration officer or adjudicator, who may release persons on conditions (such as promises to appear at hearings, and bonds).

Detention may be in gaols or immigration detention centres. In 1997-98, just over 7,000 persons were detained. However, unlike in Australia, the duration of detention is short. The average stay in prisons was 18 days, while in immigration detention centres it was only eight days.

In addition to detaining more asylum applicants, Canada has sought to deter people from arriving in Canada through visa requirements on migrant source countries, offshore immigration officers, carrier sanctions, penalising document fraud, and a C$1,000 landing fee for refugees and migrants (which can be deferred and repaid later).

Asylum in New Zealand

New Zealand is a party to the 1951 Refugee Convention. In general, New Zealand has a strong record for protecting refugees. It is one of the few countries with an annual quota for resettling refugees (750 per year), although the program was temporarily suspended after New Zealand accepted over 300 asylum seekers from the *Tampa* in 2001. It first established formal refugee determination procedures in 1978 (much the same time as in Australia), in response to the Indochinese boat people. Its asylum procedures are relatively transparent and afford basic guarantees of procedural fairness.

Onshore asylum claims are considered by the Refugee Status Branch (RSB) of the New Zealand Immigration Service. Under s 129X of the *Immigration Act 1987* (NZ), asylum claimants cannot be removed from New Zealand while their claim is being considered. This is done in order to comply with the obligation of *non-refoulement* in the 1951 Refugee Convention and in the 1984 Convention against Torture. Asylum seekers receive 16 hours of legally aided assistance in preparing and presenting their claim. Well-qualified members of an independent body, the Refugee Status Appeal Authority, hear appeals from unsuccessful claimants, and judicial review is also available within three months of a decision. The relatively small number of judicial review applications indicates the high quality of original decision-making. The number of onshore asylum seekers is small. In 2001, almost 1,300 persons claimed asylum in New Zealand. Asylum claims in Australia and New Zealand fell by 28% by between 2001 and 2004.

New Zealand provides permanent protection, and does not return refugees to their countries when there is no longer a risk of persecution. The government has sought to involve refugees and asylum seekers in the policy-making process. Government agencies (such as education, social welfare, health and housing) provide specialised services for refugees, and a range of NGOs assist in resettlement and advocacy. All persons in New Zealand enjoy protection against discrimination, and other rights and freedoms, under the *New Zealand Human Rights Act 1993*.

Nonetheless, a number of criticisms of New Zealand's asylum system have been made. The policy of speedy processing by the Refugee Status Branch, while reducing delays and prolonged uncertainty about status, can lead to other problems, such as unrealistic pressure on claimants in preparing and presenting their case, including obtaining translators, legal assistance or mental health care. Asylum seekers awaiting a decision receive less support than resettled refugees, especially regarding employment, social services, health and education. Some services, such as mental health, are inadequate to meet the needs of some asylum seekers. Despite these problems, in 2001, the *Human Rights Act* was amended to limit scrutiny of refugee policy by the Human Rights Commission.

Other concerns include the occasionally poor quality of legal representation. The UN Committee Against Torture noted that decision-makers may also not have sufficient knowledge of international law. These problems are compounded by the failure of New Zealand to ratify the Convention Relating to the Status of Stateless Persons, making it difficult for stateless persons to receive protection. New Zealand's policy of interdiction at overseas airports may risk returning persons to persecution, and there is no monitoring of failed applicants once removed from the country. New Zealand's special relationship with its Pacific Island neighbours means that it will face special challenges in unplanned migration in the form of "environmental refugees". Nothing yet has been done to address the problem of islanders displaced by rising sea levels caused by global warming.

Detention in New Zealand

Section 128 of the *Immigration Act 1987* (NZ) allows persons to be detained pending removal from New Zealand where they have been refused an entry permit at the border. In addition, s 128B allows detention where there are reasonable grounds for believing that a person is a risk to national security or public order, although in practice this provision has not been applied because it requires a higher threshold of application ("reasonable grounds") than the wider s 128. The NZIS has issued Operational Instructions to guide officials in interpreting policy and exercising their discretion in detaining asylum seekers.

Before the terrorist attacks on the US of 11 September 2001, the New Zealand Immigration Service (NZIS) seldom detained asylum seekers. Refugee claimants were typically issued with work permits and accommodated in open reception centres or hostels. Soon after that date, however, New Zealand began to detain routinely almost all asylum seekers, with the detention rate increasing from only 5% to 94% of asylum seekers. Persons were detained regardless of individual factors such as the ability to verify identity or documentation, or their personal risk to security or of absconding. Routine detention of asylum seekers also occurred in response to other security threats in recent New Zealand history, such as during the 1990 Gulf War and the APEC Conference in 1999.

The dramatic increase in detention after 11 September 2001 was challenged in the New Zealand courts. At first instance, a judge of the New Zealand High Court held that the indiscriminate detention of all asylum seekers did not meet the legal requirement that detention be *necessary* in the particular circumstances of an individual applicant. The Court of Appeal overturned that decision in *Attorney-General (NZ) v Refugee Council* (2003). The Court confirmed that s 128 is available for detaining asylum seekers, but concluded that it was not possible to decide if the NZIS policy of detaining asylum seekers was unlawful.

The latter conclusion was due to the unusual features of the period (particularly the *Tampa* incident and the security concerns after 11 September 2001), and the absence of individual examples where detention of individuals was demonstrably unnecessary. The Court of Appeal observed, however, that if high rates of detention continued over a longer period, such a policy might be challenged by the courts. In any event, after the initial High Court judgment, a new Operational Instruction was issued which narrowed the grounds of detention, resulting in a marked decrease in detention.

A UNHCR review of asylum detention in New Zealand found that it generally complied with UNHCR Guidelines and ExCom Conclusions. However, concerns remain. Asylum seekers are detained in Auckland Central Remand Prison or the Mangere Reception Centre. Detaining some asylum seekers in prisons with criminals, rather than in separate facilities, is inappropriate for persons who are not suspected of any crime, and raises concerns for their safety. Some asylum seekers have been threatened, assaulted, robbed or intimidated by criminal inmates.

Although the Mangere facility has been described by UNHCR as an "open centre", asylum seekers cannot leave without the permission of a staff member, considerably restricting liberty. The detention of children has increased, sometimes to maintain family unity, but also to detain unaccompanied minors. Legal aid is limited where detention is concerned, such as applications for conditional release or judicial review. Access to communication facilities has also been poor in the past.

The Zaoui case

The use of "security risk" certificates against suspected terrorists has also given rise to serious concerns that New Zealand is attempting to broaden the grounds of exclusion from refugee status, and restrict procedural and human rights protections. A controversial example is the case of Ahmed Zaoui, a former university lecturer, imam (religious leader) and political candidate in Algeria. After the Algerian military cancelled democratic elections in 1992 and assumed power, Mr Zaoui fled the country, seeking refugee in France, Belgium and Switzerland. While he was sentenced *in absentia* by the military regime in Algeria, the New Zealand Refugee Status Appeal Authority (RSAA) said of the trials: "[I]t would be unsafe to rely on the appellant's Algerian convictions as evidence. It is these convictions that give Mr Zaoui a very credible reason to fear returning to Algeria". Mr Zaoui was deported by Switzerland to Burkina Faso in 1998, where he stayed until 2000 before moving to Malaysia. In late 2002 he left for New Zealand after becoming aware that Algeria was seeking his extradition.

In New Zealand, Mr Zaoui requested asylum at the airport. When interviewed he allegedly admitted being a member of an Islamic militant group (the GIA). He was transferred to prison and, after his initial refugee status appeal was declined, he appealed to the Refugee Status Appeal Authority (RSAA). In 2003 the RSAA granted Mr Zaoui refugee status and cleared him of any association with militant or terrorist groups. Despite this decision, Mr Zaoui remained in prison (in solitary confinement for his first 10 months) on the basis of a "security risk certificate" issued by the Security Intelligence Service. His lawyers received only a summary of the evidence contained in the certificate and so it was not possible to test the adverse information. Only in December 2004 was he released on bail into the care of a religious order after a decision by New Zealand's Supreme Court. The government continued to maintain that Mr Zaoui was a security risk, based on secret evidence. In June 2005, the NZ Supreme Court found that a security certificate could only be issued where it met the threshold required by Art 33(2) of the Refugee Convention – that is, that there is a serious threat to the security of New Zealand, threatening substantial harm and based on objectively reasonable grounds. In contrast, the certificate issued against Mr Zaoui was based on a much lower standard.

References and further reading

D Anker, *Law of Asylum in the United States* (3rd ed, Refugee Law Center, Boston, 1999)

N Blake and R Hussain, *Immigration, Asylum and Human Rights* (Oxford University Press, Oxford, 2003) (UK law)

C Dauvergne, *Humanitarianism, Identity, and Nation: Migration Laws of Australia and Canada* (UBC Press, Vancouver, 2005)

EU Council Directive 2005/85/EC of 1-2 December 2005 on minimum standards on procedures in Member States for granting and withdrawing refugee status

EU Council Directive 2004/83/EC of 29 April 2004 on minimum standards for the qualification and status of third country nationals or stateless persons as refugees or as persons who otherwise need international protection and the content of the protection granted [2004] *Official Journal* L304/12

EU Council Regulation (EC) No 343/2003 of 18 February 2003 establishing the criteria and mechanisms for determining the Member State responsible for examining an asylum application lodged in one of the Member States by a third-country national

EU Council Directive 2003/9/EC of 27 January 2003 laying down minimum standards for the reception of asylum seekers

EU Council Directive 2001/55/EC of 20 July 2001 on minimum standards for giving temporary protection in the event of a mass influx of displaced persons and on measures promoting a balance of efforts between Member States in receiving such persons and bearing the consequences thereof

European Council on Refugees and Exiles: <www.ecre.org>

E Feller, V Turk, F Nicholson (eds), *Refugee Protection in International Law: UNHCR's Global Consultations on International Protection* (Cambridge University Press, Cambridge, 2003)

C Harvey, *Seeking Asylum in the UK: Problems and Prospects* (Butterworths, London, 2000)

J Hathaway, *The Rights of Refugees in International Law* (Cambridge University Press, Cambridge, 2005)

Cases

Attorney-General (NZ) v Refugee Council of NZ and the Human Rights Foundation of Aotearoa NZ Incorporated & D (16 April 2003) CA107/02

Attorney-General of NZ v Zaoui [2005] NZSC 38

Čonka v Belgium [2002] ECHR 14; 34 EHRR 1298

R v Secretary of State for the Home Department; Ex parte Adan [1999] 4 All ER 774

R v Secretary of State for the Home Department; Ex parte Gashi [1999] All ER (D) 335

TI v United Kingdom [2000] INLR 211

Part 4
Conclusion

13

Imagining the Future: Control and Compassion

Key Points in this Chapter

- One way to reduce the number of undocumented arrivals to Australia is to improve the international system of protection for refugees. Australia can improve global protection by helping UNHCR; through foreign aid programs; by interpreting the refugee definition more flexibly; and by assisting internally displaced persons.
- In recent years UNHCR has addressed concerns about the international protection regime through its "Convention Plus" and "Agenda for Protection" initiatives.
- Historically, refugees arriving without authorisation have rarely been popular in countries of asylum. Australia's mixed record is not unique. Even so, Australian law has become increasingly harsh in recent years. The changes proposed in May 2006 are without precedent.
- High Court rulings in detention cases highlight deficiencies in Australia's constitutional structure that are relevant to all Australians.
- Australia still needs to improve its refugee processing system.
- Australia's mistreatment of asylum seekers and refugees is likely to do lasting damage, both to those immediately affected by mandatory detention and temporary protection, and to Australian society as a whole.
- Australia's policies are expensive in financial and social terms and do little to enhance the country's international image as a liberal democracy built on fairness and respect for the rule of international law.

A mixed score card on refugees and irregular migrants

Irregular migration – particularly the unplanned arrival of refugees or asylum seekers – is rarely welcome. To the extent that any society is defined by its membership, refugees and asylum seekers are quintessentially outsiders. Without visas, they stand outside domestic law and they frequently present with linguistic and cultural differences. The receiving society can also fail to understand the experiences of those who have suffered torture or other trauma. Many challenges face those who advocate a humanitarian response to the problem. Reciting principles of international law and chiding a society for breaching those principles and failing to follow the practices of other states can be counter-productive. In the face of popular support for restrictive policies, comparisons with other (more generous) countries may entrench a fortress mentality, fostering resentment and self-righteousness.

Australia is not unusual in having a mixed score card on the treatment of refugees and irregular migrants. At the same time, aspects of its laws and policies are strangely discordant. Australia is a relatively young country which relies heavily on migrants for its growth and development. Its history and geography have permitted strict immigration control in reality and as a national aspiration. Yet there are few countries in which the issue of immigration features as strongly in the public discourse as in Australia, both in terms of media coverage and official attention.

In July 2005, an Australian Senate committee undertook yet another inquiry into the operation of the *Migration Act* – sparked by the Cornelia Rau and Vivian Solon-Alvarez scandals. It is difficult to see what such inquiries have achieved other than allowing people to put their views "on the record". In 2000, the same committee released an extensive report identifying many flaws in the immigration bureaucracy. Not one of the committee's 43 recommendations was accepted (see below). Indeed, some later changes go in the opposite direction to the committee's recommendations. The 2005 inquiry reported in March 2006, making no less than 62 recommendations.

Senate inquiries nonetheless remain an important part of Australia's democratic process. That they repeatedly consider similar issues reflects the constancy of any movement in social progress. The lessons of history are never "learnt" but have always to be learned, just as the struggle for the respect of human rights and for equality between gender, race and creed is never "won". In spite of being ever-present, change in the way of positive reform is not easy to achieve. This is particularly so when laws and policies attract widespread popular support. As one legal advocate, Chester Porter, explains, changing peoples' minds is indeed a gentle art: see Porter (2005).

This chapter reflects on the main areas of contention in Australia's laws and policies as they affect refugees and irregular migrants, beginning with some of the structural changes to administrative processes.

Although part of a more universal trend in governance in Australia, the results in immigration have been particularly harmful. It then examines issues that have arisen both within Australia and outside the country concerning the control of irregular migration. Beginning closest to home, it focuses on problems of identifying "unlawful non-citizens", their detention and the processing of refugee claims. In the latter context the Senate inquiry of 2000 is revisited and the same committee's report of March 2006 is discussed. This is followed by a review of the "Pacific Strategy".

The chapter continues with reflections on why the treatment of refugees, irregular migrants and other migrant "outsiders" matters. Domestically, a string of immigration decisions in the High Court is a reminder of the frailties of Australia's constitutional compact – matters of concern to all Australians. After reflecting on attitudes towards refugees, this chapter finishes with some observations about forced migration and the need for a coordinated international response to the problem.

Codified control

In 2005 the scandals surrounding the detention and removal of Australian citizens and (lawful) permanent residents solicited many criticisms about the culture that had developed in Australia's immigration bureaucracy: see Palmer (2005) and Ombudsman (2005). While these critiques of the system are valuable, bureaucratic culture does not develop in isolation. The most striking feature of the administration of Australia's immigration program over the past 20 years is not so much the attitudes of the administration, but the politicisation of the bureaucracy. From the time that the *Migration Act* was "codified" in 1989 (with open-ended discretions replaced by detailed regulations), politicians have interfered increasingly in day-to-day decision-making. The *Migration Regulations* have been changed with bewildering frequency in response to every shift in the political wind – and every judicial decision with which the Immigration Minister disagreed: see Crock (1994 and 1998). Over the same period, political resentment of the courts has led to increasingly explicit attacks on the judiciary and to a steady decline in the role of truly independent review. Although the focus for successive Ministers has been on securing final control over who stays and who goes, the practical impact has been to immunise DIMA from genuine external oversight. Some would argue that it has come close to being a law unto itself.

In the politicians' quest for complete control over decision-making, the wisdom of maintaining a system of checks and balances over the exercise of power has been forgotten. Palmer and Comrie highlight how decision-making functions in DIMA have been segmented, with too little attention paid to establishing connections between the different areas of administration. Palmer uses the term "siloing" to describe the isolation of, and lack of communication between, DIMA branches. What they do not acknowledge is that this structure is mandated to some extent by the legislative scheme within which DIMA operates.

This structure has been altered incrementally to "out-source" and even privatise functions previously performed by DIMA. This trend has encouraged the different branches to focus in on their own specific tasks, rather than on their function within the administration as a whole. Such change has not occurred by accident. For politicians, the segmenting of decision-making makes it easier to control outcomes. In an area where human empathy can easily intrude to soften the hard edge of policy, it has been convenient to create a regime where no single individual has carriage of the entire process.

While a culture of rejection and denial may have developed in DIMA, officials in DIMA might have seen this as a desirable outcome for their political masters. When juxtaposed with the trend to reduce or remove judicial or other independent oversight of the entire process, it is not difficult to see how such a regime could produce monstrous results.

Problems within: identifying unlawful non-citizens

A good example of the segmentation of the administrative process is the regime governing the arrest and detention of suspected unlawful non-citizens. Chapter 9 noted that arrest and detention decisions were overseen until September 1994 by inferior courts. Those arrested were brought promptly before a magistrate and were required to be returned before the court every seven days until their immigration status was finally determined. Suspects were also given free legal assistance, providing meaningful participation in the enforcement process.

The abandonment of this approach underpins the major failings in the cases of Rau, Solon-Alvarez and many of the other 240-odd cases referred to the Commonwealth Ombudsman for investigation. If the government is serious about ensuring that the pandemic of wrongful arrests and detentions do not continue, a mechanism for supervising the work of DIMA in this area must be reintroduced. As the Federal Magistracy has specialised in immigration, the obvious solution is to return to the pre-1994 model, requiring suspects to be brought before this court shortly after their arrest.

Mandatory immigration detention

Of all of the issues raised by Australia's determination to exercise absolute control over the immigration process, the laws and policies mandating the detention of unlawful non-citizens have created the greatest public debate and anxiety. In 2005 pressure from within the government's own ranks saw the relaxation of some of the worst aspects of laws that had been in place (in practice) since 1989 (the year when the first Cambodian boat people arrived). Children and families were released and new visas allow for the conditional freedom of failed asylum seekers who had no country willing to claim them as citizens or residents. The federal Ombudsman was given jurisdiction to review the cases of any persons who had been held in detention for more than two years.

As chapter 9 acknowledged, these changes reflect a more compassionate immigration control policy. By the same token, some aspects of Australia's laws still sit uneasily with its international human rights law obligations. For example, detention arguably remains "arbitrary" for single men and women who represent no threat of any kind to the Australian community. The changes proposed in May 2006 to deflect all boat people away from Australia is another example. As explored in chapter 12, Australian policy remains at odds with that of most similar democratic countries.

Perhaps the worst aspect of immigration detention in Australia, however, is the manner in which it is carried out (see chapter 11). The regime of remote, difficult to access centres inevitably corrupts some who come into contact with it. The guards of the private company responsible for running the centres are isolated and un-supervised in their work. The detainees are alienated in every sense. Baxter in South Australia is divided into compounds that keep people apart while ensuring that detainees are always under close observation. The consequences are so demoralising that long-term detainees almost all suffer some kind of mental illness. As the case of Cornelia Rau demonstrated, however, people in the system have become so hardened to the suffering that obvious mental illness has been dismissed as "attention seeking". Some Australians have also become desensitised to the suffering inflicted by long-term detention in remote centres: there is an unquestioning acceptance that people must be detained if Australia is to be safe and secure.

Ironically, the release of children and families engendered no great protest or expressions of concern in the community. Ultimately, while the *idea* that all unlawful non-citizens *must* be detained had captured the collective Australian consciousness, the injection of some compassion did not lead to any widespread dissatisfaction with the new policy.

Refugee status determination processes

The negative effects of reducing or removing the role of the courts in the immigration process is a theme that recurs throughout this book, particularly during the refugee determination process. Again, the result is a system characterised by politicised decision-making, secretive processes and lack of accountability. One of the most disappointing aspects of the regime is the extent to which recommendations made by parliamentary committees have been disregarded by the government.

The Senate Legal and Constitutional References Committee inquiry in 2005 into the administration of the *Migration Act* did well to review the findings of the same committee in 2000. In that year, the government rejected or dismissed as unnecessary all of the Senate Committee's 43 major recommendations. This was in spite of the unanimous nature of the Senate's report and the fact that the Committee included a number of senior government Senators. Many of the systemic problems identified at that earlier time were found to either remain or have worsened in the more recent inquiry.

In 2000, the treatment of two unsuccessful asylum seekers raised serious concerns about the adequacy of the refugee determination process. One case concerned a pregnant Chinese woman who was deported from Australia while eight and a half months pregnant. Upon her return to China, her baby was forcibly aborted under China's One Child Policy. This policy is recognised in some countries (such as Canada and the United States) as a basis for refugee status, but not in Australia. The second case was that of a Somali man who was rejected as a refugee by Australia. The man made a successful complaint to the UN Committee Against Torture, which ruled that he had a valid protection claim under the Torture Convention.

Over time, Senate inquiries have been conducted into a range of other matters. In 2004, for example, concerns about the misuse of ministerial discretion was at the centre of a prolonged and politically fraught investigation by the same committee. Even so, the results of the 2000 inquiry represent the most comprehensive attempt to catalogue the areas where Australia's refugee processing regime is wanting.

The Senate Committee's most important recommendations related to measures that could be taken to make Australia's refugee and humanitarian program more transparent, fair and open. For example, the Committee suggested that the practice of keeping recently arrived asylum seekers in "separation detention" – isolated from legal advice and other asylum seekers – was unnecessarily defensive: see chapter 5. It recommended that new arrivals be told of their right to seek asylum and to be provided with information about the determination process. The Committee also recommended improving legal assistance to asylum seekers, criticising a tendency to refuse claims without an interview.

The inquiry examined the adequacy of the protection available to "near miss" cases, where applicants do not quite meet the legal definition of a refugee. Until 1989, Australia had formalised visa categories for "humanitarian" cases such as these. Today, the only option is to seek the intervention of the Immigration Minister in the exercise of a "non-compellable, non-reviewable" discretion. The Senate Committee accepted that a final discretion is important, but recommended that consideration be given to creating a humanitarian visa class that would incorporate the *non-refoulement* (no return) obligations in human rights treaties. This recommendation is pertinent given moves in Europe to formalise "complementary protection": see McAdam (2005).

In 2000, the Committee examined each stage of the refugee determination process from initial application through administrative review to judicial review. It recommended that a study be made of why so many failed refugee claimants seek review in the courts, even though so few succeed given the limited power of the courts. It suggested that improvements could be made to record-keeping, training, information about situations in other countries, and information given to applicants. The Committee suggested that alternative solutions to temporary safe haven operations should be considered; and that research be conducted into refugee determination procedures internationally. It argued further that applicants should be given reasons if refused an interview. In relation to removals, the Committee recommended that there be an inquiry into the use of sedation and restraint in detention and deportation, and that there be better informal monitoring of deportees after deportation. DIMA was also urged to improve departmental procedures to prevent asylum seekers at risk of the One Child Policy being subjected to abortion on return to China. Finally, as noted in chapter 5, a range of recommendations was made to improve decision-making in the RRT.

The Committee's report made powerful and accurate criticisms of Australia's asylum laws and procedures, and suggested important recommendations for improving the deficiencies. Again, it is a matter of regret that its report has never received the response it deserves. If anything, the changes made to the law in 2001 opposed in some ways the suggestions made by the Committee.

The Committee's Terms of Reference did not allow it to comment on mandatory detention, even though detention is a key feature of the onshore determination system. As explored in earlier chapters, detention is the root of many of the inequities and inefficiencies of the determination process. The Committee draws attention, for example, to the practice of "task force" processing that forces advisers and decision-makers to work under intense time constraints in gathering information on detainees and conducting hearings at the primary decision-making and appellate levels. It is a system that has been both costly and intrinsically unfair.

In July 2005, the coalition gained control of the Australian Senate, marking the end of an era in which the Opposition and minor parties had been able to convene hostile Senate Committees to investigate a range of issues. By way of a swansong before this occurred, the Opposition-controlled Senate Legal and Constitutional References Committee convened an inquiry in May 2005 into the Administration and Operation of the *Migration Act 1958*. That Committee delivered its report in March 2006, making some blistering criticisms of both the legislative scheme governing immigration decision-making and of the "culture" within the immigration department. This report picks up and repeats many of the criticisms made in the reports of Commissioners Palmer and Comrie, who investigated the debacles surrounding Cornelia Rau and Vivienne Alvarez-Solon respectively. Although it is unlikely that many of the 62 recommendations made in the Senate report will be accepted by the conservative Coalition government, it is interesting to see the themes that recur in this document when compared with the Senate report published in 2000. Although focused more on the administration of immigration generally, the 2006 report again devotes most attention to the regimes for determining refugee status; refugee appeals; and the exercise of the Immigration Minister's residual discretion to intervene on compassionate and humanitarian grounds.

The report calls for more accountability for ministerial interventions (recs 3, 32) and for a more systematic and open approach to be taken to applications for intervention, with applicants to be assisted through the IAAAS (recs 29-31). Again, the committee calls for onshore asylum seekers to be interviewed by DIMA officials unless they are approved on the papers (rec 4). It then makes a series of recommendations about the training of interpreters (recs 6, 7) and immigration officials (recs 12-14) and about the need to review the legislation with a view to establishing an immigration regime that is "fair, transparent and legally defensible as well as more concise and comprehensible") (recs 8-10, 16). Of equal interest are the suggestions that lawyers and advisers generally be accorded a more prominent role in interviews at both DIMA and appellate levels (recs 17-19; 22-23). The balance of the report's recommendations sets out what appears to be Labor Party policy on the detention of immigration outlaws. These include provision for 90 days' mandatory detention of unauthorised arrivals for the purpose of carrying out health and character checks.

Problems abroad: the Pacific Strategy

The problems in the processes for both detaining and determining the status of asylum seekers in Australia are magnified in the deflection policies adopted to ensure that asylum seekers do not reach Australia. The experiment of sending refugee claimants to Nauru and Papua New Guinea is an unhappy one that should not be repeated. However, funds have been allocated for the construction of an 800-bed detention centre on the "excised" offshore territory of Christmas Island. In May 2006 proposals were made to extend the practice of deflecting all unauthorised boat arrivals to offshore processing centres – even those who make landfall on mainland Australia.

The rationale is that these asylum seekers should be processed offshore, without gaining access to the procedural entitlements and rights afforded to "onshore" refugee claimants. The argument is that, on the one hand, the luxuries of Australia's onshore processing are a "lure" for asylum seekers while, on the other hand, such procedures unfairly give mobile asylum seekers an advantage over those assessed by UNHCR in refugee camps in countries of first asylum.

In 2001, then Immigration Minister Ruddock asserted (and was uncritically reported in the media) that Australia's courts had been "too soft" on asylum seekers. The Minister stated that Australian asylum procedures are among the world's most generous and are certainly more generous than those of UNHCR itself. By way of example, he asserted that an Iraqi is six times more likely to gain recognition as a refugee in Australia than in a UNHCR processing centre.

In fact, the Australian courts over that period had little or no role to play in the recognition of Iraqi asylum seekers since virtually all were accepted at first instance. In any case, chapter 3 showed that Australia's refugee recognition rates are less generous than many other Western countries of asylum. The recognition rate in Australia in the 10 years to 1999 was around 13%, compared to the average rate in major Western countries of 26%. Of greater concern, however, was the Minister's inference that fairness requires all asylum procedures around the world to be as rudimentary as those used by UNHCR in its field camps where conditions are typically primitive in the extreme.

Such views deserve careful consideration, given the seriousness of the proposal to set up Australia's own version of a US Guantanamo Bay on Christmas Island and/or deflect all unauthorised arrivals to Nauru. Before the so-called "war on terror" which transformed Guantanamo Bay into a holding centre for "enemy combatants", that US installation was used to house and process asylum seekers interdicted en route to mainland America. The US idea was also to create simplified procedures so as to ensure a speedy turn around.

The arguments about levelling the playing field for asylum seekers are worrying in many respects. First, the notion that UNHCR standards should be the benchmark for Western countries fails to acknowledge the pressures which degrade UNHCR's procedures in the field. Second, it does not take into account the different functions performed by UNHCR officers compared with those of status determination authorities in asylum countries. In many instances, the role of UNHCR is to manage refugee flows in situations of mass influx. In such contexts status determinations serve to identify the cases most deserving of resettlement in third countries. Rejection does not always equate with immediate return to the country from which an individual has fled. In asylum countries such as Australia, the stakes are much higher: with refusal comes removal and return to the place of feared persecution.

Third, it is meaningless and false to compare the refugee case loads in Australia with those in a UNHCR camp. Asylum seekers who make it to Australia by boat or plane have frequently endured hardships that ensure that only those with the most serious claims persevere. The UNHCR camps tend to house women, children and less mobile refugees, many of whom cannot meet the strict legal definition of a refugee because they lack a public or political profile.

Finally, Australia has undertaken to observe the central requirement of the Refugee Convention not to *refoule* or send back a refugee to a country of persecution. It is difficult to see how Australia can fulfil these treaty obligations in good faith if it operates two recognition systems that deliver dramatically different outcomes for similar case loads. If the simplified system results in the removal of a person who would have been recognised as a refugee under the onshore processes, Australia would be in breach of its international legal obligations.

In this context, the "excision" of territories like Christmas Island or even of the whole of mainland Australia for certain non-citizens (see chapter 7) from Australia's "migration zone" has no impact on Australia's international obligations. It means simply that the *Migration Act* no longer operates in those areas for domestic legal purposes. The most important of these - and the one that Australians find most worrying - is the inability of people on those territories to lodge valid visa applications.

Could we all be aliens? Why human rights matter

The ambivalent situation of Australian citizens who live in "excised offshore places" (or islands off the Australian coast) underscores the need for greater reflection about Australian immigration control. Despite the reassurances of the government, locals on Christmas Island, for example, complain that they now feel like second class citizens. On a visit by one of the authors in 2004, they asserted that their excision was making it more difficult to attract foreign tourists and that the flow of foreign students to the local primary school had dried up. This is a salutary reminder of how protective measures targeted against outsiders can rebound to harm the people they were designed to protect. This matter is of particular concern because of the fragility of citizenship in Australia and the absence of an entrenched legal framework to protect human rights. As explored in chapter 9, Australia is the only Western country that does not have a Bill of Rights - and it shows.

If there are historical antecedents to Australia's ambivalent treatment of asylum seekers and refugees, there are also aspects of current law and practice that are without modern precedent. For its part, the High Court is as attuned to the wishes of the (conservative) government as at any time in Australian history. The ethos of immigration control has permeated through the refugee cases to a point where the human rights and civil liberties of all Australians have been placed at risk.

The fundamental problem is that when the British colonies in Australia federated in 1901 to create a new nation, the founding fathers could not reach a consensus on the meaning of Australian citizenship. As a result, the Australian Constitution makes no mention of citizenship and (as noted earlier) contains no Bill of Rights articulating the rights and duties flowing from membership of the Australian community. Instead, express powers were given to the new Parliament to make laws for the peace, order and good government of Australia with respect to such matters as "naturalisation and aliens", "immigration and emigration", "defence" and "external affairs". Under Australian law, the formal status of "Australian citizen" was not spelt out in legislation until 1948, when the *Australian Citizenship Act 1948* (Cth) was passed. In 2006, the government proposed to replace that Act with new citizenship legislation.

In a series of cases in 2004-05, the High Court explored the effect of the decision to make Australian citizenship "a mere legal inference", as John Quick described it in 1901. The High Court responded by focusing on the express powers given to the Parliament to make laws about "aliens" and their "naturalisation". By 2005, the dominant view was that these powers (and the silences of the Constitution on citizenship) mean that the ability to confer and take away citizenship is in the hands of the Parliament. In all but one case (*In re Paterson; Ex parte Taylor* (2001), later more or less overruled), it found that the Parliament has exclusive control over who is a member of the community and how non-citizens are to be treated. The High Court has stuck to this line even in cases where the laws in question are at odds with Australia's international obligations.

As noted in chapter 10, the High Court has upheld the constitutionality of Australia's mandatory detention regime since its inception in the late 1980s. The key test cases in this area have all involved asylum seekers - the earliest in 1992 concerning asylum seekers from Cambodia. In 2004, the High Court made rulings in other cases that have broader ramifications for both citizens and non-citizen "aliens" in Australia. The first was the case of Tania Singh, a child born in Australia to asylum seeker parents from India. In that case the High Court ruled 5:2 that Singh was an "alien" even though she was born on Australian soil in circumstances where she owed allegiance to the Australian Queen. The majority of the Court confirmed that the power to confer citizenship rests exclusively with the Parliament. While all children born on Australian soil used to be citizens under Australian law (until the law was changed in 1986), the Court confirmed that the Constitution does not guarantee the status of citizen to anyone born on Australian territory: see *Singh* (2004).

The second case underscores why this ruling is of concern. Susan Walsh was born in Papua New Guinea at a time when that country was part of Australia. Accordingly, she was born an Australian citizen. When Papua New Guinea gained independence, this citizenship was revoked. In *Walsh* (2004), the High Court again ruled that the Constitution contains no guarantee of citizenship. It confirmed this ruling in later cases involving Papua New Guineans, some born in Australia.

These cases indicate why all Australians should be concerned about the way the law treats asylum seekers and refugees. Australians are conditioned to think that "aliens" are as different from them in their legal status as they are in their life experiences. Yet, if the Australian Parliament has power to make laws about naturalisation (making people citizens), it clearly has power to reverse that status. If citizenship derives from an Act of the Australian Parliament, it follows that citizenship can also be lost if Parliament so decrees.

The truth is that Australian law has now reached a point where the rigid defence of (popular) government policy is being achieved at the expense of basic notions of human rights and human dignity, loss of which ultimately impacts on all Australians. The Constitution has no Bill of Rights to act as a defence against such measures. A majority of the present High Court seems to resist using the common law and rule of law traditions to make up this deficit - quite unlike the UK House of Lords.

In some cases, the Australians affected are long-term permanent residents and individuals who have lived all their lives believing that they are Australian citizens. The High Court's interpretation of the "aliens" power means that length of lawful residence in Australia provides no guarantee against deportation should a permanent resident be convicted of a crime: see *Shaw* (2003); *Te* (2002). Long-term permanent residents who came to Australia as young as six months of age have been deported after committing crimes when they reached adulthood.

Moreover, as Vivien Solon-Alvarez and Cornelia Rau discovered in 2004, the danger in Australia's harsh laws is that lawful status may offer no protection at all where an individual is *perceived* to be an "alien" who is in breach of the law. By the time refugee activists drew attention to the plight of Cornelia Rau and she was identified by her family, Ms Rau was in a sorry state indeed. In the words of her sister, Christine Rau, to the ABC's *Four Corners* program ("Anna's Story", 4 April 2005):

> The sort of accounts that we are getting are, personally, to me so chilling and so embarrassing and so reflective of cruel behaviour that I feel humiliated for Cornelia each time I read it. And if people are routinely treated like this within the detention system, then I think there should so much be an open inquiry so that we can all look at this behaviour with disgust and say, "Let's not let it happen again."

In closing *Four Corners*' account of "Anna's story", detention centre chaplain, Father Arno Vermeeren, underscored the dangers in accepting a regime that fundamentally abuses peoples' human rights on the basis that such rights do not apply to persons labelled as outsiders. He said:

> It's an absolute tragedy and everyone's shocked and horrified that this should happen to an Australian person. But they're not shocked and horrified that it should happen to someone who's not one of us.

Ms Solon-Alvarez appears to have suffered her fate, on the other hand, because of a pervasive assumption that she was a "mail order bride" or a "sex slave". Again, she was not "one of us". In late 2005, she finally returned from the Philippines, a small, injured and embarrassing reminder of bureaucratic failure and systemic lack of compassion. Around the same time, we learned of a similar failure which resulted in a mentally ill Turkish man being wrongly deported to a life of poverty and homelessness on the streets of Turkey in 2005. Australia can and must do better than this.

Refugees in perspective

When those displaced in America by Hurricane Katrina in 2005 were referred to as "refugees" there was an immediate outcry. Lawyers and refugee advocates reminded everyone solemnly that the term "refugee" has a special meaning under international law and that these people were not outside their country of origin. What is more interesting is that the displaced people also objected vehemently to the label.

The sad truth is that the "special" term refugee has become a dirty word in Western countries of asylum. Rather than invoking sympathy and dispossession, the word has become associated with people jumping queues or draining resources. There is an element of resentment, even where countries acknowledge the need for protection. The discourse on refugees - and peoples' understanding of the law - is undoubtedly becoming more sophisticated. Even so, there are still people in Australia who believe that refugees are only those who arrive through government-sponsored humanitarian programs and that boat people are not refugees but asylum seekers - even though people have to be asylum seekers before they can be refugees. Again, it has been asked: if Australia grants protection to asylum seekers who arrive without permission, why would anyone bother to seek a visa before coming to Australia?

In spite of the more than 650,000 citizens who came to Australia as refugees, many Australians find it difficult to imagine the dispossession and terror of being a refugee. Since European settlement the "Lucky Country" has not experienced war on its soil beyond the enemy bombings of Darwin and limited submarine attacks on Sydney during the Second World War. In the order of its existence, Australia has not responded well to the disorder of asylum seekers in search of protection.

Perhaps Australians need to be reminded of the phenomenal contributions that refugees have made to the Australian community over many years. The earliest refugees added greatly to the post-war economic boom by working on huge infrastructure, building and public works projects like the Snowy Mountains Hydro-electricity Scheme. In every part of the economy, refugees have provided much needed business, technical and labour skills, in addition to stimulating demand for goods and services and paying their share of taxes.

The present humanitarian intake may be more expensive in its short-term impact because of the settlement needs of those granted visas. By the second generation, however, the gap in the labour market participation rates between refugees and general economic migrants lessens dramatically. There are now many children of the first Vietnamese boat people studying at universities and progressing to highly paid jobs, and making a valuable contribution to the Australian community.

Because they have often lost everything when they arrive in Australia, refugees have proven to be among the most hard-working, industrious and productive members of society, determined to create new lives for themselves. Countless refugee stories tell of the deep sense of gratitude felt by many refugees towards their adopted country. Many stories show how refugees feel obliged to become self-sufficient and support themselves as soon as possible after arrival, because they are too proud to rely on welfare and do not want to burden Australia financially. Some of Australia's finest leaders have been refugees, including successful business people like Sir Arvi Parvo and Sir Peter Abeles.

Apart from their economic contribution to society, refugees have helped to make Australia a more interesting, diverse and sophisticated place. Refugees have shared their cultures, stories, languages and traditions with other Australians. The presence of refugees in the community has also served as a reminder of the duty of democratic societies to stand up against persecution and protect the victims of it. Australia's acceptance of refugees is an expression of the humanitarian values that many Australians hold dear - compassion, sympathy for others and freedom from oppression.

Global solutions to refugee crises

There are many reasons why the international community should work together to meet the protection needs of people displaced from their homes by persecution and human rights abuses. The desperation of the dispossessed can threaten international and national security and fuel the exploitative activities of people smugglers and traffickers.

Australia can do (and is doing) many things to help refugees. It can continue its strong financial support of UNHCR to ensure that refugee protection is effectively coordinated at an international level. UNHCR is not funded directly by the UN but relies on the generosity of donor nations. Australia can also address proactively the root causes of refugee flows. It has done this in the Asia Pacific region by funding initiatives in East Timor and across South East Asia. In many situations, refugee crises are produced by complex long-term factors, including poverty, competition for land and resources, and unequal economic development.

The UN sets targets for foreign aid contributions by developed countries of 0.7% of a country's Gross Domestic Product (GDP). In recent years, Australia has contributed less than 0.3% of its GDP to foreign aid. This will increase after Australia announced that foreign aid would double (from the level in 2004) to $4 billion per year by 2010. However, since Australian GDP will also grow over that six-year period, Australia will still not come close to meeting its UN target, and aid will be conditional on improved governance and reduced corruption in countries receiving aid. Furthermore, in January 2005 Australia committed an additional one billion dollars to Indonesian development and reconstruction projects with a focus on areas affected by the tsunami in December 2004. Half of this amount consists of interest-free loans.

Another way in which Australia could display global leadership is in adopting a flexible and progressive interpretation of the international refugee definition. This would ensure that people in need of protection are not returned to persecution as a result of narrow legal technicalities. In Africa and Latin America, countries have accepted that victims of internal conflicts and other forms of violence should be recognised as refugees. Australian governments could also educate their population about refugee issues, rather than exploiting fear of refugees based on misinformation.

Finally, Australia could work towards a binding international legal commitment to assisting "internally displaced persons" (IDPs) - people uprooted like refugees but who do not cross an international border and never receive the protection available to refugees. There are no treaties assisting IDPs, and general treaties like the Geneva Conventions governing armed conflict may be ineffective or not enforced. Other countries and organisations have been reluctant to intervene to help IDPs, because state sovereignty has been historically more important than human rights. Encouraging consistent international rules and a coordinated approach to internally displaced persons can only help in preventing and containing refugee crises.

Finding the balance between control and compassion

The abuses in immigration detention and at the hands of the immigration bureaucracy in the name of immigration control are in many respects aberrations. Australia has had and continues to have good credentials as a country that upholds the human values of compassion, fairness, justice and protection of the weak. Many aspects of Australia's refugee policies have reflected these values. Asylum has been granted to those in need, regardless of whether they entered Australia without permission.

The continuing threat of terrorist attacks may well justify Australia's moves to increase its defences against terrorist incursions. Such moves should not, however, sacrifice the civil liberties of citizens or the protection needs of victims of terror and oppression. Although the post-2001 border protection arrangements are crafted in principle to avoid the *refoulement* of refugees, they nevertheless send a clear message that refugees are not wanted in Australia, no matter how deserving.

If any lessons are to be learned from the years that followed the *Tampa* affair in 2001, it is that fear is a powerful tool in the hands of politicians: see Marr and Wilkinson (2003). Insofar as this emotion is heightened by ignorance and lack of understanding, this book hopes to make people less fearful of refugees and asylum seekers, by providing an introduction to a complex but very human area of law and policy. Once again, it collects and makes accessible accurate information about irregular migration, asylum seekers and refugees, explaining the legal, administrative and political procedures governing refugee protection in Australia within a global perspective.

Sadly, the shift in asylum policy in Australia away from compassion in the name of immigration control is not peculiar to this country. Refugees in many other places have found the going increasingly tough. Former UN High Commissioner for Refugees, Ruud Lubbers, explained the central dilemma in these terms:

> In Pakistan, I visited the infamous Jalozai camp, where thousands of Afghans are crammed together in inhumane and unsanitary conditions. When this camp appears on television screens in industrialised countries,

> there is – rightly – shock, sympathy and condemnation. But when one of these Jalozai Afghans is found hiding under a Eurostar train or arrives in a wealthy country on a leaky fishing vessel, they will suddenly cease to be an object of sympathy and fall into that sweeping category of people branded "bogus and illegal" … a modern day version of the plague-rat.

Australia has seen the human impact of failing to find the correct balance between control and compassion in the enforcement of immigration law. The experiences of Cornelia Rau and Vivian Solon-Alvarez attest that it is not just refugees and asylum seekers who stand to lose.

References and further reading

Commonwealth Ombudsman, "Inquiry into the circumstances of the Vivian Alvarez Matter", Report of the Commonwealth Ombudsman of an inquiry undertaken by Mr Neil Comrie, AO, APM (Report No 3 of 2005), <www.comb.gov.au/publications_information/special_Reports/2005/alvarez_report03.pdf>

Mary Crock, "Administrative Law and Migration Law: Actions and Reactions", PhD Thesis, Melbourne University, 1994

Mary Crock, *Immigration and Refugee Law* (Federation Press, Sydney, 1998)

Jane McAdam, *Complementary Protection and Beyond: How States Deal with Human Rights Protection* (UNHCR, Geneva, 2005): <www.unhcr.ch>

David Marr and Marian Wilkinson, *Dark Victory* (Allen and Unwin, Sydney, 2003)

Mick Palmer, "Inquiry into the circumstances of the immigration detention of Cornelia Rau Report" (July 2005), <www.minister.immi.gov.au>

Chester Porter, *The Gentle Art of Persuasion: How to Argue Effectively* (Random House, Sydney, 2005)

Senate Legal and Constitutional References Committee Report, *Administration and Operation of the Migration Act 1958*, 2 March 2006, <www.aph.gov.au/senate/committee/legcon_ctte/migration/report/index.htm>

Senate Legal and Constitutional Reference Committee, *A Sanctuary Under review: An Examination of Australia's Refugee and Humanitarian Determination Processes,* June 2000

UNHCR, "Convention Plus at a Glance": see <www.unhcr.ch>

UNHCR, "Agenda for Protection": see <www.unhcr.ch>

Debbie Whitmont, "Anna's Story", ABC TV (Four Corners), 4 April 2005: <www.abc.net.au/4corners/content/2005/s1335386.htm>

Cases

MIMA, Re; Ex parte Dang and Re Minister for Immigration and Multicultural Affairs; Ex parte Te (2002) 193 ALR 37

MIMA, Re; Ex parte Meng Kok Te (2002) 193 ALR 37

Patterson, Re; Ex parte Taylor (2001) 207 CLR 391

Shaw v Minister for Immigration and Multicultural Affairs (2003) 218 CLR 28

Singh v Commonwealth (2004) 209 ALR 355

Walsh v Minister for Immigration and Multicultural Affairs (2001) 116 FCR 524

Index

The Future of Insurance Regulation and Supervision

The Future of Insurance Regulation and Supervision

A Global Perspective

Edited by
Patrick M. Liedtke
Secretary General and Managing Director, The Geneva Association, Switzerland

Jan Monkiewicz
Professor of Financial Management, Warsaw University of Technology, Poland

palgrave
macmillan

First published 2011 by
PALGRAVE MACMILLAN

Palgrave Macmillan in the UK is an imprint of Macmillan Publishers Limited, registered in England, company number 785998, of Houndmills, Basingstoke, Hampshire RG21 6XS.

Palgrave Macmillan in the US is a division of St Martin's Press LLC, 175 Fifth Avenue, New York, NY 10010.

Palgrave Macmillan is the global academic imprint of the above companies and has companies and representatives throughout the world.

Palgrave® and Macmillan® are registered trademarks in the United States, the United Kingdom, Europe and other countries.

ISBN-13: 978-0-230-29269-7 hardback

This book is printed on paper suitable for recycling and made from fully managed and sustained forest sources. Logging, pulping and manufacturing processes are expected to conform to the environmental regulations of the country of origin.

A catalogue record for this book is available from the British Library.

Library of Congress Cataloging-in-Publication Data
The future of insurance regulation and supervision : a global perspective / edited by Patrick M. Liedtke, Jan Monkiewicz.
p. cm.
Includes index.
Summary: "Written by leading academics, researchers and insurance industry experts, this book offers a diversified perspective on how the regulatory and supervisory framework for the insurance sector will develop over the coming years. It is supported by The Geneva Association, the world-leading insurance think-tank of the private industry"—Provided by publisher.
ISBN 978-0-230-29269-7 (hardback)
1. Insurance--State supervision. I. Liedtke, Patrick M. II. Monkiewicz, Jan. III. Title.

HG8111.F88 2011
354.8'5—dc22

2011007800

10 9 8 7 6 5 4 3 2 1
20 19 18 17 16 15 14 13 12 11

Printed and bound in Great Britain by
CPI Antony Rowe, Chippenham and Eastbourne

Contents

Part VII: International Issues

List of Tables, Figures and Box

Tables

Figures

Box

Preface

Denis Kessler

A re-regulation move has closely followed the statement on which most commentators agree: enforced regulation failed to prevent the crisis that started in 2007. This crisis started as a financial crisis, through the sub-prime mortgages segment. Monoliners were also rapidly called into question in the autumn of 2007. From this specific starting point, the situation evolved into a major financial crisis that spread around the world, affecting the global system. The financial crisis evolved into an economic crisis, with a sharp recession. In turn, the economic crisis led to a social and political crisis. The sovereign debt crisis which appeared in 2010 is a clear example of the consequence of the difficulties that began in 2007. These three stages, and the order in which they arose, are typical of the way in which crises have evolved throughout history. From this point of view, the 2007–10 crisis is typical and, in fact, resembles many other crises that have punctuated world history.

Optimal regulation rather than maximal regulation

The question of regulation typically arises as part of the third stage, alongside political and social considerations. The fundamental need for regulation arises from the fact that governments have a particular responsibility with regard to the insured: governments must guarantee, in the successful conclusion of insurance contracts. This means supervising not just the quality, fairness and comprehensibility of the insurance contracts sold by insurance companies, but primarily supervising insurance companies' solvency.

The primary aim of supervision is to protect consumers, who are considered weak compared to powerful insurers, or unable to make a rational and fully informed selection of the best insurance product and the most solvent company. Moreover, because insurers receive money from policyholders (that is, premiums), before paying claims, consumers face two additional risks:

- a risk of mismanagement of their money, if it is not well invested or if premiums are insufficient because of initial miscalculation; and
- a risk of abuse by insurers who might take the money and disappear or, even worse, build so-called 'Ponzi schemes'.

The supervision of insurers' solvency is a 'second best' solution that substitutes a supervisory system operated by the public authorities when confronted with market imperfections. It is a 'second best' solution in that it comes at the expense of economic efficiency. Therefore it is about reducing the risks of mismanagement and abuse mentioned above, whilst keeping the insurance market sufficiently efficient and open to competition and new entrants.

It is important to bear this in mind because it helps us to avoid misunderstanding the ultimate goals of insurance supervision, which should not be to limit the role of the market in terms of allocating resources in the most efficient way and to fight against market forces, but to promote the market and help market forces to balance. One should always be wary of introducing 'maximal' regulation, which would be so stringent and heavy that it would dramatically reduce efficiency and competition between insurers ... at the expense, at the end of the day, of the insured's best interests.

Thus, good supervision is a matter of balance and not of safety at all costs. Optimal supervision, which should be the true goal of any government intervention, corresponds to an economic meeting point between two forces: the first leaving the greatest room for manoeuvre to the market and the second limiting opportunities for abuse as much as possible. There are indeed competing demands – minimum rates on one side, maximum security on the other – and the role of governments is to find the optimal point between what appears to be a very difficult tradeoff. By choosing this optimal point, governments represent a collective utility function in which the degree of public risk-aversion plays a key role.

A unique crisis requires a unique response

The recent crisis had an important feature that makes it totally unique: it was the first global crisis. Initially it seemed that the fates of emerging economies would be unconnected to those of established economies. But we soon discovered that this was a sweet illusion: world economies are in fact closely correlated, and the shock waves were felt across the globe. This unique crisis should have inspired a unique and globally coordinated response. This view is expressed very well by Eric Denters' contribution on 'Global Financial Architecture and the Insurance Sector' (Chapter 3).

Unfortunately there was no globally coordinated response, with most governments reacting in a very protective manner, mainly if not exclusively focusing on their own national interests. This is a typical 'prisoner's dilemma' situation, where cooperation would have yielded better results than individual struggle. But uncertainties led the actors of the crisis to trade a global solution for national or even protectionist measures. In the banking sector, it is clear that each government intervened only to save their own credit institutions, as can be seen when studying the various bailout schemes implemented since 2007.

A regulatory system that takes the specific features of each industry into account

Lack of global coordination has not been the only obstacle on the road to effective regulation. Another significant looming risk is that of amalgamation: the illusion that one solution fits all industries. Governments have focused on reforming the 'financial services industry', ignoring the fact that this 'industry' in fact is comprised of several very different segments. When it comes to regulation, one should not adopt a 'one size fits all' approach.

Confusion between the banking and insurance industries led to some fairly damaging solutions. For example, the catalyst that played a key role in the dissemination of the crisis was the liquidity crisis. Lack of liquidity – due to an incredible confidence crisis among financial institutions – transformed the financial crisis into a potential systemic crisis. The financial system was on the brink of virtual collapse as trust vanished, and banks stopped lending money to each other. This liquidity trap could only be avoided through large-scale action by the central banks.

It is well known that the insurance industry does not rely so heavily on liquidity. In fact, the insurance industry is a net provider of liquidity and resources to other economic agents. For this reason, the insurance industry is not prone to creating systemic risk. Furthermore, insurance contracts cannot be cancelled as easily as many banking or deposit contracts. Bankruptcy can happen in a day. When an insurance company is becoming illiquid, it is because it is for long insolvent and not because of independent liquidity problems. In actual fact, insurance and reinsurance provide stability to the world economy thanks to their shock-absorbing capacity and very high resilience. This fact has unfortunately been overlooked by governments and regulators. An efficient regulatory process should bear this detail in mind, and build on it. If the true target of regulation is to provide stability, policy-makers should be doing everything they can to promote insurance as a key way to limit fluctuations.

Inadequate regulation could create the next crisis

The dangers involved in inadequate or suboptimal regulation are far worse than just being unable to anticipate the next crisis. The key issue here is that inadequate regulation creates loopholes, which transform themselves into arbitrage opportunities for economic agents. For this reason, regulation should be 'forward-looking', rather than trying to address past crises. Wing-mirror driving is a dangerous exercise. As Rob Curtis points out in his contribution 'Solvency as a Focal Point of Prudential Regulation: Supervisory Lessons and Challenges' (Chapter 6), the regulatory toolbox should include new tools, and not focus purely on quantitative aspects such as solvency.

The new regulatory framework should very much be forward-looking and focused on anticipating future trends. In this perspective, new regulations should incite the development of active risk management at the level of each insurance and reinsurance company. Each time that a risk emerges and evolves, regulators should send appropriate messages to the insurance companies to call their attention to the risk and urge them to take such adverse developments into full consideration.

Some global regulation already rests on a very prospective view of each insurance company's development. This is really the optimal situation. Regulation should be as close as possible to the business plan and risk profile of each company and try to assess if the capital management of each company is fully consistent with its business plan. Moreover, it is the responsibility of each insurance or reinsurance company to define its specific risk appetite, and therefore the implied probability of loss and ruin. Once the risk appetite has been defined, the regulatory process should assess whether or not the corresponding level of capital has been secured. From this perspective, the role of internal models appears crucial. It is indeed the internal model that enables a company to check whether or not the level of capital is aligned with the risk appetite and the risk profile of a given company. It is very likely that future regulation will use each company's specific internal model, which is rooted in its specific portfolio of risks and assets. In this respect, the Solvency II approach is relevant and promising.

Get over the desire for revenge

After such a crisis, there is clearly a bitter taste in the mouths of all economic agents: companies, regulators, governments, and public opinion. They all think that the crisis could have been avoided, and that others played a key role in its creation. From this point of view, bankers were largely the victims of a finger-pointing exercise. Although this type of reaction is understandable, it is overly simplistic. Focusing on bankers allows us to avoid questioning the role of public authorities and governments.

More fundamentally, however, it would be illusory to aim for a fluctuation-free environment and an absolutely stable world. Modern societies live in a philistine 'petit-bourgeois' dream of comfort and certainty. One should consider instead that cycles are consubstantial with economic and financial markets. Flattening cycles is already difficult; eradicating them is pure fantasy.

The future of regulation lies in providing an optimal framework for economic activities in order to reduce the amplitude of cycle oscillations. The insured should of course be protected from mismanagement by companies and from the irrational and foolish behaviour of managers. Ultimately, however, the insured are responsible for choosing one insurance company over another. In most cases, difficulties for an insurance company will lead to run-off or a portfolio transfer. And more and more countries have implemented guarantee funds to cope with the total failure of insurance companies. A regulatory system that is too prescriptive would create new arbitrage opportunities, and eventually lead to a new crisis. Any regulation should aim to temper competition, not to eradicate it: otherwise innovation would stop and, all things being equal, rates would increase. Regulation is a question of striking the right balance and right incentive, and not a question of maximum cautiousness that would be the source of financial imbalances and that would give the wrong incentive with regard to risk transfer between economic agents.

The Geneva Association has been at the forefront of economic thinking in terms of understanding the role of insurance, and has been an active source of proposals to Governments, regulators, policy-makers and all interested agents. This book on the future of regulation belongs to this tradition, which is at the heart of The Geneva Association's strength and reputation. The views in this book are expressed by some of the most renowned academics and economic actors. I truly believe that they will have a positive impact on the re-regulatory shift we are currently witnessing. Let us hope that the strong messages conveyed by all the contributors are taken into account in the drafting and implementation of the new regulations!

Notes on Contributors

Manuel Aguilera-Verduzco is President of the Mexican Insurance and Surety National Commission (CNSF). He is responsible for the supervision of the Mexican insurance and surety markets and has participated in reforms, particularly regarding the modifications to the regulatory scheme of health insurance and pensions derived from the Laws of Social Security. He is a board member of the supervisory bodies in charge of the surveillance of the Mexican financial system: the Banking and Securities National Commission (CNBV), the Retirement Savings System National Commission (CONSAR) and the National Commission for the Protection of Financial Services Users (CONDUSEF). On an international level, he is Chair of the Insurance and Private Pensions Committee of the Organisation for Economic Co-operation and Development (OECD), Chair of the Latin American Insurance Supervisors Association (ASSAL), Chair of the IAIS Implementation Committee and a member of the Executive Committee of the International Association of Insurance Supervisors (IAIS).

Julian Arkell is an unincorporated sole consultant on international trade and services policy issues. He has worked on aid-funded capacity building projects to advise the governments of Caricom, Egypt, Ghana, Jordan, Maldives, Pakistan, Sri Lanka, Swaziland, Tajikistan, Thailand, the UAE, Ukraine and Vietnam. He has also completed projects for the ACP Countries, the Commonwealth Secretariat, the European Commission, SADC and the Islamic Development Bank. He worked at Shell-Mex & BP Ltd and Robert Matthew, Johnson-Marshall & Partners. He was a founder member of the Fees Committee of the Royal Institute of British Architects and Chair of the Working Party of the European Community Services. He is the organiser of the PROGRES annual international seminars on the regulation and supervision of insurance services in Geneva, and has contributed articles on trade and investment issues for the *PROGRES* Newsletter. Other publications include *Barriers to Global Insurance Business Operations: The Situation in Brazil, China, India, Mexico and Russia*. He is Officer of the Order of the British Empire by Her Majesty the Queen, for services to British Invisibles.

Philippe Brahin is Head of Group Regulatory Affairs at Swiss Re and a member of Swiss Re's Risk Management Executive Team. Previous responsibilities include the production of Swiss Re's financial reports and content management on strategic topics and he was Financial Analyst in Alternative Investments. Prior to joining Swiss Re, Philippe was Deputy Director for International Affairs at the French Insurance Association (FFSA) and he also worked for the California Department of Insurance.

Peter Braumüller is Managing Director of the Austrian Financial Market Authority, responsible for insurance and pension supervision. He is also Chair of the Executive Committee of the International Association of Insurance Supervisors (IAIS). Moreover, he is teaching insurance supervision law at several universities and has published various books and articles on supervision-related topics. He is a certified actuary with the Austrian Actuarial Association. Previous positions include Director for Insurance Supervision at the Austrian Ministry of Finance and Officer for Financial Services in the EFTA Secretariat in Brussels, Belgium.

Rob Curtis works for KPMG, UK, and is Chair of the Solvency and Actuarial Issues Subcommittee of the International Association of Insurance Supervisors (IAIS) which is tasked with designing and implementing international solvency standards and guidance. Prior to joining KPMG, he was responsible for international and domestic prudential insurance policy at the UK Financial Services Authority (FSA), Head of Group Internal Capital Assessment at Aviva plc and Project Director of the Capital and Risk Management Transformation Programme at Royal and SunAlliance. Other former roles include working in Australia for 15 years, first as an underwriter and business analyst and later for Australian regulator APRA managing the supervision of insurers, banks and pension funds. He is Honorary Fellow of the Faculty of Actuaries, Edinburgh, UK.

Erik Denters is director of the LL.M. Program in International Business Law at VU University, Amsterdam, the Netherlands. He has been a consultant for the United Nations, visiting researcher at the IMF and is currently involved in consultancy projects on trade and investments in Asia. He has an extensive academic background and is author of *Law and Policy of IMF Conditionality*. He has been a visiting scholar at various universities in Europe and Asia where he taught on international monetary law, and trade and investment law.

Martin Eling is Professor of Insurance and Director of the Institute of Insurance Science at the University of Ulm, Germany. He is also Research Fellow at the Independent Institute, Washington, DC, USA. Previously, he was Visiting Professor at the University of Wisconsin-Madison, USA. His research interests include risk management, regulation, asset liability management, and empirical aspects of finance and insurance. He has published articles in leading international journals such as the *Journal of Risk and Insurance*, the *Journal of Banking and Finance* and *Insurance: Mathematics and Economics*.

Michel Flamée is Vice Chairman of the Banking, Finance and Insurance Commission (CBFA) and Professor at the Economic and Financial Law Centre of the Free University of Brussels, Belgium. He is also former Chair and member of the Executive Committee of the International Association of Insurance

Supervisors (IAIS). In the capacity of Board Member of CEIOPS (level III within the Lamfalussy structure) and as member of the EIOPC (level II within the Lamfalussy structure), he has been heavily involved with the international repositioning of the Belgian supervisor at a both European and global level and in the setting up of the Solvency II directive. Prior to joining the CBFA, he was a practising lawyer at the Brussels Bar working in commercial law, company law, IP, IT law and Mergers and Acquisitions. Since then, he has been conferred the title Honorary Advocate. His teaching and research interests include financial and economic law and he has numerous publications in this domain.

Yasuhiro Hayasaki is Deputy Commissioner for International Affairs at the Financial Services Agency of Japan. His main responsibilities are the insurance regulation from an international perspective and issues relating to systemically important financial institutions (SIFIs). For many years, he played a key role in the area of financial stability matters at the Bank of Japan. His professional experience includes dealing with Japan's financial crisis during the late 1990s and the global financial turmoil which emerged in 2008.

Aerdt Houben is Director of the Financial Stability Division at the Central Bank of the Netherlands (DNB). The division's prime task is to prepare timely and accurate assessments of macro-prudential risks in the Netherlands and to formulate policy proposals aimed at safeguarding financial stability. Prior to taking up this position, he headed the Supervisory Strategy Department during the integration of prudential supervision on banks, insurance companies and pension funds within DNB. Before this, he was Head of its Monetary Policy Department, including during the period with the introduction of the euro. He has also worked in the Policy Development and Review Department of the IMF. He is a member of the Banking Supervision Committee of the European Central Bank, the Committee on the Global Financial System at the Bank for International Settlements (BIS) and the Analytical Vulnerabilities Group of the Financial Stability Board.

Nadège Jassaud is Senior Financial Stability Expert at the Monetary and Capital Market Directorate of the IMF. From 2007 until 2010 she was Deputy Head of the Financial Stability Division at the Bank of France and from 2005 to 2007 Head of the Macro Prudential Unit at the Autorité de Contrôle Prudentiel. From 1998 to 2005 she was off-site and on-site examiner (of which one year was on the insurance side) and she also spent one year seconded at the ECB within the Supervisory and Financial Stability Division on stress testing and crisis management.

Bradley L. Kading is President and Executive Director of the Association of Bermuda Insurers and Reinsurers (ABIR). ABIR is an association of 23 of Bermuda's market-leading Class 4 insurers and reinsurers. Prior to joining ABIR, he was Senior Vice President and Director of State Relations for the Reinsurance Association of America, RAA. Before this, he was Vice President and Director of Government Affairs for the Alliance of American Insurers in Chicago.

Denis Kessler is Chair and Chief Executive Officer of Scor Se, France. Previously, he was Chairman of the Fédération Française des Sociétés d'Assurance (FFSA), CEO and Executive Committee member of the AXA Group and Executive Vice-President of Mouvement des Entreprises de France (MEDEF).

W. Jean Kwon is Professor at the School of Risk Management of St John's University, UK. He is also a Chartered Property Casualty Underwriter (CPCU) and listed in the Fulbright Senior Specialist Pool. He gained experience as educator at Georgia State University, USA, and Nanyang Technological University, Singapore, as insurance regulator with Monetary Authority of Singapore and as industry specialist with the American Institute for CPCU/IIA. He helped to establish Asia-Pacific Risk and Insurance Association (APRIA) and organise the first and second World Risk and Insurance Economics Congress (WRIEC). This is a once-in-five-years academic forum jointly organised by APRIA, ARIA, EGRIE and The Geneva Association. He has written several books, including the 2009 Kulp-Wright Book Award-winning *Risk Management and Insurance: Perspectives in a Global Economy* (co-authored with Harold D. Skipper).

Patrick M. Liedtke is Secretary General and Managing Director at The Geneva Association, Switzerland. He is also Chairman of the Silver Workers' Institute and Director of the Applied Services Economic Centre (ASEC) in Geneva. He is Editor-in-Chief of *The Geneva Papers on Risk and Insurance: Issues and Practice*, and Editor of the *Insurance and Finance* newsletter. Moreover, he is Surveillance Board Member of IT Future AG, Frankfurt and Zwiesel Kristallglas AG, Zwiesel, Germany. His memberships include Advisory Council of Deutsche Insurance Asset Management (Deutsche Bank), Board of European Group of Risk and Insurance Economists (EGRIE); Club of Rome, World Academy of Arts and Sciences of the Advisory Committee of the Centre for Risk Management and Decision Processes (WCRMDP) at The Wharton School of the University of Pennsylvania, USA, and the International Advisory Board of the China Center for Insurance and Social Security in Beijing.

Monica Mächler is Vice Chair of the Board of Directors of FINMA. Prior to this, she was Director of the Swiss Federal Office of Private Insurances (FOPI) and worked at the Zurich Financial Services and Zurich Insurance Company, Switzerland. She is a member of the Executive Committee and Vice-Chair of the Technical Committee of the International Association of Insurance Supervisors,

IAIS. She is also a member of several expert commissions of the Confederation such as the Zimmerli Commission on the implementation of integrated financial supervision legislation, the Zufferey Commission on financial market supervision, and the Schnyder Commission on revision of the Insurance Supervision Act. Moreover, she is Lecturer in International Business Law at the University of Zurich. She has written many articles on financial market law and international private law.

Leila Madeiros is Vice President and Corporate Secretary of the Association of Bermuda Insurers and Reinsurers (ABIR). Previously, she was Deputy Director of Policy, Research and Communications at the Bermuda Monetary Authority (BMA) directing the formulation and dissemination of appropriate policies, strategies and information for the BMA. In addition, she served in various capacities as a Bermuda insurance regulator with the Registrar of Companies Department.

Donato Masciandaro is Full Professor of Economics and Chair in Economics of Financial Regulation at Bocconi University, Italy. He is also Head of the Department of Economics and Director of the Paolo Baffi Centre on Central Banking and Financial Regulation. Moreover, he is Board Member of SUERF. Previously, he was Visiting Scholar at the IMF as well as Consultant at the United Nations. His work covers three main topics: central banking, financial regulation and supervision, and illegal financial markets. His two most recent books are *Designing Financial Supervision Institutions: Independence, Accountability and Governance* (edited with M. Quintyn) and *Black Finance: The Economics of Money Laundering* (with E. Takats and B. Unger).

Jan Monkiewicz is Professor of Financial Management at Warsaw University of Technology, Poland. He is also on the editorial board of *Wiadomosci Ubezpieczeniowe* (Insurance Digest) and Editor of the *PROGRES* newsletter of The Geneva Association. Previously, he was Chair of the Insurance and Pension Funds Supervisory Commission, CEO of PZU S.A., the largest Polish property insurer, and President of the PZU Życie S.A. Supervisory Board and Management Board. After the political and economic transformation process in Poland began, he joined the Polish government administration. He served, among others, as Secretary of State responsible for the coordination of banking and insurance reforms.

Marek Monkiewicz is Lecturer at the Faculty of Management at Warsaw University, Poland. He is also Head of the Development and Analysis Department at the Polish Insurance Guaranty Fund. He gained experience at Brokerage House Bain Hogg, London, UK, Daewoo General Insurance Company, and the British Prime Minister's Office. He is the author and co-author of several books on insurance guarantee schemes and MTPL insurance, including *Insurance Guarantee Schemes on a World Markets* and *MTPL Insurance in Europe and in Poland: Current Problems*.

Marc Quintyn is Division Chief Africa at the IMF. He has worked most of his career on monetary and financial sector issues in surveillance and programme missions, FSAPs, and technical assistance work in all parts of the world. Before joining the IMF, he was Assistant Professor of Money and Finance at University of Ghent, Belgium. Other previous roles include Economist at the Research Department of the National Bank of Belgium and Professor at the University of Limburg, Belgium. He has published numerous books, papers and articles on European monetary and financial integration, monetary policy, and more recently on financial sector reform and institutional and governance aspects of banking regulation and supervision and central banking.

Marcelo Ramella is Assistant Director Research at the Bermuda Monetary Authority (BMA) and Visiting Fellow at London School of Economics and Political Science, UK. He is also National Public Accountant in Buenos Aires, Argentina. He has a long-standing research interest in innovative practices, especially processes of social and institutional legitimating of innovation.

Przemysław Rymaszewski is Project Manager and Research Assistant at the Institute of Insurance Economics at the University of St Gallen, Switzerland.

Sebastian Schich is Principal Economist at the Financial Affairs Division of the Directorate of Corporate and Financial Affairs of the OECD. He also serves in OECD's Financial Markets Committee and Insurance and Private Pensions Committee, and has represented the organisation in various forums. Previously, he worked as an economist in the Economics Department of the OECD, the Deutsche Bundesbank, and the United Nations Conference for Trade and Development (UNCTAD), as well as an investment manager at Deutsche Bank.

Hato Schmeiser is Chair for Risk Management and Insurance and Managing Director of the Institute of Insurance Economics, University of St Gallen, Switzerland. Prior to these positions, he was Professor for Insurance and Risk Management at the University of Münster, Germany. His main research interests include individual financial planning, dynamic financial analysis, option pricing and regulation of financial firms.

Sharon Tennyson is Associate Professor at the College of Human Ecology, Department of Policy Analysis and Management, Cornell University, USA. Previously, she was Faculty Fellow and Project Coordinator of the Program on Pharmaceutical Policy Issues in the same department. Other former positions include Assistant Professor in the Department of Insurance and Risk Management at The Wharton School of the University of Pennsylvania, Research Fellow at the Networks Financial Institute, Indiana State University and President of the Risk Theory Society, all in the USA. She was Associate Editor of the *Journal of Risk and Insurance* and worked on the Editorial Boards of the *Journal of Insurance Regulation* and *Insurance Markets and Companies*.

Ian Tower is Technical Specialist in the Department of Monetary and Capital Markets of the IMF. Based in Washington, he is responsible for insurance sector issues, with particular regard to insurance regulation. Ian is involved in the IMF's surveillance work, both the Financial Sector Assessment Programme (FSAP) and Article IV consultations, and in technical assistance. He is seconded to the IMF from the UK Financial Services Authority, where he was most recently responsible for the supervision of many of the retail insurance companies. He had previously led the FSA's initial work on its integrated prudential rulebook and headed its specialist unit responsible for evaluating risk management at banks, insurance companies and investment firms. Ian started his career at the Bank of England, where in addition to a period as a banking supervisor, he worked on European economic and financial issues and on the oversight of clearing and settlement systems.

Mark Teunissen is Senior Economist of the Financial Stability Division at the Central Bank of the Netherlands (DNB). Before this, he was an economist in the Monetary and Economic Policy Department and the Supervisory Policy Department of DNB. He has also worked in the Corporate Communication Division and the Economics Department of the ING Group.

Karel Van Hulle is Head of Insurance and Pension Unit and Directorate-General 'Internal Market and Services' at the European Commission. His main responsibility is the preparation of a new solvency regime for insurance and reinsurance companies (Solvency II). Other areas of work include life and non-life insurance, reinsurance, insurance mediation, motor insurance, insurance guarantee schemes and pension funds. Moreover, he represents the European Commission within the Committee of European Insurance and Pensions Supervisors (CEIOPS) and the Technical Committee of the International Association of Insurance Supervisors (IAIS). Previously at the European Commission, he was Head of Unit for Accounting Standards, Head of Unit for Financial Reporting and Company Law and Head of Unit for Accounting and Auditing. In that capacity he was closely involved with harmonisation in the fields of accounting, auditing, and company law both at EU and global level and served as the Commission's observer with the International Accounting Standards Committee (IASC), the Consultative Advisory Group of the International Auditing and Assurance Standards Board (IAASB), the European Financial Reporting Advisory Group (EFRAG) and the financial reporting working party of the Committee of European Securities Regulators (CESR). He was Secretary of the High Level Group of Experts on Company Law which prepared the Commission's 2003 Action Plan on Company Law. He started his career in the legal department at the Belgian Banking Commission and served as the first secretary of the Belgian Accounting Standards Committee.

Therese M. Vaughan is CEO of the National Association of Insurance Commissioners (NAIC), USA. In this capacity, she oversees the operations of the NAIC in its efforts to support U.S. insurance regulation and serves as its chief spokesperson in Washington. Prior to her current position, she was Robb B. Kelley Distinguished Professor at Drake University, USA, where she focused on the regulation and management of financial institutions. Other former roles include Iowa Insurance Commissioner and NAIC President. She is the co-author of two college textbooks on insurance and Past President of the American Risk and Insurance Association (ARIA).

Alexander Warzilek is Coordinator of Insurance Supervision at the Division of International Affairs and European Integration of the Austrian Financial Market Authority. Furthermore, he represents Austria in various Committees of the IAIS and the Committee of European Insurance and Occupational Pensions Supervisors (CEIOPS). Before joining the FMA, he was Assistant for Private Law at the Universities of Graz and Lucerne, Switzerland. His publications include *Personality Rights against Invasions by Mass-Media* (co-edited with Helmut Koziol).

Paul Windels is Financial Analyst at the Banking, Finance and Insurance Commission and Assistant Professor in Finance and Risk Management at the Hogeschool-Universiteit Brussel, Belgium. He is a Certified Internal Auditor and Certified Financial Services Auditor. His research interests include European and international developments in financial sector supervision, accounting and auditing. His research has been published in international journals in management, accounting and insurance.

Wei Zheng is Associate Professor of Risk Management and Insurance and Vice Chair of the Department of Risk Management and Insurance at the School of Economics, Peking University, China. He is also Secretary General of China Center for Insurance and Social Security Research (CCISSR) at the same university. His academic focus is on social security, catastrophic risk management, insurance growth and international insurance comparison. He has won numerous awards including China National Award, Beijing City Award and Peking University Award for Teaching Excellence, Beijing City Award and Peking University Award for Social Science Research, and 2008 Shin Research Excellence Award by the

International Insurance Society and The Geneva Association. He is a member of the Board of Governors of Asia Pacific Risk and Insurance Association, the Board of Directors of Insurance Institute of China, the Youth Committee of China Health Management Association, and the Expert Evaluation Committee of China Central Government Procurement. Furthermore, he is Independent Director of the Board of Directors of the Bank of China Insurance Company and a member of the Editorial Board of *The Geneva Papers on Risk and Insurance: Issues and Practice* and the *Asia-Pacific Journal of Risk and Insurance* (APJRI).

Acknowledgements

This study would not have been conceived and completed without the intellectual and logistical support of many individuals. We should particularly mention Dr Monica Mächler from Swiss FINMA, Brian Atchinson from IMSA in the US, Professor Michel Flamée from the Belgian CBFA, Ian Tower from the Bank of England and Dr Marcelo Ramella from the Bermudian Monetary Authority, who not only encouraged the idea of launching the study but also commented extensively on the initial structure of the volume and provided valuable advice on possible contributors. Katsuo Matsushita from Japan was extremely helpful in handling our Asian logistical challenges in the implementation phase, while Dr Marian Małecki secured the skilful coordination of the whole project and the work of numerous authors. Special thanks go to our colleagues at The Geneva Association who supported the project through their kind cooperation. Finally, particular words of appreciation are due to Andrzej Klesyk, CEO of PZU, for his generous institutional support.

Patrick M. Liedtke
Jan Monkiewicz

Acknowledgements

[illegible]

The Future of Insurance Regulation and Supervision

Patrick M. Liedtke and Jan Monkiewicz

Introduction

The last few years were extremely challenging and busy for all those concerned with financial regulation and supervision. These highly sophisticated and apparently esoteric issues suddenly became the subject matter of a heated political debate in public as well as private discussions and actions taken in the midst of the soaring financial crisis. They also seemed to inspire much of the systemic reforms recently undertaken worldwide. This regulatory explosion which always appears after major failures in the existing financial infrastructure that seems to be challenging the existing regulatory paradigms is nothing new. It has happened many times before. The bigger the failure, the more sweeping are the reforms proposed and implemented. The important new element this time is perhaps a global reach of the current considerations indicating a high degree of interdependence of various local solutions and intensity of the debates and actions. This demonstrates how much contemporary economies are interlinked and depend on the health of the financial system, its constituent parts and its regulatory and supervisory framework which is supposed to provide the necessary preconditions to accomplish it.

Most of the ongoing discussion and activities on current and future regulatory and supervisory framework is centred around banks and the banking sector, disregarding other financial intermediaries even though their economic role is quite substantial. The insurance sector alone represents in premium income worldwide over 7% of global GDP and has over 11% of the world financial assets under its management. Its role, however, goes far beyond what the simple financial market indicators suggest and which may in this context be very misleading. It is so because the insurance industry is about risk-taking and pooling, thus providing risk coverage to the interested parties, and not about financial operations aimed at producing some return. The money involved in insurance operations is substantially lower than the economic value of the risk transferred which is behind this money probably on average by a coefficient

1:500 – 1:1,000. It is impossible today to imagine a modern society and economy without having insurance in place. Replacing insurance (that is, collective risk management) with individual prudence (that is, individual risk management) would be much more costly and absolutely inefficient.

This asymmetry in interest about regulatory and supervisory issues in the current discussion to the benefit of banking is well grounded, as it was the banking sector in which the recent crisis exploded and it was the banking industry which recorded most of the losses worldwide and needed so much taxpayers' money to be kept alive.

The result of this asymmetrical focus of interest on banking issues and banking-specific problems is, however, an asymmetrical application of banking-specific concepts and solutions to other parts of the financial systems which, like insurance, performed quite well during the crisis. This might be detrimental to their development prospects and finds no real justification. This also gives the unjustified impression that the only source of regulatory and supervisory wisdom is located in the banking sector. It is true that most of the regulatory and supervisory innovations of the financial industry have so far originated in the banking sector – suffice it to mention deposit insurance, consolidated supervision, the use of supervisory colleges and the like. However, at the same time it was the insurance sector which paved the way for the application of the solvency concept, enterprise risk management and risk-based supervision with the development of the US risk-based capital (RBC) model back in the 1990s. This concept has been successfully applied thereafter in the banking world through Basel principles.

Poor knowledge and understanding of the solutions applied and the specificity of non-banking financial undertakings prevent the proper use of their potential for the benefit of the banking industry.

The insurance companies that make up part of the financial sector community by and large have quite specific properties and have a very distinct business model compared to the banking sector which, due to its complexity, is difficult for outsiders to understand. As a matter of fact, it was thanks mainly to the insurance companies' business model that they performed so well during the last financial crisis. The fundamental elements of this business model encompass up-front financing (reversed production cycle) which permits insurance companies to avoid wholesale funding, long-term contractual relations which stabilise their performance, application of cash outflow mitigating devices, and strict matching of the maturity of assets and liabilities which limits the dangers of liquidity pressure. As a result, the regulatory and supervisory set-up in insurance needs to be tailored to the specific features of this industry and cannot and should not simply copy the solutions worked out for the banking, securities or pension industry, no matter how attractive they look like. What is important is to have the solutions which reflect the way insurance undertakings operate, take into account the products they offer and the risks they are exposed to.

It was with this idea in mind that the present book was conceived. Facing a tsunami of publications on regulatory issues applying banking-specific concepts and proposing banking-relevant solutions, we felt that there is a need to restore some equilibrium into this picture. We strongly believe that there is a need to share with the public thoughts and ideas on the current developments and future challenges in insurance regulation and supervision. Some of these developments and challenges are clearly cross-sectoral in nature. They are affecting banking, securities, pension and insurance companies – think of the issues of market discipline, corporate governance or compensation packages. Some others are completely different. The idea of building up special purpose provisions to address the growing risk of operations and procyclicality phenomena is probably well justified and an innovative solution for banks, but is absolutely wrong for insurers who already apply technical provisions precisely to do this job. Living wills are a sensible idea for some parts of the financial sector and banks in particular; however, they are irrelevant for insurers with the special characteristics of their resolution regimes.

Regulation in the meaning of law-making and supervision in the meaning of monitoring, control and enforcement are two pillars of the public oversight. They are separate in nature but very much dependent on each other in substance. For a long time supervisory and regulatory functions in world insurance practice were attached to the same institutions. However since the 1980s they have become separated. Regulation remained clearly associated with the political structures of the state and thus continues to reflect political perspective and interests, whereas supervision becomes more and more technical in nature. To do its job properly it needs, similar to central banks, to be immune from direct political pressure and influence. However, having said this, we have to note that regulation and supervision are like twins: they have to align with each other. The effects of best regulation may vanish if the supervisory functions are not implemented properly. Therefore the two are treated jointly in their interaction in the subsequent debate in this book.

This book is a collection of chapters prepared by leading experts in the respective fields with expertise frequently difficult to match. Some of them represent the academic community, some others the business and public sectors. They represent a broad variety of experience and come from different parts of the globe, thus reflecting the local perspective. The intention of this book is to offer an analysis of the factors and forces impacting insurance regulation in the coming decade. The financial crisis we are currently going through has produced among other things a whole spectrum of regulatory observations and possible regulatory responses. Most of these proposals until now simply suggested quick recipes to answer the politically timely questions addressed as a rule to some parts of the regulatory system and not to its entirety, thus causing more noise and chaos than clarity. They are also, to a greater extent, locally oriented. Their value is therefore short-lived and limited. Once the dust has settled, most of them will disappear. This book, we hope, is different. First, it concentrates on the strategic and policy-oriented perspectives. Second, it concentrates on issues, problems and challenges rather than on normative prescriptions. It is based on scientific-theoretical grounds instead of managerial or journalistic observations. Third, it is offering a global perspective because we are living today in a globalised world and one cannot disregard it. Of course, one has to take due account of the differences in development levels, social values, cultural heritage, and so on. To do so the book is addressing both global issues as well as providing the major markets perspective, indicating the interaction between the two approaches. Only by interaction between global and local interests and demands might optimal solutions emerge. We know very well by now that solving global regulatory and supervisory issues is both a technical as well as a political task.

Part I

The Global Framework

1
Insurance Activity as a Regulatory Object: Trends and Developments and their Appreciation in the Context of Post-Crisis Global Markets

Patrick M. Liedtke

Introduction

Insuring risks in a modern economy is a multi-dimensional and very complex undertaking. As described in greater detail in a contribution to *The Geneva Papers on Risk and Insurance: Issues and Practice*,[1] it is a highly sophisticated financial business that interacts with many aspects of our lives. The importance of the insurance industry for an economy can only in part be measured by the number of its employees in a given country, the assets under management, or its contribution to the national GDP. It actually plays a more fundamental role in the workings of a modern society, being a necessary precondition for many activities that would not take place were it not for insurance. Insurance is a key component of economic development and an important driver for growth. It should therefore not be surprising that all countries around the world regulate insurance companies rather heavily and have placed the activities in their insurance markets under close supervisory control.

However, even ambitious regulation and tight supervision can fail, as the credit crisis has shown – in this case, especially in the banking sector, but the point is generally valid for all regulated activities. The impact of the problems first arising in the US mortgage sector and then engulfing the banking sectors of most developed and many emerging countries also resulted in an extremely challenging and busy period for all those connected to the insurance industry. And while most insurance managers were busy trying to minimise the impact of the crisis on their business and their clients, those concerned with financial regulation and supervision became hyperactive as well, often driven by policy-makers who were worried that the impact on insurance could be worse than it ultimately turned out to be. Suddenly, highly sophisticated and complex issues became the subject matter of a heated political debate in public as well as private discussions. Key actions taken in the midst of the soaring financial crisis gained in relevancy, especially where they were not only concerned with immediate fire-fighting but meant to make a longer-lasting contribution to more stable and resilient financial systems. The credit crisis and its consequences have doubtless inspired much of the systemic reforms undertaken recently worldwide. This directly provoked a regulatory explosion that seems always to appear after major failures in an existing financial infrastructure. Hence the proactive addressing of problems that seem to be challenging the existing regulatory paradigms is therefore nothing new, even though some observers seem to be surprised at the speed and intensity with which this has and still is occurring. However, we would posit that the bigger the failure, the more sweeping are the reforms proposed and subsequently implemented. Consequently, given that the world was faced with the most devastating financial crisis since the Great Depression, it should not be surprising that we are going to experience a regulatory and supervisory overhaul that will be commensurate with the extraordinary dimension of the crisis.

What might come as a surprise, however, is how the insurance industry has been and is drawn into some regulatory and supervisory discussions where it should play no (or at least a much less prominent) role, as the key problems emanated from other parts of the financial services sector. And it is equally surprising how much insurers are excluded from other discussions where they are very much affected by the outcome but are considered to play no significant role. In this regard, there is something new in the current process, an important new quality to our current endeavours to set the financial services sector right: the global reach of the current considerations. Never before have so many (often sweeping) reforms been undertaken that affect not only the banking sector but also other parts of the financial services sector, such as insurance, the social systems and of course our real economy. The present discussions demonstrate how much contemporary economic systems are interlinked and the high degree to which they depend on the well-being of the financial system, its constituent parts and the regulatory and supervisory framework that is supposed to provide the necessary stable preconditions for its operation.

Insurance as a regulatory object

Insurance markets do not operate independently of the rest of the economy. On the contrary, like traditional horizontal activities such as energy, telecommunications or banking, insurance penetrates the modern economy on many levels. Today, in all advanced and emerging markets, insurance plays a key role in the efficient and sustainable development of the economy, harbouring expertise that is unavailable elsewhere. It is often the precondition for (economic) action, facilitates new ventures and is intertwined with the most basic human needs and aspirations. The availability of insurance has important positive effects and externalities that go far beyond the purely financial. It is not only a tool for addressing the immediate risk assessment and risk management challenges before us; it can also be a powerful mechanism to discover and incentivise the right behaviour.

Due to this strong connection with other parts of the economic system, insurance regulation also depends on regulatory action taken elsewhere. Any significant change in the way a modern economy is set up and governed will have an impact on how the associated activities can be insured or influence relevant parameters that will affect the risk transfer among concerned parties. Regulating general economic issues such as contractual obligations, operating procedures or fiscal aspects for all participants in a modern economy will determine the insurance framework as well. In a similar manner, general financial regulation as a whole affects insurance. When general norms for accounting, auditing, financial reporting or business relations between financial intermediaries are laid down, the insurance industry – barring any special carve-outs – will have to adhere to them as well. As a consequence, insurance regulation can be understood as a subset of the regulation that affects all economic activities and a subset of the general financial services regulation. Figure 1.1 shows this in a stylised way.

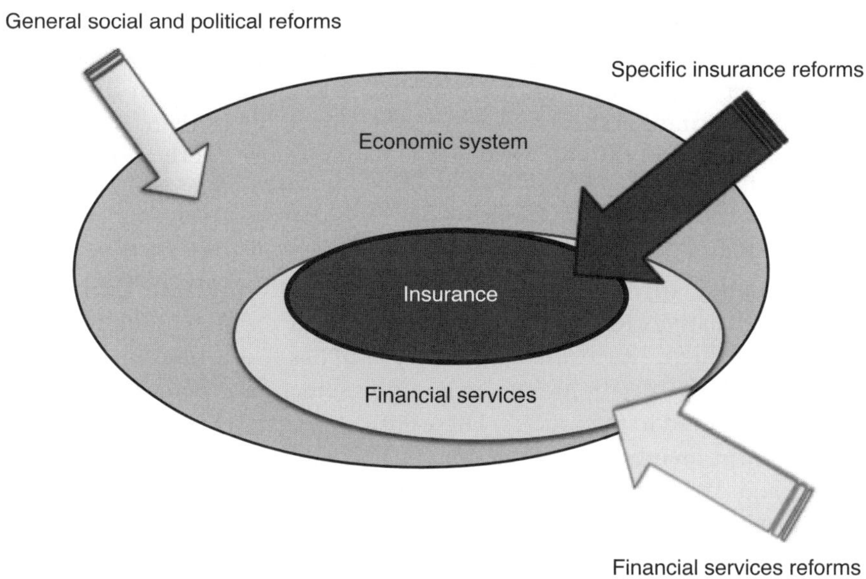

Figure 1.1 Situating insurance and its regulatory environment

This set-up has important consequences for the development of insurance regulation. In order to appreciate the full impact of changes to the way in which the insurance sector will function in the future, it is not enough to exclusively look at the specific changes in insurance regulation. We need to comprehend where societal trends are moving in order to better recognise how the economic system will be influenced in its future development. And we will have to take any general reforms of the financial services sector into account as it will impact the insurance sector, too.

What complicates matters further is the sheer number of institutions that are involved in the process to devise any regulatory reforms that affect the insurance industry. By one unofficial expert count, there are between 350 and 400 entities worldwide that are directly involved in the process – and this does not include any of the bodies that have an indirect impact, such as those setting construction norms that affect the way in which property risks are insured or those devising technical standards that define risk profiles in engineering. But even if there were only half as many, it would still be way too much for a clear and transparent process that would follow the Skipper-Klein principles mentioned later on in this chapter. Just making oneself familiar with all the proposals, calls for comments, draft papers and White Papers, consultations, discussions and proposals is bordering on the impossible, and any interested party constantly risks missing out on a pertinent element or being surprised by some new development.

This is not made easier by a high degree of interdependence of various local solutions that are discussed in a different environment than the international ones. There is a constant balancing act between what is happening on a national level and what happens on an international, read global, one. In the case of the European Union, matters are even more convoluted as there is a layer of (limited) regional authority in between the nation states and their sovereignty and the truly international fora. The current intensity of the debates and the sometimes fierce reactions to certain proposals are explained by this additional element of stress.

Unfortunately, this multitude of institutions not only exists on the side producing initiatives for insurance-related reforms – which alone would be challenging enough. The insurance industry itself has also created an impressive number of trade associations, expert groupings, technical bodies, and so on, that all are involved in the process. These entities are often overlapping in their mission and/or membership, sometimes even rivalling in their goals and are often enough no more than loosely cooperating. The result is a challenging environment in which a cacophony of voices is the rule rather than the exception.

The rationale behind insurance regulation

So what is the rationale behind the regulation of insurance activities and why do we need to regulate them in the first place? There are many excellent articles on the basic principles of insurance regulation, and the International Association of Insurance Supervisors (IAIS) and its national members habitually put out papers in which they justify the interference in what would otherwise be free markets.[2] The short answer to the above question is that regulators want to ensure competitive, solvent and fair markets in which all key stakeholders are adequately protected. To achieve this, a fine balancing act is necessary: the various objectives have to be pursued in such a way that risk transfers can take place in an efficient way and that access to risk transfer markets is open to interested parties. Regulators should ensure that quality, reasonably-priced products and services are available from reliable insurers.

During the financial crisis, solvency considerations for insurers became an issue that had many financial supervisors deeply unsettled. The collapse first of Lehman Brothers and then AIG[3] had them worried about the resilience of the financial system and its key constituents. For the insurance industry, AIG – long heralded as the world's largest insurer despite its true operations as a financial conglomerate and its aggressive and ultimately fateful risk-taking on the non-insurance side – became the showcase on how close insurance was to the centre of the problems in the banking sector. It was and remains to this day a key reference point for financial regulators when they consider new actions to regulate especially large internationally active entities. One therefore has to understand that the current wave of regulation is driven chiefly – as is to be expected and true to most regulatory waves preceding it – by the latest experiences from the financial crisis.[4]

There are some additional basic aspects that can further help situating the current reform debates. First is the desire of all relevant stakeholders not to be caught off guard again. This applies not only to the regulators and supervisors and their political masters but also to the insurance industry, with its clients, its investors and bond-holders, and many business partners. All these parties generate a lot of energy to put things right. However, their interests are not always fully aligned and are sometimes even openly opposed. While supervisors would strive for more solvency capital to better protect insurers against mishaps, the companies might regard too high a solvency ratio as detrimental to their profit-generation capacity. While clients appreciate capital buffers for their added layer of protection, they do not like paying higher insurance premiums to finance them. While policy-makers like to set frameworks under which many insurance products are available to many parties, supervisors do not always appreciate complexity and convolution in the marketplace as it makes their job more difficult.

It is obvious that every new wave of regulation produces winners and losers, hence competition among the parties concerned is fierce. This competition takes place not only among insurance companies of differing types, sometimes pitting large against small, specialist against generalist, national against international, or mutuals against publicly traded companies. The competition also occurs among supervisors who want to be seen in control of things, especially following some of the more spectacular failures that occurred during the credit crisis. Regulators and policy-makers vie for attention and have to be careful not to engage in a competition for who comes up with the most punishing rules. And for politicians this is a chance to shine, to build more political capital and maybe even to get an important reform project named after them, thus receiving the public recognition so important for winning the next election. In consequence, activism rather than cool objectivity is a constant danger and the objective of properly conceived regulation becomes entangled in special interests and cluttered with ulterior motives.[5]

In their 1999 paper,[6] Skipper and Klein came up with a set of principles that insurance regulation should follow: adequacy, impartiality, minimal intrusiveness, and transparency. It is hard enough for regulators to meticulously follow these principles at the best of times. In the current environment, it would be very naive to assume that they will not be at least partially violated in the process of dealing with the aftermath of the crisis and preparing a new framework under which financial services and insurance companies in particular will operate.

Regulatory debates in a complex environment

An added complexity for new regulatory initiatives arises from the fact that the financial sector is very heterogeneous. This is true not only regarding the difference in business models between banks, insurers and other financial intermediaries. It applies equally to differences in national regulatory and supervisory approaches that are quite dissimilar even among highly developed economies, not to mention the gulf between them and emerging markets or the least developed countries. Also, the insurance world itself is home to very distinct approaches to dealing with risks; notice the variation in methodologies employed and instruments used by life companies and non-life companies. And then there are different organisational set-ups, such as publicly traded companies that have dissimilar funding, and governance structures to mutual companies where the policy-holders are the owners of the operation.

The problem here resides chiefly in two areas. One is that the complexity of such a heterogeneous population of entities to be regulated and then properly supervised requires a very deep appreciation of the differences. It then demands a high sophistication when it comes to drafting and implementing new rules so that any unintended consequences can be minimised. The other is that it almost forbids the use of 'one-size-fits-all' approaches and the extension of rules designed for one specific part of the financial services sector to all (any) others. This results in much more complicated and lengthy processes for regulatory initiatives than many regulators and policy-makers would like. Indeed, it seems to run counter to the natural reaction of politicians to address problems swiftly and in a comprehensive way. It also requires more substantial communications efforts to ensure broader support for reforms. The more complex the reform, the more difficult it is to sell to voters and to convince the affected constituents that it is in their best interest.

In the current context, this sets the bar very high, especially for the insurance sector that cannot rely on a large population that is familiar with its complex business.[7] This puts insurance at a disadvantage as the risk of misinterpretation, misunderstanding and just plain confusion during any key discussion about the future rules and norms that should (and also those that should not) be applied to its business is a significant factor. Ceteris paribus this has to lead to suboptimal solutions. The insurance industry is very concerned about this issue and The Geneva Association has pointed it out many times.[8]

The institutional way forward on a global scale

In the following sections, the three most relevant institutions that are determining the longer-term future of insurance regulation will be discussed: the International Association of Insurance Supervisors (IAIS), the Group of Twenty (G20) and the Financial Stability Board (FSB).

The IAIS

Despite the fact that there are so many institutions actively involved in setting the pace of the current and coming reforms, there are some institutions that from a global perspective have more weight and/or impact than others. In terms of direct insurance regulation and supervision, the IAIS plays the central role. The organisation was established in 1994 and represents insurance regulators and supervisors of some 190 jurisdictions in over 130 countries, constituting over 95% of the world's insurance premiums. Its key 'objectives are to:

- cooperate to contribute to improved supervision of the insurance industry on a domestic as well as on an international level in order to maintain efficient, fair, safe and stable insurance markets for the benefit and protection of policyholders
- promote the development of well-regulated insurance markets [and]
- contribute to global financial stability.'[9]

The last point only recently entered the central brief of the IAIS at a high level and is a reflex of the experience of the credit crisis as well as the push of the political masters behind the IAIS to strengthen its role in this respect.

The IAIS is fully involved in all relevant discussions about the future regulatory framework under which the industry operates. Through its more than 120 observers and open hearings it interfaces closely with the insurance industry.

However, it lacks the real power of a true standard-setter in the sense that it can only describe best practices and provide key principles, known as Insurance Core Principles (ICPs), for the regulation and supervision of insurance markets. It can neither push through binding agreements nor enforce the application of its standards in the home markets of its members. Despite this limitation, it has a de facto influence of very significant proportions and is the key insurance supervisory body that represents insurance expertise in the Joint Forum, the FSB and other relevant international bodies that deal with financial issues. The IAIS is also central for bringing together the key national authorities that exert direct control over the industry and it sets the agenda for the development of regulatory developments in insurance on the international level.

The ICPs act as the benchmark for any insurance supervisory regimes and, according to the IAIS, should be used when establishing a supervisory regime or for identifying areas in existing regimes that need to be improved. There are currently 28 essential principles which are organised under seven distinct categories: (1) conditions for effective insurance supervision; (2) the supervisory system; (3) the supervised entity; (4) ongoing supervision; (5) prudential requirements; (6) markets and consumers; and (7) anti-money laundering and combating the financing of terrorism.[10] The following paragraph from the ICPs document is noteworthy as it underlines the close connection between insurance regulation and larger financial services concerns: 'Public authorities concerned with issues of financial stability are urged to provide the necessary support to the supervisory authority so that it can meet the principles and the criteria set out herein.'[11] It also bears testimony to the anxiety of IAIS members to secure the necessary resources to carry out their tasks.

The G20

From a political point of view, the most important current source for international regulatory initiatives is the G20. The G20 is a self-organised group consisting of the finance ministers and central bank governors from 19 countries plus a special seat in the European Union. It describes itself as:

> the premier forum for our international economic development that promotes open and constructive discussion between industrial and emerging-market countries on key issues related to global economic stability. By contributing to the strengthening of the international financial architecture and providing opportunities for dialogue on national policies, international co-operation, and international financial institutions, the G-20 helps to support growth and development across the globe.[12]

The members of the G20 represent about two-thirds of the world's population and approximately 85% of global national product.

The G20 was originally created as a response to the financial crises of the late 1990s. A key motivating factor was the growing recognition that key emerging-market countries with increasing global economic and financial relevance were not adequately included in the core of global economic discussion and governance. Following the full eruption of the credit crisis in 2008, it was the forum of choice for the leaders of the largest economies around the world (both developed and developing) to tackle the problems that the crisis created. The members wanted to strengthen international cooperation in the face of the largest financial emergency since the Great Depression. In the process, the G20 has become the source of many important concerted actions comprising a wide array of measures, such as the introduction of unprecedented expansionary macroeconomic policies in member countries, the push for significant enhancements of international financial regulation (mostly concerning banking but also affecting the wider financial services sector), and the expansion of resources to strengthen the international financial institutions. One key step was the transformation of the Financial Stability Forum (FSF) into the Financial Stability Board (FSB), which is discussed in the next section.

Today, the G20 acts as a key source and driver of a new wave of regulation in the international sphere that is relevant to many countries beyond the 20 members. And although to date no major projects have seen full implementation in all Member States, many highly relevant projects exist where broad international agreement has already been reached, such as: dealing with tax havens/non-cooperative jurisdictions (cf. the Global Forum on Transparency and the Exchange of Information), new compensation rules (FSB Principles, national legislation), the establishment of macro-prudential watchdogs (the European Systemic Risk Board (ESRB), the FSB), the overhaul of capital requirements (Basel III, Solvency II), the creation of a global liquidity standard (liquidity coverage ratio), the market infrastructure for derivative contracts (central counterparty clearing, (CCP)) and the regulation of rating agencies (International Organization of Securities Commissions (IOSCO) code of conduct, EU regulation on credit rating agencies). Further projects are aimed at improving the current status quo but still require some more development; they include: the introduction of counter-cyclical capital buffers, resolution regimes for large banks ('too big to fail'), further development of accounting rules (International Financial Reporting Standards (IFRS) 9, IFRS 4 Phase II), deeper and more comprehensive bank regulation (contingent capital, capital surcharge), special hedge fund regulations (Alternative Investment Fund Managers Directive (AIFMD), Dodd-Frank Act), and fees and levies such as the financial crisis responsibility fee or bank levy.[13]

The G20 is without doubt very important, but it has two potential weaknesses with regards to its future development: First, it has no specific democratic legitimisation beyond the decision of its members to cooperate and there is no objective and widely accepted mechanism to decide on who should be allowed to participate in the group. Second, now that the credit crisis seems to have evolved out of its most threatening phase, the interests of its members in the post-crisis setting are starting to diverge. As long as the common menace of a global collapse of the world's financial system united the members in their efforts and concentrated the minds of those that had to take the key decisions on a common goal, cooperation was easier. It will be interesting to see how the G20 will develop in the future, as the global financial markets and the world economy are in need of a body that takes the lead in determining under what rules nation states and the different markets can and should collaborate.[14] In any case, for the present and the immediate future, anyone trying to understand where the regulatory discussions are heading will have to pay close attention to the G20 and its initiatives.

The FSB

In the area of financial services regulation, there are many very relevant bodies, but one of them has become the central focal point for overcoming the problems linked to the credit crisis: the FSB. The FSB, established in April 2009, is the successor organisation to the Financial Stability Forum (FSF) which itself dates back to 1999. As a consequence of the spectacular failure of the previous set-up of global financial market regulation and supervision, the realisation of the disastrous shortcomings of the former system of financial cooperation among the large economies and in particular among the banking sector supervisory authorities, and in the face of an inability to deal adequately with financial systemic risk on a global level, the leaders of the G20 countries called for a larger membership of the FSF in November 2008. As the FSB writes,

> A broad consensus emerged in the following months towards placing the FSF on stronger institutional ground with an expanded membership – to strengthen its effectiveness as a mechanism for national authorities, standard setting bodies and international financial institutions to address vulnerabilities and to develop and implement strong regulatory, supervisory and other policies in the interest of financial stability.[15]

Today, the FSB brings together three groups of experts on international financial matters: (a) national authorities responsible for financial stability in significant international financial centres, namely treasuries, central banks, and supervisory agencies; (b) sector-specific international groupings of regulators and supervisors engaged in developing standards and codes of good practice as well as the international financial institutions charged with surveillance of domestic and international financial systems and monitoring and fostering implementation of standards; and (c) the committees of central bank experts concerned with market infrastructure and functioning. Together they aim to address vulnerabilities in the global financial system and to develop and implement strong regulatory, supervisory and other policies in the interest of financial stability.

However, from an insurance point of view it is disappointing that this body, which should cover all parts of the global financial system in a comprehensive way, has incorporated only very limited insurance expertise in its structure. While all member countries send general finance experts from their finance ministries (who usually have a strong banking and sometimes securities background, but mostly lack specific insurance expertise), from the supervisory authorities tasked to look after the whole financial services sector (again, most experts have a banking or securities background and generally much less training in and exposure to insurance) and from their central banks (exclusively concentrated on banking issues and not insurance), there is only one specialised body in insurance that sends its chairman to the FSB; this is the IAIS. None of the six members that form the subgroup of 'international organisations' and none of the other five members that, besides the IAIS, form the member subgroup of 'international standard-setting bodies and other groupings' has any specialised in-depth expertise when it comes to insurance matters.[16] This is surprising as insurance holds approximately 11% of world assets and accounts for 7% of world GDP.[17]

From a strictly systemic risk point of view, one can understand the decision of the G20 and the FSB to react in a way that could be understood as benign neglect towards insurance. After all, insurance was not at the source of the financial crisis,[18] nor do core insurance activities represent sources for systemic risk to the global financial system.[19] However, in terms of how the expert discussions on financial stability and future organisation of systemic risk develop, the lack of a wider base of insurance expertise at the FSB is a concern. It is a concern for the insurance sector – supervisors, industry and markets participants alike – in two distinct ways: one is that the role of insurance companies that can act as stabilisers in many distress scenarios for financial markets is at risk of not being taken sufficiently into account. The questions as to when insurers stabilise financial markets and when they might act as multipliers of potentially destabilising developments require deep familiarity with the complex insurance business.[20] The other is that it is more likely that without adequate insurance expertise present, FSB discussions that apply strictly to banking or securities issues suddenly start influencing insurance markets in a way that nobody took into consideration properly at the outset. This would be an unnecessary contamination risk, potentially spreading a problematic situation (or even some negative effects of a well-intended solution) to the insurance sector.

So while the FSB is trying to tackle many important issues connected with financial stability, it also has to remedy an institutional shortcoming as regards the proper representation of insurance. Going forward, it will be crucial to ensure that any initiatives for financial stability have the intended effects for all relevant market participants and all financial intermediaries and are not just geared towards the needs and requirements of banks and their specific operations. Insurance regulators, supervisors and the industry must strive to advise the FSB as best as possible in its work to minimise any danger of it devising inferior or even deficient solutions.

Key aspects to watch

The following is a list of key aspects that need to be watched carefully, as each point will have a major impact on how the regulation of financial services in general and insurance in particular will develop. Insurance as a regulatory object is strictly dependent on which setting it is carried out in and under what conditions the discussions are organised that lead to future rules and norms that define how markets are structured and the framework under which insurance companies operate. We would posit that the following key issues are of special relevance in this context:

1. *The crisis has made everybody more aware of true globalisation and its consequences.* While for several decades following the Second World War the global interaction of businesses has readily increased and the openness of national economies[21] has grown, the term 'globalisation' came to describe a new phenomenon of tight integration of markets on the world level and the appearance of global companies with production facilities and service centres in many different countries. What has not followed in an equally dynamic manner are the governance structures on the world level needed to direct globalising economies and the political and civil institutions required to accompany them. Both are needed in order to provide the same stable framework that has characterised the national (and some regional) approaches for market-oriented systems. Following the credit crisis, there is a new and stronger awareness that an overhaul of global governance – at least as far as economic and financial markets are concerned – is urgently needed.
2. *Neoclassical capitalism and the Anglo-Saxon financial hegemony are questioned.* For several decades, mainstream economic thinking has been strongly influenced by neoclassical economic theories and their derivatives. The most dynamic economic and financial developments resulted from a set of paradigms that are now being scrutinised in ever more detail in order to discover more possible shortcomings than the ones that led to the most recent crisis. The impacts of behavioural economics and other more progressive theories have begun to exert a direct influence on how the current generation of policy-makers regard market performance, efficiency, resilience and limitations. Together with the increased relevance of emerging markets for the world economy, this is expected to lead to a (somewhat) reduced importance of the financial centres in the Anglo-Saxon world.

3. *A new focus for national and international policies, and a binding of resources.* The near collapse of the world's financial system in October 2008 led to an immediate shift in attention of all major governments. Following the rescue actions, the question on how to deal with financial stability and systemic risk became the central concern for all G20 countries. This has led to a crowding out of other issues, such as climate change, trade negotiations, and so on. While one would expect that the less threatening the situation in the world financial markets appears, the more energy will be available again for other projects, it is obvious that the challenges for safeguarding the global financial system against future threats will require many years of unrelenting effort to produce acceptable solutions. Until this is achieved, the challenges for financial stability and systemic risk will require constant attention and hence reduce the capacity of all involved governments to take on other projects at the same time. In addition, there will have to be a continued and sustained struggle against any potentially appearing tendencies for protectionism as some countries could try to isolate their economy from financial havoc happening elsewhere through inappropriate measures, which would have a detrimental effect on world trade and future growth. This will also bind resources which are then not available for other initiatives.
4. *The creation of new, or revamping of current, institutions to deal with financial stability*. Although a lot has already happened in this respect (for example, the establishment of the G20 and the reorganisation of the FSF into the FSB), more activity is expected. In many countries and regions around the world, governments are getting ready to establish systemic risk councils and boards that are going to be tasked with regional or local financial stability monitoring. Other organisations such as the International Monetary Fund or the World Bank are adapting their operations to be more useful in the future to avoid financial instability and to combat it whenever it might appear. This will ultimately lead to an institutional landscape that will be very different from what was in place before the credit crisis. It will also have an influence on how and where key decisions for the world financial markets will be taken and what kind of regulation and supervision will be applied to financial institutions and, of course, insurers.
5. *International reform projects pushing national agendas*. As has been evident over the past two years, it is increasingly an international agenda that drives national agendas for regulation and supervision, rather than the other way around. The G20 as a key source for regulatory projects and a driver of institutional change has clearly established an international platform that directs the focus of national governments. Reform projects such as Basel III, Solvency II (which is increasingly not only a European project but growing into an international benchmark) or International Financial Reporting Standards reforms have not only a global quality to them but also establish

a mechanism of the international influencing and determining the national. As the trend of first conducting key discussions about regulatory reforms in international fora continues, it will have increasing consequences for the economic and political environments in all countries.

6. *A higher relevance of politicians and public servants for economic issues*. With laissez-faire capitalism (that postulated minimal governmental intervention and a soft touch for regulation and supervision as key principles) coming to an end, a new group of persons will require more relevance: government officials. As central banks have greatly increased their balance sheets, as governments and their agencies have massively augmented their debt burden, as regulators and supervisors are vying for more control over the financial and economic systems, the officials in control of these institutions all exert more direct control over markets. Many decisions that will be taken by policy-makers and public servants now have a more immediate impact on the economy and, following the new wave of regulation, this is set to increase. Market participants will have to pay closer attention to these decisions, to who takes them and why, and to how they will possibly affect the markets in which they are active.

Conclusion

As we noted at the beginning of this chapter, insurance activities are crucial to the proper functioning of modern economies. These activities are now conducted in an environment that is changing in a very dynamic way as new reform projects come online, new institutions are established and existing bodies take on different functions or develop additional responsibilities. For the whole sector it will be a constant challenge to ensure that it is fully informed about any discussions that will significantly affect its operations – even if these discussions take place outside the traditional bodies that are normally associated with the sector; that its expertise is adequately represented and listened to – even if this means that insurance expertise has to actively promote its place at the table; and that the capacity to digest the changes being mandated remains at all times sufficient.

Notes

1. See Liedtke (2007).
2. The IAIS sets out principles that are fundamental to effective insurance supervision. Principles identify areas in which the insurance supervisor should have authority or control and form the basis on which standards are developed. The latest version of the core principles is available from the IAIS website, www.iaisweb.org. The IAIS also publishes guidance papers on insurance regulation and supervision and many technical documents.
3. For further information on the AIG rescue see United States Government Accountability Office (2009).

4. It is especially instructive to read the Dodd-Frank Wall Street Reform and Consumer Protection Act, which was introduced and later signed into law in July 2010 as 'An Act to promote the financial stability of the United States by improving accountability and transparency in the financial system, to end "too big to fail", to protect the American taxpayer by ending bailouts, to protect consumers from abusive financial services practices, and for other purposes.' A comprehensive summary of this act can be found at http://banking.senate.gov/public/_files/070110_Dodd_Frank_Wall_Street_Reform_comprehensive_summary_Final.pdf
5. James Schiro, for example, writes: 'The process of designing new regulation is not always perfect. Too often regulators react to political pressure or regulation emerges through litigation and not in response to sound economic criteria' (Schiro, 2006).
6. See Skipper and Klein (1999).
7. Many insurance trade associations around the world have as one of their briefs to educate policy-makers and the wider public about insurance issues. Especially active and well-developed on the consumer side is the Insurance Information Institute in the US; see www.iii.org.

   Since the credit crisis highlighted in an especially drastic way the problems associated with a lack of proper understanding of the complexities of insurance operations even by regulatory and supervisory authorities for the financial sector, The Geneva Association (www.genevaassociation.org) has made a special effort to address this issue. It now provides more papers, analytical studies, reports and other texts in order to raise the quality of the most relevant discussions about insurance issues that influence the framework of insurance markets. For creating efficient and resilient markets it is vital that public policy-makers fully understand the unique role played by insurers in managing risk, the issues affecting the industry, both from financial and market conditions, and the special nature of insurance regulation.
8. See the various newsletters of The Geneva Association on regulation and supervision, called PROGRES, or the ones published by its Insurance and Finance Programme. All available from www.genevaassociation.org
9. See the mission of the IAIS, www.iaisweb.org
10. IAIS Insurance Core Principles and Methodology of October 2003, cited as per latest available modified version of 7 March 2007, downloadable from www.iaisweb.org/view/element_href.cfm?src=1/94.pdf
11. Ibid.
12. See the mandate of the G20, www.g20.org/about_what_is_g20.aspx
13. For more detailed information, see the current projects on the G20 website.
14. For some, the International Monetary Fund (IMF), founded in 1945 and comprising more than 180 members, would be a more appropriate international body to steer global economic and financial affairs. However, at this time it is clearly the G20 which is the source of most initiatives to deal with the economic and financial problems on the global level. Depending on how both the G20 and the IMF develop, the prominent role of the G20 could diminish in favour of the IMF, or maybe even a third body.
15. www.financialstabilityboard.org/about/history.htm
16. Compare the list of member institutions of the FSB, www.financialstabilityboard.org/members/links.htm
17. For a detailed statistic on world insurance premium income see Swiss Re (2010).
18. The role of insurance and how it fared through the credit crisis is extensively discussed in Liedtke (2010). Downloadable from www.genevaassociation.org/PDF/Geneva_Reports/GA-2010-Geneva_report[3].pdf

19. For a detailed discussion of this issue see The Geneva Association (2010). Downloadable from http://www.genevaassociation.org/PDF/BookandMonographs/Geneva_Association_Systemic_Risk_in_Insurance_Report_March2010.pdf

    The IAIS wrote in its position statement on key financial stability issues of 4 June 2010 that 'there is little evidence of insurance either generating or amplifying systemic risk, within the financial system itself or in the real economy'. Downloadable from www.iaisweb.org/view/element_href.cfm?src=1/9364.pdf
20. According to the IAIS (2010), 'There are also some circumstances where insurers may amplify risk, for example life insurers reacting to downturns in equity markets, or where they may disrupt for a period a segment of the real economy through an unexpected withdrawal of capacity.' However, the IAIS also insists that 'An effective regime of regulation and supervision can mitigate these possibilities', which is why appropriate specialised insurance expertise is so important.
21. The openness of an economy is defined as imports plus exports divided by (twice) the GDP of the economy. According to OECD (Organisation for Economic Cooperation and Development) figures, this measure has increased for almost all nations over the past 50 years.

Bibliography

Baltensperger, E. et al. (2008) 'Regulation and Intervention in the Insurance Industry – Fundamental Issues', *Geneva Report* no. 1, February.

Ferro, G. (2010) 'Insurance Regulation and the Credit Crisis. What's new?' UADE and CONICET paper, February.

FSB (2010) 'The History of the FSB', www.financialstabilityboard.org/about/history.htm

G-20 (2010) 'The Mandate of the G20', www.g20.org/about_what_is_g20.aspx

IAIS (2003) 'Insurance Core Principles and Methodology of October 2003', 7 March 2007.

IAIS (2010) 'Position Statement on Key Financial Stability Issues', 4 June.

Liedtke, P. (2007) 'What's Insurance to a Modern Economy?', *The Geneva Papers on Risk and Insurance: Issues and Practice*, 32(2).

Liedtke, P. (2010) 'Anatomy of the Credit Crisis – An Insurance Reader', *Geneva Report* no. 3, January.

Schiro, J. (2006) 'External Forces Impacting the Insurance Industry: Threats from Regulation', *The Geneva Papers on Risk and Insurance: Issues and Practice*, 31(1).

Skipper, H., and R. Klein (1999) 'Insurance Regulation in the Public Interest: The Path Towards Solvent, Competitive Markets'. Paper prepared for the Coordinating Committee on International Insurance Issues Coalition of Service Industries, Center for Risk Management and Insurance Research, Georgia State University.

Swiss Re (2010) 'World Insurance in 2009', *sigma* no. 2/2010.

The Geneva Association (various years) PROGRES Newsletters on regulation and supervision (several issues) and Insurance and Finance Newsletters (several issues).

The Geneva Association (2010) 'Systemic Risk in Insurance – An Analysis of Insurance and Financial Stability'.

United States Government (2010) Dodd-Frank Wall Street Reform and Consumer Protection Act, signed into law in July 2010.

United States Government Accountability Office (2009) 'Federal Financial Assistance – Preliminary Observations on Assistance Provided to AIG', GAO-09-490T, March.

Van Rossum, A. (2005) 'Regulation and Insurance Economics', *The Geneva Papers on Risk and Insurance: Issues and Practice*, 30(1).

World Bank and IMF (2005) *Financial Sector Assessment – A Handbook.*

2
The Economic Rationale for Insurance Regulation

W. Jean Kwon

Market imperfections and societal risk management

Like individuals and businesses, governments attempt to maximise their welfare.[1] They commonly set guidelines and regulations to lead and control, respectively, individual or business behaviours and to lead their economic activities so that they in the aggregate help the government achieve societal welfare goals. Achieving the goals, however, does not necessarily mean that government helps its citizens maximise their own welfare. It is because citizens have their own preferences and utility functions. For example, one may believe that introduction of the mandatory public pension programme does society good, but what his or her neighbour believes and the neighbour's right often differ. Because of this and other types of differences in individual preferences, coupled with other reasons discussed in this chapter, there is no such thing as a *societal* utility function.

We find an alternative from economic theory. Efficient allocation of resources suggests that citizens should undertake risk management and other activities as long as the marginal benefit is greater than the marginal cost of each activity.[2] Theory suggests that the law of supply and demand is desirably the only one governing capital market operations. It would be so if the market were perfectly competitive.

As per gauging (marginal) benefits at the societal level, we can employ the concept of 'willingness to pay' (WTP).[3] This concept generally relies on market prices. Are you willing to pay the £100 price of a fine art exhibition? If you are, presumably you have concluded that the benefits of attending the exhibition exceed the ticket price. If not, the price is 'too high' considering the benefits. On its face, this approach seems reasonable. However, two issues arise despite the universal attempt to markets as competitive as possible.[4]

The first is the issue of fairness and social justice. For example, what if you are a poor citizen for whom £100 spent on the ticket means that you must eat bread and peanut butter for a week? What if you are rich and do not need to sacrifice your appetite for quality food to attend the exhibition? One may conclude that it is 'fair' to ration art exhibition tickets based on the WTP doctrine. What if it is healthcare that is being rationed based on the same doctrine? Should only rich citizens have access to healthcare? In the competitive (Pareto efficient) market, society's scarce resources are allocated such that no one in society can be made better off without making someone else worse off. However, society (government) may not necessarily prefer a Pareto efficient allocation of its resources if it results in some people having no access to a necessity, for example, universal health insurance, public education and public assistance.

Governments universally pursue concepts of fairness. Economics offer little support for these issues except when they involve externalities. Social justice and compassion and other noneconomic factors also play a role. People generally agree that efforts should be made to rectify extreme inequality of wealth or opportunity. Nevertheless, there is much less agreement as to what constitutes 'fair' and to the extent to which greater equality needs to be pursued for its own sake. These issues are complex because they are intertwined with culture and social values, which are not only abstract but also dynamic.

The second issue relates to the rigorous conditions required of the efficiency model in making decisions at the societal level. In economics, we evaluate tradeoffs using the concept of opportunity cost. For example, would you spend £5,000 for the additional cost for a hybrid car for better fuel efficiency or invest the same amount for better retirement life? The market says, in effect, that both options carry an equal value and the cost to society of each option is identical. But is this really correct? What if the car manufacturer managed to secure permission to hold the factory nearby an ecologically sensitive wilderness area? The production process can result in the destruction of wildlife and the pollution of the grounds and nearby streams. The £5,000 price of the hybrid model does not necessarily include the cost of preserving the delicate environment and making right any damages done by the manufacturer; that is, the opportunity cost of the hybrid car is higher than its price. Thus, besides the direct costs for manufacturing vehicles, the manufacturer is imposing costs on other people and society for which they pay nothing. In reality, market prices of some goods and services are below what they would be if all opportunity costs were included. With the price too low, more will be produced and sold, hence imposing even more costs on others and society and using more of society's scarce resources than is justified.

Market imperfections

Market imperfections reduce societal welfare and can greatly affect the quality of the decisions that the government makes to manage risk. We group the causes of market imperfections into: market power, externalities, free-rider problems and information problems.

Market power

Several conditions can give rise to market power – the ability of one or a few suppliers or buyers to influence the price of a product or service. Governmentally created barriers to entry, economies of scale and product differentiation/price discrimination often create monopolistic or oligopolistic markets. In fact, most market power is facilitated by government actions. In financial services, for example, governments commonly impose national licensing requirements (an entry barrier), such as minimum capitalisation, fitness qualifications and, in some jurisdictions, detailed operating plans. Governments also tend to govern when and how insurance companies can be dissolved (an exit barrier). Problems of market power could thus be alleviated by reducing government intervention.

Economies of scale – another entry barrier – can afford a firm market power. In the market with scale economy effects, the larger the entity the more efficiently it can operate, thus putting new entrants at an immediate competitive disadvantage. Of course, whether a firm possesses market power from scale economies depends on its size relative to its market. Even a monopolist or oligopolist is unable to exercise market power in a contestable market because entry barriers are low and exit is easy in the market. In such a market, the mere threat of competition from possible new entrants may be sufficient to cause existing firms to behave as if the market were competitive.

Product differentiation occurs when one firm's goods are preferred by some consumers over its competitors'. All other factors held constant, insurers in a freer market are likely to differentiate their products based on product quality, service, location, reputation or other effective attributes. In a stringently regulated market (for instance, a market where a substantially large number of insurers produce similar but not identical products), they are likely to engage in monopolistic competition, thus wishing the ability to influence price. When firms offer identical products at different prices to different groups of customers, we observe price discrimination. Generally, governments prohibit price discrimination in insurance markets unless insurers justify price differences statistically.

Externalities

We have already dealt with a case (the hybrid car manufacturer) involving an externality – the benefit or cost observed when production or consumption of a particular good has direct and uncompensated effects on others and society. Externalities can be positive or negative. Societal risk management is particularly concerned about negative externalities. With negative externalities, the price can be lower than the true economic costs of production, too much of the good or service are produced or consumed, and too little effort and resources are devoted to correcting or reducing the externality. Conversely, with positive externalities, the price becomes too high, too little of the good or service is produced or consumed, and too little effort and resources are devoted to enhancing the externality. All other things being equal, we observe more frequently problems of negative externality when property rights are not well established or widely dispersed, thus precluding effective actions by citizens against the wrongdoer.[5] Government action is often required to minimise or solve the problems.

Free-rider problems

Some public goods – products and services that the public collectively consume – carry extensive positive externalities. A public good is what the public collectively consume and carries the attribute of non-rival consumption – one person's consumption of the good does not reduce its availability to others. When such products and services are available to others at low or no cost, they can bring about a free-rider problem. Left to itself, a competitive market is not likely to provide as much public goods as society wants. Government action – for example, taxation – is often required to solve the problem.

Information problems

Information problems occur when consumers or suppliers lack sufficient information to make an informed purchase or sales decision, respectively. When we purchase goods, we commonly do so largely on good faith, not as truly informed buyers.[6] We hope that some agency (usually the government) monitors the transactions to protect our interests and rights. Thus, markets that suffer information problems often are regulated, especially if the goods involved are important elements of our lives or the economy.

Information problems can be classified broadly into asymmetric information and non-existent information. Problems of asymmetric information can be further classified into:

- the so-called 'lemons' problem (the buyer knowing less than the seller about the seller's product or service);
- the agency problem (the buyer knowing less about the agent's actions than the agent);
- the adverse selection problem (the seller knowing less than the buyer about the buyer's situation); and
- the moral hazard problem (the propensity of one party of a contract altering its behaviour when risk is transferred to the other party).

An obvious solution is minimising, desirably eliminating, any information gap in business transactions. Contrary to the costless information assumption of the competitive market model, it costs to secure more thorough information in the real market. Tradeoffs are thus inevitable between the marginal cost incurred to become better informed and the additional cost inherent in making decisions with less information. Government actions are required when consumption of certain goods affects the public or the economy.

In many instances, the desired, complete information simply is unattainable. This kind of uncertainty leads citizens to take alleviating actions intended to reduce their exposure to the risk. Environmental factors – such as inflation and new laws – indeed present great uncertainty to the public and can render their decision-making suboptimal. Some citizens are so completely ill informed – for example, planning for financial security – that they will not or cannot protect their own best interests. Government actions are called for the creation of various safety nets for the citizens in the market.

As alluded to above, market imperfections can and do result in prices not reflecting the true economic costs. This finding suggests that no society should rely exclusively on competition to ensure adequate management of societal risk. Not surprisingly, governments have introduced scores of laws, regulations, guidelines and standards to ameliorate problems related to market imperfections. We also reiterate here that social benefits and costs often do not align with private benefits and costs. When this misalignment is substantial, society has economic justification for interfering in private decisions.

Regulation of private-sector financial services

The preceding section was mainly related to 'social regulation' and government intervention at the societal level. In this section, we focus on 'economic regulation', especially in insurance and other financial services.[7]

Private financial institutions sell a wide array of services. They are also financial intermediaries as they bring together providers and users of funds. Insurance companies (inclusive of those in the reinsurance market), depository institutions and securities firms comprise the three leading classes in the financial intermediation market.[8] Other types of institutions also exist. There are mutual funds and pension funds, which are more specialised, often large intermediaries. There is a range of other, often smaller, specialised intermediaries – such as finance companies, real estate investment trusts and mortgage companies.

We summarise below the role and importance of each type of these financial institutions.

- Insurance companies specialize in selling individuals and businesses contingent claim contracts that are payable to the contract holder (or its designee) upon the occurrence of a covered loss event. Particularly, life insurance products worldwide increasingly embed savings or investment elements on top of the traditional payment assurance of a fixed or variable sum in the event of death, incapacity or loss of health. As life insurance benefits generally are of long-term debt obligations, holders of the funds –

that is, life insurers – are major providers of long-term investment capital in many economies.

- Depository institutions – most commonly commercial banks – take in funds principally as short-term deposits and make them available as loans to individuals and businesses. They are critical to the implementation of a nation's macroeconomic policy and their activities have considerable spillover effects in the economy.
- Securities firms, also known as investment banks, are involved more with direct intermediation (bringing together security issuers and investors) than with portfolio intermediation (management of security portfolios). They perform underwriting (packaging, pricing and selling of new debt or equity issues), investing (managing assets for institutional or private investors), market making and trading (working as either agent or principal) and custodial servicing (including mergers and acquisitions (M&A) service).[9]
- Mutual funds are pools of managed assets offering investors convenient access to the securities markets. In the US, funds are sold predominantly through securities brokers or directly to the public at no sales commission charges. In Europe, funds are sold predominantly through banks. The number of mutual funds worldwide continues to grow rapidly, as do assets under management.
- Private pension funds – of both employer-provided plans and individual accounts – specialise in managing diversified portfolios of assets dedicated to providing retirement income plan to participants. Pension fund assets might be managed by the fund itself or another financial intermediary or by the individual. Most pension assets are subsumed within the total assets of their managing intermediary, be it a bank, mutual fund or life insurer. Pension funds generally are considered parts of corporations or government agencies and not separate entities, so do not appear in listings of large financial intermediaries worldwide. Nonetheless, we know that the growth in private pension funds worldwide has been enormous, fuelled by ageing, more affluent populations, favourable tax treatment and revenue-starved public pension plans.
- A financial conglomerate is a group of companies that are under common management control and their predominant activities involve significant services – production, distribution or both – in at least two of the insurance, depository services and securities markets. Along with the structures like bancassurance, allfinanz and universal banking, financial conglomerates convey some notion of financial service convergence or integration.[10] Increasingly, non-operational companies own all or the majority of the shares in separately incorporated, capitalised sectoral subsidiaries.

All financial intermediaries, on the one hand, issue their own claims – that is, underwrite risks – whether in the form of insurance policies, savings accounts, collateral and non-collateral loans, security underwriting, and so on, to clients and receive funds for doing so. They invest these funds in stocks, bonds and other income-generating instruments. Since their investment is not confined to the sector to which the savers belong, the funds can flow to the most productive sectors in an economy or abroad for possibly largest productivity gains. On the other hand, a financial intermediary may not underwrite all of the financial services it sells. Where permitted, some sell the services underwritten by other firms (for example, bancassurance).

Financial intermediation averts the need for savers to locate investors directly, and vice versa. Hence, their services are essential to society. In theory, however, financial intermediaries would not exist in a perfectly competitive market because individuals and businesses in the market would have perfect information, incur no transaction costs and deal directly financial transactions with each other.

Conversely, savers in the real world afford less-than-perfect information and can experience net marginal benefits from engaging in transactions involving a financial intermediary. Customers often do not have the ability or resources to collect adequate information about the transactions they wish to engage in. Neither are they effective in monitoring the management of the invested firms. Financial intermediaries solve information asymmetry problems and agency problems by conducting research to help their clients make informed decisions and by monitoring the management of the firms in which their clients invest. Moreover, financial intermediaries assist their clients to create and monitor an investment portfolio in line with their individual risk appetite. What distinguishes insurance business from most other financial services is that insurers' underwriting processes are likely subject to greater possibilities of adverse selection and moral hazard than other types of financial institutions.

Theories of regulation

Several theories attempt to explain the reason for regulation – some more or less as a hypothesis and some other with empirical evidence. This section summarises key theories.[11]

First, *public interest theory of regulation* – referred to recently as *normative analysis as a positive theory* – suggests that regulation exists to serve the public interest. Under this theory, government seeks to prevent or make right significant societal or consumer harm resulting from market imperfections and to ultimately maximise economic efficiency in the market. This premise presumes that government is capable of correctly identifying market failures and functioning for the overall public good and that it is indifferent to conflicts in general and specific interest group pressures.[12] Empirical evidence, however, tends to be inconsistent with this theory, thus making it more a hypothesis than a theory with a practical application (Viscusi et al., 2005).

Capture theory assumes that regulation is in response to the industry's demand for regulation or the regulator becomes controlled by the regulated over time. This theory, too, lacks the support of empirical evidence. Neither does it successfully explain why regulation does not support other interest groups (stakeholders) in the regulated industry.

Stigler (1971) introduces the *theory of economic regulation*. His theory advances the capture theory by attempting to answer why there is regulation and what industries are likely regulated. Notably, the key resource of government is 'the power to coerce', and regulation is use of the power to restrict the decisions of its citizens and businesses (or economic agents in the aggregate). Regulation, he theorises, is acquired by and is designed primarily for the benefit of the regulated and in return regulators receive financial and political support so that they can continue to stay in office. In other words, the special interested groups demand regulation and tend to be well organised and financed, and the regulatory agency is created by the captured legislatures. Stigler proposes the following regulatory policies: direct monetary subsidy, control over new entry, control over substitutes and complements, and price control.[13]

Posner (1974) modifies Stigler's theory and proposes the *equilibrium-based theory of regulation*. He suggests that there exists 'the product of coalitions between the regulated industry and the organized consumer group, the former obtaining some monopoly profits from regulation [and] the latter obtaining lower prices (or better services than they would in an unregulated market – all at the expense of unorganized, mostly consumer, groups'. He also contends that the groups that can attain regulatory objectives share a common interest, lack the ability to establish a cartel on their own and are geographically concentrated.

Peltzman (1976) suggests the *self-interested theory of regulation* – also known as the Stigler-Peltzman Model and *maximisation of political support theory* – under which regulators carry on regulatory activities to maximise their political support.[14] Under one circumstance, they would exhibit pro-industry biases to gain industry financial and other backing. Under the other circumstance, regulators would participate in activities that appeal to voting consumers (for example, price suppression) to gain their political support, even if the long-term effects were detrimental.

Joscow (1974) assumes that regulators (for example, in the electric utilities industry) wish to minimise the conflicts and criticism subject to legal and procedural constraints. Under this *minimisation of conflict theory*, the public will not be concerned with pricing as long as nominal prices are not rising and the regulated firm wishes to maximise long-term profits. However, economic analysis offers that the behaviour of the firm cannot be explained by a single variable.

Meier (1988) criticises that Stigler's theory is based on the assumed presence of mutual benefit exchange between the regulator and the regulated, but not all industries demand regulation. Further, many government agencies (for example, the Federal Aviation Administration and the Environmental Protection Agency) do not reflect the interest of the regulated. Regarding the US insurance industry, he concludes that 'capture' does not occur because the industry is too segmented to reach common policy goals, that state governments are not in full harmony – in tools and objectives – when it comes to insurance regulation and that the federal government (or Congress) continues to threaten state governments if they fail to perform their duties. In sum, Meier finds evidence for *political theory of regulation* under which regulation is shaped by the bargaining among multiple private interest groups – the regulated industry, consumers, the regulator and political elites (courts and the legislative body) – within the existing political and administrative structure. Each of these four groups has its own specific goals in the regulatory process and the influence of each group depends on the resources it can mobilise. These groups are not necessarily homogeneous, so bargaining outcomes depend on the particular issue on the table.

Consumers – even after factoring in the growing presence of consumer activist groups – tend not to be as well organised, financed or informed as do other interest groups. Protection of consumers, especially those in the markets with complex products, from the potential harm by other interest groups is justified, at least in theory, under the public interest theory.[15]

Rationale for regulation

Development and maintenance of a sound financial market environment is important in every society. At the same time, we observe that the financial intermediation process is imperfect. Government thus can play at least two important roles in the market. First, it can play the role of supplier when the private market fails to, or does not wish to, provide financial security against certain risky circumstances that its citizens face (for example, risk of natural catastrophe).[16] Even when the private sector is willing, the government may decide to be the supplier of the security (for example, social security and national healthcare insurance). Second, government attempts to minimise the chances that the economy or consumers in the private sector are harmed because of market imperfections. Regulation is the most typical tool it uses to manage the risk, provided that government intervention is limited to the circumstance under which market outcomes are, for some reason, unacceptable. In examining financial services regulation, therefore, we should be clear about the scope, role and types of financial intermediaries in the private market.

Recall that the imperfections in the financial services market are closely related to information asymmetry, market power and negative externality. Clearly, the information asymmetry in the market is the basis for most insurance and securities regulation, and, to a lesser extent, for banking regulation. Private financial institutions seek to create market power using market segmentation and product differentiation, generating scale and scope economy effects and scores of other strategies. This potential market power motive in the market gives another justification for government regulation.[17]

Negative externality in the private financial services market rises, among others, from the possibility of systemic risks. We can broadly identify two types of systemic risks in the market. First there is 'risk of cascading failure', meaning that the failure of one institution is the proximate cause of the failure of other institutions or even market collapse. An example is one bank's default on its short-term credit obligations to another bank, precipitating other bank failures. Bank regulation in principle and, to a lesser extent, securities and insurance regulation aim to minimise the risk of cascading failure.

The second type is the risk of 'runs', referring to the circumstance that a significant number of creditors (depositors) simultaneously attempt to withdraw their money and, often, in full. Such runs can be an event confined to a bank and its affiliates caused by a loss of confidence in the institution, often done with great haste by a real or imagined fear of insolvency. Capital, solvency and market conduct regulation in insurance and banking markets, along with the creation of guaranty fund and deposit insurance schemes, respectively, is in line with government's attempt to minimise this risk.

Government imperfections

Government intervention in a market for economic risk management would be justified if *all* the following three conditions are met: (1) actual or potential market imperfections exist; (2) the imperfections do or could lead to material economic inefficiency or inequality; and (3) the intervention can ameliorate the inefficiency or inequality. Conversely, no government intervention is warranted if at least one of the above conditions is not satisfied. More specifically, no government intervention is justified even when the market exhibits imperfections but they do not lead to meaningful inefficiency or inequality.

Even if the imperfections could lead to such inefficiency or inequality, government intervention will not be justified if the actions do not ameliorate the imperfection. In fact and as alluded to above, there is no guarantee that government accurately assesses the imperfections. Government intervention can make matters worse and, retrospectively speaking, the proper government response would have been no action, even for inefficient markets.

Even if all three conditions are met, government intervention still may fail. As *market* failures exist, so do *government* failures. White (1996) groups the causes of the failures as follows:[18]

- Policy-makers experience difficulty in identifying problems that are to be solved or implementing otherwise worthy goals.

- Agency problems exist in the government such that government employees who are agents for the public (the principal) have no strong or direct incentive to carry out laws and regulations fully and fairly. Besides, the overall compensation for civil servants is of less quality in many countries than for agents in the private sector, an environment sometimes leading to laxity in performance and even abuse (for example, bribery).
- The regulated company or industry engages in *economic rent-seeking activity*.[19] Such activity is not only non-productive but also decreases market efficiency and social welfare.
- Finally, and related to rent-seeking activity, there is the problem of capture. The regulated (for example, the producer) can be well financed and has substantial knowledge about interest in the regulation, whereas its consumers are not so well informed or organised. The regulator, because of its self-interest or ignorance, then may act in favour of the producer's perspective. Further, some government employees either are or hope to be closely allied with the regulated industry when they have or anticipate employment in the industry. This 'revolving door' problem is associated with capture.

Regulation of insurance and other financial services

Generally, regulatory intervention falls into three categories. First, *prudential regulation*, which is concerned with the financial condition of the financial intermediary, has evolved primarily because of problems of information asymmetry and negative externalities (especially in the banking industry). Second, *market conduct regulation*, referring to government-prescribed rules covering inappropriate practices in the market, has been developed mainly because of information problems. Finally, *competition policy (antitrust) regulation*, which is concerned with actions of the financial intermediary that substantially lessen competition, is primarily in response to problems of market power. Of the three types of regulation, prudent regulation remains the most critical one in government oversight of the financial services market operations.

Details of financial institution regulation, particularly prudent regulation, vary greatly cross countries as well as cross industries.[20] Nevertheless, some generalisations can be drawn in the extent of the activities that governments permit within a financial conglomerate. In a survey of 33 countries plus EU Member States, the Institute of International Bankers (2010) finds that the majority, especially the largest states, permit financial conglomerates to undertake banking, insurance and security activities. It also finds that the majority of governments allow joint banking and securities activities, with most permitting banks to undertake securities activities within the bank itself. Several others require some or all securities activities to be undertaken through subsidiaries or affiliates. See Table 2.1 for detailed classification of the countries.

Table 2.1 Regulation of financial conglomerates (2010)

Consolidated supervision applied to bank subsidiaries and affiliates of domestic and non-domestic financial groups		Consolidated supervision applied to bank subsidiaries and affiliates of domestic financial groups but not to bank subsidiaries and affiliates or unincorporated branches/agencies and affiliates of non-domestic financial groups	Consolidated supervision is not applied to either domestic or non-domestic financial groups
And to unincorporated branches/agencies and affiliates of non-domestic financial groups	But not to unincorporated branches/agencies and affiliates of non-domestic financial groups		
Argentina	Australia[8]	Czech Republic	Chile
Brazil	Austria[9]	Denmark[15]	
Canada[1]	Bahrain	Germany	
China	Belgium	Turkey	
France	Bermuda[10]		
India	Cayman Islands[11]		
Indonesia	Finland		
Ireland	Hong Kong[12]		
Israel	Korea[13]		
Italy	Latvia		
Japan	Norway		
Luxembourg	Poland		
Netherlands	Singapore[14]		
Panama	United Kingdom		
Philippines			
Romania[2]			
South Africa[3]			
Spain[4]			
Sweden[5]			
Switzerland[6]			
United States[7]			

Notes:

1. The Office of the Superintendent of Financial Institutions (OSFI) oversees the operations at the federal level, while certain entities within a financial group (for example, securities and insurance companies) may also be subject to supervision by provincial agencies.
2. For the EU non-domestic branches, reliance is placed on home country supervision. For the non-EU non-domestic branches, the Romanian legislation provides in principle for the same treatment as for institutions that are Romanian legal persons.
3. Consolidated supervision extends to all the companies in a banking group, including the controlling company, its subsidiaries, joint ventures and companies in which the controlling company or its subsidiaries have a direct or indirect participation.
4. As far as subsidiaries, affiliates or branches of non-domestic banks are concerned, consolidated supervision refers to their respective 'Spanish sub-groups'.
5. Regarding affiliates of banks within the European Economic Area (EEA), the Swedish authority has a shared responsibility with the home country supervisor. After notification to the Swedish supervisor a home country supervisor may conduct an on-site exam at an affiliate location in Sweden.
6. Swiss Banking law requires the Swiss Federal Banking Commission to exercise consolidated supervision over bank subsidiaries and affiliates of domestic financial groups. Bank subsidiaries and affiliates of non-domestic financial groups and unincorporated branches/agencies of non-domestic financial groups are only allowed in Switzerland if they are subject to consolidated supervision by their home country banking authority.

Notes to Table 2.1 *continued*

7. Under the Gramm-Leach-Bliley Act of 1999 and the International Banking Act of 1978 the US Federal Reserve Board makes determinations regarding the capital strength of the non-domestic banking organisation that seeks to become a 'financial holding company' or engage in other non-banking activities permissible for bank holding companies.
8. The Australian Prudential Regulation Authority (APRA) supervises locally-incorporated authorised deposit-taking institutions (ADIs) (including their overseas branches and subsidiaries) on a consolidated basis. APRA also supervises foreign-owned locally-incorporated ADIs (and their subsidiaries and any overseas branches) on a consolidated basis. Foreign banks operating as branches in Australia (foreign ADIs) are subject to supervisory oversight on the branch operations in Australia. APRA does not supervise on a consolidated basis unincorporated branches, agencies and affiliates directly owned by non-domestic financial groups, but requires such entities to be subject to adequate consolidated supervision by the parent supervisors of the foreign ADI operating in Australia.
9. Within the European Union (EEA countries) reliance is placed on home country control; non-EU countries: The Austrian Banking Act stipulates that a non-EU non-domestic branch is treated in principle in the same way as an independent credit institution is treated. Thus, the Austrian branch is obliged to fulfil the Austrian regulatory and supervisory provisions independently. The situation of the entire bank will not be taken into account. However, legally the branch is not deemed to be independent.
10. Bermuda does not license branches of overseas banks. Consolidated supervision is applied to the licensed entity and to any subsidiaries or affiliates.
11. The Cayman Islands Monetary Authority (CIMA) supervises locally incorporated authorised institutions on a consolidated basis, covering their subsidiaries as well as local and overseas branches. The CIMA will also require that branches of foreign incorporated banks are under adequate consolidated supervision in their home country. This is one of the minimum authorisation criteria that will be assessed at the time of authorisation and on an ongoing basis thereafter.
12. The Hong Kong Monetary Authority (HKMA) supervises locally incorporated authorised institutions on a consolidated basis, covering their subsidiaries as well as local and overseas branches. The prudential requirements and supervisory approach applicable to foreign bank branches are broadly the same as those for authorised institutions incorporated in Hong Kong. The HKMA will also require that branches of foreign incorporated banks are under adequate consolidated supervision in their home country. This is one of the minimum authorisation criteria that will be assessed at the time of authorisation and on an ongoing basis thereafter.
13. As far as subsidiaries, affiliates or branches of non-domestic banks are concerned, consolidated supervision refers to their respective Korean sub-groups.
14. The Monetary Authority of Singapore (MAS) supervises Singapore-incorporated banks on a consolidated basis, taking into account the operations of their domestic and overseas branches and subsidiaries. The MAS does not supervise on a consolidated basis unincorporated branches, agencies and affiliates of non-domestic financial groups but takes into account, among other things, the adequacy of consolidated supervision exercised by parent supervisors for the foreign banks' operations in Singapore and overseas in considering applications made under the licensing and regulatory processes.
15. If the parent company is located abroad only the sub-group is encompassed by the consolidated supervision.

Source: *Global Survey 2010*, Institute of International Bankers, p. 9.

Insurance regulation as well as banking regulation is largely to monitor financial and operational soundness, thus to prevent insolvencies, in the market. Differences exist, however, in that the insurance monitoring is ultimately to protect the policy-holders and claimants of defunct insurers whereas the banking counterpart is to prevent systemic risks – cascading failures and runs.

Every jurisdiction has an agency charged with overseeing and supervising its insurance marketplace. More specifically, government regulatory policy typically takes place at three levels. The legislative body commonly enacts laws to establish the country's broad legal framework. The judiciary enforces insurance laws and resolves disputes arising from insurance transactions. The state's executive branch carries out regulatory oversight. Because of the complexities in insurance business, policymakers commonly delegate this authority to a ministerial department, a (de facto) central bank or another government agency. The governing body may work with or further delegate its duty to a subordinate government agency (commonly, the Office of Commissioner) or a quasi-government agency.[21]

At the international level, the task of coordinating the work of national insurance regulators falls to the International Association of Insurance Supervisors (IAIS), formed in 1994. The IAIS promotes cooperation among insurance supervisors, sets international standards for insurance regulation and supervision, provides training for members and coordinates work with other financial services sector regulators and intergovernmental organisations. The IAIS represents more than 190 jurisdictions, with more than 120 observers. The IAIS issues principles, standards and guidance papers on issues related to insurance supervision.

The barriers among and distinctions between the main financial services sectors have begun to erode. This convergence raises the chance of market imperfections and systemic risk. This issue is no longer limited by national boundaries. With the continued globalisation of financial services, all stakeholders have become aware of the importance of coordinated and effective supervision of all industries in financial service. Several developments have already been made.

At the initiative of the Basel Committee, a group of banking, securities and insurance regulators examined in 1993 issues relating to supervision of financial conglomerates. The Tripartite Group, established in 1995, addressed cross-sectoral issues associated with integration on an international level. The Joint Forum on Financial Conglomerates, founded in 1996, took forward the work of the Tripartite Group. The Joint Forum consists of an equal number of bank, securities and insurance supervisors representing the Basel Committee, the International Organization of Securities Commissions (IOSCO) and the IAIS.

A few other regional economic associations and regulatory organisations exist. They include but are not limited to the International Network of Pensions Regulators and Supervisors (established in 2000), the Financial Stability Forum (1999), the Financial Sector Assessment Program (1999) and the Islamic Financial Services Board (2002).

Conclusions and future prospects

The Asian and other financial crises of the late 1990s and the recent global credit crisis brought forceful attention to how inadequate financial services regulation adversely affects national regional and global economies.[22] They called for closer attention of the local regulatory authorities – especially in countries with a sector-based regulatory structure – to the financial service sector as well as for enhanced regulatory coordination and cooperation internationally.

We have observed a rise in the use of a disclosure-based regulatory environment internationally. Risk-based prudential regulation – particularly Solvency II and risk-based capital (RBC) regulation – is increasingly supplemented by rules requiring broad disclosures of a company's finances, risks and strategies to not only stakeholders but also the public at large. We also observe a high degree of support, more or less as an outcome of the global credit crisis in the late 2000s, for a common international financial system with standardised international rules. Representatives of regulatory authorities and central banks in numerous countries share their knowledge and experience at the bilateral and international levels.

We also examined why government has a critical role in societal risk management and economic risk management. Social risk management deals with fairness and social justice and we expect more regulation than less in this perspective. For purposes of private-sector financial services regulation, this role has evolved primarily from imperfections in the market. Of course, many of such markets become less regulated in terms of price and product but none are perfectly competitive. As such, government continues to intervene with market activities. It is important to note that market failures are not indictments of the market and insolvency is an inevitable byproduct of the capital market system.

Various theories attempt to explain the reason for regulation. None does so completely as the market is dynamic and continues to evolve. Nevertheless, one fundamental philosophy should remain as a common denominator for all regulations. That is, regulatory efficiency and neutrality.

Potential non-neutralities may arise within a local economy if financial intermediaries are subject to different regulatory authorities. In the US insurance market, for example, we observe the federal government agency plus 51 state regulators – some appointed and other elected – attempting to achieve their own goals which are not necessarily achieving regulatory efficiency.[23] At the same time, the regulated financial intermediaries may attempt to benefit from regulatory arbitrage when they can select among different regulators. Creating subsidiaries, altering corporate ownership and creating a holding company structure can be some of the examples.[24]

Just as there are market failures, so too are there government failures. Not all government interventions are directed toward rectifying social justice and fairness or market failures. Even among the interventions that are so aimed, not all are effective. Like the market, government actions also should be evaluated through an economic lens.

Notes

1. This chapter is based in part on selected sections in Skipper and Kwon (2007).
2. The net marginal benefit of a regulatory measure at the societal level can be estimated by the net benefit discounted by an assumed social discount rate: $\sum_{i=0}^{T} \frac{R_t - C_t}{(1+r)^t}$, where T is the life of the regulation, R_t revenues (benefits) at time t, C_t cost of regulation at time t, and r social discount rate.
3. Two other commonly used alternatives are the human capital approach and the direct cost approach.
4. The OECD (1998) observes that the primary public policy interest in insurance regulation relates to concerns over the willingness and ability of policy-holders to observe and monitor the financial soundness of their insurance companies, especially when insurance is made compulsory.
5. The Coase theorem suggests that the markets in which property rights are unambiguous and there are no transactions costs generate efficient outcomes, even with externalities. If this truly happens, government need not concern itself with any negative externalities – at least from a societal efficiency standpoint and individual self-interest leads its citizens to an efficient outcome.
6. Contracts in insurance and other financial services usually are of utmost good faith. However, this fact does not warrant that buyers, especially individuals and small businesses, are not well educated consumers.
7. Economic regulation refers to the government control of firm behaviours in a market with imperfections, whereas social regulation refers to the control of firm and consumer behaviours with respect to health, safety and environmental implications in a market. Unlike the case of economic regulation, we do not observe any move toward deregulation in the social regulation regime. In fact, the move in the regime is toward more stringent regulation.
8. The financial intermediation process includes several ancillary services such as financial advice, credit cards, brokerage and trust management.
9. When an investment bank assumes the role of the principal, it holds an inventory position in an underlying security, thus bearing the risk of future price fluctuations. This is an important distinction from a risk management perspective.
10. The integration can be in the form of product integration (for example, unit-linked annuity, variable life insurance, securitisation of a bank's asset or liability portfolios, and catastrophe bonds and other alternative risk transfers) or advisory integration (for example, risk management consultants, financial planners and attorneys offering liability, financial and legal risk management programmes) that does not necessarily require any supply-side integration or even cooperation. The product convergence trend continues, making advisory integration more complex, and regulation of the market more complicated.
11. See Bhattacharya et al. (1998) for a summary of the economics of bank regulation and Pacces (2000) for securities market regulation.
12. McDowell (1989) contends that insurance is sui generis in many ways and is business clothed with a public interest, thus calling for development of a regulatory model just for insurance itself.
13. One may compare this to what Viscusi et al. (2005) propose: price control, quality control and market entry and exit control.

14. Peltzman models this theory using $M = nf - (N - n)h$, where M denotes the regulatory objective of maximizing a political majority, n the number of voters in the beneficiary group, f net probability that a beneficiary grants support to the regulator, N the total number of potential voters, and h the net probability that the one who is taxed (every non-n) opposes the regulator. See D'Arcy (1982) for evaluation of this model.
15. Of course, it is not easy for government to recognise the cases where an interest group's public interest arguments mask conflicting self-interest and private motivations.
16. Government risk bearing is not discussed in this chapter but readers may find the works by Flannery, Stiglitz and Connolly – all found as chapters in Sinderman (1991) – interesting.
17. The reader may recall that government itself would hinder competition when it creates or preserves market power, for example, by creating market entry or exit barrier.
18. Specific to the cases of non-bank financial institutions, Carmichael and Pomerleano (2002) offer the following reasons: anticompetitive behaviour, market misconduct, information asymmetry and systemic instability.
19. Any payment to a factor of production in excess of the minimum required to bring forth or retain its service is referred to as 'economic rent'. Economic rent can be thought of as excess profits.
20. Carmichael and Pomerleano (2002) propose four main components of the regulatory framework for financial institutions. They are: (1) objectives (the reason for regulation and the societal expectation related to it); (2) structure (the desirable structure of the regulatory agency); (3) backing (the political, legal and financial backing for the regulator to effectively carry out their duties); and (4) implementation (the instruments and techniques for actual carrying out of regulatory objectives).
21. One or more industry associations bridge the regulator and the regulated in a number of countries.
22. See Harrington (2009) and Grace (2010) for an evaluation of the recent credit crisis and its impact on the insurance industry.
23. The 51 regulators include the one for Washington, DC. The US also has regulators governing insurance matters in the jurisdictions and territories.
24. Carmichael and Pomerleano (2002) contend that heavily regulated parent companies could reduce their regulatory burden by shifting business into an unregulated subsidiary in a number of Asian countries and the resulting regulatory arbitrage contributed to the Asian economic crisis in the late 1990s.

Bibliography

Bhattacharya, Sudipto, Arnoud Boot and Anhan Thakor (1998) 'The Economics of Bank Regulation', *Journal of Money, Credit and Banking*, 30(4),745–70.

Carmichael, Jeffrey, and Michael Pomerleano (2002) *The Development and Regulation of Non-bank Financial Institutions* (International Bank for Reconstruction and Development).

D'Arcy, Stephan (1982) 'An Economic Theory of Insurance Regulation'. PhD dissertation, University of Illinois at Urbana-Champaign.

Grace, Martin (2010) *The Insurance Industry and Systemic Risk: Evidence and Discussion*, Policy Brief (2010-PB-02) (Networks Financial Institute).

Harrington, Scott (2009) 'The Financial Crisis, Systemic Risk and the Future of Insurance Regulation', *Journal of Risk and Insurance*, 76(4), 785–819.

Institute of International Bankers (2010) *Global Survey 2010*.

Joscow, Paul (1974) 'Inflation and Environmental Concern: Structural Change in the Process of Public Utility Price Regulation', *Bell Journal of Economics and Management Science*, 4 (Autumn), 375–427.

McDowell, Banks (1989) *Deregulation and Competition in the Insurance Industry* (Quorum Books).

Meier, Kenneth J. (1988) *The Political Economy of Regulation: The Case of Insurance* (State University of New York Press).

Organisation for Economic Cooperation and Development (1998) *Competition and Related Regulation Issues in the Insurance Industry* (OECD).

Pacces, Alessio (2000) 'Financial Intermediation in the Securities Markets: Laws and Economics of Conduct of Business Regulation', *International Review of Law and Economics*, 20, 479–510.

Peltzman, Sam (1976) 'Toward a More General Theory of Regulation', *Journal of Law and Economics*, 19(2), 211–40.

Posner, Richard (1974) 'Theories of Economic Regulation', *Bell Journal of Economics and Management Science,* 5 (autumn): 337–52.

Sinderman, Mark (ed.) *Government Risk-Bearing* (Proceedings of a Conference Held at the Federal Reserve Bank of Cleveland, May).

Skipper, Harold D., and W. Jean Kwon (2007) *Risk Management and Insurance Perspectives in a Global Economy*, 1st edn (John Wiley-Blackwell).

Stigler, George J. (1971) 'The Theory of Economic Regulation', *Bell Journal of Economics*, 2 (Spring), 3–21.

Viscusi, Kip, Joseph E. Harrington, Jr., and John M. Vernon (2005) *Economics of Regulation and Antitrust* (MIT Press).

White, Lawrence J. (1996) 'Competition versus Harmonization: An Overview of International Regulation of Financial Services', in Claude E. Barfield, ed., *International Financial Markets: Harmonization versus Competition* (AEI Press).

3
Global Financial Architecture and the Insurance Sector

Erik Denters

Introduction

The crisis in the global financial system that unfolded in 2008 has also affected the stability of institutions that operate in the periphery of financial markets. The insurance industry, pension funds and other institutional investors have suffered considerable losses as consumers of financial products created by the banking sector (Impavido and Tower, 2009; Schich, 2009). In addition, the insurance market is particularly vulnerable as poorly understood credit risks were transferred from banks to insurers. Insurers who concentrated exclusively in financial guarantees and credit default swaps writing were mostly affected. In the aftermath of the financial collapse, the crisis has further spread among sovereign actors. In an attempt to rescue financial institutions from insolvency, governments have bailed out (or even nationalised) financial institutions. As a result, institutions and highly indebted states now both create an insecure and instable environment in which investors have to operate

This chapter outlines the efforts made by governments, operating individually and jointly, to create stability in the international financial system. It also suggests that firmer international cooperation is required. Stability is required for institutional and individual investors that expose their investment portfolios to financial markets. A regulatory and supervisory system that monitors and manages risks in financial markets is a means to create stability.[1]

The causes of the financial crisis have been analysed elsewhere (FSA, 2009; Arner 2009). Deeper roots of the crisis may be found in the development of financial markets since the 1980s. Traditionally, banks were holding deposits, attracting savings and lending money. In this market place there is a common interest that risks must be known and restrained. Voluntary and mutual self-restraint may be explained because banks lend and borrow to each other. They are willing to do so as long as each bank is satisfied that its counterpart does not take excessive risks in its financial operations. Should a bank take higher risks than is acceptable for its peers, it will no longer be eligible for interbank lending. In this system of self-regulation a gentle form of supervision would be adequate.

In recent years financial markets have changed drastically. Next to traditional banking, hedge funds, investment banks and institutional investors have dealt in innovative and high-leveraged financial products. In this heterogeneous financial service industry, the absence of self-restraint may easily disturb mutual confidence. Once confidence is gone, financial institutions cease lending and borrowing. For economies that thrive on credit and rely on fresh capital from investors, lack of confidence has destructive effects.

Innovation in financial markets has also touched upon the insurance industry. Whereas traditional insurance is still the predominant business model, the line to be drawn between banking and insurance has become blurred where both activities are employed simultaneously by a single institution. Bank-assurance conglomerates ('bancassurance') sell insurance products in combination with financial products. Insurers may also perform wholesale banking operations alongside traditional insurance activities. Finally, monoline insurance companies may concentrate exclusively on providing financial guarantees by offering insurance associated with debt obligations (ECB, 2009).

Financial markets as a common good

Why do governments supervise financial institutions and why do governments bail out insolvent financial institutions? The reason lies in the fundamental role financial markets play in creating stability in the international financial system. Financial stability is a sine qua non for prosperity, both nationally and internationally. Financial stability refers to an environment that would prevent a large number of financial institutions from becoming insolvent and failing to provide key financial services such as deposits and investments for savers, loans and securities to investors, and payment services (IMF and World Bank, 2005, p. 4).

Financial markets operate as intermediary between lenders and borrowers, debtors and creditors, consumers and producers or buyers and sellers. Their essential function both on the domestic and international level is twofold: absorb and discharge financial resources, and create and maintain an infrastructure that transfers financial resources between parties. A calamity that ceases access to credit or invalidates the payments system would have devastating consequences for global welfare. Financial markets may therefore be considered a common good as they provide a service that is indispensible for all who produce, consume, trade and invest. This may even be true for subsistence farmers that grow coffee, bananas or cacao. If their produce cannot find its way to the world market due to a non-functional financial system, their livelihood will be threatened.

De Bettignies and Lépineaux (2009, p. 161) argue that the concept of common good[2] is broad and not restricted to environmental concerns:

> Although very general in its essence, the concept of the global common good can be approached through a variety of ways, material and immaterial: access to the means of existence, peace and solidarity among nations, scientific knowledge, philosophical works, artistic heritage, biodiversity, a healthy climate, political rights, social justice, shared economic prosperity, access to information and culture ... All these elements represent as many conditions, aspects or partial expressions of the global common good, which exceeds and includes them in its universal perspective.

Common to all these areas is that the states interfere to promote or protect rights and values. States protect culture, science, political rights, biodiversity and other essential areas by controlling these directly or indirectly, subsidising those who protect common goods, or by enforcing legal instruments to protect common goods.

It is arguable that a functioning financial system is in the same league as other essential immaterial goods (Feichtner, 2007).[3] The concept of common good applied to the financial system means that financial institutions do not own the system. The system is owned by humanity as a whole and financial institutions are merely caretakers of the system. When caretakers are unable or unwilling to preserve and maintain the system, substantial interference is justified. Preservation of the system should be the focus of interference, not protection of institutions that constitute the financial system.

Modes of regulation

The approach taken by governments operating individually and jointly to regulate and supervise banking activities rests on three levels: micro-prudential, cross-border micro-prudential and macro-prudential.

First, frameworks have been developed for supervising individual institutions. In the banking sector the Basel Committee on Banking Supervision has adopted the Basel II framework including standards on capital adequacy for individual banks.[4] As Basel II provides for regulation of individual banks to be implemented by domestic supervisors, it primarily focuses on micro-prudential regulation. The objective of Basel II is to secure international convergence on supervisory regulations governing the capital adequacy of internationally active banks. Importantly, the Basel Committee membership reflects a global representation[5] and thereby attempts to harmonise standards on a global level.[6] A similar global arrangement for regulating the insurance industry is absent. Only the EU has adopted a framework that harmonises regulatory and supervisory standards through its Solvency II Directive.[7] The main purposes of Solvency II are to promote a single insurance market and to secure an adequate policy-holder protection. Both Basel II and Solvency II follow a similar pattern by employing three pillars in supervision: (i) quantitative requirements (capital or solvency requirements); (ii) qualitative and governance requirements; and (iii) disclosure requirement including transparency requirements.

Second, since regulation is essentially exercised within domestic jurisdictions,[8] supervisors must cooperate on cross-border supervision of financial institutions that operate in multiple jurisdictions. Cooperation takes shape in supervisory colleges. Colleges are permanent but flexible structures for cooperation and coordination among the national supervisors involved in the supervision of significant institutions. Supervisory colleges are neither supranational institutions, nor decision-making bodies; they are merely designed to share prudential information about a particular financial institution (CEBS, CEIOPS and IWCFC, 2009; Duncan, 2010).

The composition of a college depends on the institution to be supervised. In the case of a banking or insurance group, a parent institution in country A with branches in countries B, C and D would bring together the supervisors of the four countries involved. For this purpose the supervisors would conclude an agreement on information sharing, sharing and delegation of tasks, on-site examinations and responding to crisis situations.

Basel II does not provide for colleges but the Basel Committee has proposed to identify best practices concerning colleges (Basel Committee, 2010). The EU has proposed legislation on the establishment of colleges on banking supervision, as a subdivision of the European Banking Authority. Supervisors may agree, according to a model agreement of the Committee of European Banking Supervisors (CEBS, 2007) on the exchange of information, developing a common understanding of the risk profile of a Banking Group, developing a coordinated view on supervision and risk assessment, and coordinating major decisions taken by individual authorities as far as possible and practicable. Solvency II has firm provisions on colleges supervising the European insurance market. Colleges 'should all have access to information available with other supervisory authorities within the College and they should be involved in decision-making actively'.[9]

Third, the financial crisis has revealed that the management of systemic risk is fundamental for stability. Therefore, macro-prudential supervision is aimed at assessing systemic risks. Systemic risk defines the chances for a materialisation of systemic crisis. A systemic crisis may be defined as a

> systemic event that affects a considerable number of financial institutions or markets in a strong sense, thereby severely impairing the general well-functioning (of an important part) of the financial system. The well-functioning of the financial system relates to the effectiveness and efficiency with which

savings are channelled into the real investments promising the highest returns. (de Bandt and Hartmann, 2000, p. 11)

The last element has more generally been referred to as 'the potential to have serious negative consequences for the real economy'. This element is less precise as 'real economy' as opposed to some other economy is difficult to define. Moreover, a serious crisis in the financial services industry will likely emerge as a serious crisis on all levels of the economy.

In determining systemic risks there may be two approaches: one views the financial system as a whole, top-down from a certain distance in order to have a clear view of the conglomerate of financial markets. A comparison may be made with a satellite view of a land area where a general decline, for example desertification or deforestation, is apparent. This information may not be clear when standing on the ground. It is unlikely, however, that a satellite-view approach will be workable for determining systemic risk in financial markets unless there is a toolbox available to look at financial markets from above. A second approach determines systemic risk bottom-up by selecting a number of systematically important institutions. In that sense systemic risk flows from the danger of contagion caused by insolvency of individual financial institutions. Approaching systemic risks bottom-up would be less abstract and more down to earth (IMF et al., 2009).

By identifying the systemic risks that systemically important institutions pose, it will be possible to develop a conceptual and analytical framework on which policy decisions can be made. The International Monetary Fund (IMF) and the Financial Stability Board (FSB)[10] have produced criteria for national authorities to identify systemically relevant institutions:

- *Size*. The importance of a single component for the working of the financial system generally increases with the amount of financial services that the component provides.
- *Lack of substitutability*. The systemic importance of a single component increases in cases where it is difficult for other components of the system to provide the same or similar services in the event of a failure.
- *Interconnectedness*. Systemic risk can arise through direct and indirect interlinkages between the components of the financial system so that individual failure or malfunction has repercussions around the financial system, leading to a reduction in the aggregate amount of services.

In addition to these institutional features, a well-functioning financial system rests on three pillars. First, there is a need for surveillance and analysis to monitor the impact of potential macroeconomic and institutional factors (both domestic and external) on the soundness (risks and vulnerabilities) and stability of the financial system. Second, supervision and regulation must manage risk and vulnerabilities, protect market integrity and provide incentives for risk management and good governance of financial institutions. Third, infrastructures must be created to secure legal certainty (insolvency regimes, creditor rights), market liquidity, and promote transparency and corporate governance (through adoption of codes and standards).

In support of this approach, the G20 has assigned the FSB and the IMF to report on recommendations 'to strengthen oversight and supervision, specifically relating to the mandate, capacity and resourcing of supervisors and specific powers which should be adopted to proactively indentify and address risks, including early intervention' (G20, 2010).

On the regional level some additional steps have been taken. In the EU the Larosière Group has suggested the establishment of a European Systemic Risk Council (ESRC) that would bring together national supervisory bodies, overseeing insurance companies, pension funds and securities traders (De Larosière Group, 2009). These bodies must cooperate and provide information to the ESRC. The council's objectives would be to provide oversight over the financial markets by making recommendations on macro-prudential policies and issue risk warnings when market failures pose a threat. Other proposals make similar suggestions or even propose a supranational supervisor (Speyer and Walter, 2009; Bini Smaghi, 2009).[11] Along the same lines, systemic risks councils could be set up in financially relevant regions such as in Latin America and South East Asia. Major actors such as the US and China could set up their own risk councils.

Predicaments of the current regulatory system

The current international regulatory and supervisory system is deficient to the extent that regulation and supervision is primarily exercised by domestic institutions. There are two inherent deficiencies.

Complexity and risks

Complex financial products are engineered by technicians who apply econometric models using mathematics, statistics and other disciplines. Understanding the ingenuity and risks associated with complex financial products requires highly trained human resources. In addition, the ceaseless innovation of markets – including financial products – means that supervisors always lag behind the latest technology. It is unlikely that adequate capacity is available because 'those who understand the market best are likely to be employed in the markets in positions that pay far more than those funded by the public purse' (Eatwell and Taylor, 2000). Salaries in the public sector may never match the remuneration packages that commercial parties may offer. Even if there is some degree of capacity available, there is always the threat that staff employed at supervisory bodies consider their position as a stepping stone for a more financially rewarding future. This would discourage a confrontational stance towards financial institutions to be supervised.

Complexity combined with absence of transparency even more conceals risks. Financial institutions have little interest to reveal the intricacies of a complex financial product when competitive gains are at stake and development costs cannot be recovered on third parties through licenses or otherwise. A complex financial product may be compared to an invention for which a patent may be acquired, except that patents of financial products are not or poorly protected by international agreement. However, the US offers some protection (Hunt, 2010). Whereas there is no or inadequate 'patent-like' protection for innovative financial products, there is little incentive to reveal the particulars of innovative financial products.

Provided that supervisors would fully understand financial products, the next step would be to measure risk in systemically important institutions and, subsequently, to understand how risks build up across institutions. Measuring risk is a science and difficult to understand by supervisors. Supervisors may argue that measuring risks is a difficult but a manageable task. In a Joint Central Bank Research Conference on Risk Measurement and Systemic Risk, scholars and officials from the European Central bank, the Bank of Japan and the Federal Reserve System met in 2005 to discuss innovation in financial markets and the assessment of systemic risk across financial markets and countries. Despite the high-level participation at the conference, none of the contributors anticipated the size and depth of the financial crisis that was about to erupt in 2008. The conference summary states that initial empirical evidence showed that financial innovation reduces risk in financial markets and that 'recent resilience may give policy makers cause for comfort'. However, it also admits that innovation may cause problems for supervisors and specific concerns are raised concerning the increasing use of credit risk transfer (that is, the credit default swaps). In addition, supervisors need to understand that 'problems may have shifted towards risks where policy makers may have relatively little experience, such as herding, mis-pricing of risk, the allocation of new risks outside the banking system, and the interaction of financial innovation with market participants' incentives' (ECB et al., 2007). Indeed, these conditions and events all have contributed to the collapse of the financial system in 2008.

Probably because of uncertainty about the risks associated with financial products, there is a general benevolent attitude of supervisors towards institutions. Roger W. Ferguson, vice-president of the Board of Governors of the Federal Reserve System, argued at the conference that regulators should only step in when markets are unable to consider risks themselves and that 'policymakers should have a bias toward trusting financial markets to manage the introduction of new products and the development of new institutions smoothly and without undue stress to the financial system'. However, only when 'financial firms may not consider the effects of their decisions on the stability of other firms or on the broader financial markets' or 'lack the incentives and ability to learn about and manage the risks induced by financial innovations ... policymakers may need to work with markets and their participants, and on occasion regulate them, to achieve the desired outcomes. However, policymakers should, wherever possible, avoid premature regulation that could stifle innovation' (ECB et al., 2007).

Active lobbying by the financial industry may encourage a benevolent attitude. Lobbying may be more successful when policy-makers and supervisors are uncertain about the activities of financial markets. There is an understandable tendency to trust those who have a surplus of knowledge. The IMF suggests that the 'political influence of the financial industry can be a source of systemic risk' and proposes to contain lobbying activities (Igan et al., 2009).

States as stakeholders and supervisors

A second major predicament is that states have dual roles: they have sovereign powers to prescribe and enforce laws to regulate institutions, but they also have a considerable financial stake in the markets. This raises questions about the ability of state-controlled supervisory bodies to supervise institutions in a fair and equitable way.

A number of developments have blurred the traditional distinction between sovereign and commercial actors. First, governmental involvement in the financial sector has increased substantially since the credit crisis (*The Economist*, 2010b). States have taken emergency measures in order to save the financial sector and to mitigate economic downturn. In the EU this includes guarantee schemes, recapitalization measures, state loans, the acquisition of impaired assets and even nationalization (Petrovic and Tutsch, 2009). The US Treasury, through the TARP (Troubled Asset Relief Program), purchased hundreds of billions of dollars worth of shares of preferred stock from hundreds of financial institutions (US Congressional Budget Office, 2010). In addition, a large chunk of the mortgage market in the US is run by two state-funded agencies, Fannie Mae and Freddie Mac (*New York Times*, 2010). In China the banking industry is essentially run by the state. The world's three largest banking institutions are currently located in China. These banks are state-owned and the 'Communist Party diktat' is de facto equivalent to 'macroprudential supervision' (*The Economist*, 2010a).

Another aspect is that states increasingly depend on financial markets when government bonds are issued. Budget deficits in industrialised countries have skyrocketed and uninterrupted access to capital markets is vital for survival. Obviously, highly indebted states with poor credit ratings have little interest in imposing regulations on institutions to acquire high graded sovereign bonds only. 2009 and 2010 have witnessed a general trend towards downgrading sovereign bonds.

Finally, sovereigns act – albeit to a limited extend – as commercial parties through sovereign wealth funds. Sovereign wealth funds compete with commercial financial institutions (International Working Group of Sovereign Wealth Funds, 2008). Sovereign Wealth Funds have been recognised as well-established institutional investors and important participants in the international monetary and financial system. China's trade surplus is channelled through the market and thereby China competes with commercial parties. It is unclear whether sovereign wealth funds will operate on a level playing field with privately run financial institutions.

In sum, states heavily participate in financial markets as guarantors, lenders, borrowers, debtors and creditors. The intense involvement of states in the financial sector, directly or indirectly, obscures the role of states as supervisors and casts doubts on the ability of state institutions to function as supervisors.

Designing a supervisory system

The objectives of a supervisory system are monitoring and managing risk profiles of financial markets (IMF, 2009). Provided that the markets operate internationally and supervisors have limited capacities and resources, a system need to be designed that will span multiple jurisdictions, is dynamic and draws on know-how available in the markets. The system also needs to cover the various branches of the financial market: banking, insurance and securities industries.

The system needs to cover multiple jurisdictions in order to supervise cross border operations of individual institutions and to signal systemic risks. Cross-border operations are monitored by supervisory colleges, discussed above. Systemic risks councils, regional and global, need to track the behaviour of financial institutions across multiple jurisdictions, understand the associated risks and give early warning signals when risks are building up.

The system must be dynamic too. In a rapidly changing world, risk assessments are subject to continuous changing perceptions, and, accordingly, supervisory practices must be frequently readjusted. When institutions engineer new high-risk products or ignore market risks, a supervisor must respond instantly without having to wait for legislative action. A law describing static rules and principles is therefore inappropriate. In innovate markets legislators may not anticipate the financial engineering of advanced banking. They also may not foresee the emergence of the so-called 'shadow banking system' or similar behaviour to escape supervision (*The Economist*, 2008).

There is a need for an authority that 'continuously adapts the scope and content of regulations to the changing structure of international markets and the changing character of firms' (Eatwell and Taylor, 2000, pp. 194, 195). Only a supervisor with discretionary regulatory powers may effectively monitor financial markets. Therefore, a supervisory system cannot be based on elaborated rules only, but must also rely on principles concerning governance.

Currently, a principle-based approach has been adopted in Basel II and Solvency II. The Basel II framework acknowledges that 'the supervisory review process of the Framework is intended not only to ensure that banks have adequate capital to support all the risks in their business, but also to encourage banks to develop and use better risk management techniques in monitoring and managing their risks'. Accordingly, a 'sound risk management process is the foundation for an effective assessment of the adequacy of a bank's capital position' and 'supervisors should assess the degree to which internal targets and processes incorporate the full range of material risks faced by the bank' (Basel II, Part III, Second Pillar).

Solvency II also adopts a principle-based approach. As a general governance requirement, 'Member States shall require all insurance and reinsurance undertakings to have in place an effective system of governance which provides for sound and prudent management of the business'. The system must provide for 'an adequate transparent organisational structure with a clear allocation and appropriate segregation of responsibilities and an effective system for ensuring the transmission of information'. Insurance companies must have 'written policies in relation to at least risk management, internal control, internal audit and, where relevant, outsourcing' and the 'supervisory authorities shall have appropriate means, methods and powers for verifying the system of governance of the insurance and reinsurance undertakings and for evaluating emerging risks identified by those undertakings which may affect their financial soundness'. To be able to perform this task Article 41 stipulates that 'the Member States shall ensure that the supervisory authorities have the powers necessary to require that the system of governance be improved'.

A principle-based supervisory system offers a number of features:

- a high degree of generality;
- performance should be measured in qualitative not quantitative terms;
- principles are purposive, expressing the reasons behind the rule;
- principles describe behavioural standards, such as the requirement of integrity, due diligence and reasonable care.

A principle-based supervisory system may be beneficial for an institution as it enables innovation in financial engineering and thereby enhances competition. For supervisors this system provides them with flexibility, facilitates innovation of supervisory methods and enables them to develop regulatory practices on which the market may rely. Flexibility would also include modulation in the degree of supervision. Financial institutions that are systemically important or 'too big to fail' should be subjected to firmer supervision.

A principle-based system has disadvantages too. It may fail to provide certainty and predictability, and opens up an opportunity for arbitrary or retroactive measures. In addition, Black (2008) discerns a number of 'paradoxes', such as diverging interpretations of principles ('principles can be general yet precise'), uncertainty of what is expected by the supervisor due to the opaque language of principles ('principles can facilitate communication but can also hinder it') or uncertainty whether a particular behaviour is in compliance with what is expected by the supervisor. Another worry is the costs in human resources associated with principle-based supervision. Judging the quality of governance and assessing and understanding risk is a burdensome task.

Whereas principle-based supervision may have some drawbacks, the risk of arbitrariness and costs must be balanced, however, against a pressing need to secure what may be considered a public good, that is, a stable financial system. Financial markets are caretakers of this public good and must be willing to accept rigorous measures to preserve the system.

If a principle-based system is put in place there will be shared responsibility for interpretation and application of standards. Financial institutions need to think through the application of relevant principles in specific circumstances. Supervisors have the responsibility to give guidance. In light of shared responsibility, frequent and reflective consultations should take place between the supervisor and financial institution (Black, 2008, p. 17). This means reasoned interchanges and direct conversations as to the meaning and application of principles. When a principle-based system is applied, the financial institution should be represented by risk management officers next to compliance officers. A dialogue need not be confrontational, but also may be merely informative based on past performance of the financial institution. Guo (2010, p. 5) also recognises the need for dialogue but sees this as a bargaining process, because effective supervision depends upon the information and expertise held by financial market actors.

The IMF has considerable experience with principle-based supervision of macroeconomic and monetary policies of sovereign actors. Article IV of the Fund's Articles of Agreement requires member countries to collaborate with the Fund on monetary matters. Collaboration takes place through so-called Article IV annual consultations between member countries and IMF staff on how to pursue objectives of monetary and economic policies. Article IV is entitled 'Obligations Regarding Exchange Rate Arrangements' and stipulates that member countries must follow general policies. These policies require that member countries 'shall endeavour to direct its economic and financial policies towards the objectives of fostering orderly economic growth with reasonable price stability' and 'seek to promote stability by fostering orderly economic and financial conditions and a monetary system that does not tend to produce erratic disruptions'. The phrasing reveals general behavioural standards and purposive principles. Furthermore, the general policies are supplemented by more precise rules. To oversee compliance with general policies the Fund shall 'exercise firm surveillance' and 'adopt specific principles for the guidance of all members with respect to those policies'. Specific principles are elaborated in decisions in the Fund's Executive Board that may adopt such decisions when it sees fit to do so.[12] Characteristic of the Fund's principle-based system approach is therefore laying down broad behavioural standards in a basic legal document and giving further shape and impetus through the adoption of specific principles by the decisions of an implementing body.

There are some fundamental differences between overseeing sovereign countries and commercial financial institutions. First is the prohibition of discrimination between member countries of the IMF. The Fund is expected to give its members the same treatment in similar conditions. In the case of supervision over systemically important financial institutions there would not be such prohibition and the degree of supervision may be adjusted depending on the size and past performance of the financial institution. Some institutions may only need a light supervisory touch because of the willingness to be fully transparent or having a good track record. Other institutions which have failed to conduct their business with due care and diligence and failed to implement an adequate risk management system may need a more rigorous approach.

Second is the lack of authority of the IMF to impose binding decisions upon its membership as Article IV reflects only soft law. The vagueness of the language in Article IV makes it impossible to make firm decisions based on generally formulated policies (Gold, 1983). Reports based on Article IV consultation are often received with appreciation but ignored when policies must be given shape (*Financial Times*, 2009a). This is different in the context of commercial institutions. Nothing prevents regulators and supervisors of financial institutions from imposing binding laws and, eventually, sanctions.

Challenges

The predicaments of the current supervisory system suggest that an international institutional framework must be assigned to coordinate and direct supervision over markets. Institutions created in this framework would be able to oversee the financial markets, overcome jurisdictional obstacles, defeat destructive interests, override state-centred interests and pool knowledge on the complexities of financial markets. Cooperation should address each mode of supervision: micro-prudential, cross-border micro-prudential and macro-prudential.

Micro-prudential supervision, national and cross-border, will continue to be a primary responsibility of domestic supervisors but should be coordinated by international agreement. This is also expressed by the G20. In its communiqué of 2 April 2009, the G20 stated: 'we each agree to ensure our domestic regulatory systems are strong. But we also agree to establish the much greater consistency and systematic cooperation between countries, and the framework of internationally agreed high standards, that a global financial system requires.' The G20 appears not to aim at an international authority or to allocate responsibility on the international level. It merely underscores the need for international standards and better coordination between domestic supervisors, and international cooperation must be able to satisfy such needs. An international institution should therefore endorse principles and regulations and take stock of best practices that will be implemented by domestic supervisors. Here the distinctions between regulation and supervision become relevant. Regulatory power may emerge from international cooperation and thereby ensure consistency and cooperation, whereas supervision is exercised on a domestic level. International regulatory standards are already promoted by institutions such as the International Organization of Securities Commissions (IOSCO), the International Association of Insurance Supervisors (IAIS) and the Basel Committee, joined in the FSB (FSB Charter, 2009).[13]

Macro-prudential supervision is the pièce de résistance when it comes to overseeing global markets. It elevates supervision on an aggregated level and requires firmer international involvement. Macro-prudential supervision should ensure that all financial activities that may pose systemic risks are appropriately overseen. In essence, macro-prudential supervision involves collecting and analysing aggregate data, and giving early warning signals when data reveal a threat to the system. Analysis will reveal systemic risks and the extent that failure could cause disruption to key financial markets and loss of confidence. Macro-prudential supervisors will need to asses interconnectedness and the size of institutions and take into account leverage and funding mismatches.

A dedicated macro-prudential supervisory system is currently non-existent. The IMF has taken some steps towards assessing financial markets stability within the jurisdiction of members. The Financial Stability Assessment Programme (FSAP) began in 1999 as a joint IMF-World Bank project and has gained a high profile. The FSAP's objective is to achieve an integrated analysis of stability of domestic financial markets using a wide range of analytical tools and techniques (IMF Executive Board, 2000). FSAPs are integrated in the IMF's Article IV consultations and are therefore limited to assessment within the jurisdiction of members. FSAPs have paid limited attention to global and regional linkages (IMF, Independent Evaluation Office, 2006). Another deficiency is that assessments under the FSAP are on a voluntary basis only.[14] Lacunae in reporting practices may be an explanation why the financial crisis was so poorly anticipated. Until 2009 the US failed to subject itself to FSAP oversight.

A new framework for macro-prudential supervision – towards a World Financial Organisation

The current framework for regulation and supervision over financial markets is a patchwork of national regulators and supervisors. To the extent that regulators cooperate within standard-setting bodies (Basel Committee, IOSCO, IAIS) their authority is unclear. Domestic supervisors may implement the regulations of standard-setting bodies but they may also decide not to do so. It is also unclear how standard-setting bodies relate to the IMF, which is responsible for overseeing monetary and financial policies of member countries. In addition, political fora such as the G20 issue communiqués on managing the financial system. G20 communiqués may contradict views of decision-making bodies within the IMF. Even when ideas and initiatives from various sources converge, they lack a firm and high-level political commitment. In the final analysis there is a pressing deficiency of global authority for the management of the financial system.

A new framework would recognise that there are two major actors in the financial system: states and financial institutions. Both continuously interact: states attempt to regulate and supervise institutions or even act as market participants themselves; institutions respond to states' economic policies and are habitually driven by regulatory arbitrage. Supervision over the financial system must serve stability and establish a balance between interests of sovereign actors and financial institutions.

The authority to exercise macro-prudential supervision might be placed within the existing framework of the IMF. IMF departments have suggested creating a new International Monetary and Financial Board (IMFB) that would operate on a ministerial level (IMF, 2010). The Board would take important binding decisions that are currently within the power of the Fund's plenary body, the Board of Governors. The high-level representation and limited size of the IMFB could make the Fund's role more significant in industrialised countries and restore the symmetrical treatment of all members (Gold, 1980).[15] The IMF treaty would need to be amended as it does not provide for a coordinating role as suggested. The proposal could be extended by also shifting the Fund's mandate towards firm macro-prudential supervision over both sovereign and commercial actors.

More ambitious is the proposal to establish a high-level and overarching global economic council to oversee 'the proper functioning of the global economy and the stability of the international financial system by providing close political support and strategic guidance to all financial institutions'. The council would supersede informal fora such as the G20 and have universal representation along the lines of the IMF and World Bank. The council would have 'decision-making powers, not inside but above the Fund. It would also be responsible for political supervision of the other international institutions, including the World Bank, the Financial Stability Board and the World Trade Organization' (Adams and Sadun, 2009). This proposal is reminiscent of calls for an economic security council (EU Observer.com, 2009).

A council could be institutionalised by taking the shape of a World Financial Organisation (WFO). The WFO as an intergovernmental organisation, operating alongside the World Trade Organization, would recognise that regulating finance and trade are complementary functions. Complementarity implies that a stable financial system is a precondition for trade liberalisation. Both the WTO and the WFO would share a common objective, that is, the promotion of national and international prosperity.

The WFO would adopt a two-tier approach by focusing on both states and financial markets. It would consider the interaction between macroeconomic policies of governments and behaviour of financial markets. Addressing both spheres makes sense because macroeconomic policies (including balance of payments, reserves, foreign indebtedness, exchange rate policies, liberalisation of capital movement) strongly affect the behaviour of financial institutions. Conversely, financial institutions' behaviour may have a deep impact on the macroeconomic performance of states.

The WFO would operate on a ministerial level and be able to exercise high-level political authority. It would accept global membership of states, and, if appropriate, regional organisations for economic cooperation. Its decision-making body would be limited in size and composed of ministers that represent constituencies and a limited number of large members. A minister representing a constituency would act on behalf of a group of smaller members. Decision-making should be based on consensus, but arrangements for a weighted voting system may be an option of last resort.[16]

The WFO would be more than just an intergovernmental organisation. It would also extend its authority over standard-setting bodies, systemic risk councils (provided they exist) and national supervisors. These bodies and councils should be accountable to the WFO. The WFO could incite standard-setting bodies to develop regulations and give directives to councils and supervisors. Financial organisations such as the IMF and the World Bank would be subordinate to the WFO. The WFO would streamline their activities, create a hierarchy and allocate responsibilities. The WFO might also decide when early warning signals should be followed by swift and decisive political action. (See Figure 3.1.)

The WFO's fundamental strength would lie in its ability to oversee the financial system as a whole and to give political clout to decisions. The rationale of the WFO would be the ability to take responsibility for the preservation and integrity of the financial system. Its institutional arrangements should be designed to make peer pressure constructive.

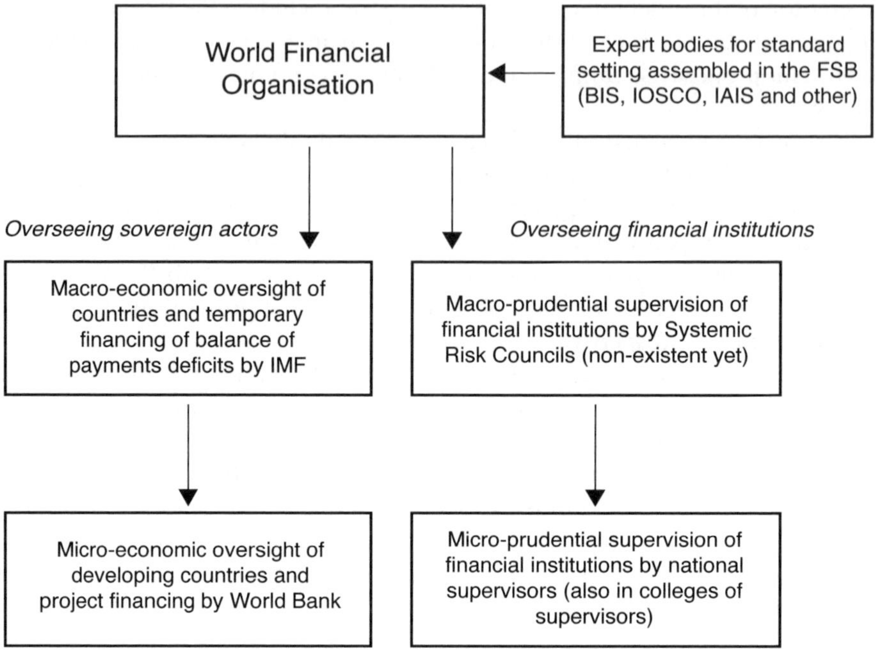

Source: Author's compilation

Figure 3.1 World Financial Organisation

Conclusion

Stability of the international financial system is vital for a sustainable international economic system. Stability paves the way towards prosperity, nationally and internationally. Because of its paramount importance, the financial system must belong to the domain of common goods. A common good cannot be owned exclusively by financial institutions or any other identifiable group; instead it belongs to humanity as a whole. Two consequences flow from this concept: financial markets must be firmly supervised to protect its integrity and stability, and any actor who abuses the system for its own purposes is liable towards other users. An abuse may be a deliberate act to conceal transparency, take excessive risks or bet against the economic downfall of another actor in the market. A sovereign actor may also abuse the markets by manipulating the exchange rate of its currency in order to gain an unfair competitive advantage over other countries.[17]

State agencies are the most obvious supervisors over markets, but some impediments are inherent. States may not be able to supervise a financial institution operating internationally because of jurisdictional obstacles. Colleges of supervisors are an attempt to remedy this. States may also lack the capacity to understand what financial institutions think and do. Moreover, states are actors on the markets themselves. They have an interest to conceal or manipulate information that may endanger their financial standing. Adequate supervision may also be compromised when a state is under threat of insolvency. How then could a supervisory agency insist that its financial institutions lend to solvent debtors only? Finally, states have a high interest in financial institutions, either by subsidisation or by nationalisation.

We conclude that a supervisory system that exclusively relies on domestic supervisors is deemed to be deficient and to serve national interests only. There must be an intergovernmental institution that oversees markets and exercises high-level political authority over existing supervisors. The proposed WFO constitutes an institutional framework for cooperation on the stability of financial markets. The WFO would legally and politically dominate existing institutions, including the IMF and World Bank.

Notes

1. A distinction should be made between regulating and supervising markets. Regulators create rules aimed at financial institutions; their main objective is to foster financial stability and to protect those who use financial services. Overseeing compliance with regulations is the responsibility of supervisors. A supervisor who finds that a financial institution does not meet legal requirements may decide to enter into a dialogue or reprimand a non-compliant institution. In literature, 'regulation' and 'supervision' are often used indiscriminately.
2. The notions of 'community interest' and 'common goods' are phenomena from previous centuries. The common good of mankind (*bonum commune humanitatis*) was developed by Francisco Suárez (1548–1617), a member of the Spanish School. Suárez held the view that international law was exclusively aimed at the conservation of justice and peace between states in order to preserve the common good of mankind. As can be inferred from contemporary doctrine, the concept has widened, beyond peace and security.
3. Feichtner recognises this for the world trading system. 'A functioning legal system which creates security and predictability in international trade relations may, however, itself be regarded as a common good.' This also applies to the international financial system. Without an effective financial system the world trading system cannot exist. Financial stability is also recognised as a global public good by the Committee on IMF Governance Reform (2009).
4. In September 2010 the Committee agreed to increase the tier one capital ratio from 2% to 7%, thereby attempting to make banks more resilient in times of economic distress. Tier one is the safest kind of asset a bank can hold, including equity and retained earnings.
5. Membership includes Argentina, Australia, Belgium, Brazil, Canada, China, France, Germany, Hong Kong, SAR, India, Indonesia, Italy, Japan, Korea, Luxembourg, Mexico, the Netherlands, Russia, Saudi Arabia, Singapore, South Africa, Spain, Sweden, Switzerland, Turkey, the United Kingdom and the United States.

6. Basel II, 'Directive 2006/48/EC of the European Parliament and of the Council of 14 June 2006 relating to the taking up and pursuit of the business of credit institutions'. *Official Journal L 177/1*, 30 June 2006.
7. Solvency II, 'Directive of the European Parliament and of the Council on the Taking-Up and Pursuit of the Business of Insurance and Reinsurance', PE-CONS 3643/6/09 REV 6, 25 November 2009.
8. Accordingly, cross-border banking will be supervised on a consolidated basis 'adequately monitoring and, as appropriate, applying prudential norms to all aspects of the business conducted by the group worldwide'. Principle 25 of the 2006 Core Principles for Effective Banking Supervision of the Basel Committee on Banking Supervision explains that 'consolidated supervision requires cooperation and information exchange between home supervisors and the various other supervisors involved, primarily host banking supervisors. Banking supervisors must require the local operations of foreign banks to be conducted to the same standards as those required of domestic institutions.'
9. Consideration 113 of Solvency II Directive. See also Chapter III of the Directive on Measures to Facilitate Group Supervision.
10. The FSB is the key institution in this process. According to its Charter the FSB is mandated to 'assess vulnerabilities affecting the financial system, identify and oversee action needed to address them; promote co-ordination and information exchange among authorities responsible for financial stability; monitor and advise on market developments and their implications for regulatory policy; advise on and monitor best practice in meeting regulatory standards; undertake joint strategic reviews of the policy development work of the international Standard Setting Bodies to ensure their work is timely, coordinated, focused on priorities, and addressing gaps; set guidelines for, and support the establishment, functioning of, and participation in, supervisory colleges, including through ongoing identification of the most systemically important cross-border firms; support contingency planning for cross-border crisis management, particularly with respect to systemically important firms; and collaborate with the IMF to conduct Early Warning Exercises to identify and report to the IMFC and the G20 Finance Ministers and Central Bank Governors on the buildup of macroeconomic and financial risks and the actions needed to address them.'
11. A similar proposal has been to create 'A European System of Financial Supervision (ESFS), modelled on the European System of Central Banks [that] would comprise a new EU-level institution – a European Financial Services Authority. This system would supervise those systemically relevant financial institutions that operate on a pan-European basis, and it would be the final authority for interpreting and implementing EU financial market rules whenever there is a conflict between national regulators.'
12. Article XII of the IMF's Articles of Agreement authorises the Board to take decisions provided the authorisation is delegated by the Board of Governors. The Board has made 25 decisions in relation to Article IV.
13. Though not a formal institution and absent of legal personality, in 2009 the FSB adopted a Charter. Article 1 states the FSB's objectives: 'The Financial Stability Board (FSB) is established to coordinate at the international level the work of national financial authorities and international standard setting bodies (SSBs) in order to develop and promote the implementation of effective regulatory, supervisory and other financial sector policies. In collaboration with the international financial institutions, the FSB will address vulnerabilities affecting financial systems in the interest of global financial stability.'

14. Formally, assessments under the FSAP are a 'technical service' (under Article V Section 2 of the IMF's Articles of Agreement) which may be requested by Fund members and is therefore voluntary. Materially, members may feel the need to subject themselves to FSAP assessments so as to demonstrate the relative strength of their banking sector and thereby gain access to capital markets.
15. The equal treatment of creditor and debtor members has been a long-standing problem in the IMF.
16. This is essentially the institutional model employed within the Bretton Woods institutions.
17. This is also prohibited under the IMF Articles of Agreement, Article IV Section 1(iii).

Bibliography

Adams, Timothy, and Arrigo Sadun (2009) 'Global Economic Council Should Oversee All', *Financial Times*, 16 August.

Arner, Douglas (2009) 'The Global Credit Crisis of 2008: Causes and Consequences', *The International Lawyer* 43(91), 91–136.

Basel Committee (2010) 'Consultative document, Good Practice Principles on Supervisory Colleges', www.bis.org/publ/bcbs170.pdf.

Billio, Monica, Mila Getmanski, Andrew W. Lo and Loriana Pelizzon (2010) 'Measuring Systemic Risk in the Finance and Insurance Sector'. *MIT Sloan School Working Paper.*

Bini Smaghi, Lorenzo (2009) 'Move to Strengthen ECB Gains Support', *Financial Times*, 13 February.

Black, Julia (2008) 'Forms and Paradoxes of Principles Based Regulation', LSE, *Law, Society and Economy Working Papers*, http://ssrn.com/abstract=1267722.

CEBS (2007) 'Template for a Multilateral Cooperation and Coordination Agreement on the Supervision of XY Group', 27 December, www.c-ebs.org/getdoc/863e6b2e-5047-4dc1-b746-78a89dd2e36c/Template_December-2007.aspx.

CEBS, CEIOPS and IWCFC (2009) 'Colleges of Supervisors – 10 Common Principles', 27 January.

Committee on IMF Governance Reform, 'Final Report', 24 March, www.imf.org/external/np/omd/2009/govref/032409.pdf.

De Bandt, Olivier, and Philipp Hartmann (2000) 'Systemic Risk: A Survey', *ECB Working Paper* No. 35.

De Bettignies, Henri-Claude, and François Lépineux (2009) 'Can Multinational Corporations Afford to Ignore the Global Common Good?', *Business and Society Review*, 114(2), 153–82, 161.

De Larosière Group (2009) *Report of the High-Level Group on Financial Supervision in the EU*, http://ec.europa.eu/internal_market/finances/docs/de_larosiere_report_en.pdf.

Duncan, Alford (2010) 'Supervisory Colleges: The Global Financial Crisis and Improving International Supervisory Coordination', http://ssrn.com/abstract=1545291.

Eatwell, John, and Lance Taylor (2000) *Global Finance at Risk: A Case for Global Financial Regulation* (The New Press).

ECB (2009) 'Credit Default Swaps and Counterparty Risk', www.ecb.int/pub/pdf/other/creditdefaultswapsandcounterpartyrisk2009en.pdf.

ECB, Bank of Japan and US Federal Reserve (2007) 'Fourth Joint Central Bank Research Conference, 8–9 November, in Co-operation with the Committee on the Global Financial System', April.

The Economist (2008) 'Barbarians at the Vault', 15 May.

The Economist (2010a) 'Great Wall Street', 10 July.

The Economist (2010b) 'The Global Revival of Industrial Policy', 7 August.

EU Observer.com (2009) 'Merkel and Sarkozy Call for Global Economic Security Council', 9 January.

Feichtner, Isabel (2007) 'Community Interest', *Max Planck Encyclopaedia of International Law*.

Financial Times (2009a) 'Top Nations "Water Down" IMF Reports, Rays Regulator', 10 February.

Financial Times (2009b) 'Bernanke Calls for Powerful Regulator', 11 March.

FSA (2009) 'The Turner Review – A Regulatory Response to the Global Banking Crisis', www.fsa.gov.uk/pubs/other/turner_review.pdf.

FSB Charter (2009), www.financialstabilityboard.org/publications/r_090925d.pdf.

G20 Toronto Summit Declaration, 26–27June 2010.

Gold, Joseph (1980) 'Symmetry as a Legal Objective of the International Monetary System', *New York University Journal of International Law and Politics*, 12(3), 423–78.

Gold, Joseph (1983) 'Strengthening the Soft International Law of Exchange Arrangements', *American Journal of International Law*, 77, 443–98.

Guo, Huachun (2010) 'Systemic Risks and the Legalization of Accountable Transnational Financial Regulation', paper presented at the Society of International Economic Law (SIEL), Second Biennial Global Conference, University of Barcelona, http://papers.ssrn.com/sol3/papers.cfm?abstract_id=1629208 .

Hunt, Robert M. (2010) 'Business Method Patents and US Financial Services', *Contemporary Economic Policy*, 28(3), 322–52.

Igan, Deniz, Prachi Mishra and Thierry Tressel (2009) 'A Fistful of Dollars: Lobbying and the Financial Crisis', IMF, www.imf.org/external/pubs/ft/wp/2009/wp09287.pdf.

IMF Executive Board (2000) 'Summing Up by the Acting Chairman – Financial Sector Assessment Program – A Review – Lessons from the Pilot and Issues Going Forward'. Executive Board Meeting 00/123, 13 December.

IMF Independent Evaluation Office (2006) 'Report on the Evaluation of the Financial Sector Assessment Program', 5 January.

MF Staff Paper (2009) 'The Perimeter of Financial Regulation', IMF Staff Position Note, 26 March, www.imf.org/external/pubs/ft/spn/2009/spn0907.pdf.

IMF Strategy, Policy and Review Department and the Legal Department (2010) 'IMF Governance Reforms', 7 July.

IMF, BIS and FSB (2009) 'Report to G20 Finance Ministers and Governors, Guidance to Assess the Systemic Importance of Financial Institutions, Markets and Instruments: Initial Considerations', 28 October.

IMF and World Bank (2005) *Financial Sector Assessment, A Handbook*.

Impavido, Gregorio and Ian Tower (2009) 'How the Financial Crisis Affects Pensions and Insurance and Why the Impacts Matter', IMF Working Paper, July.

International Working Group of Sovereign Wealth Funds (IWG) (2008) 'Sovereign Wealth Funds, Generally Accepted Practices and Principles', October, www.iwg-swf.org/pubs/eng/santiagoprinciples.pdf.

New York Times (2010) 'Federal Home Loan Mortgage Corporation', 10 May, http://topics.nytimes.com/top/news/business/companies/freddie_mac/index.html.

Petrovic, Ana, and Ralf Tutsch (2009) 'National Rescue Measures in Response to the Current Financial Crisis Legal', *ECB Working Paper Series* No. 8, July, www.ecb.int/pub/pdf/scplps/ecblwp8.pdf.

Schich, Sebastian (2009) 'Insurance Companies and the Financial Crisis' (OECD, October).

Solvency II, 'Directive of the European Parliament and of the Council on the Taking-Up and Pursuit of the Business of Insurance and Reinsurance', PE-CONS 3643/6/09 REV 6, 25 November 2009.

Speyer, Bernhard, and Norbert Walter (2009) *Europe's World* (Spring).

The Geneva Association (2010) *Systemic Risk in Insurance: An Analysis of Insurance and Financial Stability*, Appendix H, www.genevaassociation.org/Portals/0/Geneva_Association_Systemic_Risk_in_Insurance_Report_March2010.pdf.

US Congressional Budget Office (2010) 'Report on the Troubled Asset Relief Program', March, www.cbo.gov/ftpdocs/112xx/doc11227/03-17-TARP.pdf.

4
Insurance and Financial Stability

Peter Braumüller and Alexander Warzilek[1]

Introduction

Following the recent financial crisis, there have been intensive discussions on the role of insurance in the global financial system and its relationship to financial stability. The crisis was not caused by the insurance sector, but nevertheless it has had some impact on this sector. Although insurance companies are an important part of the financial system, particularly as institutional investors, and are linked to other financial institutions, the insurance sector seemed to be mainly susceptible to systemic risks from other parts of the financial system, but – in general – not generating or amplifying such risks.

The International Monetary Fund (IMF)/Bank for International Settlements (BIS)/Financial Stability Board (FSB) approach towards systemic risk is mainly banking-focused and cannot be applied to the insurance sector in the same way. There are substantial differences in the underlying business models of the insurance and banking industries. However, not all business of insurance companies is based on the traditional insurance business model and therefore regulators have to understand and carefully monitor the ways in which insurers carry out their activities.

From its inception, the International Association of Insurance Supervisors (IAIS) has included the contribution to global financial stability as one of its main objectives. It is, however, fair to say that this goal has gained much more attention over the last two years. Traditional micro-prudential supervision needs to be supplemented by macro-prudential supervision in order to identify potential stability concerns arising from the insurance sector or those affecting insurance as early as possible. Supervisors need to deploy the necessary tools to mitigate macroeconomic risks which could threaten the financial soundness of insurance companies and groups and endanger policy-holders' interests.

Insurance and its role in the global financial system

Insurance has a long tradition and plays an important role in society and the economy. It allows individuals and companies to protect themselves against adverse events and mitigates the impact of such events. Individuals or companies may not wish to bear risks to which they are exposed on their own. Through the means of insurance such risks can be transferred to insurance companies if the policy-holder is unable or unwilling to assume the negative impact of those risks possibly materialising. The uncertainty of the timing or impact of adverse events is transformed into the certainty of being protected by the regular payment of a premium. Many businesses and activities would not be respectively launched or performed without the availability of protection against the risks involved through insurance.

Insurance covers risks with different probabilities and different impacts. Risks which are too frequent might not be covered or at least not at a reasonable premium. Risks with an excessive impact might not be insurable or only with a certain limit on the maximum claim. Risks insured vary broadly. Insurance coverage may be demanded against loss of or damage to property (for example, through fire, theft, natural or man-made catastrophes), against financial loss (for example, through business interruption), or against liability towards third parties (for example, in cases of motor vehicles, aircrafts or environmental pollution). Where dangerous business activities might impact third parties, governments have made insurance mandatory, in particular in motor vehicle and air carrier liability. In these cases, the decision to take out insurance is not only based on individual preference but also required by law. Lack of insurance coverage would mean the inability to drive a car or operate an aircraft.

Personal insurance covers individual risks for example connected to death, an accident, illness or unemployment.

Retirement provision and income in old age is also an important area associated with insurance. Social security systems increasingly rely on supplementary pensions and other retirement provisions through the insurance industry. Beside the pension provided from public sources, people are more and more dependent on additional retirement income from private insurance and pension contracts.

Life insurance is part of personal insurance and was originally created to provide protection against early death in terms of support for the surviving dependants and to cover related expenses (for example, funeral costs). Certain life insurance products have expanded to include the accumulation of cash values as a method of long-term saving. In recent years, new, complex and very sophisticated life insurance products have gained substantial market share. Those products are often linked to or use banking structured products as underlying investments. In this respect, there is a certain correlation with the banking and securities sectors.

Moreover, the insurance industry is a very important purchaser of bonds and other securities. The monetary source of these investments is the premiums collected from the policy-holders. Insurers manage around US$18,700 billion of financial assets which is around 11% of the world's total (The Geneva Association, 2010, p. 7). They are among the biggest institutional investors and highly interconnected with financial markets.

Another cross-sectoral linkage arises from financial conglomerates. Some financial groups consist of banking, insurance and securities branches.

Insurance comprises a broad scale of business. Micro-insurance, for example, is related to small premiums and corresponding small claims, but the risks involved still might have significant impact on the people concerned. This socially valuable area of insurance is geared to include the poor in the emerging markets and coincides with development cooperation (see BMZ, 2009). It could be carried out by private insurers where a significant number of people are affected by the same risks.

At the other end of the scale, catastrophe insurance (for example, against hurricanes, floods or terrorism) covers risks for which a single event can lead to extremely large claims. In such a case insurers normally mitigate their exposure through reinsurance.

Beyond that insurance is part and parcel of the financial services industry. The legal structure of insurance entities can differ substantially: cooperatives and mutuals pursue a more altruistic approach, whilst stock companies operate as commercial enterprises and pay dividends to their shareholders. Profit is made in different ways: for example, through an expected profit element included in the insurance premium, through investment management (of the premiums collected) or by managing claims and expense payments efficiently.

The following figures emphasise the economic significance of the insurance sector: the global volume of premiums in 2009 added up to US$4,066 billion; on average US$3,405 and US$92 per capita were spent on insurance in industrial countries and in emerging markets respectively (Swiss Re, 2010, pp. 1, 14, 20).

In summary, insurance facilitates the economy and society to prosper but also itself contributes substantially to economic growth.

The recent financial crisis – new questions and new challenges

At the moment, we are undergoing the most serious financial crisis since the Great Depression in the 1930s and the only one since the Second World War with worldwide ramifications (Reinhart and Rogoff, 2010, p. 20; Swiss Re, 2010, p. 3; cf. also Claessens et al., 2010, p. 7).

The situation is still relatively ambiguous. The American economist and Nobel Prize winner Paul Samuelson said: 'What we know about the global financial crisis is that we don't know very much.' So let's have a look at the little of what we know so far.

Though the crisis was not started from the insurance sector, it has impacted on this sector, as we are living in a highly interlinked global financial system. The crisis and its continuing aftershocks have emphasised this fact through the rapid contagion within the global financial system, including the insurance sector. Major governmental interventions were needed to rescue banks and financial groups and to settle the markets (Claessens et al., 2010, p. 5; Swiss Committee of Experts, 2010, p. 5). Consequently, financial stability has come much more into the focus of governments as well as of supervisors. It is now clear that the contagion risks between the different financial sectors were strongly underestimated (Reinhart and Rogoff, 2009, p. 199).

The most prominent example related to the insurance sector and the current crisis was the failure of the American International Group (AIG) which is a large and complex financial conglomerate. In this case the near collapse was due to extensive banking-type activities; in particular its substantial credit default swaps portfolio and its far-reaching securities lending programme were responsible for triggering its financial troubles. In contrast, its core insurance business was operating smoothly. However, during the peak of its problems, some policy-holders lost their trust in the group as a whole and therefore wanted to cancel their insurance contracts. For the time being, interventions by the Federal Reserve Bank of New York and the US Treasury have eased the situation (www.aigcorporate.com/aboutaig/index.html; cf. also The Geneva Association, 2010, p. 87).

At this stage of the financial crisis, extensive sovereign debt caused by governmental intervention is a potential danger which could undermine global financial stability. In some cases, concerns about the countries' ability to meet their future financial obligations could lead to credit rating downgrades and cause investors to demand higher interest rates. This again may have a negative impact on the availability of short-term credit lines and as a consequence on the provision of private credit too. On the other hand, capital cash flows in a lot of emerging markets have stabilised. However, there are some concerns about the potential impact on inflation and new asset price bubbles which, fortunately, have not materialised to date (IMF, 2010a, p. xi; IMF, 2010b, p. xv; cf. also Kumar and Woo, 2010, p. 21).

Without much doubt, in the near future the most challenging problem governments are faced with is the consolidation and repair of their public budgets (IMF, 2010a, p. xii; 2010b, p. xv).

However, the global financial crisis also provides an opportunity for many financial sector regulators and policy-makers worldwide to create new and more effective regulatory and supervisory rules. Sustainable success in the coming years will depend critically on international efforts to build a stronger global economy and a well designed financial regulatory architecture (Cf. IMF, 2010b, p. xv; furthermore, IIF, 2010, pp. 13, 47, 58).

Characteristics of the insurance business model

The traditional purpose of insurance is the transfer of risk of a loss from an individual or an entity to an insurance company in return for a premium or to provide financial security in the event of death or disability.

Insurance is a hedging instrument against uncertain losses deriving from adverse events like property damage, personal injury, premature death, theft or liability claims. The key element during this process is risk diversification which can be achieved through several methods. Pooling policy-holders' risks, insuring a wide variety of policy-holder pools, underwriting in different geographic areas and diversifying across different types of risks (such as underwriting and investment risk) are the most important instruments in this context (The Geneva Association, 2010, p. 6; IAIS, 2010b, no. 3; Weiss, 2010, p. 3).

One fundamental difference between such types of traditional insurance business and banking business is the different time horizon. The insurance sector is primarily long-term oriented. Insurance contracts are designed to implement a relationship of long duration – often for many years – between the insurers and the policy-holders. Claims and benefits are delayed since premiums are generally paid in advance of insurance coverage commencing; hence liquidity risk does not often arise for insurers. This is not the case for the banking sector which is much more reliant on immediate market liquidity and price discovery and therefore subject to a fundamentally different process (The Geneva Association, 2010, p. 20). In principle, insurers do not rely on borrowed money; they do not usually make use of sustained credit lines to satisfy claims from the insured (Weiss, 2010, p. 12). The time factor affects both supervising insurers as going concerns and intervening if they get into trouble and need to be recovered or wound up (see below).

Beside diversification, there are further techniques to mitigate the insurers' risks, such as reinsurance, hedging, insurance linked securities and the use of separate accounts for certain life insurance products where the policy-holder bears most or all investment risk. Furthermore, to alleviate asset and liability mismatches, insurance entities generally are required to follow strict risk-management practices. Finally, supervisory and regulatory requirements, in particular capital and reserving regulations, help to keep insurance companies solvent (IAIS, 2010b, no. 4).

Nonetheless, occasionally insurance companies may become financially distressed or even insolvent. It is important to highlight once again the long time horizon of the financial distress of insurers. Given that claims and benefits normally only need to be paid months or even years after the inception of an insurance policy any winding up can be processed prudently and calmly. This provides regulators an opportunity to step in with caution and to minimise potential losses of the insured from the insolvency (The Geneva Association, 2010, p. 30; IAIS, 2010b, no. 5; cf. also Weiss, 2010, p. 6).

The IAIS's role in financial stability

Since the early days of the IAIS, the Association's objectives have been to enhance and facilitate supervision of the insurance industry on a domestic as well as an international level in order to maintain efficient, fair, safe and stable insurance markets for the benefit and protection of policy-holders; moreover to promote the development of well-regulated insurance markets; and to contribute to global financial stability (see Article 2 [1] of the IAIS By-Laws). In order to achieve those objectives the IAIS has committed to cooperate with international organisations, including those responsible for financial stability (Article 2 [2] [f] of the IAIS By-Laws).

It is fair to say that initially the IAIS focused more on the development and maintenance of stable insurance markets for the protection of policy-holders than on financial stability issues in a broader sense. The IAIS was involved in the work of the then Financial Stability Forum (FSF), but to a very limited extent. For many years, financial stability issues have been mainly regarded as banking-related topics with only little relevance for insurance.

As stated before, the recent financial crisis has clearly demonstrated the strong interlinkage of the insurance sector with other parts of the financial system and the widespread contagion effects that could materialize. Analysis of systemic relevance in the insurance sector has revealed that under specific circumstances and for activities remote from the typical insurance business model, systemic risk might also build up in the insurance sector (see the section below on 'Insurance and systemic risk – the IAIS's perspective').

However, the IAIS's approach towards financial stability is certainly not restricted to the area of systemic relevance. Monitoring the macroeconomic environment and analysing its possible effects on the insurance sector certainly also improves the quality and effectiveness of micro-prudential supervision of insurance companies and groups.

In 2003, when the IAIS released its Insurance Core Principles (ICPs), which are global axioms for insurance supervisors, monitoring macroeconomic developments has been implicitly taken into account. ICP 11 on market analysis states that making use of all available sources, the supervisory authority monitors and analyses all factors that may have an impact on insurers and insurance markets. It draws conclusions and takes action as appropriate (IAIS, 2003, p. 23).

Whereas the basic concept is already laid down in the present ICP 11, the IAIS is further developing its approach to macroeconomic analysis in the course of the ongoing review of the ICPs and related standards. In all likelihood, it will address the need for macro-prudential surveillance and the availability of macro-prudential tools to do so.

Financial stability has also gained in importance from an institutional perspective. In October 2009, the IAIS decided to formalise its activities in this area by transforming its Financial Stability Task Force into a permanent Financial Stability Committee reporting directly to the Executive Committee. Furthermore, the IAIS is now strongly represented in the FSB and actively contributes to the FSB's work to ensure that insurance is treated appropriately according to its particular nature.

Macro-prudential surveillance and tools in insurance

Traditionally, the focus of insurance supervision was on individual insurance entities and groups – the so called micro-prudential approach. This focus – supplemented by thorough market analysis – still forms the foundation of insurance supervision and will certainly continue to do so.

Recently, the financial crisis has accentuated the importance of surveillance of risks from a macro-prudential perspective (cf. IIF, 2010, p. 59). Risks beyond the level of the individual entity can evolve rapidly and easily cross geographical boundaries as well as financial sectors (IAIS, 2010a, p. 5). Against this background, the G20 leaders have asked regulators to put more focus on the bigger market and risk picture and to take into account system-wide risks. This will mean a major change of the present supervisory philosophy.

In one way or another most IAIS members are already carrying out macro-prudential supervisory activities, but the breadth, reach and frequency of these activities diverge substantially and the focus is often on the analysis of domestic data only (IAIS, 2010a, p. 54).

Thus the IAIS feels obliged to support and assist its members by coordinating and streamlining their approaches and by providing input on macro-prudential surveillance at a global level.

The IAIS is currently developing a framework for macro-prudential surveillance to monitor financial stability with a focus on insurance – with a very high level of support from IAIS members who welcome this initiative and recognise the leadership role of the IAIS that is needed. This task will include creating appropriate economic expertise within the IAIS and establishing a network of experts on macro-prudential surveillance.

Moreover, the IAIS is supporting cross-sectoral macro-prudential monitoring of the potential build-up of system-wide risks and is planning to develop measures for national authorities to assess degrees of system-wide risks. In this regard, the IAIS expects to contribute to the development of a global framework by building on and expanding beyond the *Global Reinsurance Market Report* (a periodic IAIS publication focusing particularly on (re)insurance issues from a global supervisory perspective; the latest issues already include improved economic analysis) and by leveraging information from other sources, such as individual supervisors, regional supervisory groups and the IMF.

In addition, the IAIS is planning to develop macro-prudential tools that can be used by supervisors to mitigate potential system-wide risks related to the insurance sector. Other duties and responsibilities of the IAIS will be the development and composition of guidance papers, good practice, standards, key risk indicators as well as advanced training and information exchange on macro-prudential issues. The IAIS should also act as a central contact point for international organisations like the FSB and the IMF as well as for peer organisations like the Basel Committee on Banking Supervision and the International Organization of Securities Commissions (IOSCO) to add to the harmonisation of the different views on macro-prudential problems (The Geneva Association, 2010, p. 75).

The IMF/BIS/FSB approach towards systemic risk

Systemic risk was at the heart of the recent financial crisis. The failure or malfunction of large and complex financial institutions and markets has had significant negative impact on the global financial system and the real economy in many countries, directly or through contagion effects. Major governmental interventions and large rescue packages were necessary to stabilise the financial system.

Consequently, the G20 identified the need to strengthen regulation and supervision of systemically important financial institutions (SIFIs) and markets and requested the IMF, the BIS and the FSB to develop guidelines in the area of assessing systemic importance.

In October 2009, the IMF, the BIS and the FSB jointly issued a report to G20 finance ministers and governors on 'Guidance to Assess the Systemic Importance of Financial Institutions, Markets and Instruments: Initial Considerations'. This report defines systemic events in broad terms. In particular, it is the disruption to the flow of financial services that is caused by an impairment of all or parts of the financial system, and has the potential to have serious negative consequences for the real economy (IMF et al., 2009, no. 7).

The references to an impairment of the financial system and negative consequences for the real economy demonstrate that – according to this definition – negative externalities become part of the risk assessment of an institution or market. Without that, risk-taking institutions would rather look to their own risk-bearing capacity and willingness and not provide for risks with possible negative effects on their environment.

A disruption to the flow of financial services means that financial services become unavailable or unaffordable. In addition, to be considered as systemic this disruption must have the potential to cause a significant negative impact on the real economy. This means that disruptions within the financial system will not be considered systemically relevant if there is no spillover to the real economy. On the other hand, significant negative effects on the economy which are not caused by an impairment of parts or the whole financial system are also outside this definition.

The assessment of systemic relevance depends on the state of the financial system overall and the economy in general. It is not restricted in geographical terms which means that institutions or markets may be systemically relevant on a national, regional or international basis. It is evident that, in the latter case, the issue of cross-border cooperation between regulators and supervisors becomes a crucial element. Aside from some institutions and markets which are particularly critical to the financial system and therefore might be more permanently regarded as systemically relevant, for most institutions and markets the assessment might differ over time. Consequently, the assessment of systemic relevance has to be carried out regularly.

It is important to mention that the IMF/BIS/FSB approach does not exclude particular types of financial institutions, markets or instruments from the scope of systemic relevance. Therefore, insurance companies could, in principle, come under the definition of systemically relevant institutions (IMF et al., 2009, no. 8).

The IMF/BIS/FSB report suggests three criteria against which systemic relevance of institutions and markets should be assessed: size, lack of substitutability and interconnectedness (Cf. also IIF, 2010, p. 12; Swiss Committee of Experts, 2010, pp. 3, 11). These rather general criteria can be qualified as first points of reference, though more details clarifying the underlying meaning of these terms are necessary.

Commonly, the importance of a single component of the financial system increases with its size, the assessment of which should be based on balance sheet totals, off-balance sheet exposures, transaction volumes and assets under management (IMF et al., 2009, no. 13). However, size cannot simply be looked at on a single entity or single group level because systemic risk might also appear where different institutions are characterised by a similar risk profile leading to all or most of them becoming distressed as a consequence of the same external event.

Anyhow, well capitalised large institutions with simple business models and exposures can also be a source of stability in times of stress (IMF et al., 2009, p. 9 fn. 6).

Another important indicator of systemic relevance is lack of substitutability. The more key the role of a financial intermediary is for the financial system and the economy, and the more unlikely it is that other market participants can step in and provide the same or similar services as a failed institution, the more systemic risk is created in the system.

The element of interconnectedness should cover cases where financial institutions or markets are interlinked in a way that financial distress of one institution might easily cause distress to other market players. To assess interconnectedness it is important to look at all possible contagion lines, including both the number and importance of links.

The criteria mentioned apply to institutions, markets and instruments. Although it is considerably more challenging to use the criteria in the context of markets and instruments it is necessary to do so in order to capture the systemic risks comprehensively (IMF et al., 2009, no. 16).

The three criteria build up a useful analytical device to structure the assessment of systemic importance, but their relevance is often greatest when they are combined in different ways (IMF et al., 2009, no. 12). Most prominently, lack of substitutability increases the relevance of size, and vice versa. Furthermore, supplementary criteria should be employed in order to complement the assessment against the three more general criteria. Those additional indicators include in particular leverage, liquidity and maturity mismatches, as well as complexity (IMF et al., 2009, no. 20).

The IMF/BIS/FSB report itself (IMF et al., 2009, no. 23) lays out the limitations of the suggested framework. They admit that excessive reliance on quantitative techniques may provide a false impression on what can be achieved in terms of precision based on existing techniques and data availability. To make a fair distinction between systemically relevant and other institutions will always comprise a certain level of discretion by supervisory authorities. The most challenging task on a global level will be to establish mechanisms through which a consistent application of the definition of systemic relevance can be achieved in practice.

Insurance and systemic risk – the IAIS's perspective

During the discussions on systemic risks following the crisis, it was pivotal for the IAIS to emphasise the specific nature of the insurance sector and its role within the financial sector and more widely the contributions insurance business makes to the economy. The IAIS – mainly through its Financial Stability Committee – has analyzed the role of insurance related to financial stability and systemic risk. These topics remain high on the IAIS's agenda.

The IMF/BIS/FSB approach on systemic relevance and systemic risk discussed above captures all kinds of financial institutions but was predominantly concerned with the banking sector. Therefore it should not be applied in the same manner to the insurance sector.

In insurance, size by itself is not the best criterion for determining the potential for systemic risk. Large insurance companies have available greater possibilities to diversify their risks and hence they are normally more robust (cf. IIF, 2010, p. 37; Swiss Committee of Experts, 2010, p. 12).

When assessing systemic risks in insurance the time factor should not be underestimated: Firstly, in contrast to banks, insurers are not dependent on wholesale funding markets which can change quickly. Secondly, insurance can often involve a significant period of time between a policy commencing and its maturity or the settlement of any claim (compared with the withdrawal of a bank deposit), which allows insurers as well as supervisors to react in a thoughtful and prudent way. In the opinion of the IAIS, the time horizon can be regarded as an additional legitimate criterion to evaluate the systemic relevance of a financial institution.

As mentioned already, insurers can also mitigate their risks by using reinsurance. On the other hand, reinsurance activities may increase the interconnectedness between insurers.

In general, we can differentiate between systemic risks arising from the insurance sector and those from another financial sector which impact the insurance sector by transmission (Weiss, 2010, p. 15).

Analysis by the IAIS shows little evidence of core insurance business either generating or amplifying systemic risk, within the financial system itself or in the real economy. On the contrary, the insurance sector often fulfils a stabilising function which diminishes systemic risk. The reason behind that is that insurance entities collect their premiums up-front and operate with a steady and strong cash-flow, most of the time on a long term basis (The Geneva Association, 2010, p. 3).

However, insurers – life insurers in particular – are significant institutional investors in capital markets and may amplify systemic risk by their reaction to downturns in equity and other securities markets. If insurers collectively hold significant positions in equities or hedging instruments and need to liquidate their positions, this can aggravate selling pressure and contribute to falling stock prices (Weiss, 2010, p. 21).

Moreover, insurers may cause disruptions to the real economy by an unexpected withdrawal of capacity, for example if insurance against catastrophes becomes unavailable after a catastrophic event. Such a withdrawal occurred after the terrorist attacks of 9/11 when terrorism insurance became unavailable (IAIS, 2010b, p. 1 and no. 12). The situation can turn particularly precarious if compulsory insurance products disappear from the market or when insurance coverage is a precondition to conduct business. This means that lack of substitutability is a highly relevant criterion to assess systemic risk in insurance.

Apart from such disruptions, under the following very specific circumstances insurers might amplify systemic risk: (1) widespread distribution of financial products which contain a minimum guarantee and/or distribution of other types of products that are similar in nature to banking products; (2) widespread (naked) derivatives trading, especially extensive distribution of credit default swaps; (3) extensive providing of financial guarantee insurance; and (4) insurers taking advantage of regulatory arbitrage to sell products or services that may be of systemic importance (IAIS, 2010b, no. 14). Finally, non-regulated entities in insurance conglomerates (as in the case of AIG) may also create systemic problems.

Nevertheless, overall it should be re-emphasised that core insurance business principally neither generates nor amplifies systemic risk, although the sector is somewhat susceptible to systemic risks generated in other parts of the financial sector.

Conclusion

The first Indian Prime Minister, Jawaharlal Nehru, said that crises and deadlocks have at least the advantage of forcing us to think. Actually a lot of interesting ideas and proposals for better regulating and supervising financial institutions have emerged in the course of the financial crisis. The process of creating new rules in this area is still ongoing. A lot of attention is rightly directed to financial stability issues and considerations about systemic risks.

The insurance industry argues that none of the main activities of insurers or reinsurers pose systemic risk (The Geneva Association, 2010, p. 4). This is not surprising, given proposals that financial institutions pay a capital surcharge or levies or at least undergo more intensive supervision based on the fact that they are systemically important (IMF, 2010a, p. xiii; Lepetit, 2010, p. 2).

To our mind a more differentiated approach would be favourable, for different reasons: Under certain conditions insurers are not only susceptible to systemic risks generated in other parts of the financial sector but may independently amplify systemic risk, for example where they may disrupt for a period parts of the real economy by an unexpected withdrawal of capacity or where their reaction to downturns in equity and other securities markets contributes to a negative spiral. Finally, non-regulated entities within a financial conglomerate and some specific insurance business (for example financial guarantee insurance) can generate or amplify systemic risk and may give rise to contagion within conglomerates or across financial sectors (IAIS, 2010b, p. 1).

Generally speaking, insurance supervisors must increase awareness of the greater potential for systemic relevance of an insurance company or group the more that the supervised entity deviates from the traditional insurance business model by engaging in banking type activities or by performing unregulated activities.

Since, under certain circumstances, systemic risks might arise in the insurance sector, insurance supervisors have to promote and facilitate macro-prudential surveillance by developing and implementing appropriate tools to be able to deal with such situations effectively.

Presumably interdependencies between the financial sectors will further increase. In fact, certain financial services have become more and more complex, diverse and global. Against this background, cross-border and cross-sectoral cooperation between national supervisors to detect, reduce and avoid financial instabilities will gain in importance.

Note

1. The views expressed in this chapter are those of the authors only.

Bibliography

BMZ (2009) *Kleine Beiträge – große Sicherheit, Mikroversicherungen in der Finanzsystementwicklung* (Bonn and Berlin).

Claessens, S., G. Dell'Ariccia, D. Igan and L. Laeven (2010) 'Lessons and Policy Implications from the Global Financial Crisis', IMF Working Paper No. 44.

IAIS (2003) *Insurance Core Principles and Methodology* (Basel: IAIS).

IAIS (2010a) *Global Reinsurance Market Report: Macroprudential Surveillance and (Re)Insurance* (Basel: IAIS).

IAIS (2010b) *Position Statement on Key Financial Stability Issues* (Basel: IAIS).

IIF (2010) *Systemic Risk and Systemically Important Firms: An Integrated Approach* (Washington DC: IIF).

IMF (2010a) *Global Financial Stability Report: Meeting New Challenges to Stability and Building a Safer System* (Washington DC: IMF).

IMF (2010b) *World Economic Outlook: Rebalancing Growth* (Washington DC: IMF).

IMF, BIS and FSB (2009) *Report to G20 Ministers and Governors, Guidance to Assess the Systemic Importance of Financial Institutions, Markets and Instruments: Initial Considerations* (IMF, BIS and FSB).

Kumar, M.S., and J. Woo (2010) 'Public Debt and Growth', IMF Working Paper No. 174.

Lepetit, J.-F. (2010) *Report on Systemic Risk: Executive Summary* (Paris).

Reinhart, C.M., and K.S. Rogoff (2009) *This Time is Different* (Princeton and Oxford: Princeton University Press).

Swiss Committee of Experts (2010) *Interim Report of the Committee of Experts Responsible for the Examination of the Risk Limitations facing Large Companies in the National Economy* (Bern).

Swiss Re (2010) 'Assekuranz Global 2009 Growth', *sigma* II.

The Geneva Association (2010) *Systemic Risk in Insurance: An Analysis of Insurance and Financial Stability* (Geneva: The Geneva Association).

Weiss, M.A. (2010) *Systemic Risk and the U.S. Insurance Sector* (Washington DC).

Part II

The Supervisory Dimension

5
The Quality of Regulation and Supervision

Ian Tower

This chapter sets out one perspective, that of a former insurance expert at the International Monetary Fund (IMF) and insurance supervisor in the United Kingdom, on the quality of current regulatory arrangements for insurance companies.[1]

Assessing quality in regulation and supervision

It is not obvious how the arrangements for insurance regulation across the world can reliably be compared and assessed. National markets in insurance, and the products developed for them, are heterogeneous, maybe more so than in banking and investment business and especially so in retail life insurance. Regulatory frameworks differ accordingly.

International regulatory standards for insurance business have been developed by the International Association of Insurance Supervisors (IAIS). However, to date at least, these have been framed in high level terms, in practice enabling countries broadly to comply with the standards using significantly different methodologies. There is no 'Basel II' (that is, a detailed benchmark for international solvency regulation) for insurance business. The IAIS has encouraged countries to undertake self-assessments of the level of their compliance with the key standards set out in the IAIS's Insurance Core Principles (ICPs) (IAIS, 2003), but these can suffer from the lack of independent evaluation, while few have been published. Nor are there yet comprehensive private sector sources for assessing the quality of insurance regulation globally.[2]

Assessing the quality of insurance regulation is also hampered by methodological issues affecting the evaluation of regulatory effectiveness generally, and not just in the financial sector. One obvious starting point, to measure quality by reference to outcomes, is subject to well-known difficulties. Positive outcomes, such as low levels of insurance company failures or limited instances of insurance consumer detriment, may indicate regulatory success but may equally be attributable to other factors, including good company management. Failures, certainly those with the highest media and political profile, tend to be blamed at least in part on weak regulation, whereas they are likely to have many and complex underlying causes.

The impact of the global financial crisis on the insurance sector was much more limited than its effect on banks. It is clear that the crisis did not emanate from insurance activities. However, there is apparently no consensus on whether this reflects fundamental features of the insurance sector business model, including limited interconnectedness with other parts of the financial sector, or effective regulation. Indeed, there is no agreement on how much further the global financial crisis would have tested the insurance sector had not governments intervened in support of banks and other markets.

The Financial Sector Assessment Programme

Against this background, it is hard to make any assessment of insurance regulation globally without relying heavily on the results of the Financial Sector Assessment Programme (FSAP). This is a joint programme of the IMF and World Bank, introduced in 1999, which has supported the efforts of the two organisations' member countries (most of the countries in the world) to promote the soundness of their financial systems and to make them resilient to major shocks.[3] The FSAP has to date been a voluntary programme – although under a decision of the IMF Board in September 2010 (IMF, 2010), it has now been made mandatory (with a frequency of every five years) for the 25 countries whose financial systems, because of their scale and interconnectedness, have the greatest impact on global financial stability.

The scope of the FSAP programme and the approach of the IMF and World Bank to assessments in practice is developing in response to the global financial crisis. For the purposes of evaluating the quality of insurance regulation, however, the key contribution of the FSAP has been, and remains, the independent judgement which it offers on the extent to which national regulatory systems comply with the IAIS ICPs.

The ICPs are comprehensive – 28 standards cover all aspects of insurance regulatory practice, including authorisation, supervision and prudential regulation as well as consumer protection issues, fraud and anti-money laundering. A number of the standards refer to institutional aspects, including the resources as well as the powers of the regulatory bodies and the need for them to be independent from government as well as free from political or insurance industry interference. One standard addresses the need for a policy, institutional and legal framework supportive of insurance regulation in addition to a well-developed and effective financial market infrastructure and efficient financial markets. These important aspects of the wider context within which the supervisory system itself operates are referred to as the preconditions for effective supervision.

IMF and World Bank assessors, who may be external experts or members of staff from the two organisations, spend typically around two weeks in the country being assessed, reviewing rules and regulations and talking to government, regulators and the insurance industry about the approach to and effectiveness of regulation. Compliance with each ICP is then scored – as 'Observed', 'Largely Observed', 'Partly Observed' or 'Not Observed'. In practice, the first two scores may be regarded as broad endorsements of the quality of the regulatory regime being assessed. 'Partly Observed' or 'Not Observed' scores both indicate serious weaknesses that would be expected to compromise the effectiveness of regulation. The approach is set out in an assessment methodology developed by the IAIS for use both in self-assessments by its members and in the IMF and World Bank FSAP work (IAIS, 2003).

The approach of course has its limitations. The time available to assessors is hardly extensive, especially where the assessment is of a large and complex market or where limited data are available. IAIS standards, as mentioned, are often high level, making it necessary for assessors to apply judgement rather than merely relying on the accumulation of factual evidence such as relevant laws and regulation. This element of subjectivity is of course desirable, if the assessment of compliance is not to become overly narrow, but it also introduces a risk of inconsistency in judgments. In practice, the IMF and World Bank mitigate this risk through careful selection of assessors from a cadre of experienced regulators and other experts, and by thorough review, both of individual draft assessments and periodically of the body of completed assessments.

The two organisations have also been careful to make themselves acquainted with the policy considerations that have informed the IAIS's development of its standards; and have worked with the IAIS on the development of the assessment approach. For example, the IMF and World Bank have worked with the IAIS over the years of the FSAP to place a greater emphasis on countries delivering effective implementation of standards, through supervision as well as rule-making. It is this cooperation with the IAIS that gives FSAP assessments of insurance regulation much of their authority.

Finally, it has to be acknowledged that publication of FSAP insurance regulation assessments is not mandatory. Increasingly, however, countries are now deciding to publish assessments and may be required to do so when members of such bodies as the Financial Stability Board and the G20.[4] Nor are all the assessments current. Until such time as all assessments are conducted with greater regularity, the evaluation of the quality of insurance regulation across a wide range of countries using FSAP results will remain constrained; and until all are published, the IMF and World Bank have an important role in undertaking cross-country assessment. Both organisations have much to contribute to future improvements in the quality of regulation by continuing to share their findings, with the IAIS, other standard-setters and more widely.

Findings from the FSAP

Analysis of the detailed findings makes it possible to draw some conclusions about the quality of insurance regulation overall as well as to identify areas of strength and weakness.

First, the overall scorings given in assessments of insurance regulation under the current IAIS ICPs, which were developed in 2003, are relatively high – more so in fact than the scores under the most recent standards for banking (the Basel Core Principles) (BIS, 2006) and securities business (the International Organization of Securities Commissions (IOSCO) Objectives and Principles of Securities Regulation) (IOSCO, 2010). This result – around three quarters of all scores at Observed or Largely Observed compared with two thirds at the equivalent Basel and IOSCO scorings – apparently gives the lie to notions occasionally voiced that the development of insurance regulation lags that of the regulation of other sectors.

In reality of course, comparability is hampered by differing samples. The latest Basel Core Principles, for example, date from 2006 and completed assessments are fewer than those made using the latest ICPs, while insurance assessments since 2003 have been weighted towards more developed countries – which tend, by reason of their greater resources, to have a more compliant regulatory framework. Nonetheless, the observation that insurance regulation is holding its own on this simple measure is sound.[5]

There are a number of areas of the detailed scorings where insurance regulation has been assessed as particularly strong. These relate to many of the core requirements and processes of insurance supervision: in particular, the quality of regulation of insurance company reserving and the adequacy of margins of solvency is assessed relatively high, as is the quality of the associated offsite supervisory process. In other words, many insurance regulators devote resources to doing well what they regard as a key function – setting minimum reserving and solvency requirements and monitoring companies' compliance through regular, detailed reporting by the companies and analysis, followed by appropriate follow-up action, by the supervisor.

This is not the same, however, as saying that all countries assessed well in this regard are applying the same level and intensity of prudential regulation in practice – or holding companies to comparable levels of solvency margin. This is much harder for IMF and World Bank assessors to evaluate given the differing national markets and the absence of detailed global solvency standards, notwithstanding the valuable high-level standards which the IAIS has developed, to act as a benchmark.

Moreover, insurance supervisors do not always make effective use of stress-testing, a practice that would shed greater light on the degree of resilience of insurance sectors to major shocks, to supplement their mainstream measures of reserving adequacy and the margin of solvency. The IMF and World Bank teams undertaking the FSAP work may therefore seek to include their own stress-testing work as part of the overall assessment of the financial strength of the insurance sector. Such stress tests have, however, to date been less often applied in the assessment of the insurance sector than they have for assessing banking sector resilience.

Also relevant to the assessment of the effectiveness of prudential regulation is the observation that in few countries is prudential regulation influenced by considerations of financial stability or the need for a macro-prudential focus. Insurance company regulation, as reflected in the formal objectives of regulators, has traditionally focused on the protection of policy-holders against failure by individual companies.

Other areas where relatively strong scoring has been observed include the broad range of powers and processes required to enforce standards effectively. Supervisors are also generally alert to the need to address insurance fraud, not only controls against insurance claims fraud but vulnerability to other forms of fraud perpetrated against the insurance company. Anti-money laundering standards are less well addressed overall, however, maybe because insurance contracts are generally seen as a lesser source of money-laundering risk than banking products, leading to relatively less focus and fewer resources being applied to insurance sector regulation in relation to anti-money laundering.

Insurance supervisors also score strongly on the sharing of information with other regulators – a key input into effective oversight of the operations of insurance companies with cross-border operations or which are parts of wider groups of insurance businesses. In other words, insurance supervisors are generally assessed to share information effectively and on a two way basis with other national and international regulators, taking into account the extent to which regulators receiving information are able to maintain its confidentiality.

Finally, insurance regulation is also scored relatively highly on the issues comprising the preconditions for effective insurance regulation. In other words, insurance regulatory systems are able to rely on sound policy, institutional and legal frameworks, effective financial market infrastructure and efficient financial markets. Key judgements in this respect are over the adequacy of the accounting and auditing framework and the availability of professional services. In practice, assessors often observe that actuarial resources available to the insurance companies are stretched. There may also be gaps in the range of financial instruments required to match all types and maturities of insurance liabilities.

There are also several areas where compliance is less evenly strong.

First, it is relatively common that assessors find institutional weaknesses at the regulator (ICP no. 3). These relate mainly to two sets of issues, the independence of the regulator from government and its available resources. Unlike banking regulation, which developed in many countries within central banks, insurance regulation has often been developed within or closely aligned to government. This has tended to affect both the scope for insurance regulators to operate free of wider government influence, if only budgetary control, while of course remaining accountable to government, and to make it harder for regulators to secure appropriate resources.

In some (but now increasingly few) countries, insurance regulators are in addition subject to reserve government powers, typically in the hands of the minister of finance, to give directions to the regulator in relation to decisions on the regulation of individual companies. Even if never used, such powers may influence insurance regulators' behaviour in relation to high profile or politically sensitive cases.

This observation on the lack of appropriate independence of some insurance regulators has not led to the IMF and World Bank advocating major institutional reform such as the creation of new or newly integrated regulatory bodies. In most countries, improvements to create the necessary degree of regulatory operational independence can be secured within existing institutional frameworks, avoiding the risks inherent in major regulatory institutional reform. The evaluation of costs and benefits of such change is best left to individual countries.

Even where the regulator is adequately insulated from political influence, it may be subject to undue industry influence. One contributing factor is often the absence of effective protection for the regulator from legal action in relation to regulatory action undertaken in good faith and through the exercise of due process. Most regulators will at some time be deterred from necessary regulatory decisions if they doubt their ability to avoid institutional or even personal liability for the results of such action. Freedom from industry influence has of course to be balanced against the need for regulatory processes to take account of industry views – through open and effective consultation and the publication of all regulatory requirements.

Inadequacy of insurance regulators' resources is another frequent observation of assessors. Determining the appropriate level of resourcing of any regulatory activity is difficult, although clear outliers may be easily identified by IMF and World Bank assessors. However, weaknesses in resourcing often relate as much to the skills as to total resources of the regulatory authority and to the effectiveness of the system by which the resources are allocated. In more sophisticated insurance markets, there is a need for high levels of regulatory skill to assess and challenge company practices, especially in reserving and risk management. Allocation of always scarce resources requires some form of risk-based methodology to ensure that resources are not wasted on less significant companies or issues while major risks, whether related to a firm, product or market, are given insufficient attention.

A second set of issues where there is relative weakness in insurance regulation is in the more qualitative aspects. The emphasis on reserving and solvency standards is not everywhere matched by attention to regulation aimed at securing good governance and effective risk management and other systems of internal control (ICPs nos 9, 10 and 18). In relation to governance in particular, some insurance supervisors see their role as monitoring compliance with general market wide corporate governance standards rather than developing their own rules and guidance on governance practices appropriate to insurance business. These may include requirements on the composition of board or the role of risk and actuarial functions or may address the particular governance arrangements called for in relation to the exercise of discretion reserved to insurance company management in certain business lines, typically life insurance savings products.

These issues are sometimes tackled by regulators through supervisory work – whereby the supervisor probes the governance and control arrangements at individual firms and takes appropriate action to remedy shortcomings. Reliance on supervision can be effective in rectifying problems at many companies. However, it cannot substitute for the clarity of regulatory expectations that only published rules and regulations can establish. In some countries, rules and regulations exist but implementation is weak – compliance is not assessed by the supervisor in practice and the use of enforcement powers in cases of serious non-compliance is limited.

Third, there are some weaknesses in relation to market analysis (ICP no. 11). While many regulators focus on analysis of core prudential reporting by companies, few are expert in the analysis of wider market developments. Supervisors may fail to observe developing trends, for example in product development.

Fourth, on-site supervisory work (ICP no. 13 – visiting companies to examine how they are managed in practice) is somewhat less well-scored than off-site work (the analysis of regulatory reports from insurance companies). In a number of countries, supervisors are still developing their approach to the assessment of risk through company visits and linking their work in this regard to their off-site analysis of company regulatory reports and other information including market analysis. Again, the rather weaker scoring of on-site work (although scores are by no means poor on average) may reflect the traditional focus of insurance supervisors on financial analysis based on company reports rather than the more qualitative aspects of supervision.

Fifth, regulators score relatively weakly on group supervision (ICP no. 17) – moving beyond the oversight of an individual insurance company to assess the risk posed by its membership of a group of companies and to set appropriate requirements in relation to these risks. IAIS standards are not fully developed in this area and much interesting and important work is being undertaken to develop and extend the current approach. Nonetheless, the existing ICP already requires supervisors to focus their group supervision on such issues as group structure and interrelationships, capital adequacy, reinsurance and risk concentration, intra-group transactions and exposures and internal control mechanisms and risk management processes. A related ICP on off-site supervision (no. 12) requires that insurance companies report financial information to regulators on both a solo company and a group basis.

Insurance supervision has traditionally focused on the solo insurance company – ensuring that it is adequately reserved with a satisfactory margin of solvency and that it is protected as far as possible, maybe even ring-fenced, from financial risk that could emanate from elsewhere in its group. This approach has risked leaving supervisors less than well apprised of developing weaknesses at group level. Typically, they do not collect regulatory data on a group wide basis or assess the group financial position to identify group wide risks such as inadequate overall capital, taking into account potential double-gearing within a group, or risk concentrations. Many supervisors now need to develop their approaches to group wide monitoring. However, as already noted, cooperation with other regulators, which is an important input into effective group supervision, is already an area where insurance supervisors score well.

Sixth, supervisory practice in relation to disclosure requirements imposed on insurance companies (ICP no. 26) is also assessed as relatively weak. This IAIS standard relates to the need for insurance companies to prepare and publish information of a type that will enable policy-holders and other stakeholders to understand an insurer's risks more fully and exercise market discipline. This is the area of regulation covered by the Basel Committee's Pillar III requirements.

As in the area of corporate governance, some insurance regulators rely on standards set by other bodies – in this case the accounting standard-setters in relation to statutory financial statements. The development of financial reporting has made much more information available through such statements; but this may not always be tailored to the needs of policy-holders specifically. In addition, the requirements may not always extend in full to insurance companies that do not have public issues of equity or debt or to the level of the individual insurance company within a group with which policy-holders have taken out their policies. Insurance supervisors need to consider what information may usefully be made available and then set requirements to ensure it is delivered.

Finally, one area of prudential standards where insurance regulators score less well is the regulation of investments. This relates in part to the absence of rules and regulations relating to such issues as the safekeeping of physical investments or attention to custody. Some supervisors continue to rely on lists of the types of asset into which policy-holders' funds may be invested, while having more limited requirements as to how those investments are to be valued or the extent of asset and liability mismatching. As on many other issues, supervisors' implementation of requirements may be weak – no effective supervision to assess compliance or enforcement action in case of serious non-compliance.

This catalogue of relative strengths and weaknesses of course leaves a number of important issues unmentioned, including authorisation of new insurance companies, requirements in relation to key functionaries such as auditors and actuaries as well as senior management, and consumer protection issues. Here practices vary and no overall conclusions are possible.

It is also important to note that the IAIS ICPs do not address aspects of the overall regulatory framework that are present in many countries. On consumer protection for example, there is no standard on the availability of a mechanism to compensate policy-holders in the event of loss due to the financial failure of the firm or on the existence of an independent process for hearing and adjudicating on policy-holder complaints against insurance companies.

Conclusion

It is not possible reliably to assess the overall quality of insurance regulation globally. We lack the body of current, comprehensive independent assessments covering a wide range of national markets. There are, however, a number of indicators that such an assessment, if possible, would rate insurance regulation as high quality. The IAIS has a wide global membership, open and consultative processes and a technical assistance programme, all of which promote the wide dissemination and adoption of good insurance regulatory practice, as set out at a high level in the ICPs. There is active attention to the development of effective supervisory standards in major regional bodies, for example in the European Union and the US. The overall scoring of assessments undertaken against the 2003 IAIS ICPs (albeit a limited sample) is broadly positive.

Equally, the sample of recent assessments sheds limited light on current practice in less developed jurisdictions in particular. It is also evident that insurance regulators are on average more proficient at those parts of their work which have traditionally been seen as the core of insurance regulation – reserving and solvency standards and the analysis and follow-up on company regulatory reports, in respect of solo insurance companies with less attention to groups.

Less well-developed are aspects of on-site supervision, qualitative standards such as governance, risk management and internal controls and group supervision. Insurance regulation will need to continue developing – to raise standards in areas already covered by the IAIS work and to extend it to new areas, including lessons from the global financial crisis such as the need for a more challenging approach to supervision[6] and for a new focus on insurance sector's contribution to financial stability. There may be a place for more detailed standards, particularly on reserving and solvency, to set a global benchmark and promote similar outcomes and increased comparability across national markets. Existing regulatory and supervisory practices, coupled with the international framework centred on the IAIS, with FSAP assessments by the IMF and World Bank, provide a sound basis for the future development of insurance regulation.

Notes

1. The chapter draws principally on a presentation by the author at The Geneva Association PROGRES conference, Montreux, Switzerland, April 2010. The author is grateful to participants at the conference for comments and questions and is particularly grateful to Craig Thorburn for comments on this chapter.
2. However, the credit rating agencies, in addition to their focus on assessing individual insurance companies, are giving increasing weight to national regulatory frameworks.
3. Information on the FSAP and its interrelationship with other aspects of the IMF's and World Bank's work is set out on the websites www.imf.org and www.worldbank.org.
4. For the published assessments, see www.imf.org/external/np/rosc/rosc.asp.
5. For a detailed cross-sector analysis of FSAP assessment scorings up to 2007, see Čihák and Tieman (2008).
6. See, for example, Viñals and Fiechter (2010).

Bibliography

BIS (2006) *Basel Committee on Banking Supervision, Core Principles for Effective Banking Supervision and Core Principles Methodology*, October, www.bis.org.

Čihák, Martin, and Alexander Tieman (2008) 'Quality of Financial Sector Regulation and Supervision Around the World', IMF Working Paper, WP/08/190, www.imf.org.

IAIS (2003) *International Association of Insurance Supervisors, Insurance Core Principles and Methodology*, October, www.iaisweb.org.

IMF (2010) *Expanding Surveillance to Require Mandatory Financial Stability Assessments of Countries with Systemically Important Financial Sectors*, International Monetary Fund, Press Release No. 10/357, 27 September, www.imf.org.

IOSCO (2010) *International Organization of Securities Commissions, Objectives and Principles of Securities Regulation*, June, www.iosco.org.

Viñals, Jose, and Jonathan Fiechter (2010) 'The Making of Good Supervision: Learning to say No', International Monetary Fund Staff Position Note, SPN/10/08, 18 May, www.imf.org.

6
Solvency as a Focal Point of Prudential Regulation: Supervisory Lessons and Challenges

Rob Curtis

Introduction

Regulators worldwide have pursued a common aim of ensuring a financially strong and stable insurance industry, able to meet obligations to policy-holders. It is therefore to be expected that solvency, or rather mechanisms for guarding against insolvency, have been a focal point of prudential regulation. Nevertheless, regulators do not share an unequivocal definition of solvency and the notion of solvency has essentially evolved in relation to our understanding of the causes of insurer insolvencies.

Insurer insolvencies are clearly not a recent occurrence, however, perhaps like no other event, the global financial crisis (GFC) of 2008–09 has brought the relationship between insolvency and regulation sharply into focus. It has served as the basis for new dialogue globally amongst regulators and industry stakeholders concerning the methods and constructs of effective regulation and supervision and how best to achieve increased insurer accountability and improved governance. A consensus would appear to be emerging that existing concepts and methodologies surrounding solvency are in need of review, and novel perspectives are required to achieve effective prudential regulation fit for the global, ever-changing and interconnected insurance market of the new millennium.

It would be wrong to suggest that it has taken the GFC to occur for insurance regulators to begin assessing the adequacy of their regulatory regimes. For the last two decades in particular, regulators around the world have been active in modernising their solvency regimes; for example, the US introduced its risk based capital (RBC) requirements with the first calculation being year-end 2003 for life risk-based capital, Canada overhauled its requirements by introducing

Dynamic Capital Adequacy Testing (DCAT) in conjunction with changes to the Insurance Companies Act in 1992, Australia introduced progressive reforms for non-life insurers from 2001 and is now currently engaged in life reforms, and finally Europe commenced the Solvency II project at the beginning of the last decade. The underlying aim of these developments has been to establish prudential standards that better reflect the risks of insurers and the risks to regulatory objectives from prudential failure. Consequently, regulators have increasingly moved away from 'tick-box' and through the use of varied risk measures have prompted insurers to improve their risk management practices and capital allocation methods.

However, have these reforms actually improved the quality of supervision and how effective has solvency been as a focal point of prudential regulation worldwide? Therefore, for the purpose of this chapter, how best can we evaluate the role of solvency? Firstly, a fundamental review of the way we assess solvency is required. Increasingly, many supervisors have focused largely on the main risk categories, and whilst this is certainly needed, this focus may well have been to the detriment of even more important solvency aspects such as understanding the business strategy, and board and senior management plans and activities. An exploration of past insurance failures and near misses reinforces these points and assists in understanding better future solvency analysis needs. Furthermore, this chapter will argue that issues concerning culture, insurer management behaviour, ethics and values also now need to be considered. We then need to fundamentally review how we conduct supervision to reflect better the changing environment we now find ourselves in the post-GFC, with particular emphasis on creating a truly global framework for supervision enabling effective group supervision to be conducted worldwide.

This chapter will not undertake a critique of different regulatory measures currently used throughout the world, as to attempt such an analysis would immediately invite political criticisms from different quarters. Instead, it will provide a strategic and policy-oriented perspective by challenging existing notions of solvency, and will analyse whether solvency, and its role within prudential regulation worldwide requires further innovation than exists in current and proposed frameworks. As part of this policy perspective a number of important themes will be explored including, the increasingly globalisation of the industry, the need to develop mechanisms to better supervise insurance groups and the extent to which regulatory aims will be served by greater convergence and commonality.

Recent trends within solvency assessment

Supervisors have used a variety of regulatory tools in undertaking their prudential supervision and generally many of these measures have focused on basic premia and claims tests. During the 1990s and onwards, quantitative risk-based or formulaic methods designed primarily as factor charges against an insurer's assets and liabilities began to emerge as the primary measure of assessing solvency.[1] Whilst different jurisdictions have applied a variety of different methodologies, the majority have involved a number of various risk factors being tested and examined across different components of the insurer's balance sheet. Such standard formulae or risk-based methodologies are now the primary supervisory and reporting tool worldwide to assess the solvency and financial condition of an insurer. In order to consider the effectiveness of these measures this paper will reflect, not on the actual methods used per se in calculating solvency requirements, but on what it is that is being reported and reviewed by supervisors and further the outcomes being sought by supervisors.

The 'bread and butter' core risks of solvency analysis, namely insurance risk, credit risk, market risk, liquidity risk and operational risk, have very often been consumed by automated processes by many regulatory authorities as part of their response to the increasingly digital age. This coincided with adoption of electronic reporting procedures and submissions, which have now become commonplace, and meant that supervisors needed to respond quickly with timely analysis to the receipt of such large volumes of data. Supervisors certainly do not want to receive information if they are going to be unable to review the material for fear of being in receipt of information which may later prove embarrassing if an insurer was to experience solvency difficulties. So, in response, supervisory authorities set on ensuring new IT systems were capable of producing automated return analysis, key ratios and tests to assist supervisors as tools in their review process.

However, given what we have now learnt as a result of the GFC, an open question to bear in mind is whether supervisors, by focusing so intently on such methods, inadvertently stopped undertaking proper solvency assessments? A number of further questions are also provoked: did supervisors, by relying on these formulaic computations and automatically generated ratio analysis trends of financial data, become distracted from considering other 'traditional' forms of insurer examinations – the assessment of strategy, board effectiveness and senior management quality? In turn, have supervisors forgotten the basics of solvency analysis and what it means to really review and challenge insurers about their key risks? All of these questions serve the purpose for a thorough challenge of what we mean by solvency.

It is also important to underline that all supervisory assessment tools should be clearly linked to the outcomes being pursued by supervisors. Policy-holder protection has clearly been the common theme, but one may surmise whether a move by some jurisdictions to integrate conduct of business and prudential supervision roles has made the task of solvency assessment more difficult by focusing too heavily on issues such as treating customers fairly. Regulators could be forgiven such a focus since arguably conduct regulation is more conducive to intervention and also facilitates a more straightforward appraisal of performance. Furthermore, one may wonder whether a move to a principles-based environment further exacerbated the above issues for some jurisdictions, in that it led supervisors to be more reluctant to challenge firms or take a view of their business model. Indeed, how often are an insurer's senior management and board seriously challenged on their risk profiles? And when was the last time a supervisor actually demanded a change in a firm's own strategic and business plan programme, or a change in the composition of the board or senior management?

Thus to summarise, has the advent of electronic reporting, changes to supervisory structures and the ideology that enveloped many jurisdictions around the world to be 'principles-based', over time, actually hindered the supervisory review process? In turn, is there now a generation of supervisors who have lost the art of supervision itself, unable to properly undertake solvency examinations as we once knew it?

Building a solvency-driven prudential framework

The first stage in considering the prudential regulatory framework begins with what should form the key basis of any good solvency examination. The traditional method used by supervisors universally to monitor solvency has been to target the main risk classes of insurers. Although it may sound predictable, these different risks (insurance, market, credit, liquidity and operational risks) are still very much a key focus of prudential regulation and every good supervisor should aim to fully appreciate and understand them. As such, to undertake effective solvency analysis requires an initial and fundamental examination of the insurer's risk appetite and the strategic and broader governance risks is required in order to understand the insurer's activities, structure, operations and management.

Risk appetite

At its basic, risk appetite defines the level of risk a firm accepts. This is set from executive and board level and is intertwined with the company's strategy. A poor risk appetite (or risk tolerance) setting and lack of goal clarity for the insurer can cause serious issues and very much deserves regulatory attention. An insurer can choose to be either conservative or aggressive in its approach to risk. This reflects the standards and values of the board, and the degree to which they seek profit and value for the company. A key component of this appetite is the level or investment risk that the firm wishes to bear. It is also worth noting that as part of their risk appetite firms may choose to apply a different level of tolerance to different types of risk, so that they may specialise in a particular type of underwriting risk. Poor decision-making concerning the size of risk appetite can cause major underwriting and financial disruption to an insurer's financial condition. Problems can span across all risk categories. In particular this covers the main financial aspects of credit, market and liquidity risk.

Supervisors would generally assess several aspects in relation to how the risk appetite is effectively used and monitored; in particular that the risk appetite fits with the strategic direction of the company, that effective communication occurs to ensure that within the firm all relevant employees understand the level of risk appetite and do not depart from the specified strategy, and for risk appetite to be backed by a consistent reward structure for staff to help ensure risk appetite is adhered to and delivered.

Strategic risks

Strategic risks are borne from the decisions and objectives of the board and are a major focus of supervisors. Such considerations fall into two broad categories:

High-level strategic objectives

Supervisors will want insurers to have processes in place to guide decisions, have adequate metrics/statistics in place to vindicate decisions and expectations and in doing so, have an appropriate framework for responding to changes and threats to strategy. Achievability and realism of such plans come particularly under focus from most supervisors especially with regards to whether the insurer is embarking on overly ambitious underwriting or other corporate goals.

Strategic options

Supervisors also need insurers to demonstrate that the degree and nature of change in markets served, cost structures and market share have all been adequately taken into account during the strategic planning process. The ability of management to take actions quickly to respond to changes in the wider financial operating environment is also a key factor in the assessment of most insurers.

As a result of changes in strategy, supervisors are generally concerned with risks that may flow down to other aspects of the insurer's business. Such considerations may include potential for risks arising from acquisitions and mergers, human resource risks and financial capacity to deal with impending changes. Risk appetite is a significant consideration and needs to be aligned to strategy to ensure a common goal is worked towards.

Corporate governance risks

Corporate governance is a key tenet of solvency. Board composition, role and effectiveness are a very critical component of any insurer's financial condition and therefore must play a crucial role in prudential regulation. Supervisors will want to ensure that the board and various risk and auditing subcommittees have clear structures in place, that the competence of members within the insurer is assessed and improved if required to ensure knowledgeable decisions can be made, and that strong levels of direction, control and understanding of the risks of the firm can be evidenced. Solvency regimes usually expect that adherence to government regulation concerning various codes on corporate governance and other such requirements are adhered to.

Illustrative cases of insurer failures

There are numerous global examples, such as Equitable Life, HIH, and more recently AIG (to name but a few), that illustrate the fundamental importance of needing to focus on strategy, governance and risk appetite in any solvency examination. This was also the conclusion of the study undertaken by the London Working Group (LWG) in its 2002 study of insurance firm failures. The LWG report documented a causal chain arising from a trigger event to explain the potential build-up of problems within a company. It suggested, 'various causes which can lead to a particular effect may not all develop at the same time. Being the most immediate cause, the "trigger event" is often the easiest to identify; however it provides only a partial explanation for a particular effect, as it is merely the final link in a chain of causes. Only when combined with underlying and intermediate causes does the "trigger event" become a problem' (Sharma, 2002, p. 9).

Twenty-one case studies were presented to the LWG and discussed in detail. In particular, the Group examined the internal and external causes of a firm's problems and constructed a risk map of the full causal chain. Above all else, the LWG study illustrated a fundamental weakness of past prudential supervisory activities that focused on traditional forms of solvency measures without adequately appreciating how the strategy, poor board oversight, culture and insurer management behaviour can affect the ultimate financial condition of an insurer. A particular benefit arising from the study was that it formed the foundation for the Solvency II project, in which 'solvency' is established not as a narrowly defined concept consisting of simple claims and premia tests, but one that encapsulated a much wider sub-set of issues.

The following key cases amply illustrate such concerns, and highlight areas for improvements in solvency requirements worldwide.

Equitable Life

Equitable Life, being the UK's oldest mutual insurer, sold a vast number of pension policies which offered a guaranteed annuity rate (GAR)[2] to 90,000 of the 500,000 pensions it supported. It is suggested that the reason for its near failure was the fact that as a mutual insurer, Equitable faced conflicting objectives. Its customers were also its members and it needed to maintain equilibrium between payments to its customers and capital adequacy. As annuity rates fell due to lower inflation and government borrowing, GAR policies were triggered resulting in the company not holding enough capital.

A number of presenting risk issues certainly contributed to Equitable's difficulties. For example:

- *Market risk*. In effect, the inefficiency of GAR products proved to be a major mistake. However, due to the way Equitable ran its business, offering high returns, rather than increasing capital, the company was always in danger.
- *Insurance risk*. The appointed actuary within the company advised that the investments returns offered were satisfactory. In hindsight the company could not meet reasonable policy-holder expectations by a large margin.
- *Operational risk*. Staff felt unable to express their views within the company, and the management did not take appropriate note. It appears that little debate was encouraged amongst employees over the success of their policies. This input could have prevented the ultimate problem.

However, by far the greatest risk that existed with Equitable was its strategic and governance risks. The company, not being accountable to stockholders/analysts given its mutual status, became quite single-minded in its decision-making. Equitable had a policy of returning most of the proceeds from investments to the policy-holders rather than retaining capital to ward off future problems. It could be suggested that Equitable dealt with its customers to meet their expectations, as opposed to selling products based on solid technical calculations. Management were either oblivious to or assumed the GAR risk could be absorbed by reductions in bonuses, and favoured short-term gains through sales as opposed to long-term stability. In effect it was a gamble on the future. In turn, given Equitable Life's structure, it did not answer to a senior authoritative body and results were not adequately scrutinised. This led to important management decisions being made in isolation of other important stakeholders. Only when GARs were triggered and bonuses reduced, did it become clear that policy-holder expectations could not be met.

HIH

HIH provides another example of poor board and senior management oversight. HIH was put into liquidation on 15 March 2001, and represented one of the biggest collapses in Australian corporate history. As a result of the collapse, a Royal Commission was formed to investigate the problems, which lay behind the failure.

As with Equitable Life, HIH presented a number of other weaknesses in their management of various risk factors, which contributed to the firm's collapse:

- *Market risk*. HIH had risk portfolios with long tails. This gave the impression that the company was successful for a long time before its risk-taking decisions were highlighted. This is obviously a danger within the insurance industry where companies can wait for many years before risks are realised and affect capital adequacy.
- *Insurance risk*. Even six months after the liquidators entered and investigated HIH, they were unable to say how large HIH losses were to the nearest 1.5 billion Australian dollars. This explains how complex it is to calculate and account for risk. The HIH accounts were clearly badly prepared and needed to be organised given the complexity of the business. Further, the reinsurance arrangements at HIH were badly structured. It demonstrated that reinsurance does not guarantee security; it can reduce risk but also present new threats to a company, particularly if it is inappropriately structured and purchased. In addition to this it may mask problems which exist in the company which need to be addressed.
- *Operational risk*. Problems will occur if the risks, which a company faces, are not reported in a uniform way throughout the company. HIH was complex in both its structure and hierarchy. The systems in place to analyse the risks taken and the accounts of the company were not consistent. External auditors were not able to assess the danger the company was facing in July 2000. This would suggest that the accounts were not entirely accurate or that a complete breakdown in reporting had occurred.

However, by far the greatest risk to HIH was its poor governance arrangements, namely board and senior management oversight. As outlined in the HIH Royal Commission in April 2003, the fundamental problem was that HIH had been offering insurance at an inadequate price, and had not set aside enough capital to cover its future liabilities. This was worsened by poor management and lack of care taken which led HIH to acquire another insurer, FAI. This was a troubled insurance business and was purchased at a high price during a period of rapid growth.

HIH therefore encountered difficulties through its over-expansion and inadequate underwriting standards. The poor performance of the stock markets exacerbated the company's position and decreased investment portfolios. The mounting losses it was suffering then strained HIH's capacity until it became insolvent.

AIG

At the end of 2007, AIG was the world's largest insurance group and had a balance sheet of over US$1 trillion, with year ending 2007 reported earnings of US$6.2 billion. At its height, AIG employed approximately 116,000 staff operating in over 130 countries. AIG's difficulties have been well documented and it ranks as of one of the largest corporate bailouts of all time.

At first glance, AIG's difficulties are that it diversified into the trading of credit default swaps (CDSs) and it used its main business, insurance, to essentially provide the resources for its financial products trading business – AIG Financial Products Corp. (AIGFP), based in London. The firm provided protection on more than US$500 billion of debt against default by the use of over-the-counter CDSs, an activity which in the United States was not regulated. AIG covered credit events on super-senior tranches of financial obligations (normally AAA or equivalent tranches). This includes asset backed securities (ABS). A number of counterparties included hedge funds, major banks, sovereign wealth funds, money managers and other institutional investors where some sought protection from AIG in order to lower their regulatory capital requirements. The firm believed that these CDSs were very unlikely to be executed given historical default levels were extremely low. Subsequently, substantial volumes were written given the perceived risk/reward. During 2007 and 2008, however, AIGFP suffered substantial losses. This was primarily caused by a CDS portfolio of more than US$60 billion on collateralised debt obligations (CDOs) which included mortgage backed securities also including subprime mortgages. As a result of these write-downs and the loss in value of the CDOs, AIG was forced to post collateral.

Added to these difficulties was AIG's securities lending programme under many of its insurance entity's lent securities to other financial institutions outside of AIG in exchange for cash collateral. This money was then used by AIG Investments for investments in mortgage backed securities and other debt obligations. Media reports concerning the weakening state of AIG resulted in a multiplier effect where increasingly lenders were returning their securities in order to gain back their money from AIG, in turn further exasperating liquidity difficulties. Combined with these events, credit rating agencies demanded additional collateral to be posted and thus a downward spiral began within the group.

However, the CDS and securities lending arrangements are merely presenting issues. The root underlying cause of ultimate failure again resulted in poor strategic, board and senior management oversight and governance. The risk appetite levels set by AIG's board were inappropriate. In essence, AIG was an extremely complex operation which had many hundred subsidiaries. Its consolidated supervisor, the Office of Thrift Supervision (OTS), was effectively unable to efficiently monitor the group and its related complexities – particularly at the holding level and to ensure adequate oversight of its non-insurance subsidiaries. However, as was amply demonstrated, AIG's own board was unable to adequately monitor the risks to the group in its entirety, and even when it did assess its risks, it judged that the scenario needed to cause such a calamitous run was too large to take seriously. Even though AIG's problems were not as a result of its insurance operations per se, it was ironically the strength of its insurance business which provided the platform needed for AIGFP to operate. The fact that senior management allowed the market risk to grow to fatal proportions – allowing its exposures to CDSs to grow so vast and homogeneous, and management in turn deeming such risks to be manageable – only further serves to highlight management's attitude to risk. Unfortunately for AIG, this resulted in the mistaken belief that the risks would never crystallise.

Lessons learned

A common trend is discernible from these past failures, which supports the views of the London Working Group findings. In each case the insurer ultimately becomes insolvent or experiences financial difficulties because of a lack of capital due to difficulties with particular risk categories. Yet, this can perhaps blind-side those stakeholders into thinking that the actual risk categories themselves are the issue and not address the underlying causes which are primarily responsible for the failure. The more fundamental problem is that of poor risk management practice, oversight and responsibility. Indeed, one theme from the case studies is myopia by management to some of the risks from significant and sustained changes to the economic or operating environment. This can be seen in the failure of AIG and others to identify the systemic risk and substantial exposures to a change in credit risks, or the failure of Equitable to identify and manage sensibly the risk from its substantial exposures to guaranteed annuity options (GAOs) (exposed to both longevity and interest rate risk). In the case of the HIH collapse the Royal Commission noted a number of important conclusions:

- the Board of HIH was compromised by the influence of senior management, and failed to subject management proposals to sufficient scrutiny;
- the absence of strategic discussions at Board level affected its ability to operate as an effective check on management;
- there was a culture where senior management failed to bring important facts to the Board's attention;
- the Board failed to monitor systematically the performance of management and generally failed to hold executives to account in the interests of the company;
- the Board failed to ensure that the Board rather than management controlled the agenda for the Board;
- the Board was involved in a systemic failure in stewardship of the Group's assets, including executive remuneration, termination payments and 'inappropriate corporate excess'; and
- the Board failed to implement mechanisms to identify and resolve conflicts.

In recent years insurance supervisors have responded by focusing on new risk management requirements such as requiring firms to undertake their own risk and solvency assessment (ORSA), and by placing greater emphasis on the responsibility of the Board for providing oversight and for holding the management to account.[3] It represents a crucial shift of supervisory emphasis in which supervisors have sought to place the duty on the insurer to demonstrate that they fully comprehend the risks that they face and accordingly the capital that they need to hold, rather than that they simply understand how to comply with regulatory requirements. An associated development has been support by some supervisory authorities for insurers to develop internal models for regulatory capital purposes rather than rely on standard formulae.

However, the GFC has brought into relief ongoing shortcomings within the ability of the Board to ensure that the firm provides against the risks that are being taken and can retain sufficient liquidity and solvency. To some extent this provokes the question of whether the Board is in fact able to effectively fulfil its function of acting as a restraining force on the strategy of the firm and the executive management. It has been noted that 'Boards manifest considerable asymmetry of information' since they are dependent on the information reported to them by management in order to provide the controlling function over the management (Schillinger, 2009, in Johnston et al., 2010). The Board's ability to truly understand the strategy and risk profile has also been challenged (Kakabadse et al., 2010, p. 8).

Regulators clearly can and have put in place structures to help encourage Boards to form sensible judgements and to minimise the occasions of, and opportunities for, ill-judged decisions. Current corporate governance frameworks, for example, work to ensure that only suitable persons are appointed to positions of responsibility and that systems are in place to ensure that appropriate information is reported to Board level. Nevertheless, it has been argued that, from a supervisory perspective, one of the key problems has been the degree of focus on these 'structural elements of corporate governance such as the board structure and composition', whilst attention should have been given to 'role definitions and board dynamics', (Kakabadse et al., 2010, p.8). This may be taken further to enquire whether it reflects a broader theme that regulators have given systems and controls too much attention to at the expense of behaviours.

Responses to the GFC and ongoing challenges

In view of the lessons learned there is an open question of whether solvency and prudential regulation should be expanded to incorporate notions of cultural and ethics more fundamentally into the supervisory architecture. As a minimum, it is incumbent on regulators to critically assess their current approaches and the assumptions upon which these are based. This has occurred to some extent; to start with there has been a notable shift in regulatory approach, at least within the UK. The pre-GFC approach was one in which intervention would not necessarily occur to prevent a firm making mistakes, but rather would encourage good practice and monitor the firm against key solvency rules or principles so that the regulator and firm could take appropriate action if either policy-holders or the sector was at undue risk. This is captured by a recent speech by Financial Services Authority (FSA) Chief Executive Hector Sants in which he commented that the '"old style" FSA [pre-GFC] rarely intervened until there was clear evidence that something had gone wrong'. In the same speech, Sants also communicated his confidence that the FSA was now operating a more 'intensive' approach in which it will 'take a view' (Sants, 2010).

Despite strong pressure on regulators to form new frameworks, they have faced considerable challenge. The insurance sector has displayed some reluctance to engage in discussions in relation to improving regulatory standards predicated on the notion that insurance business was not the cause of the current difficulties and emerged from the crisis largely unscathed. More generally, the industry has feared a new wave of regulation which adds substantial costs to compliance, yet do not necessarily address the underlying issues or eschew the development of a subsequent financial bubble. Indeed, it would be deluded not to acknowledge the difficulties facing regulation if it is to avoid simply being 'behind the curve' and addressing the old problems. Regulators have often underlined that they were not 'zero-failure' regimes, but evidently neither were they effectively risk-based regimes, in that they did not guard against the systemic risks. Attention has also been drawn to the moral hazard element of regulation, which serves to transfer responsibility away from the industry and in particular in relation to the government bail outs and asset protection schemes (Johnston et al., 2010).

However, to suggest that prudential regulation is somehow defunct (that is, that it will always be subject to the power of market forces) would be to embrace the neoliberalist outlook which has failed policy-makers in recent years. Recent events rather serve to underline the importance of establishing effective provisions so that a subsequent downturn does not destabilise the whole of the financial system. The overall policy solution is clearly beyond the scope of insurance regulators alone. Indeed, it is for governments and policy-makers to decide on the overall role of capital in society and to decide, for example, whether there should be stricter separation of consumer facing activities and riskier activities. Nevertheless, the insurance sector should be part of this discussion as insurance business is certainly not isolated from other sectors and is also certainly not immune from risk management shortcomings (as illustrated by various case studies above). Regulators have already taken steps to move away from the neoliberal pre-eminence and the favour for 'light touch' regulation. However, based on the need to prevent a recurrence of the GFC there remains a case for more innovative solutions and reassessments. Furthermore, whilst the GFC remains a vivid memory there remains an opportunity to do so.

Forming new frameworks

Realignment of supervisory focus

One factor that needs to be considered is the role and structure of risk management and whether there is a need to enshrine its role with a distinct function or 'line of defence', which holds an aggregate view of risk across the insurer, independent of the business. In this regard, consideration could be given to benefit of formalising the role of the chief risk officer at the head of the risk management function and their accountability for risk within the organisation, as per the development of an independent chief actuary.

In terms of supplementing risk based capital requirements, much attention is now being devoted to stress testing policies. It was evident that many pre-GFC stress tests were not fit for purpose as they were not designed for the type of extreme market event that occurred. Firms' stress tests failed to consider adequately the magnitude of shocks, duration of the shock, risk concentrations and the extent of correlation (and contagion) between different positions, risk types and markets. Nevertheless, whilst there has been much discussion of their flaws and inappropriate usage prior to the crisis there has also been concurrent recognition that such tests must be an essential tool in building a resilient financial sector. The challenge for supervisors and also, importantly, firms is to set tests which are appropriately severe and broad but equally not so implausible as to be of no use. Regulators should therefore encourage firms to consider building in a more hypothetical set of assumptions for how exposures may change in light of unexpected shocks. Further significant investments in IT infrastructure are also likely to be required to provide risk information that is sufficiently granular in order to construct a comprehensive firm-wide view of stress testing.

Reverse stress testing, which identifies scenarios that are most likely to cause an insurer to fail, have also been acknowledged as an important risk management tool. The current IAIS guidance paper on the use of Enterprise Risk Management for Regulatory Solvency Purposes (2010) advises that 'the focus of such reverse stress testing is on appropriate risk management actions rather than the assessment of financial adequacy' (IAIS, 2010). This leads one to an element of focus on the banking side, that of resolvability and associated planning. Insurance failures are typically resolvable through an orderly run-off, but exceptions to this have occurred and remain plausible such that there is a case for putting in place ex ante arrangements to ensure an orderly conclusion to various scenarios. Such developments would be a helpful complement to prudential requirements, but should not be seen as a replacement and preventive action should remain integral to prudential regulation.

However, in forming new frameworks to respond to the GFC it may be necessary to further broaden our perspectives. One element, to return to a question posed above would be the notion of regulators playing a greater role in assessing behaviours or even ethics. This means considering the factors which influence behaviours; in effect, a firm's culture may not be beyond the remit of regulation.

There is a strong case for making such changes since many of the Board failings outlined above at HIH are invariably, in some shape or form, also features that unfortunately exist in many other insurance firm failures. This has led to the question as posed by Hector Sants, CEO of the FSA UK, in a speech to the Chartered Institute of Securities and Investments Conference where he asked 'whether regulators should have a role in judging culture and ethics of a firm' (Sants, 2010). Sants stated:

> when I joined the FSA, I was told by senior management that 'the FSA does not do ethics'. Since that date, we have collectively experienced the worst financial crisis in modern times. Some of the causes of the crisis were deeply rooted in behavioural issues that resulted in actions and decisions that with the benefit of hindsight, were not the 'right' ones. A firm's culture plays an important role in influencing the actions and decisions taken by individuals within firms and in shaping a firm's attitude towards their customers.

Significantly, Sants is now of the view that regulators do have the responsibility to 'police behaviours and ensure firms have the right culture' (Sants, 2010). Instilling the right behaviours and judgements within firm management and broader operatives should certainly be supervisory goals according to Sants and have significant implications regarding solvency.

However, such a determination leads one into a challenging and controversial area, in particular, how regulators would assess and make judgments on more subjective issues such as culture, behaviours and ethics. In this regard it is beneficial to refer to academic studies of corporate governance and management theories, which have revealed key areas of behavioural or cultural weakness that are not addressed by existing oversight mechanisms (be it from regulators, credit rating agencies, or auditors). Indeed, it has been demonstrated that if hubris and over-confidence are allowed to develop unchecked and become dominant features within management, then it can lead to poor decision-making and the preponderance of vested interests over the interests of the organisation (Lipman-Blumen, 2005; Pearce, 2009). It is also likely to foster a situation in which challenge to leadership is avoided as individuals' fear chastisement or being branded as negative or uncommitted, (Kakabadse et al., 2010). A further theme which has been explored, though remains controversial, is the theory of GroupThink, which has been described as an 'extreme concurrence seeking in group decision making, producing group cohesiveness, anticipatory compliance and excessive loyalty' (Janis and Mann, 1977, p. 17). This can lead to a situation where there is an absence of challenge and critical evaluation based on the sense of unanimity. Some supervisory authorities themselves may have got into this environment pre-crisis. In the absence of failure, concern turns inward to ensure internal harmony and cooperation and those speaking out or questioning the status quo may be disparaged.

Similarly, it would not appear to be particularly controversial to state that a firm ought to be aware of its culture and the impact that it can have. A culture is linked, amongst other things, to the leadership, the strategy and incentives of the firm and manifests itself in particular behaviours, which in turn influences decision-making. The recent furore over bankers' bonuses would indicate that society believed the financial sector to be lacking an appropriate ethical framework within which actions and decisions were grounded, or if such a framework was promulgated it was not adhered to. Remuneration policies did not themselves engender a financial crisis; but they have rightly received attention because they are reflective of a culture in which risk taking was encouraged and thus are indicative of the need for deeper structural reform. A number of jurisdictions either have (such as the Australian Prudential Regulatory Authority, APRA) or are in the process of introducing remuneration requirements (such as the EU), and this should begin to change attitudes. Nevertheless, further developments are necessary to embed more responsible attitudes and culture within the industry. Arguably, it is incumbent on the industry as well as regulators to be reflective of their role and responsibilities in the wake of the GFC; however, firms are unlikely to address endemic cultural weaknesses. Indeed, a recent study gathering the views of senior executives from international financial firms would suggest that the crisis has done little to change attitudes (Kakabadse et al., 2010).

It has also been argued the egregious bonus culture was reflective of a more fundamental issue that managerial capitalism had supplanted ownership capitalism in which the firm is run for the management's benefit rather than for the shareholders' (Bogle, 2005). Thus, it would seem there were major incentives for the sector to provide the maximum level of growth whilst there was not the same disincentive at the consequences of a possible downturn, because the management was not clearly accountable to the owners. As a result participants were able to reap huge rewards during the upturn and were often largely shielded from the downturn. These points do not serve to chastise the industry but rather to underline that culture and ethics were important factors in defining the attitude to risk and thus from a regulatory standpoint affected financial stability. Regulators have little choice but to begin assessing how they will respond to regulating and supervising such challenges.

One of the challenges any consideration of the regulation of culture poses is that it moves regulators further into the realm of making judgements. Historically, the regulatory role has been to monitor compliance with rules and provide determinations which can be settled, if necessary, in the courts. How regulators assess the culture of a firm is clearly a difficult question. However, Sants' intention in his recent speech was that the regulatory focus should be on shaping positive behaviour, not by prescribing a particular culture, but by recognising where there was evidence of poor management that was not conducive to the appropriate outcomes (Sants, 2010).

A global approach to the structure of solvency frameworks

In addition to the specific strategic, governance, cultural, ethical and moral issues discussed, another fundamentally important aspect that we need to reflect on as a result of what we have learnt from the GFC is the overall supervisory architecture and structure.

Group supervision

Supervisors involved in group-wide supervision need to be able to assess all relevant information on all risks the insurance group is exposed to. However, highly centralised groups make it almost impossible to adequately address the risks at a solo level and subsequently to rely on data/information received at that level. A key question is the extent of group-wide supervision in that if it is to cover all the relevant businesses that insurance companies undertake, it should include non-regulated subsidiaries and off-balance sheet items. However, this is not a straightforward exercise. If the supervisor is to have the ability to adequately monitor activities at the holding company level and, if necessary, be able to intervene, then how should such requirements be established? Do supervisors need the power to collect data at the holding company level, particularly in the case of very complex holding structures? Supervisors are, therefore, very aware of the need to recognise the possible contagion lines between different parts of an insurance group as well as group reputational risks, such as increased lapse rates and increased liquidity pressures. Another issue adding further complications is the question of financial conglomerates and the need to ensure that such groups are adequately supervised on a cross-sectoral basis in order to prevent regulatory arbitrage across sectors.

Group risk assessment

The GFC was instructive in highlighting that increased financial innovation requires supervisors to remain abreast of current market developments and be able to properly understand such products across an insurance group.

An area of particular concern relates to how supervisors address diversification/concentration risk at group level (for both assets and liabilities) and fungibility of capital and transferability of assets. Supervisors need to assess the ability of the group to transfer capital, while concurrently maintaining an adequate distribution of capital within the group. This is valid for the asset side as well as the liability side of the balance sheet. Supervisors have been under pressure from the industry to recognise diversification effects. However, of particular concern to supervisors is what happens during times of stress and whether these diversification benefits are fully available. The experience of AIG demonstrates that the implied diversification offered by its financial products unit should have been questioned as to whether it would be able to withstand the test of falling markets and negative market sentiment.

The crisis also demonstrated the need for supervisors to adequately address intra-group liquidity risk exposure, since insurers can also become subject to liquidity risk and require very high amounts of liquidity injections as evidenced by AIG. Liquidity may also be transferred from different parts of a group towards others. This can have difficult implications in the case of financial conglomerates with banking, insurance and non-regulated or under-regulated business. Therefore, group-wide supervisors need to ensure that, particularly during times of crisis, there is an adequate distribution of capital within a group.

Greater transparency

Large insurance groups can be more complex in terms of structure and organisation and thus transparency and disclosure issues become increasingly important. The supervisor's task is often exacerbated by the fact that different parts of the groups are subject to different and complex legal environments. To assist in this regard, financial groups and also possibly their intra-group transactions may need to become more transparent. Supervisors will require risks to be appropriately measured and disclosed and implicit assumptions may need to become explicit. To achieve this, disclosure rules/requirements of groups may need to be strengthened. This is also valid for complex financial products to improve transparency and prevent excessive risk taking.

Increasing corporate governance requirements and improving risk management frameworks and internal controls are key supervisory goals. Given the outcomes of AIG, this now includes remuneration policies and incentive schemes.

Comparability and convergence

It is recognised that timely development of enhanced communication and cooperation amongst supervisors involved in the supervision of a group on a group-wide basis is critical. To start with comparability, the need for supervisory colleges became apparent in light of the recent financial crisis. Thus, an area of ongoing work for the regulatory community will be to define the role of the group-wide supervisor and its interplay with other supervisors. Appropriate information sharing mechanisms will be required. It is clear that regulators and supervisors will need to strengthen their crisis management arrangement and better provide solutions during a crisis as well as aiming to prevent crises. Supervisors will need to share information and discuss cross-border threats to financial stability and the overall financial soundness of the global insurance industry.

In addition to establishing more comprehensive and better defined supervisory co-operation mechanisms there is also a strong argument for greater convergence of supervisory practice. Still today in the global insurance sector, different accounting, capital adequacy and legal regimes are applied worldwide. This has resulted in a low level of regulatory harmonisation and convergence of supervisory practice. One pertinent issue to arise from G20 and Financial Stability Board (FSB)-driven discussions has been the frequent requests to supervisors for hard data on insurance activities. However, there are no globally consistent solvency reporting or measurement tools for assessing insurer solvency amongst supervisors. This is in marked contrast to the banking sector where the Basel Committee for Banking Supervision (BCBS) established common capital requirements for all internationally active banks in 1988, which have been substantially improved to Basel II in 2004 and will now undergo further review as a result of Basel III. Similarly, the International Organization of Securities Commissions (IOSCO) also applies a common capital requirement for the trading book, on the same basis as the BCBS. Such a common benchmark requirement has been demonstrated to not only contribute to enhanced market confidence and stability but also to facilitate effective banking supervision by providing common understanding and consistent data among the supervisors.

This raises the immediate question regarding the extent of comparability and convergence that presently exists in solvency systems worldwide. The International Association of Insurance Supervisors (IAIS) has recently endorsed (October 2010) new solvency standards and guidance covering capital adequacy, investments, enterprise risk management and internal models – both at the solo (legal entity) and group level. Development of a valuation standard and guidance is also due for completion in 2011. This new suite of solvency standards essentially requires supervisory regimes to establish risk-based solvency requirements, which reflect a total balance sheet approach on an economic basis, and which address all reasonably foreseeable and relevant material risks. Currently, IAIS standards take the form of high-level principles-based requirements, and thus while they are supported by guidance papers (material on the optional approaches for application of the requirements in practice), the current structure of IAIS supervisory papers allows for flexibility in how a jurisdiction implements the requirements in practice. Therefore, it is often the case that methods and degree of implementation differ among IAIS members; that is, the principles or rules are based at the local level.

Such flexibility is not necessarily inappropriate and reflects the diverse nature of the global insurance supervisory community. However, if solvency is to be a focal point of prudential regulation worldwide, then it may be more appropriate to aim at an enhanced level of convergence. Given the scale and complexity of large insurance groups, the extent of cross-border activities and the systemic relevance of the institutions, such differentiated implementation of regulatory and supervisory requirements among IAIS members may limit the optimisation of supervision. This evidently in turn limits the protection of policy-holder interest of groups and the promotion of financial stability, and moreover could allow for regulatory arbitrage. Inconsistent standards around the world, for example, would allow for the relocation of headquarters and the transfer of significant risks within a group to a less sophisticated and under-regulated jurisdiction, which could result in a greater concentration of risks in certain jurisdictions. The lack of common supervisory standards could even trigger a 'race to the bottom' among the supervisors by giving more incentive to the insurers which are seeking less sophisticated regulation.

Further, it can be complex and resource intensive, and at times impractical, for supervisors to fully understand and assess the supervisory frameworks and practices of another jurisdiction due to the extent of the prevailing diversities in solvency requirements and supervisory practices. Thus, it can be difficult for supervisors to share information and consolidate such information to reach a common understanding of the financial and risk positions of large insurance groups.

The role of supervisory colleges only serves to underline this point. Without a common solvency language amongst supervisors and firms, the effectiveness of such colleges will be hampered. For example, the assessment of the financial condition and risk management of a large multinational insurance group will be complex if each jurisdiction imposes different requirements for risk measurement and capital determination. To illustrate, if a specific risk is valued by a risk sensitive (such as internal model-based) capital requirement in one jurisdiction, a rule-based (such as standardised or RBC approach) capital requirement in another, and other supplementing measures (such as investment limits) or qualitative (such as governance related) requirements in another jurisdiction, the scope for consolidating each jurisdiction's assessment of the risks and financial positions will be limited, and hence it may be difficult for supervisors to establish a comprehensive view of the risks which a specific insurance group is holding. Added to this scenario is the fact that a college for a large international group is almost certain to involve supervisors from different jurisdictions meaning a common language becomes even more important.

The scenario developed indicates that it may remain difficult for jurisdictions to easily access and understand the comprehensive picture of group solvency (especially when risks may be transferred within the groups to minimise regulatory cost and/or complex intra-group transactions have been undertaken within the group). In the absence of a common framework, to gain such a comprehensive picture, supervisors will have to impose their own 'additional' group-level reporting requirements to assess the financial and risk position of the group. Such a duplicative process is not only inefficient but may also result in misleading conclusions for the group level assessment as the regional knowledge and efforts of the solo supervisors may not be easily reflected in the assessment. This, in turn may result in inappropriate actions being taken.

Thus, to summarise, without convergence of supervisory practices, it will be difficult for supervisors to reach a common understanding or to establish mutually recognisable equivalence of their respective regulatory approaches and supervisory practices particularly on solvency matters.

Greater commonality

It is, therefore, very encouraging that the IAIS has commenced its ComFrame project (Common Framework for the Supervision of Internationally Active Insurers), for which one of the principal aims is to explore the extent to which a common supervisory framework can be achieved, with solvency being at the core of such requirements. The project will aim to go further than the existing IAIS supervisory papers in that actual criteria measures will be developed. Thus, coupled with the generation of reporting and supervisory review requirements the ComFrame will certainly be a key solvency development for many years ahead.

Furthermore, the current IASB/Financial Accounting Standards Board (FASB) joint project to develop a new international accounting standard for insurers is to be welcomed. In numerous jurisdictions the accounting approach represents the fundamental starting point of any assessment of solvency. Thus the various accounting approaches that currently exist are a significant impediment to greater convergence of practice.

Conclusion

This analysis of prudential insurance regulation has challenged existing supervisory practices and frameworks through an evaluation of the key components of solvency assessment, the lessons learnt from insurer failures and the broader regulatory issues that have emerged from the GFC. It has espoused the view that the global supervisory structures and architectures need to develop further if we are to fully build on the lessons learnt and establish a future regulatory framework that policy-makers, supervisors and insurers can place their faith in.

More specifically, it has posited that if solvency really is to be a focal point for prudential supervision then there are a number of key areas that we need to reflect on. Firstly, it is essential that we do not neglect the core basics of solvency assessment. Such assessment should not only be built on consideration of the main risk categories but also have regard to the risk appetite, strategic risk and corporate governance risks of the insurer. It should also be grounded in thorough supervisory scrutiny and appropriate challenge of the insurer's business plan.

Secondly, that the role of the Board and senior management is particularly crucial, and indeed through the development of ORSA and internal model requirements supervisory regimes are now engaging with how they can promote greater Board understanding and ownership of the risks that are being run and reflection on their firm's resilience and limits.

Thirdly, if we are to avoid major insolvencies in the future, there should be new areas of supervisory focus, most notably the expansion of the regulatory remit to consider cultures and behaviours within firms. Past failures have shown that poor practice in these areas has led to poor decision-making, inappropriate risk-taking and a lack of challenge. It is therefore incumbent on supervisors to consider how they can reasonably promote better outcomes in these areas without seeking to define a particular culture.

Finally, we should work towards achieving a truly global understanding of the supervisory practices. This can be accomplished by establishing group supervisory frameworks underpinned by, at the least, greater supervisory convergence, cooperation and information sharing and, in order to be wholly effective, by greater commonality of solvency assessment. The latter involves the development of a common approach to valuation and greater consistency of capital and governance requirements to facilitate comparability and avoid regulatory arbitrage. This is likely to remain an aspiration for a number of years yet, but the development of a Common Framework now provides a strong platform upon which to progress in this area and crucially displays a will to enhance global supervisory frameworks within the international community.

Notes

1. A good overview of current solvency capital requirements can be found in the Issues Paper on *Group Wide Solvency Assessment and Supervision* (5 March 2009, IAIS).
2. GARs allow policy-holders to opt for a minimum pension payout and bonus when their policy matures.
3. The ORSA requirement is now part of the International Association of Insurance Supervisors (IAIS) Insurance Core Principles on Enterprise Risk Management and will be incorporated into the Solvency II regime.

Bibliography

Beveridge, D. (1995) 'Risky Financial Gamble Guts Famed Investment Bank', *AM Cycle*, 27 February.

Bogle, J.C. (2005) *The Battle for the Soul of Capitalism* (New Haven: Yale University Press).

Bower-Space, K. (2002) 'Field of Bad Dreams, The Shrinking Crop Insurance Market', 1 June.

Bradford, M. (2003) 'Framework Offers Guidance on ERM', *Business Insurance*, Vol. 37, 8 April.

Cave, A. (2001) 'Fury Over FSA Role in Independent Failure', *Daily Telegraph*, 13 July.

Change Management (2003) 'A Board Culture of Corporate Governance – Pacific Change', 10 October.

Costello, D. (2003) 'Recent Developments in Insurance Insolvency (An Irish Slant on a Global Problem)'. Presented to the Society of Actuaries in Ireland, February.

Drennan, L., and M. Beck (n.d.) 'Corporate Governance: A Mandate for Risk Management'.

FSA (2003) 'Review of UK Insurers' Risk Management Practices', October.

Harrington, S.E. (1992) 'Policyholder Runs, Life Insurance Company Failures, and Insurance Solvency Regulation', *Regulation: Cato Review of Business and Government*, 15(2), Spring.

'The HIH Legacy: Corporate Governance and Shareholder Value' (2003) *Business and Management Practices*, 12 May.

Hughes, G. (2001) 'Reinsurance Bad Debt', Insurance Institute address, 24 January.

IAIS (International Association of Insurance Supervisors) (2010) *Insurance Core Principle (ICP) 16, Enterprise Risk Management, standards and guidance material*, October (Basel, Switzerland: IAIS).

Janis, I., and L. Mann (1977), *Victims of Groupthink: A Psychological Analysis of Conflict* (New York: Free Press).

Johnston, J., A. Kouzmin, K. Thorne and S. Kelly (2010) 'Crisis Opportunism: Bail Outs and E-SCADs in the GFC', *Risk Management: An International Journal*, 12(3) (July): 208–34.

Kakabadse, A., A. Kouzmin and N. Kakabadse (2010) 'Auditing Moral Hazards for Post Global Financial Crisis (GFC) Leadership'. Paper presented at the 10th European Academy of Management (EURAM) Conference, Rome, 19–22 May, and currently under review for the *European Management Review*.

Kenny, P. (2002) 'Thoughts for CEOs in the New Year – Challenges Facing Them Today in 2002'.

Lam, J. (2000) 'Enterprise-Wide Risk Management and the Role of the Chief Risk Officer', www.erisk.com, 25 March.

Leonard, A. (2000) 'Best's Review', *Independent Thinking*, 100(12) (April): 96.

Lipman-Blumen, J. (2005) *The Allure of Toxic Leaders: Why We Follow Destructive Bosses and Corrupt Politicians – and How We Can Survive Them* (New York: Oxford University Press).

Main, A. (2003) *Other People's Money* (New York: HarperCollins).

Masters, N. (2002) 'Insurance Companies: Waking Up to International Standards', *Balance Sheet*, 10(3) (July).

Pearce, J. (2009), 'Corporate Governance and Corporate Power: A New Way Forward', in M. Mehra (ed.), *Re-Energising Corporate Governance by Realigning the Moral Compass of the Board* (India: World Council for Corporate Governance, MM Publishing), pp. 84–98.

Phillips, L. (2002) 'Nine Threats Which Face the UK Organisations Today', 14 May.

Pretty, M. (2003) 'ReAC Film Case is No Thriller', 22 October.

Reeves-Knyght, P., N. Kakabadse, A. Kakabadse and A. Kouzmin (2011) 'When Rules and Principles are not Enough: Insiders' Vignettes and the Global Financial Crisis', *Journal of Change Management* (Special Issue on 'CSR and the Dissenting Voices of Change from the Developing World'), 11(1) (March): 45–67.

Ringshaw, G. (2001) 'Bright in £4m Personal Loan Crisis', 17 June.

Ringshaw, G. (2001) 'Where Did the £700m Go?', *Daily Telegraph*, 24 June.

Sants, H. (2010) Speech to the FSA Chartered Institute of Securities and Investments Conference, 17 June.

Sharma, P. (2002) 'Report: Prudential Supervision of Insurance Undertakings', Conference of Insurance Supervisory Services of the Member States of the European Union, December.

Veysey, S. (2001) 'Independent Collapse Probed', *Business Insurance*, 25 June.

Veysey, S. (n.d.) 'Australian Regulators Charge Adler', *Business Insurance*.

Veysey, S. (2001) 'FSA Denies "Tip off" on Independent', *Business Insurance*, 16 July.

Westfield, M. (n.d.) 'HIH: The Inside Story of Australia's Biggest Corporate Collapse'.

7 The Architecture of Insurance Supervision Before and After the Financial Crisis*

Donato Masciandaro and Marc Quintyn

Introduction

What is the current state of the insurance supervision architectures? The recent financial crisis has forcefully demonstrated that the financial services markets are deeply integrated, requiring an integrated supervisory approach. How is insurance supervision integrated into the overall regulatory setting? This chapter seeks to answer this question by proposing an index of sectoral integration – the Integration in Insurance Supervision Index – which is applied based on a large and updated database of the national supervisory settings (102 countries for the period 1998–2009). Furthermore, the results are used to evaluate the proposed reforms in the European Union (EU) and the US.

Although the financial crisis hit the insurance industry in a less dramatic way than the banking industry, the turmoil suggested the need for reconsidering the overall picture of supervision. The primary goal of insurance supervision is to monitor both the financial risk profile of each company and the systemic risk profile of the insurance markets.

In the last decade and a half, risk distribution in the financial sector has been deeply influenced by the blurring of boundaries among individual sectors, with an increasing integration of the banking, securities and insurance markets, as well as their respective products and instruments (Group of Ten, 2001). The consequences of the blurring effect on both the supervisory setting and its effectiveness are relevant.

In this context, separate supervision for banking, insurance and other financial businesses increases the risk of regulatory arbitrage, which was one of the roots of

* The views expressed in this chapter belong solely to the authors. Nothing contained in this chapter should be reported as representing IMF policy or the views of the IMF.

the crisis: the shortcomings of fragmented supervisory settings were particularly evident in the US (Coffee, 1995, 2007; Brown, 2009; Leijonhufvud, 2009; Flamée and Windels, 2009).

The lack of integration is particularly acute in the insurance sector, given the US tradition of state-based supervision. Proposals to establish a new federal insurance regulator were discussed to improve the national regime (Harrington, 2006; Scott, 2007; Tennyson, 2008) as well as to contribute to the development of international insurance standards (Brown, 2009). However, the federal regulator option has also been criticised by some (Kwon, 2007; Grace, 2009).

During the recent crisis the failure of the US insurance setting is represented by the US$160 billion bailout of the insurance giant American International Group (AIG) (Sjostrom, 2009). AIG was able to conduct regulatory arbitrage among different jurisdictions in US and in Europe, and the federal agency which failed in AIG oversight was the Office of Thrift Supervision (OTS). Why was AIG – an insurance company which conducted business in 130 countries – controlled by a minor US regulator? Because among its several holdings, AIG had a savings and loan firm – since 1999 AIG organised its federal savings bank – and OTS was a consolidated supervisor but without complete and robust information on its supervised firm.

Therefore, as it has been correctly pointed out (Eling and Schmeiser, 2010), the integration of the financial markets calls for more integration in supervision to reduce the risk of deficiencies in information flows. However, integration in supervision cannot be considered per se a sufficient condition for a safe and sound financial system. Episodes of supervisory failures have been registered in countries with different regimes as well. The reasons are quite simple.

First of all, so far no optimal model of supervision has been singled out. The emerging literature on the financial supervision architecture has tried to shed some light on the impact of the supervisory structure on the performance of the banking and financial industry. Unfortunately, despite the debate on the features of the supervisory regimes and their drivers, the empirical evidence is still very limited, probably given the fact that the wave of reforms is recent (for a survey see Masciandaro and Quintyn, 2009). Therefore it has been assessed that no 'superior' model of supervision exists (Schoenmaker, 2003, among others).

Second, it has been pointed out that at least two dimensions of integration may be identified: its breadth (sectoral coverage) and its depth (functional coverage: licensing, ongoing supervision, enforcement, etc.) (Monkiewicz, 2007a). Considering integration in all the dimensions of the supervisory activity makes it possible to highlight both pros and cons (Flamée and Windels, 2009).

Nevertheless, per se the sectoral integration in supervision can be considered ceteris paribus as a device to reduce the risks of regulatory arbitrage, which generates or amplifies the potential systemic risk spin-offs from one sector to another one. For the insurance industry more sectoral integration in supervision can mean more information for the regulator and then less risk of instability. In fact, while there is little evidence that insurance business can originate systemic risk, the insurance sector is vulnerable to systemic risks generated in other parts of the financial system (IAIS, 2009; The Geneva Association, 2010).

Furthermore, the blurring of distinctions among the different national insurance markets as well as the risk of instability spillover calls for more international coordination (Braumüller, 2007). More integration in each national setting can be a device to reduce the transaction costs in establishing and implementing the exchange of information, thus improving the odds of cooperation among insurance supervisors. In an EU-perspective, more convergence of the institutional setting could increase the likelihood of more centralised supervisory settings (Masciandaro, Nieto and Quintyn, 2009).

This chapter provides answers with respect to the current state of integration of insurance supervision into the overall regulatory architecture all around the world. The chapter is organised as follows. In the next section we describe the landscape of the financial supervision architecture before the financial crisis, highlighting the trend towards consolidation. The third section is focused on the insurance supervision shape: we propose an index to measure its sectoral integration, evaluating how the regulator responsible for insurance supervision is involved in the overall supervisory responsibility. The fourth section discusses the effects of the recent proposals for the structure of supervision in the EU and the US on the degree of integration, and the final section concludes.

The supervisory architecture before the financial crisis: the trend towards consolidation

This chapter distinguishes between regulation and supervision, focusing on the latter only. While regulation refers to the rules that govern the conduct of the intermediaries, supervision is the monitoring practice by one or more public authorities in order to ensure compliance with the regulatory framework (Barth et al., 2006).

Focusing on supervision is today easier than in the past, given that an important development of the last 15 years has been the shift towards separation of regulatory and supervisory authority (Monkiewicz, 2007a). To be even more precise, the core attention of this chapter is on micro-prudential supervision, while macro-prudential supervision is usually carried out by the central bank, and competition policy is in the hands of a specialised authority (Borio, 2003; Kremers et al., 2003; Čihák and Podpiera, 2007; Herring and Carmassi, 2008).

In the last decade many countries have reformed the structure of their financial supervision. We present a dataset consisting of an heterogeneous sample of 102 countries, belonging to all continents (Masciandaro and Quintyn, 2009). Table 7.1 describes all the relevant features of the 102 supervisory regimes in the sample.

In the ten years since 1998, 64% of the countries included in the sample – 66 out of 102 – chose to reform their financial supervisory structure by establishing a new supervisory authority and/or changing the powers of (at least) one of the already existing agencies.

Table 7.1 Supervisory architectures in 102 countries (2009)

Countries	Banking sector (b)	Securities sector (s)	Insurance sector (i)	Model
Albania	CB	SI	SI	Hybrid
Algeria	CB, B1, B2	S	–	Hybrid
Argentina	CB	S	I	Silos
Australia	BI	BI, S	BI, S	Peaks
Austria	U, CB	U	U	Unified
Bahamas	CB	S	I	Silos
Bahrain	CB	CB	CB	Unified
Belarus	CB	S	I	Silos
Belgium	U	U	U	Unified
Bolivia	B	SI	SI	Hybrid
Bosnia	CB, B1, B2	S1	–	Hybrid
Botswana	CB	SI	SI	Hybrid
Brazil	CB	CB, S	I	Hybrid
Bulgaria	CB	SI	SI	Hybrid
Cameroon	B	Ss (**)	I (	Silos
Canada	BI	Ss (**)	BI, Ss (**)	Hybrid
Chile	CB, B	CB, SI	SI	Hybrid
China	B	S	I	Silos
Colombia	U	U	U	Unified
Costa Rica	B	S	I	Silos
Croatia	CB	SI	SI	Hybrid
Cyprus	CB	S	I	Hybrid
Czech Republic	CB	CB	CB	Unified
Denmark	U	U	U	Unified
Ecuador	BI	S	BI	Hybrid
Egypt	CB	S	I	Silos
El Salvador	BI	S	BI	Hybrid
Estonia	U	U	U	Unified
Finland	U	U	U	Unified
France	CB, B1, B2	CB, S	I	Hybrid
Georgia	U	U	U	Unified
Germany	U, CB	U	U	Unified
Ghana	CB	S	I	Silos
Greece	CB	S	I	Silos
Guatemala	BI	S	BI	Hybrid
Haiti	CB	–	Is (**)	Silos
Hungary	U	U	U	Unified
Iceland	U	U	U	Unified
India	CB	S	I	Silos
Iran	CB	S	I	Silos
Ireland	CB	CB	CB	Unified

Countries	Banking sector (b)	Securities sector (s)	Insurance sector (i)	Model
Israel	CB	S,I	I	Hybrid
Italy	CB, S	CB, S	I	Hybrid
Jamaica	CB	SI	SI	Hybrid
Japan	CB, U	U	U	Unified
Jordan	CB	S	I	Silos
Kazakhstan	U, CB	U	U	Unified
Kenya	CB	S	I	Silos
Korea	U	U	U	Unified
Kyrgyzstan	CB	S	I	Silos
Latvia	U	U	U	Unified
Lebanon	B, CB	CB, B	I	Hybrid
Libya	CB	SI	SI	Hybrid
Lithuania	CB	S	I	Silos
Luxembourg	BS	BS	I	Hybrid
Macedonia	CB	S	I	Silos
Madagascar	CB	CB	–	Unified
Malaysia	CB	S	CB	Hybrid
Malta	U	U	U	Unified
Mauritius	CB	SI	SI	Hybrid
Mexico	BS	BS	I	Hybrid
Moldova	CB	SI	SI	Hybrid
Montenegro	CB	S	I	Silos
Morocco	CB	S	I	Silos
Namibia	CB	SI	SI	Hybrid
Netherlands	CB, S	CB, S	CB, S	Peaks
New Zealand	CB	S	I	Silos
Nicaragua	U	U	U	Unified
Norway	U	U	U	Unified
Pakistan	CB	SI	SI	Hybrid
Panama	B	S	I	Silos
Peru	BI	S	BI	Hybrid
Philippines	CB, S	CB, S	I	Hybrid
Poland	U	U	U	Unified
Portugal	CB	S	I	Silos
Romania	CB	S	I	Silos
Russia	CB	S	I	Silos
Rwanda	CB	CB	CB	Unified
Saudi Arabia	CB	S	CB	Hybrid
Singapore	CB	CB	CB	Unified
Slovak Republic	CB	CB	CB	Unified
Slovenia	CB (.33)	S (.33)	I (.33)	Silos
South Africa	CB (.33)	SI (.66)	SI	Hybrid
Spain	CB, Bs (**)	CB, S	I	Hybrid
Sri Lanka	CB	S	I	Silos
Sweden	U	U	U	Unified
Switzerland	U	U	U	Unified
Tajikistan	CB	CB	I	Hybrid
Tanzania	CB	S	I	Silos

Table 7.1 continued

Countries	Banking sector (b)	Securities sector (s)	Insurance sector (i)	Model
Thailand	CB	S	I	Silos
Trinidad Tobago	CB	S, CB	I, CB	Hybrid
Tunisia	CB	S	I	Silos
Turkey	B	S	I	Silos
Ukraine	CB	S	I	Silos
UAE	CB	S	I	Silos
Uganda	CB	S	I (.33)	Silos
UK	U	U	U	Unified
USA	CB, B1, B2, B3, Ss**	S, S2, Ss**	I, Is (**)	Hybrid
Uruguay	CB	CB	CB	Unified
Venezuela	B	S	I	Silos
Vietnam	CB	S	I	Silos
Zimbabwe	CB	S	I	Silos

Notes: The initials have the following meaning: B = authority specialised in the banking sector; BI = authority specialised in the banking sector and insurance sector; CB = central bank; G = government; I = authority specialised in the insurance sector; S = authority specialised in the securities markets; U = single authority for all sectors ; BS = authority specialised in the banking sector and securities markets; SI = authority specialised in the insurance sector and securities markets.
* (b) = banking or central banking law; (s) = security markets law; (i) = insurance law.
** State or regional agencies, or self-regulated agencies.

Source: Author's compilation.

The reform trend is even more evident when we add a regional and country–income perspective. Figure 7.1 provides a breakdown by country groups and shows that the European, the EU and OECD countries count for, respectively, 82%, 77% and 73% of the countries that have undertaken reforms. Therefore, the shape of the supervisory regime was in the past decade a relevant issue in particular in the more advanced countries, especially Europe.

Figure 7.2 summarises the state of affairs. The supervisory regimes are grouped taking into account the three main models of supervision that theory so far proposed: the vertical (silos) model, which follows the boundaries of the financial system in different sectors of business, and where every sector is supervised by a different agency; the horizontal (peaks) model, which follows the difference among the public goals of regulation, and where every goal is supervised by a different authority (Taylor, 1995); and the unified model, where a single authority supervises the entire financial system in pursuing all the public goals. We do not consider the model by function, which follows the functions performed by banking and financial firms, given its very limited historical use.

In several cases – 36 countries, 35% of our sample – the supervisory regime still follows the vertical model, with separate agencies for banking, securities, and insurance supervision. The classic silos model worked well in a structure of the

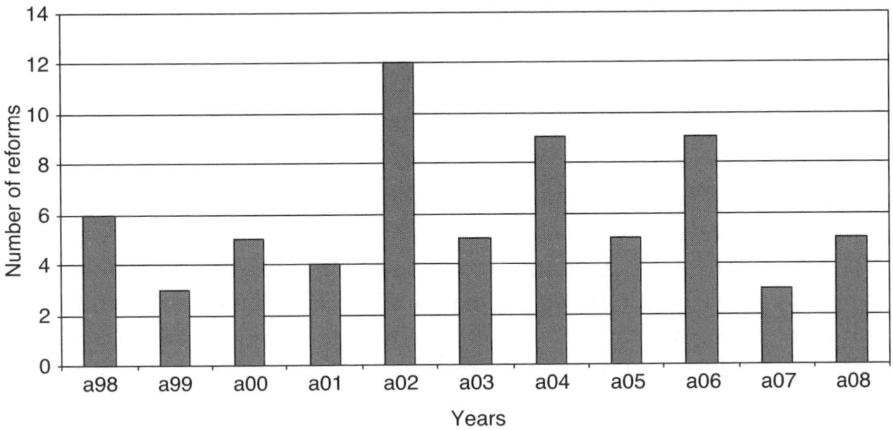

Source: Author's compilation.

Figure 7.1 Reforms of the supervisory architectures per year (1998–2008)

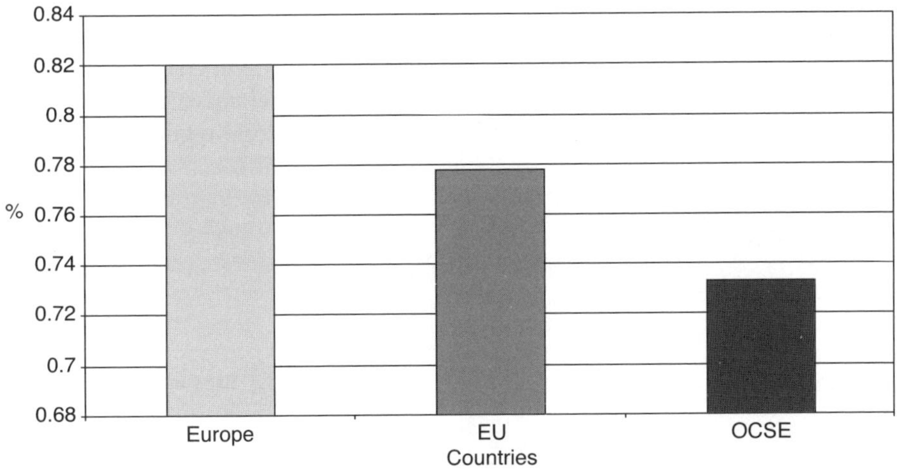

Source: Author's compilation.

Figure 7.2 Reforms of the financial architectures (1998–2008, %)

financial industry where a clear demarcation existed between banking, security markets and insurance companies. The insurance supervision is delegated to a specialised authority.

In another 24% (24 countries), a new regime of supervision has been established with the introduction of a single authority, where the supervision covering banking, securities and insurance markets is completely unified. The single supervisory regime is based on just one control authority, which acts as a monopolistic agency on the overall financial system, including the insurance sector.

The small 'peaks' group consists of two countries – Australia and the Netherlands, 2% of our sample – that adopted the so-called horizontal model, which groups supervision aimed at preserving systemic stability in one peak, and the conduct of business supervision in another. Both the unified model and the peaks model represent examples of the consolidation process that seems to dominate the reforms of the supervisory architectures.

Finally, other countries are characterized by hybrid supervisory regimes, with some supervisors monitoring more than one segment of the market and others only one. We bring them all together in a residual class (40 countries, 39% of our sample). The group is comprised of countries such as France, Italy and the US, where the structure of supervision can be better described using history or law legacy rather than an economic framework.

The evolution in the supervisory regimes becomes clearer if we focus our attention on the 66 countries that implemented reforms in the period 1988–2008 (Figure 7.3): the weights of the three main regimes (unified, silos and hybrid) become substantially equal – respectively, 30%, 33% and 33%– while the peaks regime is the least common one (4%). In other words, 40% of the sample (20 countries) adopted an innovative regime of supervision – unified or peaks regime – while the remaining 60% (31 countries) chose a 'conservative' approach, that is, maintaining the more traditional regime (silos or hybrid regime).

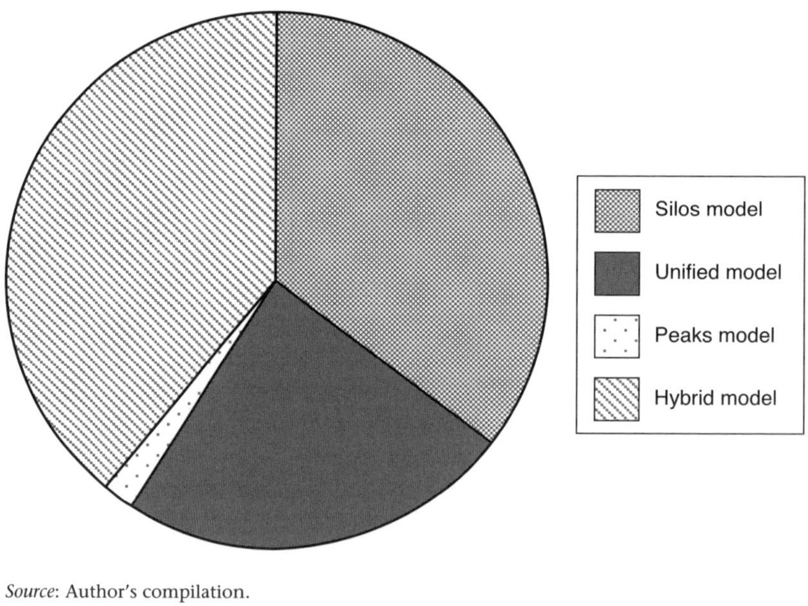

Source: Author's compilation.

Figure 7.3 Models of financial supervision architectures (102 countries)

Our data explain the reason why the recent literature on the economics of the financial supervision architectures zoomed in on the consolidation trend in reforming the supervisory architectures all around the world (Barth et al., 2002; Arnone and Gambini, 2007; Čihák and Podpiera, 2007).

Is it possible to measure the consolidation process? This is where the Financial Supervision Unification (FSU) Index comes in (Masciandaro and Quintyn, 2009). This index was created through an analysis of which, and how many, authorities in each of the examined countries are empowered to supervise the three traditional sectors of financial activity: banking, securities markets and insurance. Figure 7.4 shows the distribution of the FSU Index. On the one hand there are countries (44) with a low degree of supervisory consolidation (Index equal to 0 or 1). On the other, there are countries (27) that established a unified supervisor or that adopted the peaks model, with a high level of supervisory consolidation (the Index takes the value 6 or 7).

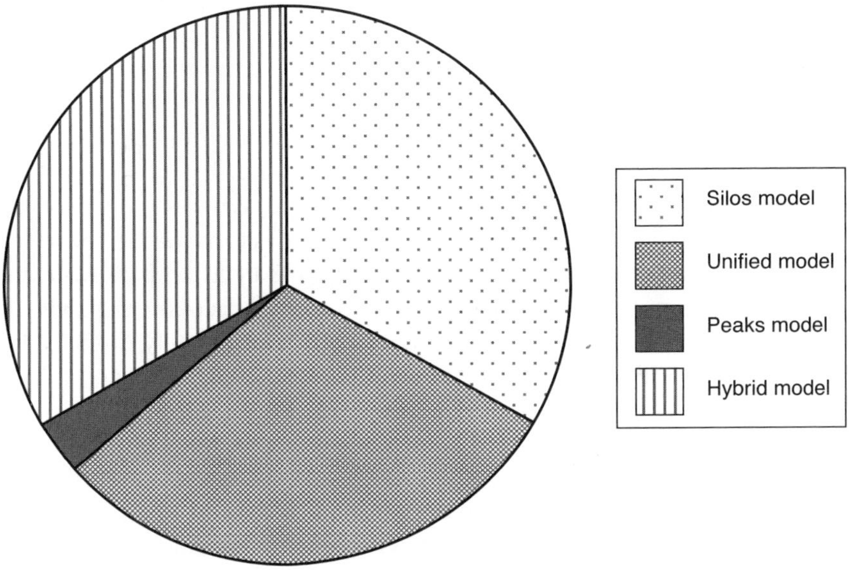

Source: Author's compilation.

Figure 7.4 Model of financial supervision regimes after the reforms (66 countries)

The integration of the insurance supervision

The analysis of the evolution of the financial supervisory architectures highlighted a trend toward consolidation, particularly evident in the industrialised countries, and even more so in Europe. From the point of view of the insurance industry the consolidation process produces different levels of integration of its supervision in the general supervisory setting. This section is focused on the sectoral integration, that is, how the insurance regulator is involved in the supervision of the overall financial system.

Zooming in on sectoral integration we can evaluate how the regulator in charge of the insurance industry can potentially gain in terms of information and then be more able to prevent or to face the risks of instability. We guess that the recent financial market turbulence demonstrated once again that sectoral integration can be considered a potential tool to improve the market monitoring. The same is not automatically true for other kind of integration, that is, technical integration – complete convergence of the supervisory toolkit used – and organic integration – complete unification of principles and standard (Monkiewicz, 2007a). In other words we can have an insurance regulator that benefits from the information gain from the sectoral integration and at the same time can be flexible in terms of both technical and operational integration. The possibility of technical and operation flexibility is crucial, given that, despite the convergence process among different banking and financial firms, there are structural differences at work that preserve the specificity of the insurance industry (Beltratti and Corvino, 2007).

From a qualitative point of view the level of integration of the insurance supervision into the other segments of financial supervision depends on the type of the supervisory model that each country has adopted. Where the supervisory regime follows the vertical model, with separate agencies for banking, securities and insurance supervision, the level of integration is likely to be low. If the regime of supervision is governed by a single authority, where the supervision covering banking, securities and insurance markets is completely unified, the level of integration is likely to be high. In the other cases – peak model and hybrid model – we can just presume an intermediate level of integration. Is it possible to be more precise in our evaluation? Is the consolidation index introduced in the above section useful?

In measuring the level of integration the consolidation index is not sufficient. It has been designed to be consistent with its own aim – measuring the degree of consolidation of the supervisory powers – using subjective weights in differentiating some cases (for example, in giving more relevance to supervision on both banking and securities industries) or in evaluating other situations (for example, the degree of consolidation when there are at least two supervisors in one sector, or when a supervisor is in charge in more than one sector). The presence of the subjective weights becomes a shortcoming when the aim is to calculate the level of supervisory integration of a given industry as such, which in our case is the insurance industry.

Therefore we need to introduce a more robust indicator to measure both the consolidation and the integration levels. We can use the Financial Supervision

Herfindahl Hirschman (FSHH) Index (Masciandaro and Quintyn, 2010), which is a measure of the level of consolidation of the supervisory powers that we derive by applying in a novel field the classical index proposed by Herfindahl and Hirschman (Hirschman, 1964). We use the FSHH index to calculate the degree of supervisory consolidation.

The robustness of the application of the FSHH to analyse the degree of concentration of power in financial supervision depends on the following three crucial hypotheses.

First of all, it is possible to define both the geographical and institutional dimension of each supervisory market: therefore in each country (*geographical dimension*) we can define different sectors to be supervised (*institutional dimension*). In other words in every country each financial market forms a distinct market for supervision. So far it is still possible to identify both the geographical dimension (that is, the existence of separate nations) and the institutional dimension (that is, the existence of separate markets) – notwithstanding the fact that the blurring of the traditional boundaries between banking, securities and insurance activities and the formation of large conglomerates diluted the definition of the intermediaries (Masciandaro and Quintyn, 2008). Then, in each sector we can define the distribution of the supervisory powers among different authorities – if more than one agency is present – and consequently their shares without ambiguity. For each sector, the greater the degree of supervision consolidation falls, the greater the number of authorities involved in monitoring activity.

Second, we consider the supervision power as a whole, that is, given different kinds of supervisory activity (banking supervision, securities markets supervision, insurance supervision) there is perfect substitutability among them in terms of supervisory power and/or supervisory skills. The supervisory power is a feature of each authority as agency, irrespective of where this supervisory power is exercised (*agency dimension*). Therefore, in each country and for each authority, we can sum the share of the supervisory power it enjoys in one sector with the share it owns in another one (if any). For each authority the greater the degree of supervisory power, the greater the number of sectors over which that agency exercises monitoring responsibility.

All three dimensions – geographical, institutional and agency – have both legal foundations and economic meaning.

Finally, we prefer to adopt the FSHH Index rather than the classic Gini Index to emphasise that the overall number of authorities matters. In general, the use of the FSHH index rather than other indices of concentration – as the entropy index – gives more weight to the influence of the unified authorities, which is, as we stressed above, the main feature of the recent evolution in the shape of the supervisory regimes.

We calculate the FSHH Index by summing up the squares of the supervisory shares of all the regulators of a country. For each country the FSHH Index is equal to:

$$H = \sum_{i=1}^{n} s_i^2$$

where s_i is the share of supervisory power of the authority i and n is the total number of authorities. For each authority i, we consider that in each country there are three sectors to supervise (each sector has the same importance) and that in each sector we can have more than one authority (each authority has the same importance). We use the following formula:

$$s_i = \sum_{j=1}^{m} s_j; \text{ and } s_j = \frac{1}{m}\frac{1}{q_j}$$

where m is the number of sectors where the authority i is present as supervisor and q is the number of authorities involved in supervision in each sector j. In other words if in one sector there is more than one authority, the supervisory power is equally divided among the incumbent supervisors.

The new methodology can be used to construct an index of the supervision integration in insurance: the Integration of Insurance Supervision (IIS) Index. The intuition is quite simple: the greater the share of the supervisor in charge of insurance, the higher the odds that the insurance supervision will be integrated into the overall regulatory organisation. In other words the integration of insurance supervision is likely to be the maximum where a unified supervisor is in charge, while the integration is likely to be low where a multiple authority model is implemented. Our index can precisely gauge the degree of integration.

To construct the IIS Index we just have to take the share of the insurance supervisor in each country, which can range from 0 to 1. We calculate the IIS Index for the 102 countries of our sample, with information updated to 2009 (Table 7.2), providing an original perspective on the state of the integration in the insurance industry.

First of all, Figure 7.5 shows that the two most frequent regimes are polarised: on the one hand, we have the maximum level of integration (IIS index = 1) where the supervisory regime is the unified one (24% of the sample); on the other, we have a relative low level of integration (IIS index = 0.33), usually where the supervisory setting is organised using the silos model (44% of the sample). The polarisation in the integration is clearly an effect of the consolidation process we described in the previous section.

Table 7.2 Supervisory architectures in 102 countries: the IIS Index (2009)

Countries	IIS	Countries	IIS
Albania	.66	Lebanon	.33
Algeria	0	Libya	.66
Argentina	.33	Lithuania	.33
Australia	.50	Luxembourg	.33
Austria	.82	Macedonia	.33
Bahamas	.33	Madagascar	0
Bahrain	1	Malaysia	.66
Belarus	.33	Malta	1
Belgium	1	Mauritius	.66
Bolivia	.60	Mexico	.33
Bosnia	0	Moldova	.66
Botswana	.66	Montenegro	.33
Brazil	.33	Morocco	.33
Bulgaria	.66	Namibia	.66
Cameroon	.33	Netherlands	.50
Canada	.49	New Zealand	.33
Chile	.49	Nicaragua	1
China	.33	Norway	1
Colombia	1	Pakistan	.66
Costa Rica	.33	Panama	.33
Croatia	.66	Peru	.66
Cyprus	.33	Philippines	.33
Czech Republic	1	Poland	1
Denmark	1	Portugal	.33
Ecuador	.66	Romania	.33
Egypt	.33	Russia	.33
El Salvador	.66	Rwanda	1
Estonia	1	Saudi Arabia	.66
Finland	1	Singapore	1
France	.33	Slovak Republic	1
Georgia	1	Slovenia	.33
Germany	1	South Africa	.66
Ghana	.33	Spain	.33
Greece	.33	Sri Lanka	.33
Guatemala	.66	Sweden	1
Haiti	.5	Switzerland	1
Hungary	1	Tajikistan	.33
Iceland	1	Tanzania	.33
India	.33	Thailand	.33
Iran	.33	Trinidad Tobago	.16
Ireland	1	Tunisia	.33
Israel	.49	Turkey	0
Italy	.33	Ukraine	.33
Jamaica	.66	UAE	.33
Japan	1	Uganda	.33
Jordan	.33	UK	1
Kazakhstan	1	USA	.16
Kenya	.33	Uruguay	1
Korea	1	Venezuela	.33
Kyrgyzstan	.33	Vietnam	.33
Latvia	1	Zimbabwe	.33

Source: Author's compilation.

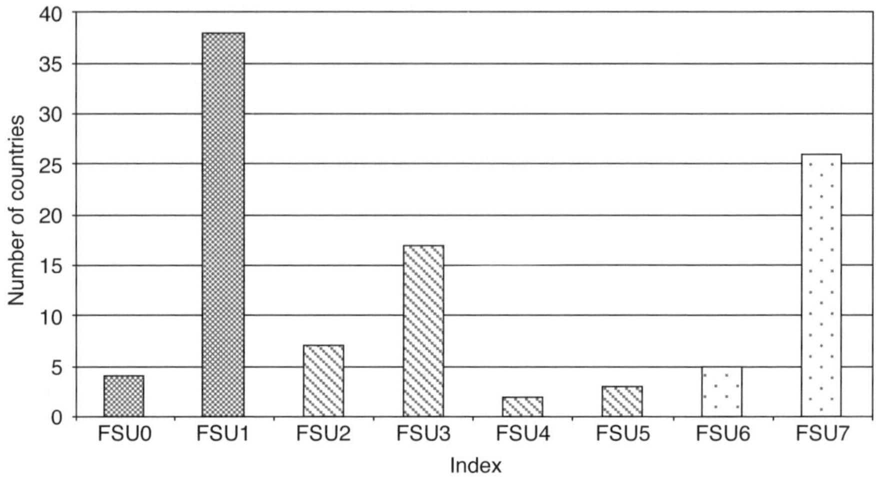

Source: Author's compilation.

Figure 7.5 The Financial Supervision Unification Index

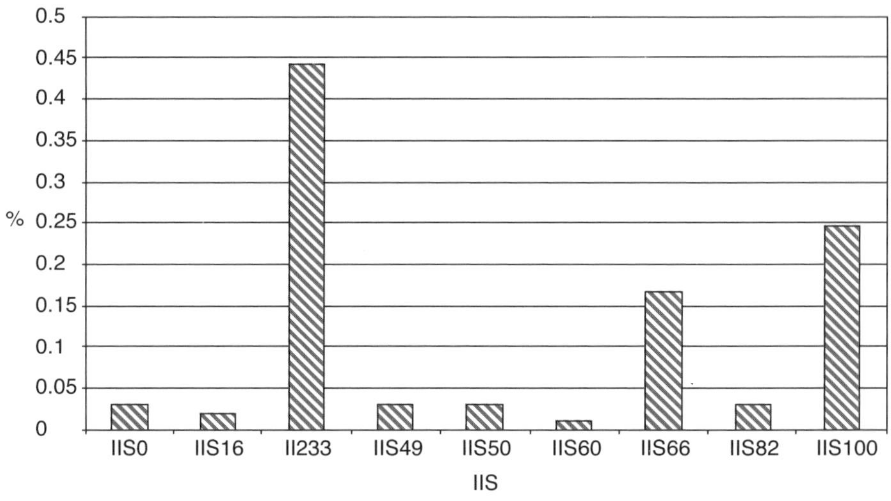

Source: Author's compilation.

Figure 7.6 Integration in Insurance Supervision Index

Second, given the overall degree of consolidation, the level of integration of the insurance supervision can be different. In fact you can have countries with the same number of authorities, but the insurance regulator is differently involved in the overall supervision.

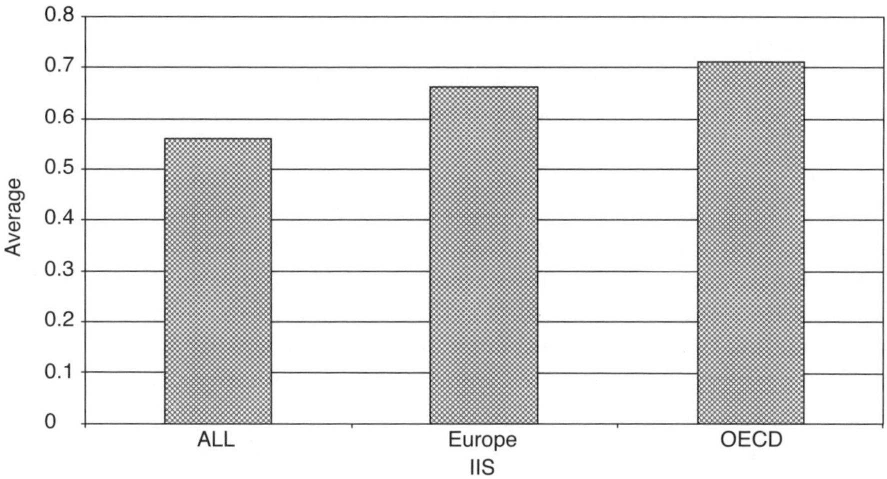

Source: Author's compilation.

Figure 7.7 Integration in Insurance Supervision: different country sample

Third, the trend toward insurance supervision integration can be studied according to country – income and regional adherence. Figure 7.6 offers this perspective: it shows that on average the degree of integration is greater if we take the industrial countries as a whole, rather than the European region; these two groups score best with respect to the overall sample. Again the result is consistent with what we noted in describing the consolidation of the overall regulatory setting.

Is the integration process still valid? Evaluating the proposed reforms in Europe and the US

After the crisis, the concern for the stability of the financial industry has caused renewed attention to the supervisory regimes. Policy-makers in several countries wondered and are wondering if they need to reshape their supervisory regimes. In this section we will review the recent proposal of reforms, wondering if the trend so far evident – integration of insurance supervision – is still valid.

Starting with the European Union, following years of debate and slow action on this front, European supervisory reform has been centre stage since the middle of 2008. In response to the financial crisis, the EU Commission mandated in late 2008 a group of experts under the chairmanship of Jacques de Larosière to present recommendations for supervisory reform on Europe.

The group presented its report in early spring of 2009. The report proposed a strengthening of the Level 3 committees of the Lamfalussy framework in a first stage (Recommendation 20). In a second stage, an integrated European System of Financial Supervision (ESFS) should be established (Recommendation 21). At a later stage, only two authorities would emerge (a peak model): one for banking and insurance supervision and any other issue relevant for financial stability, and the other for conduct of business and market issues across sectors (Recommendation 22).

The proposal by the Commission (European Commission, 2009) in fact collapses stages 1 and 2. For micro-prudential supervision, the ESFS is a three-layered structure, with a Steering Committee, three European Supervisory Authorities (ESAs) and the national supervisory agencies at the bottom layer. The three ESAs emanate from the existing Level-3 authorities in the Lamfalussy framework, with traditional sectoral responsibilities: the European Banking Authority (EBA), the European Insurance and Occupational Pension Authority (EIOPA), and the European Securities Authority (ESA). The proposal of the Commission received the full support of ECOFIN (Economic and Financial Affairs Council) in June 2009 and at the time of writing this chapter, it is under discussion in the European Parliament.

The proposed framework, consisting of three sectoral authorities at the supranational level, belongs to the category of the silo approach to supervision. The Commission (section 4.3) recognises that many member countries have different architectures, but states that at the European level this silo approach was the most evident one. In other words, in the name of continuity, given the Lamfalussy framework, European policy-makers chose a conservative approach instead of an innovative one. The European project is neutral with respect to the incentives towards integration both at supranational and national levels. The trend towards integration seems to be interrupted.

To add clarity, let us recall that at the national level in Germany the grand coalition government in 2008 threatened to dismantle the unique financial supervisor (BAFIN) in favour of the Bundesbank, while in June 2010 the UK government unveiled a reform of the bank supervisory system that will consolidate power within the Bank of England. The two proposed reforms will reduce the degree of integration of the insurance supervision, provided that the power of the supervisor in charge in the insurance markets will be reduced.

Regarding the US, the recent Dodd-Frank law covered a new architecture for financial supervision. Two new authorities are proposed: the National Bank Supervisor and the Consumer Protection Agency. The National Bank Supervisor will supervise all federally chartered banks, incorporating two so far existing authorities: the Office of Thrift Supervision and the Office of the Comptroller of the Currency. The Consumer Financial Protection Agency will protect consumers across the financial sector from unfair and abusive practices. Finally the law proposed the creation of a federal insurance office at the Treasury Department.

The Dodd-Frank law confirmed the hybrid US regime with many authorities, with some supervisors monitoring more than one segment of the market (such as the Federal Reserve or the new Consumer Protection Agency) and others only one. Therefore the US law does not follow the trend toward consolidation and integration, notwithstanding the fact that it was evident during the crisis that the fragmented supervisory setting can be incapable of monitoring the integrated, interconnected and complex reality of US financial markets (Leijonhufvud, 2009). The Dodd-Frank law prefers to bid on interagency cooperation, instead of agency consolidation.

What is our overall evaluation? In the above sections we demonstrated that before the crisis the trend in the changes in supervisory structures seemed to be characterised by two intertwined features: the observed consolidation of supervision goes hand in hand with the integration of insurance supervision.

But this is not the case with the EU-level and US proposals. The policy-makers chose to maintain supervisory regimes where the authorities are multiple: the silo regime in the EU and the hybrid regime in the US, with no integration of the insurance supervision. How can this be explained?

A political economy explanation of the conservative behaviour of the politicians can be put forward. Notwithstanding the crisis, in both cases politicians evaluated the expected benefits in reducing the fragmentation to be smaller than the expected gains of political and bureaucratic consensus in maintaining the status quo. In Europe, by adopting the silo approach, every existing national supervisor automatically maintains his/her position also at the supranational level, while every kind of consolidation at the European level could imply a delicate design of the governance rules of the new institutions. The same is true in the US. In other words, by adopting the conservative approach the national political consensus is more likely to be achieved. In fact the same Commission recognised that its proposal is clearly opposed to solutions such as full centralisation, on which there is no consensus (section 4.3).

A recent empirical paper (Dalla Pellegrina and Masciandaro, 2008) stressed the point, showing a possible relationship between the choice to maintain a multiple authorities regime with low integration and weak governance practices. In terms of the relationship between weak governance and supervision, the study interprets the latter as a possible way of compensating lobbies (vested interests) with power, in a set-up where rent-seeking behaviour involves reciprocal string-pulling. Hence, the more a politician is a rent-seeking agent, the larger the pool of institutions (or alternatively, the number of leading positions) he/she will need to create in order to please all interests in terms of power and future cooperation.

Conclusion

The worldwide wave of reforms in supervisory architectures that we have been witnessing since the late 1990s leaves the interested bystander with a great number of questions regarding the key features of the emerging structures. This chapter has tried to provide answers with respect to the evolution of the degree of sectoral integration of insurance supervision. Inspection of a unique and updated database using a new index of supervisory integration highlights a trend in both overall supervisory consolidation and integration of the insurance supervision.

In the face of the financial turmoil, what are the lessons from the past that can be useful for the future? The starting point is to recognise that in these years financial markets have grown bigger and more complex almost everywhere. How can we best supervise the ever-changing markets, which are becoming increasingly complex and intertwined with each other? The general formula for an effective supervision is always the same: it is necessary to have exhaustive and up-to-date information. But it is the application of the classical formula that is today tricky. In markets that were fundamentally static and segmented – banks, the stock exchange, insurance – a simple 'photograph' of the situation every now and then was sufficient; the vertical model was the natural and effective answer to every market, including the insurance industry. Nowadays, to have exhaustive and up-to-date information it is necessary to explore in depth the innovative models of supervision – the unified model and the horizontal model – and the degree of integration.

However, the economic rationale for modifying the supervisory settings is not always sufficient. First of all, the shape and the timing of supervisory reforms are not easy to detect. For example, before the crisis, the pros (Mayer, 2006) and the cons (Monkiewicz, 2007) of the need of reforming EU insurance supervision had already been discussed. Second, politics matter as well. To stress the role of politics and politicians it is fundamental to understand where, why and how reforms about the supervisory structure can emerge, and also in the case of the insurance sector (Perry, 2010). Why do politicians take action? When are they going to do it? In order to find the answer to these questions more research is still warranted.

Bibliography

Arnone, M., and A. Gambini (2007) 'Architecture of Supervisory Authorities and Banking Supervision', in D. Masciandaro and M. Quintyn (eds), *Designing Financial Supervision Institutions: Independence, Accountability and Governance* (Cheltenham: Edward Elgar), p. 262-308.

Barth, J.R., D.E. Nolle, T. Phumiwasana and G. Yago (2002) 'A Cross Country Analysis of the Bank Supervisory Framework and Bank Performance', *Financial Markets, Institutions & Instruments*, 12(2): 67–120.

Barth, J.R., G. Caprio and R. Levine (2006) *Rethinking Bank Regulation. Till Angels Govern* (Cambridge: Cambridge University Press).

Beltratti, A., and G. Corvino (2008) 'Why are Insurance Companies Different? The Limits of Convergence Among Financial Institutions', *The Geneva Papers*, 33: 363–88.

Borio, C. (2003) *Towards a Macroprudential Framework for Financial Regulation and Supervision?*, Bank of International Settlements Working Papers, No. 128 (Geneva).

Braumüller, P. (2007) 'Cross Border Exchange of Information and Cooperation Between Insurance Supervisors', *The Geneva Papers*, 32: 30118.

Brown, E. (2009) 'The Development of International Norms for Insurance Regulation', *Brooking Journal of International Law,* 34: 954–97.

Čihák, M., and R. Podpiera (2007) 'Experience with Integrated Supervisors: Governance and Quality of Supervision', in D. Masciandaro and M. Quintyn (eds), *Designing Financial Supervision Institutions: Independence, Accountability and Governance* (Cheltenham: Edward Elgar), pp. 309–41.

Coffee, J. (1995) 'Competition versus Consolidation: The Significance of Organizational Structure in Financial and Securities Regulation, *Business Lawyer,* 50.

Commission of the European Communities (2009) 'Communication from the Commission. European financial supervision', COM (2009) 252 final, 17 pp.

Dalla Pellegrina, L., and D. Masciandaro (2008) 'Politicians, Central Banks and the Shape of Financial Supervision Architectures', *Journal of Financial Regulation and Compliance,* 16(4): 290–317.

Eling, M., and H. Schmeiser (2010) 'Insurance and the Credit Crisis: Impact and Ten Consequences for Risk Management and Supervision', *The Geneva Papers,* 35: 9–34.

Flamèe, M., and P. Windels (2009) 'Restructuring Financial Sector Supervision: Creating a Level Playing Field', *The Geneva Papers,* 34: 9-–23.

Grace, M.F. (2009) *A Re-examination of Federal Regulation of the Insurance Industry,* Networks Financial Institute Policy Brief, No. 2 (Indiana State University).

Group of Ten (2001) *Consolidation in the Financial Sector* (Basel: Bank for International Settlements).

Harrington, S.E. (2006) *Federal Chartering of Insurance Companies: Options and Alternatives for Transforming Insurance Regulation,* Networks Financial Institute Policy Brief, No. 2 (Indiana State University).

Herring, R.J., and J. Carmassi (2008) 'The Structure of Cross-Sector Financial Supervision', *Financial Markets, Institutions and Instruments,* 17(1): 51–76.

Hirschman, A.O. (1964) 'The Paternity of an Index', *American Economic Review,* 54(5): 761–2.

IAIS (2009) *Systemic Risk and the Insurance Sector* (International Association of Insurance Supervisors) (October).

Kremers, J., D. Schoenmaker and P. Wierts (2003) 'Cross-Sector Supervision: Which Model?', in R. Herring and R. Litan (eds), *Brookings Warthon Papers on Financial Service,* pp. 225–43.

Kwon, J., (2007) *Uniformity and Efficiency in Insurance Regulation,* Networks Financial Institute Policy Brief, No. 2 (Indiana State University).

Leijonhufvud, A. (2009) 'Curbing Instability: Policy and Regulation', *CEPR Policy Insight,* 36: 1–8.

Mayes, D. (2006) 'Cross Border Financial Supervision in Europe: Goals and Transition Paths', *Sveriges Riskbank Economic Review,* 2: 58–89.

Masciandaro, D., M. Nieto and M. Quintyn (2009) *Will They Sing the Same Tune? Measuring Convergence in the new European System of Financial Supervisors,* International Monetary Fund Working Paper Series, No. 9.

Masciandaro, D., and M. Quintyn (2008) 'Helping Hand or Grabbing Hand? Politicians, Supervisory Regime, Financial Structure and Market View', *North American Journal of Economics and Finance*, 19(2): 153–74.

Masciandaro, D., and M. Quintyn (2009) 'Reforming Financial Supervision and the Role of the Central Banks: A Review of Global Trends, Causes and Effects (1998–2008)', *CEPR Policy Insight,* 30: 1–11.

Masciandaro, D., and M. Quintyn (2010) *Measuring Financial Regulatory Architectures and the Role of the Central Banks: The Financial Supervision Herfindahl Hirschman Index*, Paolo Baffi Centre Research Paper, No. 55.
Monkiewicz, J. (2007a) 'Consolidated or Specialized Financial Market Supervisors: Is There an Optimal Solution?', *The Geneva Papers on Risk and Insurance: Issues and Practice*, 32: 151–61.
Monkiewicz, J. (2007b) 'The Future of Insurance Supervision in the EU: National Authorities, Lead Supervisors or EU Supranational Institution?', *The Geneva Papers on Risk and Insurance: Issues and Practice*, 32: 393–400.
Perry, R. (2010) 'Insurance Regulation: Lessons from a Small Economy', *Southern Methodist University Law Review*, 63.
Schoenmaker, D. (2003) 'Financial Supervision: From National to European?', *Financial and Monetary Studies*, NIBE - SVV, 22(1) (Amsterdam).
Scott, H. (2007) *Optional Federal Chartering of Insurance: Design of a Regulatory Structure*, Harvard Public Law Working Paper, No. 7.
Sjostrom, W.K. (2009) 'The AIG Bailout', *Washington and Lee Law Review*, 66: 943–91.
Taylor, M. (1995) *Twin Peaks: A Regulatory Structure for the New Century* (London: Centre for the Study of Financial Innovation).
Tennyson, S.L. (2008) *State Regulation and Consumer Protection in the Insurance Industry*, Networks Financial Institute Policy Brief, No. 3 (Indiana State University).
The Geneva Association (2010) 'Systemic Risk in Insurance. An Analysis of Insurance and Financial Stability', Report of The Geneva Association Systemic Risk Working Group, March.

Part III

The Market Dimension

8
The Role of Market Discipline in the Insurance Industry

Martin Eling

Motivation

The aim of this chapter is to evaluate the role of market discipline in supervision of insurance companies. Market discipline is an important new facet of regulation in both banking and insurance. Traditionally, regulation of financial services companies focused on capital requirements and other strict rules, for example, on asset allocation, but regulators have now begun to incorporate market-based elements into regulatory regimes. Most important in this context is the incorporation of market discipline as one of the three pillars of both Basel II and Solvency II.

Market discipline is often understood as the influence customers, brokers, auditors, rating agencies and investors have on firm behaviour, and regulators hope that it can work to create a strong and solvent financial services industry (see Eling and Schmit, 2009). The underlying idea is that a transparent market will require less overt regulation as market participants themselves force appropriate insurer behaviour. However, the extent to which market discipline can be relied on for successful regulation depends on the strength of its influence.

In this chapter, we take a broad perspective and look at how market discipline is implemented in different countries as well as in different sectors of the financial services industry, thus providing a global overview of market discipline as it exists and is implemented in both banking and insurance. We highlight recent efforts to strengthen market discipline undertaken in the European Union, the United States, Japan, Switzerland and New Zealand. The analysis demonstrates that currently there is already a very broad spectrum of disciplining measures in use, ranging from extended disclosure requirements (as being developed in the European Union) to regulatory systems that rely completely on market discipline (in New Zealand no explicit regulatory model is provided; instead, external ratings are used). We also critically review these different approaches in light of the recent financial crisis.

Furthermore, we consider the role of market discipline in different lines of insurance, finding that the significant differences between lines of business – for example, judgement-proof buyers, guarantee funds, product and business complexity – result in significant differences in the way market discipline works across these lines. This investigation leads us to conclude that market discipline might be appropriate in some areas of the industry, whereas strict government regulation may work better in other segments.

Overall, the goal of this analysis is to provide an overview of the role of market discipline in different sectors of the financial services industry. Based on this overview, policy implications are derived. For example, we find that there are many ways to enhance market discipline and that, sometimes, a bundle of these measures is most appropriate in one jurisdiction or for one line of business, but that the same set of measures will be inappropriate for another area or a different line of business. This analysis will prove helpful to academics and practitioners engaged in searching for existing schemes of market discipline. The overview of market discipline around the world, which highlights recent efforts and potential instruments in the EU and other countries, will also aid regulators across the world when designing their own regulatory systems. Throughout our discussion, special emphasis is placed on the situation in the United States, as well as in Germany, which is one of the largest insurance markets in the world outside the United States.

The remainder of this chapter is structured as follows. In the second section, we discuss the characteristics of market discipline, including significant drivers and impediments. In the third section, evidence for market discipline is presented, first in the financial services industry in general and then specifically focusing on different insurance markets. We also analyse the role of market discipline in different lines of insurance. The final section contains conclusions.[1]

Characteristics of market discipline

There is no clear and accepted definition of market discipline either in banking or insurance. The few papers from insurance literature on market discipline (Zanjani, 2002; Epermanis and Harrington, 2006; Eling and Schmit, 2009) typically focus on the risk sensitivity of customer demand. Epermanis and Harrington (2006), however, point out that the term can also be used more broadly to encompass incentives for risk management provided by capital markets. This is a broader definition of market discipline, including not only customers, but also investors from capital market.

In banking, market discipline is understood as the ability of market participants to accurately assess the condition of a firm (monitoring) and their ability to impact management action in a way that reflects those assessments (influencing) (see Eling, 2010). Simply transferring this definition to insurance may not be appropriate, however, since monitoring in the insurance industry is fundamentally different from monitoring in banking and other sectors of the financial services industry. Much more than in banking, intermediaries such as brokers and agents, as well as rating agencies, reinsurers and other insurers,[2] screen the financial strength and service quality of insurers. It thus appears that there are many market participants willing to monitor risk taking in the insurance industry, but it is not clear whether they have sufficient information to conduct such monitoring. The second aspect, the influencing component, is also difficult to evaluate since we do not know whether market participants have enough market power to influence management decisions.[3]

In banking, there is a great deal of market discipline in stock and bond markets because the equity and debt of most large banks is traded on capital markets (see, for example, Baer and Brewer, 1986; Avery, Belton, and Goldberg, 1988; Sironi, 2003). Much market discipline can thus be observed with traded debt, such as yields on subordinated debt. The insurance sector, however, is fundamentally different as many insurers are mutuals, not stock companies. Furthermore, many of the insurers that are organised as stock companies are not traded on the stock market, thus making effects on stock prices difficult to observe. There is also hardly any traded debt in the insurance industry, since the reserves of the policy-holders are in general the major part of the insurers' liabilities. For example, in Germany it is prohibited to have debt other than the reserves for policy-holders and only very restrictive exceptions are allowed from this general rule (for example, with hybrid instruments). This environment makes it unlikely that we will see significant market discipline on insurance capital markets for either equity or debt as we do in banking.

An important result of this analysis is that we need to distinguish between market discipline conducted by investors and market discipline conducted by customers. The role of investors in disciplining insurance companies will not be comparable to the power investors hold in the banking industry, but market discipline by customers might play a more important role in the insurance industry, for example, considering lapse of life insurance contracts or future premium growths. Harrington (2004) and Nocera (2005) denote these two aspects as product market discipline, which is customer driven, and capital market discipline, which is investor driven. Product market discipline encompasses the extent to which demand by policy-holders is sensitive to insolvency risk. The risk sensitivity of customers might motivate insurers to manage their risk. For example, Wakker et al. (1997) show that an increase in default risk greatly reduces customer willingness to pay. Product market discipline might also be much easier to observe in the insurance industry, for example, in light of the above-mentioned role of intermediaries. Market discipline in insurance can thus be defined as monitoring and influencing conducted by customers, investors, and intermediaries (see Eling, 2010, for more details on this definition).

Based on this definition, how can market discipline be measured? There are, of course, many theoretical options for measuring both investor market discipline (stock prices, bond yields) and customer market discipline (premium growth). The insurance sector also provides additional measurement options, for example, lapse. But, as discussed, measuring market discipline in insurance is more difficult than in other sectors, since many proxies (stock prices, bond yields, price of insurance per unit of coverage) are not available and these practical difficulties significantly reduce the efficiency (or even the possibility) of employing market discipline to regulate insurance companies.

Furthermore, it is important to emphasize that market discipline is strongly affected by outside factors, which can either facilitate or impede it. A number of these drivers and impediments to market discipline are summarised in Figure 8.1. We use Figure 8.1 as a starting point for our international comparison of insurance markets. Hess and Feng (2007) develop a comparable framework for banking and base their ideas on Flannery (2001). This framework is adapted and extended to the insurance industry in Eling (2010).

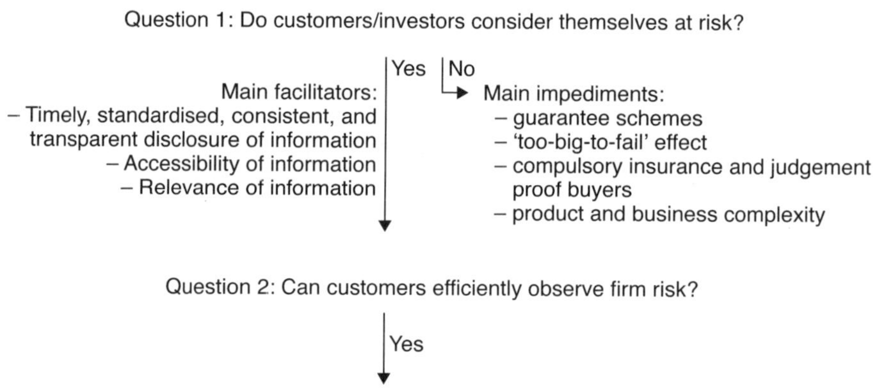

Source: Author's compilation.

Figure 8.1 Drivers and impediments to market discipline

There are basically two questions that need to be answered when analyzing market discipline. The first question is whether customers feel themselves at risk. Various aspects of the insurance industry decrease customer risk sensitivity, such as guarantee schemes (including implicit guarantee schemes from too-big-to-fail bailouts), judgement-proof buyers in the case of compulsory insurance (e.g., auto liability),[4] and product and business complexity that hamper market transparency (see Harrington, 2004). Risk sensitivity is positively affected by timely, standardised and transparent disclosure of information. If customers do not feel themselves at risk there is no reason to believe that market discipline will exist. But even if this question can be answered 'yes', we need to answer a second question: do customers efficiently observe risk? Again, for this aspect, timely, standardised and transparent disclosure of relevant information will be highly relevant. In the next section, various aspects of Figure 8.1 are discussed in more detail.

Evidence for market discipline

The role of market discipline in different fields of the financial services industry

In banking, market discipline became a part of the regulatory agenda in the 1980s when regulators recognized that regulation was becoming more complex, both with regard to the products as well as with regard to the integration of financial services from different fields and countries. Moreover, market discipline has been one of the Basel II pillars for several years now. Thus, there is much more evidence on market discipline in the banking literature than there is in the insurance literature. Although there are important differences between banking and insurance, looking at how market discipline works in the banking industry can provide some insights into its potential effects in the insurance industry. Eling (2010) provides a broad review of the evidence on market discipline found in the banking literature. Here, we briefly summarise the main aspects of that paper and then concentrate on aspects important for the insurance industry.

The banking literature documents evidence for market discipline over the last decades across a variety of measures and countries. Examples include the consideration of stock prices (for example, Baer and Brewer, 1986), the analysis of debt (for example, Avery, Belton, and Goldberg, 1988; Sironi, 2003), and consideration of deposit growth (Park and Peristiani, 1998). Results from the banking literature make it clear that investors in bank stocks have a strong incentive to monitor the firm's risk since the debt-holders are often secured by safety nets. Like every other type of insurance, safety nets create moral hazard incentives and consequently reduce market discipline. Several researchers in the banking field, such as Billett et al. (1998) and Demirgüç-Kunt and Huizinga (2004) document these effects. Moreover, Flannery and Sorescu (1996) show that reducing safety nets increases market discipline.

Several other aspects highlighted in the banking literature might also be of relevance to the insurance industry. The banking literature shows that the strength of market discipline depends on product line. For example, Morgan and Stiroh (2001) show differences for credit card, commercial, and industrial lending, all of which carry a penalty in terms of higher spreads. These differences might be relevant in light of the significant institutional differences in different lines of the insurance industry. Sironi (2003) found differences in market discipline depending on ownership structure, that is, less discipline was found for government-owned institutions. This is an important finding in light of the traditional separation of stock, mutual, and public companies in the insurance industry and the resulting differences in agency conflicts (for example, expense preference hypothesis; managerial discretion hypotheses; see Eling and Luhnen, 2010). Pop (2006) finds international differences in market discipline and argues that much work needs to be done, especially in Japan and certain European countries, to level the playing field so that market discipline can operate. We will thus analyse differences in insurance market discipline for different countries.

Although the insurance literature on market discipline is not nearly as well developed as the literature in the banking sector, there are a few papers from the 1990s that offer some implications with regard to market discipline. Among these are Sommer (1996), Phillips et al. (1998) and Cummins and Danzon (1997), all of which document a negative relationship between proxies of property-casualty prices and firm risk, a result that is consistent with market discipline. Also, certain experiments from behavioural insurance might be interpreted as evidence for market discipline. As mentioned, Wakker et al. (1997) show that policy-holders are risk sensitive to at least a certain extent in that an increase in default risk severely affects their willingness to pay. Similar experimental evidence is found in Albrecht and Maurer (2000), Zimmer, Schade, and Gründl (2009) and Zimmer, Gründl and Schade (2009). Furthermore, Fenn and Cole (1994) and Brewer and Jackson (2002) find that life insurers with risky assets experience larger stock price declines than do those with less risky assets during downturns in the real estate and bond markets.

Four studies that more explicitly test for market discipline are Zanjani (2002), Epermanis and Harrington (2006), Baranoff and Sager (2007), and Eling and Schmit (2009). Baranoff and Sager (2007) consider the number of policies written in life insurance and observe reduced product demand when ratings decline. Zanjani (2002) finds a positive relationship between policy-holder lapse rates and insurer default risk. Epermanis and Harrington (2006) consider insurer ratings in a property/casualty context and observe significant premium declines following rating downgrades, particularly for firms that had low ratings even before the downgrade. They also note the concentration of premium declines in commercial lines, which tend not to be protected by guarantee associations. Eling and Schmit (2009) analyse market discipline in the German insurance market using Epermanis and Harrington's (2006) research design and find premium declines, as well as increased lapse rates, following rating downgrades. Their findings are consistent with Epermanis and Harrington (2006), but are less significant than the results reported for the US market, leading the authors to conclude that market discipline in the German insurance market is not as strong as it is in the United States.

Several studies analyse market discipline in fields other than financial services. For example, Dangl et al. (2008) develop a model to analyse market discipline in the mutual fund industry. In their model, investors update their beliefs about the manager's skills based on observed portfolio returns. Investors can then move capital into or out of the fund and the company can fire the manager. Introducing the firing aspect lends credence to empirically documented work finding a positive relation between manager tenure and fund size or an increase in portfolio risk before manager replacement and a risk decrease thereafter. Moreover, for investment products in New Zealand, Hess and Feng (2007) document that more risky institutions have to offer higher interest rates. Overall, disciplining effects are thus theoretically modelled and empirically documented in the mutual fund industry.

The role of market discipline in different insurance markets

Overall, it thus appears that market discipline is reasonably strong in most insurance markets, but that there is some variation due to legal form (Liu et al., 2005), line of business (Epermanis and Harrington, 2006), and between countries (Eling and Schmit, 2009). All these results are confirmed on a broader empirical basis in the banking sector. We now focus on the international dimension and summarize experiences with market discipline in different countries. We conducted a web-based research involving the web pages of more than 100 regulators. The research started with the web page of the Asian-Pacific Risk and Insurance Association, which has links to insurance regulators and supervisors (see www.scicollege.org.sg/APRIA_Relsites.asp). All listed web pages were systematically scanned for transparency requirements in order to identify different approaches to market discipline. Some of the links were defunct, and in these cases, the web pages of the regulators were manually searched. Relevant keywords included, for example, 'transparency', 'disclosure requirements' and 'market discipline'.

Detailed results of this search are available upon request; in short, the results vary by country to a significant degree. In many cases, rules refer to both banking and insurance, since the regulators for banking and insurance are integrated in one financial market supervision authority. Many of the disclosure requirements also refer to accounting rules and are applicable not only to financial services companies, but to all reporting companies, including companies from other industries. Some of the results are surprising; for example, the high level of awareness on the topic of transparency in some African countries such as Ethiopia. All cited documents were posted on the web page of official organisations; a minor fraction of the information was obtained from advisory firms such as KPMG (all references are available from the authors upon request). In the following, we highlight the main results for five insurance markets: the European Union, the United States, Japan, Switzerland and New Zealand. Based on this discussion, potential policy implications are discussed in the final section.

The European Union

Regulators in the European Union are currently developing new regulatory rules for risk management and capital adequacy. A first set of new rules was introduced in 2002 under the name Solvency I. These, however, were only relatively minor modifications of original rules enacted in the 1970s. The introduction of new risk-based capital standards (Solvency II) now appears likely to occur at the end of 2012 or the beginning of 2013. One of the three pillars of Solvency II explicitly addresses market discipline. The current plan for the third pillar is that there will be two reports required from insurers (see CEIOPS (Committee of European Insurance and Occupational Pensions Supervisors), 2009). The first one, the Solvency and Financial Condition Report (SFCR), is to be made available to the public; the second, the Report to Supervisors (RTS), will be submitted to the regulator only and not be made available to the public.

The SFCR is an annual report and is to be made public three to four months after the end of the business year. The target audiences for this report are regulators, financial analysts, rating agencies, insurers, and reinsurers, as well as shareholders, policy-holders, and other investors. The SFCR will have a standardized structure so that a comparison with other insurers is possible. The report will contain information on business and performance, system of governance, risk management, regulatory balance sheet, and capital management. The content of the SFCR builds on existing international financial reporting standards (IFRS) disclosure as a reference framework, thus highlighting the goal of harmonisation between Solvency II and IFRS.

The RTS has the same structure as the SFCR, but is more detailed and will be disclosed only to the regulator. It will be required every five years, but may be requested more often if the regulator deems such to be necessary. The RTS contains several pieces of information not required by the SFCR, such as a business continuity plan, legal and regulatory issues affecting the business, future anticipated solvency needs, and additional disclosure explaining results of internal risk models. Both the RTS and the SFCR are to contain a qualitative report as well as quantitative data, including quantitative reporting templates, where necessary (see CEIOPS, 2009). The reporting templates are an especially promising element, seeing as standardised delivery of information facilitates market discipline.

Overall, CEIOPS has developed (a) reporting requirements based on the information supervisors need to adequately supervise undertakings (the RTS) and (b) disclosure requirements that will reinforce transparency and market discipline (the SFCR), while avoiding unnecessary administrative costs on the part of insurers (see CEIOPS, 2009). The additional disclosure will provide market participants with a comprehensive view of the insurer's risk situation. Good risk management can then be rewarded by the market and risky behaviour sanctioned.

Solvency II is still a moving target, since the implementation measures have not yet been published and continue to be the subject of discussion. It is likely that the rules will be comparable to those discussed above, but not guaranteed. Another aspect worth mention is that, originally, it was planned that coordination should be sought where appropriate with IFRS and other relevant disclosures. This would have eased the financial burden on insurers resulting from different reporting requirements. Unfortunately, however, the IFRS 4 standard on valuation of insurance liabilities is still under development so it is unclear whether harmonisation of IFRS and Solvency II, and other relevant disclosures (for example, question whether the different disclosure requirements will be one consistent set of rules or be comprised of different standards). The success of market discipline depends, however, on a stringent and standardised set of disclosure requirements.

The United States

The US insurance industry has been subject to several runs by policy-holders over the last decades, for example, Mutual Benefit and Executive Life in 1991. Executive Life was the largest life insurance company in California until problems from junk bond investments led to its insolvency in April 1991. In general, the flexibility of money can vary across countries. For example, in Germany, there are numerous financial disadvantages to terminating a life insurance contract, such as significant lapse costs and no participation in the terminal bonus. These financial disadvantages, which limit incentives to terminate life insurance contracts in Germany, do not always exist in other countries. Indeed, a terminal bonus is uncommon in the United States. The flexibility of invested money might thus be higher in the United States, thus market discipline might also be higher.

With regard to insolvency risk, Swiss Re (2000) documents that the number of insolvencies in the United States is significantly higher than in other developed insurance markets such as, for example, Germany or Switzerland. This aspect might also be important because US investors are used to an insolvency, which may not be the case in every insurance market. A negative experience might raise awareness of and enhance the willingness to provide information about the insurer's financial situation. As documented above, an important requirement for market discipline is that investors and customers consider themselves at risk. Given the lack of insolvency experiences, the awareness of insolvency risk might be limited, for example, in the German market, but quite high in the United States.

There are a number of other aspects that might lead us to expect market discipline to be relatively strong in the United States compared to other markets.

For example, the United States has a market-based corporate governance regime instead of the control-based regime found in many continental European countries and Japan. The US system has, for example, a one-tier board of executive and nonexecutive directors and bad manager performance is typically regulated by investors via their influence on stock prices and a reduction in manager compensation. Germany is an example for a control-based regime, that is, two-tiered boards of directors consisting of a managing board and a supervisory board. Ownership is typically more concentrated than in the US so that large block-holders can take the lead in monitoring the firm. Often, these large block-holders are banks, while in the United States stock free-float is higher on average.

This environment would lead one to expect stronger market discipline in the United States than in Germany and, indeed, this expectation is supported by empirical evidence in Eling and Schmit (2009). Eling and Schmit (2009) analyse market discipline in the German insurance market using the same methodology and the same type of data as Epermanis and Harrington (2006) used for the US market. They find that on average premium declines in property-casualty are 2–4% after rating downgrades in Germany, a number significantly lower than the corresponding 4–12% documented for the United States.

With regard to solvency regulation, the United States has had a system of risk-based capital (RBC) standards in place since 1994. The RBC standards have two main components. The first is an RBC formula that establishes a minimum capital level, which is compared to the actual level of capital. The second is an RBC model law that grants automatic authority to the state insurance regulator to take certain actions based on the company's level of impairment (see NAIC, 2005). US insurers are required to report the RBC and their available capital in their annual statements; however, the detailed calculations are confidential (see Klein, 2005, p. 143).

Recently, and in light of the development of Solvency II in the European Union, US regulators have put forward a Solvency Modernization Initiative. The chief features of this initiative deal with capital adequacy and international harmonisation of solvency rules, as well as covering accounting standards, group supervision, valuation issues in insurance, and reinsurance (to date, reinsures are not subject to the US RBC standards). Although market discipline is not mentioned explicitly in these chief features, it is implicitly considered under the harmonisation of solvency rules and accounting standards that might enhance market transparency.

Moreover, a major component of the US Solvency Modernization Initiative is the so-called Insurance Financial Solvency Core Principles. According to Principle 1 of these, entitled 'Regulatory Reporting, Disclosure and Transparency', insurers are required to file standardised annual and quarterly financial reports that will be used to assess insurer risk and financial condition. The reports are to contain both qualitative and quantitative information and must be updated as necessary to incorporate significant common insurer risks (see Solvency Modernization Initiative (EX) Task Force, 2010, p. 29). The fact that disclosure and transparency play so prominent a part in the new Insurance Financial Solvency Core Principles emphasises that US insurance regulators also see an increasing role for market discipline in future regulation.

Japan

Japan is also currently developing a new regulatory framework consisting of four pillars. Better regulation is chief among the purposes of this effort; indeed, 'enhancing dissemination of information' is mentioned explicitly. Regulators would like to develop an environment where people and interested parties throughout the world can easily access basic information and data on Japanese regulation and the country's view of and stance on current issues. To this end, the regulators intend, among other things, to promote translation of financial-related laws into English and to participate actively in symposiums and other public events both at home and abroad.

Moreover, not only is transparency on the part of financial institutions encouraged, but the regulator itself also intends to become more transparent. The fourth pillar of the new Japanese framework is called 'Improving the Transparency and Predictability of Regulatory Actions'. To this end, the Japan regulator has compiled and published its inspection manuals and supervisory guidelines. The inspection and supervisory policies are also published for each operational year. In addition, the regulator has published criteria for administrative actions and posted 'Questions & Answers' regarding the interpretation of rules (see www.fsa.go.jp/en/policy/iqfrs/br1.html for more information).

Switzerland

Switzerland introduced a new risk-based capital system in 2006, the Swiss Solvency Test (SST). The SST is comparable to Solvency II in that determining capital requirements is a two-level process. The first level is a rules-based minimum capital similar to the Solvency I rules in the European Union. The second level is a required 'target capital' based on market value. The SST also includes a quality assessment that focuses on internal processes and risk control (similar to Pillar II of Solvency II; see Swiss Federal Office of Private Insurance, 2007).

Swiss market disclosure and transparency requirements, however, are very modest at the moment. For example, and in contrast to the US RBC Standards and Solvency II, there are no rules dealing with publication of risk-related information. Only the statutory accounting standards (Swiss local GAAP) provide some rules for risk reporting (see Eberle and Aeppli, 2007). Furthermore, some insurers are subject to the International Financial Reporting Standards, thus making them subject to more disclosure requirements than other insurers.

Moreover, the Swiss Financial Market Supervisory Authority (that is, the regulator for insurance companies in Switzerland) has no explicit rules regarding risk reporting or disclosure.

Recently, Swiss regulators have started to consider how to embed market discipline in the Swiss regulatory framework, but it is too soon to tell how this consideration will manifest. Given, however, that one aim of the SST regulations will be similar to the reporting requirements introduced for Solvency II. This outcome is all the more likely considering that Swiss regulators are hesitant to impose any additional burdens on their insurance companies, most of which are doing business in the European Union and thus would need to comply with two systems if the SST is not compatible with Solvency II.

New Zealand

The regulatory system in New Zealand is unique in that no solvency model is provided and no specific level of equity capital is imposed by the regulatory authority. Insurers are required to comply with the Fair Insurance Code, the Insurance & Savings Ombudsman Scheme, and the Insurance Council's Solvency Test. The Fair Insurance Code sets minimum service standards for insurance companies and describes the responsibilities of insurance companies and customers. The Insurance & Savings Ombudsman Scheme requires that all insurers submit to independent review in case of complaints. Finally, the Insurance Council's Solvency Test requires all insurers to obtain a rating from an approved rating agency, register the rating with the Registrar of Companies, and disclose the rating before entering into or renewing a contract of insurance (see www.icnz.org.nz for more details on New Zealand's regulatory environment). Among the approved rating agencies are Standard & Poor's, AM Best, and Fitch (as of 15 June 2010).

Although New Zealand is a relatively small country and so its insurance market is not directly comparable to that of the European Union or the United States, their approach is interesting because it is so different from that of any other country. The regulatory system relies completely on market discipline: rating agencies only and no additional public authority conduct the monitoring. This approach does not impose any additional burden on insurers (for example, reporting requirements) and is thus less costly than other regulatory frameworks. However, the system is not without its flaws. Rating agencies have been criticised for the lack of transparency in their rating methodologies (see Doherty et al., 2007), especially during the recent financial crisis. The publicly available information on rating procedures is basically found in advertising material and thus can hardly be considered objective. An insurer's rating might be of some use in comparing companies, but it is difficult to understand why an insurer received the rating it did. Furthermore, mainly due to recent failures of rating agencies to provide adequate information (during the US financial crisis most obviously, but also previously in the case of the Enron and Worldcom scandals), the concentration of market power in a small number of rating agencies has been cause for some concern (see Doherty et al., 2007).

Overall, the approach implemented in New Zealand is an interesting alternative to the extensive and costly set of rules implemented in all other countries discussed in this chapter. Nevertheless, it is questionable whether completely relying on rating agencies is the best way of ensuring a safe and sound insurance industry.

The role of market discipline in different lines of insurance

In this section we consider organisational differences between lines of insurance business (life, health, property-liability, reinsurance) and their effect on market discipline. There are a number of reasons to expect differences in market discipline depending on the line of business. First, in the case of compulsory insurance (for example, auto), the judgement-proof problem (see the second section of this chapter for a definition) impedes market discipline. Second, if the government or a privately organised fund guarantees all insurance claims and benefits, there is no reason to expect market discipline. Reducing coverage, however, could be quite conducive to market discipline. Third, differences in lines of business due to products and business complexity will also affect the degree of market discipline when we think about transparency. It is far easier to compare differences between insurers when it comes to a standardised product such as, for example, motor insurance, than it is when the insurance product, or the business line offering it, is more complex, as, for example, in commercial insurance. Fourth, an increase in financial leverage increases company risk. Life insurers typically have a much higher leverage than do non-life insurers and this might affect the risk sensitivity of investors.[5] Finally, market discipline could be stronger in commercial lines compared to personal lines. Policy-holders in personal lines have less resources and competence (for example, in terms of being able to understand financial reports) to conduct efficient monitoring than do policy-holders in commercial lines, which are usually larger and have more resources. On the other hand, however, personal line insurance decisions directly affect an individual's own wealth, whereas commercial insurance decisions do not usually have much of a personal impact on the decision maker. This situation can create moral hazard problems for commercial insurance, which lowers the efficiency of monitoring for this type of insurance. Nonetheless, evidence indicates that market discipline in commercial lines is stronger than in personal lines (Epermanis and Harrington, 2006).

Table 8.1 summarises the differences between lines of business and their expected influence on market discipline. Table 8.1 makes it clear that there are important differences between lines of business that need to be recognised when assessing market discipline. Each line of business, however, has characteristics that both facilitate and impede market discipline, so we cannot conclude that market discipline will always be stronger in life insurance, for example, than it is in property liability, health or reinsurance. Furthermore, significant differences between countries can be identified when considering lines of business. We highlight these, again considering Germany and the US as two examples.

Table 8.1 Differences between lines of business and expected influence on market discipline

	Life	Health	Property-liability	Reinsurance
Contract duration	Typically, many years (MD ↑)	Germany: many years (MD ↑), US: one year (MD ↓)	Usually one year, but renewal on a rolling basis (MD ↓)	Usually one year (MD ↓)
Customers	In general, personal (MD ↓)	In general, personal (MD ↓)	Personal + commercial (MD →)	Commercial (MD ↑)
Guarantee schemes	Some coverage (MD ↓)	Some coverage (MD ↓)	None (MD ↑)	None (MD ↑)
Compulsory insurance	None (MD ↑)	Germany: yes (MD ↓), US: no (MD ↑)	In some liability lines (MD ↓)	None (MD ↑)
Complexity	In general, high (MD ↓)	In general, high (MD ↓)	In some lines, high, in some, low (MD →)	In some cases, high, in some, low (MD →)

Source: Author's compilation.

For example, the willingness of customers to monitor might depend on contract duration and amount. A life insurance policy running for many years and involving a large sum may provide stronger motivation for monitoring than a small one-year liability contract. Incentives to monitor might vary over time as well, for example, monitoring (or comparison shopping) may be very important prior to signing the contract, but not during the contract since significant lapse costs reduce the incentive to terminate the contract. Here, the flexibility of money might be higher in the United States compared to other countries (for example, Germany) since the financial consequences of terminating are not severe. Another difference between Germany and the United States is that in Germany health insurance is a type of life business involving a saving and dis-saving process and individual policy-holder reserves, while in the United States health insurance is more like a short-term property-liability contract without a reserve. Another important difference is that health insurance is compulsory in Germany, whereas it is not (yet) in the United States. We can thus identify lines-of-business-specific differences between the Germany and US insurance industry and can expect complementary differences in market discipline.

It seems likely that market discipline will be stronger for reinsurance than it is for primary insurance given the absence of guarantee schemes, compulsory insurance, and in light of the fact that only commercial customers buy reinsurance. We might also intuitively expect market discipline in life/health to be stronger than in property liability, but it is very difficult to confirm this in any concrete way. It is thus not possible to derive clear hypotheses regarding market discipline for different lines of business, but it is important to keep in mind that there are no doubt significant differences between them. Perhaps the safest and most general conclusion that can be drawn from this discussion is that some markets will do best when subjected to strict government regulation and some will do best under market discipline.

Conclusion

The results of the country comparison reveal institutional differences, for example, with regard to governance mechanisms, regulatory requirements, and insolvency experiences that affect market discipline. For example, we see differences in facilitators and impediments to market discipline that lead us to conclude that market discipline is less developed in Germany than it is in the United States. The country comparison also clearly shows that the importance of market discipline is increasing all over the world. For example, US regulators have included disclosure and transparency in the first principle of their new Insurance Financial Solvency Core Principles, a clear indication of how important market discipline is to them.

Another important result revealed by our analysis of different lines of business is that market discipline might be very effective in some areas of the industry, but far less so in others; indeed, some lines of business may be best served by strict government regulation. Unfortunately, however, sometimes it is just those lines of business least in need of market discipline that experience the strongest form of it. For example, the reinsurance market is subject to a great deal of market discipline due to its very nature since insurers and rating agencies very carefully monitor reinsurance companies.

Comparing different lines of business, we would also expect more market discipline in reinsurance than in insurance because reinsurance only covers commercial business, while insurance covers both commercial and personal lines. From a regulatory point of view, purchasers of commercial lines are less in need of protection than purchasers of personal lines. An implication for policymakers is thus that when comparing personal and commercial insurance, it appears that market discipline is weakest where it is most needed, and strongest where it is least needed.

There are many ways to enhance market discipline, the easiest of which is to strengthen and enforce disclosure requirements. Note, however, that *more* information is not necessarily *better* information; customers and investors must be able to understand the information and be able to use it in comparison shopping.

Thus, timely, standardised, and consistent disclosure of relevant information to all market participants is the most important facilitator of market discipline. Also costs need to be taken into account since every disclosure requirement will impose a financial burden, possibly leading to market exit in the case of smaller insurers. Moreover, market discipline is strongly affected by outside factors, which can either facilitate or impede it. Recently, government rescue efforts and direct intervention in the insurance and, especially, banking markets have created a great deal of market distortion with a consequent and significant effect on market discipline. These interventions have raised some complicated, but highly interesting, questions regarding moral hazard, the role of guarantee funds, the structure of rescue operations, the obligations of the firm being rescued, and the impact of intervention on competition.

Other impediments to market discipline revolve around guarantee schemes and compulsory insurance. Legal form can also be an obstacle to effective market discipline. Insurers listed on the stock market are subject to more extensive reporting requirements than are mutual insurers. Liu et al. (2005) document that agency effects are more common among mutual insurers, which generally have lower informational requirements than do stock insurers. These results can be interpreted to mean that relying on market discipline is appropriate in some areas, that is, formal regulation of these areas will be to everyone's advantage. In particular, formal regulation is likely to be the more effective in the presence of informational deficits (that is, with mutuals). Market discipline will be more effective when information is generally available (that is, with stocks).

Notes

1. This chapter builds on and extends results derived by Eling (2010) and Eling and Schmit (2009). The section on definitions, drivers, and impediments summarises some results presented in Eling (2010). The institutional comparison of Germany and the United States is analyzed on the basis of empirical data in Eling and Schmit (2009). We extend these papers by adding a broad international analysis. For the sake of brevity, however, we refer the reader to Eling (2010) and Eling and Schmit (2009) for more information on certain aspects.
2. Considering the post-insolvency assessment funding mechanisms of many guaranty funds and potential contagion effects of financial problems among insurers, insurers have an incentive to monitor each other; see Downs and Sommer (1999).
3. From a theoretical point of view, there are a number of reasons that cast doubt on the ability of market participants to influence managers. Among these are asymmetric information, costly monitoring, principal-agent problems, and conflicts of interest among stakeholders. See Eling (2010).
4. Harrington (2004) mentions the judgement-proof problem as an impediment to market discipline. Under a compulsory insurance regime (for example, auto liability, workers' compensation or professional liability) individuals with few assets to insure might simply buy the cheapest insurance they can find, with no regard to insolvency risk.

The combination of compulsory insurance and judgement-proof buyers reduces the risk sensitivity of demand.

5. Due to differences in the business model (asset accumulation processes, less stochastic insurance business) life insurers typically hold less capital in relation to their total liabilities than non-life insurers. This results in a higher leverage, here defined ratio of debt to equity. For example, in 2008 in Germany the ratio of debt to equity was 4 for property-casualty insurers and 63 for life insurers. See BaFin (2010).

Bibliography

Albrecht, P., and R. Maurer (2000) Zur Bedeutung der Ausfallbedrohtheit von Versicherungskontrakten – ein Beitrag zur Behavioral Insurance, *Zeitschrift für die gesamte Versicherungswissenschaft*, 89: 339–55.

Avery, R.B., T.M. Belton and M.A. Goldberg (1988) 'Market Discipline in Regulating Bank Risk: New Evidence from the Capital Markets', *Journal of Money, Credit, and Banking*, 20: 597–610.

Baer, H., and E. Brewer (1986) 'Uninsured Deposits as a Source of Market Discipline: Some New Evidence', *Federal Reserve Bank of Chicago Economic Perspectives*, September: 23–31.

BaFin (2010) Statistik der BaFin – Erstversicherungsunternehmen '08, available at: www.bafin.de.

Baranoff, E.G., and T.W. Sager (2007) 'Market Discipline in Life Insurance: Insureds' Reaction to Rating Downgrades in the Context of Enterprise Risks', Working Paper.

Billett, M.T., J.A. Garfinkel and E.S. O'Neal (1998) 'The Cost of Market Versus Regulatory Discipline in Banking', *Journal of Financial Economics*, 48: 333–58.

Brewer, E., and W.E. Jackson (2002) 'Inter-Industry Contagion and the Competitive Effects of Financial Distress Announcements: Evidence from Commercial Banks and Insurance Companies', Federal Reserve Bank of Chicago Working Paper No. 2002-23.

CEIOPS (2009) 'CEIOPS Advice for Level 2 Implementing Measures on Solvency II: Supervisory Reporting and Public Disclosure Requirements', CEIOPS-DOC-50/09, October.

Cummins, J.D., and P.M. Danzon (1997) 'Price, Financial Quality, and Capital Flows in Insurance Markets', *Journal of Financial Intermediation*, 6: 3–38.

Dangl, T., Y. Wu and J. Zechner (2008) 'Market Discipline and Internal Governance in the Mutual Fund Industry', *Review of Financial Studies*.

Demirgüç-Kunt, A., and H. Huizinga (2004) 'Market Discipline and Deposit Insurance', *Journal of Monetary Economics*, 51: 375–99.

Doherty, N.A., A. Kartasheva and R.D. Phillips (2007) 'Competition Among Rating Agencies and Information Disclosure', Working Paper.

Downs, D., and D. Sommer (1999) 'Monitoring, Ownership, and Risk-Taking: The Impact of Guaranty', *Journal of Risk and Insurance*, 66: 477–97.

Eberle, R., and D. Aeppli (2007) *Swiss GAAP FER, KPMG Fachempfehlungen zur Rechnungslegung*, 5th edn (Zürich).

Eling, M. (2010) 'What Do We Know About Market Discipline in Insurance?' Working Paper.

Eling, M., and M. Luhnen (2010) 'Frontier Efficiency Methodologies to Measure Performance in the Insurance Industry', accepted for publication in *Geneva Papers on Risk and Insurance*.

Eling, M., and J. Schmit (2009) 'Is There Market Discipline in the European Insurance Industry? An Analysis of the German Insurance Market', Working Paper.

Epermanis, K., and S. Harrington (2006) 'Market Discipline in Property/Casualty Insurance: Evidence from Premium Growth Surrounding Changes in Financial Strength Ratings', *Journal of Money, Credit, and Banking*, 38: 1515–44.

Fenn, G.W., and R.A. Cole (1994) 'Announcements of Asset-Quality Problems and Contagion Effects in the Life Insurance Industry', *Journal of Financial Economics*, 35: 181–98.

Flannery, M.J. (2001) 'The Faces of "Market Discipline"', *Journal of Financial Services Research*, 20(2/3): 107–19.

Flannery, M.J., and S.M. Sorescu (1996) 'Evidence of Bank Market Discipline in Subordinated Debenture Yields: 1983–1991', *Journal of Finance*, 51(4): 1347–77.

Harrington, S. (2004) 'Market Discipline in Insurance and Reinsurance', in Claudio Borio et al. (eds), *Market Discipline Across Countries and Industries* (Cambridge, MA: MIT Press).

Hess, K., and G. Feng (2007) 'Is There Market Discipline for New Zealand Non-Bank Financial Institutions?' *Journal of International Financial Markets, Institutions and Money*, 17: 326–40.

Klein, R.W. (2005) *A Regulator's Introduction to the Insurance Industry*, 2nd edn (Kansas City, MO: National Association of Insurance Commissioners).

Liu, Q., K. Epermanis and L. Cox (2005) 'Agency Conflicts and Market Discipline: Evidence from Guaranteed Investment Contracts', Working Paper.

Morgan, D.P., and K.J. Stiroh (2001) Market Discipline of Banks: The Asset Test, *Journal of Financial Services Research*, 20(2): 195–208.

National Association of Insurance Commissioners (NAIC) (2005) 'Risk-Based Capital: General Overview', available at: www.naic.org.

Nocera, G. (2005) 'Market Discipline and Insurance Pricing: A Microeconomic Model', Working Paper, Bocconi University, Milan.

Park, S., and S. Peristiani (1988) 'Market Discipline by Thrift Depositors', *Journal of Money, Credit & Banking*, 30: 347–64.

Phillips, R.D., J.D. Cummins and F. Allen (1998) 'Financial Pricing in the Multiple-Line Insurance Company', *Journal of Risk and Insurance*, 65: 597–636.

Pop, A. (2006) 'Market Discipline in International Banking Regulation: Keeping the Playing Field Level', *Journal of Financial Stability*, 2: 286–310.

Sironi, A. (2003) 'Testing for Market Discipline in the European Banking Industry: Evidence from Subordinated Debt Issues', *Journal of Money Credit & Banking*, 35: 443–72.

Solvency Modernization Initiative (EX) Task Force (2010) Documentation of 2010 Spring National Meeting, Denver, CO, 25 March.

Sommer, D.W. (1996) 'The Impact of Firm Risk on Property-Liability Insurance Prices', *Journal of Risk and Insurance*, 63(3): 501–14.

Swiss Federal Office of Private Insurance (2007) *Swiss Quality Assessment (SQA)* (Bern).

Swiss Re (2000) 'Solvency of Non-Life Insurers: Balancing Security and Profitability Expectations', *Swiss Re Sigma*, No. 1/2000.

Wakker, P.P., R.H. Thaler and A. Tversky (1997) Probabilistic Insurance, *Journal of Risk and Uncertainty*, 15(1): 7–28.

Zanjani, G. (2002) 'Market Discipline and Government Guarantees in Life Insurance', Working Paper, Federal Reserve Bank of New York.

Zimmer, A., H. Gründl and C. Schade (2009) 'Market Discipline by Enforcing Transparency of Insurers' Solvency Levels? Results on the Optimal Corporate Risk Strategy of Insurance Companies', Working Paper, Humboldt-Universität zu Berlin.

Zimmer, A., C. Schade and H. Gründl (2009) 'Is Default Risk Acceptable When Purchasing Insurance? Experimental Evidence for Different Probability Representations, Reasons for Default, and Framings', *Journal of Economic Psychology*, 30: 11–23.

9
Insurance Group Supervision: Addressing the Emergence of Adverse Network Dynamics

Monica Mächler

Introduction

With the announcement by the International Association of Insurance Supervisors (IAIS) on 1 July 2010 to initiate the development process of a Common Framework for the Supervision of Internationally Active Insurance Groups (ComFrame) (IAIS, 2010c),[1] a multilateral approach has been formally launched. This multilateral approach helps to overcome limitations that exist with the currently practised approaches to insurance group supervision. These range from no insurance group supervision at all, to shareholding-centred insurance group supervision, to unilateral comprehensive insurance group supervision and to regional comprehensive insurance group supervision (Mächler, 2010).

Several factors have contributed to the decision of the IAIS to start building ComFrame. They include developing

- 'methods of operating group-wide supervision of Internationally Active Insurance Groups (IAIGs) in order to make group-wide supervision more effective and more reflective of actual business practices',
- 'establishing a comprehensive framework for supervisors to address group-wide activities and risks and also set the grounds for better supervisory cooperation in order to allow for a more integrated and international approach', and
- 'fostering global convergence of regulatory and supervisory measures and approaches'.

The IAIS goes on to clarify that 'ComFrame does not directly address systemic risk per se.' It is, however, the belief of the IAIS that 'when ComFrame is implemented and functional, supervisors will have improved tools and means to address and, where possible, mitigate risk that may affect insurers' (IAIS, 2010c).

These statements beg the question of what insurance group supervision can and should do in order to address and, where possible, mitigate *risks that are specific to (insurance) groups*. As set out by the IAIS, a multilateral framework for insurance group supervision aims to overcome the existing fragmentation among jurisdictions in the supervision of internationally active insurance groups. It also aims to enhance communication among regulators as well as between regulators and supervised insurance groups, thereby contributing to the effectiveness and efficiency of supervision. But how this leads to transcending the traditional legal entity-focused and micro-prudential approach and, if so, to covering new areas, needs to be explored. In this regard, it is important to clarify the objectives of insurance group supervision in respect of risk mitigation as this impacts the remit, role and instruments to employ for group supervision.

For the purposes of this chapter, the term 'insurance group' refers to a group of companies that is based on shareholding or contractual links providing for control or substantive influence on decision-making and where the activities of the group – or at least a substantial part thereof – centre around insurance. As used here, the term 'group supervision' captures the act of regulating or supervising the group as a group of companies (including related parties under certain circumstances). In this context the distinction between micro- and macro-prudential approaches is also important. 'Micro-prudential regulation concerns ... itself with the stability of individual entities and the protection of individuals' (Persaud, 2009, p. 2). Micro-prudential supervision is typically attended to by supervisors (BIS, 2001, p. 2 et seq.). 'Macro-prudential regulation' in turn 'concerns itself with the stability of the financial system as a whole' (Persaud, 2009, p. 2). Sometimes it is also referred to as 'macro-prudential analysis' (BIS, 2001, p. 160 et seq.). 'Macro-prudential surveillance' is used to address the monitoring of the impact of macroeconomic developments and the analysis of aggregated data resulting from the individually supervised insurance entities and groups (ibid.).

This chapter is divided into four sections. In the first section the objectives of current approaches to insurance group supervision are reviewed and categorised. What the structure and the underlying dynamics for the evolution of insurance group specific risks are, is explored in the second and third sections. In the final section, conclusions and ideas for next steps forward are offered regarding the regulatory and supervisory remit and role as well as the instruments that can be used to reach the policy goals discussed.

Objectives of insurance group supervision articulated to date

Where approaches to insurance group supervision exist to date, the objectives articulated are often based on those used in insurance supervision in general that typically go hand in hand with the traditional legal entity-focused supervisory approach. The goals of protecting policy-holders and beneficiaries, sometimes also of safeguarding the proper functioning (Article 5, Swiss Financial Market Supervisory Act), are often transposed into a group context and combined the stability of the financial market (European Parliament, 2010).

Sometimes a risk focus is explicitly articulated. As mentioned before, reference to addressing and mitigating risk through insurance group supervision was made in the IAIS release of 1 July 2010 (IAIS, 2010c). The Joint Forum as part of its 2009 Review of the Differentiated Nature and Scope of Financial Regulation (Joint Forum, 2010, Recommendation 5) highlights the need, among other things, to enhance group regulation and supervision so as to better identify and address the risks stemming locally and across-borders from groups. No particular reference to group-related risks can be found in the most recent regional comprehensive approach to group supervision, namely in the Solvency II Directive that was issued in furtherance of, among others, the Insurance Groups Directive (European Parliament et al., 1998). Recital 16 of the Solvency II Directive confirms the protection of policy-holders and beneficiaries to be the main, generally applicable objective. Furthermore, financial stability and fair and stable markets should also be fostered without thereby undermining the primary objective (Wandt and Sehrbrock, 2010, p. 689 et seq.). Regarding insurance group supervision, recital 95 only sets out that those 'measures concerning the supervision of insurance and reinsurance undertakings in a group should enable the authorities supervising an insurance or reinsurance undertaking to form a more soundly based judgment of its financial situation' (European Parliament et al., 1998). Other recitals describe techniques to be applied.

In recent policy discussions regarding the supervision of general insurance groups led by the Australian Prudential Regulation Authority (APRA) in 2008, the emphasis was put on the fact that 'associations and dealings with other members of an insurer's corporate group may expose the insurer to contagion risk' (APRA, 2008, p. 11). In another discussion paper dated 2010 regarding conglomerates, the APRA further deepened these considerations:

> Being part of a wider group can alter the risk profile ... Financial inter-relationships may expose the general insurer to contagion risk from the financial weakness of another entity within the group. Management and policy decision at the group level may influence the type and level of risks assumed at the entity level. Subsidiaries may end up bearing risks beyond those that they would normally assume if they were operating as independent entities. (APRA, 2010, p. 9)

The Bermuda Monetary Authority, when submitting its bill on insurance group supervision earlier in 2010, set out the following:

> Despite the complexities surrounding group-wide supervision, it is important for the Authority to form a comprehensive view of the overall risk exposure of these groups, especially as they affect the regulated entities operating within Bermuda. Additionally, this view will enable the Authority to better assess the prudential situation of its insurers, and assist in mitigating any potentially adverse impact on the Bermuda financial market system, and the wider Bermuda economy. (Bermuda Monetary Authority, 2010, p. 8)

The US National Association of Insurance Commissioners (NAIC), having engaged in the Solvency Modernization Initiative, intends to include 'certain prudential features' into the shareholding-centred approach reflected in the Insurance Holding Company System model legislation. This initiative intends to address enterprise risk, governance and internal control reporting in addition to the exchange of information and the participation in supervisory colleges (NAIC, 2010c, Notes 17–22). Public interest and protection of policy-holders seem to be upheld as purposes of the insurance holding company system supervisory regime (Article 2, Insurance Holding Company System Model Regulation with Reporting Forms and Instructions) (NAIC, 2010a, 2010b). In Switzerland, where unilateral comprehensive insurance group supervision has been practised since 2006 based on the new Insurance Supervisory Law (Article 64 et seq., Swiss Insurance Supervisory Law), the bill issued at the time of the legislative process very drily set out that there was a need for expanding the group supervisory regime in order to lay the grounds for more convergence and better cooperation amongst regulators (Swiss Federal Council, 2003, p. 3903).

Outside of the circle of standard-setters, legislators, regulators and supervisors, The Geneva Association as a private insurance industry research organisation has identified insurance group supervision as one of several preventive measures that allow for addressing risks affecting the insurance sector. Group supervision would be instrumental to assess 'the consolidated risk exposure and the capital position of the group in line with its economic reality, rather than its legal structure covering insurance and non-insurance activities' (The Geneva Association, 2010, p. 72 et seq.). This should also include – as an example – substantive derivatives trading. According to The Geneva Association, a seamless cooperation amongst regulators with clearly defined roles should complete this approach.

When insurance groups and/or conglomerates encounter challenges – whether or not they stem from insurance activities – heavy critique and expectations are voiced. Usually these comments relate specifically to the risks that have materialised. A prominent example is the case of AIG where the conglomerate supervision was formally attributed to the Office of Thrift Supervision, but the risks inherent to the group could not be effectively addressed (see Gerth, 2008, for many others).

To summarise, the objectives of insurance group supervision as articulated to date centre around the following aspects:

- Protection of policy-holders and beneficiaries
- Safeguarding the proper functioning of markets and financial stability
- Assessing the financial soundness of an insurance group
- Addressing the risks of an insurance group in a group-wide context with a particular focus on contagion risks
- Enhancing communication, information exchange and cooperation between regulators and supervisors and with insurance groups
- Increasing effectiveness and efficiency in supervising insurance groups
- Fostering convergence.

The first four objectives relate to activities and risks of insurance groups. The remaining objectives cover more the communication and cooperation mechanisms among regulators and supervisors, addressing the question of how to render group supervision more effective and efficient.

The discussion here will focus on the activity and risk-related objectives. The impression arises that approaches to group supervision as articulated to date address some important elements of groups, but do not enough clearly express and thus do not fully justify why groups should be regulated and supervised in addition to the traditional regulation and supervision of legal entities. *There also remains a doubt whether they look at group supervision only from an empirical supervisory perspective applying traditional categories, or whether they really are concerned with the underlying challenges posed by the existence of insurance groups.*

In attempting to address these questions it becomes evident that there are two different aspects to be distinguished: One relates to the structure of a group forming the basis for the development of risks, namely the group as a network, the other one to the specific dynamics that allow group specific risks to evolve.

Insurance groups as networks

Interrelations between closely coexisting entities are often analysed with the help of the so-called 'Network Theory' (Temple-Gugerell, 2009). Network Theory has undergone considerable development with the work of Katz and Shapiro (1985) and Economides (1996). Networks consist of nodes that are connected to a varying degree by many edges (Tempel-Gugerell, 2009). Such networks may develop positive or negative externalities (Hammond, 2009). Network Theory has been applied to many phenomena in mathematics, in natural and social sciences as well as in technology, and increasingly also in economics and in the interrelations amongst the financial markets participants (ibid.).

Translated for the reality of insurance groups, the nodes represent the few or many companies forming the group. In contrast, the *intra-group shareholding, transactions* (such as loans, intra-group reinsurance, contingent capital, guarantees and the like) and *non-contractual exposures* (including the combination of businesses and their risk profiles, external market conditions, competition, and other factors) combined with the *group internal governance processes* (such as governance structures including corporate and management governance, risk management, internal controls, internal and external audit and similar arrangements, often supported by the identity of corporate office holders) represent the 'edges'. The degree and intensity of group-internal interlinks differs from one group to the other.

(Insurance) group networks are driven by common top corporate bodies. Their impact reaches regularly much further than only to the top company and affects the way of doing business throughout the group. The group networks are used to derive economic efficiencies and synergies that could not be reached through the separate operation of individual companies. This includes also transferring risk from one legal entity to another. Such efficiencies, synergies and risk transfers are often implemented without being confined to national boundaries. Some group managements use these structuring elements less intensively, obviously other than shareholding lines, but maintain the self-sufficiency of the legal entities to a considerable extent, whereas others create dense webs through huge numbers of interlinks, making individual entities very dependent from the group context. This creates complexities that in turn are challenging to manage.

Group networks may serve to transport effects from one legal entity or node to other legal entities. Oftentimes, positive effects are transported in (insurance) groups of companies when they achieve efficiencies and diversifications, ultimately benefitting their policy-holders and beneficiaries as well as the general economy. Successful insurance activities enable the economy to grow by pooling risk and allowing investors to grow businesses while mitigating risks potentially resulting from such business activities. Further positive effects may also result for other stakeholders such as shareholders and employees. However, negative externalities can be transported through such webs, too. They warrant regulatory attention and, sometimes, action. What are the causes of such adverse dynamics?

The potential for adverse dynamics in insurance group networks

Causes for adverse developments in insurance groups are not easy to capture in a systematised way. Some roots may be found internally within the group, others externally. Sometimes they emerge in an isolated manner, but most of the time they result from combinations of various factors. Oftentimes, positive effects turn under specific circumstances gradually into negative ones which highlights the need for a continued monitoring. Furthermore, some activities seem to be more prone to the evolution of adverse dynamics than others. Many of these features could be applied to groups with very different financial services businesses; what is the most specific element in the insurance sector in this context is the use of group internal reinsurance.

Possible scenarios of adverse dynamics can be described in a qualitative manner without claiming to be precise nor to be complete. Such scenarios where adverse network dynamics may evolve with a greater likelihood could include:

- use of intra-group transactions including corporate structures,
- intra-group exposures resulting from the interrelations or even contagion effects between the businesses of the group,
- disconnection between the strategies and the financial resources of the group, and
- governance processes not apt to identify and address or mitigate particular group risk and stress situations.

They will be the subject of the following considerations.

Use of intra-group transactions and of certain corporate structures

Numerous intra-group transactions are, among other purposes, designed to reallocate risk within the group: with an intra-group guarantee one legal entity of the group backs certain risks of another entity. The same holds true with a group internal reinsurance contract whereby risks from one insurance carrier are assumed by another one. Corporate structures may help to implement such goals through enhancing capital and tax efficiencies. A relatively simple example relates to the question of which entity owns the shares of whom. In the area of financing and risk transfer, much more complex corporate structures are conceivable and found.

These steps may be designed to alleviate the burden of a particular entity or it may provide it additional capacity to do business. They are usually the result of contractual agreements, though sometimes not all elements are properly documented. In general there is the expectation that these transactions be done at market conditions. Failing this, they may not qualify for specific purposes, such as for tax requirements. It is possible that one legal entity enters into a multitude of such reallocation transactions with other group parties. The typical situation is the one of a holding or a subholding company providing guarantees, but also group internal reinsurance carriers might develop such accumulations. This creates webs of intra-group transactions.

Under certain circumstances such reallocations may create or hide risks. One first set of risks may result from the lack of transparency on who bears which risk or benefits from what protections, or who provides which protections. There may also result considerable risk from increasing complexities. Other risks may relate to the separation of management responsibilities and balance sheet attribution. Different individuals assume underwriting responsibilities, management roles and corporate and financial responsibilities. Additional operational risk may stem from the characteristics of transactions entered into and from insufficient due diligence. Some of these failings may adversely affect enforceability.

Intra-group exposures resulting from the interrelations or even contagion effects between the businesses of the group

Another area where adverse group dynamics may materialise can be found in the combination of businesses in groups. Some groups of companies sometimes pursue only one type of business, but others have a portfolio of businesses that differs either marginally (for example, different general insurance product lines) or considerably (for example, general and life insurance), or are totally different as in the case of conglomerates (for example, insurance, banking, capital markets activities, securities dealing and other activities).

Despite the fact that in many instances the combination of different businesses may lead to synergies and positive diversification benefits, there are also situations where the combination of certain businesses may lead to considerable financial or managerial stress for the group and thus have considerable adverse effects (Darlap and Mayr, 2006). Such combinations may be the result of conscious decisions, such as mergers and acquisitions, or arise inadvertently over time. Intra-group transactions may play a role here, but also factual impacts of varying risk patterns. Often it involves not only two legal entities of the group but several ones in the same business segment or geography, or the group as a whole. Adverse effects may in particular materialise when the business conduct and the risk profiles of the various businesses are very different. This is for instance the case when one part of the group has huge amounts of external leverage, while other parts have little leverage, or when one part of the group pursues capital markets activities combined with short term refinancing, while others do more traditional insurance business. Behaviour of corporate office holders such as identity of persons or de facto corporate bodies may increase those exposures.

Disconnection between the strategies and the financial resources of the group

In many situations groups are very conscious of the need to align the strategies they pursue with their financial position. Sometimes, however, distortions occur. These may result from insufficient overview of the potential obligations of the group. In other instances, they may stem from misjudgements in the way business is done, such as in respect of underwriting and reserving or investment allocation. There may also be market influences that go beyond the control of the individual enterprise which can only be coped with through adequate prudence and financial safety buffers. In addition, there may exist organisational, structural or mental impediments or unwillingness that inhibit addressing effectively a recognised risk. All these dynamics can be such that they come to jeopardise the financial stability of parts of the group or the group as a whole.

Governance processes not apt to identify and address or mitigate particular group risk and stress situations

Depending on how centralised or decentralised they are, groups try, to a varying degree, to align the behaviour of group companies. They rely on managerial processes, corporate governance, risk management, actuarial processes, internal controls, internal and external audit and other similar processes. Whether the alignment becomes effective or not depends largely on the corporate culture regarding the monitoring and compliance approach.

Adverse effects of such processes may be the result of not identifying and monitoring certain risks, behavioural barriers to address particular blind spots, herding effects and many other possible patterns. The identity of corporate office holders may increase these risks. A particular concern may arise if the processes do not provide for prevention or mitigation of group stress situations. Such a fall off the corporate radar may particularly happen during periods when the group is enjoying financial success. Certain combinations of businesses and a dense web of intra-group transactions may further block the flexibility to address financial stress situations that would merit a reorientation and may include scaling down, running off certain businesses or divestitures. Such a lack of flexibility may badly affect the recovery potential of insurance groups in stress situations.

Conclusions for insurance group supervision and the way forward

Regarding the *purpose* of insurance group supervision, the above considerations and examples demonstrate two aspects. First, they show that the potential for adverse developments can be substantial if not properly attended to. This justifies *group specific regulatory and supervisory intervention*. Second, regarding the purpose of insurance group supervision it is clear that *monitoring and attending to the emergence of adverse network dynamics* require the most direct consideration. Policy-holder protection, financial stability, and safeguarding the proper functioning of the market and financial stability, while of relevance, should not be the first concern, but be the indirect point of orientation.

Such effects cannot be identified and attended to by considering legal entities only. These trends only become clear with a comprehensive view of the group and its entities of the group whatever purpose they pursue. For the concept of insurance supervision this means that there are *two parallel roles:* one for attending to the risks related to the individual insurance company and one for attending to the adverse network dynamics of insurance groups. They complement each other in that each covers different aspects, but fertilises and improves the effectiveness of the other.

What does this mean in practice for the *regulatory and supervisory tools* to be applied in insurance group supervision? Among many others, three aspects merit highlighting. First of all, addressing adverse network dynamics requires a broad understanding by all the involved parties of the groups under consideration and their internal and external functioning, and ongoing supervisory monitoring. This relates to the groups themselves as well as to the supervisors. The structures used need to be clear and manageable. Particularly important is also the assessment of intra-group transactions and exposures. Changes in business strategy and business mix warrant close attention. The interdependence of the group with the group-external environment should also be put on the radar. Thus, an *integrated assessment of the risks stemming from the individual group structure and the group businesses and business mixes* is key. It is important to realise that this monitoring and assessing of individual groups does not equal macro-prudential surveillance where impacts of the macroeconomy on the insurance sector and trends across the entire insurance population are watched (IAIS, 2010d). Regarding systemic risk, the situation is different. Individual insurance groups, particularly if they substantially engage in banking and capital markets activities or under other specified circumstances, may also become of systemic importance (Cummins, 2009; IAIS, 2009, 2010a; The Geneva Association, 2010; Radice, 2010).

Second, the resulting *quantitative and qualitative regulatory requirements* need to be reflective of the risks arising from those network effects. There will be groups where these network effects internally and externally play such a significant role that it makes the network aspects in respect of complexity all the more important. At the same time, with other groups there may be some nuances or considerably less complexity and thus fewer networks effects to address. This continuum may also change over time or as a result of business developments. Those changes may emanate from the business as such, for example when geographic expansion takes place or when new products are introduced. It may also result from changes in the external environment, such as from the capital markets. The requirements should touch on quantitative elements such as reserving, investing, asset liability matching and economic capital for the group as a whole, be it assessed on a consolidated or on a group-wide basis with a granular methodology. The qualitative elements will have to address the complexities resulting from the network through managerial processes, corporate governance, actuarial processes, internal controls, internal and external audit and related processes. They all should be reflective of the group specific risks and have to be complemented with agile recovery and resolution mechanisms.

Third, it is of paramount importance to overcome national boundaries to the maximum extent possible. Terminology needs to be harmonised and communication needs to be enhanced in order to approach the group-internal and group-external networks. Cooperation and information exchange between regulators needs to be enhanced (IAIS, 2007). In this regard a *multilateral approach* (World Economic Forum, 2009) as now being developed under ComFrame has the largest potential of reaching countries that are home or host states to international insurance groups. This will allow to derive synergies in an effective and efficient supervisory process related to insurance groups.

Focusing on these key points is instrumental for addressing the potential adverse network dynamics that can materialise within insurance groups.

Note

1. Earlier work on insurance group supervision is reflected in Insurance Core Principle 17 and in IAIS (2008a, 2008b).

Bibliography

APRA (2008) 'Response to Submissions, Prudential Supervision of General Insurance Groups', available at www.apra.gov.au/General/upload/DP-Prudential-Supervision-of-GI-Groups-April-2008.pdf.

APRA (2010) Discussion Paper, 'Supervision of Conglomerate Groups', 18 March, available at www.apra.gov.au/Policy/upload/Discussion-paper-Supervision-of-conglomerate-groups-March-2010.pdf.

BIS (2001) Marrying the macro- and micro-prudential dimensions of financial stability, BIS Papers No 1, Monetary and Economic Department, March, available at www.bis.org/publ/bppdf/bispap01.htm.

Bermuda Monetary Authority (2010) Consultation Paper on the Bermuda Monetary Authority's Proposed Insurance Groups Regulatory Framework, February, available at www.bma.bm/uploaded/473-100205_Consultation_Paper_on_Insurance_Groups_Regulatory_Framework.pdf.

Cummins J.D. (2009) 'Do Insurance Companies Pose Systemic Risk?', NAIC Winter 2009 National Meeting, Perspectives on Systemic Risk, available at www.naic.org/.../091203_systemic_risk_symposium_cummins.ppt.

Darlap, P., and B. Mayr (2006) 'Group Aspects of Regulatory Reform in the Insurance Sector', *The Geneva Papers*, 31: 96–123.

European Parliament et al. (1998) Directive 98/78/EC of the European Parliament and of the Council of 27 October 1998 on the supplementary supervision of insurance undertakings in an insurance group, OJ 350/1, available at http://eur-lex.europa.eu/LexUriServ/LexUriServ.do?uri=CELEX:31998L0078:EN:NO.

European Parliament (2010) Directive 2009/138/EC of the European Parliament and of the Council on the taking-up and pursuit of the business of Insurance and Reinsurance (Solvency II), OJ L 335/1, available at http://eur-lex.europa.eu/LexUriServ/LexUriServ.do?uri=OJ:L:2009:335:0001:0155:en:PDF.

Economides, N. (1996) 'The Economics of Networks', *International Journal of Industrial Organization*, 14(2) (March).

Gerth, J. (2008) 'Was AIG Watchdog Not Up to the Job?', *MSN Money Insight*, available at http://articles.moneycentral.msn.com/Investing/Extra/was-aig-watchdog-not-up-to-the-job.asp.

Hammond, R.A. (2009) 'Systemic Risk in the Financial System: Insights from Natural Science', in *The PEW Charitable Trusts, Financial Reform Projects, Briefing Paper No. 12.*

IAIS (2007) *IAIS Multilateral Memorandum of Understanding on Cooperation and Information Exchange (MMoU)* (Basel, Switzerland: International Association of Insurance Supervisors), available at www.iaisweb.org/__temp/IAIS_MMoU.pdf.

IAIS (2008a) *Principles No. 3.4 on Group-Wide Supervision.* (Basel, Switzerland: International Association of Insurance Supervisors) (available at http://iaisweb.org/__temp/7__Principles_No__3_4_on_Group-Wide_Supervision.pdf.

IAIS (2008b) *Guidance Paper No. 3.7 on the Role and Responsibilities of a Group-wide Supervisor.* (Basel, Switzerland: International Association of Insurance Supervisors), available at http://iaisweb.org/__temp/18__Guidance_Paper_No__3_7_on_the_role_and_responsibilities_of_a_group-wide_supervisor.pdf.

IAIS (2009) *Systemic Risk and the Insurance Sector*, 28 October, available at www.iaisweb.org/__temp/Note_on_systemic_risk_and_the_insurance_sector.pdf.

IAIS (2010a) *Position Statement on Key Financial Stability Issues*, 4 June, available at www.iaisweb.org/__temp/IAIS_Position_Statement_on_Key_Financial_Stability_Issues.pdf.

IAIS (2010b) 'IAIS Approves Development of a Common Framework for the Supervision of Internationally Active Insurance Groups', 19 January, available at www.iaisweb.org/__temp/19_January_2010__IAIS_approves_development_of_a_Common_Framework_for_the_Supervision_of_Internationally_Active_Insurance_Groups.pdf.

IAIS (2010c) 'IAIS initiates development of ComFrame', 1 July, available at www.iaisweb.org/__temp/IAIS_initiates_development_of_ComFrame.pdf.

IAIS (2010d) 'Macroprudential Surveillance and (Re)insurance', *Global Reinsurance Market Report*, Mid-year edition, 26 August, available at www.iaisweb.org/__temp/IAIS_GRMR_mid-year_report_2010.pdf.

Joint Forum (2010) *Review of the Differentiated Nature and Scope of Financial Regulation, Key Issues and Recommendations*, January, available at www.bis.org/publ/joint24.pdf.

Katz, M.L., and C. Shapiro (1985) Network Externalities, Competition and Compatibility, *American Economic Review*, 75(3) (June): 424–40, available at http://idv.sinica.edu.tw/kongpin/teaching/io/KatzShapiro1.pdf.

Klauer, I. (2007) 'Gruppen und Konglomerate', in J. Waldmeier (ed.), *Versicherungsaufsicht* (Zurich/Basel/Genf, Switzerland: Schulthess).

Mächler M. (2010) 'Evolution of Insurance Group Supervision', in C. Kempler, M. Flamée, C. Yang and P. Windels (eds), *Global Perspectives on Insurance Today* (New York: Palgrave Macmillan).

NAIC (2010a), Insurance Holding Company System Model Regulation with Reporting Forms and Instructions, Model #450 8/5/10 – As Adopted by Financial Condition (E) Committee, available at www.naic.org/documents/committees_pending_final_action_ins_holding_co_ex_100604.pdf).

NAIC (2010b) Insurance Holding Company System Regulatory Act Model #450 8/5/10 – As Adopted by Financial Condition (E) Committee, available at www.naic.org/documents/committees_pending_final_action_ins_holding_co_sys_reg_act_ex_100604.pdf).

NAIC (2010c) *Solvency Modernization Initiative, Roadmap*, 16 August, available at www.naic.org/documents/committees_ex_isftf_summer_ntlmtg_meeting_smi_roadmap.pdf.

Persaud, A. (2009) 'Macro-Prudential Regulation', in *The World Bank Crisis Response*, Note No. 6, July, available at http://rru.worldbank.org/documents/CrisisResponse/Note6.pdf.

Radice, M.P. (2010) 'Systemische Risiken im Versicherungssektor, Betrachtungen mit Fokus auf die schweizerische Assekuranz', in *FINMA Working Papers*, June, available at www.finma.ch/d/finma/publikationen/Documents/wp_juni2010_systemische-risiken-im-versicherungssektor_20100628_de.pdf.

Swiss Federal Council (2003) Botschaft zu einem Gesetz über die Aufsicht über Versicherungsunternehmen (Versicherungsaufsichtsgesetz, VAG) und zur Änderung des Bundesgesetzes über den Versicherungsvertrag vom 9. Mai 2003, BBl 2003, 3789 et seq., available at www.admin.ch/ch/d/ff/2003/3789.pdf.

Swiss Insurance Supervisory Law (2006) Bundesgesetz vom 17. Dezember 2004 betreffend die Aufsicht über Versicherungsunternehmen (Versicherungsaufsichtsgesetz, VAG), SR 961.01, available at www.admin.ch/ch/d/sr/9/961.01.de.pdf.

Tempel-Gugerell, G. (2009) 'Introductory Remarks', in European Central Bank, 'Recent Advances in Modeling Systemic Risk Using Network Analysis', ECB Workshop, 5 October, available at www.ecb.int/press/key/date/2009/html/sp091005_1.en.html.

The Geneva Association (2010), *Systemic Risk in Insurance – An Analysis of Insurance and Financial Stability*, Special Report of The Geneva Association Systemic Risk Working Group, Geneva, February, available at www.genevaassociation.org/PDF/BookandMonographs/Geneva_Association_Systemic_Risk_in_Insurance_Report_March2010.pdf.

Wandt, M., and D. Sehrbrock (2010) *Regelungsziele der Solvency-II-Rahmenrichtlinie, Festschrift zum fünfzigjährigen Bestehen, Schweizerische Gesellschaft für Haftpflicht- und Versicherungsrecht* (Zürich, Switzerland: Schulthess).

Weber, R.H., and P. Umbach (2006) Versicherungsaufsichtsrecht (Bern, Switzerland: Stämpfli).

World Economic Forum (2009), The Future of the Global Financial System, A Near-Term Outlook and Long-Term Scenarios, A World Economic Forum Report in Collaboration with Oliver Wyman available at http://www.weforum.org/pdf/scenarios/TheFutureoftheGlobalFinancialSystem.pdf.

10
Credit Default Swaps: Towards Tighter Regulation of the 'Shadow Insurance Sector'

Nadège Jassaud and Sebastian Schich*

Introduction

Credit default swaps (CDSs) have brought considerable benefits by allowing credit risks to be tailored to risk preferences more precisely than is possible with traditional credit risk instruments, such as bonds and loans. CDSs have thus contributed to the development of more complete markets and have increased the capacity of the financial system to allocate credit risk to those most willing and, hopefully, best able to bear it.

Recent events have drawn attention, however, to the weaknesses of this market segment, which may have amplified the depth of the financial crisis. In particular, the limited disclosure in this lightly regulated segment has fuelled broader market uncertainty and complicated the assessment of risk concentrations by regulators and market participants.

The chapter is structured as follows. The first section describes the similarities and differences between insurance contracts and CDSs, and section 2 the role of different types of financial institutions, including banks and insurance companies, in CDS activities. The final section then explains the main features of current regulatory reform efforts and concludes.

An insurance-like instrument at the core of credit risk transfers

The recent financial crisis was preceded by a massive transfer of credit risk and a substantial build-up of leverage. Much of this development has relied on an insurance-like financial instrument: credit default swaps. The market has grown rapidly since its inception in the 1990s. In December 2007, gross notional amounts of CDSs reached a record-high, at US$60 trillion.

* The views expressed herein are those of the authors and should not be attributed to the IMF, its Executive Board, or its management.

Similarities between CDSs and insurance contracts

Insurance against the risk of default

A CDS is a derivative instrument, which protects the protection buyer against the risk of default (or specific pre-defined credit events) during the term of the contract. The protection seller receives a fee in exchange for this promise. Similarly, an insurance contract can be viewed as a derivative contract where the underlying asset is the value of losses experienced by the insured. In a March 2009 *Financial Times* article, Eric Dinallo, the former New York Superintendent of Insurance, characterised a CDS as 'an insurance policy'.

Beyond this common insurance function, the payment mechanisms of both instruments have similar features: the spread times the notional amount in the case of a CDS is analogous to an insurance premium, and the net value received by the protection buyer resembles the payment of an insurance claim. A stylised representation of the cash flows associated with a CDS is provided in Figure 10.1.

As in any form of insurance, premiums on a CDS increase when perceived (credit) risks rise and decrease when these risks decline. If a default or credit event occurs, the CDS seller will make a prearranged payment to the buyer of the contract in exchange for the underlying bond (reference obligation) or by a simple cash settlement. These mechanics are represented in stylised form in Figure 10.2.

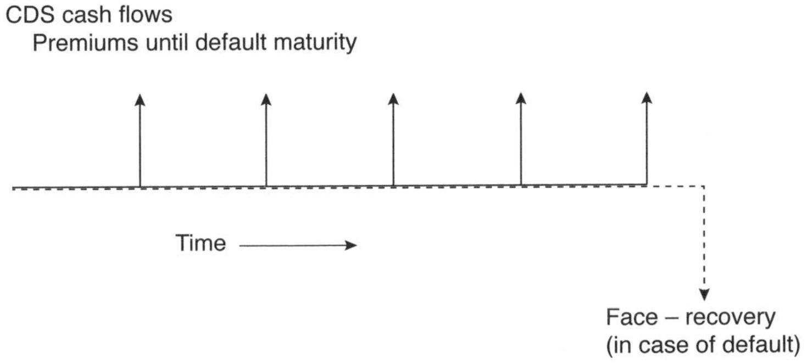

Source: Author's compilation.

Figure 10.1 Cash flows associated with a CDS contract

Protection against skewed risks

Many of the payoff distributions encountered in general insurance are skewed, with long tails to the right. Similarly, but unlike the payoffs from other bilateral over-the-counter (OTC) contracts like interest rate swaps, those associated with CDSs are (heavily) skewed.

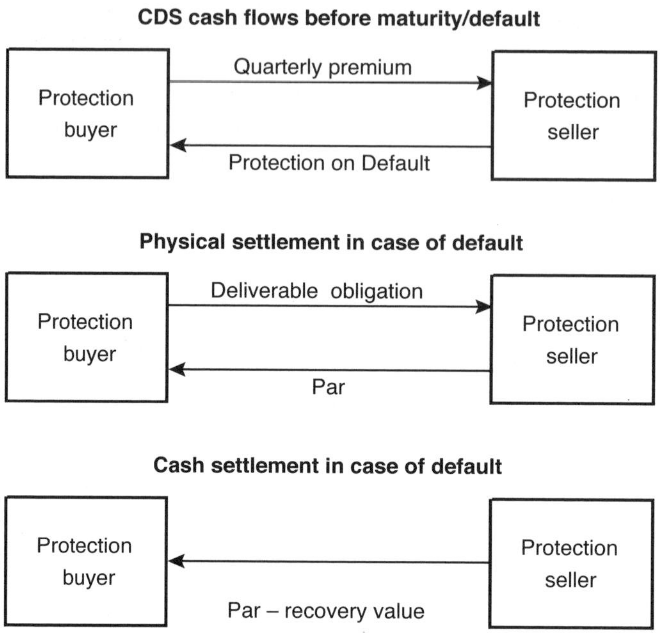

Source: Author's compilation.

Figure 10.2 Mechanics of a CDS contract in case of default

In normal times, selling protection is attractive, as the protection seller receives a regular premium payment from the buyer of protection, while credit events appear remote. Once a credit event occurs, however, the protection seller is obliged to pay the protection buyer the loss given default, which can be in extreme situations, close to the notional amount of the CDS contract when the recovery rate is low.

This increase in potential future loss exposure is referred to as 'jump-to-default risk' (for an example see Figure 10.3). In practice, this risk is extremely difficult to manage, although, typically, one or both parties to a CDS contract post collateral.

Collateral is assets provided to secure an obligation. This risk mitigation technique is used to secure repos, securities lending and derivative transactions, like CDS. The party who owes an obligation to another party posts collateral, typically consisting of cash or securities, to secure the transaction. The amount of collateral varies according to the risk at stake, that is, the value of the underlying credit risk.

However, one issue, as highlighted by the recent financial crisis is that a sudden deterioration of the underlying credit risk may force the protection seller to post significant and immediate amounts of collateral (as a result of so-called margin calls), triggering its own default.

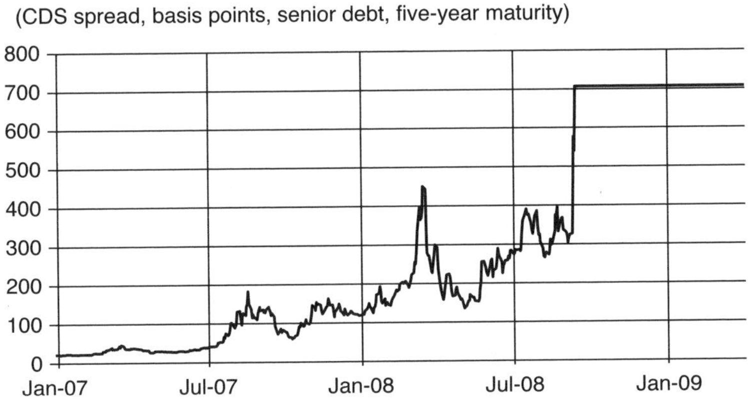

Source: Author's compilation.

Figure 10.3 Materialisation of jump-to-default risk during the Lehman Brothers' default

The situation is different from that of other derivatives, where required payments triggered by the materialization of risks are usually only small fractions of the total notional amounts of the contract. Thus, the loss distribution profile in proportion to notional value for a CDS is very different from that (for example) of an interest rate swap (Figure 10.4). The 'potential future exposure' describes how much the value of the given contract might change over the remaining life of the contract. An estimation of such exposure using Monte Carlo-based simulations is shown in Figure 10.5, illustrating the strong non-linearity of the loss distribution under CDS contracts.

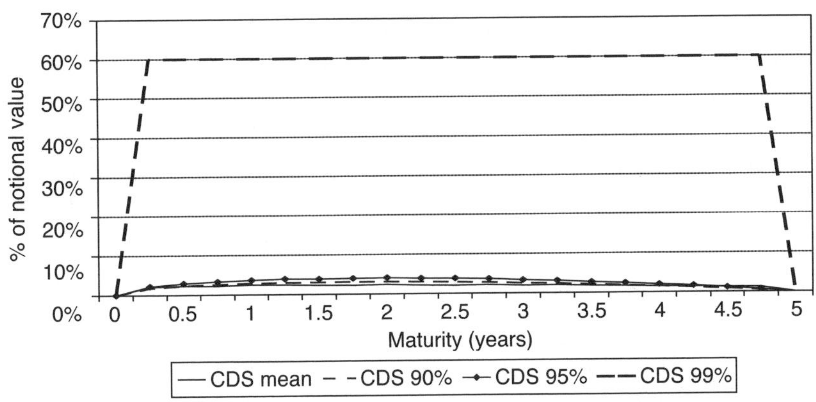

Source: ECB (2009).

Figure 10.4 Expected potential exposure: five-year CDS (percentages of total notional value)

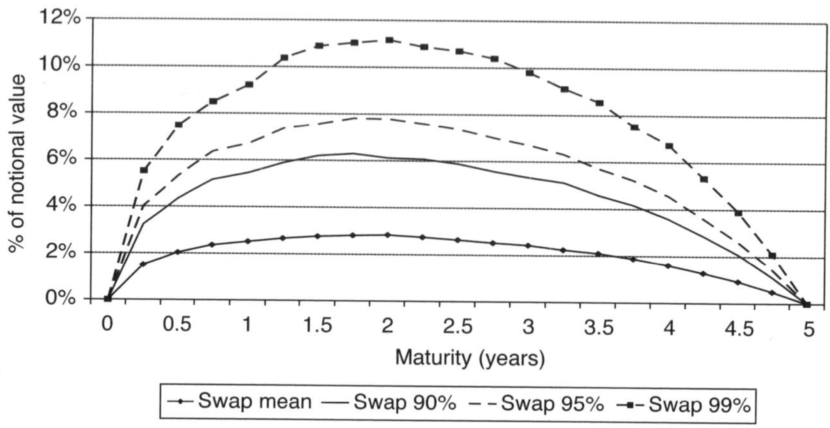

Source: ECB (2009).

Figure 10.5 Expected potential exposure: five-year interest rate swap (percentages of total notional value)

CDS specificities compared to insurance contracts

No insurable interest in CDSs

The similarities described above notwithstanding, there are also considerable differences between typical traditional insurance contracts and CDSs. In particular, the former provide indemnity against the losses *actually* suffered by the policy-holder. In contrast, the buyer of a CDS does not need to own the underlying security nor to suffer a default to qualify for 'compensation'. The set of credit events triggering compensation payment is determined on a bilateral basis between the buyer and the seller of protection, making the CDS a very flexible financial instrument. These features have contributed significantly to the rapid development of the CDS market, although they also have the potential to create undesirable incentives. In particular, in the case of so-called 'naked' CDSs (where the holder does not own the underlying instrument), the CDS protection buyer may have a comparatively higher interest in the trigger event occurring as, for example, compared to the situation of an owner of an insured property.

Concentration in CDS markets

Unlike some other financial markets segments, such as e.g. markets for corporate bonds, the CDS market presents a high degree of concentration in terms of particpants. For instance, half of all CDS trades are concentrated among the five largest dealers[1] (Figure 10.6) and on the whole, most of the CDS trades remain traded within the dealers' community (Table 10.1) (the CDS dealers are usually the largest investment banks). Under those circumstances, each of these dealers runs significant counterparty risk, and the failure of just one protection seller would leave protection buyers with considerable uncovered future exposures, that is, until all CDS contracts are replaced. As most of the dealers' CDS trading is done on a 'matched-book' basis, the loss of protection on one side could significantly increase overall risk exposure. Equally important, the failure of a major protection buyer will expose its counterparties to earnings shortfalls on unsecured net derivative receivables and could result in potential disputes over the valuation of the less liquid CDS contracts.

* Same percentage is true for net notionals, in terms of concentration.
Source: DTCC, 17 April 2009 – special ECB request, based on gross notional.

Figure 10.6 Concentration of CDS trades among top five and top ten market participants

Table 10.1 Percentage of dealers' trades versus 'non-dealers' in CDS markets

		SELLER	
		Dealer	Non-dealer
BUYER	Dealer	86%	14%
	Non-dealer	99%	1%

Source: DTCC, June 2010.

Significant presence of correlated risks in CDS markets

Before the recent crisis, some financial institutions, including banks, AIG, and financial guarantors, built up significant net exposures in CDSs. Many major protection sellers figured also as main references in CDS contracts, thus creating a chain of interconnected risks. For example, among the top ten most traded non-sovereign reference entities, nine were financial institutions, seven of which major CDS dealers (Table 10.2). As a result, there were situations where the credit quality of a CDS reference entity tended to be correlated with the CDS counterparty's own ability or willingness to pay. This situation, referred to as 'wrong way risk', implies that the effectiveness of the 'insurance function' is lessened.

Table 10.2 Top ten corporate reference entities (net notional amounts, in US$ trillion)

Top ten non-sovereign references entities (net notional amounts)		
General Electric	Conglomerate	11.1
Bank of America	Dealer	6.0
Goldman Sachs	Dealer	6.0
Deutsche Bank	Dealer	5.7
Berkshire Hathaway	Financial	5.4
JP Morgan	Dealer	5.3
MBIA	Financial	5.3
Morgan Stanley	Dealer	5.2
Wells Fargo	Dealer	5.0
Citigroup	Dealer	4.5

Source: DTCC, June 2010.

'Wrong way risk' may also characterise the markets for sovereign CDSs, which witnessed a very significant increase in activity. The question that arises in this specific context is whether financial institutions can effectively insure the country risk of mature economy governments with credit default swaps, particularly since their own financial health may be closely linked to that of their sovereigns, and perhaps even depend on the latter, as a result of government support provided.

Opacity and light regulation of CDS markets

The lack of transparency reflects the privately negotiated, bilateral nature of OTC derivatives, which are (currently) not generally subject to public disclosure requirements. It is now widely acknowledged that this lack of transparency contributed to the depth of the recent crisis in several ways: it made it difficult for market participants to judge the extent of ultimate risk borne by other market participants, complicating the operation of discipline; and it also made it more difficult for regulators to assess systemic risk. This situation also reflects the large number of unregulated entities: a CDS seller does not need to be a regulated entity, unlike insurance companies[2] or banks. Table 10.3 provides a stylised overview of some similarities and differences between CDS and credit insurance contracts.

Table 10.3 Similarities and CDS specificities

Similarities	CDS Specificities
• Insurance function • Tail risk	• Flexibility and liquidity (no need for an insured underlying, nor the materialisation of a default) • Concentration and counterparty risk • Correlated exposures • Low transparency and regulation

The role of banks and insurance companies in CDS markets

The case of financial guarantors

The primary business of financial guarantors was bond insurance. That business was viewed as virtually default-free; it focused on bonds issued by municipalities, on which defaults have historically been very rare. Essentially, these companies lend the issuers their own credit rating, which traditionally was the top-notch triple-A rating – a practice called 'credit enhancement'. Buyers of municipal bond tend to be high-credit-quality investors, and the availability of bond insurance provided by a triple-A rated bond insurer allowed these investors to do minimal, if any, credit research before investing in such bonds (Schich, 2009).

In 1997, the New York State Insurance Department, which is the primary regulator for most United States financial guarantors, allowed CDSs under insurance law, provided that (inter alia) the duration of the CDS did not exceed five years and the security referenced was rated at least investment grade. Since then, financial guarantors have increasingly granted protection in the form of writing CDSs rather than in the form of traditional bond insurance contracts ('insurance wraps'). This evolution reflects a fundamental change in their business model.

At year-end 2007, major financial guarantors provided between 10% and 30% of the total credit protection sold in the form of CDS contracts (Table 10.4). Unlike CDS dealers, these insurance companies sold CDS protection but hardly ever bought CDS protection. Compared to the size of their balance sheets (total assets), the amount of written CDSs ranged between two to five times their total assets, contributing to the dramatic leverage of those companies (Figure 10.7). As the crisis and the credit quality outlook for these guarantors worsened, it became increasingly clear that their thin capital cushions were insufficient to cover the potential defaults on these instruments. As a result, the financial guarantors were significantly downgraded and some of them went into run-off mode.

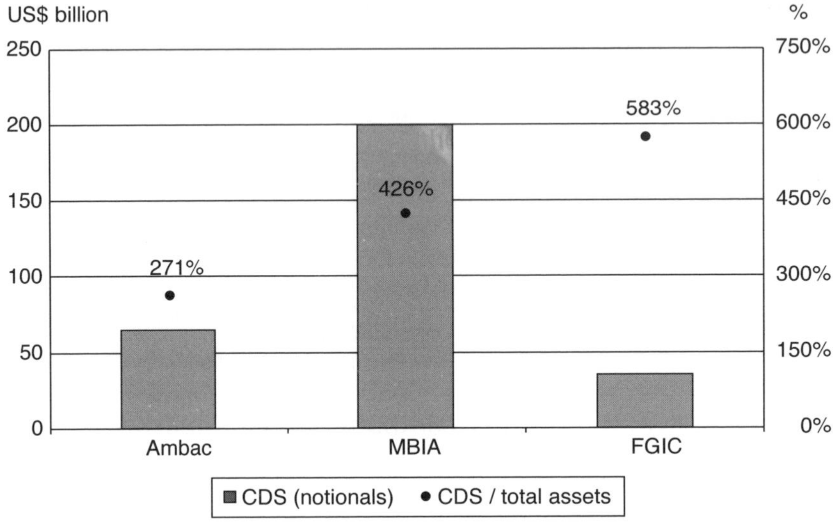

Source: Authors' calculations based on company financial statements.

Figure 10.7 CDSs sold by financial guarantors in absolute and relative terms (notional amounts in US$ billion and as of total assets in percent, as of end 2007)

Table 10.4 Credit protection sold by financial guarantors through CDSs (US$ billion and percentages, as of end 2007)

US$ billion, 31.12.2007	Ambac	MBIA	FGIC
Insured assets	524	678	314
of which:			
insurance contracts	88%	71%	89%
CDS	12%	29%	11%

Source: Authors' calculations based on company financial statements.

The role of general insurance companies

The activity of general insurance companies in the CDS market appears relatively limited, with the notable exception of AIG.

According to most recent BIS data (based on surveys of OTC trades of leading global banks from G10 countries), insurance companies (even including financial guarantors) accounted for less than 1% of the banks' counterparties at the end of 2009: the notional amount bought and sold by entities from that sector totalled about US$331 billion (Table 10.5), compared to a global CDS market of US$32 trillion.

Table 10.5 CDSs bought and sold by banks in G10 countries

(notional amounts outstanding, US$ billion, at end December 2009)

Total CDS contracts bought and sold by reporting dealers	32,700
To/from	
Reporting dealers*	17,700
Banks and security firms	9,949
Insurance and financial guarantee firms	331
Other financial institutions (hedge funds)	3,100
Non-financial institutions	1,600

* G10 BIS sample reporting banks.

Source: BIS.

A glance at the balance sheets of the ten largest insurance-dominated financial groups confirms this broad picture. Figure 10.8 shows that very few large insurance companies have written CDS contracts, with the notable exception of AIG and, to a lesser extent, AXA, through its asset management company. CDS data for Generali, Aviva and CNP are not disclosed, however. The aggregate amounts of CDSs written and bought are not very large in terms of these companies'

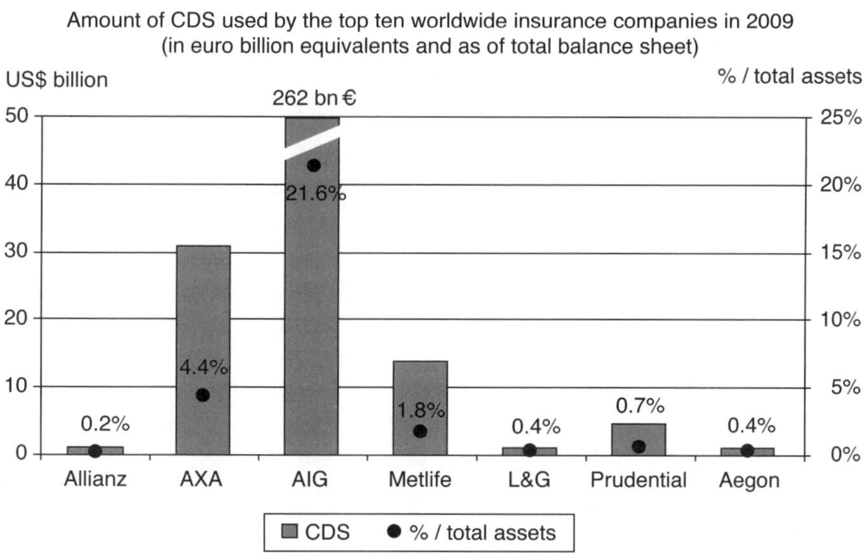

Notes: Percentage numbers refer to percentage as of total assets (right-hand axis). Otherwise, the data refer to absolute amounts expressed in (billion) euro equivalents (left-hand axis). Separate data on amounts 'sold' and 'bought' are available for AXA, Prudential and L&G. Before the crisis, hals of AIG's assets consisted of CDS notionals.

Source: Authors' calculations based on company financial statements.

Figure 10.8 Credit protection sold and/or bought by the ten largest insurance companies

total consolidated balance sheets, typically not exceeding 1%. This situation is likely to reflect the regulatory environment. Both in the United States and Europe, general insurance companies are not allowed to use CDSs for speculative purposes. Then, the use of these instruments is permitted only for the purpose of hedging, replicating, or embedded in structured products, under strict quantitative investment rules.

The only general insurer which sold credit default protection through derivatives in *significant* amounts in such relative terms was AIG. On 30 September 2008, when AIG received public support, the company's aggregate notional amount of CDSs sold was equivalent to US$372 billion on a net basis. Incidentally, AIG sold such protection through its Financial Products unit, AIGFP, a non-regulated subsidiary.

A 'shadow insurance' sector dominated by banks?

Basel II provides for lower capital charges for credit risk mitigation instruments than did Basel I. Perhaps reflecting this difference, and because of the lower capital charge assigned for trading book activities in banking regulations, banks have stepped up their CDS activity. While the percentage of CDS gross notionals to total assets amounted to only 1% in the insurance sector, this same ratio was about 100–200 times larger for EU banks.[3] Even though gross notional amounts are not the best risk metric, as they do not take into account netting agreements, for example, offsetting contracts,[4] they provide, however, the most widely used turnover measure and size yardstick (see Figure 10.9).

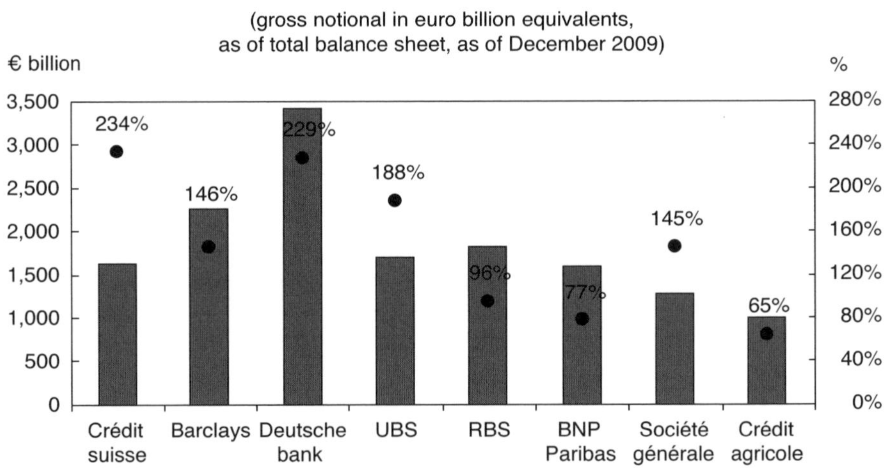

Notes: Percentage numbers refer to percentage as of total assets (right-hand axis). Otherwise, the data refers to absolute amounts expressed in (billion) Euro equivalents (left-hand axis).

Source: Authors' calculations based on company financial statements.

Figure 10.9 Credit protection sold and/or bought by largest EU banks

The dominant role of banks in CDS markets was also reflected in the list of counterparties for which AIG provided credit protection through CDS contracts. The public support provided to AIG facilitated payments by that entity to its (bank) counterparties, equivalent to about a third of the common equity of the latter (Table 10.6).The notional value of outstanding CDS contracts fell by about US$32 trillion from its peak (Figure 10.10), reflecting to a large extent the multilateral 'trade compression',[5] a practice which reduces gross exposure by redundant trades. Nonetheless, the market is still considerable in size; it is equivalent to one third of the banking assets and twice those of the insurance sector (Figure 10.11).

Table 10.6 Payments to major AIG counterparties 16 September to 31 December 2008

AIG's main counterparties, December 2008 (US$ billions)

Institution	Notional	Negative mark to market value
Société Générale	16.4	8.4
Goldman Sachs	14	8
Deutsche Bank	8.5	3.6
Merrill Lynch	6.2	3.4
Calyon	4.3	2.4
UBS	3.8	2
Deutsch Zentral Genossenschaftsbank	1.8	1
Barclays	1.5	1
Bank of Montreal	1.4	0.6
RBS	1.1	0.6

Source: ECB (2009).

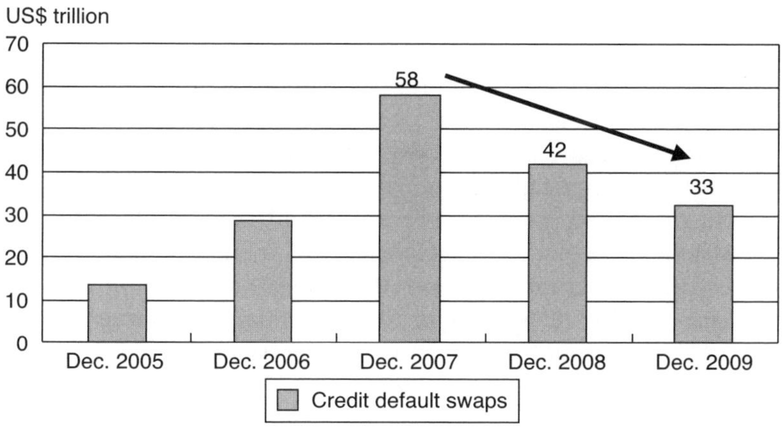

Source: BIS.

Figure 10.10 Gross notional amounts outstanding of CDS (US$ billion)

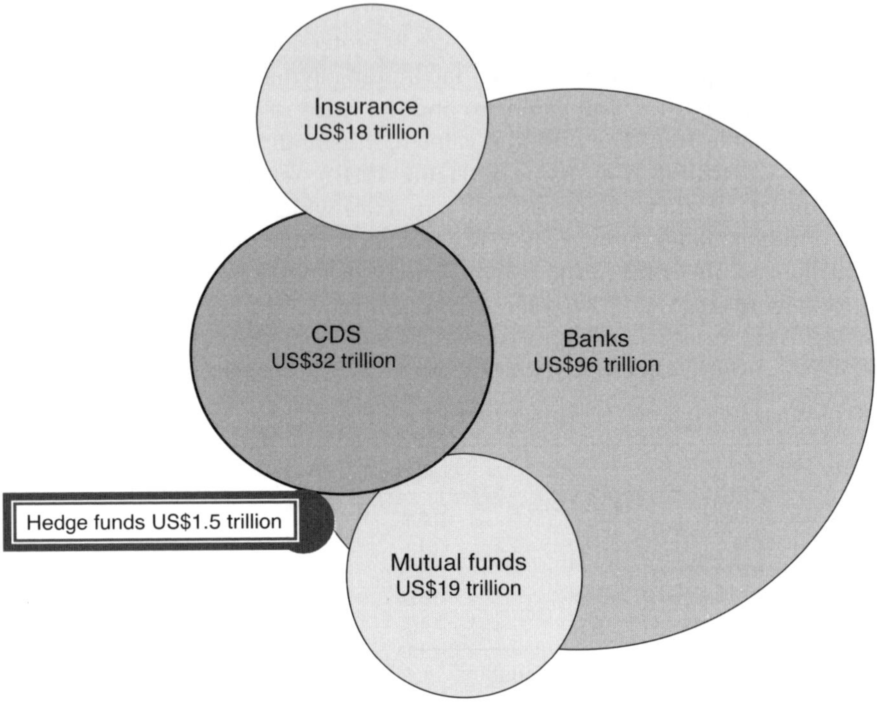

Source: Authors' estimates based on BIS, the *Banker*, and IFSL.

Figure 10.11 An (imperfect) measure of relative size of CDS markets

Global strengthening of CDS regulation

In September 2009, at the G20 Pittsburgh Summit, policy-makers agreed that 'all standardised OTC derivative contracts should be traded on exchanges or electronic trading platforms, where appropriate, and cleared through central counterparties by end-2012 at the latest'. Moreover, OTC derivative contracts should be reported to trade repositories. Non-centrally cleared contracts should be subject to higher capital requirements. Recent legislative actions and proposals in the United States (Dodd-Frank Act adopted in July 2010) and Europe (legislative proposal made in September 2010; see EU Commission, 2010) are consistent with that agreement. Also, the Basel Committee on Banking Supervision is also revising its banking regulatory capital calculations so as to better capture market and counterparty risk of banks' OTC trades and encourage the use of central clearing, and these changes should affect the market for CDSs in a more indirect way.

Mandatory clearing through central counterparties

Clearing through a central counterparty (CCP) is going to be mandatory for standardised contracts. A CCP is a separate legal entity which interposes itself between the buyer and the seller. This process allows the CCP to mutualise credit risk. Risk is mitigated through two key features. First, a CCP typically requires the posting of initial collateral to cover potential exposure, with more collateral to be posted for positions whose market value is volatile or negative. Second, a CCP is supervised and is required to have a regulatory specified minimum capital, and adequate burden-sharing arrangements and risk management in place.

Several new CCPs for CDS were introduced since 2009 (3). The gross notional volume of CDSs cleared through such CCPs had surpassed the US$10 trillion by mid 2010,[6] incidentally almost entirely through one single company, that is, ICE Group (Table 10.7).This group consists of two regional clearinghouses, ICE Trust in the United States and ICE Clear Europe. Each one is a separate legal entity with its own risk pool; the trades at one entity cannot be offset against those at the other. Both clearinghouses, however, use the same margining methodology, default procedures, and have largely the same dealer-banks as clearing members.

Table 10.7 CDS clearing providers

Name of clearing house	Location	Regulated by	Launch date	Gross notionals-Eq Bn US$ (mid 2010)
ICE US Trust	US	NY Fed, NY State Banking Dept	Already launched	6,000
CME	US	CFTC and FSA	June 2010	0.05
ICE Clear Europe	UK	FSA	March 2009	3,700
LCH Clearnet SA	France	College of European regulators	March 2010	15.5
Deutsche Börse (Eurex)	Germany	BaFin, Bundesbank and FSA	July 2009 (stopped in September 2010)	Inactive
NYSE Euronext (BClear)	UK	FSA	December 2008 (stopped in July 2010)	Inactive

Mandatory CDS reporting using trade repositories

Standardisation and clearing of *all* CDS contracts is neither possible nor desirable, as it might considerably hamper the hedging function offered by this type of this instrument. Transparency can be increased otherwise, however. Currently, reporting of OTC derivatives, including CDSs, is not mandatory. As a result, policy-makers, regulators and market participants only have a limited understanding of market developments. With the envisaged new regulations, trades in CDSs will have to be reported to central data stores, known as trade repositories. Trade repositories maintain an electronic database of derivative transactions. Regulators will have access to these repositories, which should facilitate the identification of exposures and potential accumulation of risks at an early stage. In the case of CDS instruments, there is one single trade repository that collects and records information about trades: it is located in the US and managed by the Depository Trust & Clearing Corporation (DTCC), a private company, which is supervised by the Federal Reserve Bank of New York. Its coverage is an estimated 95% of all volumes outstanding contracts at the 14 largest CDS dealers. Access to this infrastructure should allow regulators and supervisors to obtain relevant information that facilitates their micro- and macro-prudential oversight.

Increased bank capital charges for CDS activities

In addition to the above-mentioned initiatives regarding clearing and reporting of derivatives trades, the Basel Committee on Banking Supervision (BCBS) will require banks to set aside more capital (BCBS, 2010)[7] with regard to market and counterparty risk arising from derivative transactions, which includes CDS transactions.

Following the outbreak of the financial crisis in mid 2007, an important source of both losses and the build-up of leverage were the positions that were accounted for in banks' trading books.[8] A main factor contributing to that concentration of exposure was that the Basel capital framework for market risk (dated from 1996) did not adequately capture some important risks when accounted for in the trading book. In response to this insight, the Basel Committee now plans to supplement the current value-at-risk based trading book framework with an incremental risk capital charge, which includes default risk as well as migration risk, for unsecuritised credit products. For securitised products, including synthetic ones (that is, those based on CDS), the capital charges of the banking book will apply with a limited exception for certain so-called correlation trading activities, where banks may be allowed by their supervisor to calculate a comprehensive risk capital charge subject to strict qualitative minimum requirements as well as stress-testing requirements. These measures will reduce the incentive for regulatory arbitrage between the banking and trading books. The new regime will also introduce a stressed value-at-risk. Banks will have to calculate a value-at-risk taking into account a one-year observation period relating to significant losses, which must be calculated in addition to the value-at-risk based on the most recent one-year observation period. This additional requirement will also help reduce the procyclicality of the minimum capital requirements for market risk.

The second important change in the BCBS reform which is likely to affect the CDS market is related to the treatment of counterparty risk. As discussed in the second section of this chapter, CDSs involve a significant level of counterparty risk.

A new capital charge will be introduced in relation to exposure to counterparty risk, which addresses the following problem: banks' exposures to mark-to-market losses under derivatives and repo arrangements (arising as a result of a deterioration in counterparty credit quality short of actual default) was not adequately captured under current Basel rules. The envisaged new rules account for this effect through the so-called credit valuation adjustment. An additional capital charge will indeed be applied where banks identify that an exposure to a counterparty gives rise to specific wrong-way risk. Banks will also be required to adopt more rigorous collateral risk management practices and to perform stress tests. Finally, to encourage the use of central clearing, the new BCBS requirements will assign a lower risk weight to positions centrally cleared as opposed to non-centrally cleared trades (OTC-traded derivatives). Table 10.8 summarises the major changes with respect to counterparty risk. In addition, to reflect the risks that those large OTC derivative dealers' books pose to their counterparties and to the financial system as a whole, the IMF has also proposed to apply a direct charge on the amount of so-called 'derivative payables' (that is, the amounts of derivatives owed to others) (IMF, 2010; Singh, 2010).

Table 10.8 Selected proposed changes to improve counterparty risk management

Issue	Suggested measure
Price fluctuation risk coverage	• The *credit valuation adjustment* (CVA) is a framework for adjusting the market value of a bank's exposure in response to changes in counterparty credit risk. • To better capture CVA losses, methods of assessing additional capital charges have been proposed.
Correlation in interbank exposures	• Banks adopting the Internal Risk Based approach, will have to increase risk weightings on exposures to other large financial firms (this is via a multiplier to correlation assumptions, a key parameter in calculating required capital).
'*Wrong-way*' risk	• A new capital charge will be added to cover situations where the credit quality of a counterparty is correlated with the exposure to the counterparty.
Weaknesses regarding *stress testing*	• Banks will have to include a stress period in calculating the potential exposure at risk and to conduct stress tests monthly and reporting results to senior Management.
Incentivising centrally cleared operations (CCP) and penalising non-centrally cleared ones	• The new regime will increase the incentives to use CCPs for OTC derivatives.
Tighter standards for collateral management	• Margin periods (the time needed to unwind trades and rebuild positions in the event of a counterparty default) will be extended and quality of assets pledged as collateral enhanced (to limit illiquid collateral).

Source: Authors' compilation.

Concluding remarks and open issues

CDSs tend to complete financial markets, as they offer a less costly and more flexible alternative to traditional credit insurance and facilitate the transfer of credit risk. As a result of these features as well as comparatively light regulation, the market for CDSs grew rapidly in the last decade.

However, recent events have drawn attention to the weaknesses of this market. In particular, the limited disclosure in this lightly regulated segment together with the presence of significant counterparty credit risk resulting from the limited use of collateral to mitigate such risk have fuelled uncertainty, which in turn has likely amplified the depth of the financial crisis.

Soundly run and properly regulated CCPs should help reduce counterparty risk and limit the systemic risk associated with the potential for cascading counterparty failures. CCPs, by interposing themselves between the CDS buyers and the CDS dealers, assume all the contractual rights and responsibilities, as well as risks. They facilitate counterparty risk mitigation and, because they collect information on contracts cleared in one place, they can also lead to improved transparency. CCPs concentrate credit and operational risk, however, and their own failure could have systemic implications. Thus, CCPs need to adopt very prudent risk management procedures and be subject to effective regulation and supervision, so that their full benefits could be realised.

Notes

1. The DTCC defines a 'dealer' as a 'large' user, while 'non-dealers' are defined as indirect or smaller participants.
2. In 2000, the New York Insurance Department's Office of General Counsel issued an opinion, exempting CDSs from insurance regulation in the US.
3. For US banks, different accounting standards make it difficult to compare leverage-type ratios.
4. Unlike financial guarantors, CDS dealers usually are on both sides of the trades, they sell and buy CDSs. The offsetted notional, which better reflects the residual amount at risk is so-called 'net notional'.
5. When market participants hold simultaneously long and short CDS positions on the same underlying entity these trades are in effect offsetting each other and can be terminated or reduced on a multilateral basis. It helps reduce the open interest amounts of outstanding redundant CDS positions. TriOptima and Creditex offer those services.
6. CDS clearinghouses had surpassed $15 trillion in cumulative gross notional value and 400,000 transactions in January 2011.
7. At the time of writing, the rules were to be finalised by the end of 2010. Implementation is going to be phased in, till 2019.
8. The trading book is a specific portfolio in a bank's prudential account, which consists of positions in financial instruments and commodities held either with trading intent or in order to hedge other elements of the trading book.

Bibliography

Banque de France (2010) 'Derivatives, Financial innovation and Financial Stability', *Financial Stability Review*, 14.

BCBS (2010) 'Basel III: A Global Regulatory Framework for More Resilient Banks and Banking Systems', December, www.bis.org/publ/bcbs189.htm.

ECB (2009) 'Credit Default Swaps and Counterparty Risk', www.ecb.int/.../creditdefaultswapsandcounterpartyrisk2009en.pdf.

EU Commission (2010) 'Proposal for a Regulation of the European Parliament and of the Council on OTC Derivatives, Central Counterparties and Trade Repositories', ec.europa.eu/internal_market/.../derivatives/20100915_proposal_en.pdf.

IMF (2010) 'Making Over-the-Counter Derivatives Safer: The Role of Central Counterparties', *Global Financial Stability Report*, www.imf.org/external/pubs/ft/gfsr/2010/01/pdf/chap3.pdf.

Pittsburgh Summit (2009) Leaders' Statement, http://www.pittsburghsummit.gov/mediacenter/press/index.htm.

Schich, S. (2009) 'Insurance Companies and the Financial Crisis', *OECD Financial Market Trends*.

Singh, M. (2010) 'Collateral, Netting and Systemic Risk in the OTC Derivatives Market', IMF Working Paper 10/99 (Washington DC: IMF), www.imf.org/external/pubs/ft/wp/2010/wp1099.pdf.

11
The Regulation of Global Reinsurance Markets: The Current State of Affairs and Future Challenges

Philippe Brahin

Introduction

Reinsurers manage and provide coverage for the world's largest and most complex risks. Diversification is the main tool required in order to perform this crucial and demanding role. This can be achieved by underwriting different types of risk in each market as domestic insurance carriers or national pools with limited range of exposures cannot achieve optimum diversification, which requires access to risks originating in geographically different markets. This imperative suggests that the business model of reinsurers work effectively if access to global primary insurance markets is not restricted and capital is fully fungible. Most reinsurers generate only a fraction of their premium income in the respective home markets. Primary insurers and, ultimately, their policy-holders benefit through more secure cover and more affordable rates if reinsurers are permitted to operate on a global scale with utmost capital efficiency.

As the financial crisis has demonstrated, the quality of financial services regulation matters greatly to the effective protection of individual and corporate assets as well as to the stability of financial markets and the real economy at large. A progressive and modern regulatory regime requires that regulators recognise the specific characteristics of the reinsurance business model and the regulatory implications arising from it in order to maximise the industry's contribution to financial stability and economic growth.

Reinsurance, primary insurance and banking – understanding the differences

The business model of insurance and reinsurance is fundamentally different from that of other financial services providers. Banks rely on short-term deposit and short-term credit funding. In contrast, insurers and reinsurers are funded by upfront premiums, giving them strong operating cash flows. In general, premium payments cannot be withdrawn on demand or prematurely. Therefore, insurers and reinsurers are not susceptible to a 'liquidity panic' – a well-known phenomenon in the banking industry, a recent example being the 'run' on Northern Rock in September 2007. Insurance liabilities mature over a long timeframe and insurers do not need to suddenly liquidate assets. As a consequence, although insurers and reinsurers recognise the need to manage their liquidity positions under normal conditions and stressed scenarios, undertaking tend to be less exposed to liquidity risks and regulation focuses on ensuring that insurance providers control risk exposures and hold capital resources to meet adverse outcomes.

There are significant differences between primary insurance and reinsurance, too. Most insurance policies are sold to households, individuals and small businesses and the main objective of regulators is to protect these parties. Governments strive to protect the legitimate interests of policy-holders by imposing standards on the conduct of business and the financial strength of insurers. Conduct of business requirements vary but can include selling and claims practices, policy provisions and premium rates. In contrast, the case for strict oversight of reinsurance transactions is intuitively less compelling as both parties – the primary insurer and the reinsurer – are sophisticated and knowledgeable entities. Another major difference to primary insurers is that reinsurance is often transacted on a cross-border basis. This gives local insurers access to a competitive global market with efficient risk and capital structures. Open reinsurance market regimes are essential to the interests of the reinsurer and the insured.

Current regulatory regimes in reinsurance – addressing regional differences

Main regulatory objectives in reinsurance

The fact that reinsurance contracts are agreements between sophisticated parties does not mean that they should not be subject to regulation. Regulators are well aware that in case a primary insurer does not access to adequate reinsurance or is not able to recover reinsurance proceeds from its reinsurers, the financial stability of the insurer could be threatened, leaving policy-holders exposed. Safeguarding the financial health of ceding companies is, therefore, one of the objectives of reinsurance regulation.

Regulators have two complimentary approaches. They place requirements on insurers to monitor their risk exposure as insurers cede their risks to reinsurers to secure capital efficiency. Regulators encourage primary insurers to consider the security of their reinsurance cover by reference to the treaty terms and conditions and to the regulatory position and financial strength ratings of the counterparty.

The other approach is for regulators to supervise reinsurers directly and place capital requirements on them.

The reinsurance industry has proven its resilience by consistently meeting claims following the major insured disasters of modern history; examples that spring to mind are Hurricane Andrew in 1992, and the terrorist attack on the World Trade Center on 11 September 2001, as well as Hurricanes Katrina, Rita and Wilma in 2005 and the Chile earthquake of 2010. Throughout the financial crisis as well, reinsurers continued to operate as usual, meeting their obligations to cedants respectively and providing steady capacity.

The fact that, in the history of reinsurance, only a few insolvencies have been attributable to a primary insurer's inability to recover reinsurance proceeds speaks to the effectiveness of reinsurance business model and regulation.

Since the mid 1990s there has been an increasing political and regulatory focus on reinsurance. Following a spate of severe natural and man-made catastrophes, the losses of which were largely absorbed by reinsurers, the reinsurance industry is under increasing scrutiny. Reinsurance as a contributor to the stability of insurance markets started featuring on the strategic agenda of institutions such as the International Association of Insurance Supervisors (IAIS), the Organisation for Economic Cooperation and Development (OECD), the Financial Stability Forum (today the FSB), and the World Trade Organization (WTO). The respective activities led, for example, to OECD recommendations and IAIS standards on the cross-border provision of reinsurance services, laying out certain criteria according to which supervisors should evaluate the effectiveness of reinsurance cover as well as the security and soundness of selected reinsurers.

The European Union Reinsurance Directive (RID)

Against this backdrop, towards the late 1990s, the EU's fragmented approach to regulating reinsurance companies appeared to be increasingly anachronistic. The RID was enacted as a response, creating a common EU framework of reinsurance regulations as well as a model of an international mutual recognition system applicable to reinsurance regulatory regimes. It came into force in December 2005, more than eleven years after the enactment of the Third Generation of Directives which created a single market for primary insurers. The RID established a similar regulatory environment for EU-based reinsurers: a single reinsurance market in the EU countries plus Norway, Iceland and Liechtenstein, with a reinsurer's home-country licence entitling it to trade throughout all Member States ('single passport').

The RID is based on the proven principles governing EU integration policies. First, it stipulates a minimum harmonisation of certain basic rules which must meet the Directive's requirements. Second, these basic rules and the resulting regulations are mutually recognised across all Member States. Third, supervisory responsibility for branches resides with the parent company's home country authorities.

More specifically, the Directive's requirements comprise the introduction of a solvency regime as well as principles governing the investments of assets covering technical reserves, the abolition of separate capitalisation requirements for branches – which allows for significantly improved capital fungibility and efficiency – the dismantling of legally prescribed deposit requirements as well as unrestricted market access for third-country reinsurers if their home-country regulatory regime is deemed equivalent. These concepts are carried over to Solvency II.

Solvency II – a new global benchmark for insurance and reinsurance regulation

In early 2008, the European Council, together with the European Parliament, approved a joint compromise on the Solvency II Framework Directive, paving the way for the new pan-European approach to assess solvency requirements. When fully implemented, insurers and reinsurers in the European Union will operate under one of the world's most progressive insurance and reinsurance regulatory regime.

The new solvency rules are intended to establish a more risk-sensitive capital regime in a comprehensive risk management framework, which is highly supported by global reinsurers.

A key component of Solvency II is that the use of internal risk models will be permitted to determine the required capital. Many global reinsurers have developed advanced and integrated risk models to price their business, allocate capacity and steer their strategy.

Solvency II is also based on an economic view and takes into account the company's total balance sheet. Under the directive, the company's whole balance sheet should be calculated based on the market-consistent valuation of assets and liabilities.

Major differences between Solvency II and Solvency I system are that the new approach will assess accumulation potential, explicitly recognise diversification benefits and appropriately recognize risk mitigation techniques, such as reinsurance. Diversification is a fundamental principle of reinsurance. Under Solvency II, insurance companies will be required to check whether their available capital is sufficient to sustain rare, large-scale events, taking into account co-dependencies between risk factors, that is to say, their accumulation potential.

For instance, a hurricane can trigger claims in several lines of business at the same time: not just in property insurance, but also in liability and life business. A pandemic would impact life insurance business, but could also cause losses in the company's investment portfolio. Conversely, Solvency II will recognise diversification benefits when there is less than total co-dependence. Because a hurricane in Florida is not co-dependent with an earthquake in Japan, diversification reduces the cost of taking on risk and improves the efficiency of the capital deployed. Reinsurers are specialised in underwriting extreme events and the resilience of the sector has been demonstrated over the last period. Through advanced enterprise risk management and experienced risk modelling, reinsurers have demonstrated their ability to underwrite and absorb large risks. The Solvency II framework is consistent with global reinsurers approach to manage risk portfolio and allocate capacity. The new EU solvency regime is expected to appropriately recognise reinsurance as an effective risk-mitigating instrument.

The US reinsurance modernisation framework

The current reinsurance regulatory regime in the US presents two specific features, which require to be modernised: first, there is no supervision at national or federal level, but at individual state level; and second, special collateral requirements apply to foreign, non-licensed reinsurers.

The efforts to reform the US reinsurance regulation have accelerated over the last years. The National Association of Insurance Commissioners (NAIC) has acknowledged the case for fundamental reform of the statutory collateral rules with the adoption in 2009 of a reinsurance regulatory framework modernisation. The NAIC is also engaged in a comprehensive review of its regulatory system in the context of the Solvency Modernization Initiative (SMI). Reinsurance regulatory modernisation is an integral part of the SMI. Also some states have adopted or introduced revised state credit for reinsurance laws.

The enactment of the Frank-Dodd Act in July 2010, which establishes the Federal Insurance Office (FIO), also contains important improvements in the regulation of reinsurance. The FIO will monitor all aspects of the insurance industry to identify gaps in regulation. In this regard, the FIO will provide regular reports on the US and global reinsurance market. The FIO will also coordinate efforts and develop policy on prudential aspects of international matters. Under the Act, the US government will be authorised to negotiate international agreements on prudential matters. The FIO will have the power to pre-empt state laws which are inconsistent with a covered agreement.

The Frank-Dodd Act also addresses states' extraterritorial regulation of credit for reinsurance and solvency regulation of US reinsurers. The Act prohibits a state in which a US ceding insurer is licensed but not domiciled to deny credit for reinsurance if the ceding insurer's domestic state recognises credit for reinsurance. The Act also makes the US reinsurer's state of domicile the sole regulator of the reinsurer's financial solvency and no other state may require additional information.

Finally, the ongoing developments of Solvency II regime in the EU and particularly the discussions on equivalence between the US and EU regimes have encouraged state regulators, the NAIC and the US government to promote the reform.

The implementation of the reinsurance reform is poised to benefit the US market by improving access to global reinsurance capacity. In a competitive marketplace, lower capital and regulatory costs for (foreign) reinsurers will translate into more attractive premiums, terms and conditions for US households and firms.

Systemic risk and macro-prudential surveillance

The recent financial crisis has highlighted the importance of making the financial system more resilient. The crisis has triggered the creation of new macro-prudential institutions, such as the European Systemic Risk Board (ESRB) in the EU and the Financial Stability Oversight Council (FSOC) in the US. Although the focus is on banking activities, insurance and reinsurance are included in the new macro-prudential framework.

Some supervisors and policy-makers have raised the concern that substantial losses at one or more of the major reinsurers could generate a wide impact on the financial system. Various studies have analysed the potential for systemic risk under extreme circumstances, assessing the possibility of a very large reinsurance shock (sudden failure of one or some major reinsurers) and its impact on the real economy.

The G30 report initiated by the FSB on the topic of systemic risk in 2006 found that the reinsurance industry was unlikely to be a significant source of financial systemic risk. The Geneva Association report of 2010 on systemic risk in insurance came to the same conclusion. The G30 report identified three potential channels through which failure of a large reinsurance company could theoretically lead to adverse effects on the real economy: its impact on the primary insurance industry, the banking sector and the capital markets.

In the event of a reinsurance company failure, primary insurers would have to meet their obligations themselves, instead of through the related reinsurance recoverables. Since only a limited share of total insurance premium is ceded to reinsurers, the effect on the primary insurance sector would be modest.

A reinsurance failure could also affect the primary sector through its investment exposure to reinsurers' equities and bonds, but such exposures are relatively small. The effect of a reinsurance shock on capital markets is also likely to be very limited, since reinsurers' debt, equity, and credit derivative holdings represent only a small fraction of the global market.

A reinsurer's failure would probably lead to higher costs for the insurers in replacing the lost covers; this would be only a short-term effect, however, due to the low market entry barriers and overall strong capitalisation of the reinsurance industry.

Thus, the failure of a large reinsurer would be unlikely to cause widespread insolvencies in the primary insurance market and would have only a minor effect on the financial system and the real economy. Nevertheless, macro-prudential surveillance is essential to monitor the vulnerability of the financial system and identifying the emergence of systemic risks. Global reinsurers welcome the creation of macro-prudential institutions. As a shock absorber, the reinsurance sector plays an important role in the global economy. Global reinsurers adopt long-term investment strategies, providing insured manufacturing and services corporations with essential risk capital. It is therefore critically important that governments secure the business proposition of reinsurers and the benefits of large, cross-border institutions by adopting a tailored approach to micro-supervision, particularly through comprehensive group supervision, as well as macro-prudential surveillance focused on monitoring risk activities.

Reinsurance regulation in the emerging markets

Restrictions to reinsurance market access, although limited in traditional markets, are particularly prevalent in emerging markets. As mentioned before, such restrictions are particularly harmful in reinsurance as reinsurers need to write business on a global basis to be able to diversify their portfolio. Any barriers to accessing international markets impair reinsurers' capacity to absorb peak risk in an economically viable and socially responsible and reliable way. Examples of such restrictions include regulations preventing foreign reinsurers from establishing branches or subsidiaries in a country, equity participation caps and compulsory cessions to 'national' reinsurers and tax penalties for the cedant. Such barriers to market access undermine the role of reinsurance as a highly efficient and effective tool for global risk diversification and absorption.

For international diversification to work, reinsurers need the ability to use their global resources to pay local claims. Restrictions on the free flow of capital for reinsurers curtail their ability to move capital to cover major events. Deposit requirements which compel reinsurers to maintain funds within the country to cover their potential liabilities to ceding companies are an example. Such policies lead to a fragmentation of reinsurers' capital base, requiring companies to maintain larger capital funds than otherwise would be needed. The servicing of that capital adds to the cost of reinsurance and ultimately results in higher premiums for local insurers and policy-holders. As discussed in the US context, such restrictions are not limited to emerging markets.

In general, however, the trend towards liberalising reinsurance market access and modernising regulatory regimes is unstoppable. More and more countries recognize that reinsurance market restrictions ultimately run counter to efforts to accelerate their integration into an increasingly globalised and interconnected world economy. The dismantling of compulsory domestic cessions in China and the abolition of the national reinsurance monopoly in Brazil testify to a generally more open approach to global reinsurance markets and players.

Towards a global regime of mutual recognition – dismantling remaining barriers to market access

A highly effective way of lowering or even dismantling barriers to reinsurance market access is a multilateral regime of mutual recognition. For example, according to Article 50 of the EU Reinsurance Directive, the EU can decide to accept a non-EU country's supervision of reinsurers in place of Member States supervising the EU activities.

Also the Solvency II Directive establishes a framework for recognition of equivalence of supervisory regimes. Reinsurance will be a prime beneficiary of the Directive considerations on equivalence and the overall standardisation of solvency regimes. In this context, reinsurers encourage a flexible, principle-based approach to supervisory recognition. Ultimately, the equivalence process will strengthen worldwide, open and fair reinsurance markets.

Along similar lines, the IAIS is developing international standards and the benefits of mutual recognition are compelling: reinsurers would profit from reduced compliance costs, fewer barriers to market access, greater certainty of the regulatory process and a more efficient allocation of capital. At the end of the day, more reinsurance capacity will be available to primary companies which should ultimately translate into tangible benefits for policy-holders, too.

The increasing convergence of solvency regimes towards a risk-based approach is expected to be a major enabler for the various moves towards mutual recognition. Traditionally, capital requirements for reinsurers have been either the same as those of primary insurers or more liberal, given the fact that reinsurers deal with sophisticated counterparties. Currently, there is a global trend towards capital requirements which are more closely aligned with a (re)insurer's specific risk profile: in addition to insurance risks, risks emanating from financial market exposures, counterparties and operations need to be underpinned by capital.

There is increasing recognition that solvency capital alone is not adequate defence and that there is a vital role for enterprise risk management (ERM). We have seen increasing focus on ERM within firms and increasing demand for firms to demonstrate the quality of their ERM to supervisors. In the US the NAIC has introduced a solvency modernization initiative and ERM is a central part of the EU's Solvency II through the Own Risk and Solvency Assessment process in Pillar II.

Conclusion

The global reinsurance regulatory landscape is undergoing fundamental changes. In 2005, the European Union established a single reinsurance market, based on home-country control and a system of mutual recognition. In the US, a reinsurance modernisation initiative is underway, expected to overcome the current fragmentation of the country's reinsurance supervisory regime and to dismantle collateral requirements which discriminate against foreign providers regardless of their financial strength and credit credentials. In emerging markets, global reinsurers and policy-holders benefit from increasingly more open market access regimes, with China and Brazil being the most relevant examples.

These developments reflect policy-makers' growing confidence in the basic economics of reinsurance as a highly efficient, effective and secure way of diversifying ever increasing insured loss potentials – provided it is permitted to operate on a truly global basis. The global reinsurance system has repeatedly proven its resilience: In recent history it has withstood three major 'Black Swan' events: 9/11, Hurricane Katrina and the near meltdown of the global financial system following the demise of Lehman Brothers in September 2008.

Against this backdrop, policy-makers worldwide evermore recognize reinsurers' role as capable and reliable managers of the largest exposures presented by an increasingly complex and interdependent global risk landscape. And they also understand that any barriers imposed on global reinsurers would ultimately harm their national economies. Insurers, reinsurers and regulators should make every effort to establish a suitable global market place for reinsurance services: regulatory convergence and mutual recognition will be key to this.

Bibliography

Carter, R.L. (2000) *Reinsurance*, 4th edn (Euromoney Institutional Investor).

Evans, A.M. (2007) 'The EU Reinsurance Directive', *The Geneva Papers*, 32.

G30 (2006) *Reinsurance and International Financial Markets.*

IAIS (2008) *Guidance Paper on the Mutual Recognition of Reinsurance Supervision.*

IAIS (2010) *Global Reinsurance Market Report*, mid-year 2010.

Laws, T. (2009) Reinsurance Regulation in the U.S. – An Opportunity to Move into the 21st Century, *Journal of Reinsurance*, 16.

Swiss Re (2005) *Understanding Reinsurance*, 2005.

Swiss Re (2010) *The Essential Guide to Reinsurance*, 2010.

Swiss Re (2010) sigma, *Regulatory Issues in Insurance*, March.

The Geneva Association (2010) *Systemic Risk in Insurance: An Analysis of Insurance and Financial Stability* (Geneva: The Geneva Association).

Vogelgesang, R., and M. Kubicek (2007) 'Towards a Global Approach to Reinsurance Regulation', *The Geneva Papers on Risk and Insurance: Issues and Practice*, 32.

Part IV

Stakeholder Protection

12 Challenges and Approaches to Consumer Protection in the Insurance Industry

Sharon Tennyson

Introduction

Insurance markets are important in both the micro- and macroeconomies of most developed nations. At the microeconomic level, insurance facilitates risk-taking by both individuals and firms. Providing indemnification for losses increases the marginal productivity of capital by removing the need for holding large contingency funds, and in this way leads to a more efficient allocation of resources (Ćurak et al., 2009). This supports risk-averse individuals in making large purchases such as real estate, and encourages innovation by firms in risk-producing activities (Ward and Zurbruegg, 2000). At the macroeconomic level, insurance premiums amount to nearly 10% of gross domestic product (GDP) in the average Organisation for Economic Cooperation and Development (OECD) country in 2007 (OECD, 2010). Insurance as a percentage of GDP is typically less in developing countries, but many of these markets are growing at a rapid pace. Insurance market development has been shown to be related to overall economic development, and is a driver of economic growth (Outreville, 1990; Ward and Zurbruegg, 2000; Ćurak et al., 2009).

Although unfettered competition is generally thought to be the best way to promote market development, in insurance as in other financial services it has long been recognised that uninhibited competition may in fact hinder the market. The intangible nature of financial products leads to markets which rely heavily on trust and consumer confidence. Because of complexity and uncertainty, it is not possible to contractually specify firm behaviour in every possible state of the world. This contractual incompleteness reduces consumer demand for services. Legal and/or regulatory safeguards are therefore essential to promoting healthy financial markets.

As it has developed in the modern regulatory context, consumer protections in insurance markets focus primarily on safeguarding consumers from unfair practices, misrepresentations, or unwarranted risk in insurance transactions. Specific regulatory concerns include the design of insurance contracts, including contractual language; insurer selling methods, sales materials and advertisements; insurer underwriting and insurance coverage denials; insurance pricing; and claims payments. Regulator actions may take on several dimensions, including promoting market transparency, restricting specific behaviours, and facilitating consumer redress.

Despite many common elements of consumer protection regulation across jurisdictions, regulators have considerable discretion regarding the scope and form of consumer protection, and regulatory philosophies vary. Traditional regulatory approaches focus on establishing rules that insurers and intermediaries must adhere to in their dealings with consumers. More progressive regulatory approaches focus on establishing principles for market conduct and good faith dealings with customers, and requiring firms to establish internal standards and procedures for complying with those principles. In some cases industry self-regulatory bodies, rather than government agencies, have primary responsibility for defining and enforcing industry standards.

Furthermore, the decisions of government regulators or self-regulatory bodies make up only one portion of consumer protection oversight of insurers. The most basic consumer protections for insurance consumers are the general legal protections that assure that insurance contracts will be honoured. Insurance firms are also subject to statutory or common law principles that prohibit fraud, deception and unfair trade practices. State or national legislatures may also pass bills specific to the insurance sector to supplement these general protections, and the courts may afford additional protections specifically to insurance consumers. Insurance supervisory authorities oversee the enforcement of these laws and usually have the authority to make additional regulations. The relative importance of administrative, legislative and judicial oversight of consumer protections in insurance markets varies across jurisdictions and across areas of regulatory concern.

The global financial crisis has undermined trust in financial institutions and reduced faith that market discipline alone can effectively regulate the behaviour of firms. As a result, strengthening consumer protections has become a cornerstone of financial regulatory reform proposals. These events provide a timely opportunity to examine the purpose and design of consumer protections in insurance markets, and to consider alternative approaches. This chapter considers consumer protection regulation in insurance markets, describing regulatory approaches and evaluating regulations in the context of rationales for providing consumer protections. The chapter is organised as follows. The next section discusses the rationales for providing consumer protections in insurance markets. The major approaches to consumer protection regulation are then described, and similarities and differences across jurisdictions are considered. The final section of the chapter discusses the challenges faced in designing and implementing effective and efficient consumer protection regulations.

Objectives of consumer protection

Correcting information disparities

A primary objective of consumer protection regulation is to enhance the transparency of the insurance contracting environment by reducing information asymmetries faced by consumers. An insurance contract provides a financial guarantee of payments from the insurer if the policy-holder experiences specific adverse events. While its premise is simple, insurance contracts themselves are complex. Events that will trigger payments may occur in the distant future but must be specifically defined in ways that allow insurers to accurately price the product and verify losses that occur. Due to the complexity of this promise, complete contracts are difficult to write and it is a practical impossibility to assure that policy-holders are as well informed as insurers in making the transaction.

For example, the quality characteristics of an insurance policy include the strength of both the insurer's ability and willingness to pay losses and the breadth of loss events covered under the policy in relation to the potential size and scope of losses. These quality characteristics are difficult to know with certainty due to the contingent nature of the claim payment services provided, and the fact that these services are provided in the future. Additionally, product differences are often manifested in details regarding investment strategies and returns, the definition of insured events, or the amounts of coverage extended for specific events. Finally, product quality has an individual component because the quality of an insurance product includes the appropriateness of the product for the purchaser's needs.

The quality of an insurance contract also depends on the insurer's claims payment services. This aspect of quality may be particularly difficult for consumers to observe because it can change after the purchase of the contract and varies across contracts based on insurer decisions. Insurance claims can be complex and policy language cannot fully anticipate all of the nuances of a loss. Claim settlement disputes may arise between insurers and policy-holders due to differences in beliefs about the validity of a claim under the terms of the insurance policy, or the value of compensable losses experienced. Specific disputes cannot be anticipated and contracted over at the time of policy purchase.

Perhaps equally important, an insurer may gain financially by refusing to pay a claim or by reducing payment for a claim. For example, an insurer may attempt to deny or may strategically delay settlement of a particular claim for the purpose of coercing the policy-holder to accept a reduced settlement amount (Sykes, 1996). Similarly, an insurer may develop a strategy of routinely denying or underpaying small claims, based on the calculation that small claimants will have little incentive to invest in the costs of disputing the decision (Tennyson and Asmat, 2011). Insurers cannot make a fully binding commitment in the insurance contract that prevents them from (ever) denying payment of a legitimate claim.

On the other hand, competitive market forces should work to protect consumers from problems associated with information disadvantages. If consumers lack confidence that a firm provides products and services that meet quality expectations, consumer willingness to purchase will be greatly reduced. However, such reputation constraints may work only imperfectly in insurance markets. Because poor quality is difficult to discern even after purchase, and/or is realised only with a significant time lag, market discipline may not yield sufficiently large or timely penalties to overcome market failures.

Insurance prices may also not yield a reliable signal of insurance quality. Price comparisons are complicated since insurance premium rates differ across individuals. The premium rate will depend upon individual risk characteristics, which may vary with a variety of factors including sex, age, marital status, medical history, condition of insured property, place of residence, type of business, and financial history (Iuppa, 2006). Thus it is difficult for consumers to distinguish price differences based on quality differences from those based on risk differences.

The emerging field of psychology and economics provides an additional set of reasons that competitive market forces may not provide sufficient consumer protections in markets such as insurance.[1] The perspective of this field is that regulation may be necessary because of cognitive limitations and psychological biases in consumers' risk decisions. Evidence from experimental and empirical studies suggests that consumers do not have a good feel for probabilities, do not treat losses and gains symmetrically, and tend to overestimate emotionally-laden loss events while underestimating low-probability loss events. In the insurance context these tendencies may lead to: a focus on short-term costs (low premiums) while ignoring the reduction in longer-term services accompanying them; poor choice of deductibles and contract limits; and the failure to purchase insurance that should be valued or the purchase of insurance that has little value under rational expectations (Kirsch, 2002).

Promoting access to insurance

In some jurisdictions, the objectives of consumer protection regulation also include promoting insurance affordability and availability for consumers. These objectives are pursued through regulations that restrict market-determined premium rates either directly (as through rate regulation) or indirectly (as through restrictions on premium rating factors). Such restrictions may be applied only in selected markets, and often have a particular focus on protecting access for high-risk consumers. Most observers agree that these regulations are more typically addressing social policy objectives than market failures.

Economic theory does not provide a rationale for restrictions on market-determined prices if insurance markets are competitive. If insurance markets are concentrated or insurance pricing is determined by cartels, price-reducing regulation may be justified. It should be noted, however, that this has not often been the situation in price-regulated insurance markets. Many studies of the impact of price regulation, undertaken in earlier time periods when regulation was more common, indicate that regulation often raised insurance premium rates and appeared to facilitate cartel pricing and entry barriers (Joskow, 1973; Finsinger, 1986).

Insurance price regulation has become less pervasive over time, and where it is imposed it has shifted toward an emphasis on lowering prices. The current regulatory rationale is not to counteract monopoly power, but more generally to enhance insurance affordability or price equity. Even in competitive insurance markets not every consumer faces low insurance prices or prices that he/she finds affordable. Moreover, a fundamental requirement of competitive insurance pricing is that prices reflect the expected value of a consumer's insured losses. Consumers who face greater accident risk face higher insurance premiums to reflect the greater risk they impose on the insurance system. This is the characteristic of insurance pricing which generates regulatory interest in restricting market prices. Tempering differences in prices across consumers reduces price disparities and attempts to put insurance within the reach of all consumers. Consistent with this idea, insurance markets in which price regulation is most common are those in which insurance is mandatory or in which universal insurance coverage is thought to be socially desirable (Tennyson, 2007).

An added factor contributing to regulatory pressure is that insurance pricing is not perfectly correlated with risk. Insurers must set premiums based on observable characteristics that they find to be correlated with loss experience. Insurers may also adjust premiums over time based on observed loss experience since this provides a signal of the expected value of future losses. Because premium variation is more readily visible than risk variation, high prices or large price differences across consumers may lead to the perception that insurance premiums are unfairly determined or unfairly discriminatory. This often leads to consumer demand for price regulation (Blackmon and Zeckhauser, 1991; Jaffee and Russell, 1998).

Concerns about price discrimination also lead to regulatory restrictions on rate classifications. In many jurisdictions regulations limit insurers' ability to charge different insurance premiums to consumers with different characteristics. Restrictions on rate classification lead to coarser rating matrices, and thus to less premium variation than would exist under open competition. This may also facilitate social objectives regarding rate equity, and may serve other objectives including risk-spreading, income redistribution or premium stability (Pauly, 1970;

Abraham, 1985; Blackmon and Zeckhauser, 1991). Limiting premium variation across consumers leads to premium cross-subsidies from low-risk to high-risk consumers. However, cross-subsidies are inefficient forms of risk-spreading or redistribution if they distort insurance decisions.

The potential distortions from classification restrictions are well known. Consumers who receive insurance premium subsidies face less than the true marginal cost of insurance and may purchase more insurance than is socially desirable, and those who face premium overcharges may purchase less.[2] Nonetheless, there are market circumstances in which premium cross-subsidies from low risks to high risks represent a constrained efficient outcome (Crocker and Snow, 1986). One important circumstance is when market imperfections lead some consumers to fail to purchase insurance, and the uninsured impose negative externalities on other market participants (Shavell, 1986). In this case an efficiency argument for regulated premium cross-subsidies may arise. Cross-subsidies reduce premiums for high-risk consumers, promoting universal coverage by facilitating insurance purchase among this group (Picard, 2008). Social gains may be realised because greater insurance purchase by high-risk consumers reduces the external costs borne by others.

This reasoning provides a theoretical justification for regulated rate cross-subsidies, but achieving social gains depends on two important assumptions. The first is that the price elasticity of low-risk consumers' demand for insurance is not too great. Otherwise, low-risk consumers may drop out of the insurance market in large numbers as a result of paying cross-subsidising premiums. This market unravelling will create efficiency losses. The second is that cross-subsidies do not have noticeable effects on other decisions that increase the risk of loss. For example, insurance premium subsidies may not distort decisions to participate in insured activities and may reduce incentives to prevent or avoid losses. If these responses occur greater risk-taking and higher loss costs will result, working against regulatory goals, and create efficiency losses.

Approaches to consumer protection

We observe substantial heterogeneity across countries in the protections offered to consumers in insurance markets. Although a common set of basic consumer protection mechanisms exist in all countries, differences across jurisdictions arise in definitions and standards for even these common protections. Establishment of international regulatory standards is promoted in international forums including the International Association of Insurance Supervisors (IAIS) and the OECD, but progress toward standardisation has been modest (Brown, 2009). Similarly, the efforts of the European Union (EU) to harmonise insurance regulation among member nations, and efforts of the National Association of Insurance Commissioners (NAIC) to harmonise regulation across the US states, have been only partially successful. This section of the chapter describes the major forms of consumer protection regulations in insurance markets, and the similarities and differences in regulations across countries.

Prudential regulation – to maintain the financial safety and soundness of insurers – is universal, and arises in direct response to problems of unobservable quality. Rules that require insurers to maintain adequate capital and regulatory oversight of capital and risk-taking are traditional approaches, but definitions, restrictions and oversight philosophies differ across countries. For example, solvency supervision is harmonised within the EU under Solvency I and will change substantially with the adoption of Solvency II in 2013, but the US risk-based capital approach remains distinct (Eling et al., 2009). Brown (2009) notes that IAIS principles are more in line with those of Europe, but that for some countries adopting IAIS standards would require substantial changes in insurance solvency regulation. Many observers predict that Solvency II will become the international standard, and it remains to be seen whether solvency regimes will converge or continue to evolve separately.

In some jurisdictions guaranty funds provide added backing to prudential regulation. Guaranty funds provide payment of claims or continued insurance coverage to consumers in the event that their insurance provider becomes insolvent. This is a way to pool the risk of insurer insolvency, since most funds are financed via assessments to insurers. The role and need for guaranty funds is less clear than that of prudential regulation, and guaranty funds are not universally provided. All US states provide guaranty for both life and non-life insurance. However, only ten countries among 24 recently-surveyed OECD countries provide relatively complete guaranty protection schemes for non-life insurance, and seven do so for life insurance (OECD, 2008). Less than half of the EU countries have any form of insurance guaranty scheme and many that exist are limited in scope (Oxera, 2007). Funding mechanisms for guaranty funds also differ across countries, with some operating on a post-assessment basis and others on a pre-assessment basis.

Guaranty funds are rarely accessed in those jurisdictions that provide them. For example, a recent study of guaranty funds in the European Union finds that reports that guaranty fund payouts amount to far less than 1% of premiums per year in the typical country (ibid.); total payouts are similarly small in the US, even though insurer insolvencies are relatively more frequent (Oxera, 2007). Guaranty funds are therefore more correctly seen as mechanisms to enhance consumer confidence in insurance markets, by increasing the credibility of the insurance promise. One potential downside of guaranty funds is that moral hazard may be created. Insurance consumers may reduce their monitoring of insurer safety in response to the existence of a guaranty fund, although this effect seems unlikely to be dramatic. Of larger concern is that guaranty funds may lead to greater risk-taking among insurers or to greater regulatory forbearance among regulators, resulting in more frequent insolvencies and higher costs per insolvency (Lee et al., 1997; Grace et al., 2005; Oxera, 2007).

Efforts to increase market transparency and reduce transactions costs are important elements of consumer protection in insurance. Insurers along with firms in other industries are subject to laws governing unfair, misleading or deceptive practices of sellers. In addition, most countries have in place specific legislation regarding insurance contracts, in which the rights and responsibilities of insurance firms and consumers are delineated. The extent to which these laws provide additional protections to consumers of insurance contracts varies. In the United States and Canada protections are stronger than in most other jurisdictions. However, many countries – including Australia, China and countries in the European Union – are moving toward strengthening consumer protections provided in insurance contract law by expanding the duties of insurers, the rights of insurance consumers, and the mechanisms to enforce fair treatment of consumers.

Insurers' duty to disclose important contract terms and explain to consumers the terms and conditions of policies is an important area of regulatory oversight. Most countries have provisions governing communications and advertising, requiring, for example, that communications must be fair, clear and not misleading and cannot omit material facts (Joint Forum, 2008). Among the 73 countries that provided information to the IAIS in 2010,[3] about two thirds require insurers to provide the definition of each policy benefit, the premium for each benefit, the law applicable to the contract, means of terminating the contract, and arrangements for handling complaints (IAIS, 2010). Some jurisdictions specifically impose 'plain language' requirements, but others do not. However, legal standards of contract law in common law countries and in some civil law countries often hold insurers to a higher standard of contract clarity – ruling against insurers in disputes over unclear policy language (Law Commission and Scottish Law Commission, 2010).

The actions of insurance intermediaries (sales agents) come under separate regulatory scrutiny. The intermediary is an important source of information for consumers, and a potential remedy to consumer information disadvantages. However, intermediaries are also in a position to exploit consumers' lack of information for their own financial gain. To protect consumers from high-pressure sales tactics or mis-selling, 48 of the 73 countries reporting data to the IAIS mandate a 'cooling-off' period (within which the policy-holder may withdraw from the contract) for life insurance policies; 27 mandate a cooling-off period for non-life policies (IAIS, 2010). Intermediaries are additionally required to adhere to codes of ethical conduct, are subject to training requirements, and in some cases to tests for competence and necessary skills, but standards vary across jurisdictions. Licensing requirements and standards also vary.

Some jurisdictions, including the EU, the US, Canada, Japan and Australia, require agents selling products that have an investment component to provide impartial advice, and to offer products that are suitable to a customer's needs and risk tolerance. The Basel Committee (Joint Forum, 2008) notes, however, that suitability requirements for insurance companies are generally less comprehensive than for banks and securities dealers. From among 90 financial services firms surveyed, insurance companies collected less information from consumers before making an investment recommendation, and were less likely to keep a record of recommendations made, than other investment companies (ibid.). The allowable forms of compensation to intermediaries may also be regulated, and/or intermediaries may be required to reveal to consumers potential conflicts of interest arising from the nature of their compensation. However, disclosure of intermediary compensation was provided by only 40% of life insurers surveyed (ibid.).

Regulating through disclosure requirements is consistent with the information-based rationale for consumer protection, since economic theory points to disclosure as the most direct solution for information failures. However, if consumers have difficulty making effective use of disclosures, direct restrictions on products and seller behaviours may produce better market outcomes (Trebilcock, 2003; Schwarcz, 2009). For example, product standardisation may facilitate consumer comparison shopping and simplify the information consumers need to make informed choices (Grace and Scott, 2009). Some observers argue that the complexity of insurance products and potential for services to vary across consumers and over time make reliance solely on disclosure problematic in insurance markets (Tennyson, 2010; Rees et al., 1999).

Consistent with this idea, research suggests that many consumers do not understand insurance disclosures, and most consumers do not read them (Cude, 2005). Survey evidence also suggests that consumers have a poor understanding of policy language and terms (NAIC, 2010; OECD, 2008). Particularly since the global financial crisis, many countries are working to strengthen disclosure regulation in financial markets. Improving the effectiveness of disclosures may be achieved through the design of better disclosures and through consumer education (Rutledge, 2010).

Countries that treat issues of insurer market conduct on a par with those in other industries are more likely than others to rely primarily on information disclosure to protect consumers in insurance transactions. For example, disclosure requirements appear to be the most stringent in the EU and Australia (Joint Forum, 2008), where direct regulation of prices and products are less prevalent. This belies a belief that market discipline can be effective in insurance markets, and recognition of the efficiency costs of restricting competitive market forces.

Prior to the EU's Third Generation Insurance Directive in 1994, prices and products in some European insurance markets were closely regulated and competition was limited (Eling et al., 2009). For example, Rees and Kessner (1999) note that in the German life insurance market contracts were standardized, premiums were regulated and all firms had to offer the same guaranteed interest rate. Insurance markets in Italy, France, Spain and Portugal were also highly regulated (Farny, 1999). Since 1994, direct regulation of insurance premium rates has been eliminated in the EU, and markets have been opened to cross-border competition. Some indirect restrictions on prices remain in individual EU countries, however, especially in private passenger automobile insurance and health insurance (Eling et al., 2009).

In other jurisdictions, including the US and Canada, we observe a greater focus on direct regulation of insurance prices and products. Policy forms and insurance products are subject to regulatory prior approval. Product restrictions including mandated coverage provisions may be enforced. According to the IAIS, 58 of the 73 countries reporting data in 2010 mandate policy content of some non-life classes of insurance, and 30 mandate policy content in some life insurance classes. Additionally, 29 countries require regulatory approval of all life and pension products prior to market launch, and another eight require prior approval of some pension or life annuity products. Nineteen countries require prior approval of all non-life products, and another 14 countries require approval of selected non-life products (IAIS, 2010).

Regulation of insurance premium rates may be imposed through the direct setting of insurance rates by regulators, or by requiring prior approval of rates introduced by firms. IAIS data show that 15 of 73 countries reporting data require prior approval of rates in all life insurance classes, and five countries require prior approval of selected life insurance classes. In non-life insurance, regulatory prior approval of rates is required for all classes in eleven countries and for selected classes in ten countries (ibid.). Premiums may also be indirectly regulated by regulating insurers' risk classification practices or by limiting expense charges, for example. Premium and underwriting restrictions may also be accompanied by requirements to offer insurance, presumably to counteract insurers' incentives to avoid insuring consumers who are unprofitable under the rating restrictions.

Residual markets (or high-risk pools) organised by government or private sector pooling arrangements may also be set up to provide insurance to consumers who are unable to obtain coverage from a private insurer at market rates. High-risk pools deal with the problem of insufficient capacity in the private insurance market by offering insurance (usually at subsidised rates) to consumers unable to obtain insurance elsewhere. Associated losses from the pool are funded by loss-sharing among private insurers or through the general tax burden. Government-backed risk-pooling arrangements are offered in many countries throughout the world for catastrophe risks such as terrorism and natural hazards. The need for risk-pooling arrangements in other risk areas is generally small except when restrictions on market pricing lead to voluntary market shortages. For example, in some US states and Canadian provinces with strict regulation of automobile or homeowners' insurance pricing, residual market mechanisms can be important and have sometimes grown to insure a large fraction of the market (Grabowski et al., 1989; Grace and Klein, 2009; Derrig and Tennyson, forthcoming).

Although insurance contract laws and regulations aim to prevent consumer harms, systems must also be established to make remedies available when something goes wrong. Facilitating consumer compensation for harms strengthens market discipline by providing consumers with cost-effective redress mechanisms in the event of contract disputes. In many countries a financial services or insurance ombudsman office (within or separate from the regulator) is empowered to adjudicate consumer disputes with insurance companies (CCIR, 2004; Schwarcz, 2009). Although systems differ across countries, Schwarcz (2009) notes that ombudsman programmes combine insurers' internal complaint handling, state-provided complaint handling, and arbitration into a coordinated system. An important element of an ombudsman's role in mediating disputes between insurers and consumers is that the ombudsman is legally empowered to bind insurers to its decisions.

An alternative avenue for consumer redress is through private lawsuits against insurers. The private legal avenues available to policy-holders to pursue actions against their insurers for bad faith in claims settlement are particularly well developed in the United States and Canada, where a consumer whose claim has been unfairly denied or delayed may often recover for all harm or injuries sustained, and punitive damages may also be awarded.[4] These damages extend far beyond those available in other countries. In most countries punitive damages are not allowed, and in some countries (including England) no compensation beyond the insurance payment and interest due may be awarded (Law Commission and Scottish Law Commission, 2010). Making it more likely that policy-holders may be granted large damages awards will provide insurers with added incentives to engage in fair and efficient claims settlement practices. However, this may also affect insurance contracting in ways that are not socially beneficial. For example, it may create incentives for policy-holders to initiate questionable bad faith actions or reduce the willingness of insurers to vigorously challenge suspicious claims (Tennyson and Warfel, 2008).

Challenges in providing consumer protection regulation

Consumer information disadvantages in insurance transactions lead to the potential for insurer misrepresentation of products or manipulation of product quality. An important implication of persistent information asymmetries is that consumer confidence in the honesty of service providers and the quality of products is essential to the functioning of insurance markets. If consumers lack confidence that insurers provides products and services that meet quality expectations, consumer willingness to purchase will be greatly reduced. Consumers' recognition of their information and decision-making disadvantages may also undermine confidence in the market, reducing beneficial exchanges. For these reasons, legal and regulatory restrictions on insurers' market conduct are important not only to protect consumers but to promote the efficient functioning of markets and continued trade in insurance.

There are nonetheless a number of important challenges in providing effective and efficient consumer protections in insurance markets. Regulations may reduce freedom of competition in markets but as we have seen competition may not provide effective consumer protections. Choosing regulations that produce the most protection for the minimum market distortion is the key regulatory challenge. Preserving efficient markets requires recognition that regulations restrict competition and generate unintended consequences. Preserving regulatory effectiveness requires trading these against the costs of consumer information and the costs to markets of loss of consumer confidence. Moreover, because regulatory restrictions are both costly and imperfect, one must consider whether regulation can deliver benefits in excess of its costs.

Direct restrictions on products and prices lead to efficiency costs in markets. But imposing fewer direct restrictions may necessitate a higher degree of monitoring and higher regulatory enforcement costs (Trebilcock, 2003). As previously noted, reputation constraints are not likely to be sufficient to ensure that market outcomes will maximise consumer benefits. For exactly these reasons statements of principles are not sufficient to ensure appropriate behaviours by all firms and intermediaries. Detection and enforcement is therefore especially important and poses particular challenges under principles-based regulation, and represent a potential weakness in such systems. Self-regulatory organisations may also possess insufficient enforcement authority or resolve. The insurance industry has an incentive to monitor the actions of individual firms and sales agents to prevent actions that undermine industry reputation. However, governments may be interested in stronger regulations and generally have stronger enforcement mechanisms available.[5]

Consumer insurance literacy – or the lack thereof – poses another real challenge to consumer protection regulation. Consumers of insurance appear to be relatively poorly informed. Research suggests that most consumers are not very effective insurance shoppers and lack good understanding of insurance policy terms and requirements. Research on consumers' acquisition of insurance knowledge suggests that word-of-mouth and informal sources are the dominant information-gathering strategies, and that consumers switch insurance providers much less frequently than would be optimal. These shortcomings weaken market discipline and create pressure for direct regulatory intervention into insurance markets.

The political economy of consumer protection regulation creates additional challenges. Regulating for reasons of social policy, such as fairness and redistribution, is difficult to do in a manner that continues to promote a healthy insurance market. Responding to calls for greater regulation in the aftermath of the financial crisis also raises challenges, since regulatory over-reaction is common in such circumstances. Markets are dynamic while regulations are static. Due to regulatory inertia and the rise of new interest groups, regulations tend to remain in place even as circumstances change (Coate and Morris, 1999). Thus, remaining relevant is a final challenge. These considerations are important as recent events make clear that the failure of regulations to adjust to changing market conditions can have very negative effects.

Notes

1. See the discussions in Camerer et al. (2003), Thaler and Sunstein (2008) and Barr et al. (2008).
2. See the discussions in Pauly (1970), Abraham (1985) and Harrington and Doerpinghaus (1993).
3. The IAIS has over 140 member countries, but not all countries report data on insurance supervision to the IAIS database. Although all US states and the NAIC are members of the IAIS, only the NAIC and the state of Oklahoma provided data to the IAIS; thus, there is little double-counting of US laws in the database. The data reported here do not double-count US responses.
4. Legal standards for insurer bad faith liability vary by state in the US. See Tennyson and Warfel (2010) for an in-depth discussion of first-party insurer bad faith law in the US.
5. Governments may be interested in stronger regulations because their focus is on maximising aggregate benefits rather than benefits to the industry. In perfectly competitive markets there is no conflict between those two goals; however, once we deviate from perfect competition there may be.

Bibliography

Abraham, K.S. (1985) 'Efficiency and Fairness in Insurance Risk Classification', *Virginia Law Review*, 71: 403–51.

Barr, M.S., S. Mullainathan and E. Shafir (2008) 'Behaviorally Informed Financial Services Regulation'. New American Foundation Working Paper, October.

Blackmon, B.G., Jr, and R. Zeckhauser (1991) 'Mispriced Equity: Regulated Rates for Auto Insurance in Massachusetts', *American Economic Review*, 81: 65–9.

Brown, E.F. (2009) 'The Development of International Norms for Insurance Regulation,' *Brooklyn Journal of International Law*, 34(3): 953–97.

Camerer, C., et. al. (2003) 'Regulation for Conservatives: Behavioral Economics and the Case for Asymmetric Paternalism', *University of Pennsylvania Law Review*.

CCIR (Canadian Council of Insurance Regulators) (2004) *Risk-Based Market Conduct Regulation*.

Coate, S., and S. Morris (1999) 'Policy Persistence', *American Economic Review*, 89(5): 1327–36.

Crocker, K.J., and A. Snow (1986) 'The Efficiency Effects of Categorical Discrimination in the Insurance Industry', *Journal of Political Economy*, 94: 320–44.

Cude, B. (2005) 'Insurance Disclosures: An Effective Mechanism to Increase Consumers' Market Power?' *Journal of Insurance Regulation*, 24(2): 57–80.

Ćurak, M., S. Lončar and K. Poposki (2009) 'Insurance Sector Development and Economic Growth in Transition Countries', *International Research Journal of Finance and Economics*, 34: 29–41.

Derrig, R.A., and S. Tennyson (forthcoming) 'The Impact of Rate Regulation on Claims: Evidence from Massachusetts Automobile Insurance', *Risk Management and Insurance Review*.

Eling, M., R.W. Klein and J.T. Schmit (2009), *Insurance Regulation in the United States and the European Union: A Comparison, Policy Report* (Oakland, CA: The Independent Institute).

Farny, D. (1999) 'The Development of European Private Sector Insurance over the Last 25 Years and the Conclusions That Can Be Drawn for Business Management Theory of Insurance Companies', *Geneva Papers on Risk and Insurance*, 24(2): 145–62.

Finsinger, J. (1986) 'A State-controlled Market: The German Case', in J. Finsinger and M.-V. Pauly (eds), *The Economics of Insurance Regulation: A Cross-national Study* (New York: St Martin's Press).

Grabowski, H., W.K. Viscusi and W.N. Evans (1989) 'Price-Availability Tradeoffs of Automobile Insurance Regulation', *Journal of Risk and Insurance*, 56: 275–99.

Grace, M.F., and R.W. Klein (2009) 'The Perfect Storm: Hurricanes, Insurance, and Regulation', *Risk Management and Insurance Review*, 12(1): 81–124.

Grace, M.F., and H. Scott (2009) 'An Optional Federal Charter for Insurance: Rationale and Design', in Grace, M.F., and R.W. Klein (eds), *The Future of Insurance Regulation in the United States* (Washington: Brookings Institution Press).

Grace, M.F., R.W. Klein and R.D. Phillips (2005) 'Insurance Company Failures: Why Do They Cost So Much?' Working paper, Center for Risk Management and Insurance Research, Georgia State University.

Harrington, S.E., and H.I. Doerpinghaus (1993) 'The Economics and Politics of Automobile Insurance Rate Classification', *Journal of Risk and Insurance*, 60: 59–84.

IAIS (2010) Insurance Laws Database, www.iaisweb.org/index.cfm?pageID=53.

Iuppa, A. (2006) *Insurance Regulatory Reform*. Testimony before the US Senate Committee on Banking, Housing and Urban Affairs, 11 July.

Jaffee, D.M., and T. Russell (1998) 'The Causes and Consequences of Rate Regulation in the Auto Insurance Industry', in David F. Bradford (ed.), *The Economics of Property-casualty Insurance* (Chicago: University of Chicago Press).

Joint Forum (2008) *Customer Suitability in the Retail Sale of Financial Products and Services* (Basel: Bank for International Settlements).

Joskow, P. (1973) 'Cartels, Competition and Regulation in the Property Liability Insurance Industry', *Bell Journal of Economics and Management Science*, 4: 375–427.

Keeton, W.R., and E. Kwerel (1984) 'Externalities in Automobile Insurance and the Underinsured Driver Problem', *Journal of Law and Economics*, 27: 149–79.

Kirsch, L. (2002) 'Do Product Disclosures Inform and Safeguard Insurance Policyholders?' *Journal of Insurance Regulation*, 20(3): 271–95.

Klein, R.W., and J.W. Schacht (2001) 'An Assessment of Insurance Market Conduct Surveillance', *Journal of Insurance Regulation*, 20(1): 51–93.

Law Commission and Scottish Law Commission (2010) *Insurance Contract Law: Damages for Late Payment and the Insurer's Duty of Good Faith*, Issues Paper 6 (London).

Lee, S., D. Mayers and C.W. Smith, Jr (1997) 'Guaranty Funds and Risk-Taking: Evidence from the Insurance Industry', *Journal of Financial Economics*, 44: 3–24.

NAIC (2010) *New NAIC Insurance IQ Study Reveals Americans Lacking in Confidence, Knowledge of Insurance Choices*. Press Release, 6 April.

OECD (2008) *Improving Financial Education and Awareness on Insurance and Private Pensions* (Paris: OECD).

OECD (2010) *Insurance Statistics Yearbook* (Paris: OECD).

Outreville, J.F. (1990) The Economic Significance of Insurance Markets in Developing Countries, *Journal of Risk and Insurance*, 57(3): 487–98.

Oxera (2007) *Insurance Guarantee Schemes in the EU: Comparative Analysis of Existing Schemes, Analysis of Problems and Evaluation of Options* (Oxford).

Pauly, M.V. (1970) 'The Welfare Economics of Community Rating', *Journal of Risk and Insurance*, 37: 407–18.

Picard, P. (2008) 'National Disaster Insurance and the Equity Efficiency Trade-off', *Journal of Risk and Insurance*, 75: 17–38.

Rees, R., and E. Kessner (1999) 'Regulation and Efficiency in European Insurance Markets', *Economic Policy*, 14(29): 363–98.

Rees, R., et al. (1999) 'Regulation and Efficiency in European Insurance Markets', *Economic Policy*, 14(29): 365–97.

Regan, L.S., S. Tennyson and M.A. Weiss (2008) 'The Relationship Between Auto Insurance Rate Regulation and Insured Loss Costs: An Empirical Analysis', *Journal of Insurance Regulation*, 27: 23–46.

Rutledge, S.L. (2010) 'Consumer Protection and Financial Literacy: Lessons from Nine Country Studies', Working Paper, Europe and Central Asia Region, Financial and Private Sector Department, World Bank.

Schwarcz, D. (2009) 'Redesigning Consumer Dispute Resolution: A Case Study of the British and American Approaches to Insurance Claims Conflict', *Tulane Law Review*, 83: 735–812.

Shavell, S. (1986) 'The Judgment Proof Problem', *International Review of Law and Economics*, 6: 45–58.

Smith, E., and R. Wright (1992) 'Why is Automobile Insurance in Philadelphia so Damn Expensive?' *American Economic Review*, 82: 756–72.

Sykes, A.O. (1996) '"Bad Faith" Breach of Contract by First-Party Insurers', *Journal of Legal Studies*, 25: 405–44.

Tennyson, S. (1997) 'The Impact of Rate Regulation on State Automobile Insurance Markets', *Journal of Insurance Regulation*, 15(4) (Summer): 502–23.

Tennyson, S., (2007) *Efficiency Consequences of Insurance Rate Regulation*, Policy Brief 2007-PB-03 Networks Financial Institute.

Tennyson, S. (2010) *Rethinking Consumer Protection Regulation in Insurance Markets*, Policy Brief 2010-PB-07, Networks Financial Institute.

Tennyson, S., and D. Asmat (2011) 'How do "Bad Faith" Laws Affect Insurance Settlements?' Working paper, Cornell University.

Tennyson, S., and W.J. Warfel (2008) 'The Emergence and Potential Consequences of First Party Insurance Bad Faith Liability', *Journal of Insurance Regulation*, 28(2): 3–20.

Tennyson, S., and W.J. Warfel (2010) 'The Law and Economics of First Party Insurance Bad Faith Liability', *Connecticut Insurance Law Journal*, 16(1): 203–42.

Tennyson, S., M.A. Weiss and L. Regan (2002) 'Automobile Insurance Regulation: The Massachusetts Experience', in J. David Cummins (ed.), *Deregulating Property-Liability Insurance: Restoring Competition and Increasing Market Efficiency* (Washington DC: AEI-Brookings Joint Center for Regulatory Studies).

Thaler, R., and C.R. Sunstein (2008) *Nudge: Improving Decisions about Health, Wealth and Happiness* (London: Penguin Books).

Trebilcock, M.J. (2003) 'Rethinking Consumer Protection Policy', in C.E.F. Rickett and T.G.W. Telfer (eds), *International Perspectives on Consumers' Access to Justice* (Cambridge: Cambridge University Press).

Ward, D., and R. Zurbruegg (2000) 'Does Insurance Promote Economic Growth? Evidence from OECD Countries', *Journal of Risk and Insurance*, 67(4): 489–506.

Weiss, M.A., L. Regan and S. Tennyson (2009) 'Incentive Effects of Automobile Insurance Rate Regulation on Loss Costs and Accident Frequency', Working paper.

13
Insurance Guarantee Funds and their Relation to Solvency Regulation

Przemysław Rymaszewski and Hato Schmeiser

Introduction

The change in the way of thinking about the regulation of financial markets which took place within the recent two decades was to some extent revolutionary. The globally ascending trend towards integrated prudential regulation and supervision as well as the pursuit to enhance market discipline will most probably remain the main fundament of leading future regulatory frameworks covering insurance, banking, and pension fund sectors. However, the recent crisis has revealed that there is still much effort to be made in order to ensure sustainable stability of international financial markets (see, for example, CEIOPS, 2009b; The Geneva Association, 2010; IIF, 2010). Simultaneously, an increased interest in guarantee funds which offer protection against possible insolvencies of financial institutions has arisen. Those institutions, currently intensively discussed (see, for example, CEIOPS, 2009a; European Commission, 2010), are only one of many possible approaches for the organisation of companies' institutionalised run-off within the insurance industry.

Even though insurance guarantee funds have already been applied as a policy-holder protection measure in several countries (see, for example, for an overview, Oxera, 2007; Schmeiser and Wagner, 2010), leading regulatory frameworks, those being currently developed or already in place, do not explicitly consider the existing guarantee funds as an essential part. This even in spite of the potential interactions between guarantee schemes and regulatory systems.[1] In this chapter, we discuss the interdependencies between different designs for guarantee funds and present regulatory frameworks based on market consistent valuation of an insurer's balance sheet. We argue that, if the legislator decides to introduce an insurance guarantee fund, the occurring reciprocal effects constitute the need for an enhanced regulatory approach extended by guarantee fund issues. However, there is no easy answer regarding the calculation of risk-based premiums within insurance guarantee funds. Hence, the risk of cross-subsidisation between different insurance companies remains for countries that have introduced insurance guarantee funds within their regulatory frameworks.

The remainder of this chapter is structured as follows. In the next section insurance guarantee funds are put in the general context of orderly run-off solutions for insurers. In the third section we focus on the main goals of insurance regulation and supervision and evaluate to what extent current solvency frameworks may theoretically be able to support those objectives. Furthermore, we analyse whether different designs for insurance guaranty funds can be applied in order to facilitate the achievement of the introduced regulatory goals. In the fourth section we analyse different aspects concerning a potential holistic approach to solvency regulation including insurance guarantee fund's issues in case they are introduced. The final section concludes.

Solutions for failing insurers

In this section we present the arguments often raised against and in favour of predefined and continuously updated plans for the case of a company's default within the financial industry. We define a concept for an orderly run-off as a predefined and institutionalised plan for supervisor reactions to insurer insolvency that is different from liquidation procedures employed in other, non-financial sectors. In addition, we describe different basic organisational forms of insurance guarantee funds and provide an overview of potential winding-up solutions within the insurance industry.

Run-off solutions in general

The recent financial crisis has shown that the lack of an economically funded concept for an orderly run-off of systemically relevant financial institutions may lead to extensive problems in times of serious financial distress (see, for example, IIF, 2010). On the one hand, if no – at least general – plan for a controlled resolution of a financial institution exists, governments and regulators may be unprepared and, hence, less effective in the abatement of the negative economic phenomena resulting from a company's default as well as the adverse financial conditions (see European Commission, 2010). On the other hand, the example of recent major bailouts within the banking industry shows that in the case of substantial market distortions it is often the taxpayer who has to cover the costs resulting from the solvency threatening difficulties of the financial institutions. A similar approach not only can provide inappropriate incentives for diverse market participants, but in some cases can also be seen as inefficient from the economic point of view. Using public funds to support any mismanaged financial intermediaries can lead to vital misallocation of economic resources. A regulatory requirement for a continuously updated and clearly predefined framework for a controlled winding-up of a financial institution may be applied to solve some of the underlying problems connected with potential default events of financial service providers. This is a particularly important issue in case of the so-called 'too big to fail' companies, where a collapse would be exceptionally drastic for the entire economic system.

Whether the same arguments are relevant also within the insurance sector depends strongly on its systemic relevance: a matter which is currently intensively discussed (see below, 'Stability of the financial system'). If this is the case, the systemic character of the insurance industry can also be seen as an argument in favour of a controlled resolution approach for insurance companies. Depending on its specific structure and funding, a guarantee scheme based on transparent rules and accompanied by an efficient liquidation process of an insurer's assets might be applied as one possible solution for the organisation of an orderly, industry-financed run-off of an insurer facing a default. Its introduction can provide specific incentives within insurance markets and, hence, among others influence financial market stability. However, a potential disadvantage might be seen in the fact that institutionalised run-off solutions can cause serious wealth transfers between different policy-holder groups (see, for example, Rymaszewski et al., 2010).

In the following we do not explicitly discuss solutions other than insurance guarantee funds which can also be applied in order to deal with insurers' defaults. Besides diverse forms of state-funded methods of treating insurance failures as bailouts or nationalisations, one might also think of obligatory private sector solutions as additional reinsurance of policy-holders' claims (organised in the form of an insurance pool or conducted by several reinsurance companies) as well as capital market-oriented methods based on, for example, collateralised debt obligations or credit default swaps (see, for example, Schmeiser et al., 2010).

Main economic characteristics of insurance guarantee funds

Insurance guarantee funds are either private or state sector-based institutions, the main goal of which is to protect policy-holders from a (partial) default of their contingent claims against insurance companies. Their organisation differentiates depending on the country of origin.[2] In general, if an insurer goes bankrupt, an insurance guarantee fund secures the interests of the policy-holders either by continuation or by an immediate termination of their contracts. In the former case, insurers' claims are either transferred to an external agent or wound up by the fund itself. In the latter case, insureds receive cash compensation.

Depending on the jurisdiction, different funding methods are applied in order to cover the costs of insurance guarantee funds' activities, inter alia, compensation payments to policy-holders, transfer payments covering the difference between the market value of an insurer's assets and liabilities, costs connected with winding-up an insurer's claims, and administrative costs. Those actions are primarily financed by the insurance industry via charges either incurred ex ante or post-assessed based on the realised costs. However, often diverse forms of governmental contributions, inter alia, tax deductions of incurred fees, are in place. This is particularly interesting with regard to the fact that funds are often designed as defined benefit schemes with regard to the amount of the realised claims covered, frequently with caps. In many cases insurance guarantee funds' coverage is restricted to specific classes of insurance contracts; for example, it excludes commercial customers expected to be more knowledgeable than retail clients. Often legally independent funds are applied to separately cover life and non-life lines of business.

Congruence with goals of insurance regulation

Consumer protection is often mentioned as the supreme goal of insurance regulation and supervision.[3] However, since policy-holders as well as some of the remaining stakeholders (for example, society, employees) are particularly interested in the efficiency of the insurance markets, issues such as stability, lack of disruption, and competitiveness within the insurance industry can also be seen as important for the regulator (see Meier, 1991, and European Commission, 1999). In the following, we investigate in which way current solvency frameworks are intended to support the essential goals set by the insurance regulation. In addition, we analyse how differently designed insurance guarantee funds can facilitate or disrupt their achievement.

Stability of the financial system

Safeguarding the stability of the banking sector is one of the widely recognised reasons for its regulation. This is mainly due to the high interlacement of banks implied by their intense reciprocal borrowing and lending, hence causing a potential instability of the entire system. In this manner, liquidity problems implied, for example, by a bank run affecting one of the market players, can rapidly result in difficulties for other institutions within the banking industry. Those can significantly jeopardise the development of the economy and lead to momentous political and social problems.

On the one hand, Harrington (2009), CEA (2010), The Geneva Association (2010), and Radice (2010) argue that the interconnections among diverse insurance companies can be expected to be much weaker than those between banks due to their different business model, hence insurance companies can be a source of systemic risk only if they extensively conduct quasi-banking activities. On the other hand, a significant part of research conducted in this field seems to support the assumption that an insurer's insolvency may still cause significant problems for the entire financial sector (see, for example, Fenn and Cole, 1994; Angbazo and Narayanan, 1996; Polonchek and Miller, 1999).

Allen and Carletti (2006), as well as Allen and Douglas (2006), show that strong relationships between the banking and insurance sectors can lead to an opposite contagion and increase the risk of financial crises. This even despite the fact that insurance companies face the lapse risk (an insurance counterpart of a bank run) only to a restricted extent. Bernier and Mahfoudhi (2010) analyse the possible contagion effects within the insurance industry induced by post-assessed insurance guarantee funds.

In the following, we analyse the market stabilising incentives, the establishment of which is followed by the current insurance prudential regulation and supervision, and compare them with the similar impact of an insurance guarantee scheme's design.

Restrictions on insurers' risk-taking

The aim of prudential insurance regulation and supervision is to lower insurers' default probabilities. In this way, the restricted insolvency likelihood of every single insurance company operating on the market limits the probability of market-wide financial distress. Risk-based capital requirements such as those currently in place or still being developed (for an overview, see, for example, Eling and Holzmüller, 2008; IAIS, 2009; Klein and Wang, 2009), which link mandatory solvency capital to the amount of risk borne by an insurer, might be able to support this goal. On the other hand, risk-inadequate capital requirements may lead to improper incentives for insurers and possibly increase their appetite for risk-taking. This can happen if shareholders interpret their position in the insurance company solely as a call option on a company's assets with its liabilities as a strike price.[4] In such a setting and given asymmetric information, management of a publicly traded insurer can increase a company's market value by raising the volatility of its assets (see, for example, Merton, 1977; Cummins, 1988).[5] If the policy-holders are not perfectly informed about the actual solvency level of the firm, they might not be able to demand lower insurance premiums for the increased risk.[6] This in spite of the decreased value of their wealth position, which is due to the higher value of the default put option they are short of in favour of the company's shareholders (see, for example, Doherty and Garven, 1986; Butsic, 1994). Due to equity capital costs for the additional solvency capital, which is intended to reduce a company's risk, risk-adequate capital requirements directly penalise the insurer for taking additional risks.

Analogous considerations can be derived with respect to the risk-adequacy of an insurance guarantee fund's charging and payoff system which, if properly designed, can provide similar incentives for the insurers as the risk-oriented solvency capital requirements (see Cummins, 1988). On the one hand, a truly risk-oriented insurance guarantee fund requires charges closely linked to a company's risk profile. On the other hand, in order to ensure a sincere risk-orientation, fund premiums should be paid solely by the participating companies and disbursed in advance (see Rymaszewski et al., 2010, for an exemplary payoff scheme ensuring the self-supporting character of an insurance guarantee fund). Both postulates aim at avoiding a situation where the insurers do not entirely internalise their potential insolvency costs, either by transferring the costs to an external agent (for example, the government and thus the taxpayers) or by going bankrupt. In case the fund charging system is not in this sense risk-adjusted, insurers may still increase their market value by taking additional risks. Lee et al. (1997) call this possible effect a risk-subsidy hypothesis. Given a scarce congruence between a company's risk profile and an insurance guarantee fund's charges, if the outcomes of an insurer's actions are favourable, a firm's shareholders receive the entire profit resulting from taking additional risks (or at least a part of it). However, in the case of the company facing a default, the firm's owners enjoy the limited liability of their stake and any deficit of assets over the company's liabilities is absorbed by the guarantee fund and partially by policy-holders.[7]

In general, a self-supporting insurance guarantee fund, as one of the possible solutions for an orderly run-off of an insurance company, may have a further positive impact on the stability of the financial markets, irrespective of the applied premium principle. Since the existence of an insurance guarantee fund effectively financed by the insurance industry should in most cases lower the negative outcomes of an insurer's default faced by its policy-holders, the incentive for the government to bailout an insolvent insurer is likely to decrease. If the management of an insurance company anticipates this fact, it may account for it and accordingly change its risk-taking behaviour.

Influence on monitoring

The management of a company may under certain conditions increase its market value by taking additional risks only if the market is not free of frictions; in particular, if there is no information asymmetry between the market participants. Hence, reduction of friction with regard to information owned by different market players may be used to reduce the potential incentive towards extensive risk-taking. For this reason enhanced reporting requirements are an integral part of many modern solvency frameworks, which thereby aim to support market discipline (for example, Solvency II and the Swiss Solvency Test).

The impact of an insurance guarantee fund on the scale of information asymmetries in an insurance market depends inter alia on its charging and payoff structure. If the policy-holders bear only a part of insolvency costs – and are aware of this fact[8] – they might have less incentive to monitor their own insurers compared to the setting without an insurance guarantee fund. Hence, even within markets characterised by perfect information and with self-supporting but risk-inadequately designed insurance guarantee funds in place, single policy-holders are likely to have less incentive to avoid very risky protection providers. This is due to the fact that stakeholders (in particular, policy-holders and/or shareholders) of less risky insurance companies, at least partially, pay for their hazardous choice. Such a decrease of monitoring incentives is even stronger if there is an external agent covering a part of the policy-holder deficit in case it occurs. However, if the policy-holders still bear at least a part of the insolvency costs, the incentive to monitor the insurance company of their choice may weaken but never entirely disappear (see Cummins and Sommer, 1996).

Further monitoring effects may arise if the fund charges are not incurred upfront, but post-assessed based on the sum of realized policy-holder deficits. In such a setting, stakeholders of all insurance companies might be particularly interested in monitoring their rivals, since the bankruptcy costs are borne by the surviving members of the industry. Lee et al. (1997) describe this phenomenon as monitoring hypothesis. Nevertheless, the impact of this effect mainly depends on the level of market discipline within the considered market. The introduction of a post-assessed insurance guarantee fund may have a positive effect on the stability of the financial system due to additional monitoring incentives, only if markets are relatively incapable of disciplining the insurers.[9]

The current situation

To the best of our knowledge, all currently existing insurance guarantee fund schemes charge premiums not (directly) linked to insurers' risks.[10] None of the schemes in place fulfils the previously defined postulates for a severe risk-orientation. Even in cases when the premium charges are incurred up-front (as currently done in, for example, France, Germany and Denmark; see Oxera, 2007, p. 39), there are no examples of insurance guarantee funds charging risk-adequate premiums. In most cases the premiums charged by a guarantee fund are calculated in relation to the premiums earned by an insurer or the amount of its technical reserves. In particular, the former approach may have an adverse influence on the stability of insurance markets characterised by a high level of market discipline. Since in such cases the less reliable insurers earn lower premiums than the solvent firms, the fund charge calculation is an exact inverse of the postulated risk-adjusted approach (see Sommer, 1996). However, current discussions on the design of insurance guarantee schemes within the European Union allow us to surmise that the future harmonised approach within the European market is likely to be based on risk-adjusted, mainly ex ante charged contributions (see European Commission, 2010).

Several empirical studies conducted in the US confirm that similar insurance guarantee funds with risk-inadequate charging and payoff schemes may increase the instability of the financial system. Lee et al. (1997) find a significant impact of the risk-subsidy effect within the property-liability insurance market. They do not find any significant influence of the monitoring effect. Similar results for guarantee funds effectively funded by taxpayers within the US life insurance market are presented by Brewer-III et al. (1997). Downs and Sommer (1999), as well as Lee and Smith (1999), arrive at similar conclusions. In a prior study Munch and Smallwood (1980) do not confirm a significant causal dependence between the introduction of an insurance guarantee fund and a company's default likelihood.

Avoidance of market failure

In an extreme case, information asymmetries between both parties of an insurance contract may lead to a situation when nearly all suppliers of insurance have a strong incentive to exit the market.[11] Since the economic and social costs of a similar market failure concerning insurance supply can be substantial, it is of interest to the economy that prudential regulation and supervision aim at appropriately addressing this issue. Due to the fact that current solvency frameworks formally follow the goal of constraining insurers' default probabilities, the insurance companies are to some extent restricted to a minimum quality level of products they offer. Hence the probability of market failure induced by the problem of adverse selection decreases if the policy-holders believe in the effectiveness of governmental regulation. The threat of market failure resulting from adverse selection is also likely to contract due to the enhanced reporting requirements associated with regulatory schemes.

The probability of a market failure induced by the phenomenon of adverse selection may also decrease if the introduced insurance guarantee fund provides incentives leading to a restricted range of product quality on the insurance market and the insureds perceive the efficiency of this constraint. Additional incentives towards risk reduction can be achieved by the introduction of insurance guarantee funds charging risk-adjusted premiums. Depending on the premium principle used to derive the fund charge, it is possible to reduce insurers' willingness to take additional risk. An additional market disciplining mechanism mitigating the impact of adverse selection can be based on the publication of fund charges paid by the insurers.[12]

Consumer protection

The general idea that customers of financial service providers need some kind of protection is mainly motivated by the existence of information asymmetries between both parties signing an insurance contract. Nevertheless, despite the fact that an insurer is also generally affected by missing information (for example, about the true behaviour of a policy-holder), the main focus of insurance safety nets lies with policy-holders, who are assumed to be the less knowledgeable contract partners. However, even if the insurance markets were free of information asymmetries between the insurers and their clients, possible claims of ex ante unknown third parties would still be involved and may need particular care.

In this context, the role of solvency frameworks in protecting the interests of insurers' customers is based on the reduction of information asymmetries between policy-holders and the insurer as well as limitation of risks borne by the insurers. The latter effect might result from the fact that within markets with asymmetric information an increase of insurer's risk does not stringently lead to a decrease of the insurance premium. This even in spite of the increased value of the insurer's default put option which the policy-holders are short in, but the value of which they cannot perfectly observe. Hence, restrictions on insurers' risk positions as well as increased market discipline might be applied to prevent the relatively risk-averse insureds from choosing an insurance company with a risk profile which is not congruent with their preferences.

Protection of policy-holders as well as third-party claimants against the negative outcomes of an insurance company's insolvency is broadly acknowledged as the main goal of the introduction of an insurance guarantee fund (see, for example, Krogh, 1972; Oxera, 2007). It is intended to guard the insureds against the risk resulting from the pure randomness which is an integral part of insurance business. As a so-called last-resort measure, an insurance guarantee fund at least partially covers the costs resulting from default events, whose probability of occurrence can be reduced by the prudential regulation and supervision only to a predefined small, yet still positive, level. Hence policy-holder collectives of insurers participating in an appropriately designed insurance guarantee fund should theoretically enjoy only unsystematic wealth transfers in case the insurance company of their choice suffers a positive deficit of assets over claims.

In contrast, systematic wealth transfers between the policy-holders of different insurance companies can be caused by the fact that the fund payoff structure depends on the joint default distribution of all insurers participating in the insurance guarantee scheme. In this manner, we generally cannot exclude that systematic cross-subsidisation between the insureds of different insurance companies takes place. Rymaszewski et al. (2010) show that in the practically relevant case of incomplete markets and heterogeneous insurance companies systematic wealth transfers between diverse insurers cannot be avoided. Hence some of the policy-holders might be disadvantaged by the introduction of an insurance guarantee fund, if it does not significantly lower the extent of agency problems described above. Even if pooling of risks within an insurance guarantee fund leads to positive diversification effects, allocating them back to the participating insurers is in general not possible in a non-arbitrary way. Therefore, we cannot rule out the possibility of some policy-holder groups being better off than the others.

Thereby, the investigation whether insurance guarantee funds in individual cases support the goal of consumer protection depends on the regulator's exact definition of this objective. If the major aim of insurance guarantee funds' introduction is understood solely as securing the policy-holders in extreme bad states of nature, every payoff structure financially supporting the insureds given insurer's default and characterised by a positive (or neutral) influence on the agency issues can be recognised as in line with the goal of consumer protection, despite the potential cross-subsidisation problems. However, in our opinion, analysing the introduction of an insurance guarantee fund without accounting for wealth transfer issues influencing the entire financial position of the policy-holders is not sufficient, since it generally disregards a possibly substantial part of hedging costs borne by (some of) those insured.

Competition

Lack of competition within the insurance sector may under certain circumstances have an undesirable effect not only on the wealth position of policy-holders but also on the entire economy. Joskow (1973) argues that deficiency of competition within insurance markets may lead to inefficient capital allocation and restricted insurance supply. Furthermore, a decreased level of competition is likely to lower insurers' incentives to monitor their rivals, which may result in a restricted level of market discipline.

On the one hand, we can assume that insurance regulation has a restrictive impact on the level of competition, since insurance companies are limited in the possibility to compete with each other with regard to the safety level they offer. The effect may be similar if solvency requirements include binding market access restrictions; for instance, with regard to the minimum capital requirements.[13]

On the other hand, there are several arguments why the introduction of solvency frameworks, which follow recent developments in the field of risk management and regulation, might have a positive influence on competition within insurance markets. Enhanced reporting standards may have a desirable impact on the disciplining capabilities of the financial markets, hence an auxiliary influence on the level of competition. Furthermore, converging regulatory rules between different jurisdictions – as within the future Solvency II framework – might be expected to lower the market access barriers for insurance providers willing to enter a market within a different cognisance as well as support a level playing field between competing insurers (see European Commission, 2010). Hence harmonisation of regulatory systems is likely to strengthen competition.[14]

In general, insurance guarantee funds, as institutions securing an orderly run-off of an insurance company, are expected to ease a market exit of an inefficient and uncompetitive insurer. This is mainly due to the fact that the introduction of an insurance guarantee fund allows a reduction of the social and political costs of an insurer's insolvency. However, if the premiums of an insurance guarantee fund are charged ex ante, there might be constellations in which the possibility of a new market entry is restricted, depending on the premium principle applied to derive them – for instance, if there are floors for the fund charges implied by an insurance guarantee fund's fixed costs.

Ligon and Thistle (2007) discuss the potential influence of insurance guarantee funds effectively underwritten by the government on the organisational structure within the insurance industry. They prove that under certain conditions it might be rational for an insurance provider to offer different insurance products within separate monolines rather than a multiline company. However, the influence of this effect on the level of competition is difficult to assess without a loss of generality.

The discussed issues connected with an insurance guarantee fund's risk-orientation show that the interactions between the goals of solvency frameworks and the shape of insurance guarantee funds are not limited to the matters of the risk-based solvency capital and the fund's premium calculation as well as the resulting incentives to prevent excessive risk-taking. Moreover, the resulting monitoring incentives are to some extent directly linked to the efforts aiming at supporting the self-disciplining capabilities of financial markets, which are made in order to increase their stability. In our opinion, both aspects justify the need for the integration of insurance guarantee funds into solvency frameworks.

A holistic view on solvency issues

Possible interactions with the supervisory process

In general, current solvency frameworks aim at providing a holistic approach to solvency measurement, inter alia, they are expected to account for the intra-group effects and interactions between different business lines (see, for example, FOPI, 2004, 2006; European Parliament, 2009). Nevertheless, they incorporate the strategies for an orderly run-off (in case an insurance company goes bankrupt) as their integral part only to a restricted degree. They do not explicitly aim at addressing the applied institutionalised run-off solutions, as insurance guarantee funds. This even in spite of the potential interactions between both concepts.

For instance, both Solvency II and the Swiss Solvency Test account for issues of a potential company's run-off only in regard to the market consistent estimation of the insurer's assets and liabilities. Such an approach, allowing for a market value margin over the best estimate of the insurer's liabilities, is expected to ensure that a company's claims are covered with an appropriately high probability, either by the company itself or by a third party willing to take over the insurance company's portfolio under the current market conditions. However, in this manner policy-holders are still potentially exposed to a total or partial default of their contingent claims. A similar market-oriented insurance regulation as the only measure of consumer protection would make the insureds' financial position default-free only if there was no possibility of a so-called jump-to-default and given a continuous supervision of insurer's activities.

An extended view on an insurance company's solvency can fill the gap not covered by the current solvency frameworks which aim at substantially restricting and not entirely neutralising insurers' default probabilities. We have argued that, depending on their design, insurance guarantee funds may either support or disrupt the achievement of the goals followed by prudential regulation and supervision. The significance of this effect – proven in several empirical studies (see above, 'Stability of the financial system') – is dependent not only on the specific guarantee fund payoff structure but also on the level of market discipline within the insurance sector. From the perspective of a supervisory authority, integration of the issues connected with the existence of insurance guarantee funds in their current form in the regulatory process would allow a comprehensive view to be gained on the incentives for the insurers and the policy-holders implied by both elements of an insurance safety net. In case inconsistencies occur, an extended approach may facilitate their detection and provide additional instruments to address them.

In particular, an analysis of the interrelations between guarantee funds' charging and payoff systems and risk-based capital requirements may deliver essential insights into the influence of insurance guarantee funds on insurers' default probabilities. This specific dependence is particularly important since the introduction of an insurance guarantee fund in general leads to an increase of an insurer's insolvency likelihood. This phenomenon is due to the fact that insurance companies are charged premiums, which are used to cover deficits faced by policy-holders in case of a default.

Moreover, in our opinion and for similar reasons, in case the local regulatory system does not include an institution comparable to an insurance guarantee fund, however, a different institutionalised strategy for an insurer's run-off exists, the regulator should always be aware of and systematically analyse the potential interactions between the solvency frameworks and the appointed resolution approach.

Explicit consideration of insurance guarantee funds and/or other run-off solutions is particularly important within different jurisdictions aiming at the development of a harmonised system of insurance regulation, for example, Solvency II within the European Union. Different resolution approaches applied within each Member State may otherwise be contradictory to the aspired compatibility of comprehensive regulatory systems, even despite the congruency of the solvency capital requirements.[15]

Interactions with regard to premium calculation

In general, the introduction of an insurance guarantee fund on incomplete financial markets (almost) certainly causes wealth transfers between the participating collectives of policy-holders (see Rymaszewski et al., 2010). This effect is determined by the general impossibility of allocating diversification benefits resulting from the pooling process to the participating insurance companies. In this context, we face a problem similar to the capital allocation issue intensively discussed in the literature within the last few years (see, for example, Phillips et al., 1998; Myers and Read, 2001; Sherris, 2006; Gründl and Schmeiser, 2007; Ibragimov et al., 2010; Zanjani, 2010) that cannot be solved by a premium principle based, for example, on the risk of a single insurer, that is, oriented on an insurer's loss distribution (for example, value-at-risk). The degree of cross-subsidisation depends, inter alia, on the applied scheme for the fund charge calculation.[16] Nevertheless, if the establishment of an insurance guarantee fund is likely to lead to a decrease of agency costs, its introduction may still be beneficial for the policy-holders. This is caused by the fact that agency problems can at least partially be restricted by a risk-based fund premium calculation (see above, 'Stability of the financial system').

Derivation of the guarantee fund's premium based on the standard or internal models used for calculation of the risk-based capital requirements can be seen as one of the possible solutions to adjust the charges paid by insurers to the risk they are bearing. One possible advantage of a similar approach are the potential economies of scope lowering the direct costs of an insurance guarantee fund's establishment. However, a simple adoption of the models used for solvency capital requirement calculation within the insurance guarantee fund charging system might in some cases be problematic. This is due to the fact that the solvency frameworks aim at reducing the default probability of a single insurer, and hence account mainly for the insurer-specific risk. In the context of an insurance guarantee fund, the important advantage of which can be seen in pooling of the default risks, the risk contribution of an insurer to the underlying portfolio might be the relevant factor for the premium calculation. This is the case if the payments of an insurance guarantee fund made to an insurance company depend not only on its own realised deficit, but also on other insurers' shortfalls. This is always the case if an insurance guarantee fund is organised as a self-supporting institution, which implies that the available funds are restricted. Thus, if the solvency frameworks do not appropriately account for the interdependencies between assets and claims of all insurers participating in an insurance guarantee fund – particularly if those interrelations are significant – a simple adoption of models applied within the solvency frameworks may insufficiently account for pooling issues.

On the other hand, allowing for a diverse method of premium calculation might deliver a different view on company's risk-profile, and hence reduce the model risk within the regulatory process.[17] If the model applied for the purpose of fund premium calculation explicitly allows for interdependencies between assets and claims of the participating insurers and adjusts for an insurer's risk contribution to an insurance guarantee fund's portfolio, the insights from fund charge estimates can be of use within the entire supervisory process.[18]

An enhanced analysis of the interrelations between the portfolios of different insurers may have a positive effect on the financial market's stability. Since the current regulatory frameworks explicitly aim at constituting an integral part of an insurer's risk-management system, implementation of complementary risk-assessment models may result in further advantages from an insurer's perspective.

Conclusion

The recent financial crisis has shown that default events of systematically relevant financial institutions can be a realistic threat to the economy. Insurance guarantee funds with their different – currently applied and notionally thinkable – designs are one possible and presently broadly discussed solution to resolve failing service providers within the insurance industry. Since the introduction of an insurance guarantee fund is connected with diverse incentives for market participants interacting with the goals of prudential regulation and supervision, we find it adequate and important to analyse the effects of their establishment and subsistence on the functionality of the current solvency frameworks. In this way, a permanent analysis of issues related to currently in-force insurance guarantee funds into systems of solvency supervision can be applied to support the congruence of actions within both schemes. In this chapter we have discussed which aspects insurance guarantee funds may support or disrupt the achievement of the goals followed by the insurance regulation. In case a different institutionalised resolution approach is employed within the insurance industry, the effects of its implementation should also be accounted for. A similar integrated approach can be used to facilitate the comprehensiveness of the view on issues relevant for insurance regulation, and hence, support the holistic treatment of insurance business, which is the major objective of modern solvency frameworks.

Notes

1. For instance, the premium charged by the insurance guarantee fund influences the solvency level of the insurer.
2. See, for example, Brewer-III et al. (1997), Feldhaus and Kazenski (1998), Oxera (2007) and Bernier and Mahfoudhi (2010), for an overview of the existing insurance guarantee funds within diverse jurisdictions.
3. See, for example, European Commission (1999) and FOPI (2004) for the motivation behind the development of the Solvency II framework and the Swiss Solvency Test, respectively. IAIS (2009, p. 7) mentions consumer protection as the ultimate objective of group-wide solvency assessment and supervision.
4. Due to the fact that a bankrupt insurer remains always insolvent, shareholders of an insurance company may theoretically see their stake within the firm as a barrier option; see, for example, Black and Cox (1976). Since the value of such an option might under certain conditions decrease in the underlying volatility, the shareholders

of an insurer might have less incentive towards risk-taking compared to the valuation based on a plain (European) call.

5. Lee and Smith (1999) suggest that a similar effect occurs if an insurer intentionally under-reserves its claims.
6. A similar effect might occur in a market with perfect information if the policy-holders cannot renegotiate their contract in case the insurer changes his risk profile. However, this issue might become less important in a multi-period context, where the insureds can account for the insurer's behaviour in the subsequent periods (see, for example, Axelrod and Hamilton, 1981).
7. Hence the impact of the risk-subsidy effect is likely to depend on the legal structure of the insurer and can be expected to be less significant in the case of mutual insurance companies, where the equity and policy-holder stakes are inseparable. In their empirical study, Lee et al. (1997) do not find any significant influence of the insurance guarantee fund introduction on the risk-taking behaviour of mutuals.
8. The European Commission (2010) claims that policy-holders are able to understand the relevant information with regard to insurance guarantee funds only to a restricted extent.
9. For empirical evidence of market discipline with regard to the price of insurance see, for example, Sommer (1996), Cummins and Danzon (1997) and Phillips et al. (1998). Fenn and Cole (1994) find evidence of market discipline with regard to the prices of insurance companies' stocks.
10. See Oxera (2007, p. 34), for an extensive overview over the insurance guarantee fund schemes within the European Union. US regulation concerning the life insurance sector can be found in Brewer-III et al. (1997, p. 305). See Lee and Smith (1999) for a description of the US-based property-liability guarantee fund system. Within the German life insurance guarantee fund scheme, charges depend on companies ranking according to their financial capacity, defined as equity relative to solvency margin. Oxera (2007) classifies this approach as risk-based. However, in our opinion a similar method of premium calculation cannot be seen as plenary risk-oriented under the currently valid Solvency I regulatory framework.
11. Akerlof (1970) shows, in an example of a market for second-hand cars, that given asymmetric information it may be disadvantageous for sound suppliers to remain active within the market, if the customers do not perceive the above-average quality of their products. For issues connected with information asymmetries within insurance markets see, for example, Rothschild and Stiglitz (1976). An empirical investigation on asymmetric information within insurance markets was conducted by Chiappori and Salanié (2000).
12. In fact, the problem of adverse selection can additionally be alleviated if the insurers were explicitly allowed to use the information about premium payments as a signalling instrument; see, for example, Spence (1973).
13. This matter is at least partially allowed for within the Solvency II framework by the principle of proportionality, which is aimed at ensuring that the regulatory framework reflects the nature, scale and complexity of insurance business – in particular, it appropriately addresses the issue of small and less risky insurance companies (see European Parliament, 2009, p. 9).
14. Note the possible impact of enhanced competition on the stability of the international financial markets, which can change due to the increased interlacement of the financial markets.

15. Harmonisation of insurance guarantee schemes within the EU is postulated by de Larosière et al. (2009) and the European Commission (2010), as well as recommended within the Solvency II Directive (see European Parliament, 2009).
16. A non-arbitrary solution for premium calculation is possible only under the assumption of perfect financial markets (see Cummins, 1988; Duan and Yu, 2005). However, Rymaszewski et al. (2010) show that within the contingent claim approach a self-supporting insurance guarantee fund does not bring any benefits for policy-holders.
17. See Rymaszewski et al. (2010) for an alternative, utility-based method for guarantee fund premium calculation. For different risk-oriented solutions within the banking sector see, for example, European Commission (2008).
18. As a practicable approach, under the assumption of well diversified asset portfolios correlations between insurers' assets can be derived from the adequate market data. However, such a method can hardly be applied for insurers' claims.

Bibliography

Akerlof, G.A. (1970) 'The Market for Lemons: Quality Uncertainty and the Market Mechanism', *Quarterly Journal of Economics*, 84: 488–500.

Allen, F., and E. Carletti (2006) 'Credit Risk Transfer and Contagion', *Journal of Monetary Economics*, 53: 89–111.

Allen, F., and G. Douglas (2006) 'Systemic Risk and Regulation', in M. Carey and R.M. Stulz (eds), *The Risk of Financial Institutions* (Chicago).

Angbazo, L.A., and R. Narayanan (1996) 'Catastrophic Shocks in the Property-Liability Insurance Industry: Evidence on Regulatory and Contagion Effects', *Journal of Risk and Insurance*, 63: 619–37.

Axelrod, R., and W.D. Hamilton (1981) 'The Evolution of Cooperation', *Science*, 211: 1390–6.

Bernier, G., and R.M. Mahfoudhi (2010) 'On the Economics of Postassessments in Insurance Guaranty Funds: A Stakeholders Perspective', *Journal of Risk and Insurance*, 77(4): 857–92.

Black, F., and J.C. Cox (1976) 'Valuing Corporate Securities: Some Effects of Bond Indenture Provisions', *Journal of Finance*, 31: 351–67.

Brewer-III, E., T.S. Mondschean and P.E. Strahan (1997) 'The Role of Monitoring in Reducing the Moral Hazard Problem Associated with Government Guarantees: Evidence from the Life Insurance Industry', *Journal of Risk and Insurance*, 64: 301–22.

Butsic, R.P. (1994) 'Solvency Measurement for Property-Liability Risk-Based Capital Applications', *Journal of Risk and Insurance*, 61: 656–90.

Chiappori, P.-A., and B. Salanié (2000) 'Testing for Asymmetric Information in Insurance Markets', *Journal of Political Economy*, 108: 56–78.

Comité Européen des Assurances (CEA) (2010) 'Insurance: A Unique Sector. Why Insurers Differ from Banks', available at www.cea.eu.

Committee of European Insurance and Occupational Pensions Supervisors (CEIOPS) (2009a) 'CEOIPS Input to the European Commission work on Insurance Guarantee Schemes', available at www.ceiops.eu.

Committee of European Insurance and Occupational Pensions Supervisors (2009b) 'Lessons Learned from the Crisis: Solvency II and Beyond', available at www.ceiops.eu.

Cummins, J.D. (1988) 'Risk-Based Premiums for Insurance Guaranty Funds', *Journal of Finance*, 43: 823–39.

Cummins, J.D., and P.M. Danzon (1997) 'Price, Financial Quality, and Capital Flows in Insurance Markets', *Journal of Financial Intermediation*, 6: 3–38.

Cummins, J.D., and D.W. Sommer (1996) 'Capital and Risk in Property-Liability Insurance Markets', *Journal of Banking & Finance*, 20: 1069–92.

de Larosière, J., L. Balcerowicz, O. Issing, R. Masera, C. McCarthy, L. Nyberg, J. Pérez and O. Ruding (2009) 'Report of the High-Level Group on Financial Supervision in the EU', available at http://ec.europa.eu.

Doherty, N.A., and J.R. Garven (1986) 'Price Regulation in Property-Liability Insurance: A Contingent-Claims Approach', *Journal of Finance*, 41: 1031–50.

Downs, D.H., and D.W. Sommer (1999) 'Monitoring, Ownership, and Risk-Taking: The Impact of Guaranty Funds', *Journal of Risk and Insurance*, 46: 477–97.

Duan, J.-C., and M.-T. Yu (2005) 'Fair Insurance Guaranty Premia in the Presence of Risk-Based Capital Regulations, Stochastic Interest Rate and Catastrophe Risk', *Journal of Banking & Finance*, 29: 2435–54.

Eling, M., and I. Holzmüller (2008) 'An Overview and Comparison of Risk-Based Capital Standards.', *Journal of Insurance Regulation*, 26: 31–60.

European Commission (1999) 'The Review of Overall Financial Position of an Insurance Undertaking', available at http://ec.europa.eu.

European Commission (2008) 'Risk-Based Contributions in EU Deposit Guarantee Schemes: Current Practices', available at http://ec.europa.eu.

European Commission (2010), 'White Paper on Insurance Guaranty Schemes', available at http://ec.europa.eu.

European Parliament (2009) 'Directive of the European Parliament and of the Council on the Taking-up and Pursuit of the Business of Insurance and Reinsurance (Solvency II)', available at http://register.consilium.europa.eu.

Federal Office of Private Insurance (FOPI) (2004) 'White Paper of the Swiss Solvency Test', available at www.finma.ch.

Federal Office of Private Insurance (2006) 'Technical Document on the Swiss Solvency Test', available at www.finma.ch.

Feldhaus, W.R., and P.M. Kazenski (1998) 'Risk-Based Guaranty Fund Assessments', *Journal of Insurance Regulation*, 42: 42–63.

Fenn, G.W., and R.A. Cole (1994) 'Announcements of Asset-Quality Problems and Contagion Effects in the Life Insurance Industry', *Journal of Financial Economics*, 35: 181–98.

Gründl, H., and H. Schmeiser (2007) 'Capital Allocation for Insurance Companies – What Good Is It?', *Journal of Risk and Insurance*, 74: 301–17.

Harrington, S.E. (2009) 'The Financial Crisis, Systemic Risk, and the Future of Insurance Regulation', available at www.naic.org.

Ibragimov, R., D. Jaffee and J. Walden (2010) 'Pricing and Capital Allocation for Multiline Insurance Firms', *Journal of Risk and Insurance*, 77: 551–78.

Institute of International Finance (IIF) (2010) 'Global Approach to Resolving Failing Financial Firms: An Industry Perspective', available at www.iif.com.

International Association of Insurance Supervisors (IAIS) (2009) 'Issues Paper on Group-Wide Solvency Assessment and Supervision', available at www.iaisweb.org.

Joskow, P.L. (1973) 'Cartels, Competition and Regulation in the Property-Liability Insurance Industry', *Bell Journal of Economics and Management Science*, 4: 375–427.

Klein, R.W., and S. Wang (2009) 'Catastrophe Risk Financing in the United States and the European Union: A Comparative Analysis of Alternative Regulatory Approaches', *Journal of Risk and Insurance*, 76:, 607–37.

Krogh, H. C. (1972), 'Insurer Post-Insolvency Guaranty Funds', *Journal of Risk and Insurance*, XXXIX, 431–450.

Lee, S.-J., D. Mayers and C.W. Smith (1997) 'Guaranty Funds and Risk-Taking Evidence from the Insurance Industry', *Journal of Financial Economics*, 44: 3–24.

Lee, S.-J. and Smith, M. L. (1999), 'Property-Casualty Insurance Guaranty Funds and Insurer Vulnerability to Misfortune', *Journal of Banking & Finance*, XXIII, 1437–1456.

Ligon, J.A., and P.D. Thistle (2007) 'The Organizational Structure of Insurance Companies: The Role of Heterogeneous Risks and Guaranty Funds', *Journal of Risk and Insurance*, 74: 851–62.

Meier, K.J. (1991) 'The Politics of Insurance Regulation', *Journal of Risk and Insurance*, 58: 700–13.

Merton, R.C. (1977) 'An Analytic Derivation of the Cost of Deposit Insurance and Loan Guarantees. An Application of Modern Option Pricing Theory', *Journal of Banking & Finance*, 1: 3–11.

Munch, P., and D.E. Smallwood (1980) 'Solvency Regulation in the Property-Liability Insurance Industry: Empirical Evidence', *Bell Journal of Economics*, 11: 261–79.

Myers, S.C., and J.A.J. Read (2001) 'Capital Allocation for Insurance Companies', *Journal of Risk and Insurance*, 68: 545–80.

Oxera (2007) 'Insurance Guarantee Schemes in the EU: Comparative Analysis of Existing Schemes, Analysis of Problems and Evaluation of Options', available at http://ec.europa.eu.

Phillips, R.D., J.D. Cummins and F. Allen (1998) 'Financial Pricing of Insurance in the Multiple-Line Insurance Company', *Journal of Risk and Insurance*, 65: 597–636.

Polonchek, J., and R.K. Miller (1999) 'Contagion Effects in the Insurance Industry', *Journal of Risk and Insurance*, 66: 459–75.

Radice, M.P. (2010) 'Systemische Risiken im Versicherungssektor? Betrachtungen mit Fokus auf die schweizerische Assekuranz', FINMA (Swiss Financial Market Supervisory Authority), Working Paper.

Rothschild, M., and J. Stiglitz (1976) 'Equilibrium in Competitive Insurance Markets: An Essay on the Economics of Imperfect Information', *Quarterly Journal of Economics*, 90: 629–49.

Rymaszewski, P., H. Schmeiser and J. Wagner (2010) 'Under What Conditions Is an Insurance Guaranty Fund Beneficial for Policyholders?', *Journal of Risk and Insurance*, forthcoming.

Schmeiser, H, and J. Wagner (2010) 'The Impact of Introducing Insurance Guaranty Schemes on Pricing and Capital Structures', Working Paper, University of St Gallen.

Schmeiser, H., J. Wagner and A. Zemp (2010) 'A Proposal for a Capital Market-based Guaranty Scheme for the Financial Industry', Working Paper, University of St Gallen.

Sherris, M. (2006) 'Solvency, Capital Allocation, and Fair Rate of Return in Insurance', *Journal of Risk and Insurance*, 73: 71–96.

Sommer, D.W. (1996) 'The Impact of Firm Risk on Property-Liability Insurance Prices', *Journal of Risk and Insurance*, 63: 597–636.

Spence, M. (1973) 'Job Market Signaling', *Quarterly Journal of Economics*, 87: 355–74.

The Geneva Association (2010) 'Systemic Risk in Insurance: An Analysis of Insurance and Financial Stability', available at www.genevaassociation.org.

Zanjani, G. (2010) 'An Economic Approach to Capital Allocation', *Journal of Risk and Insurance*, 77: 523–49.

14
Government Intervention in Insurance: An Examination of the Risk of Moral Hazard[1]

Michel Flamée and Paul Windels

Introduction

The multiplicity of government support actions during the financial crisis has meant the return of stronger government intervention in the free market economy, particularly in the financial sector. Restoring financial stability, ensuring lending to the real economy and dealing with the systemic risk of possible insolvency have been advanced as the main purposes of government interventions. Through different support measures such as guarantee schemes, recapitalisation measures and impaired asset schemes governments have become directly involved in the operations of the financial industry (hereafter 'the industry'). In several cases, governments have become important shareholders in financial institutions, potentially exerting an influence on the organisation's strategy. These actions were, for the most part, not planned or carefully prepared but were taken at a time of crisis out of necessity in order to preserve the stability of the financial system.

Governments are not determined to continue to play a leading role in the industry, but the regulatory and market implications of their support actions should not be neglected. A well-known risk is that individual support actions may lead to distortions of competition. For instance, measures taken by a state to support institutions operating within its national financial market may favour these institutions to the detriment of others operating within that state. Broader support actions such as guarantee schemes and asset relief schemes may trigger undesired effects such as an erosion of market discipline and inappropriate risk behaviour by management. There is also the risk of maintaining financial institutions or activities that would not be profitable without state aid. Furthermore, extensive state support may expand the risk of moral hazard from 'too big to fail' institutions to the wider economy. In order to ensure that government support measures do not generate unnecessary distortions of competition between financial institutions operating in the market, competition authorities have requested or imposed a number of compensatory measures.[2]

By contrast to potential anti-competitive effects, the inherent risk of the moral hazard of extensive state intervention was more difficult to contain. A number of related explanations can be provided. First, during the unfolding crisis a Keynesian approach to crisis management involving extensive state intervention in the economy not only appeared to be necessary but quickly became generally accepted. This approach had worked during the Great Depression and was considered as a straightforward measure to resolve a systemic crisis. Second, in view of a threatening new reality of major financial collapses there was really no alternative but to provide massive government support to financial institutions which could endanger the stability of the financial system.[3] Third, proponents of far-reaching government support justified the need for government to play an enhanced role in the economy by pointing, for instance, to shortcomings – or failures – of the free market system. In their view, the issue of moral hazard was considered merely as a theoretical problem which was overrated and even dangerous (for example, Summers, 2007). Last but not least, the overall financial stability framework provided no specific measures to deal with the risk of moral hazard.

The term 'moral hazard' originally comes from the insurance sector. It occurs when the behaviour of the insured party changes in a way that raises costs for the insurer because the insured party does not assume the full consequences and responsibilities of its actions.[4] In finance, moral hazard arises if those that take the risks come to believe that they will not have to carry the full burden of losses and therefore have a tendency to act less carefully than they would otherwise. For instance, a misalignment of incentives can encourage managers to become more interested in the pursuit of short-term gains with restricted interest or responsibility for potential long-term costs. This behaviour can be created by expectations that there will be a bailout by governments or central banks in case of a crisis situation (for example, Summers, 2007). With hindsight, moral hazard may have played an important role in the events leading up to the crisis. Researchers have documented failures in risk management, corporate accountability, corporate governance and public policy as contributors to the financial crisis while referring to the underlying problem of moral hazard (for example, Brown, 2008; Dowd, 2009).

However, the moral hazard problem itself should not be restricted to crisis situations as governments intervene in financial markets in different ways. In addition to the implementation of financial regulations (that is, prudential regulations, financial market regulations, consumer protection rules), governments exert an important influence on financial markets, for instance, through the establishment of competition rules, consumer protection schemes such as insurance guarantee funds and direct market participation including public investments, quasi-public financial institutions and nationalisations. Academic research, mostly on the banking sector, has pointed to the potentially distortive effects of different public interventions on organisational behaviour and market discipline. These market-distortive effects, which are generally grouped under the common flag of moral hazard, have not received much attention. With a focus on the insurance sector, this chapter presents an analysis of the moral hazard problem related to a number of government interventions and proposes different prudential measures as a possible response.

Government interventions, regulatory environment and moral hazard

In the literature, several determinants of moral hazard have been examined, that is, factors which contribute to a misalignment of incentives by executives and investors creating inappropriate risk behaviour. Generally, firm-specific factors such as the extent of external monitoring (for example, by creditors), the relationship between management and stockholders, the firm's level of franchise value and governance arrangements (that is, the ownership structure and the remuneration structure) have been examined as elements which may have an adverse impact on firm incentives, regulatory costs and market discipline (for example, Jensen and Meckling, 1976; Brewer et al., 1997). Next to this, a number of government interventions have been identified which may equally affect a firm's willingness to increase risk and, as such, contribute to moral hazard. Some of these interventions merit more profound reflection from a prudential supervisory perspective.

Government bailouts and nationalisations

The extension of government safety nets to systemically important financial institutions (SIFIs), and in extensu to numerous other financial and non-financial institutions in difficulties, has marked a turning point in attitudes to financial liberalisation. Whereas at the onset of the crisis critics still pleaded for a severe restriction on government bailouts and nationalisations (for example, Wolf, 2008), the significance of the unfolding events changed these attitudes as drastic measures were required to prevent a complete financial meltdown. Suddenly, a wide range of institutions, including internationally active insurance and reinsurance companies, were considered as systemically important or 'too big to fail'. The micro-systemic impact and risk of contagion associated with the failure of such an institution could endanger the stability of the financial system.

One should, however, recognise that in the course of the crisis it had become increasingly difficult for supervisors to make a reliable estimate of the probability and impact of a failure of an internationally active insurer or reinsurer.

Several explanations could be advanced, ranging from poor harmonisation of regulatory frameworks, through a lack of sufficient and reliable information, to unwillingness to engage in supervisory cooperation or exchange of information, and most certainly a lack of preparedness to see realised unthinkable scenarios. The International Association of Insurance Supervisors (IAIS) has determined a number of factors that can be taken into account in the assessment of a systemic threat posed by an insurance or reinsurance company. However, great uncertainty as to the evolving financial situation of large groups has resulted in a huge loss of efficiency while at the same time complicating crisis management. Hence, one could assume that certain institutions were considered 'too big to let fail' because this was the only workable assumption.

The increasing willingness of national governments to adopt crisis support measures can be justified from a financial stability perspective but contains a number of inherent problems. First, extensive government support requires a very strong government and may be less effective in resolving crises that affect a large number of institutions at the same time. The recent problems with smaller European jurisdictions could be considered as a case in point. Second, government intervention through bailouts and nationalisations are temporary crisis measures but are not effective in controlling the probability of individual failures (Nier, 2009). Third, extensive government support disturbs the level playing field in the global financial market, as particularly large financial institutions in larger jurisdictions may gain undue advantage (James, 2010). Within the EU, competition authorities have enforced anti-competitive measures to mitigate this risk. Fourth, the reactions and expectations of different government bodies, including competition authorities, prudential supervisors and national governments, in relation to bailouts and nationalisations may be inconsistent, thereby increasing moral hazard.

Indeed, the budgetary impact of rescue measures on individual states' finances has become a concern. But an equally important problem is that through the numerous bailouts and nationalisations during the crisis, moral hazard has become visible. Worldwide, governments have intervened on a massive scale, and this can only enhance the expectations of the industry regarding government support in future crisis situations. Research has documented the detrimental effect of support expectations on market discipline, a consequence that lies at the heart of the moral hazard problem (for example, Nier and Baumann, 2006). In order to address the immanent risk of moral hazard prudential measures should more explicitly minimise and condition the expectations of a government bailout or nationalisation in a crisis situation and develop sanctions with a deterrent effect to those who would confide in such measures. Thus, more research is needed to appreciate the risk of moral hazard related to government bailouts and crisis interventions, in order to draw correct conclusions regarding the factors which can mitigate this risk.

Insurance guarantee funds

Insurance guarantee funds guarantee as a last resort the rights of policy-holders and beneficiaries in the event of the failure of an insurance company. Generally, a guarantee fund will intervene by compensating the financial losses of the claimants or by securing the continuation of the insurance contracts. The adoption of insurance guarantee funds traditionally reflects the view that the private market has proven inadequate as a risk-sharing mechanism for certain types of policy-holders. Many types of insurance, such as liability insurance, are purchased to fulfil legal obligations toward future claimants who are a third party in the contracting process. As the buyers of these products have no direct self-interest in the insurance coverage, they will likely be motivated to buy insurance from the least expensive insurer. At this point, incentive conflicts arise between the buyers of insurance and the third-party claimants who will be affected in case of insurer insolvency. Once a guarantee fund has been introduced, buyers will be indifferent as regards high-risk and low-risk insurers. Then, the costs of insurer insolvencies are borne by the insurance system (and possibly the state) rather than by the individual policy-holders and third-party claimants.

However, insufficient attention has been paid to the impact insurance guarantee funds have on firm incentives to increase risk-taking, the aggregated level of risk in the insurance system and the cost of insurer failures (for example, Buser et al., 1981; Cummins, 1988). In order to understand this, first a regime without guarantee fund protection has to be considered. Under this regime, policy-holders' funds are at risk and policy-holders would have considerably more incentive to buy coverage from safe insurers. There would be less incentive to choose a company which offers the lowest premium for insurance coverage or relatively high interest rates on investment products, regardless of its safety (Harrington, 1991). Other parties such as agents, brokers and providers of mortgage loans would also be expected to pay more attention to the soundness of insurers. This preference for safety would motivate companies to be prudent by developing moderate risk-taking, holding more capital and obtaining high ratings by external analysts. Insurance companies would be sensitive to the interests of their stakeholders and put a strong emphasis on confidence building. As a result, the financial health of insurance companies would be driven largely by public demand (Dowd, 2009).

Through the introduction of insurance guarantee funds policy-holders' and insurers' incentives are likely to change. With a comprehensive insurance guarantee fund in place, policy-holders are less concerned with the safety of their insurance company and less motivated to assess competing insurers' financial strength. Policy-holders may still have some incentive to hold risk-taking in check depending on the amount of coverage and the payout time of the guarantee fund in the event of liquidation of a failed company (Sommer, 1996). However, recent developments on deposit guarantee and investor compensation schemes at the European level increasingly focus on augmenting the minimum coverage amount and shortening the payout time, thus further diluting the incentive for due private monitoring (European Commission, 2009). As a result, if not accompanied with counterweighting deterrent measures, market discipline to ensure the safety of institutions is strongly reduced. High-risk insurance companies will be less constrained to keep risk and leverage at acceptable levels for their customers. Previously prudent insurers will suffer from competitive pressure from high risk insurers and will be tempted to take on more risks in order to be able to compete. In the end, the total cost of insurer insolvencies may be considerably higher than in a regime without insurance guarantee funds.

Competition policy

The regulation and supervision of competition is concerned with market concentrations and actions by market participants which impede, restrict or distort competition. Certain competition objectives relating to consumer protection, for instance, to reduce information asymmetries between sellers and buyers of financial products, are comparable to traditional conduct of business regulations. However, competition authorities are not so much concerned with financial stability but focus instead on market-distortive effects, caused, for instance, by a major shift in the financial markets. Recent crisis events have illustrated the complex relationship between the objectives of competition rules (that is, preservation of a free market and reduction of market distortions) and the objectives of prudential regulation (that is, consumer protection and mitigation of systemic risk) (Flamée and Schuermans, 2006). In the resolution of the crisis, competition measures were taken to mitigate unfair competition rather than to contribute to the objective of minimising systemic risk. Although some objectives of competition policy and prudential regulation converge, recent developments in the financial sector have increasingly called into question the relationship between competition, financial consolidation and stability.

The Financial Stability Board (FSB) and other international institutions have indirectly pointed towards the risks of financial consolidation and the problem of moral hazard. Through the emergence of 'too big to fail' institutions and the lack of substitutability of certain actors, the financial system can become exposed to increased systemic risk. Even if greater competition may contribute to higher efficiency, the inherent risks of far-reaching financial consolidation should not be minimised, given the high costs of financial instability in a crisis situation. A key problem is that efficiency gains by competition are difficult to predict and to measure, while empirical data on the costs of financial instability are quite clear (for example ,IMF, 2009). In view of the huge risks financial instability can pose to the global economy, the impact of competition measures on financial stability deserves more careful consideration and examination by researchers, competition authorities and prudential supervisors.

Prudential regulation

From a prudential point of view, insurance regulation has been introduced to prevent financial difficulties which could endanger the viability of insurance companies and to sustain a sound operating sector that protects and maintains the confidence of policy-holders. Prudential rules aim at protecting the rights of the insured and of third parties affected by the execution of insurance contracts, and to that end determine the principal conditions and rules governing the commercial activity of insurance undertakings. These rules include, for instance, the conditions for obtaining authorization as an insurance company and rules governing the activities of the insurance business. Over the past years, the traditional focus of insurance supervision on policy-holder protection has broadened into a general concern for financial stability in view of the expansion of insurers into global financial markets (IMF and World Bank, 2005). In this respect, prudential measures to support the broader policy objective of financial stability need to be further developed.

The implications for financial stability arising from an insurer's failure can be catastrophic, but even in the absence of failures, a weakened financial system can have an impact on the economy at large (CEIOPS, 2010). Since the costs of these impacts are unlikely to be internalised by individual institutions in their risk management, prudential regulation is needed to mitigate systemic risk (Nier, 2009). In this regard, prudential regulations have evolved over the past years from a rules-based approach to a principles-based approach to regulation. The application of a rules-based approach to regulation has been recognised as consistent and transparent but can also create moral hazard. For instance, rules-based requirements are largely based on static considerations such as year-end company results and only to a limited degree take into account organisational behaviour or evolutions in the environment of the institutions. As these requirements are not aligned with the nature and full scale of risks undertaken, companies may be tempted to increase their risk-taking significantly. At the same time, prudential supervision may not be very effective since companies will merely try to comply with regulations by adapting their reporting to the formal expectations of the supervisor.

Despite the recent shift toward a principles-based approach of regulation in many countries, some remarks can be made with respect to current design of prudential requirements in the insurance sector. First, prudential capital requirements focus predominantly on the occurrence of micro-systemic risk in an attempt to reduce the probability of failure to an acceptable level. With a few notable exceptions,[5] the build-up of macro-systemic risk has not received much attention by prudential supervisors. Second, risk-based capital frameworks such as Solvency II are based on the assumption of the same probability of failure across all financial institutions. This probability of failure reflects the desired level of financial stability irrespective of the potentially systemic consequences of individual failures which are statistically considered as acceptable. Third, prudential capital requirements are usually based on risk estimations of models with a short time horizon, while systemic risk in the insurance sector develops over a longer term. Fourth, prudential requirements are implemented by way of precaution but do not attempt to control the impact of systemic risk once a crisis emerges. Lastly, there is a continuing debate on whether prudential capital requirements are an effective means to impose constraints on the use of financial leverage (Hellmann et al., 2000).

Differentiated nature and scope of financial regulation

International financial regulation, and its review and assessment by supervisors, is sector specific which results in a differentiated nature of supervision for the banking, insurance and securities sectors.[6] With the emergence of truly global financial institutions active in numerous jurisdictions around the world and offering a multiplicity of financial services under sometimes very different legal frameworks, financial regulation has been stretched to its limits. These financial groups, through networks of legal entities and structures, blur the boundaries among the sectors and present challenges for the application of financial regulation and supervision. Sometimes differences in the nature of regulation among the different financial sectors are warranted due to specific characteristics of each financial sector. However, differences in regulation combined with a legal entity approach to supervision also create the potential for regulatory arbitrage and gaps in the regulation of a group as a whole. To the extent that 'regulatory optimisation' may lead to significant cost savings, financial conglomerates may be tempted to significantly increase their risk appetite as such creating the moral hazard problem.

A number of key differences have been identified among the regulatory frameworks of the banking, securities and insurance sectors that have no objective justification. For instance, the emphasis placed on group-wide supervision varies significantly in the three sectors. Whilst the Basel Committee on Banking Supervision (BCBS) has always placed a strong focus on consolidated supervision, the IAIS only recently increased its attention for group-wide supervision and the International Organization of Securities Commissions (IOSCO) has not developed any requirements in this regard. Comparable differences exist with regard to the development of a global capital framework within each sector. At present, a uniform and global capital framework only exists for the banking sector whereas different capital requirements are applied within the insurance and securities sectors across jurisdictions. Strong variations in the regulation of the different sectors have also been found with respect to business conduct and consumer or investor protection. Next to differences in the legal or regulatory framework across financial sectors, differences in the implementation of regulations by supervisors can result in significant differences in practice. As a natural response, financial groups active in different financial sectors try to create synergies and take advantage of these differences in the regulatory, supervisory or fiscal environment.

The Joint Forum (2010) has also indicated a number of differences in regulatory treatment which can create problems for supervisors in capturing and assessing the full spectrum of risks of financial groups, and the impact and cost that these may impose on the financial system. These differences relate, for instance, to the consideration of unregulated entities when calculating group capital adequacy, the assessment of intra-group transactions and exposures, and the supervision of unregulated parent holding companies or other unregulated companies that are higher in the hierarchy of ownership. In order to address these differences appropriately, the nature and scope of financial regulation should be expanded so that all risks undertaken are effectively managed by the regulated entities and supervised by the appropriate authorities.

Quasi-public financial institutions

Fundamental questions have risen regarding the business model of quasi-public financial institutions, that is, financial institutions that are private but partly publicly owned, backed by a government or otherwise financed by a government, such as the government-sponsored entities in the US and a number of banking and insurance companies in the EU (for example, Nier, 2009). The crisis has shown that moral hazard incentives can be particularly strong for financial institutions which can benefit from implicit or explicit government guarantees. Across the globe, the losses for quasi-public financial institutions have been huge, and in many cases extensive government intervention was necessary to rescue the failing institutions. The theoretical explanation is that many of these institutions had engaged in more aggressive risk-taking because the potential gains and losses were asymmetric (Harrington, 2009). In good times, high profits could be realised, while in bad times the losses would be borne by other parties, including taxpayers. Quasi-public financial institutions could also enjoy a competitive advantage as implicit government guarantees lowered their financing costs. This may have contributed to the development of high leverage positions and more risky underwriting and investment strategies.

Given their specific business model, quasi-public financial institutions are able to pursue public policy objectives or objectives that otherwise would not be delivered by private institutions. An example is the objective to increase the availability of motor liability insurance at acceptable premium levels for all categories of drivers within a given population. However, the attainment of public policy objectives through private institutions may create adverse incentives which can result in significant losses to the government. A key problem is that market discipline for these institutions is structurally weak. Traditional mechanisms which promote prudence, safety and soundness in insurance companies, including market and supervisory control, become less efficient. For instance, supervisory action may become more difficult when the management of the sponsored institution enjoys the implicit backing of the government. When market and regulatory discipline is weak, companies' incentives to fulfil market expectations, for instance, regarding capital requirements diminish and management has greater discretion for potentially undesirable actions. A growing untransparency of company actions over time only exacerbates the problem of moral hazard.

The loss of market efficiency for quasi-public financial institutions may be difficult to overcome from a supervisory perspective. Structural changes in the business model such as a nationalisation, a complete privatisation or a specific regulatory framework with direct and strong powers of oversight and resolution are required to address the moral hazard problem of these organisations (see, for example, Nier, 2009).

Reflections on measures to reduce moral hazard

In the wake of the crisis, several policy measures have been proposed as a means to promote sound and safe insurance markets including, for instance, the establishment of a systemic risk regulator, the adoption of tougher capital requirements, the introduction of limitations on the scope of financial institutions' activities and drastic changes in the design of government guarantees. Given the incentive problems associated with different government interventions, it should be recognised from the outset that some regulatory responses may not help to encourage market discipline or improvements in firms' risk management. In fact, the result could be that some measures would again lead to undesirable distortions in companies' decisions and provide incentives for them to circumvent the requirements in innovative ways (Harrington, 2009). Therefore, in the elaboration of policy responses to strengthen the resilience of the financial system, due consideration should be given to the impact each of these measures may have on market efficiency and organisational behaviour.

Enhancing group-wide supervision

Whilst the crisis may not be very instructive on the ideal structure of financial supervision, it highlights the need for more targeted supervision of large complex institutions, sometimes active in diverse financial services and with potential systemic implications. In this regard, there seems to be no good argument for excluding insurance, or any other type of financial activity, from the scope of this oversight, as the crisis has shown precisely the risks and problems caused by partial and limited oversight carried out by different supervisory authorities for these groups. In other words, the problem is not whether or not to include insurance groups within the scope of systemically important financial institutions but how to organise and improve the supervision of these large and complex cross-border groups which necessitate the involvement and cooperation of a large number of supervisors. Next to the question of the structure of supervision, a key challenge relates to the development of supervisory instruments and regulations which can effectively take into account the complexities and particularities of cross-border and cross-sector groups. In this light, the enhancement of an adequate framework for the supervision of cross-border groups has been recognised internationally as a priority.

The most feasible approach to overseeing cross-border insurers and reinsurers is likely based on a minimum set of compatible supervisory principles and practices. The basic assumption is that restricted convergence of company-level regulations would not be problematic if these regulations were supplemented with a harmonised approach to supervision of cross-border groups. The arrangements for the supervision of cross-border groups should also be enhanced with respect to the functioning of the supervisory colleges, including modalities for ongoing coordinated supervision of the group and procedures for cooperation in crisis situations. In this perspective, the IAIS has begun to develop a common assessment framework for the supervision of international insurance groups (ComFrame). Through a group supervision framework which looks beyond the pursuit of company-level regulations, supervisors should gain a group-wide perspective from which to examine key elements such as group solvency, group risk management and intra-group risk exposures. The purpose will be to integrate the role and experience of each local supervisor within a coherent group-wide approach to avoid duplication or divergence of action. Consideration will be given to establishing harmonised, firm-wide requirements of supervisory reporting in order to improve group-wide risk assessments while reducing the administrative burden for groups.

Strengthening the macro-prudential focus on systemic risks

At different national and international levels, financial sector reforms have been initiated with the aim of developing and integrating the macro-prudential dimension into financial sector supervision. At the European level, reference can be made to the new European System of Financial Supervision and the development of a European Systemic Risk Board (ESRB). At the national level, comparable reforms have been proposed to foster the integration of micro- and macro-prudential supervision and enhance the supervisory focus on financial stability. For instance, in France, Belgium and the UK the responsibility for micro-prudential supervision has been entrusted to the central bank in addition to its macro-prudential activities. However, at the international level, the supervision of systemic risks has not yet been formalised in a clear mandate and delegated to an existing or new authority such as, for instance, the International Monetary Fund (IMF), the FSB or the Bank for International Settlements (BIS).

In order to improve supervision of systemic risks, the scope, objectives and outputs of the expected macro-prudential activities will need to be carefully identified with due consideration for the different financial sectors. In the elaboration of this important work, the entire set of macroeconomic factors and international trends which could lead to a decrease of financial stability should be taken into account. For instance, periodic macro-prudential analyses could indicate heightened risks from negative market trends, unsound market practices and poor risk estimations for certain types of activities. In order to give appropriate consideration to these analyses, macro-prudential authorities should receive sufficient powers to require direct supervisory actions from their micro-prudential colleagues in case of emergency. Micro-prudential supervisors should be able to integrate the raised concerns into their assessments and to implement appropriate measures to mitigate detected risks. Micro-prudential actions could include, for instance, additional requirements such as heightened capital requirements, a liquidity premium or a modified weighting of risks.

Macro-prudential analyses should also regularly examine the systemic importance of the different financial sectors as a whole in view of their key role within the economy. With regard to the insurance sector, the examination of systemic risks should include both a cross-sectional dimension (that is, the way in which particular market developments can be perceived among firms) and a time dimension (that is, how long it would take for an event to impact on the real economy). Macro-prudential actions to deal with any systemic risk relating to insurance activities should focus on the insurance sector as a whole and should be predominantly of a regulatory nature. The adopted macro-prudential approach may differ from the approach in the banking sector in view of the distinct business model of insurance in comparison with banking. It goes without saying that macro-prudential analyses could be complemented in a meaningful way by industry analyses in order to approach potential systemic events in the most appropriate way. Industry involvement in global financial stability analyses could be regarded as an effective means to reduce moral hazard when systemic risks develop.

Improving micro-prudential risk assessments

Micro-prudential risk assessments which are used to determine regulatory capital requirements need to be improved. For instance, current prudential measures insufficiently take into account the instability of today's financial markets and the development of extreme risks which could become of a systemic nature. In the same vein, the risk of illiquidity of the financial markets is insufficiently considered in present risk models or in any other prudential measures. As a result, losses due to extreme market events are not measured consistently or covered by companies' own funds. Although periodic stress tests are used to examine extreme market shocks, these tests only partially replicate extreme loss scenarios accompanying a systemic event such as a liquidity squeeze. From this perspective, an additional set of prudential measures has become indispensable to make a complete and correct risk assessment of financial activities. These measures should give specific consideration to the probability and impact of extreme market events on the individual company's activities, investments and available capital to absorb extreme losses.

Based on their risk assessments, micro-prudential supervisors should have at their disposal appropriate means to discourage and correct the development of systemic risks which could endanger the stability of the financial system. General consent seems to have been reached on the use of temporary regulatory and supervisory measures to encourage changes in behaviour in view of reducing the build-up of systemic risk. For instance, micro-prudential supervisors should receive powers to limit, on a temporary basis, the volume of certain systemic activities or the development of new complex activities (Lepetit, 2010). Other powers could relate, for instance, to the possibility of intensifying the extent of supervisory reporting, imposing higher capital requirements or limiting the exposure to a single counterparty as regards the company's own funds. Another area requiring increased supervisory attention concerns the analysis and avoidance of regulatory arbitrage between different regulated and unregulated financial sectors (for example, de Larosière Group, 2009; Lepetit, 2010). The possibility of differential regulatory treatment of financial sectors may lead to an underpricing of risks and, consequently, to an unnatural accumulation of risks. Adequate supervision of cross-sectoral activity should focus on emerging complexities such as the creation of bridges between regulated and less regulated institutions for the transfer of risks and the adoption of business techniques which may endanger macroeconomic stability.

All in all, the ongoing developments in the financial markets require a more pro-active and integrated form of financial supervision. Integrated risk-based supervision assesses the business of an insurance company, its risk profile and the macroeconomic context. This requires a forward-looking approach based on a complete picture of an insurer's financial and operational position in the key business areas. Macro-prudential analyses that focus on emerging macroeconomic and macro-financial developments need to be incorporated into company-level analyses in order to examine new forms and dynamics of risk accumulation. In the same vein, regulatory requirements should become forward-looking, in line with the evolving business models and risks on both a company basis and an aggregated level. A comprehensive analysis of capital adequacy should use both quantitative and qualitative information elements which together provide a longer time horizon for analysis.

Implementing a national policy for systemically important financial institutions

The FSB has advanced a framework of high-level principles to guide the development of national policies aimed at dealing with SIFIs. Specific measures will need to be developed to address the negative externalities created by institutions that may impose significant rescue costs on societies. On the one hand, system-wide initiatives should reduce structural system-wide risk by mitigating the potential for spillovers from SIFI failures. These initiatives include efforts to improve the effectiveness of resolution frameworks and their interaction in a cross-border context, measures to reduce contagion risk through improved financial infrastructures, and efforts to enhance the intensity and quality of the supervisory framework for SIFIs. On the other hand, more targeted institution-focused initiatives should force SIFIs to internalise the externalities they impose on the system, in line with their contribution to the build up of systemic risk. These measures should increase a firm's loss absorption capacity and reduce its probability of failure, while providing incentives to reduce the degree of systemic risk. For instance, SIFIs would be subjected to additional prudential requirements such as capital and liquidity surcharges, more stringent requirements for the quality of capital, additional constrained leverage or the mandatory holding of contingent capital.

The proposed approach entails the concept of 'constrained discretion' which establishes a clear set of principles, defines the necessary set of tools, and requires all national authorities to put in place some effective combination of actions, but with a degree of national discretion over the application of different tools. Specifically, the approach would require all authorities with SIFIs operating in their jurisdictions to develop an explicit SIFI policy, drawing on a globally defined mix of policy tools. Next to this, a global standard for the definition of higher capital and liquidity requirements for SIFIs would be established (for banks this work would be done by the Basel Committee) from which deviation is allowed only if alternative policy levers are in place to reduce systemic risk. Processes would need to ensure that all jurisdictions have made reasonable tradeoffs in their detailed application of SIFI principles. Variations from the globally defined standard could be justified, for instance, by the resolvability of specific institutions. In this regard, several factors could be considered such as the credibility of the institutions' resolution and recovery plans, the interconnectedness of the institution, the implications of group internal legal structures for resilience and resolvability and the progress of national authorities in establishing a crisis resolution framework.

Developing crisis resolution regimes

At different international levels, the importance of sound crisis management and resolution methods has been underlined (for example, de Larosière Group,

2009). At present, national provisions for crisis management differ significantly between jurisdictions, rendering a quick reaction and a smooth cooperation in an emergency situation very difficult. In order to progress towards an efficient and harmonised system of crisis resolution, an overarching set of procedures for the orderly recovery and liquidation of financial institutions should be instituted at the international level. These procedures should take the form of a coherent set of international principles and standards to be implemented by individual jurisdictions in their national crisis regimes. These measures should not only ensure the continuity of financial sector activity and the reduction of systemic risk in crisis situations but should also improve coordination between financial supervisors in the resolution of cross-border firms. As a first response, the FSB has established crisis management groups for a number of large, complex financial groups. These crisis management groups are responsible for initiating processes for the development of recovery and resolution plans, and are driven forward mainly by home supervisors, in cooperation with host supervisors.

A related challenge consists in the development of burden-sharing plans, that is, plans which define the modalities of financing crisis resolution plans. In this regard, particular consideration should be given to the involvement of the private sector in the resolution of a crisis in order to minimize the risk of moral hazard. For instance, crisis resolution plans should not be financed through the development of a permanent guarantee fund but through a crisis resolution mechanism supported by the financial sector which could be activated in exceptional circumstances. In this light, the European Commission has indicated that it supports the establishment of ex ante resolution funds, funded by a levy on financial institutions. As an integral part of the crisis resolution framework, these resolution funds should allow a failing financial institution to be unwound in a timely and orderly manner, while minimising the risk of contagion and financial instability. However, to avoid the risk of moral hazard, these funds should not be regarded as an insurance against failure or for bailing out failing institutions. Therefore, the financing of the resolution funds would be based on the 'polluter pays' principle, those responsible for causing the financial crisis will pay the costs of a future crisis.

Introducing risk-based insurance guarantee funds

An insurance guarantee fund could be seen as an effective means to allow for a controlled run-off of insurance companies, one that should minimise financial instability. This is possible because insurers, unlike banks, are less susceptible to insurance runs and related liquidity problems. However, previous research has indicated that the design of insurance guarantee funds may significantly condition companies' incentives for safety (for example, Cummins, 1988). In particular, if the premium to finance the guarantee fund does not reflect insurer risk, an incentive may be created for more risky firms to increase risk-taking as the market value of equity increases. These firms may consider the guarantee fund as 'a put-option-like subsidy' (Eling and Schmeiser, 2010), which allows them to charge lower premiums in order to attract policy-holders. As a result, market discipline will diminish for high risk insurers while the burden on regulatory monitoring will increase due the heightened level of risks and insolvencies in the insurance markets. In order to minimise the risk of moral hazard, an insurance guarantee fund should be designed to achieve a sound balance between providing incentives for safety to insurers and protecting consumers for losses in the case of insurer insolvency (Harrington, 1991). In this view, the financing of the guarantee fund should be based on risk-based premiums in a competitive market instead of flat volume-based premiums. The guarantee fund premium would then vary directly with the risk of the firm and reduce the potential for distortions in the firm's asset and liability portfolios (Cummins, 1988).

A number of related measures could be envisaged to reduce the moral hazard risk of insurance guarantee funds. For instance, incorporating all stakeholders into the financing of the fund may be considered, in order to enhance market discipline in the insurance market. Next to insurance companies and the government, which should act as a lender of last resort, policy-holders could be required to bear a small percentage of the loss in the event of insolvency, for instance through a system of co-payments (that is, fixed deductibles, minimum floors, percentage reductions or caps). However, the implementation of this measure may be less feasible from a political perspective. As another measure, clear restrictions could be imposed on the scope of protection provided by insurance guarantee funds. For instance, commercial insurance could be excluded from coverage, as could investment risk on the part of the policy-holder. Net worth limitations could be applied with regard to the value of claims to exclude excessive benefits from cover. With regard to financing, a combination of ex ante and ex post funding may be preferred, allowing insolvency cases to be handled relatively quickly while incentivising companies to moderate their risk-taking. To this end, risk-based premiums could be used based on the insurers' volume of risks and liabilities. Over time, a greater harmonisation of guarantee protection systems, and the possible development of a mutual support regime, could contribute to a level playing field between the financial sectors.

Analysing the impact of competition on financial stability

Apart from recent exceptional interventions from competition authorities, the impact of competition measures on financial sector stability has not received much attention from a prudential perspective. By contrast, a significant body of research has analysed the relationship between competition and financial stability. Several studies have indicated that, when confronted with increased competition, financial institutions intentionally take on more risk and moral hazard is exacerbated (for example, Smith, 1984; Keeley, 1990; Repullo, 2004).

A related assumption is that in more concentrated markets large financial institutions become more easily subject to regulators 'too big to fail' policies, creating an incentive to take on higher risks (for example, Caminal and Matutes, 2002; De Nicolo et al., 2004). Other studies are built around the so-called 'franchise value' hypothesis (for example, Keeley, 1990): lower levels of competition allow financial institutions to earn higher profits, so that their franchise becomes valuable and going bankrupt costly to them. In such an environment companies with greater market power will protect their franchise value by generating larger capital buffers and the adoption of more prudent, low-risk strategies (Hellmann et al., 2000; Matutes and Vives, 2000). Through stronger competition, market power (and franchise value) would be reduced which could magnify the agency problem between the shareholders of the institution and the government protection fund.[7] To the extent that there is a government protection fund in place, shareholders or managers acting on their behalf become more prone to risky actions. Shareholders then profit from the rewards of the additional risk taken on while the cost of failure is borne by the government protection fund.

However, several studies have shown that the empirical relationship between competition and financial stability is not straightforward (for example, Carletti and Hartmann, 2003). There is no direct or automatic causal relationship between financial institutions' market position and their risk behaviour. Several competing hypotheses have been advanced to provide evidence that higher market concentration does not necessarily lead to more instability but may offer significant opportunities to improve the efficiency of the system (for example, Beck et al., 2006). For instance, essential conditions have been delineated such as the implementation of vigilant prudential supervision and a government safety net which plays a restricted but effective role (Mishkin, 1999). In other words, the relationship between competition and financial stability should not be regarded in terms of a simple tradeoff. There may be a number of qualifying factors, such as the extent of prudential supervision, which could have a profound impact on stability and should be integrated into the analyses. Therefore, current studies have started to focus more directly on the relationship between competitive behaviour of financial institutions and the risk of a crisis (Claessens and Laeven, 2004; Schaeck et al., 2006). The development of a theoretical framework to weigh the costs and benefits of competition versus financial stability and to define an optimal balance for policy could be regarded as an important research objective (for example, Allen and Gale, 2004).

From a practical perspective, a careful balance needs to be found between competition concerns and financial stability objectives. Certain competition measures can be beneficial to economic growth and financial stability in the short term while being counterproductive or even dangerous in the long term. Therefore, the impact of competition policy on financial sector growth and risk behaviour should be monitored more closely as certain market developments may have far-reaching consequences for financial stability. For instance, the negative externalities from financial consolidation and heightened competition deserve proper attention in financial stability analyses. Likewise, the risks of insufficient competition in certain jurisdictions should be carefully monitored. The lack of substitutability of dominant market players and low levels of competition in certain market segments have been recognized as important weaknesses which may have contributed to the accumulation of systemic risks (Lepetit, 2010). To this end, stronger forms of cooperation need to be developed between macro-prudential supervisors and competition authorities in order to achieve the common objective of healthy competition in a stable financial market.

Enhancing market discipline through public disclosure

Systemically important insurance and reinsurance companies require stronger government guarantees and tighter regulation because of the greater risk of adverse effects on the economy. These government measures reduce systemic risk and deter insurance runs but at the same time increase the risk of moral hazard. Thus, there is a policy tradeoff to be made (Harrington, 2009). In order to reduce moral hazard to an acceptable level, market discipline should be sufficiently strong for institutions to be safe and sound. Market discipline therefore has an important complementary function next to prudential regulation and should be integrated within the prudential framework. This has been recognised, for instance, in the Basel framework for banking supervision and in the Solvency II framework for insurance supervision in the EU. In these models, explicit attention is paid to supervisory reporting, public disclosure and market discipline under pillar three, next to a strong focus on quantitative requirements under pillar one and qualitative requirements under pillar two. These prudential frameworks have as general objectives to avoid undercapitalised financial institutions, to enhance incentives for internal risk management and to foster market discipline through public disclosure (for example, more pressure from rating agencies, capital markets).

Every insurance company should also maintain the possibility of disclosing on a voluntary basis any information or explanation on important actions or their financial condition which is not already required to be disclosed from a legal or prudential perspective. In this regard, considerable emphasis should be placed on promoting increased transparency and fairness to consumers, next to investors and other financial market participants. Indeed, consumers could be considered an important part of the monitoring system and a powerful engine to influence organisational behaviour. At present, the assumption that market discipline from retail markets is relatively strong could be called into question. Until recently, not much attention has been given to the role consumers can play in fostering market discipline. Insurance regulation has traditionally focused on protecting policy-holders' rights in existing policies (Bell and Keller, 2009).

Financial supervisors should, however, undertake more initiatives to foster market discipline by retail markets. These initiatives could focus, for instance, on the enhancement of consumer information, bilateral communication and financial education.

Conclusions

During the global financial crisis, far-reaching government interventions have been required at different national and international levels to support the financial sector, to protect the rights of depositors and policy-holders, and to ensure financial stability. As a result of these massive crisis interventions a heavy economic burden has to be borne by today's taxpayers and future generations (European Commission, 2010). As a response, policymakers, regulators and industry stakeholders alike have been proposing diverse measures for regulatory repair. However, recent events not only have shown that failures in the financial sector may cause a lot of external costs to others, but also that the risk of moral hazard has been seriously underestimated in the design of the overall financial stability framework. Consequently, more consideration should be given to the possible impact of each policy measure on market efficiency and organisational behaviour. The design of new prudential requirements should not only take into account the distinctive nature of insurance markets but should also target the risk of moral hazard itself.

Research has shown clear incentive problems relating to extensive government interventions in the financial sector, for instance through bailouts and nationalizations, comprehensive guarantee arrangements and the establishment of quasi-public financial institutions. Likewise, it has been recognised that regulatory and competition measures, if not well designed, may not help to encourage market discipline or improvements in firms' risk management. Not only does the relationship between competition and financial stability deserve more careful examination. Caution should also be exercised in the development of new prudential regulations to avoid that these measures again would lead to undesirable distortions in companies' decisions or provide incentives for them to circumvent the requirements. More extensive research is required to offer a well-founded answer to the complex and neglected question of moral hazard from a prudential perspective. The international institutions in charge of financial stability could contribute to these analyses in a meaningful way.

In order to enhance stakeholder involvement, profound impact assessments combined with extensive stakeholder consultations should become a best practice for regulatory development, as it is the case at the European level (for example, Mather and Vibert, 2006). Taking into account the risks and benefits of financial regulation, the prudential framework should target key risks in a balanced way, that is, any new requirements should be proportionate to the perceived risks in each financial sector. In this respect, a risk-adequate pricing of prudential requirements could offer the best guarantee that sound risk management and governance processes are implemented in the organisations. Furthermore, recent problems cannot be tackled only through an increase in risk-based quantitative requirements. There is also a need to strengthen the so-called pillar two requirements, that is, the qualitative supervisory requirements which focus on the implementation of sound governance principles and adequate control mechanisms within the organisations. This is, of course, the most delicate part of supervisory work as it involves an examination of the organisations' functioning and its management. In order to make professional examinations, the quality of financial sector supervision, including the development of a skilled staff, deserves proper attention.

In order to get a real grip on industry evolutions and risks prudential actions should unfold in a business context, and not only in a legislative environment. Sometimes, strong prudential requirements may be necessary to avoid excessive risk-taking but these measures should always be carefully considered, in relation to companies' business models and with respect for creativity and financial innovation. The importance of increased prudential action, for instance, in relation to group-wide supervision, should certainly not be minimised against the backdrop of the increased moral hazard which is occasionally advanced by the industry as an important risk. However, a strong dialogue between regulators and the industry can in many cases lead to a public-private win-win situation.

Notes

1. The views expressed in this chapter are solely those of the authors.
2. This was, for instance, the case in the European Union.
3. In particular, the failure of Lehman Brothers and the heightened risk of a financial meltdown had put a different perspective on crisis resolution.
4. For example, when holders of automobile insurance tend to drive less carefully, thereby increasing the risk of an accident for the insurer.
5. For example, counter-cyclical capital requirements for banks were implemented in Spain in 2000.
6. The following draws heavily on the Joint Forum report, *Review of the Differentiated Nature and Scope of Financial Regulation: Key Issues and Recommendations* (2010).
7. In this view, the government protection fund could be seen as a 'lender of last resort'.

Bibliography

Allen, F., and D. Gale (2004) 'Competition and Financial Stability', *Journal of Money, Credit and Banking*, 36: 453–80.

Beck, T., A. Demirgüç-Kunt and R. Levine (2006) 'Bank Concentration, Competition, and Crises: First Results', *Journal of Banking and Finance*, 30: 1581–603.

Bell, M., and B. Keller (2009) *Insurance and Stability in the Reform of Insurance Regulation* (Zurich: Zurich Financial Services).

Brewer, E., T.S. Mondschean and P.E. Strahan (1997) 'The Role of Monitoring in Reducing the Moral Hazard Problem Associated with Government Guarantees: Evidence from the Life Insurance Industry', *Journal of Risk and Insurance*, 64(2): 301–22.

Brown, B. (2008) 'Uncle Sam as Sugar Daddy', *MarketWatch*, 19 November.

Buser, S.A., A.H. Chen and E.J. Kane (1981) 'Federal Deposit Insurance, Regulatory Policy, and Optimal Bank Capital', *Journal of Finance*, 36: 51–60.

Caminal, R., and C. Matutes (2002) 'Market Power and Bank Failures', *International Journal of Industrial Organisation*, 20: 1341–61.

Carletti, E., and P. Hartmann (2003) 'Competition and Stability: What's Special about Banking?' in P.D. Mizen (ed.), *Monetary History, Exchange Rates and Financial Markets: Essays in Honour of Charles Goodhart*, Vol. 2 (Cheltenham: Edward Elgar).

Claessens, S., and L. Laeven (2004) 'What Drives Bank Competition? Some International Evidence', *Journal of Money, Credit and Banking*, 36: 563–83.

Committee of European Insurance and Occupational Pensions Supervisors (CEIOPS) (2010) 'Note on Components of Systemic Risk of Insurance Business Models', February.

Cummins, J.D. (1988) 'Risk-based Premiums for Insurance Guarantee Funds', *Journal of Finance*, 43(4): 823–39.

De Nicolo, G., P. Bartholomew, J. Zaman and M. Zephirin (2004) 'Bank Consolidation, Internationalization and Conglomerization: Trends and Implications for Financial Risk', *Financial Markets, Institutions and Instruments*, 13: 173–217.

Dowd, K. (2009) 'Moral Hazard and the Financial Crisis', *Cato Journal*, 29(1): 141–66.

Eling, M., and H. Schmeiser (2010) 'Insurance and the Credit Crisis: Impact and Ten Consequences for Risk Management and Supervision', *The Geneva Papers on Risk and Insurance: Issues and Practice*, 35: 9–34.

European Commission (2009) Directive 2009/14/EC of the European Parliament and of the Council of 11 March 2009 amending Directive 94/19/EC on deposit-guarantee schemes as regards the coverage level and the payout delay, available at http://ec.europa.eu/.

European Commission (2010) 'Bank Resolution Funds', Communication from the Commission to the European Parliament, the Council, the European Economic and Social Committee and the European Central Bank, available at http://ec.europa.eu/.

Flamée, M., and P. Schuermans (2006) 'Europese controle: wondermiddel voor het oplossen van toezichtconflicten in de verzekering? Een blik achter de schermen', *Bull. Ass. - De Verz.*, 12: 78–84.

Harrington, S.E. (1991) 'Should the Feds Regulate Insurance Company Solvency?', Cato Review of Business and Government, *Regulation*, 14: 53–61.

Harrington, S.E. (2009) *The Financial Crisis, Systemic Risk, and the Future of Insurance Regulation*, NAMIC public policy paper (Indianapolis: National Association of Mutual Insurance Companies).

Hellmann, T., K. Murdock and J. Stiglitz (2000) 'Liberalization, Moral Hazard in Banking and Prudential Regulation: Are Capital Requirements Enough?', *American Economic Review*, 90: 147–65.

IMF (2009) 'Fiscal Implications of the Global Economic and Financial Crisis', IMF Staff Position Note 09/13 (Washington, DC: International Monetary Fund).

IMF and World Bank (2005) 'Evaluating Financial Sector Supervision: Banking, Insurance and Securities Markets', in *Financial Sector Assessment: A Handbook* (Washington, DC: IBRD/WB/IMF).

James, H. (2010) 'Why Big Banks Will Get Bigger', Project Syndicate, available at www.project-syndicate.org/commentary/james36/English.

Jensen, M. and Meckling, W. (1976) 'The Theory of the Firm: Managerial Behavior, Agency Costs and Ownership Structures', *Journal of Financial Economics*, 3: 305–60.

Joint Forum (2010) *Review of the Differentiated Nature and Scope of Financial Regulation: Key Issues and Recommendations* (Basel: BCBS, IAIS and IOSCO).

Keeley, M. (1990) 'Deposit Insurance, Risk and Market Power in Banking', *American Economic Review*, 80: 1183–200.

de Larosière Group (2009) *Report of the High Level Group on Financial Supervision in the EU*, 25 February.

Lepetit, J.F. (2010) *Rapport sur le risque systémique* (Paris: Conseil National de la Comptabilité).

Mather, G., and F. Vibert (2006) *Evaluating Better Regulation: Building the System*, European Policy Forum, September, City of London Research Series.

Matutes, C., and X. Vives (2000) 'Imperfect Competition, Risk-taking and Regulation in Banking', *European Economic Review*, 44: 1–34.

Mishkin, F.S. (1999) 'Financial Consolidation: Dangers and Opportunities', *Journal of Banking and Finance*, 23: 675–91.

Nier, E.W. (2009) 'Financial Stability Frameworks and the Role of Central Banks: Lessons from the Crisis', IMF Working Paper 09/70 (Washington, DC: International Monetary Fund).

Nier, E., and U. Baumann (2006) 'Market Discipline, Disclosure and Moral Hazard in Banking', *Journal of Financial Intermediation*, 15: 333–62.

Repullo, R. (2004) 'Capital Requirements, Market Power, and Risk-taking in Banking', *Journal of Financial Intermediation*, 13: 156–82.

Schaeck, K., M. Cihak and S. Wolfe, (2006) 'Are More Competitive Banking Systems More Stable?', IMF Working Paper 06/143 (Washington, DC: International Monetary Fund).

Smith, B. (1984) 'Private Information, Deposit Interest Rates, and the "Stability" of the Banking System', *Journal of Monetary Economics*, 14: 293–317.

Sommer, D.W. (1996) 'The Impact of Firm Risk on Property-Liability Insurance Prices', *Journal of Risk and Insurance*, 63: 501–14.

Summers, L. (2007) 'Beware Moral Hazard Fundamentalists', *Financial Times*, 23 September.

Wolf, M. (2008) 'The Rescue of Bear Stearns Marks Liberalisation's Limit', *Financial Times*, 25 March.

15
The Systemicness of Insurance Companies: Cross-Border Aspects and Policy Implications[1]

Aerdt Houben and Mark Teunissen

Introduction

The last two decades have witnessed an ongoing internationalisation of the insurance sector, which has now become a truly global segment of the financial industry. This has brought substantial benefits in terms of risk diversification, economies of scale and financial technology transfers, thereby augmenting the insurance industry's contribution to a smooth functioning of the real economy. At the same time, however, this internationalisation has created cross-border risks, both at the level of individual institutions and of the broader stability of financial sectors, which in terms of supervision and burden sharing are still partitioned along national lines. These cross-border fault lines have come to the fore during the current financial crisis and have raised issues on the adequacy of the international crisis management and resolution framework governing multinational insurance companies.

This chapter examines the systemicness of insurance companies, with special attention to cross-border aspects and implications for supervision and crisis management. The chapter is structured as follows. In the second section, the internationalisation of (re)insurance is analysed on the basis of the costs and benefits of cross-border insurance operations. Against this background, the third section assesses the systemic implications of cross-border risks in the context of national and regional supervisory structures. The fourth section then discusses the current national and international frameworks for insurance supervision and crisis management, including an overview of the related institutional shortcomings with specific examples from the recent crisis period. The fifth and final section draws policy lessons, both from the recent experiences and from the proposals being developed for the banking sector. The case is made to limit the activities of insurance groups that may generate systemic risk, to develop crisis resolution frameworks that allow for an orderly wind-down of failing insurance companies, to strengthen regulation and consolidated supervision of cross-border insurance groups, including through closer cross-border cooperation and more information sharing between supervisors, and to include major insurance groups in the macro-prudential frameworks currently under development.

Internationalisation of the insurance industry

The state of play

In recent years the insurance business, like other financial services, has become increasingly international. This can be readily illustrated by the market share of foreign insurance companies in local markets. As shown in Figure 15.1, this share has increased substantially between 2000 and 2008 in the life insurance sector, most prominently in the UK, but also in the EU, Japan and Australia, and the US. Canada is an outlier, as the foreign market share has declined. Several local markets – particularly in Central and Eastern Europe – are now dominated by foreign insurance companies (European Commission, 2009a). In the non-life sector, a strong increase is evident in the US and especially continental Europe, but the picture is uneven as Japan, Australia, Canada and the UK actually experienced declines, though this development was marginal in the latter two countries and the foreign market share still constitutes nearly 40% and 50% respectively (Figure 15.2).

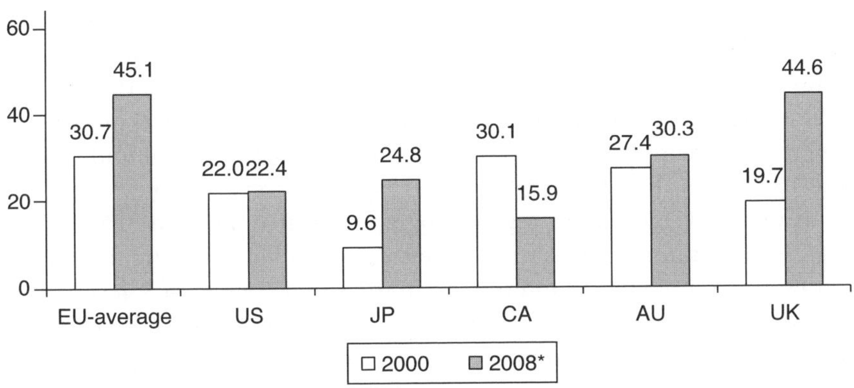

EU-average of 11 countries: AU, CZ, DE, HUN, IT, LUX, NL, POL, POR, ES, SW (IT not included in 2000).
*For AU, CA, JP and UK data for 2007.
Source: OECD.

Figure 15.1 Increasing share of foreign life insurance companies in local markets (%)

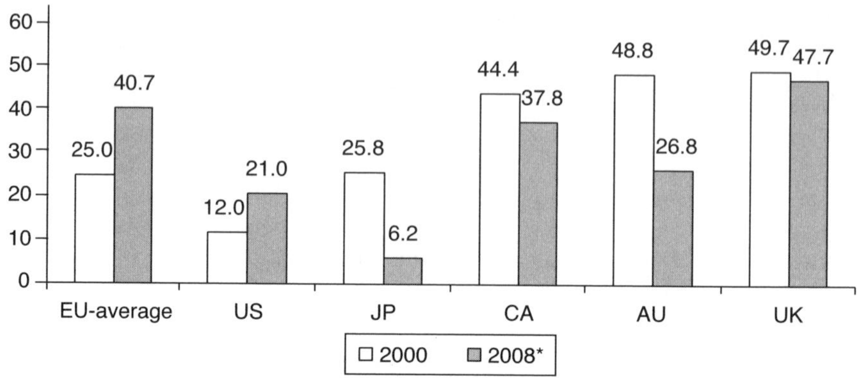

EU-average of 11 countries: AU, CZ, DE, HU, IT, LUX, NL, POL, POR, ES, SW (IT not included in 2000).
* For CA, JP, UK data for 2007.
Source: OECD.

Figure 15.2 Increasing share of foreign non-life insurance companies in local markets (%)

A second indicator for the ongoing internationalisation can be derived from the geographical distribution of individual insurance companies' gross written premiums. To map this out, we look into the geographical income distribution of 18 large European insurance companies (including two reinsurers) which – based on indicators such as turnover, gross premiums and total assets – belong to the largest in Europe. Together, these insurers had a premium income of €508 billion in 2008, representing 45% of European premium income and 18% of global premium income. Based on the geographical sources of premium income and the classification in Table 15.1, our analysis shows that of these 18 insurance companies, seven have a European orientation, five are truly global players and six still rely on their home market as their primary source of premium income (Figure 15.3). This strong dependence on foreign markets is also evident from these insurers' (weighted) aggregate geographical income distribution: their total gross premium income is more or less equally divided among their home countries, the rest of Europe and the rest of the world (Figure 15.3, last bar).[2]

A third – albeit more indirect – indicator of the ongoing internationalisation is the correlation between the share price developments of different insurance groups. Figure 15.4 shows that for a group of large insurers, this correlation has increased substantially over the last decade. An increase is also visible in the share price developments of other non-financial companies, but is smaller and correlations remain at a lower level. Although insurance companies' increased correlation could result from common shocks to their balance sheets,[3] it may also indicate that, over time, these companies have become more interconnected.

In combination with the increased reliance of insurers on foreign markets for generating premium income, this indicates that insurance markets have become more integrated across national borders.[4]

Table 15.1 Geographical orientation of major insurance companies (2008)

	Criterion	Insurer
National	Less than 50% of premium income generated abroad	CNP (FR), Ergo (DE), Eureko (NL), Helvetia (CH), Legal & General (UK), Mapfre (ES)
European	More than 50% of premium income generated abroad and premium income generated in Europe exceeds income from the rest of the world	Allianz (DE), Axa (FR), Aviva (UK), Generali (IT), Scor (FR), Zurich Financial Services (CH), Prudential (UK)
Global	More than 50% of premium income generated abroad and premium income generated in the rest of the world exceeds income from Europe	ING (NL), Munich Re (DE), Swiss Re (CH), Aegon (NL), Hannover (DE)

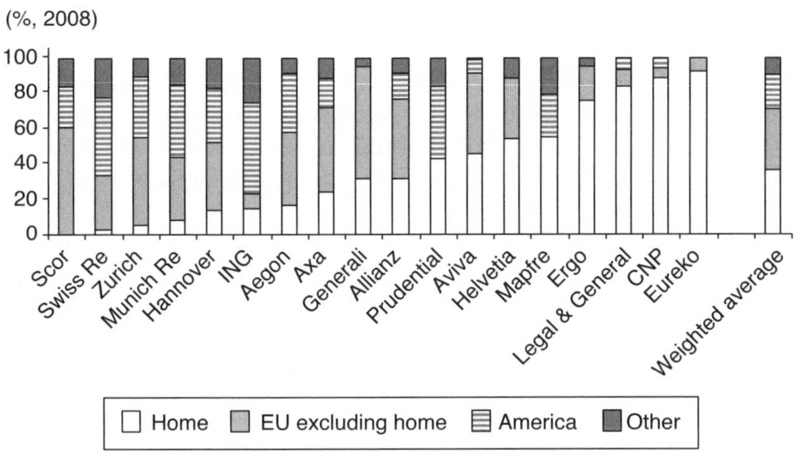

* America: US and Latin America.
Source: Annual Reports.

Figure 15.3 Distribution of premium income across regions

What are the driving forces behind this internationalisation in insurance? In general terms, prime factors are the removal of regulatory barriers to market entry, the advances in information technology and the privatisation of social security schemes. In Europe, the creation of the single currency and the Single Market in financial services has clearly been an important driver of the ongoing

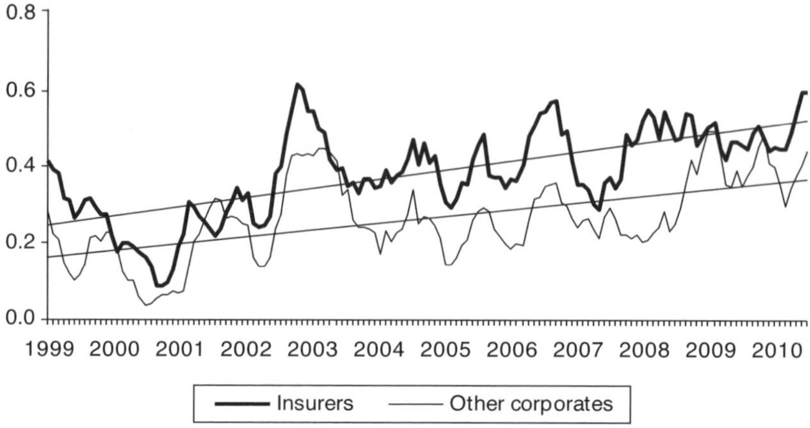

The average correlation for the category 'Insurers' has been calculated for Aegon, AIG, Allianz, Axa, Aviva, CNP, Generali, Legal & General, Zurich Financial Services and Swiss Re. The category 'Other Corporates' comprises 26 corporates.

Source: Datastream and own calculations.

Figure 15.4 Increasing correlation of insurance companies' share prices

financial integration. Indeed, for the 18 insurance companies analysed earlier, the aggregate premium income generated in other European countries is roughly equal to the premium income from their home market (Figure 15.3, last bar).

Beyond this, more than 90% of Western Europe's local insurers do not hold a dominant position on their saturated home markets and view external expansion as key to raising their growth potential (Boston Consulting Group, 2008). Specifically, in light of population ageing, insurers increasingly focus on retirement services and asset accumulation. As the US is, globally, the largest market for pensions and life insurance, it is not surprising that many European insurers have expanded their activities in the US. For instance, the two major reinsurance companies Swiss Re and Munich Re generate around 40% of their premium income in the US. And Dutch ING is currently one of the largest providers of retirement services and life insurance in the US,[5] while AEGON is the seventh largest life insurer, generating around 70% of its annual profits in that country.

However, the financial crisis has put a brake on the internationalisation trend over the last couple of years. Merger and acquisition activity in the European insurance sector has been subdued, as potential acquirers have lacked the financial capacity to continue their cross-border expansion (European Commission, 2009a). Overall, this internationalisation trend has nevertheless had a material impact on the organisational structure of insurance companies (IAIS, 2009a; Schoenmaker et al, 2008). First, from the 1990s, insurance *groupings* have been on the rise. Currently, most internationally active insurers are organised in a group structure, with each individual entity having its own legal identity, incorporated in its own local jurisdiction according to its national legal framework, but as part of an umbrella grouping. Second, over the past 10–15 years, large internationally active insurance groups increasingly conduct enterprise risk management (ERM)[6] and capital management on a group wide basis, complementing the risk and capital management programmes applied at individual entity levels. Third, a group-wide approach has emerged in the development of internal models.

Benefits and risks of cross-border insurance operations

The internationalisation of the insurance industry and the proliferation of cross-border insurance groupings has brought substantial benefits for insurance companies. At the same time, the emergence of international insurance groups has created novel risks for the individual insurance entities, the home supervisors, as well as the authorities of host jurisdictions in which insurers operate (IAIS, 2009a). These risks have come to the fore during the financial crisis.

Benefits

Economies of scale and scope. Operating within an international group structure allows entities to access and share greater technical resources and expertise. This specifically applies in the areas of asset and risk management, as evidenced by the roll-out of complex retirement products such as variable annuities by different entities within a group. In practice these products have typically been developed in countries such as the US and Japan and then rolled out in European markets. This has often involved central product development teams working closely together with local businesses and leveraging on best practices and experiences within the group. While economies of scale in the asset and risk management business of life insurers are significant, differences in national tax systems, regulations and social law make it more difficult to realise operational synergies.

Risk diversification. The centralisation of risk management functions that has accompanied the internationalisation of insurers has generally strengthened their risk management capacity. Next to allowing earlier adoption of state-of-the-art risk management tools and skills, it creates opportunities for risk diversification through risk transfers and pooling between group entities. The associated capital savings are larger in the non-life business, where claims are less correlated. By contrast, diversification benefits are smaller across geographies in life insurance, as the dominant longevity risk is a global phenomenon.

Funding and capital management. Being part of a large international insurance group provides individual entities with broader sources of financing, for instance through intra-group funding and better access to securities markets, thereby lowering funding costs. Moreover, centralised capital management contributes to an efficient distribution of capital within the group, helping to balance the different requirements of regulators, rating agencies and shareholders on a group wide basis.

Risks

Contagion risk. Within a group structure, an insurer is exposed to financial weaknesses in other group entities through financial, reputational and operational risks. In case of financial distress within a certain entity, group policy is likely to require other entities to take actions, for instance by providing financing, some form of insurance or upstreaming dividend. As such, this may result in individual insurance entities bearing risks beyond those they would carry on a stand-alone basis. The upstreaming of capital in 2007 by insurance entities within the pressured Fortis Group, outside the scope of national host supervisors, provides a powerful example.

Complexity. An insurance group that expands across different jurisdictions, fiscal and supervisory domains becomes more complex, potentially involving a myriad of legal entities interwoven through multiple intra-group transactions and operational platforms. A clear example is American International Group (AIG), which – pre-intervention – consisted of some 70 US insurance companies and 175 non-US companies and insurers, conducting business in 130 countries (Harrington, 2009). Cross-border expansion creates opacity, making it difficult to discern the linkages between a group's different parts and to get a clear understanding of its overall risk position.

Risks for local markets. An individual insurance entity may be of limited significance within a group, but nonetheless substantial in its local market. By consequence, certain business decisions (such as reducing capital allocated to a local entity which may limit its growth potential, or phasing out of certain product groups) may be sensible from the group perspective, but problematic for the local market in which it operates. This partly explains the focus of the current *solo* supervisory framework on individual entities (see below, 'Current Framework for Insurance Supervision and Crisis Management').

A framework for assessing systemic relevance of insurers

The emergence of large cross-border insurance groups raises the quintessential question whether and under what circumstances insurers generate or amplify systemic risk.[7] Traditionally, the insurance sector is regarded as a relatively stable part of the financial system. Contrary to banks, insurers have a negative duration gap on account of their long-term liabilities, often coupled to lengthy payout procedures and penalties for premature liquidation of policies. As a result, insurers are less vulnerable to liquidity risks than banks which have the opposite balance sheet structure, with short-term deposits and long-term assets. Consequently, while bank failures usually take the form of abrupt illiquidity, insurance failures are slow moving acts and stem from a gradual deterioration in solvency. Thus, systemic problems in the insurance sector are less acute and tend to unfold over a long time horizon (Brouwer, 2004; IAIS, 2009b). Furthermore, insurers are less systemically relevant in periods of market turbulence or in case of their eventual failure. First, contrary to banks, insurers do not operate in interbank markets and do not participate in payment systems, significantly reducing contagion risks to other financial institutions and consumers. Second, insurers often transfer residual risks on their balance sheet to other parties. For instance, investment risks may be passed on to policy-holders (as reflected in the rapid growth of unit-linked products over the past decade) and certain tail risks may be reinsured. Third, insurers commonly have a long-term investment horizon since they receive premiums upfront for policies that run over many years. They can thus hold a substantial share of their investments to maturity, which alleviates the propagation of systemic shocks.

Overall, the insurance sector may generally be viewed as having a stabilising influence on financial markets and the economy at large. But this is changing. Amplified by the internationalisation of the industry, there is increasing interaction between insurers on the one hand and financial markets, banks, other insurance companies and businesses and households on the other. This sectoral interaction provides a framework to map out the systemic importance of insurers (see Figure 15.5).

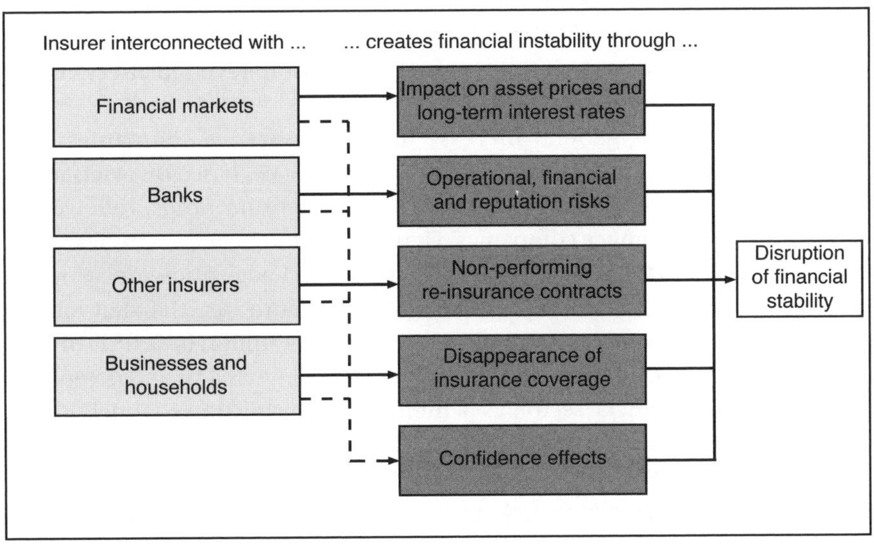

Figure 15.5 Framework for assessing systemic risk of insurance companies

Interconnectedness with financial markets

The relevance of insurers for financial stability has increased in line with the growth of the sector over the last decade. In fact, euro area insurers' financial assets roughly doubled in the decade to 2008, rising from 35% to 50% in terms of euro area gross domestic product (GDP). This is driven by a high income elasticity of demand in both life and non-life insurance. The former reflects population ageing and ongoing reforms in pension systems that encourage a higher allocation of savings to life insurers (and pension funds). The latter reflects the financial deepening and more advanced risk management that comes with economic growth. As these trends are likely to endure, the insurance sector may be expected to continue expanding in the coming years.

In this context, as large insurers are generally more diversified both geographically and across business lines, it has been argued that the risks to which the components of large insurers are exposed are mainly idiosyncratic and therefore largely uncorrelated (The Geneva Association, 2010). Along this line of thinking, the total risk of these larger institutions is less than the sum of their individual parts and their size is not viewed as a risk to financial stability. However, since these diversification benefits are generally captured by shareholders through capital relief, the financial system at large may well have less risk absorbing capacity and therefore be less resilient. Moreover, the question is whether these diversification benefits actually hold up in times of stress, when correlations between different risk types shoot up. In fact, although the relationship between size and stability is not clear-cut, Figure 15.6 and Figure 15.7 indicate that in normal times large insurers indeed do tend to be more stable than smaller companies, but that this relationship reversed after Lehman Brothers' failure in September 2010.

Accompanying this general increase in size, insurance companies have become large investors in financial markets. On aggregate, based on assets under management, the largest investors worldwide are pension funds, followed by mutual funds and insurance companies (Figure 15.8). Moreover, a significant part of the assets under management of private equity and hedge funds are owned by insurance companies (Schich, 2009). Focusing on the euro area, the total value of insurers' investment assets amounted to a colossal €4.4 trillion in 2008. Through their investment portfolios, insurers influence financial markets, and potentially the stability of the financial sector, via a number of transmission channels. Given the sheer size of their asset portfolios, fund reallocations or the unwinding of positions can sway market developments. Indeed, herding behaviour among insurers can – in the extreme – affect financial stability by destabilising asset prices. This could be the case when insurers reach their minimum solvency requirement and become pressed to engage in fire sales.

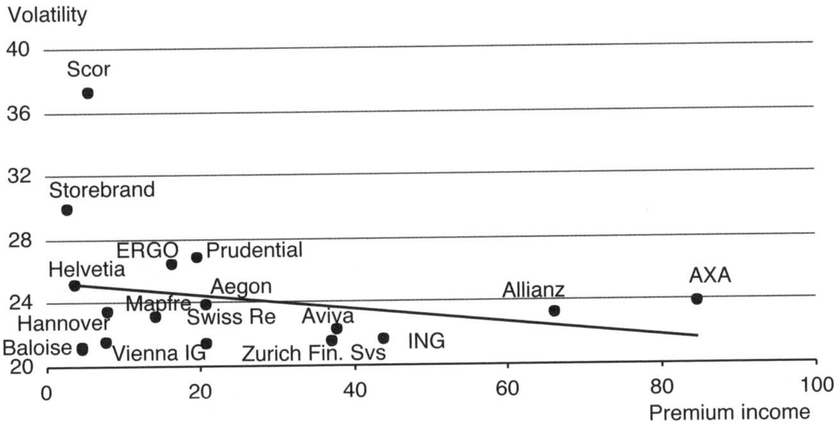

Premium is measured for 2008. Volatility is measured by the average of the 65 daily moving standard deviation for the period 2003–2008 (based on period September–February for each year – ending February 2008 – and subsequently annualised). Sampo coincides with Baloise.

Source: Isis, Datastream.

Figure 15.6 Relationship between size and volatility: 2003–1H2008 (in EUR bn and % respectively)

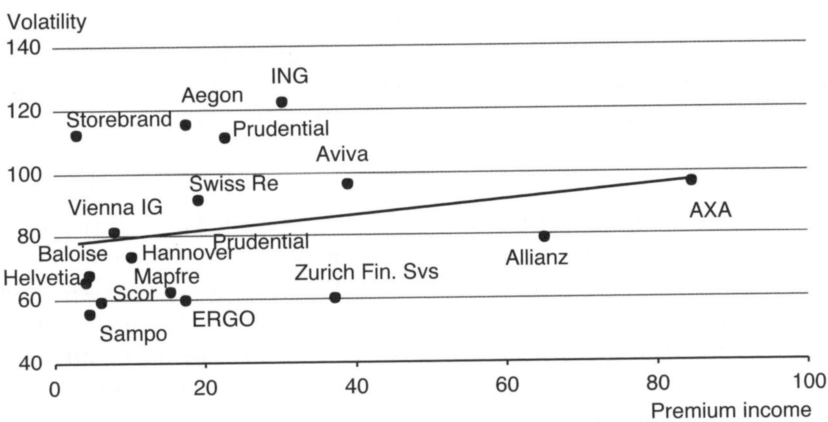

Premium is measured for 2009. Volatility is measured by the annualised average of the 65 daily moving standard deviation for the period September 2008–February 2009.

Source: Isis, Datastream.

Figure 15.7 Relationship between size and volatility: 2H2008–2009 (in EUR bn and % respectively)

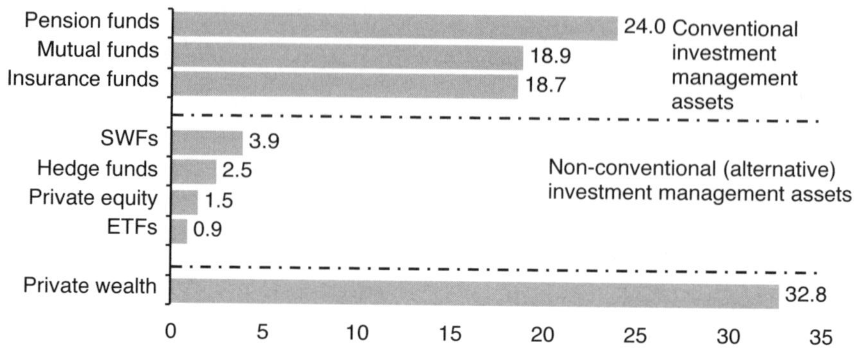

Source: IFSL.

Figure 15.8 Total assets under management within selected financial entities (in US$ trillion, 2008)

The impact of insurers' investment behaviour is primarily felt in the debt and other fixed income securities markets, where changes in their positions (in the case of euro area insurers comprising over €2 trillion) can impact long-term interest rates and prices in the secondary markets. The flip side is that insurers are important for the provision of financing to both governments and firms. Specifically, around 20% of debt securities issued by euro area governments is held by euro area insurers and pension funds. This adds up to close to 15% of euro area insurers' assets, against just 7.5% for euro area banks.

Besides investments in debt securities and equities, the insurance sector has been a key player in the provision of credit default swaps (CDSs).[8] In principle, insurers are well positioned to offer this kind of credit protection given their long-term investment horizon. However, the size of CDS exposures, the speed of CDS price adjustments and the interconnectedness created by CDS contracts within the financial sector have added a systemic dimension to the insurance sector. While the involvement of insurers in the credit derivatives market varies significantly across institutions, experience has shown that this kind of derivatives trading may quickly transmit losses beyond an individual entity into the broader financial markets, particularly when insurers operate on a global scale (The Geneva Association, 2010).

The collapse of AIG illustrates this point. In the run-up to the crisis, AIG had become by far the largest seller of credit protection among insurers. During the summer of 2008, AIG's net notional CDS exposure amounted to nearly US$450 billion, or a third of the group's total assets and five times its shareholders' equity. Rating downgrades and declines in the values of collateralised debt obligations on which it had written credit default protection, forced it to post large amounts of collateral. In turn, this created severe liquidity and solvency problems, with potential knock-on effects that put the stability of the global financial system at risk. This ultimately required intervention on an unprecedented scale by the US authorities. Whether an insurance company could be systemically relevant was no longer an open question.

Interconnectedness with banks

From a financial stability perspective, the interconnectedness of insurance companies with banks is important, as problems in the insurance sector can then be relatively easily transmitted to the banking sector (and vice versa). A number of linkages can be identified. A first – obvious – one is through direct ownership. Indeed, over the last decade direct ownership links between banking groups and insurance undertakings increased and many financial conglomerates emerged. According to the European Commission, 67 financial conglomerates are currently active in the EU, including AXA, BNP Paribas, Allianz, ING, Generali, Swiss Re, AIG and Citigroup (European Commission, 2009b).[9] Notwithstanding the potential benefits from combining banking and insurance in one group (particularly commercial benefits such as cross-selling, network sharing and economies of scale, as well as diversification benefits), there are also contagion channels within these conglomerates. For instance, there may be reputational risks between entities, particularly when a common brand name is used, and operational risks when back-offices are integrated. Besides this, financial risks may spread between entities within a group. In practice, while no business model offered full protection during the recent strains, the bancassurance model has generally been less resilient than solo banking or insurance models. Indeed,

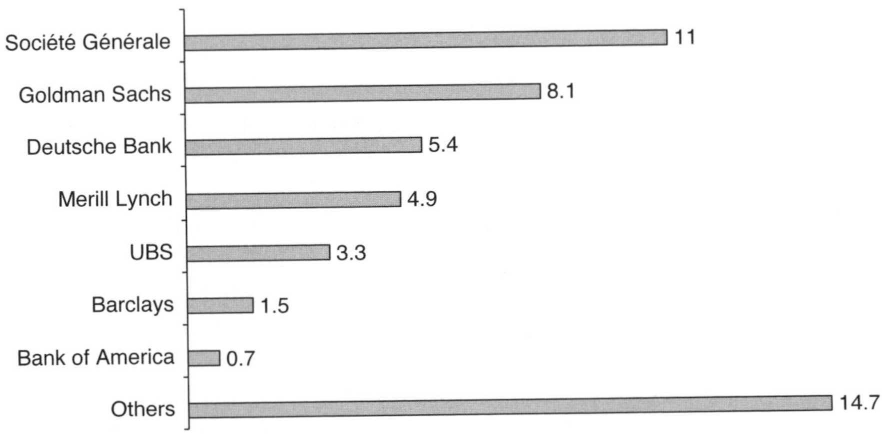

Source: The Geneva Association (2010).

Figure 15.9 Impact of AIG bailout on major banks (settlement of AIG CDS deals with major banks (US$ bn))

the severe impact of the financial crisis on some financial conglomerates has highlighted the transmission of financial risks within such diverse groupings.

Second, insurance companies are an important source of funding for the banking sector, implying that a (sudden) withdrawal of funding or capital could strain banks' ability to refinance themselves. Indeed, euro area insurance companies and pension funds hold 10% of debt securities and 8% of shares issued by euro area banks (ECB, 2009).[10] Third, insurance companies have also increasingly engaged in financial transactions with banks, including through credit risk transfers, which has increased the linkages between the sectors. As an extreme example, Figure 15.9 shows how interconnected AIG was with major banks through its CDS trading – and consequently how AIG's bailout protected these banks from severe losses – underscoring the systemic impact a failure of AIG could have had.

Interconnectedness with other insurers

If an insurer is an important reinsurer or counterparty to other insurers, financial difficulties can spread within the sector when reinsurance hedges or other mutual contracts are not delivered upon. Thus, financial problems may spread to other (primary) insurers and may force them to cut back on their underwriting or to withdraw from capital markets. Given the international consolidation of the reinsurance industry in recent years, the potential for a reinsurer to cause a systemic event within the primary insurance sector has increased. Since reinsurers cover the market's peak exposures and generally come into play when primary insurers are already under strain, a failing reinsurer could well drag troubled primary insurers with relatively high reinsurance exposures down with it (Brouwer, 2004).

Interconnectedness with businesses and households

Insurers underpin the stability of household and business balance sheets. When insurance market capacity declines or temporarily disappears, for instance due to the failure of an insurer in a concentrated market, this may impact domestic activity and undermine the stability of the financial system. Specifically, activities requiring insurance coverage may then come to a halt, which in turn may disrupt production in certain sectors. Although most insurance markets have several suppliers and fallout is generally quickly substituted by new capacity, there may be situations where this does not readily occur. For instance, when the financial crisis spread to the real economy and the number of commercial counterparty defaults increased, trade credit insurance became more expensive and coverage was reduced and occasionally even withdrawn. This had a direct negative impact on businesses' ability to engage in international commerce (CEIOPS, 2010). Another example is the sharp decline in aviation insurance cover immediately after the 9/11 terrorist attacks, which forced public authorities to set up government sponsored aviation insurance schemes (IAIS, 2009b). Also, in the run-up to the hurricane season, demand for disaster coverage often far outstrips supply, leading businesses with hurricane exposures to cancel projects or run the risk of inadequate insurance cover.

Loss of confidence

In addition to these transmission channels, the actual or prospective failure of a large, prominent and trusted publicly-listed insurance company can precipitate a loss of confidence in the solidity of the domestic financial system, which may infect other fundamentally sound and viable financial institutions. The experience of the Dutch financial sector in 2008 provides a case in point. Due to severe financial problems at Fortis/ABN Amro, the Dutch authorities were ultimately compelled to take over the (systemic) Dutch entities of Fortis, including ABN Amro, in early October. These developments clearly showed how wavering market

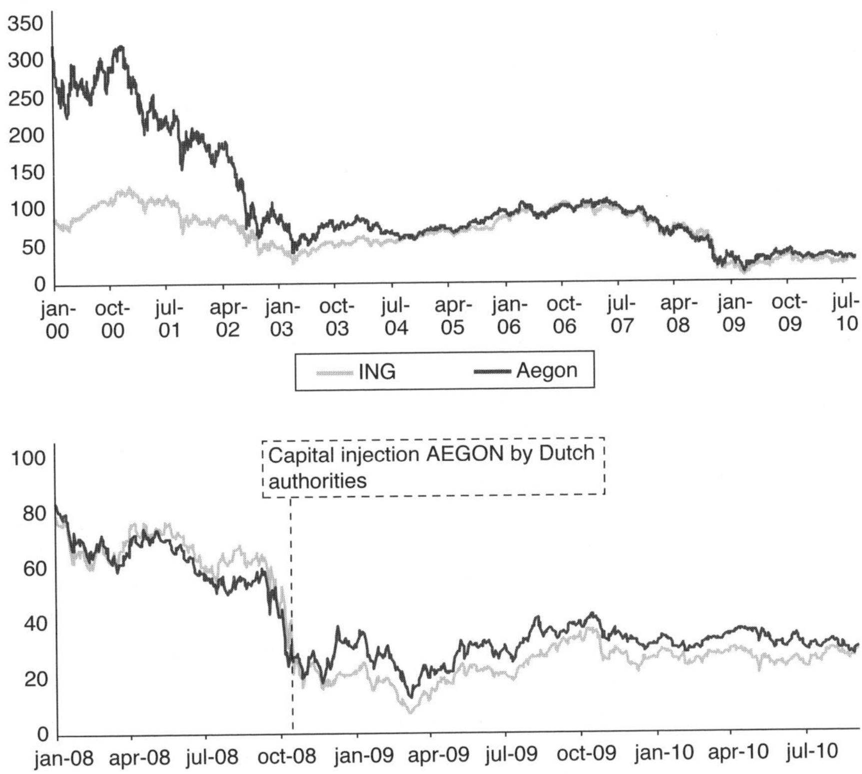

Source: Datastream

Figure 15.10 Synchronised shareprice developments of AEGON and ING (index 1 January 2007 = 100)

confidence in a particular financial institution could contaminate other financial players in the same region, as evidenced by a Benelux markdown in share prices and CDS contracts. Indeed, although two other Dutch financials, Aegon and ING, are fundamentally different in terms of their business models, activities and strategy,[11] markets no longer distinguished between the two institutions when the system came under extreme financial stress. In essence, they were placed in the same category of troubled institutions, as illustrated by their synchronised share price movements during 2007 and 2008 (Figure 15.10). As such, the Dutch authorities' decision to strengthen the capital base of Aegon later that month was driven by the precautionary principle, that is the imperative to preserve trust in both the institution and the Dutch financial sector at large, at a time when the stability of the financial system was deeply questioned.[12]

In sum, contagion risks involving the insurance sector have risen on account of the increased interdependence between insurers on the one hand and the broader financial industry and the real economy on the other. From the perspective of their assets, insurers have become major investors in financial markets and counterparties to banks. From that of their liabilities, they are connected to the global reinsurance market and provide protection to households and businesses which may not be easily substituted for. Moreover, depending on the liquidity of markets and the underlying state of the economy, in situations of extreme stress the fate of major insurers may impact confidence in the financial sector as a whole.

Current framework for insurance supervision and crisis management and its shortcomings

Current framework for insurance supervision and crisis management

Traditionally, the supervision of insurance companies has been based on the stand-alone, or *solo* assessment of the risk and solvency positions of each separate legal entity within a group. The rationale behind this solo supervision is the protection of policy-holders' rights in each separate entity. A group approach to insurance supervision was launched in Europe in 1998 with the Insurance Groups Directive. This approach supplements the solo supervision with an assessment of the group as a whole, by taking account of group relations that impact the financial position of the individual licensed entities. This relates, for instance, to intra-group exposures and risk transfers. Thus, solvency requirements are applied to all relevant entities, as well as to the aggregated group (solo *plus*). Insurance companies within financial conglomerates are also subject to the 2002 EU Directive on the Supplementary Supervision of Financial Conglomerates, which introduced additional supervision of regulated entities in groups that straddle more than one financial sector. The Directive provides for such supplementary supervision by focusing on risks of double gearing (multiple use of capital), contagion, management complexity, risk concentration and conflicts of interest. In so doing, the Directive fosters prudential supervision on a group-wide basis and establishes a framework for coordination between the supervisory authorities of different financial sectors and EU Member States.

Next to these regulatory developments, the growth of cross-border groups has led to numerous cooperation agreements between supervisors. Underpinning these agreements, international organisations involved in insurance regulation, such as the International Association of Insurance Supervisors (IAIS), the Joint Forum and the Committee of European Insurance and Occupational Pensions Supervisors (CEIOPS), have developed principles, standards and guidance on cross-border cooperation. In particular, within the EU, the so-called Helsinki Protocol entered into force in 2000 as a direct follow-up to the Insurance Groups Directive.[13] This Protocol specifies cooperation between national supervisory authorities as a prerequisite for the appraisal of cross-border insurance groups and provides a practical framework for such cooperation, especially by creating Coordination Committees of supervisors. Furthermore, in 2008, a Memorandum of Understanding (MoU) on Cooperation between the EU Financial Supervisory Authorities, Central Banks and Finance Ministries on cross-border financial stability was adopted. This MoU establishes procedures for sharing information and assessments, including during the management and resolution of cross-border financial crises. Finally, at the global level, the IAIS adopted a Multilateral Memorandum of Understanding on Cooperation and Information Exchange in 2007, establishing a formal basis for cross-border cooperation and information exchange among authorities supervising a group and its individual entities. The aim of all these guidelines is to ensure that information is readily shared and that supervisory authorities' decisions and policy measures are mutually consistent.

Lessons from the crisis

How have these arrangements performed during the crisis? A number of substantial lessons have come to the fore.

Systemic relevance. First, the crisis has shown that insurance companies may indeed become 'too important to fail'. While some supervisory authorities (or governments) exercised forbearance by temporarily exempting insurers from prevailing capital requirements or mark-to-market accounting practices, in those countries where no exemptions were provided, a number of insurers needed to be rescued with government support (OECD, 2010). In particular, the US Troubled Asset Relief Program (TARP) was extended to insurers which have bank or thrift holding companies. Several large insurance groups – including AIG, Hartford Financial and Lincoln National – applied for and eventually received financial assistance through TARP. In Belgium, Fortis and Ethias and, in the Netherlands, ING, Aegon and SNS REAAL received capital support from the government, and

Fortis Insurance Netherlands (ASR) came fully into state hands.[14] As a result, the perimeter of 'too important to fail' organisations has been broadened beyond banks. This has raised challenging policy questions on how to reduce or control the systemic features or activities of such companies.

Intra-group relations. The importance of intra-group relations and the potentially devastating implications of non-supervised parts of a group have been overlooked (CEIOPS, 2009a). This risk proved greatest for insurers with complex, cross-border operational and legal structures, such as AIG. Indeed, the crisis has underscored that complex and opaque group structures limit the ability of supervisors, shareholders and other stakeholders to grasp the relevant risks and hamper the ability to engineer an orderly wind-down. A related lesson is that reputational risks for insurance groups stemming from unfavourable events within specific entities of a group or from the external situation of the financial sector can indeed be significant.

Holdings. In Europe, holding companies that are not separately licensed insurers fall outside the scope of supervision. However, these holdings have in some cases harboured high risk investments, including structured products (CEIOPS, 2009a). Also, a holding structure creates room for double leverage, with equity in subsidiaries (partly) financed through debt at the holding company level, possibly eroding the subsidiary's solvency position. Experience has indeed shown that, without insight in a holding company's operations, it is difficult for supervisors to understand relations between a group's entities, and consequently to gauge the overall risks.

Supervisory cooperation. Despite the various coordination mechanisms that have been set up, genuine and effective cooperation between national supervisors during the crisis was limited. The solo supervision framework does not include an obligation for supervisors to share information and this made it difficult to obtain a clear overview of insurance groups that ran into difficulties. Moreover, Coordination Committees did not function as expected – and in some cases never actually came together during the crisis – and relevant decisions such as the ring-fencing of assets were taken on a national basis.

Non-EU entities. Beyond the EU, with the current international regulatory framework, supervisors depend on voluntary information from foreign supervisors and from the institution itself for their oversight of foreign entities. At the same time, however, these foreign entities may become a source of financial problems for the group as a whole. Even with good cooperation between the home and foreign supervisors, this limited oversight of some entities – also on account of different supervisory standards – may impede the relevant group supervisor from taking timely pre-emptive measures during an emerging crisis. This applies for instance to the supervison of EU groups' branches or subsidiaries in the US.

Reporting and solvency frameworks. The crisis has highlighted shortcomings in the reporting and solvency frameworks for insurance companies within the EU.

In particular, the current reporting requirements are not risk-based and, given the minimum of yearly accounts with a half year lag, do not generate meaningful and up-to-date supervisory information. Similarly, the crisis has highlighted the inadequacy of solvency requirements, as a few insurance companies with solvency reserves well above the required minimum ended up receiving public support. In this respect, the loss absorbing capacity of insurers' capital may be hampered by the existence of intangible or deferred assets, such as goodwill and deferred tax assets and particularly deferred acquisition costs.

Supervisory capacity. Prior to the crisis, insurers were generally not deemed systemically relevant. In combination with the risk-based approach applied by most supervisors, this often resulted in a parsimonious allocation of supervisory capacity. It is telling that, following the crisis, many countries have substantially expanded their supervisory capacity for the insurance sector.

In sum, the crisis has laid bare shortcomings in the supervision of insurance companies, notably regarding the lack of formal rights to conduct group-wide supervision, the inadequate solvency and reporting requirements, and the ineffective cooperation amongst supervisors in a cross-jurisdictional and cross-sectoral context. Although solo supervision will remain the core of insurance supervision – given the legal obligations to policy-holders at the legal entity level – the growing internationalisation and interconnectedness of the insurance industry and the emergence of systemically relevant players make it increasingly important to complement this supervision with a comprehensive overview of the group as a whole, including its strategy, financial and solvency position, legal structure, risk and capital management as well as governance processes (IAIS, 2009c). In particular, consolidated (upward) supervision will allow supervisors to gain better insight in issues like double gearing, intra-group contagion and the build-up of systemic risks. Furthermore, information sharing and cooperative decision making between supervisors need to be strengthened.

Policy recommendations

The crisis has shown that, at times, insurance companies may have the potential to destabilise the financial system and may then be considered 'too important to fail'. In these circumstances, in line with the proactive precautionary principle governing systemic risks, public authorities will not allow such an insurer to fail. This has been evident in recent practice, where next to banks quite a few insurers have received state support. However, such government interventions create moral hazard, disturb the competitive playing field and burden public finances. As a result, priority should be given to (see below) limiting the activities of insurance companies that may generate systemic risk, fostering the scope for their orderly wind-down, strengthening the regulatory and supervisory framework for cross-border insurers and including insurers in macro-prudential oversight (see also OECD, 2010; CEIOPS, 2009b; Impavido and Tower, 2009; IAIS, 2010a, 2010b).

Reducing the systemicness of insurance companies

The prolonged financial strain since 2007 is changing the structure of the insurance industry in a manner that seems to be reducing its systemic relevance. Most notably, the financial crisis has led to a process of de-conglomeration whereby several financial conglomerates have initiated the separation of their banking and insurance operations. The driving factors behind this structural shift are competitive requirements related to state support, contagion problems within the group and, most fundamentally, doubts about the advantages of the bancassurance business model. This has contributed to a 'back to basics' approach currently visible within both the banking and the insurance industry. In addition, specific concentrations in the insurance sector (especially AIG and monoliners) have been addressed through restructuring and supervisory measures.

The 'Too Important to Fail' issue may be further mitigated in the insurance sector through various policy measures that are currently under debate for banks (Box 15.1). In particular, measures should be taken to limit insurers' propriety trading in (naked) derivatives and credit default swaps. Focusing insurers' activities on insurance proper, rather than on business more akin to asset managers or hedge funds, will reduce systemic risk in the sector. Beyond this, a capital surcharge could be introduced based on an insurance company's contribution to systemic risk. Conceptually, this contribution could be determined on the basis of a progressive quantitative measure, reflecting for instance an insurer's size and interconnectedness with other parts of the financial sector. At the same time, supervisors could be given the discretion to lower this capital surcharge, depending on the degree to which an insurance company is able to 'bail in' its creditors or can be easily wound down in a crisis. The merits and practical feasibility (including the data challenges) of such a framework for the insurance sector deserve to be fleshed out.

Fostering an orderly wind-down of failing insurers

In the final analysis, in absence of far-reaching restrictions on the size and activities of financial institutions, the situation may once again arise that authorities face the threat of insolvency at a large internationally operating insurance company that is tightly interwoven with other parts of the financial sector. A resolution framework that allows for an orderly wind-down of such a company would then mitigate the risk of systemic disruption, exert discipline on the firm's financiers and other stakeholders, and minimise costs of public support.

Several measures can increase the scope for the orderly wind-down of a large, complex insurance company. First, major insurance companies with tight linkages to other parts of the financial system should develop contingency plans and procedures for crisis situations, in line with the development of the so-called recovery and resolution plans ('living wills') of major international banking groups. Generally, these recovery and resolution plans should provide a *going concern* plan, spelling out potential activities to scale down and non-core business lines to sell, as well as a *gone concern* plan identifying actions to achieve an orderly wind-down should the de-risking plans prove insufficient. This should be less difficult for insurance than banking conglomerates, given the tighter legal entity requirements in insurance as well as the more limited liquidity and payment systems risks.

Second, supervisory authorities should have a full range of resolution instruments, including the power to transfer part or all of a failing insurer's business to another insurer. They should also be able to take control of part or

Box 15.1 Policy initiatives to reduce systemic risks in banking

When weighing policy options for the insurance industry, it is useful to look at the various proposals being developed to address the financial stability concerns stemming from large, systemically relevant cross-border banks. These proposals are being drawn up in groups such as the Financial Stability Board (FSB) and the Basel Committee on Banking Supervision (BCBS) and comprise:

- Increasing overall capital and liquidity requirements, with greater increases in the capital requirements for trading activities, (re-)securitisation and counterparty credit risks. While these increases apply to all banks, they tax elements of interconnectedness and activities primarily undertaken by the larger institutions, and will thus have a larger impact on systemically relevant banks ('Basel III').
- Setting direct limits on the size of systemically important banks and on propriety trading and certain investment banking activities ('Volcker rule').
- Introducing regulatory capital or liquidity surcharges for individual institutions depending on their systemic importance, measured by indicators such as size or interconnectedness.
- Emphasising stand-alone subsidiaries along geographic or business lines, and tighter liquidity requirements for foreign branches, thereby lowering interconnectedness and increasing national financial sector resilience and resolvability ('local autonomy').
- Developing recovery and resolution plans, including contingency funding and de-risking plans, as well as wind-down scenarios ('living wills').
- Strengthening crisis resolution frameworks and instruments, in particular through the introduction of Special Resolution Regimes for banks.
- Introducing bank levies to recover or anticipate fiscal costs associated with the failure of a systemically important institution.
- Establishing cross-border crisis management groups for all systemically relevant institutions, consisting of supervisors, central banks and finance ministries.
- Enhancing international exchange of information, consultation and coordination via supervisory colleges.

all of an insurer's business, by establishing a separate asset management vehicle controlled and owned by the authorities, to which pressurised or difficult to value assets could be transferred. Ultimately, the relevant authorities should have the power to take an insurer into temporary public ownership, allowing for a restructuring of the company and its obligations, as well as the liquidation of its assets if necessary. In this context, consideration should be given to bail-in options, granting authorities going concern powers to convert contingent capital and to impose debt-equity swaps or haircuts on bond-holders, within the bounds of the losses that bond-holders would otherwise occur in case of bankruptcy. Third, as last-resort protection, internationally consistent policy-holder guarantee schemes need to be established and augmented in order to protect consumers in case of a failing insurer. In the EU, the European Commission has launched a White Paper to this end, proposing a coherent framework for insurance guarantee schemes with a minimum set of harmonised features for all EU Member States.

Strengthening the regulation and supervision of cross-border insurance groups

Recent experience has shown that, in crisis situations, cooperation between insurance supervisors is minimal. In the EU, this is being addressed through the implementation of Solvency II. This regulatory regime will come into effect at end-2012 and will fundamentally strengthen the regulation and supervision of cross-border insurance groups. Specifically, it will introduce proper group supervision in insurance, by designating the home supervisor as the group supervisor and by making the parent company subject to consolidated prudential supervision of the group as a whole. This implies that the parent company will be the key contact for the group supervisor and will be responsible for implementing governance and risk management procedures across the group, as well as for complying with group reporting requirements.

Solvency II will create a formal basis for enhanced supervisory cooperation. Each cross-border insurance group will be required to have a College of Supervisors, chaired by the group supervisor, with representatives of all supervisors of local subsidiaries and significant branches. The chair is responsible for organising College meetings and for ensuring an adequate information exchange that allows a comprehensive overview of the solvency position, risk management, governance and other compliance issues at the group level. Although the aim is to take decisions by consensus, the group supervisor has the ultimate responsibility to set the Solvency Capital Requirement for the group as a whole and to validate the group's internal model. With respect to crisis management, periodic stress tests should be conducted and emergency plans should be fleshed out, including cooperation and coordination procedures during crises as well as burden sharing arrangements. Ideally, these Colleges should also take preparatory steps in mapping out potential contagion channels, conflicts of interests and barriers to coordinated action in a crisis.

In the case of broader international insurance groups, stretching beyond the EU, the crisis has further highlighted the fragmented state of global financial regulation and the associated risks of regulatory arbitrage and competitive distortions. This fragmentation also makes it very difficult for supervisors to obtain a thorough understanding of the financial position of the group as a whole. Although extremely challenging, a coherent global regulatory framework is needed for globally active insurance companies, including common regulatory elements such as quantitative (solvency) and qualitative (corporate governance, risk management) requirements as well as agreed methods of supervision and coordination. To this end, IAIS has initiated the development of common parameters for insurance group supervision on a global footing. In particular, tools are being developed to assess group businesses and structures from an encompassing risk management perspective, with consistent supervisory requirements for insurance groups and guidance for cross-border cooperation between supervisors. But much remains to be done.

Include insurers in macro-prudential oversight

Traditionally, insurance companies have been viewed as an inherently stabilizing influence on the economy at large and as fundamentally different from banks, which are systemic by nature. However, the experiences of the financial crisis have illustrated that insurances companies may, under certain circumstances, also be systemically relevant. This change reflects the tightened interlinkages between insurance companies and banks, the increased size of insurers' positions in financial markets and the heightened importance of insurance cover for financial institutions, businesses and households. Besides this, developments in insurance markets have a cyclical impact, as financial conditions influence premium and solvency levels, and macroeconomic conditions influence underwriting standards, thereby determining the build-up of risks in the financial system. By consequence, assessments of the insurance industry and its interlinkages with other financial sectors and the broader economy should be included in macro-prudential oversight. This relates to the financial stability frameworks of national authorities as well as that of the European Systemic Risk Board, which may issue risk warnings or policy recommendations related to the insurance sector.

Notes

1. The views expressed in this paper do not necessarily reflect those of De Nederlandsche Bank.
2. This classification broadly follows Schoenmaker et al. (2008), who also find strong evidence of internationalisation in the European insurance industry. They conclude

that about 55% of the business of 25 large EU insurance groups is conducted abroad. The cross-border activities are predominantly within Europe (30% to 35%) and less so in the rest of the world (20% to 25%). Other sources (Fortune Global 500, Swiss Re) confirm this internationalisation trend at a global level: in 2008, 18 general insurance groups and 27 life insurance groups accounted for nearly half of the world's insurance premiums.

3. Such as certain catastrophic events leading to rising global reinsurance tariffs.
4. A separate analysis shows that over the same period the average correlation of share prices of global banking groups follows the same pattern as that of insurance companies, reflecting the internationalisation and integration process that has also taken place within the global banking industry over the last decades.
5. In particular, ING is the third-largest provider in the US of defined contribution retirement plans in terms of assets under management and administration.
6. ERM is the process of identifying, assessing, monitoring and controlling risks in an insurance enterprise as a whole.
7. Systemic risk can be defined as the risk of disruption to the flow of financial services that is (i) caused by an impairment of all or parts of the financial system, and (ii) has the potential to have serious negative consequences for the real economy (IMF et al., 2009).
8. Another relevant instrument class through which insurers and capital markets interact are Insurance Linked Securities (ILS). ILS are predominantly used by non-life insurers to transfer insurance tail-risks to the capital markets. The most successful ILS product is the CAT Bond, which releases funds to insurers following catastrophes without creating the obligation to repay. Life insurers use ILS for funding purposes.
9. According to EU regulations, a group qualifies as a financial conglomerate if more than 40% of its activities are financial and the group has significant cross-sector activities.
10. Based on second quarter 2009 data.
11. While both Aegon and ING are active in the US, Aegon's core business in the US is providing insurance and pension products, while ING – next to its insurance activities – also operates the country's largest direct bank.
12. See, for instance, the letter by the Dutch Minister of Finance to Parliament motivating the capital injection in Aegon, dated 29 October 2008.
13. Protocol relating to the collaboration of the supervisory authorities of the Member States of the European Union with regard to the application of Directive 98/78/EC on the supplementary supervision of insurance undertakings in an insurance group, 11 May 2000.
14. Moreover, the group of financial guarantors known as 'monoliners' – which focused exclusively on the provision of financial guarantees and CDS writing and trading – were hit hard by the crisis and effectively put out of business.

Bibliography

Boston Consulting Group (2008) 'Creating Competitive Advantage: The European Insurance Landscape'.

Brouwer, H.J. (2004) 'The Relevance of Insurance for the Financial System and European Crisis Management', speech at the Comité Européen des Assurances.

CEIOPS (2009a) 'Lessons Learned from the Crisis (Solvency II and Beyond)'.

CEIOPS (2009b) 'CEIOPS Advice for Level 2 Implementing Measures on Solvency II: Cooperation and Colleges of Supervisors'.

CEIOPS (2010) 'Note on Components of Systemic Risk of Insurance Business Models'.

ECB (2009) 'The Importance of Insurance Companies for Financial Stability', *Financial Stability Review*.

European Commission (2009a) 'European Financial Integration Report 2009', Commission staff working document.

European Commission (2009b) 'Identification of Financial Conglomerates', JFC/DOC/2009/3.

Harrington, S.E. (2009) 'The Financial Crisis, Systemic Risk and the Future of Insurance Regulation', *Journal of Risk and Insurance*, 76(4): 785–819.

IAIS (2009a) 'Issues Paper on Group-wide Solvency Assessment and Supervision'.

IAIS (2009b), 'Systemic Risk and the Insurance Sector'.

IAIS (2009c) 'Guidance Paper on the Use of Supervisory Colleges in Group-wide Supervision'.

IAIS (2010a) 'Standard on cross-border cooperation and crisis management (draft)'.

IAIS (2010b) 'Common Framework for the Supervision of Internationally Active Insurance Groups (ComFrame)'.

IMF, FSB and BIS (2009) 'Guidance to Assess the Systemic Importance of Financial Institutions, Markets and Instruments: Initial Considerations', Report to G20 Finance Ministers and Governors.

Impavido, G., and I. Tower (2009) 'How the Financial Crisis Affects Pensions and Insurance and Why the Impact Matters', IMF Working Paper 09/151.

OECD (2010) 'The Impact of the Financial Crisis on the Insurance Sector and Policy Responses'.

Schich, S. (2009) 'Insurance Companies and the Financial Crisis', *Financial Market Trends*, OECD.

Schoenmaker, D., S. Oosterloo and O. Winkels (2008) 'The Emergence of Cross-border Insurance Groups within Europe with Centralised Risk Management', *The Geneva Papers on Risk and Insurance – Issues and Practice*.

The Geneva Association (2010) 'Systemic Risk in Insurance: An Analysis of Insurance and Financial Stability', Special Report of The Geneva Association Systemic Risk Working Group.

Part V

The Developed Markets Perspective

16
Regulatory Developments in the US Insurance Sector in the Aftermath of the Financial Crisis

Therese M. Vaughan

Recent years have seen tremendous activity related to prudential regulation and supervision. The 2008 financial crisis has highlighted the need for an improved understanding of how risk is evolving in the financial system, including insurance. While the insurance sector remained relatively stable during the crisis, its continued globalisation and consolidation present ongoing challenges for insurance supervisors and policy-makers. The purpose of this chapter is to describe developments in US insurance supervision in response to these emerging issues and trends.

Overview

To appreciate the regulatory challenges in the United States and the structure of regulation, one must have an understanding of the scope and diversity of the US insurance market. Based on aggregate premium volume, the US represents over one third of worldwide insurance premiums, the largest market in the world. Over 7,000 insurers are licensed to sell insurance, ranging from multinational firms to firms that limit their sales to a small geographic area of a single state. Some firms are part of insurance groups that write coverage in virtually all areas of insurance, including life, annuities, personal property and casualty, commercial property and casualty, and health insurance. Others are highly specialised, writing coverage for only one market segment, such as jewellers or churches. Some are publicly traded, others are privately owned, and still others are mutual insurers owned by their policy-holders.

Compounding the diversity is the federalist system of government in the US, under which certain rights are reserved to the states. As a result, certain characteristics of the insured risk are defined at the state level. For example, the states have developed their own tort and compensation schemes governing worker injuries, medical malpractice and auto injury, to which insurers must respond. The size of the US also leads to different natural catastrophe challenges in different parts of the country, and states have responded to these in diverse ways. California has created a unique programme governing losses from earthquake, while central states have focused on tornadoes and hail storms, and Gulf and Atlantic coastal states have focused on hurricane problems.

The US insurance regulatory system reflects the large and diverse insurance markets in the US. Each state has the authority to supervise and regulate insurance companies that operate in that state, and each regulator places his or her primary emphasis on protecting insurance consumers. Given the number of insurers that operate across multiple states, it is not surprising that the state-based system has evolved over many decades to a strong collaborative system in which states coordinate to develop national standards and to supervise and regulate multistate insurance companies. This is particularly true in solvency regulation. The National Association of Insurance Commissioners (NAIC) serves as the central linchpin of the national system of state-based regulation, the forum for developing national standards and best practices and for implementing and fostering the necessary coordination.[1] Under the NAIC's Financial Regulation Standards Accreditation Program, states undergo periodic on-site and off-site assessments to determine the degree to which they have adopted the necessary standards and maintain appropriate supervisory practices (NAIC, 2010c). An insurer based in a state that is not accredited will be subject to enhanced supervision by the remaining states, thus providing an incentive for states to become accredited. At this time, all states and the District of Columbia are accredited.

The effectiveness of the US insurance regulatory system was demonstrated by the resilience of the insurance sector during the recent financial crisis. Aside from AIG, only two insurers received assistance under the US Treasury's Capital Purchase Program (CPP), as opposed to over 500 banks. The case of AIG, while clearly pointing to the need for enhanced supervision of systemically important financial institutions in the US, can scarcely be called a failure of insurance regulation.[2] AIG's regulatory structure included a combination of state and federal officials, and the Office of Thrift Supervision (a federal banking regulator) was assigned the role of holding company supervisor. State insurance regulators were the functional regulators of the insurance subsidiaries, which remained solvent even as AIG's Financial Products division imploded. Indeed, the insurance companies were the valuable assets used to collateralise loans from the Federal Reserve.

The US Insurance Solvency Framework

Because it has evolved over a series of decades, the US system of insurer solvency regulation is complex and multifaceted. A description can be found in The United

States Insurance Solvency Framework (NAIC, 2010b), a document that describes the US system in a comprehensive framework with underlying core principles. The mission of US regulators is to protect policy-holders/claimants/beneficiaries first and foremost, while also facilitating an effective and efficient marketplace for insurance products. As indicated earlier, each state insurance department and state insurance commissioner retains ultimate responsibility for the solvency of insurers doing business in that state.[3]

One of the most noteworthy characteristics of the US system is the remarkable multistate coordination and collaboration that has emerged over the years. States coordinate in the development of national standards, in the collection and review of data, and in the development of regulatory actions. An extensive network of committees, task forces, and working groups engages state regulators in the development of regulatory standards, tools and activities. Formal peer review mechanisms, such as the Financial Regulation Standards Accreditation Program and Financial Analysis Working Group, promote best practices.

This multistate system offers a number of benefits. Peer pressure encourages states to take appropriate regulatory action, limiting the effects of regulatory capture and forbearance, and redundancy in regulatory processes (multiple sets of eyes) makes it less likely for problems to be missed. Prompt and effective regulatory action is promoted by the fact that other states retain the right to take enforcement action if the domestic regulator fails to act. Through consensus building and compromise, regulators are driven toward centrist solutions, avoiding dramatic swings in regulatory policy as the political or economic environment changes. The evolution of best practices across the states can be shared to facilitate improvement in all states (that is, 'the laboratory of the states'). This multi-state structure, coupled with a risk-focused approach to regulation, form the foundation for the current national system of state-based regulation, and the NAIC serves as the central structure through which the necessary coordination and joint policy development can occur.[4]

The seven core principles of the US insurance solvency system are described in The United States Insurance Solvency Framework. These core principles are implemented throughout the states primarily through the states' adoption of NAIC model laws and regulations, many of which are embodied in the NAIC's accreditation programme.

The seven core principles that have been identified include:

1. *Regulatory reporting, disclosure and transparency*. Insurers file detailed financial statements on an annual and quarterly basis, and these statements are captured electronically in the NAIC's centralised financial database. The extensive data includes, among other things, detailed information on premiums written by line of business and state, reinsurance arrangements, and investments owned, bought and sold (by CUSIP number, where applicable). Central data collection

is coupled with a variety of tools designed to enhance multistate oversight, and the NAIC data is used by regulators and the market to evaluate the risk profile of insurers.

2. *Off-site monitoring and analysis*. Off-site monitoring is used for ongoing assessment of the financial condition of the insurer. The detailed NAIC financial information forms the basis for extensive analyses of trends at the company and market level. A single insurer can be compared against a peer group to identify areas in which the insurer's performance or risk profile is an outlier. These types of analyses are provided to the state insurance regulators through many off-site monitoring tools maintained by the NAIC and are used in conjunction with a state's own analysis tools and processes.

   In addition to the independent analysis conducted by state insurance regulators, the NAIC maintains a central staff to perform ongoing monitoring of nationally significant insurers, known as the Financial Analysis Division (FAD). The FAD refers potentially troubled insurers and insurance groups to the Financial Analysis Working Group (FAWG), a group of seasoned financial regulators from 16 states that provide peer review of the domestic regulator's actions. The FAWG, with the support of the FAD, also monitors industry trends in various risk areas and provides guidance for state regulators, including recommended responses to risks that have been identified. Risk areas could include, for example, capital market changes, credit crunch issues, catastrophic events, international events, anomalies with lines-of-business writings, reinsurance activities, investment strategies, and leverage. The FAWG forms a key element of the collaborative processes that exist at the NAIC.

3. *On-site risk-focused examinations*. US regulators carry out on-site risk-focused examinations in which the insurer's corporate governance, management oversight, and financial strength are evaluated, as well as the processes for risk identification and mitigation. Beginning in 2010, the accreditation programme standards require US regulators to use a revised examination approach that incorporates an enhanced risk assessment process.[5] This approach increases the review of an insurer's prospective risks, risk management, and corporate governance. Among other things, it provides for increased supervisory reliance on the work of the internal and external auditors and on documentation related to the US Sarbanes-Oxley requirements. It also emphasises the importance of evaluating the impact of insurer management.

4. *Reserves, capital adequacy and solvency*. Insurers are required to maintain reserves and capital and surplus to provide an adequate margin of safety. The US risk-based capital (RBC) system establishes regulatory capital requirements and creates a ladder of intervention – a set of increasingly strong regulatory actions to be taken as capital levels fall. RBC is primarily a factor-based approach; however, internal models are used for certain targeted risks where a factor-based approach has been determined to be inadequate. Though RBC

serves an important function in insurance regulation, regulatory action has typically occurred well before the company breaches the RBC action triggers as a result of the off-site monitoring system of analysis and examination. Where monitoring results trigger regulatory attention before RBC results do, the Hazardous Financial Condition Regulation (described below) provides the authority for regulatory action.

5. *Regulatory control of significant, broad-based, risk-related transactions/activities.* Certain significant transactions/activities affecting policy-holders' interests must receive regulatory approval. These include, for example, licensing a company to transact business, change of control of the company, the payment of material dividends, and transactions with affiliates (including affiliated reinsurance).
6. *Preventive and corrective measures, including enforcement.* When risks are identified as a result of on-site or off-site monitoring, the regulator will take preventive and corrective measures to reduce their impact to the company, thereby protecting policy-holders. The NAIC's Hazardous Financial Condition Model Regulation, a required element of the NAIC accreditation programme, provides the regulatory authority to address risky behaviours and characteristics exhibited by insurers. The regulation identifies a number of general factors that may indicate the need to take action, and provides the regulator with the authority to intervene in a variety of ways, including requiring the insurer to hold additional capital.

   The FAWG, mentioned earlier, often serves as a forum for collaboration and problem-solving with respect to potentially troubled insurers and groups. Once the NAIC staff or another regulator identifies an insurer or group in need of attention, FAWG will review the available facts, ask questions of the domiciliary or lead regulator(s), and often invite that regulator in to discuss the situation and their supervisory plan. Those discussions may lead to further requests for information, to additional discussions through regular meetings/calls, and even to recommended regulatory actions. The FAWG process, which has existed for over 15 years, is a model of a multi-jurisdictional peer review process. By engaging a variety of regulatory perspectives to assist and encourage a domestic regulator who is dealing with a troubled insurer, FAWG promotes effective and timely regulatory intervention.[6]
7. *Exiting the market and receivership.* The legal and regulatory framework defines a range of options for the orderly exit of insurers from the marketplace, including a receivership scheme that prioritises the payment of policy-holder obligations.

   Together, the variety of regulatory tools and activities embedded in these core principles create a robust regulatory system. While each state regulator is ultimately responsible for the solvency of all insurers operating in its state, regulators meet this responsibility through a high degree of coordination across the system. Insurers provide detailed information centrally. This information can be accessed by all states, and is supplemented by other market data to permit ongoing multistate monitoring of individual companies and insurance markets. Financial analysis tools, developed and maintained by individual states and by the NAIC centrally, facilitate analysis of this detailed information. Periodic on-site examinations of insurers complement the ongoing financial analysis, and these examinations often include regulators from multiple states. Accounting and capital requirements establish triggers for required company and regulatory action, although in most cases off-site monitoring has triggered action prior to breaching a risk-based capital threshold. Regulatory control of significant transactions and activities provide explicit oversight of targeted company activities, and there is a developed process for rehabilitating or winding down insurers. The NAIC accreditation programme articulates the requirements for individual states to be accredited and evaluates each state's ability to meet those requirements. Robust peer review processes, including the accreditation programme and FAWG, provide multistate review of the regulatory and supervisory processes in a given state. And all of this is developed and maintained by the states collaboratively, through NAIC processes and with support from centralised NAIC resources.

The IMF Financial Sector Assessment Program (FSAP)

In 2010, the International Monetary Fund (IMF) completed its review of the US financial regulatory system, including insurance, under the Financial Sector Assessment Program (FSAP).[7] In its Detailed Assessment Report (DAR) on insurance, made publicly available in May 2010, the IMF confirmed the effectiveness of US insurance regulation, noting that 'Strong regulation contributed to the overall resilience of the insurance sector during the financial crisis' (IMF Detailed Assessment Report (DAR) on Insurance, p. 14). From the perspective of US insurance regulators, in addition to assessing the US system against international standards, an important benefit of the FSAP process was an increased understanding by IMF and others of how states oversee the business of insurance, including the extensive collaboration among the states, and how the NAIC operates in conjunction with the states. It is a unique system for a unique market, one that is not always well understood by those outside the system.

The IMF assessed the US insurance regulatory system against 28 Insurance Core Principles (ICPs) of the International Association of Insurance Supervisors (IAIS) and found that the US observed or largely observed 25 of these international standards.[8] The IMF concluded that there is generally a high level of observance of the ICPs, and that 'Insurance regulation in the United States is generally thorough and effective, although there are areas where development is needed.' Key aspects of the US system, notably the comprehensive data collection and robust tools and processes for analysing individual insurance companies, were termed 'world leading'. The IMF also recognised the various multi-state and peer review mechanisms that exist to ensure individual states implement solvency requirements effectively.

In its report, the IMF suggested some areas for improvement, specifically related to the three ICPs that were assessed as being only 'partly observed'. Under ICP 3 (Supervisory Authority), the IMF expressed concern over the independence of US supervisors given the ability of many Governors to dismiss the insurance commissioner, although it did acknowledge the operational independence of state insurance regulators.[9] Under ICP 17 (Groupwide Supervision), the IMF encouraged enhancement of the US system of group supervision, an issue US regulators had already identified and begun to tackle.[10] Finally, the IMF identified some areas for improvement under ICP 28 (Anti-Money Laundering and Combating the Financing of Terrorism.)[11] The IMF made a number of other recommendations, some suggesting specific changes in state laws or regulations and others suggesting a more general review of regulatory policies and practices. The NAIC is reviewing the IMF's recommendations and has assigned each recommendation to a relevant NAIC committee, task force or working group to review and take into account in their relevant work plan.[12]

The Dodd-Frank Wall Street Reform Act (PL 111-203)

Countries around the globe are strengthening their systems of financial regulation in response to the recent financial crisis, and the US is no exception. In July 2010, President Obama signed into law the Dodd-Frank Wall Street Reform and Consumer Protection Act (PL 111-203). This act represents the most comprehensive overhaul of financial regulation in the United States since the Glass-Steagall Act of the 1930s. The stated objective of the measure is to 'promote the financial stability of the United States by improving accountability and transparency in the financial system, to end "too big to fail", to protect the American taxpayer by ending bailouts, to protect consumers from abusive financial services practices, and for other purposes'.

The Dodd-Frank Act creates a number of new agencies and new regulatory authorities. While a complete discussion of the statute is not possible here, its most important elements include:

- A new *Financial Stability Oversight Council (FSOC)* is created, comprised of ten voting and five non-voting members, with the Treasury Secretary as chair. The FSOC is charged with monitoring the financial services marketplace to identify potential threats to stability, recommending heightened prudential standards for activities that pose systemic risk, and identifying systemically important financial entities for heightened prudential regulation by the Federal Reserve. The FSOC will also advise Congress on domestic and international regulatory developments and make recommendations to enhance the integrity and stability of US financial markets. A new Office of Financial Research (OFR) will provide support to the Council, collecting data and conducting independent analysis of available information.

- The Federal Deposit Insurance Corporation (FDIC) is given new *Orderly Liquidation Authority*, under which it may become the liquidator for a non-bank financial institution if necessary for financial stability. This provides a legal mechanism outside bankruptcy to unwind a systemically important firm, enabling the FDIC to take over the firm, dispose of its assets, and impose losses on shareholders and creditors.

  The act contains a number of features intended to limit the use of this authority to extreme situations. Moreover, while the FDIC may provide necessary financial assistance for an orderly resolution and is empowered to borrow from the Treasury (subject to limits) to do so, there is a prohibition on taxpayer funding and a requirement that any costs be recovered from assessments on financial firms. Assessments must vary to reflect the size and risk profile of the firm.
- The act creates a new *Bureau of Consumer Financial Protection* charged with regulating consumer financial products and services, including mortgages, credit cards, and other financial products. Although the Bureau will be housed within the Federal Reserve, the Federal Reserve is prevented from interfering with its operations. Mortgage originators are subject to increased regulation.
- A new *Federal Insurance Office (FIO)* is created within the Treasury Department (discussed later). Other insurance-related provisions pre-empt certain aspects of state regulation of reinsurance and non-admitted (surplus lines) insurance.

In addition to the above, the Dodd-Frank Act strengthens the regulation of various activities and enhances regulatory authority of existing agencies. For example:

- The Federal Reserve is given specific responsibility related to systemic risk and financial stability, and it is explicitly charged to 'identify, measure, monitor, and mitigate risks' to financial stability. In addition to its existing responsibilities for regulating bank holding companies, it will regulate systemically important non-bank financial firms, and it must subject those firms to heightened prudential standards. It is also given a greater role in supervising the systemically important payment, clearing, and settlement activities of financial institutions. The President of the New York Federal Reserve, who is currently appointed by the board of the NY Fed (the majority of which is elected by member banks), will now be a presidential appointee.

- There are specific provisions aimed at proprietary trading by banks and derivatives trading generally. The 'Volcker rule' restricts proprietary trading by a bank or bank holding company and their sponsorship of hedge funds and private equity funds. With respect to derivatives, the bill provides for enhanced regulation of swaps, including credit default swaps (a particularly problematic area during the recent financial crisis), and contains provisions that promote the use of exchanges or clearinghouses. Banks must spin off their derivatives trading operations into separately capitalised affiliates, subject to a number of exceptions (for example, trading in interest rate and foreign exchange markets, and trading for risk mitigation purposes). Major swap participants (that is, entities that take significant swaps positions) are subject to enhanced regulation, including capital, registration, margin, and disclosure requirements.
- The Securities and Exchange Commission (SEC) is given increased powers in regulation and enforcement, as well as new structures intended to increase the influence of investors. There are new requirements on securitisation, including a requirement that issuers of asset-backed securities retain a portion of the credit risk of the securities. Other provisions relate to executive compensation, proxy access for shareholders, changing the definition of accredited investor and imposing a fiduciary duty on broker-dealers.[13]
- Miscellaneous provisions relate specifically to the structure of banking regulation. The Office of Thrift Supervision (which was the holding company supervisor of AIG) is abolished, and its powers are transferred to other federal banking regulators. Federal deposit insurance limits are permanently increased to US$250,000.

The impact of the Dodd-Frank Act on US insurance regulation

In many respects, the ultimate impact of the Dodd-Frank Act remains to be seen. Much of the detail is left to various rules to be developed by the existing and new regulatory agencies. While there will undoubtedly be some impact on the way insurance companies operate and are regulated, the impact will be significantly less than that for the banking and securities sectors. In several key areas, insurance is specifically exempted from the new law. Given the limited role played by insurance in the recent crisis, as well as the relatively strong performance by the US insurance regulatory system, this result is perhaps not surprising.

In a number of areas, insurance is carved out of the law:

- The business of insurance is expressly exempted from the oversight of the Bureau of Consumer and Financial Protection. State insurance regulators actively regulate insurance products, and Congress saw no need to replace or duplicate existing regulation.[14]

- With respect to the new Orderly Liquidation Authority, insurance companies will continue to be resolved under state liquidation laws and by state insurance regulators, unless the firm is deemed to be systemically risky and in need of liquidation and the state regulator fails to act within 60 days.
- The bill contains a specific provision prohibiting the SEC from regulating non-variable annuities if the state has adopted the NAIC's Suitability in Annuity Transaction Model Regulation.
- The proprietary trading restrictions of the Volcker rule have limited application to insurance companies.[15]

In other cases, changes not specifically aimed at insurance are likely to have collateral effects on the insurance sector:

- The elimination of the Office of Thrift Supervision (OTS) will affect those insurance companies that are affiliated with thrifts, including most large life insurance companies. Previously, the OTS was the consolidated supervisor of thrift holding companies. That responsibility will now move to the Federal Reserve, meaning most large life insurance groups will be subject to Federal Reserve oversight in addition to functional regulation of the insurance subsidiaries by state insurance regulators.[16]
- The impact of the change to derivatives regulation is unclear; much will be decided by the rule-making process. Insurers are active users of certain derivatives (for example, interest rate and equity-linked derivatives) in their risk management activities. The changing environment for derivatives regulation, increased capital and margin requirements on counterparties, and increased use of exchanges and clearinghouses will undoubtedly impact the cost and structure of this activity. An important question is whether, given the volume of their activity in this area, some insurers might be recognised as 'major swap participants'. There are certain exemptions in the law for end-users and for commercial hedging, but it is unclear whether these would apply to insurance companies. If they do not, and some insurers are deemed to be 'major swap participants', they will be subject to registration requirements, reporting, and capital requirements that could duplicate and potentially contradict current state regulatory requirements.
- The FSOC's mandate is defined broadly to address systemic risk, and it encompasses systemic risk that might be created by the insurance sector. Of the 15 members (ten voting and five non-voting), there are three members with insurance expertise (one voting and two non-voting).[17] One question is the extent to which any insurance companies or groups might be identified as systemically important by the FSOC. As indicated earlier, this would lead to Federal Reserve supervision and enhanced prudential requirements.

The Federal Insurance Office

One of the most significant provisions of the Dodd-Frank Act for insurance regulation is the creation of the Federal Insurance Office, or FIO, a new office in Treasury that can serve as a central resource on insurance issues. For several years, industry and state regulators have agreed that the US suffers from not having some formal function in the federal government that is charged with acquiring knowledge and understanding of this distinct sector. Many of the discussions on financial regulation within the federal government and globally tend to be bank-centric, and insurance regulators agreed that a formal federal function could help to increase understanding of insurance issues in Washington and elsewhere, and provide a clear partner for state insurance regulators to work with on emerging issues. During the drafting of the legislation, the NAIC supported a properly structured FIO.

The legislation creating the FIO also tackles the challenge of how a state-based system can function in a world of international trade agreements. The law provides that the Treasury Secretary may enter into agreements covering prudential matters in insurance, so long as they achieve a level of protection 'substantially equivalent to that achieved under state insurance regulation'. The FIO may pre-empt inconsistent state regulations, subject to the protection of certain state insurance measures and a number of due process requirements.

Other functions assigned to the FIO include:

- monitoring all aspects of the insurance industry and coordinating with state insurance regulators to obtain information;
- assisting the Secretary in administering the Terrorism Insurance Program;
- recommending insurers and affiliate entities in need of enhanced supervision to the FSOC; and
- developing federal policy on international insurance matters (including representing the US 'as appropriate' before the IAIS) and assisting the Treasury Secretary in negotiating covered agreements.

The law specifically provides that the FIO has no general supervisory or regulatory authority over the business of insurance. To further emphasise its limited role, the Director of the FIO is a career level position within the Treasury, and not a presidential appointment.

As with many aspects of the Dodd-Frank Act, the precise implications of this new body will only become clear with time. In the best case, it can serve as the focal point of a well-functioning federal/state partnership, a connection between the existing national system of state-based insurance regulation and federal policy-making, and a conduit through which the expertise of the current regulatory structure can influence federal discussion on issues that might affect insurance. Under a less optimistic (and less likely) scenario, the FIO could attempt to usurp the role of the state regulators on prudential matters in insurance, or the Congress could expand its role. Concentrating prudential policy-making in a single federal agency would diminish the effectiveness of the checks and balances in the existing state system. Furthermore, it would tend to increase political influence over prudential standard-setting, given that the FIO is not an independent agency. The NAIC has committed to working cooperatively with the FIO to achieve a strong federal/state partnership.

Non-admitted and reinsurance regulation

The non-admitted (that is, surplus lines) and reinsurance elements of the Dodd-Frank Act are aimed specifically at streamlining the current regulatory system, in which multiple states can exercise regulatory authority over a single multi-state transaction. In the surplus lines area, the bill provides that only the home state of the insured may regulate the placement of the coverage and collect surplus lines premium taxes. In reinsurance, credit for reinsurance will be determined by the domiciliary (that is, home) state of the ceding company, and nondomestic states may not impose additional requirements, so long as the domestic state is accredited by the NAIC or has substantially similar solvency requirements. In addition, the domiciliary state of a reinsurer is given exclusive authority to regulate the solvency of that reinsurer, so long as the domestic state is accredited or has substantially equivalent solvency requirements. While supporting the objective of streamlining reinsurance regulation, state insurance regulators have raised concerns over the pre-emption that is embodied in the reinsurance provisions, arguing that it eliminates a key strength of the state regulatory system – the checks and balances that constrain the behaviour of domestic regulators. This is particularly true where a state is not accredited. Regulatory requirements are only one aspect of an effective regulatory system; implementation and enforcement are equally important.[18]

The Solvency Modernization Initiative

Beyond the significant activity at the federal level, the NAIC has been engaged in its own assessment of the US solvency regulatory system. The NAIC's Solvency Modernization Initiative (SMI) began in June 2008 as a critical self-examination of the US insurance solvency regulation framework. The NAIC began by reviewing international developments regarding insurance supervision, banking supervision, and international accounting standards to consider their potential use in US insurance regulation. While US insurance solvency regulation is updated on a continuous basis, the SMI focuses on five key areas: (1) capital requirements; (2) governance and risk management; (3) group supervision; (4) statutory accounting and financial reporting; and (5) reinsurance.

The NAIC's SMI Task Force released an updated Roadmap in August 2010 (NAIC, 2010d). This document summarises the work plan for SMI through December 2012.[19] A number of ideas are currently under consideration.

Capital requirements

Capital requirements in the US have been risk-based for more than a decade, with the initial life insurance risk-based capital (RBC) formula implemented in 1993. The initial step to RBC, as often overlooked, is the development of financial data on a conservative statutory accounting basis. RBC is then largely a factor-based approach, with simple correlation assumptions, but scenario modelling is used for life insurance interest and market risk (C-3). The factors are significantly more granular than a typical factor-based system, with different factors for asset and for liability risks, credit risk factors that depend on asset ratings and concentration, and non-life factors adjusted to reflect company experience with reserving and pricing. The RBC formula is calibrated to identify 'weakly capitalised companies' and does not represent economic target levels of capital that a company should hold.[20] There is a ladder of intervention, with four thresholds triggering various levels of company and/or regulatory action.

US insurance regulators are examining the current structure of risk-based capital requirements, recognising that it will continue to be an important component of the US solvency framework. Specific areas under consideration are: calibration of the formulae and how correlation is treated; modification of the formula to include missing risks, and identification of areas where additional use of modelling might be appropriate. Some future modifications have already been incorporated into the NAIC's Capital Adequacy Task Force's work plan, including quantification of catastrophe risk in the property/casualty RBC using modelling, the improved measurement of interest rate and market risk (C-3) in the life RBC, improved measurement of asset risk in all formulas, and the impact of health reform in health RBC. In 2009, the NAIC significantly revised its approach for Residential Mortgage Backed Securities, eliminating the role of rating agencies. The new approach will be extended to Commercial Mortgage-Backed Securities in 2010.[21]

Governance and risk management

Today's corporate governance requirements for insurers largely exist in state corporate governance law, including case law. In addition, the NAIC's enhanced risk-focused surveillance process, which is a part of the accreditation requirements, requires the examiners to assess risk and the insurer's management and mitigation of risks. The SMI Roadmap calls for further study of the existing legal framework and international corporate governance principles, the development of high level governance principles, and a determination of the best avenue for implementing/enforcing them. In the risk management area, ideas under consideration include periodic risk reporting, an Own Risk and Solvency Assessment (ORSA) requirement, stress tests, and other tools for prospective solvency assessment.

Group supervision

One of the main lessons for US insurance supervisors from the recent financial crisis is the need for enhanced group supervision. Currently, insurance companies that are part of a holding company system are subject to the Insurance Holding Company System Regulatory Act and Regulation, which include a variety of regulatory reporting and prior approval requirements. These govern steps to acquire an insurer, commissioner approval of extraordinary dividends and certain material transactions (for example, large investment or reinsurance transactions, management agreements, cost-sharing agreements, tax allocation agreements and certain guarantees), examination authority (of insurer and affiliates), and receivership authority. The main thrust of holding company regulation is to prevent intercompany and other transactions that might adversely affect the insurer.

In addition to the statutory aspects of holding company supervision, states have developed ways to coordinate in their supervision of insurance groups. Following the enactment of the Gramm-Leach-Bliley Act in 1999, the NAIC identified a lead regulator for every holding company system that contained more than one insurer. The purpose was to create a more effective and efficient coordination and communication of regulatory activities among the multiple domestic regulators. The lead regulator's responsibility is to coordinate holding company analysis and information sharing among domestic regulators. Where possible, financial exams of the individual insurers are scheduled to occur simultaneously, exam processes are coordinated, and resources are shared. Note that the lead regulator primarily serves a coordination role; states do not relinquish any of their own authority.

Given the difficulties of AIG, the NAIC has concluded it is not enough to 'wall off' the insurance companies. Regulators also want to enhance their ability to look outside the insurance company, adding 'windows' so they can identify activities that create reputational risk or other risk for the insurer. The current NAIC's Holding Company Model Act and Regulation already give regulators the authority to gather information from the holding company; however, that authority hasn't always been used as aggressively as it could. The Model Regulation and Act are being strengthened and new regulatory disclosures are being added. Regulators also support enhancements to our current lead supervisor system, clarifying the responsibilities of the lead supervisor and further increasing coordination and communication. Because corporate structures do matter in the case of insolvency, this enhanced group supervision would supplement – and not replace – the current focus on the corporate walls. The concepts addressed in the 'windows and walls' approach include (1) communication between regulators; (2) supervisory colleges; (3) access to and collection of information; (4) enforcement measures;

(5) group capital assessment, and (6) accreditation (NAIC Group Solvency Issues Working Group, 2010).

As they pursue enhancements to the US system of group supervision, US regulators reject the notion that group supervision can replace the supervision of individual companies, or that individual supervisors should defer to a single group supervisor with ultimate decision-making authority. Rather, US regulators support a multijurisdictional model based on cooperation and collaboration, an approach that continues to evolve in the US. As indicated earlier, US regulators believe the benefits of a multijurisdictional approach are significant: a diversity of perspectives leads to centrist policy, multiple eyes reduce the risk that problems will be missed, and peer pressure from regulators with a responsibility to protect their own markets counteracts tendencies toward forbearance and regulatory capture. While a single all-powerful group supervisor is arguably more efficient, US regulators believe the benefits of a multi-jurisdictional model far outweigh the limited increase in costs.

A key objective of group supervision must be to examine the gaps that are created by focusing only on the subsidiary insurers and understanding the linkages throughout the group. Given the increased tendency for groups to centralise certain activities (for example, investment, aspects of risk management), there continue to be opportunities to improve efficiency through enhanced coordination and collaboration.

Statutory accounting and financial reporting (including valuation)

Unlike other lines of insurance, the valuation of life insurance reserves under statutory accounting is not principles-based. The NAIC has been developing a new principles-based valuation methodology that would replace the existing formulaic life insurance reserves. The new Standard Valuation Law was adopted in late 2009, but the Valuation Manual remains to be completed. In June 2010, the NAIC announced a study to assess the impact of the draft Valuation Manual on the industry. It is expected that this study will be completed by March 2011, and the Valuation Manual finalised by late fall 2011.

Regulators must also make significant policy decisions about the future of statutory accounting and the financial reporting system. The current statutory accounting system is effectively based on Generally Accepted Accounting Principles (GAAP), with variations that are deemed appropriate for regulatory accounting. As new GAAP standards are issued, the NAIC reviews the standards and decides whether to accept, modify, or reject them for statutory accounting purposes. The development of International Financial Reporting Standards (IFRS) by the International Accounting Standards Board (IASB) will have some impact on GAAP, particularly given the proposed convergence between GAAP and IFRS. Consequently, the NAIC has decided it needs to make some policy decisions about the future of statutory accounting and financial reporting.

Reinsurance

US credit for reinsurance laws require unlicensed reinsurer to post collateral in order for a ceding company to receive credit for that collateral. This has long been a contentious issue. Collateral requirements are generally opposed by European and other non-US reinsurers, and by the European Commission, while they tend to be strongly supported by many US ceding companies. Resolution of this issue has been complicated by the multistate regulatory system, in which companies must comply with the credit for reinsurance requirements in all states in which they do business. In 2008, the NAIC endorsed the Reinsurance Regulatory Modernization Framework, which was 'intended to facilitate cross-border reinsurance transactions and enhance competition within the US market, while ensuring that US insurers and policy-holders are adequately protected against the risk of insolvency'. One of the key elements of the framework was a partial reduction in collateral requirements for creditworthy reinsurers from approved jurisdictions. Given the challenges in adopting the Framework uniformly in all states, the NAIC also endorsed federal implementation, and drafted the Reinsurance Regulatory Modernization Act as the vehicle (NAIC, 2010d). Unfortunately, the bill failed to find the necessary support.

As indicated earlier, the Wall Street Reform Act pre-empts certain extraterritorial regulation of reinsurance and may thus create the foundation for amending collateral requirements through the state-based system. Specifically, the law prohibits a state from denying credit for reinsurance if the domiciliary state of the ceding insurer recognises such credit and is either (1) an NAIC-accredited state, or (2) has financial solvency requirements that are substantially similar. The NAIC is currently considering how key elements of the Framework might be implemented through a combination of changes to the accreditation programme and state legislative action. Regulators are also considering modernising risk transfer requirements applicable to life reinsurance.

Conclusion

As is the case with other sectors and other countries, US insurance regulators are engaged in an intensive assessment of their prudential regulatory system. At the federal level, the Wall Street Reform Act is the most significant piece of legislation related to regulation of the financial sector since the 1930s. It will have some impact on insurance regulation, although it will be significantly less than the impact on other sectors, and key aspects of the US insurance regulatory system have been preserved in the bill. To some extent, this is a reflection of the strong performance of the national system of state-based regulation during the recent crisis.

US insurance regulation is a national system of state-based regulation. Supervision embodies a variety of tools, and US regulators place particular emphasis on tools that go beyond regulatory capital requirements. Detailed financial reporting and analysis, coupled with on-site examinations, enable regulators to identify firms that are outliers along a number of dimensions and focus their resources accordingly. Robust peer review mechanisms promote regulatory action when appropriate.

While insurance regulation performed relatively well, there are opportunities for improvement in any system of supervision. The NAIC's Solvency Modernization Initiative is examining those lessons and developments in regulation in other countries and sectors as part of a process of continuous improvement of the insurance regulatory system in the US. This will undoubtedly result in enhancements, but given the already strong system, it is likely that any changes will be evolutionary, rather than revolutionary. Areas of focus include regulatory capital requirements, group supervision, reinsurance regulation, financial reporting and accounting, and corporate governance and risk management.

While US regulators continue to improve insurance regulation and supervision in the US, they also actively participate in efforts at the IAIS to improve supervision globally. Insurance supervisors around the world have recognized the need for improved transborder coordination and cooperation, particularly in the supervision of internationally active insurance groups. US supervisors have long embraced a collaborative, cooperative model to supervising firms that operate across state borders, and they believe the benefits of adopting a multijurisdictional approach are significant. These strengths include a diversity of perspectives that tends to lead to centrist policy, multiple eyes that reduce the risk that problems will be missed, and peer pressure from other regulators that counteracts tendencies toward forbearance and regulatory capture. The lessons learned by US regulators in creating a national system of state-based regulation can inform efforts to develop a global system of supervising internationally active groups.

Notes

1. The NAIC was formed in 1871, and one of its first projects was to provide for the consistent valuation of assets for insurers writing in multiple jurisdictions. Today, insurers are required to file detailed financial statements with the NAIC on a quarterly basis.
2. While AIG is widely described as an insurance group, it is in reality a complex financial entity with significant insurance operations. The failure of AIG was precipitated largely by its unregulated financial products division, which had written credit default swaps protecting a number of US and foreign banks against default of mortgage-related assets. See Harrington (2009), also Congressional Oversight Panel (2010). One of the key lessons from AIG for US insurance regulators is the need for increased focus on the

activities outside the insurance companies and the risks they pose to the solvency of the insurers. The NAIC is currently developing a system for enhanced group supervision.

3. The term 'Commissioner' is used by most states to refer to the chief insurance regulatory official, however, some states use the term 'Administrator', 'Director' or 'Superintendent of Insurance').
4. For a more complete description of the role of checks and balances in the US regulatory system and the advantages of a multijurisdictional approach to solvency regulation, see Vaughan (2009).
5. The risk-focused examination is part of a broader effort adopted by the NAIC in 2004, known as the Risk-Focused Surveillance Framework. The Risk-Focused Surveillance Framework ties together four functions, most of which had been performed previously, and coordinates them in a more cohesive manner to be applied consistently by regulators. These four elements are (1) risk-focused exams, (2) off-site risk-focused financial analysis, (3) examination of internal and external changes in the organisation, (4) and an annual supervisory plan for the insurer developed by the domestic regulator. An Insurer Profile Summary is used to 'house' summaries of risk-focused examinations, financial analysis, internal/external changes, the Supervisory Plan and other standard information. It provides an Executive Summary of an insurer's financial condition, risk profile, regulatory actions/plans and other highlights.
6. The need for enhanced peer review processes has been highlighted by the current financial crisis. According to Sir Callum McCarthy (2009), the former chairman of the UK Financial Services Authority, '(A)t present, national supervisors do not challenge each other's decisions often or fiercely enough. ... We need a better process of robust challenge, with an enforcement process that involves at least a strong element of naming and shaming.' See also de Larosière (2009): 'The present processes and practices for challenging the decisions of a national supervisor have proven to be inadequate.'
7. Established in 1999 in response to the Asian financial crisis, the FSAP is a joint IMF and World Bank programme providing an in-depth and comprehensive review of a jurisdiction's financial regulatory sector including insurance with the purpose of promoting national and international financial stability and assisting in strengthening financial systems of member countries. The IMF notes that the purpose of the FSAP is: (i) to identify the strengths and vulnerabilities of a country's financial system; (ii) to determine how key sources of risk are being managed; (iii) to ascertain the financial sector's technical assistance and developmental needs and (iv) to assist in prioritizing policy responses. To date, more than three quarters of IMF member countries have undergone an FSAP; however, 2009–10 is the first year that the US (including the NAIC and state regulators representing the insurance sector) has participated. See also the IMF website on the FSAP at www-bcc.imf.org/external/np/fsap/fsap.asp.
8. In preparation for the IMF review, the NAIC conducted a self-assessment of the extent to which the US system complies with the 28 ICPs of the IAIS. The IAIS ICPs form the basis for the IMF's assessment on the insurance sector (NAIC, 2009a).
9. State insurance regulators argue that the state-based system – in which regulators in other states maintain their ability to restrict a company's license if the domestic regulator fails to do so – is a powerful antidote to political interference and regulatory capture in the company's home state.
10. One of the main lessons of AIG for US and other insurance supervisors is the need for enhanced group supervision, and US insurance regulators are working with regulators around the world to accomplish this. In addition, a key part of the NAIC's Solvency Modernisation Initiative (SMI) (discussed in the next section) is building the

capabilities and processes to enhance the regulator's understanding of the group-wide risk profile and risks posed by a group's noninsurance entities.

11. Enforcement of AML requirements is complicated by the US bifurcated regulatory scheme. The federal government has primary jurisdiction over AML statutes, while the regulation of insurance and expertise in financial examination of insurance is the responsibility of the states. There is room for improved cooperation and coordination among regulators in this area.
12. The NAIC has committed to reviewing these recommendations both for internal purposes and to better respond to future assessments. The US will be subject to an FSAP update every few years, and FSAP assessors will assess the degree to which US regulators consider and address recommendations made in the FSAP. In addition, the Financial Stability Board (FSB) has created a program of ongoing peer review assessments constituting country and thematic reviews, and these reviews will utilize FSAP results. Note that IAIS ICPs, which form the basis for the FSAP, are being updated and the US insurance sector will be assessed in future FSAP assessments on its compliance with these new ICP standards. The NAIC is an active participant at the IAIS in the process of updating the ICPs.
13. A 'fiduciary duty' is essentially a requirement that the individual act in the best interest of the customer.
14. Section 1002(15) of the Dodd-Frank bill contains the definition of 'financial product or services', the activities that fall under CFPA authority. The business of insurance is explicitly excluded in paragraph C of the definition, where the 'business of insurance' is defined in section 1002(3) as 'the writing of insurance or the reinsuring of risks by an insurer, including all acts necessary to such writing or reinsuring and the activities relating to the writing of insurance or the reinsuring of risks conducted by persons who act as, or are, officers, directors, agents, or employees of insurers or who are other persons authorized to act on behalf of such persons'.
15. Specifically, they only apply to groups that include a bank (that is, a bank holding company) or a firm designated as systemically significant. Even then, the restrictions do not apply to investments made for the insurer general account, as long as they are subject to state regulation and the federal banking regulators have not jointly determined that the regulation does not adequately protect the bank or financial stability.
16. The Federal Reserve has long had the responsibility to regulate bank holding companies, where a holding company owned a commercial bank. There have been a few cases where these holding companies included significant insurance operations, and state insurance regulators continued to regulate the insurance companies and cooperated with the Federal Reserve to share supervisory information. Notable examples include Citigroup and MetLife.
17. The Director of the FIO and a state insurance regulator (chosen by the state regulators) are nonvoting members of the FSOC. The President will appoint a voting member with insurance experience.
18. To the extent the state is accredited, there is some multistate oversight of implementation and enforcement through the accreditation review process.
19. For up-to-date information on the NAIC's Solvency Modernisation Initiative see http://naic.org/index_smi.htm.
20. At an interim meeting in March 2010, the SMI Task Force discussed the role of regulatory capital in the US. The comments and discussion that occurred during the interim meeting highlighted an important feature of the US regulatory system. Risk-based capital is considered to be only one of a panoply of weapons in the

regulatory arsenal. For many regulators, RBC's importance was to provide a clear, undebatable threshold for regulators to take action or to assume control of the firm. The objective nature of the RBC thresholds, and the limited need to engage in debate with a company over whether a threshold was triggered, was held by many regulators to be a critical feature of the system. Other tools – including the extensive data analysis, comprehensive examination processes, and authority granted under the Hazardous Financial Condition Model Act and Regulation – were viewed to be more important in identifying and constraining risky behaviours. US regulators tend to be sceptical that the best way to identify excessive risk concentrations is to focus limited regulatory resources on assessing a firm's internal economic capital models. See NAIC (2010a) and Vaughan (forthcoming).

21. For more information on the NAIC's RMBS and CMBS initiatives, see the NAIC's website at www.naic.org.

Bibliography

Congressional Oversight Panel (2010) *The AIG Rescue, Its Impact on Markets, and the Government's Exit Strategy* (June Oversight Report), http://cop.senate.gov/documents/cop-061010-report.pdf.

de Larosière, J., et al. (2009) *Report of the High Level Group on Financial Supervision in the EU*, http://ec.europa.eu/internal_market/finances/docs/de_larosiere_report_en.pdf.

The Dodd-Frank Wall Street Reform and Consumer Protection Act of 2010, Public Law No. 111-203.

Harrington, S. (2009) *The Financial Crisis, Systemic Risk, and the Future of Insurance Regulation*, www.namic.org/pdf/090908SystemicRiskAndTheFuture.pdf>.

IMF (2010) *United States: Publication of Financial Sector Assessment Program Documentation – Detailed Assessment of Observance of IAIS Insurance Core Principles FSAP Detailed Assessment Report (DAR)*, www.reinsurance.org/files/public/IMF%20Study%20on%20US%20Financial%20Sector.pdf.

McCarthy, Sir C. (2009) 'Britain is not a Regulatory Island', *Financial Times*, 31 March.

NAIC (2009a) *IMF Financial Sector Assessment Program: Self-Assessment of IAIS Insurance Core Principles*, www.naic.org/documents/topics_iais_fsap_assessment.pdf.

NAIC (2009b) *Reinsurance Regulatory Modernization Act*, www.naic.org/documents/committees_e_reinsurance_090915_reins_ref_modernization_act.pdf.

NAIC (2010a) *Solvency Modernization Update (17 March)*. http://naic.org/documents/index_smi_update_100317.pdf.

NAIC (2010b) *The United State Insurance Solvency Framework*, www.naic.org/documents/committees_e_us_solvency_framework.pdf.

NAIC (2010c) *Financial Regulation Standards and Accreditation Program*, www.naic.org/documents/committees_f_FRSA_pamphlet.pdf.

NAIC (2010d) *Solvency Modernization Initiative Roadmap (16 August)*, http://naic.org/documents/committees_ex_isftf_summer_ntlmtg_meeting_smi_roadmap.pdf.

NAIC Group Solvency Issues Working Group (2010) *Report to Solvency Modernization Initiative (EX) Task Force on Suggested 'Windows and Walls'*, http://naic.org/documents/index_smi_group_solvency_windows_and_walls.pdf.

Polakoff, S.M. (2009) *American International Group: Examining what went wrong, government intervention, and implications for future regulation. Testimony before the Senate Banking Committee, March 5*, http://banking.senate.gov/public/index.cfm?FuseAction=Hearings.

Testimony&Hearing_ID=1655fd01-154e-48de-9fd8-2832a68f04d6&Witness_ID=ad4b84ae-b2cd-46eb-b4f4-4aa20a2f8d1a.

Vaughan, T.M. (2009a) 'The Implications of Solvency II for U.S. Insurance Regulation', *Networks Financial Institute Policy Brief 2009-PB-03*, www.networksfinancialinstitute.org/Lists/Publication%20Library/Attachments/132/2009-PB-03_Vaughan.pdf.

Vaughan, T.M. (2009b) 'The Economic Crisis and Lessons For (and From) U.S. Insurance Regulation', *Journal of Insurance Regulation*, 28(1): 3–18, www.naic.org/documents/cipr_jir_vaughan.pdf.

Vaughan, T.M. (forthcoming) 'Improving Regulatory Capital Requirements: Developments in the U.S.', in *Global Perspectives on Insurance Today: A Look at National Interests versus Globalization* (New York: Palgrave Macmillan).

17
Regulatory Challenges and Developments in the European Union[1]

Karel Van Hulle

Introduction

One of the main objectives of the European Union is the creation of a single market. The single market is all about bringing down barriers and simplifying existing rules to enable everyone in the EU – individuals, consumers and businesses – to make the most of the opportunities offered to them by having direct access to 30 countries and 500 million people.[2]

The cornerstones of the single market are the four freedoms: the free movement of people, goods, services and capital. These freedoms are enshrined in the Treaty on the Functioning of the European Union (TFEU) and form the basis of the single market framework.

For insurance, a single market means that insurance and reinsurance undertakings should be able to establish themselves in other Member States by setting up a subsidiary or a branch or to offer their services cross-border.

The completion of such a single market is still ongoing although much has already been achieved through harmonisation of sometimes very different rules and practices in Member States.[3] Harmonisation takes place through Directives. A Directive is a legal instrument, proposed by the European Commission and adopted by the Council of Ministers and the European Parliament. It is addressed to the Member States, which must implement its provisions into national law within a stated period of time. Lack of implementation or wrongful implementation or application of a Directive is controlled by the European Commission under the supervision of the European Court of Justice. If a Member State is unwilling to correctly implement Community legislation, the Commission may decide to start an infringement procedure and eventually bring that Member State before the European Court of Justice.

With the adoption of the Third Life[4] and Non-Life[5] Directives in 1992, the principle of home country control on the basis of a single passport was introduced.

Insurance undertakings, on the basis of authorisation in any one Member State, are entitled to offer their services throughout the entire EU without any price control or prior notification of terms and conditions. A distinction is made between prudential supervision which is exercised by the supervisory authority of the Member State in which an insurance undertaking received its authorisation and market conduct which can still be supervised by the host Member State authority within the limits of the so-called 'general good' principle.[6]

The reform introduced in 1992 has increased competition in Member States and has brought about a more dynamic insurance market. It is therefore no surprise that many EU insurers and reinsurers have become major players also on a global level.

A further boost to harmonisation was given with the adoption in 1999 of the Financial Services Action Plan[7] aiming at a deeper integration of the internal market for financial services in the EU. In insurance, this led to the adoption of a Directive on the reorganisation and winding up of insurance undertakings,[8] a first reform of the solvency regime,[9] the adoption of a Directive on insurance mediation,[10] of a Directive on financial conglomerates,[11] and of a Directive on reinsurance.[12]

This contribution looks at the legislative reforms that are being prepared now. It focuses first on the new supervisory architecture which the Commission proposed after the financial crisis showed serious weakness in the present cooperation between supervisors particularly in crisis situations. It will then describe the main features of the new solvency regime which is being developed in the EU and which will fundamentally change prudential supervision. Finally, a number of initiatives will be described which aim at strengthening the protection of policy-holders in the aftermath of the financial crisis.

A new supervisory architecture

There can be no doubt that the harmonisation carried out through the various Directives adopted over a period of 30 years[13] profoundly changed national laws and regulations in Member States. It must, however, be recognised that the harmonisation was not meant to lead to a uniform system of insurance supervision. Important differences therefore remain between the regulatory regimes in Member States.

The Lamfalussy structure

On 17 July 2000, the Council set up a Committee of Wise Men on the Regulation of European Securities Markets, chaired by Alexandre Lamfalussy, to develop ideas on how the decision-making process at EU level could be improved in the area of securities regulation. It had appeared that the traditional harmonisation process, based upon Directives following a minimum harmonisation approach, was suboptimal in the sector of financial services because of the dynamics of that sector. Over the years, it had also become clear that a more important role in the law-making process needed to be attributed to supervisory authorities, who are dealing on a day-to-day basis with regulated entities.

In its final report,[14] the Committee of Wise Men called for the establishment of a four-level regulatory framework in order to make the regulatory process for EU securities legislation more flexible, effective and transparent. The proposed approach was subsequently extended to banking and insurance at the specific request of the European Parliament, which also obtained a number of safeguards to ensure that its co-legislative powers would not be infringed upon by the Commission and the Council.

The regulatory framework under the Lamfalussy approach comprises four levels:

- The first level consists of principles-based legislation (usually a directive) adopted by the Council and the European Parliament.
- The second level consists of rules (directives or directly applicable regulations) adopted by the European Commission on the basis of a specific authorisation included in the level one legislation. These implementing measures are prepared by the supervisory authorities on the basis of a specific mandate from the Commission. The draft texts are discussed with and voted upon by Member State experts in the context of a regulatory committee chaired by the Commission.
- The third level contains non-binding guidelines developed by the supervisory authorities, within the context of a committee set up by a Commission decision.
- The fourth level comprises the Commission's enforcement mechanism. The Commission is expected to see to it that what has been agreed at EU level by Member States and by the European Parliament is actually implemented in national law.

Following the proposals made by the Committee of Wise Men, the Commission set up the Committee of European Insurance and Occupational Pensions Supervisors (CEIOPS)[15] based in Frankfurt and the European Insurance and Occupational Pensions Committee (EIOPC)[16] (composed of high-level Member State experts). The EIOPC set up in 2003 replaces now the former Insurance Committee.[17] Similar committees were set up in the areas of banking and securities regulation.

The structure was subsequently modified in order to give more powers to the European Parliament, which received a right of scrutiny[18] and in order to ensure that the level-three guidance from the European committees of supervisors (such as CEIOPS) is applied by supervisors (on a comply or explain basis) and that they take most decisions with qualified majority.[19]

Reform after the financial crisis

When the financial crisis broke out in 2007/08, it became immediately clear that the structure that had been set up for a closer cooperation between supervisors in the development and practical implementation of prudential legislation was not adequate for dealing with the financial difficulties of cross-border groups. Supervisors tended to look first at resolving their national problems, thereby forgetting the cross-border consequences of their actions.

This was an important reason why the Commission asked a group of high level experts, chaired by Jacques de Larosière, to develop a blueprint for a new EU supervisory architecture. The group presented its report on 25 February 2009. Building on its recommendations, the Commission set out proposals for a new European financial supervisory architecture in its Communication of 4 March 2009.[20]

These proposals were presented in more detail in a Communication of 27 May 2009:[21]

- establishment of a European System of Financial Supervisors (ESFS), consisting of a network of national financial supervisors working in tandem with new European Supervisory Authorities (ESAs). The ESAs are created by transforming the existing European supervisory committees into a European Banking Authority (EBA), a European Insurance and Occupational Pensions Authority (EIOPA) and a European Securities and Markets Authority (ESMA). This combines the advantages of an overarching European framework for financial supervision with the expertise of local micro-prudential supervisory bodies that are closest to the institutions operating in their jurisdictions;
- establishment of a European Systemic Risk Board (ESRB) in order to monitor and assess potential threats to financial stability that arise from macroeconomic developments and from developments within the financial system as a whole. To this end, the ESRB will provide an early warning of system-wide risks that may be building up and, where necessary, issue recommendations for action to deal with these risks.

It is important to note that the Commission did not propose to merge the three existing European supervisory committees into a single European Authority. It was recognised that each of the sectors represents distinct particularities and that most Member States have not yet opted for the model of a single integrated supervisor. Indeed, there still is a great deal of disagreement on what type of supervisory structure is preferable: a distinct supervisor for each sector, an integrated supervisor for all sectors, or a twin peaks system distinguishing between prudential supervision and market conduct. In the present situation, it would have been very complex and inefficient to set up one single Authority at EU level whilst keeping a different supervisory architecture at national level.

Nor did the Commission propose to completely overhaul financial supervision by transferring prudential supervision from the national to the European level. Although there are a large number of cross-border groups that might qualify for European supervision, most financial institutions are still national. Similarly, it would be difficult to transfer supervision to the European level without developing some kind of European bailout system. As long as the financial bailout remains the (financial) responsibility of Member States, it is difficult to transfer the supervision of the institutions to the European level.

The Communication also concluded that in order for the ESFS to work effectively, changes to the financial services legislation would be necessary, in particular to provide an appropriate scope to the more general powers provided for in the individual Regulations establishing the Authorities, ensuring a more harmonised set of financial rules through the possibility to develop draft technical standards and facilitate the sharing, where necessary, of micro-prudential information.

On 23 September 2009, the Commission presented its proposals for the new European supervisory architecture.[22] The proposals were accompanied by a Commission Staff Working Document[23] which sets out the likely changes that will be brought forward by the Commission in the sectoral legislation so as to take account of the creation of the new European Supervisory Authorities and the powers conferred to these Authorities in the respective Regulations. In Annex 1 to this document, the likely changes to the Solvency II Framework Directive are listed.

EIOPA

On 26 October 2009, the Commission presented a proposal for a Directive which includes the changes in the sectoral legislation following from the creation of the new European Supervisory Authorities. This proposal is commonly referred to as Omnibus 1[24] and includes proposed amendments to the regulation in banking, securities regulation and pension funds. It does not include proposals for amending the insurance legislation as the Solvency II Framework Directive (Directive 2009/138/EC of 25 November 2009) had at that time not yet been officially adopted and published. The amendments of the insurance legislation will be tabled later in a new Commission proposal that will be called Omnibus 2 (see below).

The plan is to have the European Supervisory Authorities, including EIOPA, in place by 1 January 2011. EIOPA will receive a number of new competences. The most important new competences are the following:

- the power to adopt binding technical standards (Article 7 of the proposed EIOPA Regulation). EIOPA will continue to issue guidance which is not legally binding but will also be able to develop technical standards that will become legally binding after endorsement by the Commission. The objective is to move in the direction of a common EU rulebook for prudential supervision in insurance;
- the power to ensure a consistent application of EU law in cases where a national supervisory authority does not comply with existing Community legislation (Article 9 of the proposed EIOPA Regulation);
- the power to require joint action by supervisors in the case of an emergency situation (Article 10 of the proposed EIOPA Regulation);
- the power to settle disagreements between national supervisory authorities (binding mediation) (Article 11 of the proposed EIOPA Regulation);
- the power to sit as an observer on all EU colleges of supervisors and the right to obtain all relevant information for that purpose (Article 12 of the proposed EIOPA Regulation).

Furthermore, EIOPA will receive a specific mandate to contribute to the development of a common supervisory culture. It will have the power to carry out peer reviews, will cooperate with the ESRB and will collect information (common database) which is relevant for prudential supervision from a European perspective.

The specific powers of EIOPA need to be introduced through an amendment of the Solvency II Framework Directive. A Commission proposal (to be called Omnibus 2) which was most likely to be tabled in September 2010. It will take account of the discussions that have taken place on similar amendments in other sectoral legislation (banking, securities regulation and pension funds) through Omnibus 1.

Possible candidates for binding technical standards could be supervisory reporting, disclosure and valuation of assets and liabilities, including technical provisions. Binding mediation might be foreseen for disputes concerning the approval of a group internal model between the group supervisor and one or more solo supervisors.

The negotiations on the new European supervisory architecture are still ongoing. The European Parliament wants a further increase of the powers of the new ESAs such as the power to give instructions to individual financial institutions and a strengthened role in the supervision of cross-border groups. It is expected that an agreement will be reached by the beginning of September 2010 so that the new system can enter into force on 1 January 2011.

The impact of the new supervisory architecture on the existing European supervisory committees, such as CEIOPS, will be tremendous. EIOPA will have a full time Chairperson and its staff will increase rapidly from the present number of 15 to about 90 in three years time. In practice, this means that much of the work which is done today for CEIOPS by national authorities will be carried out in the future by the staff of EIOPA. This should stimulate a more European approach to the issues thereby increasing the level of harmonisation in the direction of a single EU rulebook for insurance supervision.

A new solvency regime

From Solvency I to Solvency II

On 25 November 2009, the European Parliament and the Council adopted the Solvency II Framework Directive.[25] This text, officially proposed by the Commission on 10 July 2007, contains the basic principles for a new fully risk-based solvency regime for insurance and reinsurance undertakings, replacing the existing Solvency I requirements. At the same time, the Directive contains a recast of the most important Insurance Directives.

The present solvency regime was introduced by the First Non-Life (1973) and Life (1979) Directives. It was reviewed in 2002 after the findings of the Müller Report (1997),[26] prepared at the request of the Commission by the EU Insurance Supervisory Conference. This Report considered the present solvency regime as generally satisfactory, although it recognised certain weaknesses in the methodology and gave consideration to the need for a more risk-based approach. The new solvency rules introduced in 2002 are often referred to as Solvency I.

It was agreed that a more fundamental solvency reform was necessary and that Solvency I could only be seen as a quick fix awaiting a more radical reform of the solvency rules. Important reasons for this were that Solvency I was not sufficiently risk sensitive and that it was not capable to cope with the increased complexity of financial markets and the emergence of new risks.

The fundamental revision of the solvency regime was started by the Commission in 2000 and was carried out in two phases, whereby the first phase was devoted to an analysis and discussion of the issues and the second phase concentrated on the development of the new solvency regime. A number of studies[27] were carried out and discussions were held with industry experts, the actuarial profession and experts from Member States. The discussions also looked at the situation in other countries outside the EU (Australia, Canada, US, Switzerland) and at the work carried out at international level by the Basel Committee, the International Association of Insurance Supervisors (IAIS) and the International Accounting Standards Board (IASB). This led to the adoption by the Commission of a Framework for consultation (2004) containing the basic principles of the new solvency regime, which served as a basis for specific calls for advice addressed to CEIOPS during the course of 2005 and 2006. At the same time, three quantitative impact studies (QIS) were carried out by CEIOPS at the request of the Commission. A fourth quantitative impact study (QIS 4) was carried out in 2008 during the negotiation of the Commission's proposal in the Council and in the European Parliament.

The Solvency II Framework Directive is the first directive in the insurance field that makes full use of the Lamfalussy procedure. The objective was to draft a Framework Directive containing the basic principles of the new solvency regime to be further elaborated through implementing measures to be adopted by the Commission on the basis of a specific mandate in the Framework Directive. Further (level 3) guidance would then be developed by CEIOPS on the basis of the principles and rules developed at levels 1 and 2.

The Commission started the process by asking CEIOPS for advice on a large number of questions which were agreed beforehand with Member State experts in EIOPC and which were in line with the Framework for consultation. At all stages of the process stakeholders were consulted, both by CEIOPS before delivering final advice to the Commission and by the Commission before launching its calls for advice to CEIOPS. All documents prepared by the Commission or by CEIOPS were made available on the website of the Commission and/or the website of CEIOPS.

The Commission's proposal, which was tabled on 10 July 2007 was accompanied by an extensive Impact Assessment[28] which – based upon the information gathered from the three QIS exercises – explained why the Commission had chosen certain options and rejected other alternative options. Several outside parties, such as the insurance industry (CEA (European insurance federation) and AMICE (Association of Mutual Insurers and Insurance Cooperatives in Europe)) and the European Central Bank (ECB), contributed to the Impact Assessment. The insurance industry produced a document analysing the potential impact of the new solvency regime on insurance markets and products as well as a paper estimating the potential cost of the new regime. The ECB produced an analysis of the impact of the new solvency regime on financial stability.

Main objectives of Solvency II

Solvency II was developed in order to address a number of weaknesses in the Solvency I regime, which became very much apparent during the financial crisis at the beginning of this century:

- capital requirements under Solvency I are not sufficiently risk sensitive with the consequence that important risks at both the liability side and the asset side of the balance sheet are not captured. This leads to some insurance undertakings operating with too much capital while others are undercapitalised. Another consequence is that insurance undertakings are not encouraged to improve their risk management;
- there is no early warning mechanism under Solvency I. An insurance undertaking could therefore find itself in difficulties without prior warning;

- group supervision is not dealt with in its own right; it is considered as an activity that is merely supplementary to solo supervision;
- Solvency I is based on minimum harmonisation, thereby creating a lack of level playing field in the protection of policy-holders between Member States as some Member States went beyond the minimum requirements of the Directives and introduced more risk-based requirements;
- under Solvency I, too much importance is attached to prudence, particularly in technical provisions. This results in an inefficient allocation of capital which prevents insurers from taking on more risks;
- the Solvency I requirements are impossible to reconcile with the economic capital concepts developed by the insurance industry, thereby introducing a layer of administrative bureaucracy which neither serves industry as a management tool nor supervisors as an efficient supervisory tool;
- cooperation between supervisors is not sufficiently organised and the powers of supervisors are very different from Member State to Member State making it difficult for supervisors to communicate and to develop a common approach to supervision.

The Commission's Impact Assessment Report, which accompanies the Proposed Solvency II Framework Directive, lists the main objectives of Solvency II:

- deepen the integration of the EU insurance market by improving the harmonisation of Member States' rules and the convergence of supervisory practices;
- enhance the protection of policyholders and beneficiaries by removing the lack of risk sensitivity in the current solvency regime;
- improve the international competitiveness of EU insurers and reinsurers by adopting more modern actuarial, accounting, risk management and supervisory standards and techniques;
- promote better regulation by making full use of impact assessments and studies pre and post adoption of the new solvency regime.

In order to achieve these general objectives, Solvency II follows a number of specific objectives:

- introduction of an encouragement for EU insurers and reinsurers to improve their risk management by providing an incentive to measure and properly manage their risks through the potential of lower capital requirements;
- advancement of supervisory convergence and co-operation by introducing the same toolkit for supervisors in all Member States and by organising the cooperation between supervisors through the establishment of colleges of supervisors;

- encouragement of cross-sectoral consistency by removing the potential for regulatory arbitrage particularly in the context of financial conglomerates;
- better allocation of capital resources by making the capital requirements risk sensitive;
- promotion of international convergence by making the solvency regime compatible with current and future international standards;
- increase of transparency by introducing uniform requirements on supervisory reporting and public disclosure.

Main characteristics of Solvency II

Solvency II will apply to all insurance and reinsurance undertakings in the EU (about 5,000 companies and mutuals). However, very small insurance undertakings fulfilling certain conditions, including a level of gross premium income below €5 million, are excluded. In order to address potential problems which may result from the broad scope of Solvency II, the Directive states that its provisions should be proportionate to the nature, the scale and the complexity of the operations. The principle of proportionality applies both to the substantive rules of the Directive and to the activities of supervisors. Simplifications (for instance, in the calculation of technical provisions) are provided for small and medium-sized insurers.

Solvency II adopts the three-pillar approach of Basel II and of the Capital Requirements Directive (CRD).[29] Under Solvency II these three pillars are of equal importance and are interconnected. Much attention is usually paid to the capital requirements. However, capital is only one element and the Sharma Report (2002) showed clearly that most failures in the past were due not so much to an insufficient level of capital but very much to failures in risk management and governance. These issues are specifically addressed in Pillar 2. It could be argued that if an insurance undertaking has put in place good risk management, capital requirements will no longer be the main issue. It is therefore unfortunate that so much discussion is focused just on the required level of capital. Similarly, it is incorrect to state that Solvency II is relying too much on an insurer's risk management and modelling which is difficult to supervise. One should not forget the important disclosure aspects in Pillar 3, under which an insurer is required to justify the assumptions underlying the internal model compared with the standard formula.

Pillar 1

Pillar 1 deals with the quantitative requirements: market consistent valuation of all assets and liabilities, including technical provisions; calculation of own funds; adoption of the 'prudent person' approach to investments instead of the current quantitative investment restrictions; introduction of two capital requirements.

The Solvency Capital Requirement (SCR) should deliver a level of capital that enables an undertaking to absorb significant unforeseen losses over a one-year time horizon and should give reasonable assurance to policy-holders that payments will be made as they fall due.

The SCR can be calculated on the basis of a standard formula or on the basis of an internal model to be approved by the supervisor. The choice between a standard formula and an internal model should allow the undertaking to develop its risk management according to its own needs and risk profile. A breach of the SCR leads to supervisory intervention. It is an early warning signal. A recovery plan will have to be drawn up assuring compliance with the SCR within an agreed period of time (in principle, six months).

The SCR is designed to ensure that all quantifiable risks attached to the undertakings' assets and liabilities are taken into account and includes at least the following risk modules: non-life underwriting risk, life underwriting risk, health underwriting risk, market risk and counterparty default risk. Each of the risk modules is calibrated using a Value-at-Risk measure, with a confidence level of 99.5% over a one-year period. The chosen ruin probability of 0.5% over a one year time horizon can be viewed in two different ways. Either that a specific insurer would be expected to fail once every 200 years or that on an annual basis, one in every 200 insurers will fail.

The standard formula will be introduced through an implementing measure and is being tested in a number of quantitative impact studies before being finalised in 2011. The conditions for the approval of a partial or full internal model will be further specified in an implementing measure. Mechanisms are being introduced to ensure a level playing field between Member States in the approval of an internal model.

The Minimum Capital Requirement (MCR) represents the level of capital which must at all times be present in the undertaking: a breach of the MCR triggers ultimate supervisory action, i.e. withdrawal of the licence. The MCR is set at a confidence level of 85% and has an absolute floor specified in the Directive. The MCR may not fall below 25% nor exceed 45% of the SCR.

Own funds are classified into three tiers following the approach in Basel II. They are further divided into basic own funds and ancillary own funds whereby the basic own funds represent the difference between assets and liabilities valued on a market consistent basis as well as subordinated liabilities. Ancillary own funds are off the balance sheet items, that is, commitments which have been received from third parties and which can be called upon to absorb losses.

Pillar 2

Pillar 2 deals with the qualitative requirements and the supervisory review process.

A key element of Solvency II is an enhanced internal control, governance and risk management, as well as a self-assessment of capital needs. All insurance and reinsurance undertakings must have in place an effective system of governance which provides for sound and prudent management of the business. The governance system implies the creation of a number of functions: risk management, internal control, internal audit and actuarial function. The system must take account of the nature, scale and complexity of the business (proportionality principle). The importance of good corporate governance in financial institutions in general is stressed in a Green Paper which the Commission published recently.[30] Undertakings must regularly carry out an Own Risk and Solvency Assessment (ORSA). This should allow them to see whether their risk profile deviates from the SCR. The ORSA is an essential feature of Solvency II. It is an answer to the fear that the imposition of a standard formula, which can do no more than to reflect the position of the average European insurer or the development of an internal model by the undertaking itself, with all the subjectivity surrounding risk modelling, will detract an insurer from continuous and thorough risk analysis and management. Undertakings and supervisors will have to learn to work with the ORSA and to turn it into an efficient tool both for the undertakings themselves and for prudential supervision.

The supervisory review process should allow supervisors to step in at an early stage, thereby making up for the absence of an early warning mechanism under Solvency I. Once the SCR has been breached, supervisors will step in. They dispose of a uniform toolkit which is an important element in achieving supervisory convergence. Following the supervisory review process, supervisory authorities may in exceptional circumstances (such as a deviation from the assumptions underlying the standard formula which cannot be remedied within a specified timeframe or where the undertaking shows severe deficiencies in governance) impose a capital add-on. The capital add-on must be reviewed at least once a year by the supervisory authority. It is removed when the undertaking has remedied the deficiencies which led to its imposition.

Pillar 3

Pillar 3 deals with supervisory reporting, which is aimed at supervisors and public disclosure which is addressed to the public in general.

Insurers and reinsurers must submit to the supervisory authorities the information which is necessary for the purposes of supervision. In order to streamline that information, common templates will be developed which will be introduced as an implementing measure.

Insurers and reinsurers must also disclose, on an annual basis, a Solvency and Financial Condition Report, including, for instance, information on capital add-ons, the main differences between the underlying assumptions of the standard formula and those of the internal model used and the amount of any non-compliance with the MCR or any significant non-compliance with the SCR.

The enhanced transparency resulting from this report will contribute to market discipline.

Group supervision

The three pillars of Solvency II are covered by a roof which represents group supervision. Solvency II recognises a group as an economic entity and applies the solo solvency requirements equally to the group level. Groups will therefore have in addition to the SCR and the MCR of the solo entities making up the group, a group SCR and a group MCR with full recognition of diversification benefits. Groups will have to appoint a group supervisor who chairs the college of supervisors in which all supervisors of the entities belonging to the group (including significant branches) are represented. The group supervisor has a number of powers such as the right to approve the group internal model. Groups will need to do their own group solvency assessment (ORSA) and will have to publish a Solvency and Financial Condition Report concerning the group.

The final text of the Directive no longer contains provisions on group support. They were deleted after difficult discussions in which the European Parliament supported the Commission's position. Under the group support regime, proposed by the Commission, a parent undertaking would have been allowed to replace part of the solvency capital in one or more subsidiaries with a promise to deliver that capital. This system would have avoided that too much capital would remain blocked in subsidiaries rather than to use it more efficiently to promote further activities of the group. This issue, which was already controversial from the very beginning, became a serious stumbling block when a major financial crisis broke out during the course of 2008.

It became impossible to convince particularly host Member States (those Member States in which the subsidiaries are located) that a parent undertaking would be prepared to provide group support to a subsidiary when in addition to the subsidiary also the parent or the group as a whole would face serious financial difficulties. Supervisors of host Member States and their Ministries of Finance were also worried that – whilst the group supervisor had the right to approve the group support regime – they would nevertheless remain responsible when the subsidiary which remained subject to their supervision would fail. They were afraid that they might have to bail out the subsidiary if the parent was unwilling or unable to provide the necessary funds.

It was finally agreed by way of compromise to delete the chapter on group support from the Directive, to replace it with a chapter on groups with centralised risk management and to come back to the issue of group support at a later stage after the Commission will have submitted a report by 31 October 2015 to the European Parliament and to the Council, in which it will assess the benefit of enhancing group supervision and capital management within a group and will present, where appropriate, proposals for an amendment of the Directive.

In accordance with Article 242(2) of the Solvency II Framework Directive, the assessment must include 'possible measures to enhance a sound cross-border management of insurance groups notably of risks and asset management'.

It must also take into account new developments and progress concerning:

- a harmonised framework on early intervention;
- practices in centralised group risk management and functioning of group internal models including stress testing;
- intra-group transactions and risk concentrations;
- the behaviour of diversification and concentration effects over time;
- a legally binding framework for the mediation of supervisory disputes;
- a harmonised framework on asset transferability, insolvency and winding-up procedures which eliminates the relevant national company or corporate law barriers to asset transferability;
- an equivalent level of protection of policy-holders and beneficiaries of the undertakings of the same group particularly in crisis situations;
- a harmonised and adequately funded EU-wide solution for insurance guarantee schemes;
- a harmonised and legally binding framework between competent authorities, central banks and ministries of finance concerning crisis management, resolution and fiscal burden sharing which aligns supervisory powers with fiscal responsibilities.

The long list of items which the Commission is asked to consider before coming back with a proposal on group support shows the complexity of the issue and the lack of agreement between Member States on this issue. The introduction of an effective system of group supervision through Solvency II will contribute to a greater awareness of supervisors about the need for a closer cooperation in the case of groups. The problem is that things tend to become rather complicated in the case of cross-border groups because of differences in the legal regime, the absence of legal mechanisms and instruments that are effective on a cross-border basis, cultural differences and political sensitivities. It may well be that the future lies in organising some sort of European supervision for all or major cross-border groups (as advocated by the European Parliament). Meanwhile, some groups will no doubt consider transforming some of their subsidiaries into branches, thereby avoiding the capital problems resulting from the use of different legal entities and the need to cooperate with different supervisory authorities on solvency matters.

If an insurance group is part of a wider financial group, the supplementary supervision rules of the Financial Conglomerates Directive[31] apply. This Directive will be amended in order to take account of the experiences during the financial crisis and the changes in the capital adequacy and solvency regimes for banks and insurance undertakings. A first proposal has been tabled by the Commission for adoption in 2011. An important feature of the proposal is to ensure that the sector-specific (banking and insurance) supervision and supplementary supervision is also applied to the conglomerate's parent entity, even if that entity is just a holding company. Banking supervision would therefore remain applicable even if the banking group acquires a significant stake in an insurance business and insurance supervision will also remain applicable if the insurance group acquires a significant stake in a banking business.

Impact of the financial crisis on Solvency II

When the financial crisis broke out in 2008, the question was raised whether the overall architecture of the future solvency regime was still sound. The Commission asked all stakeholders for their views on this issue. The unanimous view expressed by the industry as well as by supervisors, by Member States and by the European Parliament was, that there was no need to fundamentally rethink Solvency II. That conclusion was not evident as questions had been raised concerning the use of fair value for the valuation of assets and liabilities and the allowance of a full internal model for the calculation of the SCR. The crisis in the banking sector had shown the risks of using fair value accounting in a disorganised manner. It also made apparent the disadvantages of relying too much on internal models, particularly if the model does not capture the tail risk and is entirely based on the positive developments of the past which are merely extrapolated into the future.

On 19 March 2009, CEIOPS published a paper, 'Lessons Learned from the Crisis (Solvency II and Beyond)'.[32] The main conclusion of the paper was that Solvency II should be adopted as soon as possible. However, CEIOPS also identified a number of issues that needed to be looked at again at levels 2 and 3 (further refinement of the existing Solvency II calibrations, both at module and sub-module levels; further strengthening of governance, risk management and internal control; the importance of the own risk and solvency assessment; the need to focus supervision more on consolidated entities than on solo entities only; the need to adopt a holistic approach to insurers' exposures to special purpose vehicles; the need to address the issue of procyclicality).

The various Solvency II working groups of CEIOPS were asked to look into these issues when developing their advice to the Commission for the implementing measures (level 2) and in developing the level 3 guidance. Specific crisis-inspired proposals were made by CEIOPS for Pillar 1 (quality of the capital, alternative forms of risk transfer, treatment of market risk, correlation between certain risks), Pillar 2 (reliance on credit rating agencies, treatment of liquidity risk, conditions for the approval of an internal model) and Pillar 3 (avoidance of possible procyclical effects of market value based disclosures).

Some changes related to the financial crisis were also introduced in the Framework Directive during the negotiations in the Council and the European Parliament: the inclusion of a specific mandate for supervisory authorities to give proper consideration to financial stability and to the potential procyclical effects of their actions; the inclusion of a symmetric adjustment mechanism in the equity risk sub-module (pillar 1 dampener); the extension of the period for the recovery of the SCR in the event of an exceptional fall in financial markets (pillar 2 dampener). As for investment in equity, Member States are allowed to apply in the equity risk sub-module the so-called duration approach to pension products, where the average duration of the liabilities exceeds an average of twelve years.

Implementing measures of Solvency II

In order to avoid divergences in the application and interpretation of the new requirements, Member States and the European Parliament have listed a large number of areas (43) where the Commission is either required (29) or invited (14) to issue implementing measures.

As soon as the Framework Directive was adopted (May 2009), the Commission asked CEIOPS to start work on the implementing measures. In its letter of 12 June 2009[33] to CEIOPS, the Commission provides detailed guidance to CEIOPS as to how the work should be organised.

CEIOPS should concentrate on those areas where the Framework Directive requires the Commission to issue implementing measures. The list of areas where the Directive provides for implementing measures is attached to the letter. The Commission also indicates a number of areas where level 3 guidance would be useful, such as on supervisory reporting (templates), capital add-ons, the system of governance and the valuation of technical provisions.

Attached to the letter is a proposed structure for the CEIOPS advice as well as a request in the form of a Call for Advice for the contribution of CEIOPS to the impact assessment that will accompany the proposed implementing measures. A detailed timetable indicates how the Commission sees the preparation and further development of the implementing measures.

The first advice for the level 2 implementing measures was delivered by CEIOPS in November 2009. The last advice was presented in April 2010.

The work of CEIOPS is supervised at level 2 by the EIOPC whose agreement is sought by the Commission before sending a Call for Advice to CEIOPS. Since November 2009, the Commission Services have organised a series of meetings with Member State experts in a working party (Solvency Expert Group) of EIOPC for a discussion of the draft implementing measures which the Commission Services have prepared on the basis of CEIOPS advice.

Whilst the implementing measures (level 2) are being prepared and discussed, CEIOPS is already working on its level 3 supervisory guidance. This guidance is not legally binding although all members of CEIOPS have committed themselves to respect that guidance on a 'comply or explain' basis.

Some of the advice delivered by CEIOPS for the level 2 implementing measures has been very controversial. Whilst CEIOPS argued that the financial crisis urged them to follow a more restrictive approach on issues such as capital, technical provisions, own funds, calibration and correlation between risks, the insurance industry complained that CEIOPS failed to look at the total impact of its advice and that the CEIOPS proposals would lead to excessive capital requirement for an industry that was not the cause of the financial crisis.[34]

Problems also arose with CEIOPS' advice (technical specifications) for the last major field test, that is, QIS 5. Here again, different views were presented by CEIOPS, industry and Member States. After examining the various points of view and after discussing their own draft with stakeholders and with Member State experts at the EIOPC meeting of 30 June 2010, the Commission Services came up with an adapted version of the technical specifications, which they submitted to CEIOPS on 5 July 2010 with a Call for Advice to launch QIS 5 between August and November 2010.

As QIS 5 is the last major test, the results are crucial for the final calibration and for other elements of the level 2 implementing measures (the calculation of own funds and of technical provisions). CEIOPS is therefore urged to ensure a high participation rate from the industry: at least 60% of the undertakings in all Member States (which means about 3000 undertakings) and 75% of the insurance groups (which means about 100 groups). In order to stimulate participation by small and medium-sized insurers, CEIOPS has been asked to make the spreadsheets user-friendly and to develop a QIS 5 user manual.

The official results of QIS 5 will be published by CEIOPS in April 2011. The Commission will examine these results carefully so as to amend where necessary the draft implementing measures. These implementing measures will in any case be accompanied by an impact assessment report. Preparation of this report has already started.

It is the intention to have the implementing measures adopted by the Commission in spring 2011. The Council and the European Parliament will then have a period of three to four months during which they can object to the text presented by the Commission. In order to facilitate the introduction of Solvency II, it has been agreed to move the original deadline of 1 November 2012 for the entry into force to 1 January 2013. This means that the implementing measures must be formally adopted by 31 December 2011 so as to allow Member States one year for the implementation of the EU legislation into national law.

In September 2010, the Commission will present its proposal for Omnibus 2, which will include a number of provisions that are of crucial importance for the practical implementation of Solvency II such as the areas where EIOPA is expected to adopt binding technical standards or to settle disputes between supervisors and the areas where transitional measures are necessary.

With the Lamfalussy architecture and the creation of EIOPA, the level of harmonisation in prudential supervision will increase tremendously. There will be very few matters on solvency where supervisors will be able to come up with 'local' requirements. Although the level 2 implementing measures are still to a large extent principle based, there will be a considerable amount of level 3 guidance, thereby making it difficult for national supervisors to depart from the approach agreed at EU level. This is further strengthened by the fact that some of that guidance may now become a binding technical standard.

Third country equivalence

Many EU insurers have important operations in third countries. In the same way, many third country insurers operate within the EU. From a Solvency II perspective, three questions arise:

- Can EU supervisors rely on the supervision exercised by third country supervisors over the activities of a third country reinsurer operating in the EU?
- How should the data concerning operations of EU insurers in third countries be integrated in the group SCR of the parent undertaking based in the EU?
- Can EU supervisors rely on the group supervision exercised by a third country supervisor concerning a third country insurer operating in the EU?

In order to facilitate an answer to these questions and to avoid that conflicting decisions would be taken by individual EU supervisors, the Solvency II Directive allows the Commission to decide whether the solvency regime of a third country can be considered equivalent with that of Solvency II.

Once an equivalence decision has been taken, EU supervisors can rely upon the supervision carried out by the supervisor of the country in which the reinsurance undertaking is headquartered, the calculation of the group solvency as regards the specific third country undertaking can be based upon the solvency requirements laid down in the third country concerned and the EU supervisors will be able to rely on the equivalent group supervision exercised by the third country supervisor.

The recognition of equivalence runs in two stages. In a first stage, the Commission needs to decide on the general criteria to be used to assess third country equivalence under Solvency II. These criteria will be included in an implementing measure which will be subject to agreement by Council and European Parliament. In a second stage, the Commission will by way of an individual decision decide on the equivalence of the solvency regime of specific third countries, using the assessment criteria that have been agreed as part of the implementing measure.

In order to prepare the process, the Commission asked CEIOPS for their advice. On 1 April 2010, CEIOPS provided final advice to the Commission on the general criteria to be used to assess third country equivalence under Solvency II.[35] As a follow-up to this, CEIOPS published for public consultation on 14 July 2010 a Consultation Paper (no. 81) with draft advice concerning the equivalence assessments to be undertaken in relation to Articles 172 (reinsurance), 227 (group solvency calculation) and 260 (group supervision) of the Solvency II Directive, in which they propose to consider Switzerland and Bermuda, in respect of the three equivalence articles and Japan for reinsurance. CEIOPS also advocate in this document the adoption of transitional measures in order to deal with a number of third countries that have not been included in the first wave. The comment deadline (13 August) has expired and CEIOPS will deliver its final advice to the Commission by the end of August. The Commission will decide by mid November 2010, after consulting other stakeholders and will then ask CEIOPS to carry out an examination of the solvency regime of the third countries that have been identified with a view to providing final advice to the Commission by the end of July 2011 in order for the Commission to take a final decision in June 2012.

The equivalence debate is important and complex. It should not be misunderstood. The Commission cannot ask CEIOPS to examine the solvency regime of all relevant third countries before July 2011. This would not be possible. On the other hand, it is not because a third country is not included in the first wave of countries to be examined, that its solvency regime is looked at as sub-standard. Indeed, it is even possible that the prudential regime of a third country has received a positive analysis from the International Monetary Fund (IMF) as part of a Financial Sector Assessment Programme (FSAP), but that it is still not considered as equivalent with Solvency II. The reason is that the analysis of equivalence has to be carried out from a Solvency II perspective and not from the perspective of satisfying the Core Insurance Principles of the IAIS. However, it is clear that some transitional regime will have to be adopted for a number of third countries, particularly when these countries have already taken measures to move in the direction of a risk-based solvency regime. There have been precedents in EU legislation in the areas of accounting, auditing and securities regulation. The equivalence process should therefore be seen as a call for further progress at international level in the area of solvency.

Policy-holder protection

Although one of the primary objectives of the solvency reform described above is the protection of policy-holders, other initiatives are being planned which aim at improving policy-holder protection from a particular point of view, for instance pre-contractual information given to policy-holders or the protection of policy-holders when an insurance undertaking has become insolvent.

Insurance mediation

During the discussions of Solvency II in the European Parliament, the Parliament specifically asked the Commission to amend the Insurance Mediation Directive

(IMD),[36] taking into account the consequences of the solvency reform for policy-holders. The implementation of the IMD has had important consequences for intermediaries throughout the EU. It establishes an internal market for insurance mediation and covers some 1 million professionals (brokers and agents) who must be registered with a competent authority and satisfy certain professional requirements. The IMD follows the minimum harmonisation approach. It has led to heavy gold-plating (introduction of more stringent requirements) in a number of Member States, thereby making cross-border operations difficult and increasing the administrative burden. CEIOPS has asked the Commission to have another look at the Directive and has made an effort to improve cooperation between competent authorities through the adoption of the so-called 'Luxembourg Protocol'.[37] Following a Commission competition inquiry into business insurance, the Commission identified in its final report published in 2007[38] a number of weaknesses in the regulatory regime for brokers particularly in the area of conflicts of interest and announced that it would look into this matter as part of a revision of the IMD.

The Commission has asked CEIOPS to prepare the groundwork for the reform and to produce a report with advice on seven different issues: the legal framework for the IMD (should there be more harmonisation using the Lamfalussy structure?); the scope of the Directive (should direct sales by insurance undertakings be included?); international dimension (how can the quality of services offered by insurance intermediaries from third countries be improved?); professional requirements (is there a need to further harmonise professional qualifications?); cross-border aspects of insurance mediation (how can cross-border provision of services be facilitated?); conflicts of interest and transparency (should the remuneration of brokers and agents be made public? How should conflicts of interest be managed?); reduction of administrative burden (is there scope for deregulation?).

CEIOPS was expected to come forward with detailed advice by November 2010. This advice, together with the input received from a consultation would be launched by the Commission by the end of September 2010, and would be used to prepare a legislative proposal that is planned for the end of 2011.

Packaged retail investment products

The amendment of the IMD must also be seen in the context of further work that is being carried out in the financial services sector to arrive at a cross-sectoral harmonisation of the rules applicable to the sale of packaged retail investment products. Many retail investment products have an insurance wrapper such as in the case of unit-linked life insurance policies whereby a portion of the premium is used to purchase life cover (the sum assured) with the balance invested in an investment fund. The return on the policy is linked to the performance of the fund. As opposed to traditional life insurance products, unit-linked policies usually do not guarantee the payment of a determined financial amount in particular in the case of death/survival, but instead an amount which is a multiple of the market value of one or several units. Therefore, by definition, the policy-holder bears the investment risk.

In its 2009 Communication on Packaged Retail Investment Products,[39] the Commission outlined important investor protection and level playing field issues in the retail investment markets which broadly cover investment funds (both UCITS (Undertakings for Collective Investment in Transferable Securities) and non-UCITS), retail structured products, and insurance-based investment products. The regulatory framework that has developed to address these problems is inconsistent and patchy and incurs a risk of regulatory arbitrage and investor detriment. The significance of these issues has been underlined by the financial crisis.

In response, the Commission committed to ensure investor protection standards are always at the appropriate level by taking a new 'horizontal' regulatory approach to the standards. This would ensure a level playing field between different types of retail investment products.

Two regulatory areas need to be addressed: rules on pre-contractual disclosures and rules on selling practices. The intention is to prepare a horizontal measure for pre-contractual disclosure for which the key investor information document (KID) being developed for UCITS could serve as a model and to have the selling practices dealt with at sectoral level, whereby the Markets in Financial Instruments Directive (MifiD)[40] rules addressing conflicts of interest and inducements, appropriateness and suitability could serve as a model.

For insurance, this reform would entail that those life insurance products which have the characteristics of a Packaged Retail Investment Product (PRIP) would in terms of pre-contractual disclosure be dealt with by the horizontal measure and that the IMD would have to be amended so as to introduce specific selling rules for PRIPs. To the extent that the MifiD rules would be found not to be suitable for an insurance product, specific alternative rules would have to be introduced.

The PRIPs project is very complex because there still is disagreement about the exact definition of a PRIP and both the MifiD rules and the IMD are at the moment being revised. The intention is to complete the project with proposals to be issued by the Commission before the end of 2011.

Insurance guarantee schemes

On 12 July 2010, the Commission published a White Paper on Insurance Guarantee Schemes[41] which sets out the Commission's views on a coherent framework for EU action on insurance guarantee schemes (IGSs) protection for policy-holders and beneficiaries. The White Paper invites all interested parties to submit comments and to provide further input on the identified options by 30

November 2010. It is accompanied by an impact assessment which is supported by a comprehensive methodological report and other annexes.

Already in 2001, after the failure of a major insurance undertaking operating cross-border, the Commission started work on insurance guarantee schemes. In 2007, the Commission asked Oxera to examine the situation in the EU. On the basis of the Oxera Report,[42] the Commission carried out a public consultation exercise in 2008 and organised a public hearing. Whilst a number of Member States supported an EU initiative in this area, there was considerable opposition from certain parts of the industry. The financial crisis changed the picture. It was difficult to justify why guarantee schemes should exist for banks and investment funds but not for insurance undertakings.

In May 2009, the Commission asked CEIOPS to give its views on the feasibility of the various design features of a possible European solution on IGS and to update the description of existing IGS in the Oxera report. CEIOPS submitted its report to the Commission on 30 June 2009 in which it advocated a solution based upon minimum harmonisation of a number of key elements.

IGSs provide last-resort protection to consumers when insurance undertakings are unable to fulfil their contractual commitments. Of the 30 EAA countries, only 12 operate one or more general insurance guarantee schemes. This means that, measured in terms of gross written premiums, one third of the entire European Economic Area (EEA) insurance market is not covered by any IGS in the event of an insurance company going bankrupt. Some 26% of all life insurance policies and 56% of all non-life insurance policies are unprotected.

The main reasons why the Commission advocates the introduction of a European regime on IGSs are: the greater awareness of consumers of the existence and limits of consumer protection guarantee schemes in all financial sectors following the financial crisis; the limited protection offered under Solvency II which does not provide for a zero failure regime; the likelihood of increased cross-border insurance activity which calls for harmonisation as not all Member States provide for an equal level of protection in case of insolvency; the lack of a level playing field between domestic and incoming insurance companies operating in the same market; the risk for market instability; the lack of a valid alternative.

The Commission proposes to introduce at EU level a coherent and legally binding framework on IGS protection, applicable to all policy-holders and beneficiaries, by means of a directive. IGSs should serve as a last-resort mechanism in each Member State. IGSs should cover not only policies issued by domestic insurers but also those sold by branches of domestic insurers established in other Member States. Both life and non-life insurance policies should be covered. The system should cover natural persons and selected legal persons. IGSs should be funded on the basis of ex ante contributions by insurers, possibly complemented by ex post funding arrangements in the case of lack of funds, which should be calculated according to the individual risk profiles of the contributors. An appropriate target level for funding should be set, with a suitable transition period. IGSs should at least and within a pre-defined period of time compensate policy-holders and beneficiaries for losses when an insurer becomes insolvent.

Conclusion

The legislative reforms which are presently underway in the EU are important and complex. Although they are not all directly related to the financial crisis, the financial meltdown during 2007 and 2008 has certainly confirmed that these reforms are necessary.

The new EU supervisory architecture is urgently needed. It is good to harmonise rules and regulations on prudential supervision but it is equally important to ensure that supervisors learn from each other and operate in a convergent manner. The tools and procedures to ensure this are not yet available and that weakness came out clearly during the financial crisis.

Solvency II will have a profound impact on the insurance industry, on supervisors and on policy-holders in the EU. A fully risk-based solvency regime combined with a market consistent valuation of all assets and liabilities will not be easy to operate. I do, however, believe that the economic risk based approach introduced with Solvency II is superior over a regime where not all risks are properly captured or where risks are hidden through smoothing devises. The complexity of the new regime will require transitional measures so as to avoid sudden changes. The new regime will also have consequences on product design, particularly in the case of long-term guarantees. The financial crisis made it clear that a number of products offered on the market today are possibly too risky in an environment with very volatile markets and low interest rates.

The ultimate goal of prudential supervision is the protection of policy-holders. Insurance products are complex. They are not always properly understood. Because the objective of insurance is to transfer the risk from the policy-holder to the insurer it is important that the policy-holder knows exactly which risks have been transferred and what service he/she receives in return for the insurance premium. Clarity about that is essential if the insurance industry is to play the important role which it must in times of uncertainty and change.

Notes

1. The views expressed in this contribution are attributable solely to the author.
2. This includes the 27 EU Member States and three countries belonging to the European Economic Area (EAA), that is, Iceland, Liechtenstein and Norway.
3. First Council Directive 79/267/EEC of 5 March 1979 on the coordination of laws, regulations and administrative provisions relating to the taking up and pursuit of the business of direct insurance other than life assurance, OJ L 228, 16.8.1979,

p. 3; Council Directive 78/473/EEC of 30 May 1978 on the coordination of laws, regulations and administrative provisions relating to Community co-insurance, OJ L 151, 7.6.1978, p. 25; Council Directive 87/344/EEC of 22 June 1987 on the coordination of laws, regulations and administrative provisions relating to legal expenses insurance, OJ L 185, 4.7.1987, p. 77; Second Council Directive 88/357/EEC of 22 June 1988 on the coordination of laws, regulations and administrative provisions relating to direct insurance other than life assurance and laying down provisions to facilitate the effective exercise of freedom to provide services, OJ L 172, 4.7.1988, p. 1; Council Directive 91/674/EEC of 19 December 1991 on the annual accounts and consolidated accounts of insurance undertakings, OJ L 374, 31.12.1991, p. 7; Directive 98/78/EC of the European Parliament and of the Council of 27 October 1998 on the supplementary supervision of insurance undertakings in an insurance group, OJ L 330, 5.12.1998, p. 1.

4. Council Directive 92/96/EEC of 10 November 1992 on the coordination of laws, regulations and administrative provisions relating to direct life assurance and amending Directives 79/267/EEC and 90/619/EEC (third life assurance Directive), OJ L 360, 9.12.1992, p. 1.
5. Council Directive 92/49/EEC of 18 June 1992 on the coordination of laws, regulations and administrative provisions relating to direct insurance other than life assurance (third non-life insurance Directive), OJ L 228, 11.8.1992, p. 1.
6. See the Commission Interpretative Communication on Freedom to provide services and the general good in the insurance sector, OJ C 43, 16.2.2000, p. 5.
7. Commission Communication on 'Financial Services: Implementing the framework for financial markets: action plan', COM (1999) 232, 11.5.1999, 32pp.
8. Directive 2001/17/EC of the European Parliament and of the Council of 19 March 2001 on the reorganisation and winding-up of insurance undertakings, OJ L 110, 20.4.2001, p. 28.
9. Directive 2002/12/EC of the European Parliament and of the Council of 5 March 2002 amending Council Directive 79/267/EEC as regards the solvency margin requirements for life assurance undertakings, OJ L 77 of 20.3.2002, p. 11, repealed by Directive 2002/83/EC of the European Parliament and of the Council of 5 November 2002 concerning life assurance, OJ L 345 of 19.12.2002, p. 1, and Directive 2002/13/EC of the European Parliament and of the Council of 5 March 2002 amending Council Directive 73/239/EC as regards the solvency margin requirements for non-life insurance undertakings, OJ L 77 of 20.3.2002, p. 17.
10. Directive 2002/92/EC of the European Parliament and of the Council of 9 December 2002 on insurance mediation, OJ L 9, 15.1.2003, p. 3.
11. Directive 2002/87/EC of the European Parliament and of the Council of 16 December 2002 on the supplementary supervision of credit institutions, insurance undertakings and investment firms in a financial conglomerate and amending Council Directives 73/239/EEC, 79/267/EEC, 92/49/EEC, 92/96/EEC, 93/6/EEC and 93/22/EEC, and Directives 98/78/EC and 2000/12/EC of the European Parliament and of the Council, OJ L 35, 11.2.2003, p. 1.
12. Directive 2005/68/EC of the European Parliament and of the Council of 16 November 2005 on reinsurance, OJ L 323, 9.12.2005, p. 1.
13. A recast version of the various Directives, together with the solvency reform, was published in 2009: Directive 2009/138/EC of the European Parliament and of the Council of 25 November 2009 on the taking-up and pursuit of the business of Insurance and Reinsurance (Solvency II), OJ L 335, 17.12.2009, p. 1.

14. Final Report of the Committee of Wise Men on the Regulation of European Securities Markets, Brussels, 15.02.2001, 117pp.
15. Commission Decision 2004/6/EC of 5 November 2003 establishing the Committee of European Insurance and Occupational Pensions Supervisors, OJ L 3, 7.1.2004, p. 30, repealed and replaced by Commission Decision 2009/79/EC of 23 January 2009, OJ L 25, 29.1.2009, p. 28.
16. Commission Decision of 5 November 2003 establishing the European Insurance and Occupational Pensions Committee, OJ L 34, 7.1.2004, p. 34.
17. See Directive 2005/1/EC of the European Parliament and of the Council of 9 March 2005 amending Council Directives 73/239/EEC, 85/611/EEC, 91/675/EEC, 92/49/EEC and 93/6/EEC and Directives 94/19/EC, 98/78/EC, 2000/12/EC, 2001/34/EC, 2002/83/EC and 2002/87/EC in order to establish a new organisational structure for financial services committees, OJ L 79, 24.3.2005, p. 9.
18. Council Decision 2006/512/EC of 17 July 2006 amending Decision 1999/468/EC laying down the procedures for the exercise of implementing powers conferred on the Commission, OJ L 200, 22.7.2006, p. 11.
19. Commission Decision 2009/79/EC of 23 January 2009 establishing the Committee of European Insurance and Occupational Pensions Supervisors, OJ L 25, 29.1.2009, p. 28.
20. *Driving European Recovery,* Communication from the Commission to the European Parliament and to the Council, COM (2009) 114 final of 4.3.2009. This document as well as all official documents referred to in this contribution can be consulted and downloaded from the Commission's website: http://ec.europa.eu/internal_market.
21. *European Financial Supervision,* Communication from the Commission to the European Parliament and to the Council, COM (2009) 252 final of 27.5.2009.
22. Proposal for a Regulation on Community macro-prudential oversight of the financial system and establishing a European Systemic Risk Board (ESRB), COM (2009) 499 final of 23.9.2009; Proposal for a Decision entrusting the European Central Bank with specific tasks concerning the functioning of the European Systemic Risk Board (ESRB), COM (2009) 500 final of 23.9.2009; Proposal for a Regulation establishing a European Banking Authority (EBA), COM (2009) 501 final of 23.9.2009; Proposal for a Regulation establishing a European Insurance and Occupational Pensions Authority (EIOPA), COM (2009) 502 final of 23.9.2009; Proposal for a Regulation establishing a European Securities Markets Authority (ESMA), COM (2009) 503 final of 23.9.2009.
23. SEC (2009) 1233 of 23.9.2009.
24. Proposal for a Directive of the European Parliament and of the Council amending Directives 1998/26/EC, 2002/87/EC, 2003/6/EC, 2003/41/EC, 2003/71/EC, 2004/39/EC, 2004/109/EC, 2005/60/EC, 2006/48/EC, 2006/49/EC and 2009/65/EC in respect of the powers of the European Banking Authority, the European Insurance and Occupational Pensions Authority and the European Securities and Markets Authority, 26.10.2009, COM (2009) 576 final.
25. Directive 2009/138/EC of the European Parliament and of the Council of 25 November 2009 on the taking-up and pursuit of the business of Insurance and Reinsurance (Solvency II), OJ L 335 of 7.12.2009, pp. 1–155.
26. *Solvency of Insurance Undertakings*, Report of the Conference of Insurance Supervisory Authorities of the Member States of the EU ('Müller Report'), April 1997, 102pp.
27. *Technical Provisions in Non-life Insurance,* Report of the Insurance Supervisory Authorities of the Member States of the EU ('Manghetti Report'), 2000, 42pp; *Study into the Methodologies to Assess the Overall Financial Position of an Insurance Undertaking from*

the Perspective of Prudential Supervision ('KPMG Report'), May 2002, 249pp; *Prudential Supervision of Insurance Undertakings* ('Sharma Report'), December 2002, 112pp.

28. Commission Staff Working Document accompanying the Proposal for a Directive of the European Parliament and of the Council on the taking-up and pursuit of the business of Insurance and Reinsurance (Solvency II), Brussels, 10.7.2007, SEC (2007) 871. This document as well as all official documents referred to in this contribution and relating to Solvency II can be consulted and downloaded from the Commission's website: http://ec.europa.eu/internal_market/insurance/solvency2.
29. CRD consists of two Directives: Directive 2006/48/EC of the European Parliament and of the Council of 14 June 2006 relating to the taking up and pursuit of the business of credit institutions (recast), OJ L 177, 30.6.2006, p. 1, and Directive 2006/49/EC of the European Parliament and of the Council of 14 June 2006 on the capital adequacy of investment firms and credit institutions (recast), OJ L 177, 30.6.2006, p. 201.
30. Green Paper from the Commission on Corporate Governance in financial institutions and remuneration policies, COM (2010) 284 final of 2.6.2010.
31. Directive 2002/87/EC of the European Parliament and of the Council of 16 December 2002 on the supplementary supervision of credit institutions, insurance undertakings and investment firms in a financial conglomerate and amending Council Directives 73/239/EEC, 79/267/EEC, 92/49/EEC, 92/96/EEC, 93/6/EEC, and Directives 98/78/EC and 2000/12/EC of the European Parliament and of the Council, OJ L 35, 11.2.2003, p. 1.
32. This document can be found on the website of the Commission referred to under footnote 28 as well as on the website of CEIOPS: www.ceiops.org.
33. A copy of this letter as well as of the response from CEIOPS can be found on the Commission's website referred to in note 28 above.
34. See in particular the brochure published by the European Insurance and Reinsurance Federation (CEA) under the title *Why excessive capital requirements harm consumers, insurers and the economy,* March 2010, 36pp.
35. CEIOPS, Technical criteria for assessing third country equivalence in relation to Articles 172, 227 and 260 (Former CP78), March 2010, 52pp.
36. Directive 2002/92/EC of the European Parliament and of the Council of 9 December 2002 on insurance mediation, OJ L 9, 15.1.2003, p. 1.
37. Protocol relating to the cooperation of the competent authorities of the Member States of the EU in particular concerning the application of Directive 2002/92/EC of the European Parliament and of the Council of 9 December 2002 on Insurance Mediation, April 2006, 15pp.
38. Communication from the Commission: Sector Inquiry under Article 17 of Regulation 1/2003 on business insurance (Final Report), 25 September 2007 and Commission Staff Working Document accompanying the Communication from the Commission, 25 September 2007.
39. Communication from the Commission to the European Parliament and the Council on Packaged Retail Investment Products, COM (2009) 204 final of 30.4.2009.
40. Directive 2004/39/EC of the European Parliament and of the Council of 21 April 2004 on markets in financial instruments, OJ L 145, 30.4.2004, p. 1, as amended by Directive 2006/31/EC, OJ L 114, 27.4.2006, p. 60; Commission Directive 2006/73/EC of 10 August 2006 implementing Directive 2004/39/EC of the European Parliament and of the Council as regards organisational requirements and operating conditions for investment firms and defined terms for the purposes of that Directive, OJ L 241, 2.9.2006, p. 26; Commission Regulation (EC) No 1287/2006 of 10 August 2006

implementing Directive 2004/39/EC of the European Parliament and of the Council as regards record-keeping obligations for investment firms, transaction reporting, market transparency, admission of financial instruments to trading, and defined terms for the purposes of that Directive, OJ L 241, 2.9.2006, p. 1.

41. White Paper on Insurance Guarantee Schemes, COM (2010) 370, 12.7.2010.
42. Oxera Report, *Insurance Guarantee Schemes in the EU: Comparative Study of Existing Schemes, Analysis of Problems and Evaluation of Options*, 2007, 279pp.

18
Regulatory Challenges and Developments in Japan

Yasuhiro Hayasaki

Introduction

The global financial landscape has dramatically changed from a period of ample liquidity and high risk appetite to that of scarce financial transactions and deleveraging since the emergence of the current financial crisis in 2008. Although Alan Greenspan, former Chairman of the US Federal Reserve Board, described the current financial crisis as a 'once-in-a-century credit tsunami' in a testimony to Congress,[1] it is considered 'the second-in-a-decade' in Japan, due to the financial crisis experienced in the late 1990s.

Needless to say, Japan is not immune from the current crisis. However, we believe that our financial system itself was relatively sound compared with those in the United States and Europe at the occurrence of the current crisis. It is partly because the country had established a resilient financial regulatory system after the crisis in the 1990s.

Viewing both the current crisis and the previous crisis in the 1990s, one can find that the two evolved in a similar fashion.

- First, irresponsible lending had been widespread prior to both crises, on the assumption that real estate prices would continue to go up.
- Second, the financial market turmoil was triggered by the decline in real estate prices or other types of collateral assets.
- Third, the adverse effect of the market turmoil spilled over to other financial activities and ultimately to the real economy.
- Finally, the turmoil resulted in a system-wide financial crisis, thereby necessitating public intervention by governments and central banks.

While a lot of similarities are observed between the two financial crises, the current crisis differs significantly from Japan's past crisis in some important aspects.

- First, the current crisis can be characterised as a twenty-first-century type of crisis, where risks are scattered through the financial markets to a wide range of investors by means of financial technology like securitisation. In contrast, in 1990s' Japan, risks were heavily concentrated in the commercial banking sector in the form of lending assets on their balance sheets.
- Second, American and European banks and institutional investors were forced to write down securitised products promptly due to mark-to-market accounting whereas, in the 1990s, Japanese banks were allowed to take time to dispose of their non-performing loans. Thus, the Japanese banks kept their deteriorating assets on balance sheet hoping that the borrowers' credit would improve.
- Third, Japan's financial crisis was contained within the border, and the impact and the loss on the real economy remained as a domestic issue. On the contrary, the financial impact and the losses resulting from the current financial crisis were immediately dispersed globally because of the widespread use of securitisation and the 'originate-to-distribute' business model. This has caused severe slowdown of the global economy, impacting Japan's financial system through the decline in share prices and the worsening of the broader economy.

During the crisis of the 1990s, the Japanese government established the necessary regulatory frameworks in order to resolve the non-performing loan problem. Through these experiences, the Japanese financial market including banking and insurance sectors learned that there needs to be a balance between both short-term measures to stabilise financial markets and medium- and long-term measures to strengthen the financial system and ultimately to vitalise the financial markets. Also, we learned how to respond properly to public sentiments.

Therefore, it seems that Japan's bitter experience in the 1990s does offer some useful suggestions as to how the authorities around the world should tackle the problems they face now.

Overview of Japan's insurance market

The life insurance market

As of 31 March 2010, 46 life insurance companies were operating in Japan, including Kampo Life (Japan Post Insurance).[2]

As of 31 March 2010, the total number of in-force policies was 199 million and the total insured amount was ¥1,403 trillion (US$15 trillion). Individual insurance, group insurance, and individual annuity are three major categories of insurance type, sharing 64%, 27% and 7% respectively, of the total insured contracts in force. While the in-force insured amount of individual life and group life decreased by 3.9% and 0.6% respectively, from the previous year, the in-force amount of individual annuities increased by 5.4%.

The background of these changes are attributable to (1) the general tendency to slim down life insurance coverage by household under the sluggish economic condition and (2) the shift of insurance needs from death benefit to longevity risk mitigation type of products due to the rapid demographic changes in Japan.

The total assets of life insurers were ¥318 trillion as of 31 March 2010 (66% of the gross domestic product (GDP)), an increase of 2.15% from the previous year. Of which, in terms of amount, 76.7% is securities and 14.7% is loans. As to the breakdown of securities, 40.2% of the total asset is invested in Japanese Government Bonds (JGBs), 13.5% in foreign securities and 5.9% (or ¥18,661 billion) in equities.

Regarding the distribution channels in Japan's life insurance market, there are three types: (1) in-house sales staff, (2) agents (including banks engaged with sales of insurance at their counters) and (3) direct sales through telephone calls or the internet. The number of in-house sales staff has declined and our record shows that it was 248,481 as at 31 March 2009. The number of agents, individual and legal entities combined, has also gradually decreased to 107,979. However, the total number of people who are employed by agents and licensed to sell life insurance has increased since 2001 and reached a total of 949,220 as at 31 March 2009, reflecting the introduction of over-the-counter sales at banks in 2001.

One of the recent major industry topics is demutualisation and listing on the Tokyo Stock Exchange of Dai-Ichi Life in April 2010. This is the first case among the major life insurers in Japan. Generally, the major benefit of a stock company is its enhanced capability in capital funding, capital management and corporate strategy while the major benefit of a mutual company is its ability to maintain consistent management without being influenced by short-sighted stakeholders.

The general insurance market

The total number of general (non-life) insurance companies in Japan was 52 as of 1 July 2010, within which 30 were licensed as domestic insurers including entities with foreign capital of over 50%, and 22 were licensed as branches of foreign insurers.[3]

The total of net premiums written by the member companies of the General Insurance Association of Japan (GIAJ) was ¥6,971 billion (US$74.8 billion) as at 31 March 2010, a decrease of 2.7% from the previous year. Voluntary motor insurance was the largest line of insurance, accounting for 49.2%. Fire and compulsory automobile liability insurance (CALI) were representing 15.1% and 11.5% respectively, at the end of the fiscal year 2009.

The reasons behind the decrease of net premiums are (1) automobile drivers' preference to choose smaller, fuel-efficient and lower carbon emission-type vehicles, (2) the sluggish economic situation, and (3) the sharp decline in the marine cargo insurance sector caused by contracted global trade during 2009.

The distribution channel has been dominated by agents, including banks, accounting for 92.3% of the total premiums, with the direct channel accounting for 7.4% and brokers accounting for 0.3%. The total number of agents has decreased from 509,619 in the year 2000 to 207,903 in 2009 due to enhanced efficiency and productivity as a result of mergers of general insurance companies. Like the case in the life insurance sector, the total number of licensed sales staff and agents has increased from 1,145,252 in the year 2000 to 2,160,029 in 2009, reflecting the introduction of licensed bank staff for over-the-counter sales of insurance.

As of March 2010, the total assets and net assets held by general insurance were valued at ¥31.5 trillion and ¥5.5 trillion respectively, representing an increase of 5.2% and 30.1%, from the year before. The increases of net assets are mainly due to higher equity prices at the end of fiscal year 2009 than that of the preceding year.

Demographic change and a lacklustre economy in Japan led the premium to a gradual decrease, affecting the general insurance market as a whole. Major general insurers decided to further integrate their operations in order to cope with the saturated domestic market demand and to seek sustainable growth opportunities in the international markets, especially emerging markets. Mitsui Sumitomo Insurance, Aioi Insurance and Nissay Dowa General Insurance integrated as MS&AD Holdings effective 1 April 2010. Also, Sompo Japan Insurance and NIPPONKOA Insurance integrated as NKSJ Holdings effective 1 April 2010. With Tokio Marine Holdings, the three major groups are expected to cover more than 80% of the general insurance market in Japan with a view to improve efficiency in business process and optimisation of strategic synergy for the benefit of the policy-holders and the customers. The regulator intends to continue monitoring on these initiatives and developments by the new three major general insurance.

Reflection on the 1990s

Deregulation and the liberalisation process

The Financial System Reform Law, enacted in June 1998, was a milestone of the deregulation in the 1990s. However, the intent of the law was not limited to deregulation. It went further to strengthen prudential framework, such as introducing an early warning measure for insurance companies and establishing a policy-holder protection system. The enactment of the Financial System Reform Law was propelled by the 'Implementation of the Japanese Financial System Reform Plan' in 1996 and the 'Report of the Insurance Council' in 1997. Also, The Japan-US Insurance Talks in the 1990s worked as accelerator of policy measures such as the reform of the rating organisation system and the introduction of differentiated rates applied to motor insurance.

Examples of deregulations and prudential measures, including a safety net, are as follows:

1. There was a revision of the Law concerning the Non-Life Rating Organisation in 1998, which abolished the obligation of member insurers to use the rates calculated by the Organisation.
2. Mutual entry into life and general insurance through subsidiary entities was allowed in 1996.
3. Both the Non-Life Insurance Policy-holders Protection Corporation and the Life Insurance Policy-holders Protection Corporation were established in 1998.
4. An Early Warning measure was introduced in 1999.
5. A ban on insurance sales by banks was partially lifted in 2001, and fully lifted in 2007.

This process and intensified competition encouraged the consolidation of the industry from 2001 to 2004, aiming at benefit of scale, operational efficiency, strengthened capital position and synergy in marketing, among others. For example, Dai-Tokyo Fire and Chiyoda Fire consolidated and established Aioi in April 2001; Koa Fire and Nippon Fire consolidated and established NIPPONKOA in April 2001; Mitsui Marine and Sumitomo Marine established Mitsui Sumitomo Insurance in October 2001; Yasuda Fire and Nissan Fire established Sompo Japan in July 2002; Tokio Marine and Nichido Fire merged in October 2004, to become Tokio Marine and Nichido Fire. As a result of the series of consolidations, the general insurance market in Japan has become highly concentrated and competitive.

The lost decade: insurance after the burst of the bubble

In the 1980s, the Japanese economy enjoyed a boom. Triggered by the Plaza Accord in 1985, the yen started its sharp revaluation against the US dollar. The Tokyo market demonstrated strong resilience and recovered faster than any other market in the world from Black Monday in October 1987. The Nikkei Average peaked in December 1989, with ¥38,915 which is now seen as the harbinger of the burst of the bubble economy. This was followed by the growth of non-performing loans in the banking sector and a lacklustre economy that has been continuing for more than 20 years.

The official discount rate (the rate at which the Bank of Japan rediscounts bills or extends loans to financial institutions) of the Bank of Japan was lowered from the 4.50–5.50% range in 1991, from the 1.75–2.50% range in 1993 to the 0.50–1.00% range in 1995 to boost the economy.

This trend has brought an extremely adverse effect on the life insurance sector, the so-called negative spread: the difference between the yield guaranteed to the policy-holders and the return expected from the investment portfolio. This situation put much stress on life insurers simply because most policies written by the life insurers were the guaranteed products. Seven life insurance companies, mostly mid-sized, became technically insolvent due to this stress and inadequate risk management (including asset liability management, ALM), or seeking higher risk-taking in their investment activities.

Table 18.1 shows seven cases of life insurance company insolvencies.

Table 18.1 Life insurance companies that have filed for bankruptcy

Name	Filed date	Procedure	Excess liabilities	Aid Amount (¥ billion)	Reduction of policy reserves (¥ billion)
Nissan Life	April 1997	Administrative	302	200	Nil
Toho Life	June 1999	Administrative	650	366	10%
Daihyaku Life	May 2000	Administrative	317	145	10%
Taisho Life	August 2000	Administrative	37	27	10%
Chiyoda Life	October 2000	Judicial	595	–	10%
Kyoei Life	October 2000	Judicial	690	–	8%
Tokyo Life	March 2001	Judicial	73	–	–

Source: Life Insurance Association of Japan.

In the general insurance sector, the Dai-Ichi Fire Mutual Insurance Company was also declared insolvent in May 2000. More than 90% of its insurance liabilities consisted of long-term savings type insurance with negative spread and this forced them to seek for higher return but risky investment.

The brighter side of these events was that in all cases except for Dai-Ichi Fire, in-force insurance contracts were transferred to reliever insurance companies, although a reduction of yield had to be introduced. Financial aid was offered by the Policy-holders Protection Corporation (PPC). In the case of Dai-Ichi Fire, insurance contracts were transferred to the Non-Life Insurance Policy-holders Protection Corporation in April 2001 and the PPC managed the run-off process since then. Regarding the Life Insurance Policy-holders Protection Corporation, it is worth noting that governmental guarantee is now offered when it requires a bank loan. In case the total maximum amount of PPC fund contributed by licensed life insurers in Japan were exhausted, the government is obliged to extend loan to life insurance PPC.

While the experience in the failure of insurance companies has not caused serious confusion or led to systemic risk in the financial market in Japan, both regulators and the industry have learned enormous and valuable lessons.

Steps towards forward-looking supervision

In December 2007, the Financial Services Agency (FSA) announced the Plan for Strengthening the Competitiveness of Japan's Financial and Capital Markets.[4] As a financial centre, even though it had many attractive aspects, Japan's financial markets had a number of shortcomings, as did many others. According to a survey which compared the competitiveness of financial centres throughout the world, Tokyo not only trailed behind such global centres as London and New York, but also lagged behind such regional rivals as Hong Kong and Singapore. Given ever intensifying global competition among markets, strengthening the competitiveness of Japan's financial and capital markets had become a pressing policy issue, to meet the needs of both domestic and foreign users and fulfil their roles sufficiently. For Japan to sustain economic growth with its declining and rapidly ageing population, there was an urgent need to boost the competitiveness of its financial and capital markets.

One of the specific measures of this plan was to incorporate 'Improving the Regulatory Environment (Better Regulation)'.[5] The FSA aimed to enhance the effectiveness, efficiency and transparency of financial regulation by improving its supervisory methods. Better Regulation centres upon the four pillars of:

- the optimal combination of rules-based and principles-based supervision;
- a risk-focused and forward-looking approach;
- regulation aimed at incentivising voluntary efforts by the private sector; and
- improved transparency and predictability of supervision.

This includes intensive dialogue with the industry with a view to sharing the principles for financial regulation, as well as close monitoring of market developments and effective supervisory response. By the mid 2000s, the environment in which we pursued the objectives of financial regulation had changed dramatically resulting in substantial progress in disposing non-performing loans dispelling uncertainties over the financial system. Meanwhile, efforts by both public and private sectors in response to the exposed problems of protecting the users of financial services and ensuring fairness and transparency in the market, made significant progress in improving the regulatory framework and the actual practices. In the phase where the lessons learnt from these experiences should be firmly incorporated and further deepened, it was crucial for each financial institution to tackle various issues based on its own efforts and responsibility. Financial regulation should also correspond properly to the changes in situation and place a greater emphasis on self-responsibility and voluntary efforts by financial institutions.

The financial crisis and its implications for Japan's insurance market

Just as the FSA's regulatory framework was entering the new stage, as mentioned above, the financial crisis in 2008 hit the global market. As stated in the Introduction, however, Japan's financial system has remained relatively stable compared to that of the US and Europe. Accordingly, the impact of these losses on capital was less severe in Japan. The exposure of Japan's financial sector to opaque, toxic assets was also significantly smaller.

The *Global Financial Stability Report* by the International Monetary Fund (IMF), released in April 2009,[6] estimated that, of the total losses of US$4.054 trillion in 2007–10 in relation to loans and securities that originated in the US, Europe and Japan, the US accounted for US$2.7 trillion, or 67%, while Europe accounted for US$1.2 trillion, or 29%, and Japan accounted for US$149 billion, or 4%. As for the comparison between the ratio of outstanding assets and the ratio of losses, the ratio of US assets to total global assets stood at 46% against the ratio of 67% for US losses to total global losses. The ratio of European assets stood at 41% against the ratio of 29% for European losses, and the ratio of Japanese assets in Japan at 13% against the ratio of 4% for Japanese losses. These figures indicated that Japan's financial sector was relatively sound, compared with that of the US and Europe.

There may be a few reasons for this relative soundness:

- It was partly because Japan's financial firms were not strongly innovation-oriented, as some critics pointed out.
- It is because they were giving priorities to improve their financial soundness rather than to enhance their profitability in the last several years. When the so-called 'originate-to-distribute' business model became widespread, it happened that Japan's financial firms were at the final stage of resolving the non-performing loan problems.
- The improvements in risk management practices of Japan's financial firms were significant. Firms became more cautious than before about investing in financial products with uncertainty on their underlying assets or associated risks. Early implementation of the Basel II framework for banks in Japan had also contributed to ensuring these practices.

Considering the difference between two crises that we faced, there are some more reasons for our relative resilience in the current crisis.

- First, the current turmoil in Japan was triggered by an exogenous shock, whereas the root causes of the previous crisis existed in the country. 'Exogenous shock' means that the current crisis stems mainly from the collapse of the housing market and the securitisation market in the US and the UK. In contrast, in Japan's crisis in the 1990s, Japanese financial firms were primarily responsible for the creation of the bubble in the domestic real estate market. Accordingly, their exposure to underperforming loans was much greater in the 1990s, while the direct impact of the current market turmoil on Japan's financial system itself was not as severe as the last crisis.

- Second, the regulatory framework and financial safety net significantly improved in Japan. In the early 1990s, the regulatory regime had in place neither sufficient effective frameworks for disclosure or provisioning with respect to non-performing loans, nor sufficiently robust schemes for deposit protection and resolution of failed banks. This provided disincentives for financial institutions to accelerate the disposal of their non-performing loans, and for authorities to proceed with resolving banks. This prolonged financial distress and the economic slump. Based on this bitter experience, the FSA has enhanced disclosure requirements, clarified the rules on write-downs and provisioning, put in place a prompt corrective action scheme, and established an early warning system that enables the supervisors to conduct intense monitoring of banks before they become undercapitalised. The deposit insurance scheme was strengthened, and a robust framework to deal with systemic risk was put in place.

As for the situation of Japan's insurance industry specifically, it is largely as sound as the banking sector. Like other financial firms, Japanese insurers have not significantly invested in complex and opaque instruments, such as asset-backed securities (ABSs), collateralised debt obligations (CDOs) and leveraged loans. The share of these instruments in the total assets is less than 2% on an aggregate basis. On the liability side, some non-life insurers have entered into reinsurance with US monoline insurers and provided financial guarantees to municipal bonds, but the losses, both realised and unrealised, are within the manageable size due to the well diversified portfolio. The established safety net for the insurance industry, as mentioned above, also helped the industry resilience.

Nevertheless, it is commonly believed that the financial crisis has hit the Japanese economy in various ways; for example, through the turmoil in the stock market and the foreign exchange market, as well as through a plunge of exports. Japan's real GDP growth rate for fiscal year 2008 was –3.7%, which was the worst since the end of the Second World War. In addition, the Nikkei dropped from the ¥18,000 level in the 2007 summer to ¥7,054 on 10 March 2009. Accordingly, the financial results of Japanese financial institutions including insurers reflected significantly reduced profits.

In these circumstances, one small life insurer, Yamato Life, went bankrupt in October 2008. Under the final rehabilitation plan, 90% of policy reserves would be covered based on financial support provided by the Life Insurance Policy-holders Protection Corporation of Japan, which would mean a 10% reduction in compensation, and the guaranteed yield was reduced to 1.0%. It should be noted, however, that the company's business structure and business model were totally different from other Japanese life insurers. Yamato Life's extremely high cost structure was more than twice as high as other insurers, and it had a much riskier investment strategy aimed at higher returns than its competitors in the last few years. Therefore, this was an exceptional case, and what is more, it never led to systemic risk.

In the crisis period, as our fellow regulators abroad, the FSA has been working on two categories of policies at the same time. One is short-term crisis management, and the other is medium-term reforms to 'redesign' the regulatory framework.

The first category of policies is short-term crisis management to cope with the ongoing financial turmoil and economic difficulties. Unlike in the US and Europe where the authorities have taken a number of extraordinary actions to stabilise the financial sectors, the policies in Japan are more focused on maintaining the function of financial intermediation in order to support economic activities. They include:

- providing the capital injection scheme, which can be used by banks to maintain a sufficient capital base in order to sustain their lending; and
- an intensive supervisory review of banks' lending practices to ensure that their financial intermediary functions work properly.

Given its relative soundness, Japan's financial sector is increasingly relied upon in preventing further deterioration of the real economy.

The second category consists of medium-term reforms to 'redesign' the regulatory framework in order to prevent the recurrence of a similar kind of crises in the future. Discussions are underway on a global basis regarding capital adequacy, procyclicality in the financial system, market integrity and transparency, and international cooperation among regulators. They are in line with the recommendations put forth by the Financial Stability Forum (FSF, later to become the Financial Stability Board, FSB) in April 2008, which were endorsed at the subsequent meetings of the G7 and the G20 leaders.

Reinforcing prudential standards

Refining the regulatory solvency margin ratio

The foundation of the modern solvency standards for insurance companies in Japan was set in April 1996, when the 'solvency margin ratio' standard was introduced. Ever since, the standard has undergone a number of revisions.

Conceptually, the solvency margin ratio is a prudential indicator which depicts an insurance company's ability to respond with its capital and reserves to counter an extraordinary event which exceeds its usual estimates. The ratio is calculated by using the following formula:

Solvency Margin Ratio = (Solvency Margin / 1/2 x Risk Amount) x 100

The 'solvency margin' is, in principle, composed of the equities and reserves to counter an extraordinary event (for example, market fluctuations, and so on).

The 'risk Amount' is represented as follows:

Risk Amount = [√{Insurance Risk2 + (Assumed Interest Rate Risks + Asset Management Risks + Minimum Guarantee Risks (life insurance company))2}] + Business Management Risks + Major Catastrophe Risks (non-life insurance company)

The utilisation of the solvency margin ratio is aimed at covering a number of supervisory objectives. As a monitoring tool, the ratio functions as an indicator to identify which insurance company needs to be closely watched. Even if the insurance company in question has a solvency margin ratio well above 200%, which is the first regulatory trigger, it may reveal weaknesses in profitability, or insufficient risk management practices in the areas of credit risk, market risk or liquidity risk. Thus the ratio is also used to enable supervisory action for early warning purposes.

Another important aspect of the ratio is its contribution to increased transparency of the risk condition of an insurer. Not only the ratio but the components of the formula of every insurance company are made subject to public disclosure, which effectively heightens the level of management and discipline in the organisation.

Before the current crisis, the Japanese insurance sector initiated steps to refine the regulatory solvency assessment measures. The FSA invited a group of industry and academic experts to study what enhancements should be made to the existing solvency assessment framework in November 2006. Based on the group's report which was published in April 2007, the FSA released a proposal to revise the framework in February 2008. The proposal was later fortified in part by the lessons learned from the current crisis, and made its way to promulgation in April 2010. This is considered as a short-term enhancement, with a potential for another set of proposals to address mid- to long-term alterations.

Under the short-term revision, a more rigorous approach is taken in the calculation method of the solvency margin ratio. This is done by restricting the surplus portion of the insurance premium reserves and deferred tax assets.

Meanwhile, a more rigorous and granular approach is taken in the measurement of risks, the denominator of the formula. Major changes in the denominator include:

- the confidence level in determining risk factors is increased to 95% under the value-at-risk (VaR);
- statistical data used as the basis of calculation (the conversion factor) for each risk are renewed;
- a strengthening of the risk conversion factor related to securitised or re-securitised products and financial guarantee insurance, as well as the installing of a new risk factor for credit spread risk to better capture credit default swap (CDS) transactions.

The solvency margin ratios of insurance companies are, in general, expected to decline as a result of these revisions. To ensure awareness of the change in the calculation formula among insurance policy-holders and market players, the implementation takes place in two steps. The recommended disclosure practice becomes effective from the term ending March 2011. The full implementation is scheduled for March 2012, at which point the solvency margin ratio calculated under the revised standard is scheduled to be utilised as a benchmark for the invocation of an early corrective measure.

As a mid- to long-term project, the FSA is examining the introduction of solvency assessments based on economic value. This is in part due to the international discussions taking place in the International Association of Insurance Supervisors (IAIS) and the other initiatives including the EU.

The FSA is also paying attention to the development in the standard setting for financial reporting, which is relevant to solvency assessment based on economic value. In view of the revision to the international accounting standards on insurance contracts by the International Accounting Standards Board (IASB), the FSA intends to advance considerations on how the supervision and accounting of insurance should be in Japan in the medium term. Furthermore, prior to the standard being finalized, the FSA will promote examination for any necessary convergence with the current international accounting standards.

In June 2010, the FSA called for a field test to be completed by the end of the year. The field test is set to capture the insurance liability based on economic value, as well as the measurement of interest rate risk based on coherent ALM of each company, under a single set of preconditions. It is notable that the FSA is requesting information on internal risk models from insurance companies which are already adopting such models. The results of the test will be utilised to assess the economic impact to the insurance market, and to capture potential issues in implementing a new prudential regime.

Consolidated prudential regulations

From the perspective of protecting the interests of policy-holders and beneficiaries, prudential standards applicable to insurance groups on a consolidated basis are scheduled to be introduced at the end of March 2012, and the details including risk measurement of non-Japanese insurance companies or non-insurance companies, calculation method of margins, and scope of the consolidated group, need to be defined before then.

Conclusion

Japan has witnessed two financial crises since the mid-1990s. Three lessons can be drawn from our experiences.

First, crises need to be prevented ex ante. It is true that mismanagement in macroeconomic policies which lead to an upswing in asset prices could be the main contributing factors of the crises. However, from a supervisor's perspective, to conduct appropriate micro-prudential supervision is a necessary step for the prevention of crises. In this aspect, refining the regulatory framework such as with the solvency margin ratio plays an important role. In addition, it is imperative to require insurance companies, through daily monitoring and on-site inspection, to develop a risk management system; how to make best use of the results of stress testing is one of the challenges in this area.

Second, in case an insurer's failure cannot be avoided, its negative impacts on policy-holders and the market economy must be contained ex post. In terms of policy-holders, Japan introduced a policy-holder protection framework and it proved to be effective in preventing uncertainties from spreading into policy-holders of not only the failed insurer itself, but also other insurers. In terms of impacts on the market economy, insurance companies do not usually rely on short-term market funding and do not need to fire-sale assets in order to meet maturities of such funding. Therefore, unlike the case of banks and investment banks, insurers' failure did not trigger turmoil in the market economy in Japan's case; the Japanese central bank never needed to provide liquidity to failed insurers.

Third, we need to take account of changes in regulatory environments. The examples of changes are (a) expanding cross-border activities of insurers, (b) developments in risk management techniques and (c) the introduction of market value-based accounting. The first factor requires national supervisors to coordinate their actions more closely. In addition, the perspective of group supervision gains importance. With regard to the second and third factors, under market value-based accounting, changes in market conditions could affect profit and capital levels of insurers more than before. In theory, this could be met by an improved risk management framework. However, in reality, it is not an easy job.

The recent global financial crisis has revealed that something unexpected could happen in the real world. It is undeniable that supervisors are not the almighty. However, it is also true that regulators/supervisors are not allowed to escape from challenges.

Notes

1. Alan Greenspan testifies before the House Oversight and Government Reform Committee on Capitol Hill in Washington on 23 October 2008. See http://oversight.house.gov/images/stories/documents/20081023100438.pdf.
2. For basic data on the life insurance market in Japan, see www.seiho.or.jp/Life Insurance Business in Japan.
3. For basic data on the general insurance market in Japan, see www.sonpo.or.jp/General Insurance in Japan Fact Book.
4. See www.fsa.go.jp/en/news/2007/20071221/01.pdf.
5. See www.fsa.go.jp/en/policy/iqfrs/br1.html.
6. See www.imf.org/External/Pubs/FT/GFSR/2009/01/pdf/text.pdf.

Part VI

The Emerging Markets Perspective

19
China's Insurance Regulation: Framework, Issues and Prospects

Wei Zheng

Overview of China's Insurance Market

The first insurance company in China was established more than 200 years ago in 1805. Since the founding of the People's Republic of China in 1949, China's insurance market has undergone three major stages: early development (1949–58), suspension (1958–79) and redevelopment (1979–present).

China's insurance market has seen rapid growth since 1979. In 2009, the gross premium income in China reached over $163 billion, accounting for 3.98% of the world insurance market, standing as the seventh in the world. The insurance density was US$121.2, and the insurance penetration was 3.27%, ranking it 64th and 44th in the world, respectively (Swiss Re, 2010).

In the submarket of life insurance, the premium income in 2009 amounted to US$109.175 billion, accounting for 67% of the gross premium income in China and 4.63% of the life insurance income in the world, raising it to seventh place in the world. The density of life insurance reached US$81.1, and penetration reached 2.19% (ibid.).

In the non-life insurance submarket, the premium income placed China ninth in the world with US$53.871 billion, taking up 33% of the gross premium income in China and 3.09% of the non-life insurance market in the world. The density and penetration in this sector were US$40.0 and 1.08% respectively (ibid.).

By the end of 2010, there were 53 property insurance companies in China, including 34 Chinese domestic ones and 19 foreign-funded ones; 61 life insurance companies, including 33 Chinese domestic ones and 28 foreign-funded ones. By the end of 2010, the total assets of the insurance industry had reached RMB 5.05 trillion, and the balance of insurance fund investment had reached RMB 4.6 trillion (CIRC, 2010c).

A brief history of China's insurance regulation

Growing along with the development of China's insurance market, China's insurance regulation has gone through three stages since 1979: the preliminary stage before 1998, regulation on market behaviour and solvency during 1998–2006, and the 'three-pillar' regulatory system from 2006.

Before 1998: the preliminary stage

China's insurance regulation was at a preliminary stage before 1998, in which the responsibility of regulating insurance market lay with the People's Bank of China instead of with an independent regulatory body. Three milestones in this stage are noteworthy: the first was in 1992, when the establishment of the Shanghai branch of American International Assurance marked the opening of China's insurance market to the outside world; the second was in 1995, when the fundamental *Insurance Law* of China was promulgated; and the third was in 1995, when China issued the *China Life Insurance Mortality Table (1990–1993)*, the first of its kind in China. The three seemingly isolated events in effect laid the foundation of openness, ruled-by-law and scientific practice for China's insurance market.

1998–2006: market behaviour and solvency regulation

In 1998, the China Insurance Regulatory Commission (CIRC), the central government organ specialising in insurance regulation, was established. After many efforts by CIRC in constructing the framework of rules and regulations, insurance regulation in China has become much more professional.

During this period, the target model of 'equal status of market behaviour regulation and solvency regulation' was formed. Before 1998, the focus of insurance regulation was on market access and market behaviour regulation; after 1998, the attention shifted to regulation on solvency, for which the initial form of a special regulatory system was launched in 2003, giving it equal emphasis with market behaviour regulation.

In addition, CIRC formulated a series of regulations for insurance companies, insurance intermediaries, reinsurance, and insurance fund investments, and launched the National Actuarial Exam in 1999. Though not flawless, these moves reflected the gradual adoption of international rationales and the initial establishment of an insurance regulation framework in China.

After 2006: three-pillar regulation

In 2006, CIRC adopted the regulatory system comprised of 'three pillars', namely the regulation of market behaviour, of solvency, and of corporate governance. The addition of the last item compared with the former framework is deemed to help reduce risk in insurance companies at the root. The birth of this system was marked by the release of *Guidelines on Regulating the Governance Structure of Insurance Companies* (CIRC, 2006).

Supplementary to the 'three-pillar' system, CIRC set up 'five defences' for risk management, which are based on internal control, focused on solvency regulation, relying on field inspection, and with regulation of insurance fund investment as the key step and Insurance Protection Funds as the shield.

With the 'three pillars' and the 'five defenses' as the main structure, a relatively complete framework of insurance regulation has been constructed in China.

The framework of China's insurance regulation

This section will elucidate two points about the insurance regulation in China – the relevant legal system and the major aspects of insurance regulation.

The legal system for insurance regulation

The legal system relevant to insurance in China is comprised of five parts (Zheng and Jia, 2009) – laws (by the National People's Congress (NPC) or the Standing Committee of the NPC), administrative regulations (by the State Council), department rules (by CIRC or other ministries), international treaties, and judicial interpretation (by the Supreme People's Court).

Laws

The most important relevant law is the Insurance Law of the People's Republic of China (hereafter referred to as the Insurance Law). Approved by the 14th session of the 8th Standing Committee of the NPC on 30 June 1995, the Insurance Law came into force on 1 October that year. On 28 October 2002, the law was amended in the 30th session of the 9th Standing Committee of the NPC. After another amendment in the 7th session of the 11th Standing Committee of the NPC on 28 February 2009, the new law took effect on 1 October that year. As the fundamental law in coordinating insurance relations, the Insurance Law serves as the core of the legal system.

The 2009 version of the *Insurance Law* consists of eight chapters (NPC, 2009): 'General Provisions', 'Insurance Contracts', 'Insurance Companies', 'Operational Rules Governing Insurance', 'Insurance Agents and Insurance Brokers', 'Supervision and Administration of the Insurance Market', 'Legal Responsibilities' and 'Supplementary Provisions'.

Other laws relevant to insurance business include the Maritime Code of the People's Republic of China, the Contract Law of the People's Republic of China, and the Company Law of the People's Republic of China.

Administrative regulations

There are two sets of administrative regulations governing insurance relations, namely Regulations of the People's Republic of China on Administration of

Foreign-funded Insurance Companies and Regulations on Compulsory Insurance for Traffic Accident Liability of Motor Vehicles.

The Regulations on Administration of Foreign-funded Insurance Companies, approved in the 49th State Council executive meeting on 5 December 2001, was implemented as of 1 February 2002. It is comprised of seven chapters: 'General Provisions', 'Establishment and Registration', 'Scope of Business', 'Supervision and Administration', 'Termination and Liquidation', 'Legal Liability' and 'Supplementary Provisions'. The purpose of the regulations is to strengthen supervision and administration of foreign-funded insurance companies. For any issues concerning administration of these companies yet not stipulated in the regulations, the Insurance Law, other relevant laws, administrative regulations and government rules are applicable. The regulations also apply mutatis mutandis to branches established and operated in Chinese mainland by insurance companies based in Hong Kong SAR, Macao SAR and Taiwan.[1]

The Regulations on Compulsory Insurance for Traffic Accident Liability of Motor Vehicles, approved in the 127th State Council executive meeting on 1 March 2006, came into effect on 1 July that year, including 'General Provisions', 'Insurance Application', 'Indemnity', 'Penalties' and 'Supplementary Provisions'. The purpose of the regulations is to ensure compensation for victims of traffic accidents involving motor vehicles, and to secure traffic safety.

Department rules

Department rules relevant to insurance mainly refer to regulatory documents formulated by CIRC about supervision and administration of insurance market, all scrutinised and approved in the CIRC chairman's office meeting. There are also some other rules jointly written and issued by CIRC and related government agencies. Over 40 department rules are effective now, including Administrative Provisions on Insurance Companies (CIRC, 2009), Administrative Provisions on the Solvency of Insurance Companies (CIRC, 2008b), Measures for the Administration of Insurance Protection Funds (CIRC, 2008a), Administrative Measures for the Information Disclosure by Insurance Companies (CIRC, 2010a) and Interim Administrative Measures for Insurance Fund Investment (CIRC, 2010b).

International treaties

The international treaty relevant to insurance is primarily the World Trade Organization (WTO) agreement signed by China. After obtaining membership of the WTO, the international treaties and practices of the Chinese government on opening insurance market were integrated into the legal system in China. The pledges concerning China's insurance industry mainly cover the establishment of insurance companies, geographical restrictions, scope of business, business permits, large-scale commercial insurance, compulsory insurance, brokerage of 'master policies', and cross-border payments in the insurance service.

Judicial interpretation

The judicial interpretations related to insurance include Interpretation I of the Supreme People's Court on Certain Issues Concerning the Application of the Insurance Law of the People's Republic of China (hereafter referred to as Interpretation I) and Provisions of the Supreme People's Court on Several Issues about the Trial of Cases Concerning Marine Insurance Disputes (hereafter referred to as the Provisions).

Interpretation I was approved in the 1,473rd meeting of the Judicial Committee of the Supreme People's Court on 14 September 2009, and came into effect on 1 October that year. It specifies the application of the new insurance law, and some issues in respect of the transition from the previous insurance law to the new one. Some other judicial interpretations will be issued with the implementation of the 2009 Insurance Law.

The Provisions was approved in the 1,405th meeting of the Judicial Committee of the Supreme People's Court on 13 November 2006, and came into effect on 1 January the following year. In compliance with the relevant provisions of the Maritime Code and the Insurance Law, the Provisions was formulated for fair trial of cases in respect of marine insurance disputes.

Major aspects of insurance regulation

Insurance regulation covers a wide range of issues. This subsection will discuss its three major aspects – market behaviour regulation, solvency regulation, and corporate governance regulation.

Market behaviour regulation

As market behaviour regulation is a crucial part of insurance regulation, the Insurance Law set a series of principles and prohibitions regarding insurance market behaviour.

It is stipulated that insurance companies should do business in fair competition, and not be engaged in illicit business. The following behaviours are prohibited for insurance companies and their staff: (1) deceiving the applicant, the insured or the beneficiary; (2) withholding important information about insurance contracts from the applicant; (3) hindering or inducing the applicant from fulfilling the obligation of disclosure; (4) offering or promising to offer rebates or other benefits to the applicant, the insured and the beneficiary beyond what is stated in the insurance contract; (5) declining the obligation of indemnity or payment; (6) making up non-existent insurance accidents or insurance contracts, or overstating the loss of an insurance accident for illicit payment or other illegal benefits; (7) embezzling, retaining, or misappropriating premiums; (8) trusting unauthorised organisations or individuals with insurance sales; (9) seeking illegal benefits for organisations or individuals using insurance services; (10) using insurance agents, brokers or appraisal organisations for illegal conduct such as fake intermediary business or false surrender; (11) tarnishing the reputation of rivals by starting or spreading slander, or disturbing the insurance market with other foul play; (12) leaking the business secrets of the applicant or the insured obtained in doing insurance business; (13) other behaviours violating laws, administrative regulations and regulations of CIRC.

The focus in market behaviour regulation changes over time. The recent focus covers six aspects: first, in property insurance, continuing the investigation on data fraud in business and finance of insurance companies, strengthening supervision of corporate entities and senior management staff; second, in life insurance, organising nationwide special field investigations for accident insurance in accordance with business standards to resolve the problems of fluctuating prices and doctored data; third, carrying out inspections on intermediary business of insurance companies; fourth, implementing market forbiddance, revoking and closing companies, forbidding related individuals from resuming insurance business for illegal practices; fifth, in statistics inspection, organising self-inspection and sample inspection, in particular for false or incomplete declaration of business and financial data; sixth, in comprehensive inspection, further guarding against false insurance companies, false policies and false claims.

Solvency regulation

Solvency regulation is the core of insurance regulation, as the central goal of insurance regulation is to protect the interests of consumers. If an insurance company is not solvent facing the claim of insurance payment, the most important interest of insurance consumers is damaged, so the central goal of insurance regulation becomes void. For this reason, solvency regulation deserves the core position among all the aspects of insurance regulation. The interests of consumers can be safeguarded, and the central goal of insurance regulation can be realised, only with effective solvency regulation.

Many achievements have been made recently by CIRC in this aspect, mainly including establishing a regulation system, improving the regulation mechanism and strengthening regulation.

First, a solvency regulation system has been established. Based on a thorough study of the systems in other countries, the Administrative Provisions on Solvency Margin of Insurance Companies and Regulation Indices was issued in 2003, mainly borrowing from EU Solvency I with allowance for the status of the insurance market in China, marking the birth of solvency regulation. Twenty-five compilation rules and explanations have come into effect in recent years. Dynamic solvency regulation has been launched, and categorised regulation has been promoted, forming a system consisting of internal risk management, solvency reporting, financial analysis and inspection, regulatory intervention and Insurance Protection Funds.

Second, the solvency regulation mechanism has been improved. Learning from the latest change in EU Solvency II, CIRC issued the amended Administrative Provisions on the Solvency of Insurance Companies in 2008, further improving the solvency regulation mechanism. CIRC set up the Solvency Standard Committee and Solvency Regulation Committee and established a solvency risk management mechanism, initially constructing a coordinated regulatory and administrative mechanism linking the headquarters of CIRC, the provincial branches of CIRC and insurance companies. The Solvency Standard Committee founded in 2007 serves as an advisory organisation specialising in solvency standards, providing consultation and demonstration for major professional issues in studying and formulating solvency regulation standards. The Solvency Regulation Committee founded in 2009 is responsible for coordinating the supervision and administration of insurance solvency.

Third, the solvency regulation has been strengthened. The risk of loss from interest rate spread plaguing the previous business of state-owned insurance companies has been gradually resolved through reform and going public, laying the foundation for solvency regulation throughout the whole industry. The number of companies with insufficient solvency was cut step by step due to stricter regulation and punishment for those companies. In particular, a Financial Crisis Working Group was established to follow closely the solvency risk of the parent companies of foreign-funded insurance companies, effectively preventing cross-border transmission of risks.

Corporate governance regulation

Since the CIRC formally launched the regulation of insurance company governance in 2006, corporate governance regulation has made significant progress. In 2009, the CIRC further established the Regulatory Committee on Insurance Corporate Governance. After several years of effort, the objectives, visions and models of insurance company governance regulation have gradually become clear.

First, to establish the work objectives of corporate governance regulation: the first objective is to prevent illegal appropriation or possession of insurance funds and to protect insurance company assets; the second is to help mediate the severe company governance conflicts and disputes and to ensure normal corporate management; the third is to promote and supervise the establishment of an internal control system in insurance companies, and to enhance decision-making, execution and risk-control capabilities.

Second, to establish rationales of corporate governance regulation: the first concept is the regulatory standards of public companies; to be exact, to supervise all insurance companies according to the standards of public companies; the second is the regulatory objectives of asset safety, to strictly monitor related-party transactions and other illegal fund transfers; the third is the regulatory approaches combining mandatory measures and guidance measures. The company shall be forced to follow the fundamental principles and compliance requirements of corporate governance. At the same time, corporate governance can be improved by the following measures: encouragement, guidance, demonstration and reasonable intervention, and so on.

Third, to construct a corporate governance regulation model applicable to the insurance industry: the first point is to regulate the acts of main shareholders on the basis of optimisation of equity structure; the second is to take the board of directors as the core and strengthen the establishment of the board of directors; the third is to improve internal control system in insurance companies, further strengthening risk prevention and enhancing executive capacity.

Major issues in China's insurance regulation

Insurance regulation involves many issues, but we will select three significant issues to discuss in this section: the first is categorised regulation, concerning the issue of how government can regulate the insurance industry more effectively; the second is information disclosure, concerning the mobilisation of social forces to supervise the insurance industry; the third is Insurance Protection Funds, concerning the subsequent handling process after the insolvency of insurance companies.

Categorised regulation

On 1 January 2009, CIRC's categorised regulation system for insurance companies and professional insurance intermediary institutions came into being.

Regarding insurance companies, CIRC will conduct a comprehensive evaluation on the classification of insurance companies at the beginning of each year according to the audited data of the previous year so as to decide which supervisory measures should be taken. On this basis, an evaluation will be conducted once every quarter so as to make corresponding adjustments to the annual evaluation results and supervisory measures. CIRC will inform insurance companies which group they belong to and the corresponding supervisory measures taken against them on a regular basis, but will not make such information public.

CIRC classifies insurance companies based on the monitoring indicators and the supervisory information obtained by the CIRC in daily supervision. The monitoring indicators of the insurance companies include five categories: solvency ratio; corporate governance, internal control and compliance risk indicators; fund application risk indicators; business operation risk indicators; financial risk indicators.

CIRC classifies insurance companies into four groups according to their degree of risk, Groups A, B, C and D, and takes different supervisory regulation measures against the four different groups of companies according to their different risk status.

Group A refers to companies which reach the solvency requirements and have no problems in corporate governance, investment and market behaviour. Against a company of Group A, no special supervisory measures will be taken.

Group B refers to companies which reach the solvency requirements but have certain risks in corporate governance, investment or market behaviour. Against a company of Group B, one or more of the following supervisory measures will be taken: holding supervisory talks; reminding it of its risks; asking it to rectify the existing problems within a specified time limit; making on-site inspections of its existing problems; and/or asking it to submit and effect a plan for preventing its failure to reach the solvency requirements.

Group C refers to companies which fail to reach the solvency requirements or have relatively big risks in corporate governance, investment or market behaviour. Against a company of Group C, in addition to the supervisory measures that will be taken against companies of Group B, one or more of the following supervisory measures will be taken according to the reason why the company fails to reach the solvency requirements: making a comprehensive inspection; asking it to submit a plan for improving its solvency; ordering it to increase the registered capital; restricting it from paying dividends to shareholders; restricting the salary and on-job consumption level of directors and senior managers; restricting commercial advertisements; restricting the new establishment of its branches; restricting its scope of business, ordering it to stop initiating new business; ordering it to assign the insurance business or ordering it to handle the ceded-out business; ordering it to auction its assets or restricting its purchase of fixed assets; restricting the channels or scope of its uses of funds; changing the person in charge and the relevant managerial person; and reporting its operation situations to the board of directors, the board of supervisors or the principal shareholders.

Group D refers to companies which are far from reaching the solvency requirements or have serious risks in at least one aspect of corporate governance, investment and market behaviour. Against a company of Group D, in addition to the supervisory measures that will be taken against the companies of Group B and Group C, CIRC can take any supervisory measures it deems necessary, such as rectification and taking over.

The risk level of a professional insurance intermediary will be evaluated based on two categories of indicators: compliance and stability. Based on its risk level, insurance intermediaries will be divided into three categories: companies subject to routine off-site inspections, companies on special watch and subject to off-site inspections, and companies subject to on-site inspections. Against companies subject to routine off-site inspections, CIRC will conduct off-site inspections on a regular basis. Against companies on special watch and subject to off-site inspections, in addition to off-site inspections, the CIRC will strengthen risk monitoring and may take one or more of the following measures: issuing a risk warning or holding regulatory interviews; increasing the frequency of regulatory reports; requiring special reports on the areas exposed to risks; requiring engagement of a qualified external accounting firm to conduct a specific audit on the information provided and submission of the audit report; conducing on-site inspections; and other regulatory measures as CIRC deems necessary. Against companies subject to on-site inspections, in addition to the regulatory measures applicable to companies on special watch and subject to off-site inspections, CIRC will conduct an on-site inspection at least once a year.

In addition, CIRC promulgated the provisions on categorised regulation of branches of insurance companies in May 2010. The Insurance Regulatory Bureau in each province will perform a comprehensive analysis and risk assessments of branches of insurance companies based on the objective information, identify the branch institution's specific regulation type and adopt relevant regulation measures according to the assessment results.

Due to the uneven qualities of insurance companies and insurance intermediaries and very limited regulation resources, implementation of categorised regulation is considered as a step in the right direction, and also accords with international practice. The establishment and improvement of the categorised regulation system would be conducive to integrating regulation resources, identifying regulation focus, strengthening regulation and enhancing supervisory efficiency.

In the next few years, another two issues concerning the categorised regulation of insurance companies will demand special attention. The first is to enhance the technical level and to systematically clean up the department rules and regulatory documents related to the categorised regulation. The mandatory clauses and prohibitory clauses stipulated in the laws and regulations concerning insurance company regulation should have sufficient causes. The second is to strengthen execution, and to attach great importance to the cultivation of 'compliance culture' in the industry. Under the precondition of ensuring the technical nature, several issues should be accomplished, including strengthening execution, strictly enforcing orders and prohibitions, and reinforcing the application of categorisation results in insurance regulation practice, helping insurance companies generate sufficient intrinsic motivation to develop in a healthy way.

Information disclosure

Although categorised insurance regulation is absolutely necessary, it is still within the scope of 'government supervision' in a narrow sense. Regarding the issue of how to mobilise social forces in insurance company supervision on a larger scale, information disclosure of insurance companies is regarded as an effective approach to tackle the problem.

Information disclosure by insurance companies means provision of information related to the insurance company's operation and management to the public. Since the insurance industry is an industry managing risk and thus has a strong relationship to the public interest, the market requires insurance companies to disclose more information than companies in other industries. Information disclosure is an important measure to tackle market information asymmetry, and improve the efficiency and transparency of the insurance market.

In May 2010, CIRC issued the Administrative Measures for the Information Disclosure by Insurance Companies, and demanded that information disclosure by insurance companies shall follow these principles: authenticity, accuracy, completeness, timeliness and effectiveness, and the company shall not provide false records, misleading statements or material omissions. The Measures also specify the contents, methods, timing and administration of information disclosure by insurance companies.

Insurance companies are required to disclose seven types of information: its basic particulars; financial accounting information; its risk management position; the operations of its insurance products; its solvency capability; material affiliated transactions; and information on material events.

Regarding the different types of information, the Measures stipulate different requirements of method and timing of information disclosure. The basic information is to be disclosed on the company's website and updated within ten business days from the date of alternation should there be any change. The annual information disclosure report is to be published on the company's website and in the newspapers designated by CIRC by 30 April each year; information on material events is to be disclosed on the company's website within ten business days from the date of occurrence of the events.

In addition, the Measures require that insurance companies should establish an information disclosure administration system, including contents and basic format of information disclosure, information inspection and release processes, division of responsibilities in information disclosure affairs, and responsibility investigation.

Among new regulatory rules on information disclosure, one of the most controversial issues is solvency information disclosure. Solvency information includes a company's actual capital and minimum capital, excess of assets over liabilities or equity gap, solvency ratio, change in solvency ratio against that of the last year's report and its causes, and so on. Since a company's solvency status is quite sensitive information, there exist different opinions on the issue of whether to disclose solvency information to the public. Those opposed to solvency information disclosure hold the opinion that solvency is a technical term in insurance regulation and insolvency does not mean that the insurance company is going bankrupt. Disclosure of such information to the public may cause unnecessary fear or confusion and amplify the insurance company's risk. Besides, as not all insurance companies are listed companies, a non-listed company is not a 'public company' and does not need to disclose solvency information. However, those in favour of solvency information disclosure hold the view that solvency is a core concept in insurance regulation and disclosure of solvency information will help consumers to make a rational choice, ensure orderly market competition and promote healthy development of the insurance industry. As social forces are mobilised to supervise insurance companies, the risk in the insurance industry is actually prevented and reduced, rather than amplified. Furthermore, an insurance company, whether listed or not, has tens of thousands of policy-holders, and in this sense, an insurance company may not be a public listed company, but is still a 'public company'. Therefore, we must set strict rules for information disclosure of a public company, including disclosure of solvency information.

In addition, as for new-type life insurance products, CIRC has more detailed information disclosure requirements. For instance, a life insurance company and its agent shall provide policy-holders, the insured, beneficiaries and the public with information regarding the features of new insurance products, insurance benefit projections, and performance history, and so on.

Insurance Protection Funds

Categorised regulation and information disclosure with regard to insurance are both important. However, even with the strictest supervision, there is no guarantee against the bankruptcy of insurance companies. Once an insurance company goes bankrupt, dealing with it involves the issue of the Insurance Protection Fund.

In China, Insurance Protection Funds can be divided into Property Insurance Protection Funds and Life Insurance Protection Funds, which are contributed to by property or life insurance companies based on a certain ratio of premiums to business incomes. To use Insurance Protection Funds, the standard process should be that, first of all, CIRC postulates risk settlement schemes and the way of using the Fund, and reports to the State Council for approval after necessary discussions with other ministries concerned.

The Insurance Law allows the use of Insurance Protection Funds under the following circumstances: (1) to provide a relief fund for the applicant, the insured or the beneficiary, if the insurance company is deregistered or goes bankrupt; (2) to provide a relief fund for the insurance company B that undertakes the life insurance contracts of A in accordance with the law, if an insurance company A is deregistered or goes bankrupt; (3) other circumstances ruled by the State Council. In September 2008, CIRC, the Ministry of Finance and the People's Bank of China co-promulgated the Measures for the Administration of Insurance

Protection Funds (referred to as the Measures below), which makes clear more specific regulations for the use of Insurance Protection Funds.

For non-life insurance, the amount of loss has to be considered. With regard to a loss of less than RMB 50,000 of a policy-holder, the Insurance Protection Fund should be granted in full. In the case of the policy-holder's loss of more than RMB 50,000, for a personal policy-holder, the relief of the Insurance Protection Fund should be more than 90% of the partial amount; for an institutional policy-holder, the relief of the Insurance Protection Fund should be over 80% of the partial amount.

For life insurance, the Insurance Protection Fund aims to provide relief to the policy assignee company. More specifically, for personal policy-holders, the amount of relief after assigned should not exceed 90% of the pre-assignment interest of the policy, and for the institutional policy-holders, the amount of the relief after assigned should not exceed 80% of the pre-assignment interest of the policy.

In accordance with the Measures, apart from deregistration or bankruptcy, the Insurance Protection Fund can be used under the circumstances that, after discussing with concerned ministries, CIRC concludes the insurance company is at significant risk and might endanger public interests or financial stability. In other words, the insurance protection can be used not only for handling the post-crisis issues of an insurance company, but also as a remedy for an insurance company during a crisis.

In addition, in September 2008, in accordance with the Measures, the China Insurance Protection Fund Ltd was officially established, in charge of the raising, management and use of Insurance Protection Funds in accordance with the Measures. The board of the China Insurance Protection Fund Ltd consists of nine directors, coming from the China Insurance Regulatory Commission, the Ministry of Finance, the People's Bank of China, the State Administration of Taxation, the Legislative Affairs Office of the State Council, and three insurance companies, respectively. The capital use of the Insurance Protection Fund abides by the principle of safety first, and the range of investment is limited to bank deposits, government bonds, central bank bills, financial bonds issued by central financial institutions, and so on.

Prospects

The growth potential of China's insurance market

How large is the potential for the mid- and long-term growth of China's insurance industry? This question is highly controversial. On the one hand, many studies from home and abroad believe that China's insurance industry has a vast growth potential, and that is why a lot of international insurance institutions enter or wait to enter China's insurance market. On the other hand, for the past few years, the growth rate of China's insurance industry has slowed down, and many domestic and foreign insurance institutions feel that China's insurance market is very competitive and some even think that some regional insurance markets show signs of saturation.

Our recent preliminary study (Zheng et al., 2010) shows that from 2010 to 2020, based on the assumption of annual GDP growth 6–10%, the annual increase range of China's life insurance premium would be 8.9–23.5%, with 12.0–19.2% as a more likely range. Besides, the annual growth range of non-life insurance would be 9.4–15.6%, with 9.6–15.1% more likely. The annual increase range of the whole insurance industry would be 9.1–21.4%, with 11.3–18.1% more likely.

To put it another way, compared with the GDP from 2010 to 2020, it's relatively easy for China's insurance industry to maintain a growth rate 3–5% higher than the GDP growth, and it's even possible to maintain a growth rate 5–8% higher than the GDP growth. However, it's rather difficult to achieve a growth rate 8–11% higher than the GDP growth, and even more difficult to achieve a growth rate 11% higher than the GDP growth.

From 2010 to 2020, the average annual growth rate of China's insurance industry (14.8%) would be appropriately twice the global rate (7.6%). By 2020, China's insurance industry might occupy 8% of the global insurance industry, which means China will be the third largest insurance market compared with the seventh in the world insurance market in 2009.

The role of insurance regulation

In a market economy, governmental regulation concerning the insurance industry is quite necessary. It is not because the development of the insurance industry needs the administrative guidance of the government, but that the insurance market may fail or malfunction just like any other market, and consumers in a market economy are the relatively disadvantaged group, whose interests need the protection from the government. In this respect, China's insurance regulation experiences the changing of regulation rationales.

Economic theory tells us that as a governmental sector, the insurance regulation institution is the agent or 'watchdog' of the public. It is costly and infeasible for each citizen to supervise the company and the market on his/her own. Therefore, the insurance regulation institution should naturally supervise the insurance companies and the market, representing the public. Moreover, consumers, the relatively disadvantaged group in terms of professional knowledge, are likely to be misled by insurance companies, and thus insurance regulation is of greater importance in protecting the interests of consumers.

We have to be aware that the potential damage of the insurance industry to the economic and social development does not lie in the slowing down of the growth of premiums, but lies in issues like incapacity on solvency, sales misleading, claim disputes, etc. If systemic problems occur in this respect, social instability might be incurred. Therefore, the increase of premiums is not the core or essence of supervision on the part of the insurance regulation institution, nor is the maintenance of industrial image. That is to say, the insurance regulation institution should re-adopt its 'supervision' role. The insurance regulation institution is the referee rather than coach, and the level of the 'players' has nothing to do with the referee, whose job is to maintain justice and fairness. The insurance regulation institution should not be worried about the disclosure or exposure of 'family scandal', but should encourage and even strive for the disclosure of scandals, since scandals are inevitable in a market economy, and it is the regulation institution's obligation and key responsibility to control and disclose scandals (Sun and Zheng, 2009). If this understanding is achieved, many relevant relations can be easily straightened out.

We emphasize that the biggest responsibility of the insurance regulation is to protect the interests of consumers. It may seem that such an emphasis is to put the insurance regulation against insurance companies. However, as a matter of fact, they are the two sides of a coin. Profoundly, it is good for the long-term development of the whole insurance industry, as to protect consumers' interests is not only good for consumers, but also good for the sustainability of the insurance industry. In the market economy, although the professional knowledge of consumers is relatively limited, the power of safeguarding their rights is enormously mighty. The healthy development of a company and an industry eventually relies on the respect for and protection of consumer interests. Recently, CIRC pointed out that 'the protection of consumer interests directly contributes to the success of the insurance industry', and 'the insurance industry should always consider the protection of consumer interests as its starting point and foothold', which gives a vivid explanation for the slogan that the insurance industry is to 'stand at the new starting point, and enter a new phase'.

International cooperation in insurance regulation

Against the overall background of economic globalization and financial crisis, the international cooperation of insurance regulation presents itself as more and more important. For the past few years, CIRC has made full use of the international cooperation of insurance regulation, and actively participated in formulating rules of international insurance regulation. Meanwhile, relying on the international cooperation platform of insurance regulation, CIRC has strengthened its link with international organizations and external supervision institutions, actively coped with the financial crisis, and achieved favorable results.

After the outbreak of the global financial crisis, the International Association of Insurance Supervisors (IAIS) launched strategic readjustments, and led the international development trend of insurance supervision. As an executive committee member of IAIS, CIRC participated in the discussion and decision-making of the strategic readjustments of IAIS without delay, and played a critical role in IAIS's strategic readjustments. At the same time, CIRC enhanced its role in participating in the formulation of the international insurance supervision rules, sent working parties to take part in IAIS's group discussion regarding the uniform rules, financial stability, corporate governance, micro insurance, and solvency, etc.

In 2006, CIRC initiated and held the 1st Asia Insurance Supervisors Forum. For the past few years, CIRC has promoted the cooperation and stable development of insurance supervision in the Asia-Pacific Regions by enhancing the communication and cooperation under the mechanism of the Forum. In addition, CIRC constantly consolidates and strengthens the cooperation with the insurance regulation institutions of staple insurance markets like America, Europe, and Japan, grasps the development trend and the risk trend of the global insurance industry in time, and thus facilitates the healthy development of the insurance industry.

In July 2010, IAIS decided to officially launch the formulation of the 'Common Framework of the International Insurance Group Supervision', in order to enhance the coherence of the supervision of these internationally active insurance groups, and the uniformity of global supervision measures. CIRC actively participated in formulating the above-mentioned Common Framework. It's predictable that along with China's economic development, China will play a more active role in the international communication and cooperation of insurance regulation in the future.

Note

1. As a supporting measure, CIRC formulated *Detailed Rules for Implementation of Regulations of the People's Republic of China on Administration of Foreign-funded Insurance Companies*. Scrutinised and approved in the commission chairman's office meeting on 15 March 2004, the *Detailed Rules* were implemented as of 15 June that year.

Bibliography

CIRC (2006) *Guidelines on Regulating the Governance Structure of Insurance Companies.*
CIRC (2008a) *Measures for the Administration of Insurance Protection Funds.*
CIRC (2008b) *Administrative Provisions on the Solvency of Insurance Companies.*
CIRC (2009) *Administrative Provisions on Insurance Companies.*
CIRC (2010a) *Administrative Measures for the Information Disclosure by Insurance Companies.*
CIRC (2010b) *Interim Administrative Measures for Insurance Fund Investment.*
CIRC (2010c) www.circ.gov.cn.

NPC (2009) *Insurance Law of the People's Republic of China*.
Sun, Qixiang, and Wei Zheng (2009) *Insurance and the Market Economy* (Beijing: Economic Science Press).
Swiss Re (2010) 'World Insurance in 2009 (updated appendix)', *sigma*, No. 2.
Zheng, Wei, and Ruo Jia (2009) *Insurance Law* (Beijing: China Development Press).
Zheng, Wei, Yongdong Liu and Yiting Deng (2010) 'Research on the Insurance Growth of China and World' (manuscript).

20

Regulatory Challenges and Developments in Latin America

Manuel Aguilera-Verduzco[1]

Overview of the Latin American insurance markets

The economic environment and insurance sector dynamics

From an economic perspective, the Latin America (LA) region (henceforth, 'the region') has proven to be an attractive destination to invest in and to develop the insurance sector. On one hand, the macroeconomic and institutional environments in the region have been strengthened and further developed in the past decade. That has built up the capacity, among other things, to weather important challenges, such as those posed by the recent global financial crisis. And on the other hand, economic growth, a large population and low levels of insurance penetration and density represent the possibility for significant potential rates of growth in this market.

The macroeconomic environment

For almost a decade, important steps have taken place in order to maintain fiscal and monetary discipline in the region. Most LA jurisdictions have achieved lower levels of public deficit, public debt and inflation; and they have in place, predominantly, flexible and less volatile exchange rates. Inflation in the region has settled below two digits for almost a decade; a positive environment for savings, investment and consumption. This situation has allowed lower premium rates growth and, therefore, the possibility of greater access to insurance products.

In 2008, gross domestic product (GDP) in the region amounted to US$4,209 billion, which is equivalent to 29.1% of the size of the economy of the United States. In 2009, these amounts decreased to US$3,869 billion and 27.1%, respectively. Nevertheless, prior to the slowdown in economic activity, primarily caused by the recent global financial crisis, the region experienced several years of economic expansion. From 1995–2008, growth rates in the region were positive.

In 2004, the highest growth level was achieved, 6.1%. However, in 2009, a 1.8% decrease in economic activity was expected, switching to the positive arena in 2010.

In 2009, the region's largest economies in terms of GDP were (in US$ billions): Brazil, 1,482; Mexico, 866; Argentina, 353; Venezuela, 301; Colombia, 229 and Chile, 150. These six economies represented 87.4% of the region's GDP. Additionally, the LA market represents an opportunity for expansion of the insurance industry, in light of the size of its population. LA's population was 557 million people in 2008 and was expected to rise to 564 million people in 2009.

Insurance sector dynamics

The region's insurance industry has maintained important growth rates for several years. Even during the recent crisis, the rates of growth have remained high and considerably above those of more developed countries. In 2001–08, premiums' average real annual growth rate was 7%. This behaviour contrasts with the 1.6% average real annual growth observed in industrialised economies. Some years, such as 2006 and 2007, the region reached growth rates above 11%, while developed countries had average rates around 3% (Table 20.1).

Table 20.1 Insurance premiums: industrialised versus LA and Caribbean countries (US$ millions)

Year	Industrialised countries	Real growth (yoy, %)	Latin America & Caribbean	Real growth (yoy, %)
2001	2,173,371	0.2	41,208	6.7
2002	2,359,175	4.8	40,103	4.4
2003	2,637,194	1.4	41,788	1.6
2004	2,871,690	1.7	49,313	10.5
2005	3,009,214	2.6	58,662	2.2
2006	3,390,180	3.1	71,428	11.2
2007	3,705,676	2.7	89,642	12.1
2008	3,756,939	–3.4	104,933	8.4
Average growth		1.6		7.0

Source: Swiss Re.

In 2008, despite the global financial crisis, the LA insurance sector had an 8.4% real annual growth. In 2009, preliminary figures point to positive annual rates of growth that do not show deterioration. Comparing the premiums' real growth rate of LA, in 2008, with the corresponding –3.4% growth in industrialised economies, an 11.8 percentage point gap can be observed (Figure 20.1).

To have a better view of the main trends and dynamics shown by insurance premiums in LA, an index (base 2001) is shown in Figure 20.2. The region reached

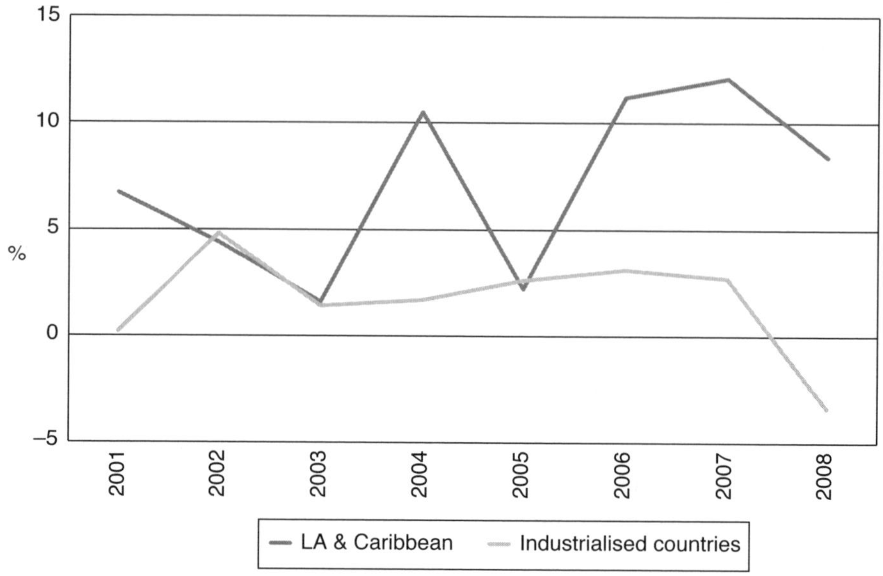

Source: Swiss Re.

Figure 20.1 Insurance premiums (real rates of growth, yoy %)

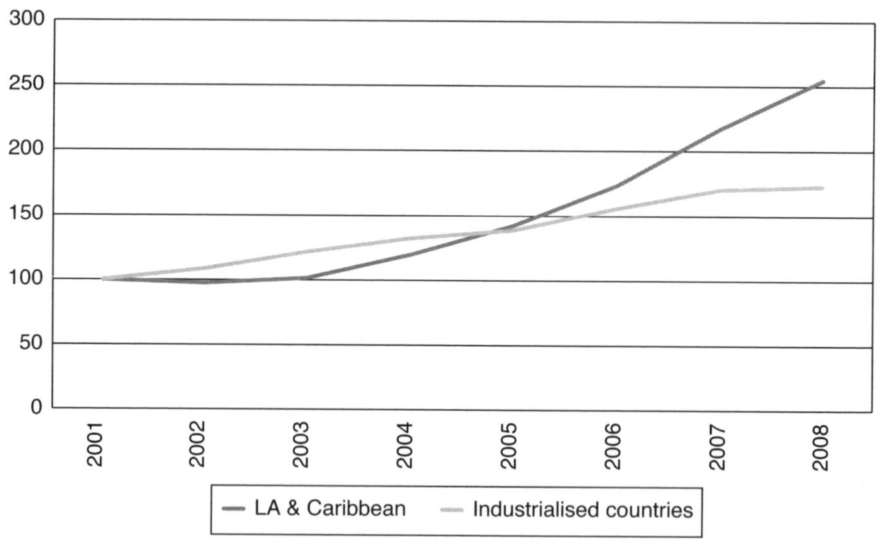

Source: Swiss Re.

Figure 20.2 Insurance premiums (index, 2001 = 100)

255 points in 2008, which is considerably higher than the 173 points achieved by industrialised countries.

In sum, data reveal an important positive dynamism in the LA insurance market, which has remained high even when facing adverse economic and financial environments.

Structure of the insurance sector

The insurance market in LA is primarily concentrated in six countries. In 2008 (in US$ billions), Brazil issued premiums of 47.5; Mexico, 15.5; Venezuela, 10.1; Argentina, 8.4; Chile, 5.8 and Colombia, 4.1. They accounted for 90% of the region's insurance market. Regarding their participation in the world insurance market, Brazil had a 1.1% share of the premiums; Mexico, 0.45%; Venezuela, 0.24%; Argentina, 0.20%; Chile, 0.14% and Colombia 0.10% (Table 20.2).

Table 20.2 Participation in the world insurance market, 2008

Country	Premiums (US$ millions)	Percentage of world market (premiums)		
		Total	Life	Non-life
Brazil	47,493	1.11	0.90	1.41
Mexico	15,498	0.45	0.33	0.6
Venezuela	10,060	0.24	0.01	0.55
Argentina	8,396	0.20	0.08	0.36
Chile	5,783	0.14	0.14	0.13
Colombia	4,106	0.10	0.06	0.15
LA	101,602	2.38	1.56	3.5
LA & Caribbean	104,933	2.46	1.64	3.6

Sources: Swiss Re (2009) and CNSF.

The number of insurance undertakings that operate in each jurisdiction of the region varies considerably. In 2008, some countries had more than 100 licensed insurers, such as Argentina (183), Brazil (119) and Mexico (100). In contrast, there were some countries that had less than 20 operating insurance undertakings: El Salvador (18), Bolivia (14), Peru (13) and Nicaragua (5).

In the past two decades, the insurance sector in LA has not been the exception in the process of liberalisation of financial markets. Several jurisdictions celebrated Free Trade Agreements which included Financial Services chapters. This commercial mechanism has opened the possibility for foreign insurance undertakings to participate in domestic markets as subsidiaries and, in some cases, as branches (Table 20.3).

The liberalisation process has been setting a more favourable stage for competition and institutional development in the region. This should increasingly contribute to the development of the insurance market and to an increased penetration of insurance products in more segments of the region's population.

Table 20.3 Insurance undertakings, 2008

Country	Insurance undertakings		
	Domestic	Foreign	Total
Argentina	179	4	183
Bolivia	14	0	14
Brazil	n.a.	n.a.	119
Chile	52	0	52
Colombia	27	17	44
Ecuador	41	2	43
El Salvador	17	1	18
Guatemala	28	0	28
Mexico	41	59	100
Nicaragua	5	0	5
Peru	13	0	13
Dominican Republic	26	7	33
Uruguay	17	0	17
Venezuela	n.a.	n.a.	50
Paraguay	n.a.	n.a.	31

Sources: ASSAL, MAPFRE, CNSF.

In addition, some LA jurisdictions are moving towards a more liberal regime with fewer entry barriers. These developments will also entail further transformation in the insurance corporate landscape, characterised by the privatisation of state-owned insurers, consolidation in some markets and higher penetration of foreign players in previously reclusive markets. In this sense, two important experiences can be highlighted. First, in January 2007, the Vice President of Brazil signed Law 126/07, opening up the local reinsurance market and thus ending a 69-year monopoly of the state-owned single reinsurer. In December 2007, the Brazilian regulator issued the new framework for the opening of the market; foreign reinsurers may now apply to operate in Brazil as authorised reinsurers. And second, before the ratification of the Central American Free Trade Agreement (CAFTA) in 2008, the Costa Rican insurance market was controlled by a government-owned insurer. On 8 July 2008, the Costa Rican Congress approved the new Insurance Market Regulatory Law 8653 8, as part of the CAFTA implementation process, ending an 84-year monopoly and opening the Costa Rican insurance market.

Regarding the insurance portfolio in the region, and considering the seven largest markets (Brazil, Mexico, Venezuela, Argentina, Chile, Colombia and Peru), in 2008 non-life business amounted to US$55.8 billion, which represented

60% of the total operations. On the other hand, life business amounted to US$37.0 billion (Figure 20.3).

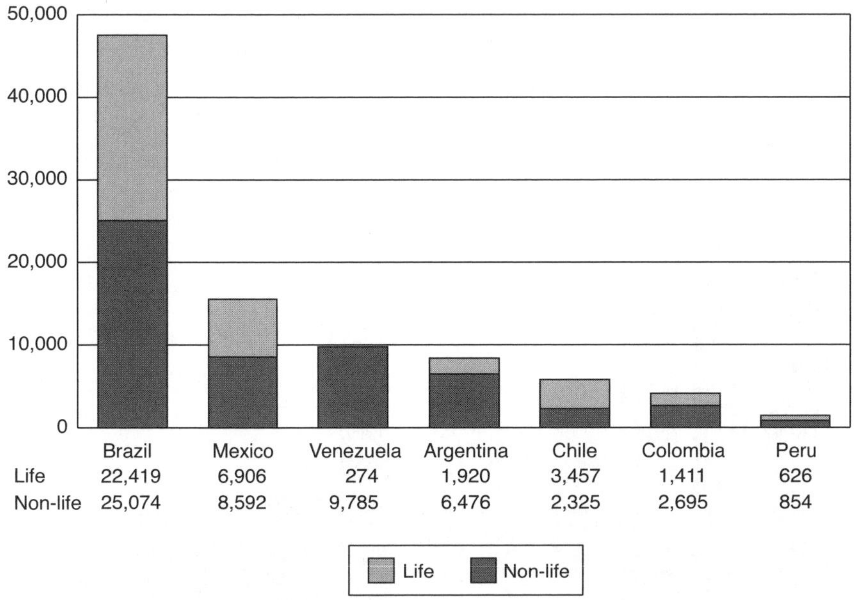

Sources: Swiss Re (2009) and CNSF.

Figure 20.3 Market size: premiums (US$ millions, 2008)

It is important to point out that Chile was the only jurisdiction with a larger portion of operations concentrated in the life sector. In 2008, the proportion concentrated in non-life in the region went from 53% to 77%. The exceptions were Chile with 40% and, in contrast, Venezuela with up to 97.3% of total portfolio.

With respect to the dynamics in both the life and non-life insurance segments, there are some interesting aspects to highlight regarding the most recent available information. Colombia's life insurance sector grew 40.9% in 2008, year-on-year, in real terms. This growth was driven, to a great extent, by an increase (above 100%) in the annuities market. Argentina's non-life insurance sector grew 22.6%, auto insurance being one of the main drivers.

Regarding the insurance market share in the region, in 2008, the non-life sector amounted to US$44.2 billion, which represented 63.9% of the total LA insurance market. The high percentage of property and casualty insurance can be explained mainly by auto insurance, which represented 24.8% of the total market share, even higher than that of accident and health insurance which accounted for 17.3%, while life insurance accounted for 36.1%.

From the competition perspective, most LA jurisdictions maintained highly concentrated insurance markets, as shown by the CR5 Index (which measures the market share concentration of the five largest insurance undertakings). The CR5 Index shows that Peru, Uruguay and Honduras are extremely concentrated insurance markets: 95%, 90% and 80% of their premiums, respectively, are issued by their five largest insurers. On the other hand, Argentina (23%), Brazil (37%) and Colombia (39%) are the jurisdictions that point to a more competitive environment (Figure 20.4).

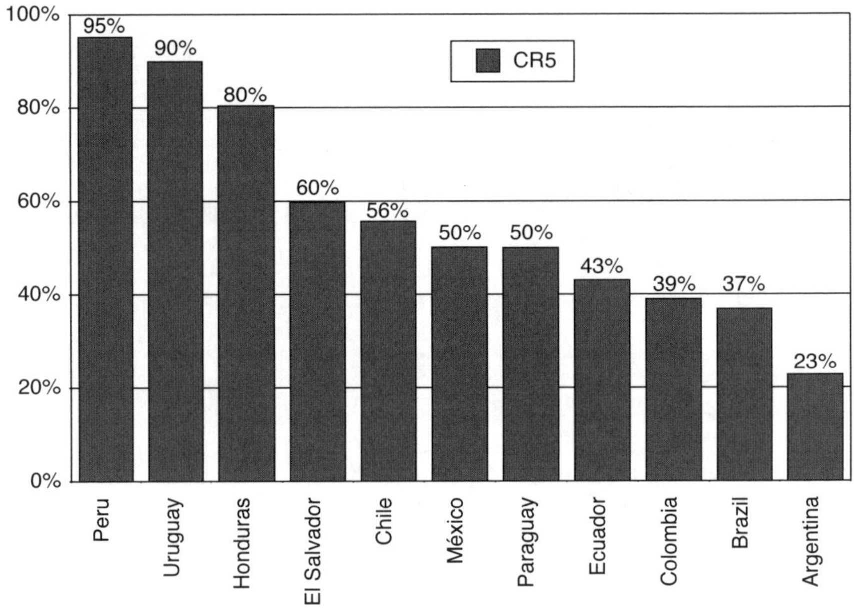

Source: AXCO.

Figure 20.4 Insurance market concentration (% of premiums)

Insurance penetration and density

In LA, the penetration index (premiums over GDP) and insurance density (premiums per capita), along with other analytical measures, point to a significant lag with respect to those observed in more developed economies.

This fact has two sides. On one hand, it means that a high percentage of the LA population lacks insurance as a protection to cover risk. And, on the other (positive) hand, it represents an important potential for growth of the insurance industry in the region. Between 2001 and 2008, the penetration index in the region rose from 2.17% to 2.53%. These levels are low and they are less than one third of the average insurance penetration observed in the industrialised economies, which has stayed at around 9% (Figure 20.5).

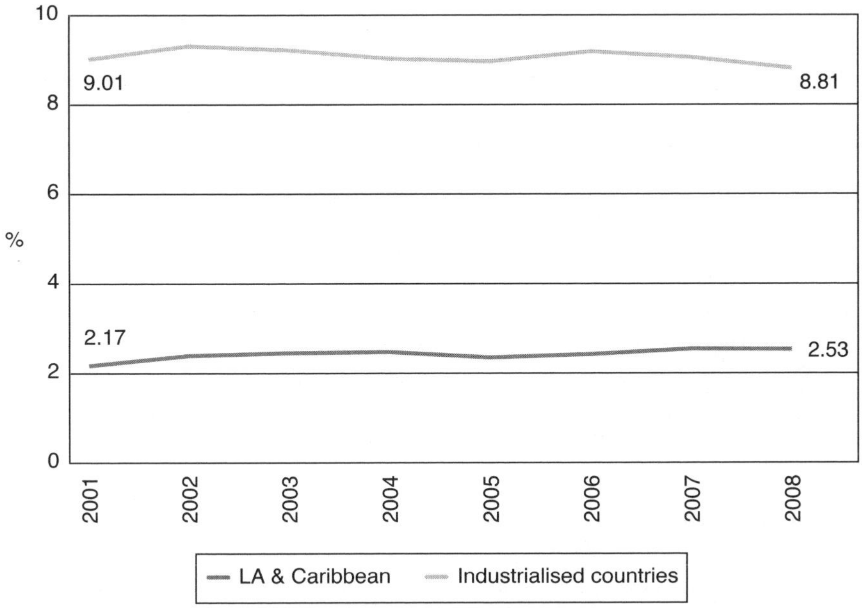

Source: Swiss Re (2009).

Figure 20.5 Insurance penetration (premiums/GDP)

However, an interesting indicator regarding the potential for growth in the region is an index that shows the trend followed by the penetration levels of LA and its comparison with the trend followed by industrialised countries (Figure 20.6). Throughout 2001–08, while the latter has been slightly decreasing (–2.2 percentage points), the former has increased significantly (+16.6 percentage points).

Comparing the penetration index among different LA jurisdictions, there are also some contrasting levels. While Chile has a ratio close to 4%, and Venezuela, Brazil and Panama have one close to 3% (above the region's average), Peru has an insurance penetration as low as 1%.

Regarding insurance density (premiums per capita), the region also shows lower levels than more developed economies and it presents a heterogeneous behaviour. While Venezuela and Chile reached densities above US$300, Colombia, Ecuador, El Salvador and Peru have densities below US$100. In the case of Venezuela, the relatively high level of insurance density in the non-life sector is mainly explained by the effect of compulsory insurance. In the case of Chile, the high

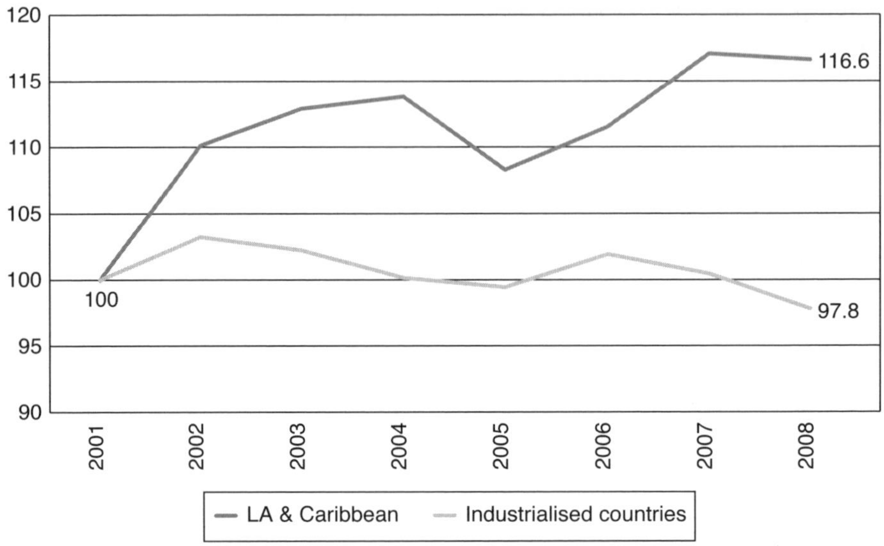

Source: Swiss Re (2009).

Figure 20.6 Insurance penetration (index, 2001 = 100)

level of insurance density in the life business is explained by the development of the annuities market linked to the social security system.

The low levels of both indexes, insurance penetration and density, are also explained by structural factors. The most important is income distribution. Insurance penetration and density are closely linked to the high inequality in terms of income distribution in the region. Analysing the Gini coefficient (which measures the degree of concentration of wealth in an economy) it is possible to conclude that the higher the income inequality, the lower the insurance penetration and density. In contrast, countries with a more sound wealth distribution have higher levels of insurance penetration and density.

There does not seem to be any middle ground; there is no evidence of bad income distribution with high levels of insurance penetration and density. Figures 20.7 and 20.8 show that LA jurisdictions are concentrated in the *high income inequality/low penetration and density* quadrant. Therefore, a great challenge is faced by the region, not only to reach higher levels of GDP growth, but simultaneously achieving a spillover effect that reaches different income segments of the population.

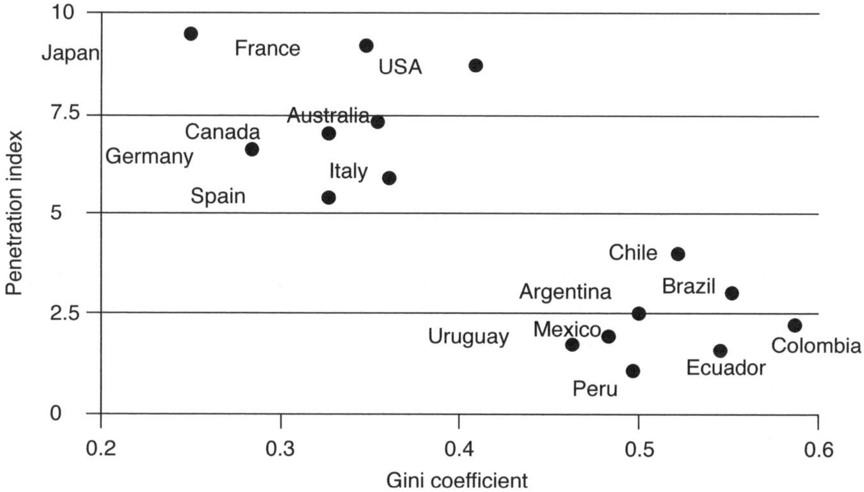

Sources: World Bank, Swiss Re.

Figure 20.7 Income distribution versus penetration in the insurance market

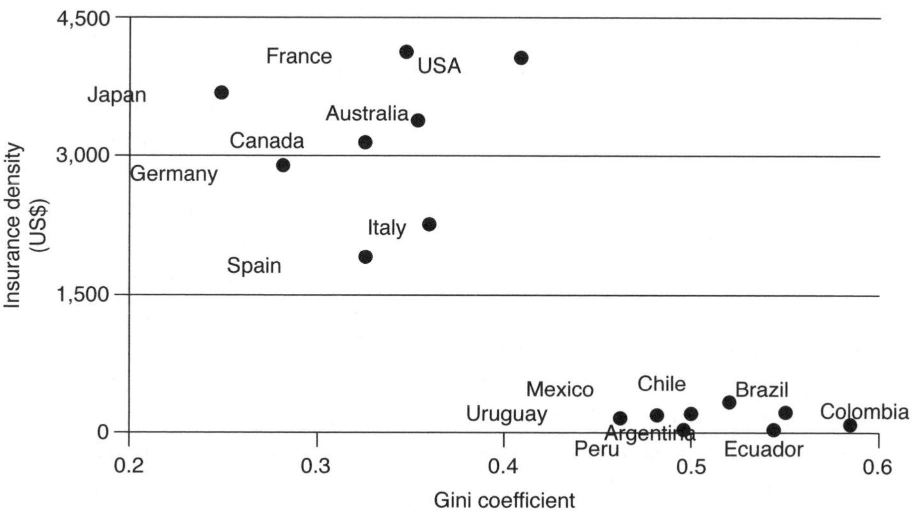

Sources: World Bank, Swiss Re.

Figure 20.8 Income distribution versus density in the insurance market

Institutional arrangements in insurance supervision

Sound and efficient regulation and supervision of the insurance market has gained importance, among other things, with the increasingly global nature of insurance activities and the emergence of complex financial products and risks. Therefore the development of the insurance market requires adapting the operating bases of the industry and the regulatory framework in order to maintain a sound basis for its development and to improve the efficiency and competitiveness in the marketplace.

Throughout the past decade, the regulatory response to globalisation and liberalisation, as well as the evolution of regulatory regimes, has been very encouraging in the LA region. Insurance supervisors have made great efforts to improve their regulatory frameworks and supervisory practices, which continue to move towards a more robust solvency regime. All this has been done in the context of the adoption of international standards and best practices, and in conjunction with other reforms in the financial sector.

Some of the recent regulatory reforms in the LA insurance markets include: (1) more dynamic open and competitive frameworks (for example, the opening of the Brazilian reinsurance market in April 2008, and the opening of the Costa Rican market to insurance and reinsurance competition in July 2008); (2) new products and commercial practices, such as micro-insurance and access to non-traditional markets; (3) coordination and collaboration among supervisors, both locally and from other jurisdictions (by signing bilateral and multilateral memoranda of understanding, and active participation in supervisory colleges); and (4) steps toward the implementation of more advanced and sophisticated solvency regimes.

Historically, most LA jurisdictions adopted a solvency framework following the rationale behind the European Union insurance solvency regime (Solvency I Directives). In this sense, when developing their regulatory frameworks, each country decided to adapt its solvency requirements, to some extent, to the requirements considered in those Directives.

Traditional insurance supervision in LA has focused on the verification of the insurer's compliance with different rules and regulations (*rules-based* supervision). However, this approach does not appropriately consider aspects such as the management and surveillance of risks that may affect the solvency, liquidity and stability of supervised insurers. Therefore, recently many LA supervisors have been moving steadily towards the implementation of a *risk-based* supervision approach, regulating insurance undertakings according to the risk inherent in their business. With this new supervisory approach, authorities will be able to focus on those risk factors that may have an impact on the solvency position of the supervised insurers.

In particular, four jurisdictions have already started a clear reform process towards a more advanced regulatory framework in the region. Brazil has recently issued new regulations for capital requirements characterised by revised capital and solvency requirements based on the risks inherent to credit, market, legal, underwriting and operating risks, incentives for insurers to develop internal risk models and the use of stochastic models in calculating economic capital. Chile has been reviewing its solvency regime, moving from one based on uniform capital requirements to a *company-based* and *risk-driven* scheme, emphasising corporate governance, risk management and transparency towards the market. Peru is advancing towards a Solvency II type framework by enhancing risk modelling, the generation of sufficient databases, strengthening institutional actuarial techniques, and incorporating Pillar II into its solvency regime. And Mexico is well advanced in the process of developing a Solvency II type framework, based on a complete new Insurance Law that was due to be sent to Congress in late 2010.

Some other jurisdictions in the region have also started the implementation of different measures in order to improve their regulatory frameworks. In Guatemala, a new Insurance Law was approved by Congress. The new law contemplates an increase to capital requirements, and it adds to the solvency margin investment and credit risks. In Nicaragua, a new Insurance Law is also in Congress. Among other things, it incorporates new concepts such as risk capital, real capital, real and non-real assets. Argentina is evaluating different alternatives to measure capital and liquidity requirements based on risk exposure in order to develop a proposal for the local insurance market. The purpose is to go through a rule-making process where the concept of risk exposure is developed, taking into consideration the proportionality and the different characteristics of the insurance undertakings. Colombia is modifying its regulation to establish capital requirements, on top of the existing ones, to account for asset risk and, for certain types of insurers, for other market risks. Finally, although El Salvador has not made any changes to capital requirements and solvency regimes over the past years, authorities are working on regulatory changes to move towards risk-based supervision according to international standards.

The evolution of insurance regulation and supervision in the region must evolve together with changes to the institutional arrangements in which insurance supervision is conducted. Currently, insurance supervision in LA is basically carried out by insurance supervisory authorities linked to their corresponding Ministry of Finance. In a few other countries, such as Uruguay and Paraguay, insurance supervision is carried out by the central bank.

In some jurisdictions, integrated financial authorities are in charge of insurance supervision (Bolivia, Colombia, Peru, Nicaragua and El Salvador). In the case of Chile, the supervisory authority supervises insurance and securities markets. In Mexico, the insurance supervisor also supervises the surety market. In Honduras,

Ecuador and Guatemala, insurance supervision is conducted jointly with the supervision of banking institutions. Finally, the countries that have an authority that exclusively supervises the insurance market are Argentina, Brazil, Costa Rica, Panama, Dominican Republic and Venezuela.

Major LA insurance markets are expected to witness sustained insurance demand in the near future. In the coming years, insurance markets will benefit from the enhanced regulation and from the improved solvency regimes that will be implemented in the region.

Main drivers for the development of insurance

The evolution of the insurance markets in LA has been driven by several factors at the macro- and microeconomic levels. At the same time, public and private initiatives have contributed to maintain high levels of growth and sound insurance markets. The drivers range from: (1) macroeconomic stability to financial culture initiatives; (2) development of insurance alternatives as micro-insurance, compulsory and standardised insurance products; (3) increased distribution channels for insurance (for example, bancassurance); and (4) development of annuities markets and insurance products with investment components.

First, on the macro side, for almost a decade, as a result of fiscal and monetary discipline, macroeconomic strength and stability have been achieved. Therefore, the insurance sector expanded during times of economic growth, and even despite the global financial crisis. With continuous GDP growth, higher per capita income can be reached, and, thus, an expansion in the demand for insurance. Additionally, low inflation levels contribute to avoiding the deterioration of insurance premiums, with a positive effect on consumers. A sustained combination of economic expansion and low inflation can be expected to trigger an improvement in insurance penetration and density, increasing the possibility of generating demand from lower-income-level consumers. Additionally, macroeconomic stability creates a propitious environment to attract foreign investment to the insurance industry in the region. This, in turn, favours a more competitive market.

Second, financial authorities have been able to rapidly adjust regulatory and supervisory schemes, when it has been necessary, to facilitate insurance development, maintaining sound and efficient markets.

Third, in a coordinated effort between financial authorities and private sector participants, financial education and literacy has been promoted. One of the main obstacles to increasing insurance penetration is the lack of knowledge and understanding about the benefits of insurance products as a means of risk protection and mitigation. Another complication is the lack of access to information regarding insurance, as well as to products that are accessible and meet the needs of lower-income segments of the population. Improvement in insurance education is a gradual process. Nevertheless, in the LA insurance markets different strategies have been implemented to help speed it up. In this sense, the main measures that different jurisdictions have implemented for this purpose are: (1) compulsory insurance, (2) micro-insurance, and (3) standardised insurance products.

The objective of *compulsory insurance* is to protect the population from specific events, predominantly those related to third-party liability. By its nature, this type of insurance introduces the population to the benefits of being insured. Nearly all LA jurisdictions have compulsory insurances. Among the many classes, the following are the most relevant: social security, civil liability, workers' compensation, aviation insurance, public transport users' insurance and automobile insurance.

Micro-insurance is another strategy to promote the demand for insurance products in the medium and long run in the region. Micro-insurance products are designed to offer protection to the low-income population, considering their particular needs. Basically, micro-insurance products are pooled to increase efficiency; have small insured sums and accessible premiums; can be paid by partial payments, and have the least possible restrictions. This type of insurance offers two main benefits: from a *social perspective*, it mitigates the effects of the materialisation of certain risks, facilitating the path towards improved standards of living; and from a *financial perspective*, micro-insurance is a means to strengthen financial education and to increase insurance penetration in the medium and long term.

Different kinds of micro-insurance products have been developed in LA, the most common are: payment protection plans, temporary life insurance, annuity and retirement insurance, health insurance, coverage for tangible assets and disability insurance. Some countries also have more complex types, such as agricultural and educational coverage. Some jurisdictions have been developing the appropriate institutional framework to implement and promote micro-insurance. Brazil established a committee to study the potential of micro-insurance and suggested possible legislation and tax codes for this specific segment. A proposed micro-insurance law is expected to be approved in the near future. In 2007, the Peruvian supervisory authority issued micro-insurance regulation for the insurance industry and its agents that includes a definition of micro-insurance and rules for claims handling. In Mexico, specific regulation for micro-insurance was issued in 2008. This regulation includes definitions, the characteristics of micro-insurance, and the requirements regarding the design and selling of these products. Nicaragua is developing a new insurance law that will strengthen the current requirements and will introduce new ones regarding micro-insurance.

Standardised insurance products represent another strategy to promote education in the insurance field and to incentivise demand for insurance products. Some LA countries, such as Mexico, have introduced this type of insurance. The motivation is that traditional insurance is a complicated financial instrument, and simpler products might be more accessible for non-sophisticated consumers. The main objective of standardised insurance products is to have 'uniform' insurance policies for the main types of risks (life, accidents, health, auto), with a clear and simple policy structure: a precise coverage, minimum restrictions, and simple requirements for claims and payments.

Another driver of the development of the insurance sector in the LA region has been *bancassurance* (the sale of insurance through the bank network). Successful bancassurance models have thus far primarily involved selling simplified products over the counter to customers. There is evidence that through bancassurance insurers can help to lower costs and maximise synergies.

Finally, the development of annuities markets and the availability of insurance products that compete with mutual funds products have been important drivers of growth in the region. Additionally, some countries, such as Guatemala and Nicaragua, are developing some projects to improve the development of agricultural insurance. And Argentina has been developing products to attend to particular insurance needs that have emerged as a result of the modification of cultural patterns and customs of certain sectors of the population, in both urban and rural areas.

The role of regional coordination efforts to support sound insurance markets and financial stability

The last couple of decades have been characterised by global market integration and liberalisation. Financial regulation has been modified to update and harmonise supervisory and regulatory practices, according to international principles and standards. Therefore, adoption of standards has become an important basis to promote global financial stability and to foster domestic economic and financial systems.

In this context, an important set of activities carried out by insurance supervisors has been related to international cooperation regarding supervision. Several associations have been created to gather supervisors from different jurisdictions: in the international arena, the International Association of Insurance Supervisors (IAIS) and, in the regional field, the Latin-American Association of Insurance Supervisors (Asociación de Supervisores de Seguros de América Latina, ASSAL).[2]

The objectives of the ASSAL are: (1) to exchange information about legislation, control methods, market characteristics and operational systems, from member jurisdictions, regarding insurance and reinsurance; (2) to harmonise policies and supervisory mechanisms; (3) to promote regional education programmes related to insurance and reinsurance; (4) to gather and release technical and statistical information; and (5) to promote cooperation among its members.

In the past decade, the ASSAL consolidated its presence in the international arena, since it has linked its activities with those of other associations and international organisations with common interests. These organisations include the IAIS and the Insurance and Private Pensions Committee of the Organisation for Economic Cooperation and Development (OECD). Additionally, a cooperation agreement has been signed with the United States' National Association of Insurance Commissioners (NAIC), and there is regular communication and cooperation with the Committee of European Insurance and Occupational Pensions Supervisors (CEIOPS).

Conclusion

The recent financial crisis drove attention towards deficiencies in the regulatory frameworks and supervisory practices. Specifically, it pointed to potential gaps in the supervision of financial groups. Additionally, it brought to the attention of the financial community the role of insurance activities in the generation and amplification of systemic risk.

All this has increased the need to improve regulatory frameworks and supervisory practices, and to enhance the cooperation and information exchange mechanisms among supervisors. In this post-crisis environment, strengthening cooperation and collaboration schemes will be one of the most important challenges for the LA insurance supervisors.

Notes

1. The author thanks Norma Alicia Rosas, Gabriela Basurto and Héctor Romero for their help in the preparation of this chapter.
2. The ASSAL was created in 1979 to join the insurance supervisors and regulators in the region. Its current members are: Argentina, Bolivia, Brazil, Chile, Colombia, Costa Rica, Cuba, Ecuador, El Salvador, Guatemala, Honduras, Mexico, Nicaragua, Panama, Paraguay, Peru, Puerto Rico, Dominican Republic and Uruguay, plus Spain and Portugal.

Bibliography

Asociación de Supervisores de Seguros de América Latina (ASSAL), Datos estadísticos http://www.assalweb.org/.

AXCO, Insurance Market Reports, https://www.axco.co.uk/axcoimr/home2.asp.

CEPAL (2009) *Anuario Estadístico de América Latina y el Caribe.*

Comisión Nacional de Seguros y Fianzas (CNSF), http://www.cnsf.gob.mx.

IMF (2008) *World Economic Outlook.*

MAPFRE (2009) *El mercado asegurador latinoamericano 2008–2009* (Madrid: Instituto de Ciencias del Seguro, Fundación MAPFRE).
Swiss Re (2002) 'El seguro mundial en el año 2001', *sigma* no. 6.
Swiss Re (2003) 'El seguro mundial en el año 2002', *sigma* no. 8.
Swiss Re (2004) 'El seguro mundial en el año 2003', *sigma* no. 3.
Swiss Re (2005) 'El seguro mundial en el año 2004', *sigma* no. 2.
Swiss Re (2006) 'El seguro mundial en el año 2005', *sigma* no. 5.
Swiss Re (2007) 'El seguro mundial en el año 2006', *sigma* no. 4.
Swiss Re (2008) 'El seguro mundial en el año 2007', *sigma* no. 3.
Swiss Re (2009) 'El seguro mundial en el año 2008', *sigma* no. 3.

21
Regulatory and Supervisory Issues and Challenges in the Russian Insurance Sector in the Aftermath of the Transformation

Marek Monkiewicz

Introduction

The peaceful dissolution of the Soviet Union back in 1991 gave birth to 15 new republics including the Russian Federation. Three of the new republics – Lithuania, Latvia and Estonia – turned immediately for association with the European Community. The remaining ones joined the Commonwealth of Independent States (CIS) (Russian: Sodruzhestvo Nezavisimykh Gosudarstv, SNG) – a regional organisation – created as a successor to the Soviet Union with some sort of Russian domination. On 18 August 2008 Georgia decided to opt out following the South Osethian War with Russia and the resulting bilateral hostilities.

The CIS was conceived as a very loose association with no real executive powers so in 2000 some CIS members decided to tighten their mutual economic cooperation by creating the Eurasian Economic Community (Belarus, Kazakhstan, Kyrgyzstan, Tajikistan and Russia). In 2003 some countries signed an agreement creating a common economic area (Russia, Ukraine, Belarus and Kazakhstan), a sort of custom duty association. In all these different settings things tend to rely foremost on the position of the Russian Federation which represents over 50% of the entire population of the CIS and nearly 80% of its gross domestic product (GDP). It is also the most wealthy country in the region with GDP per capita in 2009 of around US$15,000 compared to US$11,800 in Kazakhstan, US$11,600 in Belarus, US$10,400 in Azerbaijan, US$6,900 in Turkmenistan and US$6,400 in Ukraine (expressed in purchasing power parity, PPP) (CIA, 2010).

The demise of the Soviet Union and the emancipation of the new states coincided with the revolutionary economic and political transformation of the whole region. Its interim result was political, social and economic discontinuity, deep economic recession, soaring inflation and rising social inequalities. By the year 1998 most of the countries concerned had not even managed to match the real GDP level of 1989 and as a whole recorded negative growth rates (Kołodko, 2010, pp. 81–9). Russia was no exception.

However, the last decade has turned out to be fairly good for the CIS with an annual GDP growth rate in 2002–08 of between 5% and 8%. The recent crisis halted development processes for a while and left a severe imprint on the countries concerned with a GDP growth rate falling again to –6.6% in 2009, to recover to 4.0% already by 2010 (IMF, 2010, p. 155).

By 2008 – 20 years after the start of the transformation – only half of the CIS states reported a real GDP level to match that of 1989. This, of course, could not be so without influencing the financial markets, and insurance in particular.

Overview of the insurance market in the CIS region

Before the start of the transformation, the insurance sector of the future CIS had effectively been run by two Soviet-wide monopolistic companies – Gosstrakh and Ingostrakh. Gosstrakh had been providing insurance since 1921 and concentrated on inland risks after the set-up of Ingostrakh. Ingostrakh, on the other hand, had been operational since 1947 and focused on foreign risks – marine, aviation and export contracts, as well as reinsurance. It was active not only in the Soviet Union but also had several subsidiaries in Western Europe.

The dissolution of the Soviet Union effectively meant for the insurance world the abolition of these monopolies and the rise of their local equivalents. It also meant the withering away of the legal base for these activities. Only a few years later – in most cases by the mid 1990s – the respective laws on insurance activities came into effect.[1] In the legal vacuum in between, no special regulations existed.

The poor macroeconomic performance of the countries concerned in the 1990s was echoed in the insurance sector which tended to develop very slowly and continued to play a largely insignificant role in their socioeconomic development. Suffice it to say that in 1999 the overall premiums volume written in the CIS was estimated at US$1,456 million, of which US$1,400 million was Russia alone (ECE, 2001, p. 8).

The general macroeconomic improvement in the first decade of the twenty-first century created a more conducive environment for the insurance sector development. As a result the size of the market increased by 2006 to over US$30 billion (see Table 21.1).

However, both insurance density and penetration are still at very low levels. Russia continued its regional hegemon role, representing, in 2008, over 80% of the total market, followed by Ukraine, 12%; Kazakhstan, 5%; and Belarus, 1% (*The Insurer*, April–May 2008, p. 59).

Table 21.1 Selected characteristics of the CIS insurance market, 2006

Country	GWP* (€ mn)	GDP (€ mn)	Population (000s)	Insurance density (€)	Insurance penetration (%)
Russia	17,900.0	780,232	142,894	125.3	2.29
Ukraine	2,270.6	84,852	46,300	49.0	2.69
Kazakhstan	829.4	61,552	15,285	54.3	1.35
Belarus	204.6	29,442	9,725	21.0	0.69
Azerbaijan	76.5	15,793	8,120	9.4	0.48
Uzbekistan	31.2	12,821	27,780	1.1	0.24
Georgia	30.8	6,240	4,646	6.6	0.49
Tajikistan	16.2	2,240	7,077	2.3	0.72
Armenia	11.3	5,108	2,972	3.8	0.22
Kyrgyz Republic	2.9	2,249	5,214	0.6	0.13

* Gross written premiums.
Source: *The Insurer* (August–September 2007, p. 10).

Gross premiums written in Ukraine in 2008 reached the level of €2.6 billion, to contract to €1.8 billion a year later due to the heavy economic recession which hit the country. It is estimated that two thirds of the premiums were essentially tax arbitrage and money laundering operations. In 2009 the country hosted 469 insurance undertakings, of which 73 were in the life insurance sector. Life business represents only 4% of the premiums collected (*The Insurer*, Spring 2010, p. 56).

As for Kazakhstan, gross premiums written in 2008 reached the level of around Euro €760 million, of which one fifth were from compulsory lines. Overall assets of the insurance industry are close to €2.2 billion (National Bank of Kazakhstan, 2010b). The market hosts around 40 insurance undertakings, a number that has been stable since 2006.

The insurance market in Belorussia is very small and still largely publicly owned. In 2009 its premiums income was close to €300 million. The market now hosts 20 insurance companies, compared to 42 in 2000 (*The Insurer*, Winter 2009–10, p. 69).

A specific characteristic of the insurance market in the CIS region is the extremely low level of the life sector. In 2008 it constituted no more than 3% of the gross premiums volume in Russia, and less than 5% in Ukraine, Belorussia and Kazakhstan – the major regional markets (Swiss Re, 2009, pp. 37–9). There are various possible explanations to this fact, the most plausible of which is the extremely poor reputation of the insurance services among the population, reinforced by the frequent cases of fraudulent activities registered in the region.

The Russian insurance market – legal and regulatory framework

After the collapse of the Soviet Union its legal system ceased to exist. New states emanating from the Soviet Union were therefore compelled to hastily fill the regulatory vacuum in all areas of economic activity with new standards or just to authorise the validity of the existing Soviet acts. The insurance sector had little to take over as under the Soviet system there was little public regulation covering insurance (Mariska and Manson, 2005, p. 62). The reason for that was the state insurance monopoly exercised through two publicly owned companies: Gosstrakh and Ingostrakh. As a result, most of the technical regulation took the form of internal corporate acts, whereas the political part of the regulation was addressed in more general laws. In such a situation external experience had to be tapped – European countries in particular.

During the first phase of transformation, therefore, there was neither special legislation governing the set-up and operations of the insurance companies nor any public supervisory system put in place. The situation changed substantially, however, between 1993 and 1996 when two major pieces of legislation relevant to the insurance business came into force: the Civil Code and the law 'On the Organisation of Insurance Business in the Russian Federation'.

The Civil Code of the Russian Federation was finally adopted in 1996 and represented a seminal step in law development in Russia. It was the first ever regulation of this type in the history of Russia. It has been given a special ranking among other laws on economic activities, with the power to overrule their regulations in case of conflict. As such, its insurance-related chapters constitute the backbone of the current insurance regulation in Russia.

It contains two chapters specifically related to insurance activities – chapters 48 and 59. Chapter 48 deals with insurance, or more precisely with insurance contracts. It specifies inter alia the concept of insurable interest, indemnity, standard forms of insurance contracts, conditions for invalidating the policies, rights and obligations of the insured, and so on. Chapter 59, on the other hand, regulates the liability order, that is, it defines inter alia the principles of the responsibility for harm and calculation of damages. It foresees among other things a discount on damages compensation if the party concerned demonstrated gross negligence.

The law 'On the Organisation of Insurance Business in the Russian Federation', adopted in late November 1992, came into force in 1993. It was substantially modified in 1997 to accommodate the standards contained in the Civil Code and again in 1999 to take into account the 'Partnership and Cooperation Agreement (PCA) with the European Union' (Mariska and Manson, 2005, p. 64).

Other major amendments were introduced in 2004 in the wake of the country's preparation for the accession to World Trade Organization (WTO).

It should be noted, perhaps, that the changes introduced modified the existing law to make it more compliant with the standards introduced in the European Community. With the last amendment the law separates, effective as of 2007, life and non-life business, prohibiting new composite companies from authorisation and requiring existing composite companies to be effectively split into separate life and non-life undertakings. It also requires licensing of insurance brokers and attestation of actuaries who became responsible for the valuation of reserves. It also allows for the operation of mutual insurance societies, which were not mentioned in the old law.

The amended law substantially increases the regulatory capital requirements for both insurance and reinsurance companies. In case of non-life companies, the minimum capital required is US$1 million, whereas in case of life business it is twice as much. The reinsurers need to have a minimum capital base of US$4 million. Apart from raising regulatory capital requirements, the new law foresees at the same time the tightening of the regulations regarding the quality of capital recognised for supervisory purposes.

The amended law introduces for the first time some fit and proper requirements but only for the second line of management, excluding managing board members. Senior management, for example, including the general director, should have a higher education diploma either in economics or finance. They are also required to have a minimum of two years' experience in insurance or financial services (Mariska and Manson, 2005, p. 78). The same applies to the chief accountant, who additionally should be a Russian resident.

Key characteristics of the market

The Russian insurance market today remains fairly non-transparent and requires different analysis in statistical terms. It is so because of the development of numerous quasi-insurance operations which are used largely for tax arbitrage purposes or outright fraudulent activities. It is also the reason for and at the same time the result of the sizeable dimensions of the captive industry run largely by various industrial corporations. Last but not least, there is also the important part of the market sponsored directly by the state in which insurance companies play a purely administrative role. This in essence covers two areas: medical insurance and some special insurance for state employees. All in all, it is frequently assumed that as much as 50–70% of the premiums volume today should not be classified as real insurance operations. However, no hard data are available.

In the last few years the size of the market has been growing rapidly, with the rates of growth achieving a two-digit level. In 2008, for example, gross written premiums reached the level of nearly U$39 billion, which was more than 22.7%, in comparison to the year before. It was even more spectacular in 2007 when the premiums volume increased over 2006 by more than 27% (FSSN, 2008,

p. 3). As a result of these developments the share of insurance premiums in Russian GDP has been steadily increasing from 2.75% in 2000 to nearly 4% in 2006 (see Figure 21.1). In 2009 it fell abruptly because of a crackdown by the Russian administration on non-insurance financial schemes which used insurance-relevant packaging and were dominating the life business of the country. Immediately, a substantial part of the premiums income went.

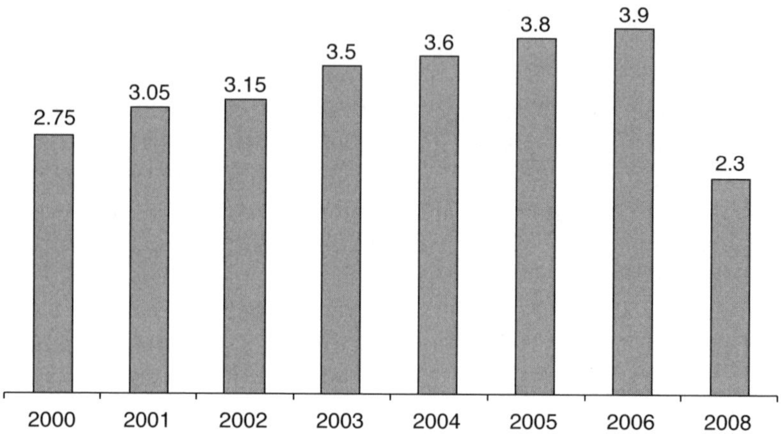

Figure 21.1 Share of insurance premium in Russian GDP in 2000–08 (%)

It is perhaps interesting to note that the share of indemnities and compensation paid out to beneficiaries (claims ratio) in 2008 reached 65%, which indicates healthy proportions in the industry finances.

A peculiar characteristic of the Russian insurance market is the extremely high level of compulsory insurance lines in the overall premiums volume (see table 21.2).

Table 21.2 Premium income structure compulsory versus voluntary (% and roubles bn)

	2005	2006	2007	2008	2009
Compulsory lines (roubles bn)	203.5	273.2	368.7	481.8	557.1
Share (%)	41.1	44.7	47.5	50.9	57.0
Voluntary lines (roubles bn)	292.0	337.4	407.3	464.4	420.4
Share (%)	58.9	55.3	52.5	49.1	43.0

Source: FSSN, respective years.

This is primarily the result of the high volume of mandatory medical insurance schemes which currently represent around 30% of the overall insurance premiums income in Russia. If we take medical insurance out of the picture, the major line of business is property insurance (around 60%), personal retail (20%), motor third-party liability (15%) and general liability (4%). Life business became extremely low, representing less than 3% of the total premiums volume in 2008 (FSSN, 2008, p. 3).

The market is fairly concentrated in terms of both geographical split and operating companies. According to the available statistics, around 60% of the premiums collected in 2008 originated in Moscow and Petersburg (formerly Leningrad). They were also the headquarters for over 60% of the total number of the registered insurance companies (FSSN, 2008, p. 17).

At the same time, the five largest companies (out of total number of 786 as of December 2008) collected nearly 28% of the total premiums volume in 2008. The market share of the 20 largest operators was over 56% (see Table 21.3).

Table 21.3 Market concentration in premium collection (excluding mandatory medical insurance) (%)

	2005	2006	2007	2008
Top 5 operators	23.9	26.5	28.3	27.8
Top 10 operators	34.0	37.5	39.0	40.6
Top 20 operators	48.9	51.9	54.4	56.1

Source: FSSN (2008, p. 5).

The unique aspect of the Russian insurance market is the relatively large number of insurance companies, in particular in view of the modest size of the insurance business. At the same time, this population is notoriously plagued by frequent withdrawals and failures. From 1984 to 2008, more than 1,500 insurance companies disappeared from the market. Some of them stopped underwriting; others had their licences revoked; yet others simply went bankrupt. No detailed figures are available, but the long-term trend is clear – the market consolidates at an accelerating pace. Between 2000 and 2008, the number of insurance companies decreased by nearly half – from more than 1,500 to 786 (see Figure 21.2). It may be a clear indication that business is getting serious and there is less space for poor insurance practices.

Most of the companies (around 65%) are limited liability companies, followed by open joint stock companies (15%) and closed joint stock companies (19%).[2] Only about 1% of the companies are municipal or state-owned.

Russian legislation has recently provided the opportunity for mutuals; however, so far the details of the legislation have not been agreed upon.

It may be worthwhile to observe that an important number of companies to date (around 40%) are captive, tied to underwriting only for their sponsors.

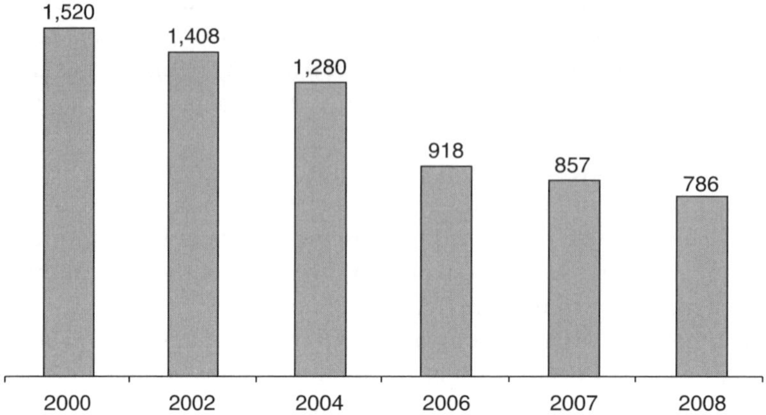

Figure 21.2 Number of insurance companies registered in Russia in 2000–08

Another 20% of the companies are believed to concentrate on tax optimisation schemes using insurance tools, so there is a widely held belief that the population of direct writers will continue to contract for some years to come.

An important characteristic of the market is the financial health of the operating insurance companies as measured by their own capital resources.

This aspect of insurance development in recent years has been given increased attention by the market regulator and supervisor as the premium volumes have increased and companies have turned to the public to write their business. All in all, between 2001 and 2008 the total share of capital available in Russian insurance increased sixfold – from 25 billion roubles to over 150 billion roubles (FSSN, 2008, p. 11). It was accomplished largely by decreasing the number of the smallest companies via increased minimum capital requirements (see Table 21.4).

Table 21.4 Distribution of insurance companies by size of authorised share capital

Authorised share capital	31.12.2004	31.12.2005	31.12.2006	31.12.2007
Up to 30 mn roubles	563	312	129	0
30–120 mn roubles	452	468	470	500
120–150 mn roubles	80	94	103	118
150–200 mn roubles	120	133	143	164
500 mn roubles to 1 bn roubles	39	38	42	41
Over 1 bn roubles	26	30	31	34
Total:	1,280	1,075	918	857

Source: FSSN, respective years.

As indicated by the figures presented in Table 21.4, between 2004 and 2007 the large population of the smallest companies with a share capital of around US$1 million each effectively disappeared entirely, and the number of those with a share capital of over US$4 million increased substantially. The insurance business is getting more serious.

Motor insurance

A new era in market development in Russia began with the introduction of compulsory motor third-party liability insurance (MTPL) in 2004. It should perhaps be noted that Russia was one of the last countries in Europe to do so. The maximum level of liability was set very low, at US$13.660, with a cap of US$7.600 for material damages and US$11.500 for personal injury. The tariff is defined by the government and has to be applied by all direct writers. Its level depends on the type of the car, age and driving experience of the driver, as well as the region within which it is used. The premium level is affected by the mandatory bonus-malus system which credits 5% for every year without accident with a maximum limit of 50% discount, and penalises each accident with a 5% increase in the tariff level but no more in aggregate than 245% (Pukała, 2008, p. 48). Effectively, the average premium is kept at a very low level of between US$60 and US$80 and is matched by an equally low coverage compensation level, which was around US$800 in 2008 (Russian Association of Motor Insurers (RAMI), 2009, p. 23).

All insurers writing MTPL (169 as of December 2008) are members of the RAMI. The Association runs two special-purpose funds to compensate the claimants in the event of a failure of the insurance company. They are financed by levies imposed on premiums. As of 2009, the Compensation Fund also compensates victims of uninsured or untraced drivers. The Guarantee Fund, on the other hand, comes into play when direct writers become insolvent.

As of 2008, MTPL insurance made up around 8.5% of the total insurance premium volume in Russia (Table 21.5).

Table 21.5 Market structure and MTPL (roubles bn)

Year	2009
Gross premiums written	977.5
MTPL	85.7
Total compensation paid	734.4
MTPL compensation	49.8

Source: RAMI (2009).

The future of the market is well secured with the rapidly growing number of vehicles. Between 2004 and 2008, the number of vehicles on the road increased from around 36 million to 43.5 million. The rise was echoed in the number of policies issued, which increased from around 26 million in 2004 to nearly 37 million in 2008 (RAMI, 2009, pp. 20–2). All in all, between 2004 and 2008, over 170 million MTPL policies were issued. It should perhaps be underlined that the introduction and take-up of this compulsory product went very well and the rate of coverage recently reached 90%.

An interesting part of market development was the introduction in 2005–08 of a modern system of direct settlement of claims and simplified reporting of road accidents. Under this system, based on French and Belgian solutions, road victims have the right to present their claims for compensation directly to their own insurer (and not to the insurer of the liable person, as is normally the case). This right may be exercised only in the absence of personal injury and when the amount claimed does not exceed defined limits (around US$800 as of December 2008). Under this system, simplified documentation of the accident may be completed without the presence of the road police – provided, however, that there are no more than two vehicles involved and if both drivers agree on the joint statement on the principal causes and circumstances surrounding the event.

Supervision of the market

Financial supervision in Russia is split conventionally among three sectoral authorities. Banking supervision is allocated to the Russian central bank (the Central Bank of the Russian Federation), capital market supervision rests in the hands of the Securities Commission, and the insurance sector is overseen by a specialised insurance supervisory authority.

Soon after the adoption of the amendments in the insurance law in 2004, supervision became the responsibility of the newly created Federal Service for Insurance Supervision (Russian: Fiedieralnaya Sluzhba Strakhogogo Nadzora, FSSN). Since then the Ministry of Finance, released from the supervisory tasks it performed between 1996 and 2004, has concentrated entirely on policy-making and regulatory issues.

To accomplish its primary objectives of law observance, legislation enforcement and successful development of the insurance business, the supervisory authority has the powers to:

- grant licences;
- define specific conditions for carrying out insurance activities;
- set policy rates, level and structure of tariffs in compulsory lines of business;
- define the solvency standards of insurers;

- regulate requirements regarding technical provisions, including their constitution as well as their subsequent allocation rules;
- specify the maximum liability level the direct writer is allowed before purchasing reinsurance coverage; and
- define rules and conditions of information disclosure and statistical reporting for supervisory purposes.

It also carries out on-site and off-site inspections and controls the market cap limits for foreign investors. Additionally, it prepares and introduces secondary regulations in insurance. The FSSN is internally split into different departments and has seven regional offices – in St Petersburg, Moscow, Rostov on Don, Samara, Yekaterinburg, Novosibirsk and Khabarovsk. The chairman of the FSSN is supported by three deputies: one for licensing and authorisation, one for ongoing supervision and one for general affairs. Its overall employment figure is round 200 officers. The regulatory toolkit of the supervisory authority includes market entry instruments, market correction instruments which are issued to prevent any breach of the law, and market exit instruments – revocation of a licence requiring the company to stop writing certain lines of business, and finally revocation of the licence.

In order to properly control insurance activities, the FSSN has authority inter alia over licensing, approving the increase of charter capital, controlling the financial soundness of insurers, maintaining their state-wide register and assessing the compliance of their operations with Russian legislation. Thus far it has emphasised activities on the market entry side, but recently its interest has shifted into market exit regulations as a result of a massive decrease in the number of insurance companies since the introduction of severe prudential regulations in 2007.

The role of foreign investors

The opening up of the financial markets to foreign competitors has a long tradition of state control. It was a cornerstone of financial market regulation in the 1960s and 1970s. Only in the 1980s and 1990s did these standards start to be replaced in the developed economies by prudential regulation. However, many countries, particularly emerging ones, still limit the access of foreign investors to their national markets. This applies in most cases to the banking and insurance industries.

There are several arguments supporting these policies – the crucial one being concerns for national autonomy and national security. It is believed that foreign entrants might skim the local markets, neglecting wide customer groups which are too poor to be taken care of. Their entry might also threaten the financial stability of the existing local companies, and last but not least lead to an overall overreliance on foreign insurance capacity. That could have a detrimental effect at a time of financial distress (for a good review of the discussion, see ECE, 2001, pp. 11–13).

These worries are counterweighted by the possible positive outcomes of market-opening. Foreign insurers may bring much-needed capital, knowledge and skills to the local industry. They could improve local customer satisfaction and the efficiency of the whole insurance market. They could also enhance the professional capabilities of the local supervisory authorities and produce some benefits to local economy (see Figure 21.3).

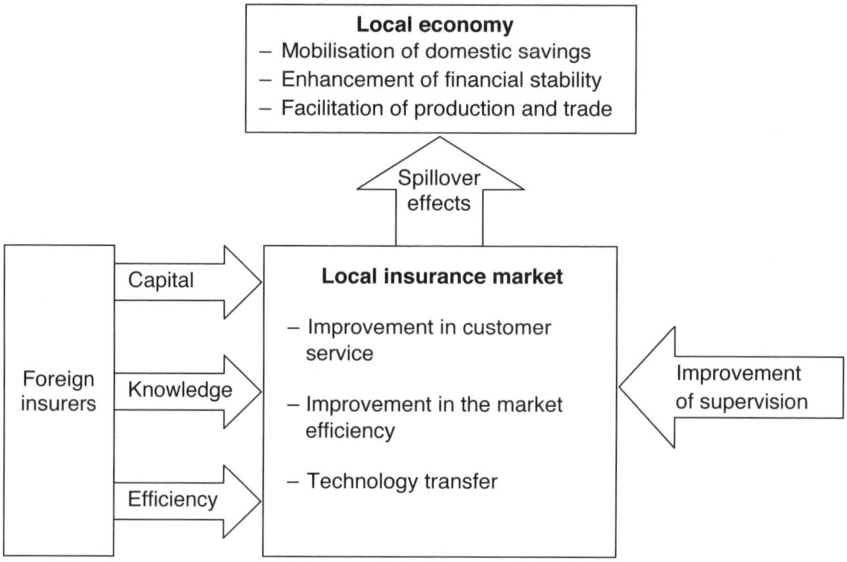

Source: Swiss Re (2000).

Figure 21.3 Benefits of market access liberalisation for emerging markets

All these arguments are present in the local debate in Russia.

Until 1999 the share of foreign investors in Russian insurance companies was limited to 49%. In 1999 this formula was changed and instead of setting the quota for individual companies a market cap of 15% was introduced. According to the new law, if this quota is exceeded, the insurance supervisor ceases to issue new licences for foreign-controlled insurance companies. Foreign-controlled insurance companies were defined as subsidiaries of foreign investors or those in which the shareholding of the foreign investors in their charter capital exceeds 49%. Since 2004 this market cap has been extended to 25%.

Foreign-controlled insurance companies are restricted from some classes of insurance business. This covers, in particular:

- life insurance;
- compulsory insurance;
- compulsory state insurance (medical insurance);
- property insurance with governmental procurement;
- property insurance of state or municipal organisations.

The current law specifies also fit and proper requirements for foreign investors in insurance. It requires an investor to be an insurance company, to be in operation at home for at least 15 years and to participate for at least for two years in insurance activity on Russian territory. Most of these restrictions are lifted for the companies headquartered in the European Union which is a direct result of the Partnership and Cooperation Agreement between Russia and EU concluded in 1994 and extended in 2004 to cover new EU Member States (see Table 21.6).

Table 21.6 Restrictions on foreign capital in Russian insurance

Restrictions that apply to a foreign-controlled insurance company	1999	2004 investors from outside the EU	2004 investors from the EU
Limit of international capital in total market capital (quota)	15%	25%	Does not apply
Prohibition of life insurance	Applies	Applies	Does not apply
Prohibition of compulsory insurance	Applies	Applies	Does not apply
Prohibition of insurance of state property	Applies	Applies	Does not apply
Investor must be insurance company established 15 years	Applies	Applies	Does not apply
Investor must have been operating in the Russian market for 2 years	Applies	Applies	Does not apply
Payment for shares must be in roubles	Applies	Applies	Does not apply
Senior staff must be Russian citizens	Applies	Applies	Does not apply
Special rules may be applied concerning solvency	Applies	Does not apply	Does not apply
Special rules may be applied concerning the creation and investment of insurance reserves	Applies	Does not apply	Does not apply
Restriction on setting up branches	Applies	Applies	Applies

Source: Moriska and Manson (2005, p. 75).

Notwithstanding these restrictions, the role of foreign capital in market development tended to quickly increase in the last decade. Between 2002 and 2008 the share of foreign investors in the share capital of the industry increased nearly sixfold, from around 2.5% to nearly 14% (FSSN, 2008, p. 13). In 2008, around 35% of the total premiums volume in insurance and around 24% in reinsurance was written by the companies with foreign participation. As of 2008, 38 insurance companies (compared to 21 in 2006) were 100% foreign-owned and collected as much as 9% of the total insurance premiums. However, it can safely be said that two-thirds of premiums are still collected by purely Russian companies.

As far as the sources of foreign capital is concerned Europe is decisively dominating the scene with the Netherlands (40%), Germany (20%), UK (10%), Cyprus (12%) and Austria (7%) playing the leading role.

Conclusion

As indicated in the preceding analysis, the Russian insurance sector has recorded substantial quantitative growth since its inception 20 years ago, and in particular during the last decade. It has also evolved considerably in qualitative aspects. Modern regulations have been implemented, the market is controlled by a strong federal agency, many poorly capitalised companies were pushed out of the marketplace. However, there are a number of challenges and issues remaining.

Probably the most important is the need to increase market safety and integrity. It requires not only enhancement of the capital requirements vis-à-vis insurance companies but also stricter rules on its quality to avoid the effect of double gearing and junk asset classes. It also requires granting the supervisory agency early intervention powers along the lines observed today in the mature insurance market. The use of stress tests, scenario analysis, early warning indicators, and so on, will provide the system with more security than it has today.

Market safety could be substantially enhanced with the establishment of the insurance compensation fund to take care of the policy-holders of the failed insurers. It is of special importance for the emerging insurance markets in which failures happen relatively frequently and this regulation of the industry is at a low level.

Another important challenge is bringing order to the marketplace by eliminating quasi-insurance operations and schemes. It will give the market much-needed transparency and remove a substantial degree of fraudulent activities. To accomplish this, some tax loopholes need to be eliminated without negatively impacting classical insurance lines.

On the other hand, bringing more order to the market requires the development of its infrastructure. It should include, in the first place, various databases which may both assist insurance companies in their underwriting activities as well as help them to combat insurance fraud. It also could include common market procedures and practices to assist in the cooperation of companies.

Last but not least, a real challenge is to bring more insurance to the people. De facto that means development of the life sector – practically non-existent today. It requires not only public assistance (via education and perhaps tax subsidies) and an increased marketing effort by the companies concerned. It may also require bringing to the market completely new product designs that will attract demand. One idea might be the application of the micro-insurance concept.

Notes

1. In Armenia it took place in 1996, Azerbeijan – 1993, Georgia – 1999, Kazakhstan – 1993, Kyrgyzstan – 1991, Turkmenistan – 1995, Uzbekistan – 1993. See Pukała (2008, pp. 178–91).
2. Open joint stock companies may offer shares to the public whereas closed may not.

Bibliography

Baling, M. (ed.) (2009) *Current Trends in the Russian Financial System* (Vienna: SUERF).

Borowski, T. (2008) *Market Analysis. Ukraine 2007. General Information and Insurance Market Overview* (Warsaw: VIG).

Central Bank of the Russian Federation (2009) *Annual Report 2008* (Moscow).

Central Bank of the Russian Federation (2009) *Banking Supervision Report 2008* (Moscow).

Central Bank of the Russian Federation (2010) *Bulletin of Banking Statistics*, No. 1(200) (Moscow).

CIA (2010) *World Factbook 2010*.

ECE (2001) *The Economic Importance of Insurance in Central and Eastern Europe and the Impact of Globalisation and e-Business*, Trade/2001/15, May.

FSSN (2008) *Doklad o sostojanii i razvitii rosijskogo rynka strakhowanija za 2008* (Moscow).

FSSN (2009) *Analiticheskaya spravka o dieyatielnosti strakhovykh brokierov za 2008 god* (Moscow).

IMF (2010) *World Economic Outlook*, April.

Ingostrakh (2008) *Summary of the Development of the Insurance Market in Russia in 2007*, April.

Kołodko, G.W. (1999) *Ekonomia i polityka transformacji* (Warsaw: Poltext).

Kolomiyets, W. (2008) 'Zakonodatielnyje i ekonomicheskije uslovija razvitija pieriestrakhovaniya v Ukrainie', Moskovskiy miezhdunarodnyj pieriestrakhovocznoj congress, 25–26 marta, 2008 goda.

Mariska, M.D., and T.B. Manson (2005) 'Reforming the Insurance Market in Russia', *Policy Issues in Insurance*, No. 10 (Paris: OECD).

Ministry of Finance of the Russian Federation, Department of Insurance Supervision (2003), *Report on Development, Regulation and Reforming of the Russian Federation Insurance Market*, June.

Mosiychuk, T. (2006) *Ukrainian Insurance Market Development. Trade and Regulation Features*, State Commission for Regulation of Financial Services Markets in Ukraine.

National Bank of Kazakhstan (2010a) *Financial Stability Report of Kazakhstan 2009*.

National Bank of Kazakhstan (2010b) *Statistical Bulletin*, No. 1(182), January.

National Bank of Ukraine (2009a) *Annual Report 2008* (Kiyev).

National Bank of Ukraine (2009b) *Bulletin of the National Bank of Ukraine*, No. 11/2009(130) (Kiyev).

Pukała, R. (2008) 'Perspektywy integracji rynków ubezpieczeniowych europejskich państw postradzieckich z rynkiem Unii Europejskiej', unpublished PhD dissertation, SGH, Warsaw.
RAMI (2009) *Annual Report 2008* (Moscow).
RAMI (2010) *Annual Report 2009* (Moscow).
Russian Polis Information Group (2008) *The Current State and the Development Prospects of the CIS Reinsurance Markets* (Moscow).
Suslov, V. (2009), 'Pidsumki diyalnosti strakhowogo rinka za 2008 rik', Vsieukrainska Narada Organiv Dierzhavnoj Vladi ta StrakhoVogo Biznesu Ukrainy, 14 kvitnya.
Swiss Re (2009) *sigma* 2/2009.
Wyer, M. (2000) *The Law of Insurance Supervision in the Russian Federation, Roundtable on Insurance in Russia* (Moscow), 15–16 May.

Part VII

International Issues

22
Insurance Regulation: Mutual Recognition, Equivalence and International Standards

Bradley L. Kading and Leila Madeiros

The rationale for international insurance solvency regulation standards

Insurance is a global business. The top 18 general insurers and the top 27 life insurers write 50% of the global reinsurance premium.[1] This simple, astonishing statistic makes the case for why international prudential regulatory standards are necessary and relevant. For the commercial insurance and reinsurance markets it is easily understood that the customers themselves have international footprints, therefore insurance buyers are looking for global insurers who can meet their needs wherever the plant or office location happens to be. This necessitates agreement on cross-border provision of services, but also licensing of subsidiary and branch operations in markets around the world. These insurers have achieved economies of scale by serving global markets, but also are able to deliver insurance products more cheaply because they are able to pool risk and capital and thus achieve the benefits of diversification. Consumer benefits from the involvement of these international insurance groups include: additional capacity on an aggregate basis; additional capacity on a per risk basis; added competition on price; and product innovation and service.

For a decade now, insurance regulators and market participants have discussed various approaches to get to a coordinated, efficient system of prudential regulation that remains consistent with goals promoting international trade. Regulators have been focused on substantive regulation, while insurers have participated to ensure that non-discriminatory cross border competition is promoted. Both groups have committed themselves to efficient, effective regulation proportional to the market being addressed; and have expressed concerns about overlapping or redundant regulatory requirements that should be avoided. One can think of various optional approaches being arranged on a spectrum: on one end you have bilateral mutual recognition agreements where jurisdictions agree to recognise each other's regulatory requirements as part of a plan to provide reciprocal market access for their domestic insurers; in the middle one can put multilateral equivalence agreements where jurisdictions are recognised based on an evaluation of adherence to regulatory principles and then non-discriminatory market access will be provided to insurance groups from the so-called equivalent jurisdictions; and at the far end one can place a framework where multiple jurisdictions apply common regulatory requirements including capital measures upon internationally active insurance groups as a means to ensure such global insurers are regulated according to the same rules with clear designation of regulatory responsibilities. This chapter, and more broadly this book, reviews these various approaches.

In the aftermath of the global financial crisis the G20 group of nations has called for better coordination of regulation of the financial services business including insurance and also for standardisation of prudential solvency regulation requirements. The goal of the G20 and other policy-makers is for international principles to be commonly applied so that there can be confidence that these major insurance groups are subject to a level of supervision that is consistent around the world so that they can be benchmarked to a common standard. The contemporary term seems to be 'equivalency' – does regulation in different jurisdictions lead to an equivalent level of policy-holder protection? The goal of policy-makers is to establish a principles-based prudential supervision standard that leads to a system of regulation that allows regulators in one jurisdiction to trust, inform, cooperate and coordinate with (as appropriate to avoid duplicative regulation) with regulators in another jurisdiction. None of this is to say that this is easy, but the basic premise is 'trust and verify' against a common set of regulatory principles. Once the principles are in place, then information sharing can occur in a way that allows regulators to understand and interpret the data that are received, and then via a process infused with cooperation, trust can then be developed that will allow for coordinated supervision to prevail. Such a coordinated system of regulation needs to be efficient and avoid redundancy and contradiction. Efficiency would result from clear designation of regulatory responsibility so that regulatory arbitrage does not occur and so that gaps in regulation are eliminated. Additional regulatory powers that lead to overlapping, redundant or contradictory regulation will detract from the regulatory goals of the standard-setters.

Global prudential standards can lead to a means for common comparison among insurers domiciled in various jurisdictions. No one is presupposing that this will lead to uniform application of legal standards. But implementation of a principles based set of standards should be sufficient to lead to a degree of regulatory deference. Deference to a designated leader in supervision of an internationally active insurance group will lead to a higher quality regulation because of better informed and coordinated regulatory action. Further work may also be focused on a global standard setting system which may include a resolution framework that allows for an allocation of assets based on a rational resolution of a troubled company's liabilities. Ultimately, though, international standard-setting which will lead to recognition of equivalent regimes will boost consumer protection. It is this goal of aiding consumers that justifies the immense time and resource commitment to try to design an international prudential regulatory regime for insurers.

The G20 has also commented that the goal of developed economics must be to respond to the financial crisis in a way that does not lead to protectionism or limitations on cross border trade. Protectionist policies, be they tax or prudential regulation in nature, would largely disturb the insurance markets in the developed world and be at cross purposes to the global regulatory standard setting effort.

The work of the IAIS and the IMF with regard to evaluation of solvency regulation systems

Global commercial insurance markets are already integrated. The logical next question is can regulation be structured in such a way to efficiently and effectively regulate such internationally active insurance groups? The International Association of Insurance Supervisors (IAIS) is recognised as the international standard setting body for the insurance and reinsurance industry and works closely with other financial sector standard-setting bodies and international organisations such as the International Monetary Fund (IMF) and the Financial Stability Board (FSB) in an effort to promote financial stability. Never has this mission been more clearly appreciated since the global financial crisis and much debate has ensued as to how these organisations could best work together to minimise both the risks and the potential impacts to the financial markets.

The IAIS was formed in 1994 to improve supervision of the insurance industry both on a local and international level in order to maintain efficient, fair, safe and stable insurance markets for the benefit and protection of policy-holders, promote the development of well-regulated insurance markets and contribute to global financial stability (IAIS By-laws, 2004). The IAIS has worked diligently over the past 15 years to develop principles, standards and guidance which represent best practices for insurance supervisors to adopt within their own regulatory systems where appropriate. The IAIS Insurance Core Principles (ICPs) and Methodology, adopted in October 2003, provide an extensive menu of principles relating to various aspects of insurance supervision that when applied in practice provide a framework for which the evaluation of solvency regulation systems can be carried out. The IAIS recognises that many regulatory regimes and legal frameworks exist across its membership but that there are fundamental elements of regulation that can be applied across regulatory regimes in order to provide base line protections for policy-holders and financial stability in the insurance marketplace.

The ICPs form the basis by which both internal regulatory and external independent assessments can be made to evaluate whether or not a particular jurisdictional insurance supervisory regime is meeting the benchmark. National supervisors can perform a self-assessment to measure their own regulatory regime against the principles in an effort to identify any weaknesses or shortfalls or to address whether or not a particular principle is appropriate given the market it regulates. This is not dissimilar to other financial sector standards set by the Basel Committee on Banking Supervision (BCBS) for banks or the International Organization of Securities Commissions (IOSCO) for investment bodies or the International Association of Deposit Insurers (IADI).

The IAIS ICPs, standards and guidance are crafted and developed through the process of subcommittees made up of participating IAIS member regulators and industry representatives and are consulted with on a broad basis and then voted on for adoption by members. The IAIS has undertaken extensive work as of late to revamp its ICPs and to create a uniform formula for designing the standards and the relevant guidance in order to provide greater clarity as to the expectations of best practice. In addition, the set of ICPs, for example, provide a vehicle by which the regulatory and supervisory regime of a country can be assessed for compliance with best practice and therefore can gain recognition for having done so. As far back as 2002, the IAIS contemplated some form of 'mutual recognition' in the adoption of its 'Principles on Minimum Requirements for Supervision of Reinsurers', on 11 October 2002, at a time when the supervision of reinsurers in some jurisdictions was minimal at best or absent altogether and there was a growing recognition with the global expansion of the reinsurance market that there was a need for internationally recognised principles for the supervision of reinsurers. Having adopted a set of detailed ICPs, the IAIS definitively established a benchmark by which insurance and reinsurance regulatory regimes around the globe could be assessed.

These efforts greatly assist the work of the IMF in conducting its assessments of the compliance of national systems with financial sector standards and codes. The IMF is heavily involved in financial sector surveillance through its Financial Sector Assessment Programme (FSAP). As of May 2010, the IMF reports that more than 150 assessments under the FSAP have been conducted.[2] The IAIS ICPs form a uniform 'exam sheet' as it were, by which the IMF can 'grade' a country's compliance with those recognised standards established by the IAIS. While there is recognition that the FSAP 'has limitations as a surveillance tool',[3] it provides an opportunity for independent assessment which can be utilised by other national jurisdictions and other organisations to make determinations regarding the level of compliance with IAIS standards and therefore whether or not that country's regime could be accepted as being equivalent or compliant with internationally recognised standards.

The work of the IAIS with regard to reinsurance regulatory equivalency assessments

In October 2007 the IAIS adopted a 'Discussion Paper on the Mutual Recognition of Reinsurance Supervision' (DP) prepared by the IAIS Reinsurance Mutual Recognition Subgroup in consultation with IAIS Members and Observers. Roughly eight jurisdictions account for approximately 90% of the worldwide reinsurance capacity. The DP suggests that mutual recognition of reinsurance supervision would facilitate the cross-border supply of reinsurance by developing a framework for efficient and effective international supervision by allowing a supervisor to recognise the quality of the supervision exercised by another jurisdiction which would in theory result in reducing unnecessary regulatory requirements. The DP summarises the benefits of mutual recognition and the standardisation of regulation and supervision to reinsurers to maybe include: reduced compliance costs; less work in seeking market access; greater certainty of the regulatory process; fewer barriers to entry in new locations and more efficient allocation of capital with the removal of regulatory barriers to the flow of capital between companies in reinsurance groups. Benefits for the supervisors are lower administrative costs by utilisation of existing comparable supervisory regimes; greater dedication of resources to domestic supervision; improved collaboration with their counterparts in other jurisdictions and less regulatory arbitrage. However, there is recognition of the risks to mutual recognition, one of which is the lack of harmonisation in the regulatory requirements set by jurisdictions. It could be argued that since the publication of the DP, other regulatory action such as the Solvency II Directive in Europe will – at least across Europe – have the effect of 'harmonizing' the regulatory approach exercised by European Economic Area (EEA) countries. And further, can be extended in practice to those countries outside of the EEA which agree to adopt the principles of Solvency II and are found to be equivalent (see below).

As mentioned above, even in the backdrop of a common set of standards, it really does come back to the basic premise of 'trust and verify', and to that end the IAIS developed a template Multilateral Memorandum of Understanding on Cooperation and Information Exchange (IAIS MMoU), adopted in February 2007. The aim of the development of the IAIS MMoU was to create a framework for improved cooperation amongst IAIS members by setting high standards for the protection of confidential information – the 'trust', and secondly, by establishing cross-border protocols and practices for expansion of international insurance business – the 'verify'. The current ongoing work by the IAIS to revise its ICPs to incorporate the IAIS MMoU principles together with the IAIS Guidance Paper on the Use of Supervisory Colleges in Group-Wide Supervision (2009) and other group-wide supervisory standards will assist in creating a regulatory equivalence assessment framework whereby jurisdictions can measure both themselves and other regulators under a common set of standards.

See below for further details of the IAIS and its efforts to create a common insurance regulation assessment framework.

Europe's Solvency II and the international regulatory equivalence framework

Europe's Solvency II provides a leading example of the development of a proposed insurance regulatory equivalency system. Embedded in Solvency II is a mechanism to recognize the regulatory regimes of so-called equivalent jurisdictions. The purpose of this is to assure better policy-holder protection in light of the predominance of global insurance groups, many domiciled outside the EU, which provide important insurance coverage to EU citizens and businesses. The directive creates a system of regulation which may lead to avoidance of duplicate regulation or contradictory regulation. It also works to enhance regulatory cooperation via a framework for group solvency calculation and group supervision. If the system results in efficient regulation then that will lead to lower insurance costs for consumers. Alternatively, if such standards do not lead to regulatory efficiencies they can lead to added regulatory costs from duplicate or contradictory regulation which will create costs that will have to be passed on to consumers.

Under the EU process, the European Commission has the power to grant equivalency. The Council of European Insurance and Occupational Pension Supervisors (CEIOPS) provides advice to the Commission and in turn carries out actions as directed by the Commission. During the time period in which this chapter was written, CEIOPS had delivered its preliminary advice, received comments from stakeholders and then published its final advice. The Commission was expected in the autumn of 2010 to provide further direction to CEIOPS with regard to the equivalence assessment criteria and methodology. Under the CEIOPS proposals, so-called third countries will be evaluated based on the outcomes associated with their prudential supervision frameworks. The jurisdictions would be expected to be found equivalent based on a measurement of principles and objectives outlined in the paper. The equivalency process will review more than 100 indicators which will be used to measure whether or not the principles and objectives are likely to be met. There is no requirement that all the indicators be met, but rather an expectation that on the whole the indicators allow an opportunity for the assessment team to conclude that the principles that are identified can be met by the regulators in the third country. The equivalency framework is divided into three sections: (1) regulation of reinsurers; equivalence under Article 172 of the level 1 text; (2) measurement of group capital requirements; in relation to Article 227 of the level 1 text, group solvency of a participating undertaking in a third country insurance or reinsurance undertaking where deduction and aggregation is used to calculate group solvency; and (3) execution of a group supervision framework, solely in relation to Article 260 of the level 1 text, third country group supervision.

Jorgen Holmquist, in his 11 June 2010 letter to Gabriel Bernadino (CEIOPS Chair), noted the following with regard to equivalence assessments:

> I fully agree with the statement made in your letter that the overarching principle should be to ensure that the third country supervisory regime ensures a similar level of policy holder and beneficiary protection as the one provided under Solvency II. Solvency II adopts an economic risk-based approach to insurance regulation and the equivalence assessment provides us with a real opportunity to converge internationally towards a risk-based approach. Consequently, it is my view that the equivalence assessments should focus on the substantive issue of whether the third country (re)insurance undertakings are subject to a risk-based supervisory regime.[4]

Embedded in the Solvency II equivalency system is also recognition that enactment of exact, identical regulatory requirements in multiple jurisdictions is not required. Rather, the measurement test is on the equivalency of outcomes associated with the regulatory regimes. Equivalency is also associated with common assessment and measurement so that comparable measures of capital, liabilities and assets can be measured across the various regulatory regimes. Another key ingredient is the principle of proportionality. Again, this principle is not well defined but rather is recognised as a flexible framework that allows regulators to evaluate the regulatory regime in a jurisdiction and assess whether the regulatory framework allows for a legitimate regulatory framework to be fairly applied to an insurance sector in such a way that is proportional to the consumer impact or economic impact of that segment.

In the Commission's advice to CEIOPS delivered in June 2010, the Commission identified five points upon which CEIOPS should make recommendations with regard to which third country jurisdictions should be first evaluated for equivalency. Those criteria are:

(a) whether the third country currently has a supervisory regime that is fully risk-based or has taken measures to move towards such a system;
(b) the materiality of an equivalence finding to EU insurance and reinsurance undertakings and their policy-holders;
(c) the number of related undertakings situated in the third country held by EU insurance and reinsurance undertakings;

(d) the importance to the insurance market in the third country of the equivalence finding; and
(e) the existence currently of mutual recognition or equivalent arrangements between third countries and Member States.[5]

CEIOPS in its March 2010 advice to the Commission entitled *CEIOPS' Advice for Level 2 Implementing Measures on Solvency II: Technical Criteria for Assessing Third Country Equivalence in Relation to Art. 172, 227 and 260*, published criteria for how CEIOPS would evaluate third countries.

'Equivalence assessments will aim to ensure that the third country regulatory and supervisory regimes provide a similar level of policyholder/beneficiary protection as the one provided under the Solvency II Directive.'[6] CEIOPS further noted: 'This stands as an overarching principle of CEIOPS' advice i.e. it must be met by the third country in relation to each of the above mentioned areas (reinsurance supervision, group solvency calculations and group supervision) for which equivalence is being assessed.'[7]

With regard to equivalence under Article 172 for reinsurance, the CEIOPS paper sets forth six principles, defines an objective and then identifies 130 indicators that would be evaluated as to whether these principles and objectives were met. The CEIOPS' advice notes: 'It should be noted that when assessing a particular principle and objective, every indicator does not necessarily need to be fulfilled in order for principle and objective to be considered observed.'[8]

The six principles and objectives that must be met by the third country include:

1. *Powers and responsibilities of the supervisory authority*. The supervisor must have the means and the 'relevant, expertise, capacity and mandate to achieve the main objectives of supervision, namely the protection of policyholders and beneficiaries regardless of their nationality or residence. They have to have the resources to fulfill their objectives which includes in particular financial and human resources.'[9] CEIOPS notes that for this principle to be met the authority has to be legally empowered to carry out this obligation.
2. *Authorisation requirements*. This objective notes that the reinsurance business must be subject to prior authorisation to ensure that the undertakings satisfy basic standards prior to becoming authorised and on a continuous basis thereafter.[10]
3. *System of governance*. This objective cites an obligation for the undertaking to have in place 'an effective system of governance ... which provides for a sound and prudent management of the reinsurance business'. Further, there must be 'adequate risk management, compliance, internal audit and actuarial functions'. There must be public financial statements to evaluate the 'financial performance'.[11]

4. *Proposed changes to the business operations and management.* This principle includes prior notice of acquisitions, an ability to analyse the acquisition, notice of disposal of qualified holding, change in management and control and definition of thresholds determining various regulatory reviews.[12]
5. *Solvency assessment.* The supervisor must ensure that the reinsurer maintains adequate financial resources to prevent 'disorderly failure', and the authority shall establish requirements for technical provisions that are calculated in a way 'that enables them to meet their (re)insurance obligations towards the ceding undertaking'. Further, 'capital requirements should be based on sound economic principles and reflect a level of eligible own funds of sufficient quality that insurance and reinsurance undertakings are able to absorb significant losses and gives reasonable assurance to policyholders and beneficiaries that payments will be made as they fall due'.[13]
6. *Supervisory cooperation, exchange of information and professional secrecy.* The third country authority must have in place the legal authority and means to coordinate with other regulators, exchange information and ensure that the supervisory parties are bound by professional secrecy.[14] This requirement is also applied to the other two subjects of regulatory equivalence.

With regard to equivalence under Article 227, insurance groups' solvency calculation, the CEIOPS paper cites two principles and objectives which apply to this equivalency assessment which is relevant to European groups which have undertakings outside of the EU.

1. *Solvency assessment.* This first objective is the same as the one described above with regard to reinsurance assessment with the addition of one noteworthy item. The additional criterion regards 'own funds'. 'There should be sufficient information on the constitution of own funds to ensure that the group supervisor is able to apply the technical principles to the group solvency assessment (e.g. the elimination of double use of eligible own funds.)'[15]
2. *Supervisory cooperation.* This is the same as principle six for the reinsurance assessment with the addition of one explanatory note. The addition states: 'Supervisory cooperation is important, in particular, to assist the group supervisor to assess the undertaking's contribution to the group capital requirement and the availability (inter alia transferability and fungibility) of own funds for the whole group.'[16]

Thus, with the CEIOPS paper, the reader begins to appreciate that the core regulatory principles can be applied broadly to each of the three areas of equivalence assessment. The principles are applied in the context of the assessment being made. So in the case of the groups' solvency calculation, the key issue for supervisors is to be able to measure 'own funds', eliminate double-counting and ensure that the regulators of the various entities have access to and share financial information to enforce the principles being applied.

The third equivalency assessment is applicable to group supervision, as defined in Article 260 of the Solvency II directive.

There are seven principles to be measured:

1. *Powers and responsibilities of a group supervisor.* This principle is the same as the first being applied to reinsurance undertakings assessment. Again, for the purpose of the groups' assessment, an additional contextual note is applied: 'Supervisors of insurers within a group must be able to form a comprehensive view of the overall group business strategy, financial position, legal and regulatory position and the risk exposure of the group as a whole, which will enable supervisors to assess and react to the prudential situation and solvency of the respective insurers within the group.'[17]
2. *Group supervision.* This objective, unique, to the groups' assessment, requires that the supervisory regime has a framework for determining which undertakings fall within the scope of supervision at group level: 'undertakings controlled (through significant or dominant influence e.g.) by the group shall be included in the scope of group supervision'; 'All parts of the group (including holdings, other financial sectors, off-balance sheets items) necessary to ensure a proper understanding of the group and the potential sources of risks within the group have to be included within the scope of group supervision.'[18]
3. *Provisions to allow 'efficient and effective supervision' through cooperation and exchange of information among supervisors.* This simply stated principle requires that effective coordination and cooperation procedures be in place to allow for successful group supervision. The item makes it clear that a simple exchange of information is insufficient to meet the objective.[19]
4. *System of governance.* This is the same as principle 3 of the reinsurance assessment, with the appropriate modifications to reference groups.[20]
5. *Business change assessment.* This is the same as reinsurance assessment principle 4.[21]
6. *Group solvency assessment.* This is similar to principle 5 of the reinsurance assessment, but again it has been modified to be appropriate to a group regulatory regime. The additional provisions relate to a requirement that 'calculation methods of the group capital requirement shall lead to a result at least equivalent to one of the two methods of the Level 1 text (consolidation method, aggregation method)'. And 'Each undertaking within the group maintains a minimum level of financial resources, below which it should not fall. This assessment should also include how non-insurance undertakings are considered as part of group supervision and how contagion risk is dealt with.'[22]

7. *Supervisory cooperation, exchange of information and professional secrecy*. This is the same as principle 6 of the reinsurance assessment and principle 2 of the group solvency calculation assessment.[23]

In July 2010 CEIOPS proposed a list of jurisdictions to the Commission that will be assessed for equivalence during a 'first wave'. It is recommending Switzerland and Bermuda for a comprehensive equivalency assessment and Japan for a reinsurance equivalency assessment.

The Commission was likely to provide its final direction to CEIOPS on which jurisdictions to assess by mid November 2010. The CEIOPS equivalence assessments of third countries would then commence in December and by recommendations would be provided to the Commission by July 2011. The Commission would consult with other parties and likely render its opinion on which third countries could be granted equivalency by mid-year 2012. The Solvency II directive's effective date is now intended to be 31 December 2012. The equivalence jurisdictions need to be identified in advance of the Solvency II effective date so that EU regulators will know how to meet the regulatory tests associated with international active insurance groups.

The IAIS's efforts to create a common insurance regulatory assessment framework

The European Solvency II project and equivalence can be viewed as an attempt to get to regulatory principles applicable to a major trading block. But can a global framework also be created? The IAIS has long recognised the need to create a common insurance regulation assessment framework since its beginnings in 1994, considering its membership of over 190 country supervisory authorities, and since 1999, which today includes involvement of 120 industry representatives referred to as 'observers'. It can be appreciated that with a huge number of constituent jurisdictions and the relevant supervisory authorities represented and the unique legal systems and markets, a common insurance regulatory framework might seem like a near-impossible outcome. However, with the increased globalisation of both the insurance and reinsurance markets, it was deemed imperative that the IAIS develop a common assessment framework, and in 2005 the IAIS took a giant step forward in reaching toward that goal by adopting a policy paper entitled 'A New Framework for Insurance Supervision: Towards a Common Structure and Common Standards for the Assessment of Insurer Solvency' ('Framework Paper')' and an associated paper, 'Cornerstones for the Formulation of Regulatory Financial Requirements' ('Cornerstones Paper').

Prior to these two papers, much of the IAIS's work had focused on a wide range of specific aspects relating to insurance supervision as evidenced in the creation and adoption of Insurance Core Principles and Methodology back in

2003 which would be used by insurance supervisors as the basic benchmark for assessing their own insurance regulatory and supervisory frameworks. However, the adoption by the IAIS of a 'new framework' in 2005 signalled a recognition that indeed not only was there a need to respond to the development of the global insurance and reinsurance marketplace and the relevant financial solvency and implications of operating across various jurisdictions, but also to determine how best policy-holder protection might be achieved in such a dynamic environment. Further to the equation was added the element of convergence across other financial sectors which would require the need for a common approach which could be 'globally acceptable' (2005 Framework Paper) and, more importantly, applied and understood across many jurisdictions. Since 2005, the IAIS has been extremely busy and prolific in developing standards and guidance that provide a principles-based approach to assessing the three areas of the common framework: financial requirements, governance and market conduct issues.

The IAIS in its work does not subscribe to the premise that all jurisdictions must have the same regulatory framework, as this would be both unrealistic and impractical given the multitude of legal and regulatory systems represented by the IAIS membership. The emphasis has been on creating a common framework based on core principles that could be implanted and embedded across the regimes of its members and therefore creating 'the major benchmark for jurisdictions in developing and updating their own solvency regimes and supervision' (16 February 2006 IAIS Roadmap for a Common Structure and Common Standards for the Assessment of Insurer Solvency). More recently, the IAIS has undergone a major project to revamp its ICPs to reflect the changes and activities of major regulatory regimes and events since 2003. With the pending implementation of the Solvency II Directive in 2013, the IAIS has also initiated a further initiative to address the treatment of globally active insurance and reinsurance groups – 'ComFrame'. ComFrame was officially launched on 1 July 2010 and is itself a further step in creating a common language and assessment framework for supervisors with oversight of groups which transpire across jurisdictional boundaries. This project is most in line with the concept of creating common regulatory requirements for internationally active insurance groups. More information on ComFrame is provided in another chapter of this book.

The path to effective international regulatory agreements

After a decade of discussion, it seems that we are on the cusp of sovereign jurisdictions entering into international insurance prudential regulatory frameworks. With the enactment of a new US federal law allowing the negotiation of international prudential insurance supervisory agreements and with the coming effective date of Europe's Solvency II, we will likely see by 2013 implementation of regulatory regimes that officially recognise the regulatory regimes of another jurisdiction. This must be considered a milestone. After much discussion of a variety of alternatives from multilateral mutual recognition agreements regarding reinsurance supervision, to bilateral agreements on solvency regulation and the IMF's FSAP of the IAIS principles for insurance supervision, it appears that the first steps will likely be taken in the European Union with the recognition of equivalent jurisdictions. This may well lead to recognition agreements (broad or narrow) between the EU and the US government in a bilateral approach to the recognition of other regulators.

The IAIS has been at work the longest on the development of international regulatory principles and it will ultimately be the body that is able to best define, promote, assess and monitor such standards. Today, international regulatory standards are being discussed by the IAIS in the ComFrame project. But prior to the implementation of the so-called ComFrame there may be bilateral or multilateral recognition frameworks. In the end, the path towards regulatory equivalency (or mutual recognition) seems logically to follow these steps: (1) enactment of common regulatory principles that are expected to lead to specific regulatory outcomes (via IAIS principles on solvency regulation); (2) cooperative arrangements amongst regulators via regulatory colleges (bilateral or multilateral agreements as envisioned by US financial services reform or the EU's Solvency II directive); (3) information and regulatory cooperation that leads to trust among regulators (via the IAIS MMoU); and (4), with practical experience and real world experience, trust is established that can lead to regulatory deference. This means regulators relying upon each other in such a way as to avoid regulatory redundancy and inefficiency and avoid contradictions in regulatory requirements. The IAIS ComFrame project seems to build upon this foundation and could be a means to propose actual regulatory requirements that would be applied by cooperative sovereign states to insurance groups that are designated as internationally active.

Inevitably, the power to implement, experiment or enforce regulatory recognition agreements can only be held by sovereign governments. International associations such as the IAIS can propose standards and regulatory frameworks, but it will not likely ever gain the legal power to enforce such agreements and compel enforcement action. That power will rest with the sovereign states who will need to be convinced that such agreements with legally enforceable powers will provide enough of a benefit to their consumers that the political risk associated with such international agreements will be accepted. The global regulatory jurisdictions will only get to this position via a process of trial and error in the coming years. Much progress has been made, much work remains to be done.

Notes and references

1. Presentation, FINMA Deputy Chair, Monica Maechler, PROGRES, The Geneva Association Conference, April 2010.

2. J. Vinals and J. Fiechter (2010) *The Making of Good Supervision: Learning to say 'No'* (Washington, DC: IMF).
3. IMF (2010) *Financial Sector Surveillance and the Mandate of the Fund* (Washington, DC: IIMF), March.
4. European Commission, Consultative Document, *Draft Call for Advice from CEIOPS, Third Country Equivalence*, cover letter, page 1 (11 June 2010).
5. European Commission, Consultative Document, *Draft Call for Advice from CEIOPS, Third Country Equivalence*, 2.1 Cfa.5, page 4 (11 June 2010).
6. Page 3, 1.4, *CEIOPS' Advice for Level 2 Implementing Measures on Solvency II: Technical Criteria for Assessing Third Country Equivalence in Relation to Art. 172, 227 and 260* (March 2010).
7. Page 3, 1.4, *CEIOPS' Advice for Level 2 Implementing Measures on Solvency II.*
8. Page 3, 1.3, *CEIOPS' Advice for Level 2 Implementing Measures on Solvency II.*
9. Page 9, 2.3.10 and 2.3.11, *CEIOPS' Advice*, formerly CP 78.
10. Page 11, 2.3.20, *CEIOPS' Advice*, formerly CP 78.
11. Pages 12 and 13, 2.3.27, 2.3.28 and 2.3.29, *CEIOPS' Advice*, formerly CP 78.
12. Page 14, 2.3.38, *CEIOPS' Advice*, formerly CP 78.
13. Page 15, 2.3.45, 2.3.46, and 2.3.47, *CEIOPS' Advice*, formerly CP 78.
14. Page 18, 2.3.56, *CEIOPS' Advice*, formerly CP 78.
15. Page 23, 3.3.13, *CEIOPS' Advice*, formerly CP 78.
16. Page 26, 3.3.23, *CEIOPS' Advice*, formerly CP 78.
17. Page 38, 4.3.31, *CEIOPS' Advice*, formerly CP 78.
18. Page 40, 4.3.40 and 4.3.41, *CEIOPS' Advice*, formerly CP 78.
19. Pages 40 and 41, 4.3.46, *CEIOPS' Advice*, formerly CP 78.
20. Pages 42 and 43, 4.3.54, 4.3.55 and 4.3.56, *CEIOPS' Advice*, formerly CP 78.
21. Page 44, 4.3.65, *CEIOPS' Advice*, formerly CP 78.
22. Page 45, 4.3.75 and 4.3.76, *CEIOPS' Advice*, formerly CP 78.
23. Page 49, 4.3.86, *CEIOPS' Advice*, formerly CP 78.

23
The Regulatory Future of International Insurance Centres: Balancing Sound Supervision, Innovation and Competition[1]

Marcelo Ramella

Introduction

> In the absence of a global financial regulator, central bank or fiscal authority, it proved difficult in the recent crisis to ensure the safety and soundness of globally active financial institutions ex ante, and almost impossible to address their liquidity and solvency problems ex post without causing further systemic disruptions.
>
> These are genuine, serious concerns. But I will argue that we can ensure that the benefits of global financial integration outweigh the costs. Keeping local problems from turning global requires both strengthening and harmonising financial supervision across borders. (Cecchetti, 2010, p. 1)

Stephen Cecchetti's reflections on the current global financial crisis capture nicely some of the key learning and future challenges emerging from recent events. Supervisory bodies operating within national-level boundaries appeared ill-equipped to address some of the problems generated by financial institutions functioning on a global scale; looking ahead, financial supervision must enhance its ability to successfully operate across national borders. On the other hand, following Cecchetti's train of thought, it must aim to achieve this while preserving 'the benefits of global financial integration'.

This chapter explores the debate at the intersection of cross-border supervision enhancement and global financial integration by looking at the regulatory future of international insurance centres. Insurance is a constitutive element of the global financial system, of which future regulation and supervision is subject to strong winds of reform; international insurance centres are, perhaps more than any other component in the insurance sector, at the very core of the debate. The chapter argues that international insurance centres are a complex phenomenon that cannot be reduced to its quantitative dimension, that is, the comparatively large amount of cross-border business written in these centres. Qualitative issues, such as the cluster-like network of services supporting their insurance sector, the political and economic stability experienced by the countries hosting the centres, and the centres' embeddedness within their local economic sphere, are key factors that have to be considered in making sense of current – and future – approaches to global insurance regulation and supervision. This is specifically critical in understanding the relationship between strengthening regulation and supervision of the global insurance business, and enabling the development of innovation and competition in the insurance sector.

The chapter is organised as follows. The first part explores the concept of the international insurance centre, looking at quantitative and qualitative elements that define and characterise them. It discusses literature on the matter generated by various academic disciplines interested in the phenomenon; it also provides examples drawn from illustrations from the international insurance centres themselves, especially from the international insurance centre of Bermuda. The second part examines current policy initiatives in relation to cross-border issues regarding insurance regulation and supervision, looking at attempts to formalise information exchange and cooperation between supervisors, as well as discussing proposals aimed at systematising the reliance by one supervisor on the work done by another supervisor (that is, the supervisory recognition debate). The chapter concludes with reflections on challenges ahead faced by the international insurance centres themselves and by the various insurance regulation policy reforms in progress.

Making sense of international insurance centres

There is no shortage of literature looking at the issue of international financial centres. The matter appears addressed from a wide variety of angles. Economists for example have considered the domestic welfare-generating potential of these centres (Park, 1982; Suss et al., 2002). Within finance studies, interest has revolved around understanding the flows of cross-border activity (Cassard, 1994). Political geography has looked at the impact of globalisation in redefining spaces and places, which appear to be more and more socially constructed (Hudson, 1998). Anthropology has taken an interest in the complexities and significations of due diligence processes (Maurer, 2005). Within sociology, Donaghy and Clarke (2003) have challenged the often homogenising impulse with respect to international financial centres, arguing that to better understand these we must focus on differences between them and not just similarities. Political theory has examined, among other things, the challenges posed by international financial centres to the concept of sovereignty (Roberts, 1995). Interestingly, the large majority of these texts focus on the banking sector. The word 'banking' is often used as a synonym of 'financial' when making reference to international financial centres (Zoromé, 2007).

Importantly, independently from the financial sector in question, that is, banking, insurance or otherwise, the word 'international' has been subject to extended debate. One such debate has probably concentrated a great deal of academic and policy attention: the concept of 'international' in relation to that of 'offshore'. While some treat the terms 'international' and 'offshore' interchangeably (Zoromé, 2007), others distinguish sharply between the two. Moreover, the concept of international is often broken down into 'onshore' and 'offshore', with the latter being characterised by a variety of – often highly critical – significations that transcend the cross-border meaning of the term international (FSF, 2000; IMF, 2000). Others argue that the negativity frequently attached to the concept of 'offshore' more often than not applies to the notion 'onshore' as well (UN, 2009). Further, according to the International Monetary Fund, so called 'offshore' centres have undergone substantial transformations during the first decade of the twenty-first century, which have derived the concept of 'offshore' from many of the controversial connotations identified in the late twentieth century (IMF, 2008a). With respect to the international versus offshore/onshore debate, this chapter focuses on the former and not on the latter. Moreover, and probably most importantly, it examines the international dimension of insurance centres, exploring it from a quantitative as well as a qualitative perspective.

Looking at the issue from a quantitative angle, an arbitrary, although useful port of entry into international financial centres in general, and international insurance centres in particular, is the work done over the past couple of decades on the matter by the International Monetary Fund (IMF).[2] The IMF proposes to group under such a banner all countries or jurisdictions providing financial services – including insurance – to non-residents, on a scale incommensurate with the size and the financing of their domestic economy. Importantly, the IMF determines the incommensurability of the financial services provided by looking at the ratio of net financial services exports to gross domestic product (GDP), and defines it as incommensurable if it falls above one standard deviation of the mean of the population of financial centres (Zoromé, 2007). In so doing, it identifies a list of 22 countries and jurisdictions spanning from Barbados to Vanuatu, from Singapore to Switzerland and the UK.[3]

Following Zoromé's logic we call international insurance centres that subgroup of international financial centres with cross-border insurance operations that are incommensurate to their domestic insurance markets.[4] In so doing, nine out of Zoromé's original list of 22 countries and jurisdictions qualify as such, that is: Bermuda, the Cayman Islands, Guernsey, Ireland, the Isle of Man, Luxembourg, Singapore, Switzerland and the United Kingdom.

The quantitatively defined list of international insurance centres derived from Zoromé's work may not be considered fully exempt from shortcomings. For example, the notion of 'centre' shows some definitional porosity. While Zoromé's study includes countries and other jurisdictions such as the Cayman Islands, it excludes places like the US state of Delaware, which has a long history of activity as an international financial centre (UN, 2009). Notwithstanding this criticism, the quantitative approach to defining an international insurance centre provides a valid tool to draw, however porous, an initial boundary around the phenomenon.

Looking at the quantitative dimension in practice and examining closely the relationship between cross-border insurance activity and GDP, Bermuda provides probably the most compelling case of an international insurance centre. Data from 2008 show aggregate gross written premiums of US$145 billion,[5] and an estimated GDP of US$6.09 billion,[6] making Bermuda a valid example of a centre where the volume of insurance is incommensurate to that of the domestic economy.[7] Figure 23.1 and Table 23.1 provide insurance and GDP data for the period 1981–2008.

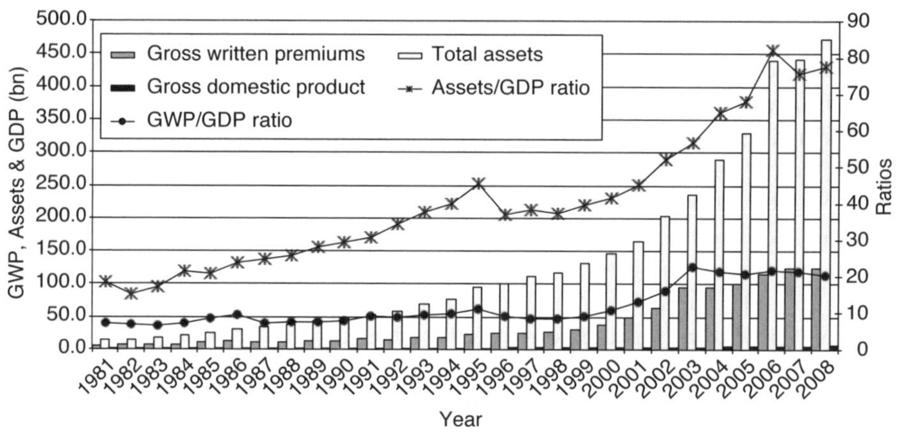

Figure 23.1 Bermuda: insurance market and GDP

In addition to the cross-border element, the literature has identified a multiplicity of qualitative elements that contribute to the notion of international financial centres. For example, Cassard (1994, p. 41) singles out the following factors: 'stable macroeconomic and political environment', 'modern infrastructure and communications network', 'proximity to a growing region', and 'high level of regulatory rectitude'. Kaufman (2000), in addition, argues that these centres also possess a 'well-educated and sophisticated workforce' serving the financial

Table 23.1 Bermuda: insurance market (US$ bn)

	Gross written premiums	Total assets	Gross domestic product	Assets/ GDP ratio	GWP/ GDP ratio
1981	5.7	14.8	0.7996	19	7
1982	6.2	13.6	0.9053	15	7
1983	6.5	17.1	1.0034	17	6
1984	7.6	22.2	1.0395	21	7
1985	10.1	24.5	1.1735	21	9
1986	12.4	30.9	1.2965	24	10
1987	10.3	34.9	1.4151	25	7
1988	11.1	38.7	1.5020	26	7
1989	12.0	44.5	1.5920	28	8
1990	13.0	48.0	1.6350	29	8
1991	15.4	52.3	1.7050	31	9
1992	15.1	58.8	1.7200	34	9
1993	17.9	69.9	1.8640	38	10
1994	18.8	76.1	1.9140	40	10
1995	23.4	95.0	2.0830	46	11
1996	25.1	99.9	2.7141	37	9
1997	25.4	111.8	2.9328	38	9
1998	26.6	116.4	3.1307	37	8
1999	30.4	131.6	3.3244	40	9
2000	38.1	146.0	3.5079	42	11
2001	48.5	165.3	3.6608	45	13
2002	63.3	204.0	3.9198	52	16
2003	94.7	236.0	4.1688	57	23
2004	95.3	290.2	4.4646	65	21
2005	100.7	329.8	4.8461	68	21
2006	115.8	440.4	5.3564	82	22
2007	124.4	442.3	5.8550	76	21
2008	123.6	473.0	6.0930	78	20

industry and the regulator. The paragraphs below provide some illustrations of these qualitative elements in practice by looking at examples from the identified international insurance centres.

Looking at the stability of the *macroeconomic and political environment*, the literature identifies sustained economic growth as well as stable macroeconomic variables, especially inflation, as conducive to the generation of international financial activity. In addition, robust, validated and well-functioning political institutions are singled out as critical factors. In this respect, and taking Bermuda as an illustration, both the Bermuda economy and political framework appear to have contributed significantly to it emerging as a large international insurance centre. In fact, regarding the former, Bermuda has one of the highest income-per-capita levels in the world and has enjoyed a long period of economic growth and low inflation. With respect to the latter, two factors appear to have played a part in Bermuda's political stability. First, Bermuda's status as a British Dependent Territory; Bermuda is the oldest self-governing British Overseas Territory. And second, Bermuda's system of government, which is based on the Westminster Model of parliamentary democracy. Extending the Bermuda example, macroeconomic and political stability are defining traits of all the other international insurance centres identified earlier: the Cayman Islands, Guernsey, Ireland, the Isle of Man, Luxembourg, Singapore, Switzerland and the UK.

There is another angle from which to approach the issue of political and economic stability in relation to international insurance. This can be understood as a relationship, one that bears a multiplicity of deeper significations. While it is the case that financial markets, especially international ones, seek stability as a condition for carrying out business, so do the governments in the centres hosting the financial markets. Further, governments often make concerted efforts in order to generate and, more importantly, to maintain the conditions of possibility for the emergence of international financial centres (Kersell, 1985; Suss et al., 2002; UN, 2009). Although this has been especially the case since the collapse of Bretton Woods in the early 1970s (Hudson, 1998), according to Palan (1998a, 1998b) the phenomenon has a longer and more complex history. The cases of Switzerland (Pearson, 2001) and the City of London in the UK (HMT, 2009) provide compelling examples of this point.

Critically, the relation between political and economic stability on the one hand, and international finance on the other, responds not just to historical developments such as the abandonment of the gold standard but should be seen as a broader trend marked by increased governmental efforts towards promoting entrepreneurship and competition at every level of society, including government itself (Foucault, 2005; Roberts, 1995; Kersell, 1985).

A further key qualitative factor contributing to making sense of international insurance centres is made up of the centre's infrastructure and networks. This encompasses physical as much as social and institutional factors, from roads, airports and information technology to clusters of support services, forums and other 'soft' networks. For example, Nachum (2003) has shown how these factors have played, and continue to play, a crucial part in the strength shown by the London wholesale insurance market, as a genuinely international centre. Concrete factors span widely and include, for example, the high concentration of knowledge within a tight geographic area, the high quality of local service suppliers, or the size and professionalism of the locally available labour force. Focusing on knowledge and its circulation Thrift (1994) highlights the value added by close-knit networks operating in the City of London. Moreover, in a study of the Bermuda insurance market, Pitt (2006) singles out the role played by supporting industries such as insurance brokers, law firms, accounting firms and others as a key factor contributing to the development of Bermuda as what he calls a 'Silicon Valley' of insurance. As an illustrative example, with over 100 actuaries and a population of approximately 64,000 people in the international insurance centre, Bermuda is home to the largest concentration of actuaries in the world (Gribble, 2006).

Another qualitative element identified in the literature is that of the location of the international insurance centre. Within this debate (see, for example, Roberts, (1995; Hudson, 1998), there are at least two elements that can contribute to better understand the phenomenon of international insurance centres: the relative location of these places, and the absolute attributes of the space hosting the centres. In the case of Bermuda, for example, its relative location can be described as just over 1,000 kilometres east of the shores of North Carolina, in the North Atlantic Ocean, or under two hours away by plane from New York City and approximately six hours away from London. It is likely that Bermuda's location has contributed to its development as a centre serving the US and London markets. For example, in 2008 Bermuda reinsurers assumed approximately half of the insurance ceded cross-border by US insurers,[8] and over a quarter of Lloyds' premiums.[9] Moreover, Rose and Spiegel (2005) suggest that the relative location of an international financial centre close to a large financial centre contributes to the competitiveness of the large centre served by the international one. Similar observations could be made of the islands of Guernsey and the Isle of Man in relation to Europe or, Singapore, in relation to Southeast Asia.

In addition to relative location there is the issue of the space as such. Again, looking at Bermuda, and in addition to the points discussed above regarding stability and infrastructure, key features that seem to have contributed to its condition of being an international centre are, for example: a comparatively high standard of living, minimal commuting times, well connected airport facilities, and subtropical climate. Or further, a survey by the Insurance Managers Association of Cayman (IMAC) identified 'weather' and 'beach' as the second and third main reasons mentioned by respondents as reasons for holding meetings in the Cayman Islands (IMAC, 2008).[10]

So far we have explored key quantitative and qualitative traits contributing to making sense of the notion of international insurance centres. We now turn the focus to the centres themselves to assess to what extent their contribution to insurance appears any different from non-international insurance centres. In this respect, there are two key interrelated elements that emerge from the literature. International insurance centres appear to have contributed to enhancing the competitiveness of insurance markets as well as to increasing the provision of insurance coverage. Regarding the former, international insurance centres have contributed to developing cost-effective insurance solutions. The case of captive insurance companies provides an illustration of this point (Cross et al., 1986; BMA, 2009). Second, international insurance centres have contributed to extending the provision of insurance coverage in critical niches. The recapitalisation of reinsurers post-9/11 or post-US 2005 Hurricane Season provide sound examples of this point (IAIS, 2009a; Ramella and Madeiros, 2007).

Moreover, and looking deeper into the issue, international insurance centres have succeeded in generating an environment that enables the development of innovative ideas that have proven to be long-lasting. Ideas span from products such as captive insurance or insurance securitisations to risk management tools, such as economic capital and catastrophe models (BMA, 2008). Importantly, within international insurance centres the transformation of innovative ideas into marketable products has taken place in comparatively short periods of time (Ramella and Madeiros, 2007). Further, and critically, at the heart of this issue there is the entrepreneurial investment made by the states themselves in creating and maintaining the conditions for international insurance centres to thrive. Such a state intervention acts as an effective counterbalance to the inherent fragility that characterises contemporary financial innovation (Engelen et al., 2010). By relying on international insurance as a key economic development driver, international insurance centres' state authorities, including regulators, appear to equip themselves with additional prudential safeguards that enable them to guard the soundness of the market as much as the welfare of their societies. The strengthened capitalisation that has characterised the Bermuda catastrophe reinsurance insurance market (IMF, 2008b), for example, provides empirical support to this claim.

To summarise, this section has proposed, from an operational perspective, a definition of international insurance centres as those jurisdictions providing cross-border insurance coverage that is relatively incommensurate to their domestic economies. Further, it has been argued that key to the understanding of international insurance centres was not just the quantitative dimension but also, and probably most importantly, the qualitative one. In this respect the section reviewed key qualitative issues related to international insurance centres. Finally it looked at the role played by international insurance centres within the overall insurance market.

Regulatory futures of international insurance centres

> Regulation is first and foremost the responsibility of national regulators who constitute the first line of defence against market instability. However, our financial markets are global in scope, therefore, intensified international cooperation among regulators and strengthening of international standards, where necessary, and their consistent implementation is necessary to protect against adverse cross-border, regional and global developments affecting international financial stability. Regulators must ensure that their actions support market discipline, avoid potentially adverse impacts on other

countries, including regulatory arbitrage, and support competition, dynamism and innovation in the marketplace. (G20, 2008, p. 2)

Given the distinct cross-border nature of international insurance centres, their regulatory futures appear tied with special intensity to the reform of global financial regulation currently underway and spearheaded by the Financial Stability Board (FSB), under the leadership of the G20. The paragraph reported above, which was produced within weeks of the bankruptcy of the Lehman Brothers financial conglomerate and the bailout of the AIG financial conglomerate, poignantly condenses a number of the most critical elements that are likely to shape the landscape of financial regulation in the years to come. Of particular relevance to international insurance centres are the inherent tensions between financial firms operating globally (in terms of borders and sectors) and regulatory bodies operating nationally and within statutorily defined sectors, and the pressures emerging from market demands for innovation-enabling rules and public demands for stability-promoting frameworks.

Looking at how these tensions, pressures and debates impact on insurance regulation and supervision in general, and on the regulation and supervision of international insurance centres in particular, this section discusses current work in progress to address these in practice. Drawing on the agenda for reform laid down by the G20, the Financial Stability Forum (FSF) and now the FSB, it examines four areas that have attracted international-level efforts by the International Association of Insurance Supervisors (IAIS) as well as regional- and national-level work (for example, Europe, the US). In particular, the initiatives discussed are the IAIS Multilateral Memorandum of Understanding, the Supervisory Colleges, the IAIS Common Framework for the Supervision of Internationally Active Insurance Groups, and finally, work done in advancing supervisory recognition.

The Multilateral Memorandum of Understanding (MMoU) of the International Association of Insurance Supervisors

In a nutshell, the IAIS MMoU, which was launched in early 2007, aims to create a global framework for cooperation among IAIS members (Oster, 2009). Through a system of cross-border cooperation protocols, it acts as a tool that establishes a formal basis for information exchange between signatory authorities regarding supervision of insurance companies where cross-border aspects arise (IAIS, 2007).

MMoU provisions include requesting and providing information on operations of insurance companies by all signatory authorities with a legitimate interest. The MMoU covers all issues related to insurance companies' supervision, such as licensing, continuous supervision and winding-up processes.

Joining the IAIS MMoU is a voluntary process. IAIS members apply to the IAIS, and are assessed through a formal IAIS procedure. Importantly, at the time of writing, only ten of the more than 140 IAIS members have become official signatories to the MMoU.[11] Of these, Bermuda and Singapore are the only international insurance centres to have done so. Further, the first three members became signatories in June 2009, providing the overall MMoU initiative with scant empirical evidence on its effectiveness in practice, an issue acknowledged by the FSB in its effort to promote global adherence to international cooperation and information exchange standards (FSB, 2010).

Supervisory Colleges

As is the case with the MMoU, Supervisory Colleges constitute another institutional arrangement that has received focused attention following the current financial crisis (G20, 2009, 2008), and which is likely to impact on the regulatory future of international insurance centres. Unlike the MMoU, the Supervisory College could be understood more as a forum for cooperation than as a formal agreement to cooperate.

Briefly put, Supervisory Colleges are ad hoc groups established with the fundamental purpose of facilitating the effectiveness of the supervision of firms belonging to a group. Supervisory Colleges provide a forum for cooperation and communication between supervisors involved in the supervision of groups. In line with current trends, the IAIS has been involved in the development of tools in support of Supervisory Colleges and published in October 2009 a 'Guidance Paper on the Use of Supervisory Colleges in Group-wide Supervision' (IAIS, 2009b).

The Common Framework for the Supervision of Internationally Active Insurance Groups (ComFrame) of the IAIS

An issue that is central to international insurance centres is the ability of these centres to engage in effective supervision of international insurance groups. On the other hand, a key area that emerged as wanting in the analyses carried out on the current financial crisis is the dearth of resources for designing and carrying out group-wide supervision, and in particular, cross-border level group supervision. In this respect, and complementing the two tools discussed above, the IAIS is currently developing a distinct, though inter-related tool, the Common Framework for the Supervision of Internationally Active Insurance Groups (IAIS, 2010).

According to the IAIS, a prime goal of the ComFrame is to generate a framework, a set of parameters that are applicable to multiple jurisdictions and go beyond national or regional regulatory approaches and that accommodate to the needs of supervisors 'hosting' companies of a group as much as the 'home' supervisor of the group. Critically, the IAIS aims to embed the ComFrame within the web of existing tools for the supervision of insurance firms and groups, including the MMoU and the Supervisory Colleges mentioned above.

Supervisory recognition

While the MMoU and the Supervisory Colleges can be understood as tools aimed to help supervisors, in particular those in international insurance centres, to cooperate with each other, and the ComFrame can be seen as a tool to operate on a specific area such as internationally active insurance groups, supervisory recognition aims at a deeper level of interaction and integration, enabling a supervisor to rely on the systems and work by another supervisor.

Supervisory recognition, discussed in detail elsewhere in this book (see Chapter 22 by Kading and Madeiros), treasures rich potential, as it provides a pathway for bridging the – often large – gap created by the global nature of financial firms and the international operation of regulatory bodies. However, going hand in hand with this potential, there is an array of conceptual and practical obstacles that have to date riddled the supervisory recognition agenda with challenges. Below, we briefly introduce and discuss three initiatives in course at present, aimed at paving the way for supervisory recognition between insurance regulation bodies.

Within the IAIS, the Mutual Recognition Subgroup of the Reinsurance Subcommittee has produced a discussion paper (IAIS, 2007) and a guidance paper (IAIS, 2008) on the matter. IAIS work focuses on developing tools for facilitating the recognition process by providing practical support, such as how to frame and conduct an assessment of the regime in place within the supervisory authority with whom recognition is sought, or how to document the process and outcome of the supervisory recognition endeavour. Critically, although the IAIS guidance has been effective since 2008, to date there have been no cases of reinsurance supervisory recognition agreements reached by IAIS members via the tools discussed.

The European Union work on mutual recognition provides a robust regional attempt to articulate in practice the reliance of one supervisory body on the work by another body. A key aspect of the work done in the European Union in relation to mutual recognition is its potential global reach. While the concept of mutual recognition[12] applies within the regional block, an additional notion – that of third country equivalence – articulates the matter between the regional block and any country outside it.

In relation to insurance supervision the passing of the Reinsurance Directive in 2005 and of the 'Solvency II' Directive in 2009 have provided a concrete framework for supervisory recognition both within Europe and between Europe and the rest of the world. Importantly, in February 2010, Switzerland became the first – and only – international insurance centre to be granted third country equivalence under the Reinsurance Directive. However, critics of the notions of mutual recognition and third country equivalence have pointed out that, independently from the intuitive appeal that these notions may have, they are not without problems, as evidenced, for example, by the relatively poor record of success in their implementation in practice (Ortino, 2007); or, as poignantly put by Nicolaïdis and Schmidt (2007): 'Would a British bus driver working in Germany drive on the left?'

Last but not least, and in relation to the US, in 2008 the National Association of Insurance Commissioners (NAIC) developed a framework, the 'Reinsurance Regulatory Modernization Framework', aimed at modernising state-based regulation of reinsurance, by establishing single-state regulation of eligible US and non-USA reinsurers, promoting mutual recognition of US and non-US regulatory regimes, and introducing modified risk-based collateral requirements.

In 2009, the framework was developed further into a national-level bill, the 'Reinsurance Regulatory Modernization Act' (NAIC, 2009), which among other things proposes the creation of the NAIC Reinsurance Supervision Review Board (RSRB) in charge of reviewing and evaluating systems of reinsurance regulation in non-US jurisdictions to determine which jurisdictions qualify as effective regulators. In so doing, the RSRB follows a similar logic to that discussed above in relation to Europe's work on third country equivalence. At the time of writing, the Reinsurance Regulatory Modernization Act is under consideration by US legislators. Importantly, some US states have unilaterally taken steps in a similar direction. For example, in 2008 the State of Florida implemented its own state-level equivalence arrangement. However, to date, there have been only two successful applications under this regime.

To conclude, the future regulatory landscape of international insurance centres appears populated by interesting promissory notes that have yet to come to fruition. Designing, articulating and implementing mechanisms of a global reach constitute impressive undertakings that do not seem to crystallise overnight. However, there are promising indications that these initiatives treasure value-adding potential, in particular in relation to strengthening cooperation between supervisors while enabling innovation and competition (Arner and Taylor, 2009).

Conclusion

This excursion into the issue of regulatory futures of international insurance centres has considered a variety of dimensions and, in so doing, has hopefully highlighted some interesting points. From a research perspective, as shown by the dearth of literature on international insurance centres in comparison to banking ones, there seems to be a need for more in-depth examination of the insurance dimension of international financial centres. This appears particularly important for a variety of reasons; to cite a few: international insurance centres have grown in size and complexity over the past decades, which has also been the case with international insurance business; insurance markets have developed more and more avenues for convergence with other financial markets (for example, cross-sectoral insurance risk transfer to capital markets via sidecars or cat bonds); as the current crisis has shown, international financial systems have proven to be vulnerable, their weaknesses and shortcomings impacting substantially on global welfare; and, international insurance regulation has come under close scrutiny and comprehensive review. These factors, among others, call for enhanced attention to be dedicated to the study of international insurance centres. This paper aims to contribute to efforts under this call. In particular, by highlighting both the quantitative and the qualitative dimensions of international insurance centres, the paper has attempted to draw attention to the complexity of the issue and to the importance of not reducing a key international finance issue to its numerical dimension.

From a policy perspective, the chapter has looked closely at some of the many initiatives in place aimed at bridging the gap between the national-level constraints of international financial regulation and supervision, and the global-level reach of international finance. This is a critical gap. According to the German philosopher Jürgen Habermas (2010a, 2010b), bridging it will necessitate not just a renewed impetus for international cooperation but also, and crucially, it will require 'history-making' individuals and a new Enlightenment offensive.

In this respect, the chapter has argued that international insurance centres are at the core of this debate. The chapter has discussed that the work done so far on enhancing and strengthening cooperation among supervisors and facilitating reliance by supervisors on the systems and work of other supervisors appear as steps in the right direction. The IAIS MMoU, the Supervisory Colleges, ComFrame, and the progress made to date on the supervisory recognition front, provide sound examples of practical tools that can help supervisors around the world to perform their duties more effectively. This appears to be of critical value to supervisors of international insurance centres. On the other hand, the scant empirical evidence on the extent to which these initiatives translate into sounder cross-border regulation and supervision, demands a call for caution. Further work is needed in refining these tools, implementing them broadly and assessing their effectiveness. Moreover, the current crisis has added both momentum as well as pressure to this process. As hosts of some of the most innovative practices in insurance, and as key contributors to the competitiveness of global insurance markets, this momentum and this pressure are probably being felt in international insurance centres with greater intensity than anywhere else.

Notes

1. The views expressed in this chapter are the author's own and do not necessarily reflect the views of the Bermuda Monetary Authority or the London School of Economics and Political Science.
2. See, for example, IMF (2000, 2002, 2003, 2004, 2005, 2006 and 2008a).

3. The full list of countries and jurisdictions emerging from Zoromé's study is as follows: Bahamas, Bahrain, Barbados, Bermuda, the Cayman Islands, China Hong Kong, Cyprus, Guernsey, Ireland, the Isle of Man, Jersey, Latvia, Luxembourg, Malta, Mauritius, the Netherlands Antilles, Panama, Singapore, Switzerland, the UK, Uruguay and Vanuatu.
4. For data on cross-border insurance coverage sold, see OECD (2009), IMF (2008a).
5. Data source: Bermuda Monetary Authority – Annual Report and Accounts 2009, available at www.bma.bm.
6. Data source: Bermuda Department of Statistics – Gross Domestic Product 2008, available at www.gov.bm.
7. In line with Zoromé (2007), we take GDP as the proxy factor to assess against the size of the relevant financial market, in our case, the insurance market.
8. Data source: Reinsurance Association of America – Offshore Reinsurance in the US Market 2008 Data.
9. Data source: Association of Bermuda Insurers and Reinsurers, available at www.abir.bm.
10. Favourable weather conditions and beautiful beaches feature prominently in the Cayman Island's Chamber of Commerce efforts to market the island as an international financial centre. See www.caymanchamber.ky.
11. Australia Prudential Regulation Authority, Australia; Bermuda Monetary Authority, Bermuda; Financial Supervisory Commission, Chinese Taipei; Autorité de Contrôle des Assurances et des Mutuelles, France; Bundesanstalt für Finanzdienstleistungsaufsicht (BaFin), Germany; De Nederlandsche Bank, The Netherlands; Financial Market Authority, Austria; and Insurance Supervisory Commission, Romania; Comision Nacional de Seguros y Fianzas, México; and Monetary Authority of Singapore, Singapore.
12. Within the European Economic Area the concept of mutual recognition goes hand in hand with that of single passport, according to which no Member State may question the authorisation granted to an insurance company by the country where the head office is located (Pasa and Benacchio, 2005).

Bibliography

Arner, D., and M. Taylor (2009) 'The Global Financial Crisis and the Financial Stability Board: Hardening the Soft Law of International Financial Regulation?', AIIFL Working Paper No. 6, Asian Institute of International Financial Law (Hong Kong: University of Hong Kong).

BMA (2008) *Survey of Economic Capital Modelling Practices in the Bermuda Insurance Market* (Hamilton, Bermuda: Bermuda Monetary Authority).

BMA (2009) *A Profile of the Bermuda Captive Insurance Market* (Hamilton: Bermuda Monetary Authority).

Cassard, M. (1994) 'The Role of Offshore Centers in International Financial Intermediation', IMF Working Paper WP/94/107 (Washington, DC: International Monetary Fund).

Cecchetti, S. (2010) 'Current efforts to enhance global financial supervision' – remarks prepared for the Federal Reserve Bank of San Francisco Asia Banking and Finance Conference, 7–8 June, 2010 (Basel, Switzerland: BIS), http://www.bis.org/speeches/sp100608.pdf.

Cross, M., W. Davidson and J. Thornton (1986) 'The Impact of Captive Insurer Formation on the Parent Firm's Value', *Journal of Risk and Insurance*, 53(3): 471–83.

Donaghy, M., and M. Clarke (2003) 'Are Offshore Financial Centres the Product of Global Markets? A Sociological Response', *Economy and Society*, 32(3): 381–409.

Engelen, E., I. Erturk, J. Froud, A. Leaver and K. Williams (2010) 'Reconceptualizing Financial Innovation: Frame, Conjuncture and Bricolage', *Economy and Society*, 39(1): 33–63.

Errico, L., and A. Musalem (1999) 'Offshore Banking: An Analysis of Macro-and Micro Prudential Issues', IMF Working Paper WP/99/5 (Washington, DC: International Monetary Fund).

FSB (2010) *Promoting Global Adherence to International Cooperation and Information Exchange Standards* (Basel: Financial Stability Board).

FSF (2000) *Report of the Working Group on Offshore Financial Centres* (Basel: Financial Stability Forum).

Foucault, M. (2005) *Nascita della Biopolitica. Corso al Collège de France (1978–1979)* (Milan: Feltrinelli).

G20 (2008) 'Declaration – Summit on Financial Markets and the World Economy', Washington, DC, 15 November.

G20 (2009) 'Declaration on Strengthening the Financial System', London, 2 April.

Gribble, J. (2006) 'Actuarial Supply and Demand'. Paper prepared for the Congress of the International Actuarial Association, Paris, 27 May to 2 June.

Habermas, J. (2010a) 'En el euro se decide el destino de la EU', *El País*, 23 May.

Habermas, J. (2010b) 'A Rare Interview with Jürgen Habermas' (interview by Stuart Jeffries), *Financial Times*, 30 April.

HMT (2009) *UK International Financial Services – the Future. A Report from UK based Financial Services Leaders to the Government* (London: HM Treasury).

Hudson, A. (1998) 'Reshaping the Regulatory Landscape: Border Skirmishes Around the Bahamas and Cayman Offshore Financial Centres', *Review of International Political Economy*, 5(3): 534–64.

IAIS (2007) 'Discussion Paper on the Mutual Recognition of Reinsurance Supervision' (Basel: International Association of Insurance Supervisors).

IAIS (2008) 'Guidance Paper on the Mutual Recognition of Reinsurance Supervision' (Basel: International Association of Insurance Supervisors).

IAIS (2009a) *Development in (Re)insurance Securitizations – Global Reinsurance Market Report, Midyear Edition* (Basel: International Association of Insurance Supervisors).

IAIS (2009b) 'Guidance Paper on the Use of Supervisory Colleges in Group-Wide Supervision' (Basel: International Association of Insurance Supervisors).

IAIS (2010) 'Common Framework for the Supervision of Internationally Active Insurance Groups (ComFrame) – First Outline of the IAIS ComFrame Project' (Basel: International Association of Insurance Supervisors).

IMAC (2008) *2008 Cayman Captive Survey* (Grand Cayman: Insurance Managers Association of Cayman).

IMF (2000) 'Offshore Financial Centers', IMF Background Paper (Washington, DC: International Monetary Fund).

IMF (2002) *Offshore Financial Centers Program: A Progress Report* (Washington, DC: International Monetary Fund).

IMF (2003) *Offshore Financial Centers Program: A Progress Report* (Washington, DC: International Monetary Fund).

IMF (2004) 'Offshore Financial Centers: The Assessment Program – An Update' (Washington, DC: International Monetary Fund).

IMF (2005) *Offshore Financial Centers: The Assessment Program – A Progress Report* (Washington, DC: International Monetary Fund).

IMF (2006) *Offshore Financial Centers: The Assessment Program – A Progress Report* (Washington, DC: International Monetary Fund).

IMF (2008a) *Offshore Financial Centers: A Report on the Assessment Program and Proposal for Integration with the Financial Sector Assessment Program* (Washington, DC: International Monetary Fund).

IMF (2008b) 'Bermuda: Assessment of Financial Sector Supervision and Regulation' (Washington, DC: International Monetary Fund).

Kaufman, G. (2000) 'Emerging Economies and International Financial Centers', Loyola University, Chicago – School of Business Administration Working Paper 001101.

Kersell, J. (1985) 'The Administration of Government in Bermuda', *Public Administration and Development*, 5(4): 373–84.

Maurer, B. (2005) 'Due Diligence and "Reasonable Man", Offshore', *Cultural Anthropology*, 20(4): 474–505.

Nachum, L. (2003) 'The Home-based Advantages and a Hierarchy of Location Advantages: Foreign and British-owned Firms in the London Wholesale Insurance Market', Working Paper No. 260, ESRC Centre for Business Research, University of Cambridge.

NAIC (2009) 'A Bill to Enact the Reinsurance Regulatory Modernization Act' (Washington, DC: National Association of Insurance Commissioners).

Nicolaïdis, K., and S. Schmidt (2007) 'Mutual Recognition "On Trial": The Long Road to Services Liberalization', *Journal of European Public Policy*, 14(5): 717–34.

OECD (2009) *Insurance Statistics Yearbook 1998–2007* (Paris: Organisation for Economic Cooperation and Development).

Ortino, M. (2007) 'The Role and Functioning of Mutual Recognition in the European Market of Financial Services', *International and Comparative Law Quarterly*, 56(2): 309–38.

Oster, A. (2009) 'IAIS MMoU as a Tool for International Supervisory Cooperation: Interim Assessment', in *Etudes et Dossiers* No. 352. The 25th PROGRES International Seminar: 'Towards Efficient Regulatory Regimes – Balancing Regulations and Market Forces', 6–7 April, Montreaux, Switzerland. Working Papers Series of The Geneva Association.

Palan, R. (1998a) 'The Emergence of the Offshore Economy', *Futures*, 30(1): 63–73.

Palan, R. (1998b) 'Trying to Have Your Cake and Eating It: How and Why the State System has Created Offshore', *International Studies Quarterly*, 42(4): 625–44.

Park, Y. (1982) 'The Economics of Offshore Financial Centres', *Columbia Journal of World Business* (Winter): 31–5.

Pasa, B., and G. Benacchio (2005) *The Harmonization of Civil and Commercial Law in Europe* (Budapest: Central European University Press).

Pearson, R. (2001) 'The Birth Pains of a Global Reinsurer: Swiss Re of Zurich, 1864–79', *Financial History Review*, 8(1): 27–47.

Pitt, W. (2006) *Bermuda: The New Capital of Insurance?* (Hartford, CT: Conning Research & Consulting Ltd).

Ramella, M., and L. Madeiros (2007) 'Bermuda Sidecars: Supervising Reinsurance Companies in Innovative Global Markets', *The Geneva Papers on Risk and Insurance: Issues and Practice*, 32(3): 345–63.

Roberts, S. (1995) 'Small Place, Big Money: The Cayman Islands and the International Financial System', *Economic Geography*, 71(3): 237–56.

Rose, A., and M. Spiegel (2005) 'Offshore Financial Centers: Parasites or Symbionts?' Federal Reserve Bank of San Francisco Working Paper Series, May.

Suss, E., O. Williams and C. Mendis (2002) *Caribbean Offshore Financial Centers: Past, Present, and Possibilities for the Future* (Washington, DC: International Monetary Fund).

Thrift, N. (1994) 'A Phantom State? The De-traditionalization of Money, the International Financial System and International Financial Centres', *Political Geography*, 13(4): 299–327.

UN (2009) *Report of the Commission of Experts of the President of the United Nations General Assembly on Reforms of the International Monetary and Financial System* (New York: United Nations).

Zoromé, A. (2007) 'Concept of Offshore Financial Centers: In Search of an Operational Definition', IMF Working Paper WP/07/87 (Washington, DC: International Monetary Fund).

24
International Trade Agreements and their Impact on the Regulation and Supervision Insurance Services

Julian Arkell

The World Trade Organization

Introduction

The World Trade Organization (WTO) is the only multilateral treaty applying a rule of law to international trade, thus providing predictability and stability under a framework for international cooperation. This is crucial for the operations of multinationals and internationally integrated supply chains operating in the growing economic interdependence of the global economy. It was during the Uruguay Round of multilateral trade negotiations, concluded in 1993, that it was agreed to form the WTO and to create the General Agreement on Trade in Services (GATS) to cover trade in services alongside the General Agreement on Tariffs and Trade (GATT) for goods.

The WTO has an influence on national policies and measures that unduly distort trade and the associated services investment, or that undermine the fundamental obligation of the non-discrimination principle. The rule-oriented WTO helps to redress geopolitical power exercised unfairly and thus assists in the essential balancing of competing policy goals. Trade is impacted by many factors that fall, however, outside the remit of the WTO such as fiscal and monetary policies, taxation, interest and exchange rates, product standards, defect liability and social and environmental regulations. The WTO dispute mechanism increases the transparency of information availability and enhances compliance with legal commitments, acting to prevent escalating tensions arising from trade conflicts – indeed during the recent financial crisis this constrained protectionist restrictions.

The WTO legal framework

The constitution of the WTO provides a framework under which its member governments enter into legal commitments, ratified by their parliaments, on the conditions applicable to the entry into their territory of goods and services products, and of services suppliers and their related investment, thus providing the legal ground rules for international commerce. WTO members have both a duty to submit to the existing body of its charter rules and a right to contribute to their modification and development: these rules cannot be altered by unilateral declaration by one state, however powerful. The commitments are essentially legal contracts that bind governments to maintain their trade policies within the specified conditions, with the goal of making the rules predictable for producers of goods and services and their exports and imports.

The WTO is independent of the United Nations (UN) and has its own legitimacy as a legal treaty derived from the support of its Members. There is no central law-making authority lying above the WTO in its specific domain, though in general there are superior rules under the members' obligations to the UN Charter that may be relevant. The WTO cannot override norms of international law from which no derogation is permissible (that is, rules of a *jus cogens* nature[1]).

The WTO entered into force on 1 January 1995. There are 153 WTO members and 30 observer governments – the latter have to start accession negotiations within five years of becoming observers. The major emerging markets have been members of the WTO from its inception in 1995, apart from China which acceded in 2001 and Vietnam in 2007: but Russia has yet to join. There are a few countries with major populations that have not yet joined and these include Iran, Sudan, Algeria, Afghanistan, Uzbekistan and Iraq, in descending size order.

The WTO legal framework has six main parts: an umbrella agreement establishing the WTO, agreements for each of three broad areas of trade (goods,[2] services and intellectual property), dispute settlement, and reviews of governments' trade policies.

The WTO is driven by its member governments, with all major decisions being made by consensus among the membership as a whole, either by ministers (who meet once every two years) or by their ambassadors and delegates who meet regularly in Geneva. Power is not delegated to the Director General and there is no board of directors (unlike the World Bank and the International Monetary Fund (IMF)). In between ministerial conferences, the day-to-day work is handled by three bodies: the General Council, the Dispute Settlement Body and the Trade Policy Review Body reporting to the Ministerial Conference. In effect they are the same, though meeting under different terms of reference. There are separate Councils for goods and services (again consisting of all members) and each has subsidiary bodies. Special committees cover issues such as trade and development, trade and the environment, regional trading arrangements, and administrative matters: also specifically on investment, competition policy, transparency in Government Procurement and trade facilitation.

The three principal 'pillars' of the WTO are the following agreements:

1. The GATT, covering trade in goods products.
2. The GATS, covering trade in services, as described in the next section.

   The GATT and GATS set out broad principles and attach extra agreements and annexes dealing with sector specific issues[3], and schedules (that is, lists) of commitments made by each member allowing specific products and service providers access to their markets. Both incorporate two fundamental principles: non-discrimination and transparency (or openness).[4]
3. The Agreement on Trade-Related Aspects of Intellectual Property Rights (TRIPS) which aims to promote the effective and adequate protection of intellectual property rights.

Among other WTO agreements there is the Plurilateral Agreement on Government Procurement, which has twelve WTO members plus the EU27 and entered into force on 1 January 1996 that can cover commitments by governments to buy insurance services, for example.

The WTO Secretariat (with 630 staff) has no management board and no autonomous powers or resources: it has to take instructions from the members in order to give support to their policies and negotiations. The extent of its research function has grown with an increasing emphasis on collaboration with external researchers and with developing country research centres. The WTO has published its annual *World Trade Reports* since 2003.

The Trade Policy Review Mechanism (TPRM) is a peer review system, which increases transparency and understanding of the trade policies and practices of members with a view to improved adherence to rules, disciplines and commitments.

The WTO acts as a forum for trade negotiations. The opening of domestic markets, or liberalisation, is progressively achieved under successive negotiating Rounds of reciprocal bargaining to lower barriers to trade. In fact though, much liberalisation over the past decades has been undertaken unilaterally, but not fully bound under the WTO.[5]

When there are conflicts of interest between members, the provisions for arbitration and dispute settlement are available on the basis of law under the Dispute Resolution mechanism. The WTO rules are enforced by the members themselves under agreed procedures they negotiated, including the possibility of trade sanctions – the latter having to be authorised by the membership as a whole. The Dispute Settlement system comprises panels of independent experts and the standing Appellate Body that deals with appeals from the decisions of panels. The five panel cases to date related to services have not involved insurance services.

The majority of WTO members are developing countries comprising a highly diverse group with very different policies and concerns. WTO agreements include numerous provisions giving developing and Least Developed Countries (LDCs) special rights or extra leniency, termed 'special and differential treatment'. The WTO devotes resources to giving trade policy related capacity building and adjustment assistance to developing countries in cooperation with the World Bank, the IMF, the UN Conference on Trade and Development (UNCTAD) and the UN Development Programme (UNDP). In general 'Least-developed countries shall be accorded substantially increased technical assistance in the development, strengthening and diversification of their production and export bases including those of services, as well as in trade promotion, to enable them to maximise the benefits from liberalized access to markets' (GATT, 1994).[6]

The Parliamentary Conference on the WTO, organised jointly by the Inter-Parliamentary Union and the European Parliament, has become a regular fixture. Sessions are organised each year as well as on the occasion of WTO Ministerial Conferences and also regionally with the aim of strengthening democracy at the international level by bringing a parliamentary dimension to multilateral cooperation on trade issues.

The WTO relationship with international organisations

The agreement setting up the WTO includes an article on the relationship with other international organisations: 'With a view to achieving greater coherence in global economic policy-making, the WTO shall cooperate, as appropriate, with the International Monetary Fund and with the International Bank for Reconstruction and Development [IBRD] and its affiliated agencies.' Memoranda of Understanding have been signed with the IMF and the World Bank, and regular meetings are held between the secretariats. The WTO jointly funds the International Trade Centre with UNCTAD.

The WTO has granted various international organisations observer status to follow the discussions, including the ACP (Africa, Caribbean and Pacific), the Organisation for Economic Cooperation and Development (OECD), the IMF, UNCTAD, the World Bank and the UN. The application for observer status at the Committee on Trade in Financial Services by the International Association of Insurance Supervisors (IAIS) is pending along with a number of other organisations due to a general political hiatus at the WTO not related to the IAIS itself. Meanwhile there is cooperation through the exchange of information when WTO officials and committee members occasionally visit the IAIS and by participation of the IAIS in relevant WTO workshops, seminars and meetings (on an ad hoc basis), though not yet in a significant way due to lack of resources.

The WTO and the private sector

The WTO Secretariat attempts to make the private sector trade associations more aware of the explicit and implicit assumptions underlying the multilateral trade agreements. Article V:2 of the 1994 Marrakech Agreement setting up the WTO states that 'The General Council may make appropriate arrangements for consultation and cooperation with non-governmental organisations concerned with matters related to those of the WTO.' This was initially carried out informally with national, regional and global trade associations, labour unions and non-governmental organisations (NGOs) and in recent years more formally by their participation in the WTO Annual Public Forums.

The GATS and its main disciplines

All WTO members are signatories to the GATS which provides the legal framework for commitments by governments relating to the entry of foreign services products and suppliers, including individuals, into their jurisdiction. It binds governments to general obligations of non-discrimination and transparency and to disciplines that apply to the conditions and limitations relating to the access for specific services suppliers, their products, subsidiaries and related investment. These disciplines apply to the legal regulations in force and thus can have an influence on the actions of regulatory and supervisory authorities and their enforcement of legal measures.

The GATS is the first set of multilateral rules governing international trade in services. It consists of three elements: the main text in six parts; annexes, including those for four sectors; and each member's specific commitments to provide access to their markets. The GATS rules are intended to contribute to trade expansion 'under conditions of transparency and progressive liberalisation and as a means of promoting the economic growth of all trading partners and the development of developing countries'. The GATS explicitly recognises the right of governments to regulate and to introduce new regulations in order to meet national policy objectives and in particular the need of developing countries to do so.

GATS Part I Scope and Definition

Article I *Scope and Definition* provides that the GATS 'applies to measures by Members affecting trade in services' (I:1). Trade in services is defined as the supply of a service which depends upon the territorial presence of the supplier and the consumer at the time of the transaction, under four 'modes' of services (I:2) – those supplied:

(a) 'from the territory of one Member into the territory of any other Member' (Mode 1 – Cross-border trade) (for example, by transport, internet, mail)

(b) 'in the territory of one Member to the service consumer of any other Member'
(Mode 2 – Consumption abroad) (for example, to tourists, repairs to ships when abroad)
(c) 'by a service supplier of one Member, through commercial presence, in the territory of any other Member'
(Mode 3 – Commercial presence) (for example, the establishment and operation of subsidiaries and branches abroad)
(d) 'by a service supplier of one Member, through the presence of natural persons of a Member in the territory of any other Member'
(Mode 4 – Presence of natural persons) (such as by professionals temporarily working abroad).

Article I:3 stipulates that the GATS applies to measures by members affecting trade in services, whether taken at the central, regional or local government level, or by non-governmental bodies exercising delegated powers. Here, '"measure" means any measure by a member, whether in the form of a law, regulation, rule, procedure, decision, administrative action, or any other form', with the very broad coverage 'in respect of:

- the purchase, payment or use of a service;
- the access to and use of, in connection with the supply of a service, services which are required by those Members to be offered to the public generally;
- the presence, including commercial presence, of persons of a Member for the supply of a service in the territory of another Member'.[7]

However, 'services supplied in the exercise of governmental authority' are exempted (Article I:3b) when 'supplied neither on a commercial basis, nor in competition with one or more service suppliers' (Article I:3c), for example, monetary policy operations, mandatory social security and taxes.

The GATS annexes

There are annexes for the Most-Favoured-Nation (MFN) Exemptions, the movement of individual suppliers and for four sectors: air transport, financial (including insurance) services, maritime transport and telecommunications.

The *Annex on Movement of Natural Persons Supplying Services under the Agreement* spells out how the disciplines apply to individuals working temporarily in a country for the purpose of supplying a service. It specifies that GATS 'shall not apply to measures affecting natural persons seeking access to the employment market of a Member, nor shall it apply to measures regarding citizenship, residence or employment on a permanent basis'.

The *Annex on Financial Services* sets out the listing of financial services and specific provisions on recognition and dispute settlement for the sector. Its second paragraph critically provides for a so-called 'prudential carve-out' in financial services. This exception states that notwithstanding any other provision of the GATS, a member shall not be prevented from taking measures for prudential reasons, including for the protection of investors, depositors, policy-holders or persons to whom a fiduciary duty is owed by a financial service supplier, or to ensure the integrity or stability of the financial system. However, such measures shall not be used as a means of avoiding the member's commitments or obligations under the GATS.[8]

GATS Part II: general obligations and disciplines

There are general obligations in Articles II, III and VI.

Article II *Most-Favoured-Nation Treatment* sets out the MFN principle. It seeks to replace the frictions and distortions of power-based (bilateral) policies with the guarantees of a rules-based framework where trading rights do not depend on the individual participants' economic or political weight. The most favourable conditions that have been conceded to any country must be extended to all WTO Members. MFN applies even if the member has made no specific commitment in a sector to provide foreign companies access to its market under the GATS, and this applies to all services, though some special temporary exemptions were allowed when the GATS came into force and since then for new Members when they acceded to the WTO.

Article III *Transparency* provides that members shall publish promptly all measures pertaining to or affecting the operation of the GATS. They should notify the Council for Trade in Services at least annually of all legal or regulatory changes that significantly affect trade in sectors where specific commitments have been made. Members are also required to establish enquiry points which provide specific information that is not confidential, to other WTO members upon request.

Article V *Economic Integration* provides that WTO members may enter into agreements to further liberalize trade in services on a bilateral or plurilateral basis, provided the agreement has 'substantial sectoral coverage' and removes substantially all discrimination between participants, recognising that such agreements may form part of a wider process of economic integration beyond services trade. It also provides for their flexible application in the event of developing countries being parties to such agreements. However, the overall level of barriers must not be raised to non-participants in the sectors covered. Otherwise, should an agreement lead to the withdrawal of commitments, appropriate compensation must be negotiated with the members affected.

The WTO Committee on Regional Trade Agreements (RTAs) was set up in February 1996 with the mandate to verify the compliance of notified RTAs with the relevant WTO provisions and consider the implications of such agreements and regional initiatives for the multilateral relationship between them.[9] Members have not been able to reach consensus on the format or the substance of the reports on any of these examinations, and this stalemate has resulted in little progress in its mandate. In launching the Doha Round of negotiations in 2001, Ministers stressed the need for a harmonious relationship between the multilateral and regional processes, and that the Round should seek to improve the relevant disciplines and procedures under existing WTO provisions and to minimise the risks related to the proliferation of RTAs.

On the less contentious procedural issues members reached formal agreement on a Transparency Mechanism for RTAs to be applied on a provisional basis pending the conclusion of the Doha Round.[10] Such transparency should help private sector exporters navigate through the maze of preferential regulatory regimes and provide tools to better assess the relationship between the WTO and RTAs.

Article VI *Domestic Regulation* mainly applies to specific commitments undertaken by Members, in that they have to:

- 'ensure that all measures of general application affecting trade in services are administered in a reasonable, objective and impartial manner' (VI:1)
- 'maintain or institute as soon as practicable judicial, arbitral or administrative tribunals or procedures which provide, at the request of an affected service supplier, for the prompt review of [ ] administrative decisions affecting trade in services' (VI:2)
- 'within a reasonable period of time after the submission of an application considered complete under domestic laws and regulations, inform the applicant of the decision concerning the application' (VI:3)
- 'not apply licensing and qualification requirements and technical standards that nullify or impair' specific commitments (VI:5)
- 'provide for adequate procedures to verify the competence of professionals' (VI:6).

Significantly, under VI:4 the Council for Trade in Services has to 'develop any necessary disciplines' so as to ensure 'that measures relating to qualification requirements and procedures, technical standards and licensing requirements do not constitute unnecessary barriers to trade in services.' These 'disciplines shall aim to ensure that such requirements are, inter alia:

(a) based on objective and transparent criteria, such as competence and the ability to supply the service;
(b) not more burdensome than necessary to ensure the quality of the service;
(c) in the case of licensing procedures, not in themselves a restriction on the supply of the service.'

Article VII *Recognition*. One of the barriers to trade expansion for service suppliers is created by the multiple licensing and certification requirements in export markets. Mutual recognition agreements are potentially in conflict with the MFN obligation under Article II. However, Article VII provides that members

> may recognise the education or experience obtained, requirements met, or licences or certifications granted in a particular country. Such recognition, which may be achieved through harmonisation or otherwise, may be based upon an agreement or arrangement with the country concerned or may be accorded autonomously ... Wherever appropriate, recognition should be based on multilaterally agreed criteria. In appropriate cases, Members shall work in cooperation with relevant intergovernmental and non-governmental organisations towards the establishment and adoption of common international standards and criteria for recognition and common international standards for the practice of relevant services trades and profession.

Importantly, the GATS does not set such standards.

Article XIV *General Exceptions*. The chief exceptions to the GATS disciplines recognise the legitimacy of higher-order policy aims, such as the maintenance of national security, the protection of public morals and order, and of human, animal and plant life or health, privacy and safety, the prevention of fraud, and the imposition and collection of direct taxes. Members may take measures necessary for such overriding policy concerns. However, the measures must not lead to arbitrary or unjustifiable discrimination or constitute a disguised restriction to trade. Article XII *Restrictions to Safeguard the Balance of Payments* allows for the introduction of temporary restrictions to safeguard the balance-of-payments.

GATS Part III: specific commitments

Article XVI *Market Access* is very flexible, allowing each member to adjust the conditions of market entry to its sector-specific objectives and constraints. Members are free to designate the sectors, and list them in their schedules of specific commitments and relating to the four modes of supply, with any limitations retained in order to reserve the right to operate measures inconsistent with full market access. These can vary widely as between sectors and there is a greater degree of flexibility accorded to developing countries.

Article XVII *National Treatment* aims for the removal of any discriminatory measures that may adversely modify the conditions of competition for foreign services or service suppliers, though limitations can be specified to provide cover for inconsistent measures, such as discriminatory subsidies and tax measures or residency requirements. This obligation applies whether or not foreign services and suppliers are treated in an identical formal legal way to their national counterparts: essentially they should in practice be granted equal opportunities to compete.

Article XVIII *Additional Commitments* enables members to schedule measures that do not have to be scheduled under the market access and national treatment articles, which includes non-discriminatory regulations and those relating to qualifications, standards and licensing.

The *Understanding on Commitments in Financial Services* is a unique legal instrument in the WTO, not formally being part of the GATS. Some 40 countries have made a high level of liberalisation commitments in accordance with the 'Understanding' which forms an optional basis for binding commitments in financial services on an alternative approach to that otherwise provided for in the GATS: these undertakings include:

- not to introduce any new non-conforming measures (a 'standstill')
- to eliminate or reduce existing monopoly rights in financial services
- to accord MFN and national treatment to any supplier established in the market for government purchases of financial services
- to permit the cross-border supply, under conditions of national treatment, of the following services:
  - insurance risks relating to maritime shipping, commercial aviation and space launching and freight, to cover any goods being transported, the vehicle transporting the goods, and any liability arising; and goods in international transit
  - reinsurance and retrocession and the services auxiliary to insurance
  - provision and transfer of financial information and financial data processing, and advisory and other auxiliary services (excluding intermediation) relating to banking and other financial services
- to permit its residents to purchase in the territory of any other Member certain financial services
- to grant the right to establish or expand within its territory, including through mergers and acquisitions, a commercial presence, under the terms of any such authorisation
- to permit new financial services to be offered by established firms
- to permit the transfer of information or its processing, or the transfer of equipment as necessary for the conduct of ordinary business
- to permit the temporary entry of certain specialist personnel
- to remove or limit any significant adverse effects of non-discriminatory measures that prevent suppliers offering permitted services, or expanding the supply to the entire territory, and any other measures that adversely affect the ability to operate, compete or enter the market

- to accord national treatment for access to payment and clearing systems operated by public entities, and to official funding and refinancing facilities, and access to self-regulatory bodies, exchange and futures markets, clearing agency, or other organisation or association which is required in order to compete on an equal basis with local firms.

GATS Part IV: progressive liberalisation, and Part V: institutional provisions

Part IV provides for successive rounds of negotiations on specific commitments, their scheduling and modification. These negotiations are undertaken in the Council for Trade in Services Special Sessions chaired by an ambassador of a member. Part V provides for consultation between members that may lead to a dispute and covers dispute settlement and enforcement. A private sector enterprise faced with any restriction or requirement voiding a specific commitment cannot raise a dispute directly with a WTO Member country, but has to convince its home country government to take up the case under the WTO dispute settlement mechanism. Part V also provides the definition of key terms including: measure, supply of a service, commercial presence, sector, supplier, consumer, natural and juridical persons, and direct taxes.

The Committee on Trade in Financial Services has a standing agenda to monitor implementation of the Financial Services Agreement of 1997 (which has not yet been ratified by Brazil and the Philippines); to provide a forum for technical discussions; to conduct studies on measures of members; and to conduct examinations of any other technical matters affecting trade in services in the sector concerned.

Preferential Trade Agreements (PTAs)

Regional and plurilateral PTAs

By 2007 the number of regional PTAs in force that had been notified to the WTO was 214 and many more were being negotiated. Among the most significant are:[11]

Table 24.1 Significant PTAs

	No. of members		No. of members
ASEAN FTA	10	ECOWAS	15
CARICOM	15	GCC	6
CEMAC	6	Mercosur	4
CIS	11	NAFTA	3
COMESA	20	SADC	12
EC	27	SATIS	10

The negotiations in PTAs can be less burdensome to conduct, particularly among like-minded countries, and cover subjects still excluded from the multilateral agenda, such as government procurement, competition policy and investment. UNCTAD sees that RTAs are easier to conclude for trade in services than at the multilateral level due to the limited set of participants, economies at similar levels of development, geographical proximity, cultural ties and reciprocity with no free riders. However, the sheer number of PTAs taken together, in effect produce barriers to liberalisation due to their complex interaction, and potential lack of compliance with multilateral obligations legally bound under the GATS. This flexibility of the PTAs is creating a maze of different regulatory regimes that undermine the principles of transparency and predictability in trade relations.

Bilateral trade agreements

Although there are hundreds of bilateral trade agreements, only about 50 include services. They mainly feature countries in the Americas and the Asia-Pacific region, with Africa remaining outside the trend. The largest countries involved are the US, Japan, China, Brazil, and from the EU – though there are no bilateral agreements between each other. There are few bilaterals between developing countries. It should be noted also that there is an increasing number of bilateral agreements between regional PTAs such as the European Community (EC) with Mercosur (the Common Market of the South); the Association of Southeast Asian Nations (ASEAN) and the Gulf Cooperation Council (GCC); and South African Customs Union (SACU) with the European Free Trade Association (EFTA) and Mercosur, which adds further complexity to trade negotiations.

Due to the sensitivities of the financial services sector there are varying liberalisation modalities in bilateral trade agreements. One modality has been explicitly to exclude the sector, though accompanied by a commitment to review the situation after the entry into force of the agreement. Others have an additional chapter or annex that clarifies or elaborates upon the more general provisions for trade in financial services.

Bilateral Investment Agreements (BITs)

Some 2,500 BITs have been signed and about 1,900 are in operation. Most cover all sectors of the economies including services, so that insurance, banking and other financial services are directly involved. The coverage of services sectors in BITs often exceeds the number of sectors inscribed in the counterpart schedules of specific commitments by WTO Members. The issue of the relationship between BITs and the GATS appears not to have been explored in the current set of WTO negotiations.

The extent of trade liberalisation achieved

GATS: the multilateral level

The multilateral trade negotiations relating to insurance services under GATS provide for specific commitments to be made by each WTO member on the restrictions and limitations applied by regulations on market access to their jurisdiction and operations within it, for insurance services and suppliers. Such measures fall within their sovereign right to regulate and this includes any standards so set. Such standards may be *sui generis*, or follow regional or international standards (such as the OECD Codes and the IAIS principles and guidelines) and may or may not be aligned with those of other members.

The typical market access barriers that can face foreign insurance services and enterprises include restrictions on cross-border supply and the temporary stay of individuals supplying services under contracts, limits on equity and direct branching, restrictions on other operations, the imposition of requirements for minimum capital invested, mandatory cessions, joint ventures, posting of collateral for large risks, local cover for imports, tax on reinsurance placed abroad and numbers of nationals on boards of directors. Further, there may, or may not, be mutual recognition agreements among members or unilateral recognition of certain legal requirements of one member by another member.

Although the countries that were founding WTO members in 1995 had made specific commitments in insurance services at the end of the Uruguay Round in December 1993, there were further negotiations on financial services that were concluded in December 1997 which resulted in an average level of liberalisation higher than other sectors – though those for insurance were lower than for banking. This reflected the high levels of bindings undertaken by the OECD countries and a few others, while since then some transition countries have joined the EU and nearly all the members acceding since 1995 were pressured into making equivalently high commitments.

The current WTO liberalisation round of negotiations was launched in Doha in 2001 as the Doha Development Agenda (DDA) and incorporated the negotiations on trade in services under the GATS that had begun in early 2000. This 'Single Undertaking' ('nothing is agreed until everything is agreed') has so far meant that the services negotiations are quiescent, due to being held hostage to the negotiations on subsidies in agriculture and tariff reductions on other goods.

Negotiations to agree on specific commitments under the GATS are arrived at by the process of bilateral requests and offers. Although the exchange of requests and offers will therefore remain ultimately bilaterally based, the Hong Kong Ministerial Declaration of December 2005 stimulated the tabling of 21 plurilateral requests by groups of Members covering 18 sectors (including for financial services), and cross-border supply (Modes 1 and 2), commercial presence (Mode 3), the movement of natural persons (Mode 4) and MFN Exemptions.

The plurilateral request in 2006 for insurance services sought the removal of limitations on:

- the right to establish new companies and to acquire existing companies
- foreign ownership (to give the freedom to establish in the form of wholly-owned subsidiaries, joint ventures or branches)
- numerical quotas and Economic Needs Tests (that use economic criteria to decide whether the entry into the market of a foreign firm is warranted) and mandatory insurance cessions
- non-discrimination in the application of laws, regulations and administrative decisions
- Modes 1 and 2 commitments in a defined list of subsectors
- national treatment, and
- transparency in the development (including consultation) and application of laws and regulations relevant to the financial services sector.

The liberalisation offers revealed in July 2008 at the so-called Signalling Conference show little sign in general of improving much on the 1997 levels of market access liberalisation.

PTAs: the regional level

The growth of regional PTAs has been rapid since 2005 and the consequent regulatory complexity is potentially raising the costs of insurance exporters and undermining the transparency and predictability of the commercial scene (Marchetti 2008, and Fiorentino 2007).[12] Although in principle each PTA has the common objective of trade liberalisation and deeper regional integration, mercantilism is not the sole driver and many include other regulatory domains, and foreign policy dimensions, that increase the regulatory complexity.

A few agreements have shown that deeper liberalisation is possible, and the Andean Common Market in Services, for example, has an aim to harmonise national policies. The ASEAN Framework Agreement on Services (AFAS) is GATS-plus. In the North American Free Trade Agreement (NAFTA) bindings are more transparent than at GATS because nothing remained unbound after negotiations were concluded, so that there is an automatic extension of benefits of any unilateral liberalisation (for example, on cross-border financial services), but the provisions on labour mobility are limited.

Other than in the EU single market and NAFTA, the actual binding of services liberalisation has not yet been very significant in the largest regional PTAs, including, for example, the Asian Free Trade Area (AFTA)/ASEAN, Mercosur,[13] the Southern African Development Community (SADC) and the South Asia Trade in Services (SATIS), each of which follows the positive listing approach. Probably even in these regional PTAs the full liberalisation of the movement of natural persons to supply services or work in foreign controlled services subsidiaries will hardly become a general reality.

The political scene

The current political situation at the WTO is in striking contrast to that preceding the Uruguay Round in September 1986 of GATT negotiations, for which the US had been the first strong advocate for the liberalisation of trade in services. Although at the launch in 2001 of the Doha Development Agenda Round there was some empathy with the US following the World Trade Center tragedy of 11 September. However, following the election of President Obama the political voice of the US was silent in Geneva with no ambassador to the WTO in post until May 2010. Although the voices of the Cairns Group on agriculture and ASEAN countries have stayed at the forefront, the 49 LDCs have in effect sought to avoid any commitments and be given unfettered access to all markets on a preferential basis. India supports the GATS negotiations, pressing hard for further opening for the Mode 4 supply of services, Brazil is no longer so averse and the voices of South Africa, Mexico and Chile have moved more centre-stage. Some developing countries even joined the plurilateral requests on services liberalisation, including Brazil, China, Colombia, Egypt, Hong Kong, India, Morocco, Pakistan, Peru, Thailand and Uruguay. China has affirmed that its accession commitments are sufficient and urges other developing countries to match them, a position being held by the similarly placed recently acceded members. Officials from the US, the EU, China, Brazil and India are exploring ways forward and this was widened to 19 countries in May 2010. However, Brazil sees the latest US position as unrealistic because it presses for much improved market access conditions for US firms. The services negotiations are anyhow being held up by those on agriculture, where India cannot agree to any conditions that would put millions of its rural people at risk, while China cannot agree to expose its cotton farmers to subsidised US imports, or give more access for wheat and corn.

How trade agreement commitments can impact regulation and supervision

It is important to underline that the term 'regulation' is viewed and employed differently in the WTO context from that in the IAIS and insurance sector contexts. For the diplomats, trade negotiators and trade analysts, regulations, or measures, are viewed as to whether they affect trade in services and can include a wide range of objectives. For insurance regulators and supervisors and financial analysts it is prudential regulation that is the main focus. There can be instances where the two aspects overlap. A certain prudential regulation, in principle excepted under the GATS 'prudential carve-out' provision, could be deployed in a way that gave market protection and thus nullify a GATS commitment.

An assessment on how commitments made under trade agreements can impact the regulation and supervision of insurance services has to take into account the negotiated disciplines embodied in the trade agreements and the level of commitments undertaken to keep insurance markets open to foreign suppliers, given the level of development of a country in both regulatory and commercial terms.

To the extent that the Financial Stability Board (FSB) will mandate stricter regulation of insurers for the supervisors to enforce, this could trigger issues relating to the existing GATS obligations and commitments. The key GATS disciplines that could condition the outcome of recent regulatory actions taken and constrain their likely evolution, are: the two non-discrimination obligations of MFN treatment and national treatment; the implicit extent of the broad exception provided in the Annex on Financial Services (that is, the 'prudential carve-out'); the disciplines on non-discriminatory domestic regulation (including the application of standards and the issuing of licences); and on preferential trade agreements. These disciplines are underpinned by the WTO legal dispute resolution mechanism.

Given there are some 50 or more PTAs that include services and because they are required to observe the GATS disciplines, it is assumed that their commitments will have a similar conditioning effect to those of the GATS on the regulation and supervision of insurance services, even where the commitments are more liberal.

Many countries have undertaken high levels of liberalisation commitments in financial services, including provisions for the mutual recognition of the measures of counterparty authorities. The larger, more advanced markets are likely to have the highest level of committed market openness for foreign suppliers, whilst the emerging markets with large potential have made generally lower commitments. The new FSB regulatory model patterns will necessarily be influenced by the governments of the large emerging markets which may continue to press to retain a larger degree of 'policy space', resulting in further trade in services liberalisation being slower and more conditional.

For many developing countries the trend in regulation has been generally moving from a rules-based to a principles-based system and from price and product control to prudential tests of soundness of the insurers. The issue will be whether this trend in regulatory approach can be expected to continue, or whether will there be a return to a more rules-based, product and price control basis, induced by new regulations mandated by the FSB.

During the financial crisis some monetary bail-out measures for firms 'too big to fail' have been taken which raises the issue of whether any foreign insurance supplier's right to non-discriminatory treatment guaranteed under the GATS or PTAs has been denied and thus the extent to which specific commitments might need to be withdrawn and costs be incurred to compensate partner countries that are adversely affected as a result. If actions taken to stem the adverse effects of the financial crisis have, for example, included disallowing branches, this might constitute the withdrawal of bound specific commitments, most likely by those countries that had undertaken higher market access commitments under the WTO 'Understanding on Commitments in Financial Services', and this could give rise to demands for compensation. It is possible that the enforcement of certain new prudential measures might constitute non-violation in cases where this resulted in commitments and obligations under trade agreements being avoided, also giving rise to the right to compensation.

The GATS and PTA negotiations on measures affecting trade in services aim in principle to make the *regulation* of national markets more open to foreigners and because the commitments are the result of reciprocal bargaining, the present situation may reflect decisions taken many years ago to make specific commitments at a lower level of market access for foreign services than is actually now applied. Thus the GATS may have had only a slight restraining influence so far on trade protectionism. It seems more likely that any new regulation of insurance services will cause governments to reduce future offers of trade liberalisation under the Doha Round rather than strengthening the disciplines to exert any significant influence over such regulatory advances.

There may be even less influence of the GATS disciplines on the actions of *supervisors* because the enforcement of national measures within a jurisdiction will predominantly be exempted by the provisions of the 'prudential carve-out' contained in the Annex on Financial Services, or be covered by GATS Article VI *Domestic Regulation* – though importantly, subject to such measures being applied in a non-discriminatory way. This would be the position also in PTAs. The trade commitments do not affect the type or level of any standards applied in a jurisdiction – indeed, for insurance there is no equivalent of the Basel I, II or III rules for banking.

The actions of the FSB in setting up Colleges of supervisors, for each large insurer and conglomerate that has regional or global operations, in order to coordinate risk and crisis management in preparation for managing cross-border insolvencies, in effect provides for mutual recognition. In future this could be significant to prevent economic spillover by enforcing the internalisation by insurers of the costs of risks. In principle such moves would be permitted under GATS Article VII *Recognition* and any similar provisions in PTAs. Within these Colleges, insurance supervisors can establish relationships of trust and work collectively across borders to control the largest insurance groups that are internationally systemic.[14] This will also have to be carried on in the context of federal/sub-federal states necessitating a degree of convergence of supervisory standards at sub-federal, national, regional and global levels.

If governments set up resolution authorities to take over insolvent firms (in order to enforce orderly winding-up procedures) and also set up consumer protection bureaus, these actions would be consistent with trade agreements, provided that the measures are applied without discrimination between nationally-owned firms and foreign-controlled firms. This conclusion also applies in cases where insurers might be required to make contributions to central funds to pay for bail outs to prevent costs falling on the taxpayers, or if risk swaps are banned such as on interest rates and credit default instruments, affecting the investment policies of insurance companies.

Notes

1. *Jus cogens* is the only real category of 'superior' rules in that treaty law cannot derogate from them. They include, for instance, anti-slavery, human rights and genocide.
2. Including certain aspects of trade-related investment measures affecting goods.
3. For GATS these include the movement of natural persons to supply services, financial services, shipping, telecommunications and air transport.
4. Discrimination is seen as arbitrary intervention by governments to reduce the rights of suppliers of goods and services from other members. Non-discrimination has two forms: most-favoured nation treatment and national treatment (as described in the section 'The General Agreement on Trade in Services and its Main Disciplines').
5. There is thus a difference under the GATS between bound regulatory measures and the rules actually applied which may be less restrictive.
6. Decision on Measures in Favour of Least-Developed Countries, Art. 2 (v), page 441 of *The Results of the Uruguay Round of Multilateral Trade Negotiations – The Legal Texts* (GATT, 1994).
7. GATS Article XXVIII *Definitions*.
8. The extent of the 'prudential carve-out' has not been resolved under GATS law and no challenges have so far been raised on its interpretation by a member.
9. WTO document WT/L/127, 7 February 1996.
10. WTO document WT/L/671, 18 December 2006.
11. ASEAN: Association of Southeast Asian Nations; CARICOM: Caribbean Community and Common Market; CEMAC: Economic and Monetary Community of Central Africa; CIS: Commonwealth of Independent States; COMESA: Common Market for Eastern and Southern Africa; EC: European Community; ECOWAS: Economic Community of West African States; GCC: Gulf Cooperation Council; Mercosur: Southern Common Market (of Latin America); SADC: Southern African Development Community; NAFTA: North American Free Trade Association; SATIS: SAARC Agreement on Trade in Services (SAARC: South Asian Association for Regional Cooperation). The SADC Protocol on Services and the SAARC Agreement on Trade in Services (SATIS) texts have not yet been signed.
12. This subsection draws on Marchetti and Roy (2008) and Fiorentino et al. (2007).
13. However, within the Mercosur, the Mode 4 commitments are significantly GATS-plus in the coverage of categories, skills and sectors, including in certain cases the removal of labour market tests.

14. Such Colleges may also be needed to cover groups of small countries where insurance is supplied cross-border because it is not commercially worth establishing subsidiaries abroad.

Bibliography

Fiorentino,R., L. Verdeja and C. Toqueboeuf (2007) 'The Changing Landscape of Regional Trade Agreements: 2006 Update', WTO Discussion Paper No. 12.

GATT (1994) *The Results of the Uruguay Round of Multilateral Trade Negotiations – The Legal Texts* (GATT).

Marchetti, J. and M. Roy (eds) (2008) *Emerging Markets of Trade in Services* (WTO/Cambridge University Press).

Index